FREEDOM FROM POVERTY

Freedom from Poverty as a Human Right

Who Owes What to the Very Poor?

Edited by

THOMAS POGGE

United Nations
Educational, Scientific and
Cultural Organization

OXFORD

UNIVERSITY PRESS

OXFORD
UNIVERSITY PRESS

Great Clarendon Street, Oxford ox2 6DP

Oxford University Press is a department of the University of Oxford.
It furthers the University's objective of excellence in research, scholarship,
and education by publishing worldwide in

Oxford New York

Auckland Cape Town Dar es Salaam Hong Kong Karachi
Kuala Lumpur Madrid Melbourne Mexico City Nairobi
New Delhi Shanghai Taipei Toronto

With offices in

Argentina Austria Brazil Chile Czech Republic France Greece
Guatemala Hungary Italy Japan Poland Portugal Singapore
South Korea Switzerland Thailand Turkey Ukraine Vietnam

Oxford is a registered trademark of Oxford University Press
in the UK and in certain other countries

Published in the United States
by Oxford University Press Inc., New York

Published jointly in 2007 by the United Nations Educational, Scientific and Cultural Organization
(UNESCO), 7, place de Fontenoy, 75007 Paris, France, and Oxford University Press, Great Clarendon
Street, Oxford ox2 6DP, United Kingdom

The moral rights of the authors have been asserted
Database right Oxford University Press (maker)

First published 2007

British Library Cataloguing in Publication Data
Data available

Library of Congress Cataloging in Publication Data
Data available

The designations employed and the presentation of material throughout this publication do not
imply the expression of any opinion whatsoever on the part of UNESCO concerning the legal status
of any country, territory, city or area or of its authorities, or the delimitation of its frontiers or
boundaries. The authors are responsible for the choice and the presentation of the facts contained in
this book and for the opinions expressed therein, which are not necessarily those of UNESCO and do
not commit the Organization.

Typeset by SPI Publisher Services, Pondicherry, India
Printed in Great Britain
on acid-free paper by
Biddles Ltd., King's Lynn, Norfolk

ISBN UNESCO: 978–9–23–104033–7
ISBN Oxford University Press: 978–0–19–922631–3
978–0–19–922618–4 (pbk.)

1 3 5 7 9 10 8 6 4 2

To Alan Gewirth 1912–2004

Foreword

This publication is a result of the first cycle of workshops for a UNESCO project on poverty launched in 2002. The project, originally proposed as *Ethical and Human Rights Dimensions of Poverty: Towards a New Paradigm in the Fight Against Poverty,* focuses on the conceptual analysis of understanding poverty within the framework of human rights. Since 2002, eleven seminars have been held, bringing together scholars from the fields of Philosophy, Economics, Political Science, and Law. The present volume gathers selected papers from a series of philosophy seminars held in six countries.

The first phase of the project aimed to foster a philosophical analysis and elucidation of understanding poverty and how it relates to human rights, basic needs, and corresponding duties. Scholars within and beyond the philosophical community were invited to produce papers which analyze the key concepts relevant to poverty and human rights, such as responsibility, violation, obligation, duty and the question of duty-bearers, accountability, indirect or direct causality, as well as the significance of solidarity, social global justice, and the minimal conditions for maintaining and preserving human dignity. This conceptual analysis has given rise to reflections on the notions of individual and collective action and identity (personal, social, and institutional). The challenge is to see how an organization such as UNESCO might galvanize the commitment of the world community by addressing the moral obligation to take action to eradicate poverty and to contribute to the full realization of the fundamental basic rights of all peoples.

Poverty is not simply a matter of material deprivation. It is a matter of human dignity, justice, fundamental freedoms, and basic human rights. But the existing paradigm apparent in various approaches to poverty reduction remains deeply questionable and largely ineffective, lacking the genuine inclusion of the above-mentioned aspects as the mobilizing force of poverty eradication. UNESCO is endowed with an ethical mandate unique to the Organization, and can address the problem of poverty in terms of moral responsibility and ethical necessity to mobilize actors in the international arena. UNESCO is also the intellectual arm of the United Nations (UN) and can take the lead in fostering the understanding of poverty in relation to legal and causal responsibilities of the world community.

The first phase of the project has thus been the conceptual development of poverty as it relates to human rights. The second phase will be to reach out to the community of non–governmental organizations (NGOs), decision-makers and the general public to nourish action with the conceptual analysis produced by the scholars and to foster strategies on combating poverty through the framework of human rights.

Pierre Sané, former Secretary-General of Amnesty International and currently the Assistant Director-General for Social and Human Sciences at UNESCO, has given tremendous support to the project through his vision and direction. This project would not have continued in its current form without his guidance. On behalf of the UNESCO Poverty and Human Rights Team, I would like to thank Thomas Pogge for his relentless efforts in giving his energy, wisdom and commitment to the realization of the present publication and to the project. He supported the project from the very beginning and has given precious advice and support to the team despite difficulties and obstacles. I would like to express my deep gratitude to the central figures of the project who gave their support and collaborated with the team: Stephen Marks, Arjun Sengupta, Paul Hunt, Christine Chinkin, Chaloka Beyani, Lucie Lamarche, Paolo Pinheiro, Miloon Kothari and Rio Hada. I would like to thank the UNESCO Team on Poverty and Human Rights, beginning with Mrs. Feriel Ait-Ouyahia, the coordinator, who worked hard to realize the project with me: Annali Kristiansen, Kristina Balalovska, Marlova Jovchelovitch Noleto, Beatrice Maria Godinho Barros Coelho, Paolo Fontani, and Firmin Eduardo Matoko. I would also like to thank Rekha Nath and David Mollica for organizing and carefully editing the final manuscript. Finally, I would like to say how grateful I am to the solid support given to me for my work by the Chief of Section, Moufida Goucha, as well as by my colleagues at UNESCO for the project: Victor Billeh, René Zapata, and Hans D'Orville.

While putting the finishing touches on his contribution to the present volume, our colleague Alan Gewirth passed away. We are grateful to his wife, Jean Laves, for her help in finalizing his essay according to his wishes.

Alan Gewirth was a great pioneer in teaching and writing about human rights who made important contributions also in medieval political philosophy, early modern philosophy, and ethics. He was born in Manhattan in 1912 and received his AB from Columbia University in 1934. After two years of graduate study there, he spent 1936–7 at Cornell and then moved to the University of Chicago as assistant to Richard McKeon. Having served four years in the army, he spent 1946–7 at Columbia on the GI Bill, receiving his Ph.D. in philosophy in 1948. He taught at the University of Chicago until he retired in 1982 as the Edward Carson Waller Distinguished Service Professor. Gewirth served as president of the American Philosophical Association and the American Society for Legal and Political Philosophy and was a Fellow of the American Academy of Arts and Sciences. His main books are *Reason and Morality* (1978), *Human Rights: Essays on Justification and Applications* (1982), *The Community of Rights* (1996), and *Self-Fulfillment* (1998). At the time of his death, he was working on a new book, *Human Rights and Global Justice*. He died on May 9, 2004, at the age of 91. We, all who have worked together on this volume, are dedicating it to his memory.

Mika Shino

Teamleader of the Poverty and Human Rights Project
Section of Philosophy and Human Sciences
UNESCO, Paris Headquarters

Contents

List of Contributors

Marcelo Alegre is Professor of Law and Philosophy at the University of Buenos Aires and Director of the University of Palermo Law School. He received a Doctorate of Juridical Science at New York University under the supervision of Thomas Nagel with a dissertation on egalitarian rights and constitutional democracy. He works in the fields of constitutional law and moral, legal and political philosophy.

Elizabeth Ashford is a lecturer in Philosophy at the University of St Andrews. She has been a Visiting Faculty Fellow in Ethics at the Harvard University Edmond J. Safra Foundation Center for Ethics and an H. L. A. Hart Visiting Fellow at the Oxford University Centre for Ethics and the Philosophy of Law. Her main research interests are in ethics and contemporary political philosophy, and her publications include 'Utilitarianism, Integrity and Partiality' (*Journal of Philosophy* 97, 2000), and 'The Demandingness of Scanlon's Contractualism' (*Ethics* 113, 2003).

Tom Campbell is Professorial Fellow at the Centre for Applied Philosophy and Public Ethics at Charles Sturt University, Canberra, as well as Distinguished Associate at the Centre for Commercial Law, Australian National University, and Visiting Professor at King's College Law School, London. He was formerly Professor of Law at the Australian National University and Professor of Jurisprudence in the University of Glasgow. His interests are in legal and political philosophy and business and professional ethics. His most recent book is *Rights: A Critical Introduction* (Routledge 2006).

Simon Caney is Professor in Political Theory at Oxford University and Fellow and Tutor in politics at Magdalen College. He is the author of *Justice Beyond Borders* (Oxford University Press 2005). He has published articles on liberalism, perfectionism, global distributive justice, human rights, humanitarian intervention, sovereignty, and national self-determination. He is currently working on global environmental justice and cosmopolitan principles of distributive justice and is writing a book provisionally entitled *On Cosmopolitanism* (under contract to Oxford University Press).

Stéphane Chauvier is Professor of Philosophy at the University of Caen, France. His main research interests are in contemporary political philosophy and theories of social justice. He has published two books and various articles on international justice and transnational migration and is currently working on the question of natural resources ownership.

Álvaro de Vita is Professor Associado of Political Science at the University of São Paulo, Brazil. His main research interests are modern theories of justice, questions of inequality and poverty, and the relation between democracy and justice. He has published *A justiça igualitária e seus críticos* [*Egalitarian Justice and Its Critics*]

(São Paulo: Martins Fontes 2007). Representative of his work are 'Individual Preferences and Social Justice' (*Brazilian Review of Social Sciences*, special issue, 1, 2000) and 'Moral Reasoning and Political Deliberation' (*RIFD. Quaderni Della Rivista Internazionale Di Filosofia Del Diritto*, special issue, 4, 2004).

Marc Fleurbaey is research director at CNRS-CERSES (Paris), a member of the Institut d'Economie Publique (Marseilles), and a Lachmann Fellow at the London School of Economics. He works in the intersection of philosophy and economics, specifically on social choice and distributive justice: fairness and inequality, prioritarianism, and egalitarianism.

Roberto Gargarella has an SJD from the University of Chicago and is a researcher at the National Research Council for Science and Technology of Argentina as well as Professor of Constitutional Theory at Universidad Torcuato Di Tella, Buenos Aires. A former John Simon Guggenheim and Harry Frank Guggenheim Fellow, he has published extensively on issues of legal and political philosophy, as well as on US and Latin American constitutionalism. His latest book is *Courts and Social Transformation in New Democracies* (Ashgate 2006).

Alan Gewirth was the Edward Carson Waller Distinguished Service Professor of Philosophy Emeritus at the University of Chicago. He was an internationally renowned scholar who made important contributions in medieval political philosophy, early modern philosophy, and ethics (especially the theory of rights). His lifelong devotion to teaching and research continued unabated after his 1982 retirement: When the University constituted its Human Rights Program in 1997, Gewirth became a charter member of its board and also developed and taught its primary course. He published two monographs in the 1990s and was at work on another, *Human Rights and Global Justice*, at his death in May 2004.

Osvaldo Guariglia is a Senior Researcher at the National Research Council for Science and Technology of Argentina and Professor *honoris causa* at the University of La Plata. A former Professor of the University of Buenos Aires, his research interests include Aristotelian, Stoic, and Kantian ethics, as well as public ethics, distributive justice and, more recently, economic and social human rights. His latest books are *Ethics and Human Rights in a Postmetaphysical Time* (Buenos Aires 2002), and *Morality: Universalistic Ethics and Moral Subject* (in Italian, Naples 2002).

Regina Kreide teaches political and sociological theory at the J. W. Goethe University in Frankfurt. She previously was Visiting Scholar at Columbia University and Research Assistant at the Goethe University. Her research interests are human rights, global justice, equality, transnational democracy, and quality of life. She is currently working on a book about problems of global justice.

Thomas Pogge is Professor of Political Science at Columbia University and Professorial Fellow in the Centre for Applied Philosophy and Public Ethics at the Australian National University. His research interests include moral and political philosophy, Kant, and global justice. His latest books are *World Poverty and*

Human Rights (Polity 2002) and *John Rawls: His Life and Theory of Justice* (Oxford University Press 2007).

Arjun Sengupta is one of India's leading economists who moved between economic research and teaching and policymaking at the highest levels. He currently serves as a Member of Parliament, as Chair of the National Commission on Enterprises in the Unorganized/Informal Sector (with cabinet rank), as the UN's Independent Expert on Human Rights and Extreme Poverty, and as Chair of the New Delhi Centre for Development and Human Rights. He has been an Adjunct Professor of Development and Human Rights in the Public Health Faculty of Harvard University and a Professor in Jawaharlal Nehru University's School of International Studies. Sengupta has also served as an Executive Director of the IMF and as administrative and technical head of the Planning Commission of India, as its Member Secretary.

John Tasioulas is Fellow and Tutor in Philosophy at Corpus Christi College, Oxford. He has been a Visiting Fellow at the Australian National University and the University of Melbourne. His research interests are in moral, legal, and political philosophy. Recent publications include 'Punishment and Repentance', *Philosophy* 81 (2006) and 'Customary International Law and the Quest for Global Justice', in A. Perreau-Saussine and J. B. Murphy (eds.), *The Nature of Customary Law: Philosophical, Historical and Legal Perspectives* (Cambridge University Press 2006). With Samantha Besson, he is co-editing a volume of new essays entitled *The Philosophy of International Law* for Oxford University Press.

Leif Wenar is Professor of Philosophy at the University of Sheffield. He has been a Fellow of the Princeton University Center for Human Values, the Murphy Institute of Political Economy at Tulane, and the Carnegie Council for Ethics and International Affairs. He has published on a range of topics in political, legal, and moral philosophy.

Introduction

Thomas Pogge

In his State of the Union Address of January 6, 1941, Franklin D. Roosevelt proclaimed that 'freedom means the supremacy of human rights everywhere'. He set forth four human rights in particular as guiding principles for a post-fascist world, 'attainable in our own time and generation'. These are still widely remembered as Roosevelt's 'four freedoms', but their content needs to be recalled:

The first is freedom of speech and expression—everywhere in the world.

The second is freedom of every person to worship God in his own way—everywhere in the world.

The third is freedom from want, which, translated into world terms, means economic understandings which will secure to every nation a healthy peacetime life for its inhabitants—everywhere in the world.

The fourth is freedom from fear, which, translated into world terms, means a world-wide reduction of armaments to such a point and in such a thorough fashion that no nation will be in a position to commit an act of physical aggression against any neighbor—anywhere in the world.

Today, none of the human rights Roosevelt proclaimed is close to being fully realized. Yet the struggle continues. The book before you addresses Roosevelt's third freedom in particular. But we understand that all four freedoms are interconnected. Where fear and hostility reign, all human rights are more easily crushed in the name of 'security'. And where freedom of speech and expression are precarious, information and debate about human rights violations are stifled. These dangers are real today, as Roosevelt's four freedoms have few active defenders among the rich and powerful anywhere. This ought not discourage the struggle for human rights. But it can and does, of course, greatly exacerbate the burden of human rights violations.

Sixty-six years after Roosevelt gave his historic speech, half of humankind are still mired in severe poverty, sharing less than 2% of a now vastly more abundant global product. And one third of all human lives still end in a premature death from poverty-related causes. This massive persistence of severe poverty is the great scandal of this globalized civilization and threatens its promised gains in peace, stability, and prosperity.

The essays collected in this volume are narrowly focused on providing a moral analysis of world poverty—more specifically, an analysis in terms of human rights. We are focusing here on *severe* poverty, or the *very* poor. This includes those living in so-called extreme poverty, for whom 'a minimum, nutritionally adequate diet plus essential non-food requirements are not affordable' (UNDP 1996: 222). But it also includes those somewhat above this extreme who live in constant peril of being rendered unable to meet their basic needs.

There are poor people in the more affluent countries who suffer social disadvantage, exclusion, and indignity on account of their grossly inferior socioeconomic position. Their 'relative' poverty falls outside the scope of our discussion, except in those exceedingly rare instances where such people are so poor in the absolute sense that their access to basic necessities is as insecure as that of the very poor in the developing world.

An exact and applicable definition of poverty is important (Reddy and Pogge 2007), for instance in tracking progress toward achieving the first of the Millennium Development Goals proclaimed by the United Nations (UN). Such an exact definition is less crucial for the more philosophical discussions of this volume. But, focusing on the monetary aspect of severe poverty alone, let me give a sense of what sort of definition would make true what I wrote above: that half of humankind are still mired in severe poverty. According to World Bank data, the global median consumption expenditure in 2001 was $925 PPP 1993 per person.[1] This means that, in 2001, half the world's population lived on more, and half on less, than what $925 could buy in the United States in 1993. To count as very poor by this standard, a family of four living in the United States in 2007 would have to be living on no more than $5,500 for the entire year (www.bls.gov/cpi/home.htm). In trying to imagine what this would be like, bear in mind that half the world's population live *below* this threshold. In fact, the poorest sixth of humankind live, on average, fully 70% below this median.[2]

Severe poverty and the powerlessness it entails are all but impossible for us affluent to imagine. Such poverty involves continuous and acute vulnerability to events over which one has no control: job loss, poor weather, illness, funeral expenses, theft, an accident, a police fine, an increase in taxes or food prices, and a wage reduction—any such event, and many more, can cut very poor persons or families off from basic necessities. The very poor are compelled to take risks. Many young women, often desperate to help their parents or siblings, leave home in hopes of better incomes. Some risk their health in factories, enduring 60-hour weeks of pressured monotony under heavy discipline—in the maquiladoras of

[1] My calculation, based on iresearch.worldbank.org/PovcalNet and World Bank 2003*a*: 235. The year 2001 is the latest for which full poverty data are available. Unless otherwise noted, '$' refers to the US dollar throughout. 'PPP' stands for 'purchasing power parities', which are further discussed in my contribution to this volume.

[2] These are the households that subsist below the World Bank's $1 per day international poverty line, defined as $392.88 PPP 1993. On average, they fall 28.4% below this line (Chen and Ravallion 2004: 152 and 158, dividing the poverty gap index by the headcount index), hence 70% below $925 PPP 1993.

Ciudad Juarez (just across the border from El Paso), perhaps, where in the last 10 years over 370 young women have been found murdered, often bearing marks of rape and torture, and many more have disappeared.[3] Others entrust their fate to traffickers who take millions of women and children far from home to be forced into abject prostitution and pornography.[4]

The very poor are typically unable to defend their civil and other legal rights effectively. They may be illiterate due to lack of schooling or preoccupied with their family's survival. Or they may be compelled by social dependency to put up with illegal treatment—as is inflicted on so many domestic servants who are enduring, far from home, sexual or other forms of severe abuse from their employers. Such horrific fates of utter humiliation and despair are suffered by millions of the very poor and yet remain completely unfelt by the more affluent. No Charles Dickens or Thomas Hardy or John Steinbeck or Toni Morrison makes these experiences vivid to us.

This volume and the seminars preparing it evolved from a UNESCO Project on Poverty and Human Rights launched in 2002 by a team of young professionals, led by Mika Shino of the Section of Philosophy. The project was developed with the guidance of Pierre Sané, who joined the Organization in 2001 as Assistant Director-General for Social and Human Sciences. At our first planning meeting in Paris in June of 2002, Sané drew a parallel between poverty and slavery, identifying as the key objective in the struggle against severe poverty its abolition in law. This thought can seem odd. One may be drawn to think of the early colonists, in Jamestown perhaps, trying to end their deprivation by passing a law against it. But reflection soon separates Sané's thought from such a pointless legislative exercise.

The legal abolition of slavery did not boil down to passing a law against it. Slavery was not some kind of rogue conduct that had been left uncriminalized and hence unpunished and undeterred. Rather, slavery was deeply embedded in the legal and social order of the United States (and other countries), enshrined in the Constitution, fugitive slave laws, and much else. Important components of the US institutional order were designed to encourage, facilitate and enforce the enslavement of black people. Ending slavery in the United States involved not the mere passing of a law against it, but a thorough restructuring of its legal system toward an institutional design that discouraged, deterred, prevented, and punished such comprehensive and permanent personal subordination.

Severe poverty today, while no less horrific than that experienced by the early American settlers, is fundamentally different in context and causation. Its persistence is not forced on us by natural contingencies of soil, seeds, or climate. Rather, its persistence is driven by the ways that economic interactions are structured: by interlocking national and international institutional arrangements. The mere fact that the poorer half of humankind consume under 2% of the global product

---

[3] cf. www.amnestyusa.org/women/juarez. Maquiladoras are export factories operated under highly favorable terms that the Mexican government maintains to attract foreign investment.

[4] cf. www.hrw.org/about/projects/traffcamp/intro.html and www.unfpa.org/gender/violence1.htm

(at market exchange rates) strongly suggests that severe poverty is wholly or very largely avoidable today. We can avoid it—not by passing laws against it but—by restructuring national and global legal systems so that everyone has real opportunities to escape and avoid severe poverty.

Some countries are far along in achieving such designs nationally, typically by complementing well-regulated markets with public outlays for education and a social safety net. In these countries, we can say, severe poverty has been abolished in law. Globalizing this achievement is more difficult, because it requires a series of reforms, each meticulously planned and carefully monitored.

While I personally share Sané's emphasis on legal and institutional reform, other contributors focus more on the contributions that individuals, corporations, government agencies, and non-governmental organizations (NGOs) can and should make to the eradication of severe poverty. The essays here assembled are therefore complementary to some extent, but also diverge on some issues concerning why severe poverty persists, how it can best be overcome, and what moral responsibilities various more privileged agents have to address it.

There is no disagreement in this volume about the deeper question whether there is a human right to freedom from severe poverty. This is deliberate. We know, of course, that this issue has been and remains controversial. This controversy led the UN to split its human rights law into two Covenants in the 1960s, a split that enabled some countries—Belize, Botswana, Haiti, Mozambique, South Africa, and the United States—to endorse civil and political human rights without having to endorse social, economic, and cultural human rights as well. Instead of revisiting this old debate, we focus on the formulation, justification, and practical implication of a human right to basic necessities. Only when a candidate human right has been given the clear and full articulation we aim for here can there be a fruitful debate about its moral plausibility. And achieving such a clear and full articulation is urgently needed for making real progress against severe poverty.

When they are vague and fuzzy, proclamations of human rights easily become a substitute for real progress. Great battles are fought, and glorious victories won, over rhetorical details that in the end make precious little difference to the real world. People used to say that it is awful, regrettable, or troubling that so many children go to bed hungry and so many mothers must watch their children die from diarrhea or some other cheaply treatable disease. Today we are more likely to say that the very poor have a human right to basic necessities, or even that their basic human rights are violated. This change of language appeals to many of us as we can now picture the poor not as shrunken wretches begging for our help, but as persons with dignity who are claiming what is theirs by right. But it is still only a new form of words, a rhetorical triumph: one in a long series of paper victories. The real task is to end severe poverty on this planet. And in this task we are failing badly, as illustrated by some 300 million premature deaths from poverty-related causes since the end of the Cold War.

Severe poverty persists on such a large scale because it is self-reinforcing, hence entrenched, in a context of great inequality: The very poor lack the resources effectively to fend for their interests while the more affluent give scant weight to these interests.

And yet, our indifference is in decline. Our debates about globalization, initially mainly fuelled by painful adjustments within the rich countries themselves, now pay increasing attention to wages and working conditions in the poor countries. And we are beginning to understand how our own corporations and governments are aggressively aggravating poverty abroad: by demanding that the poor countries spend less on education and health care in order to service their debts to us; by insisting that they extract from their populations rents for our intellectual property in drugs, seeds, compounds, production processes, and much else; by denying their goods and workers access to our vastly more lucrative markets; and by enticing and pressuring their governments to spend billions on arms imports. As British Chancellor Gordon Brown said at the World Economic Forum in Davos: 'I now sense that in 2005, hundreds, then thousands, then millions in every continent are coming together with such a set of insistent demands [to fight poverty] that no politician, no government, no world leader can ignore them' (www.voanews.com/english/2005-01-29-voa36.cfm).

Let us hope Brown's prediction will prove correct. More important, let us *make* this prediction correct. Without the popular pressure Brown foresees, the world's politicians, of rich and poor countries alike, will certainly make no real progress against severe poverty—only that rhetorical progress of summits, declarations, high-level working groups, and all that, which showcase dissimulation and hypocrisy while debasing the language ('pledge', 'undertaking', 'intolerable', 'concern', 'priority', 'regret', etc.) and enticing the unwary into believing that everything humanly possible is already being done in our behalf.

There are historical examples of how ordinary people, acting together, can moralize politics. Here Sané's parallel to slavery is instructive once more. A crucial step in ending slavery was Great Britain's nineteenth-century initiative of enforcing, unilaterally and worldwide, a ban on all maritime slave trade irrespective of a vessel's ownership, registration, port of origin, or destination. It is hard to see how this could have been perceived as being in the best interests, crudely understood, of the British commercial elite or citizenry: Britain bore the whole cost of enforcing its ban as well as additional opportunity costs from lost trade, especially with Latin America. Though implemented by the government, the British anti-slavery initiative was driven by a massive domestic mobilization of ordinary people who, inspired by a deep religious or moral revulsion against slavery, gathered into an irresistible abolitionist movement (Drescher 1986). These ordinary people of all stations—from dock workers to writers, from clerics to housewives—abolished slavery, just like that, once and for all. If they could do this, in one of Britain's finest hours, then we ordinary people from all continents can fulfill Brown's prediction and abolish severe poverty.

In the book before you, fifteen authors seek to contribute to this task by developing and clarifying the arguments that make this task morally compelling. Taking for granted that a human right to basic necessities is undeniable, we focus on the concrete claims such a right entails. Our subtitle expresses this focus: Who Owes

What to the Very Poor? The human rights of the poor do not merely remain unfulfilled, like those of the Jamestown colonists facing a severe winter. They remain unfulfilled by human choice. The persistence of severe poverty depends on human decisions at all levels—from large political decisions about the basic rules of our national or global economy to small personal decisions about consumption, savings, and NGO contributions. To make serious progress against severe poverty, human agents must change some of their decisions and ways of decision-making. But which decisions and decision procedures, by which human agents, can plausibly be criticized for contributing to severe poverty, for violating the human rights of the very poor? What is a plausible assignment of responsibilities for eradicating such poverty? And what moral constraints are there on advancing the cause of poverty eradication? This book seeks well-grounded answers to these questions, which vindicate the practical importance of the human rights perspective on poverty eradication by giving a clear sense of direction to the collective effort to end severe poverty in our time.

My opening essay argues that severe poverty should be classified as a human rights violation insofar as it is a foreseeable and avoidable effect of how the world economy is currently structured. Quite apart from any positive duty the more privileged may have to help the very poor, we have a negative duty not to harm them through our uncompensated contribution to imposing upon them a global institutional order which is so designed that it foreseeably produces avoidable human rights deficits on a massive scale. Describing how the affluent are involved in shaping and upholding the global institutional order and how this order systemically sustains world poverty, I conclude that the affluent are harming the global poor and have a shared negative responsibility to work toward the eradication of severe poverty worldwide.

By contrast, Tom Campbell argues that the issues of who causes poverty and how it comes about are not decisive in deeming it a violation of a human right. Rather, the violation arises primarily from the fact that poverty itself is a state of great misery and suffering whose worldwide eradication is today quite feasible. The fact that it can be eradicated at such low cost to the world's affluent makes its continuation especially egregious. In order to end the perpetuation of these human rights violations, Campbell offers the idea of a redistributive scheme, in the form of his Global Humanitarian Levy (GHL) that would be based on his principle of humanity and implemented globally through an organization like the UN.

Rather than addressing how poverty has come about or can be relieved, John Tasioulas examines the sense in which there can actually be a human right to be free from poverty based on interests shared by all of humanity. He contends that we can assert the existence of such a right even if it is currently unenforceable and even if the positive obligations that are correlative to it have not been fully specified and allocated to identifiable duty-bearers. He goes on to argue that the interest-based account of human rights obviates the need to choose between interactional and institutional understandings of human rights. In conclusion, he considers the ways in which such an account is and is not committed to asserting the priority of rights over duties.

Àlvaro de Vita approaches the topic from a perspective similar to mine. He emphasizes the importance of shifting part of the responsibility for severe poverty and inequality from the national to the international level. And he argues for a justice (as opposed to a humanitarian) approach that focuses on the role the international economic order plays in the perpetuation of massive inequality. Responding to those who object to any principle of international distributive justice, de Vita defends such a principle and argues that, in light of it, we can and should reshape the international order toward reducing severe poverty and inequality.

While Marc Fleurbaey agrees with de Vita that we can regard poverty as a violation of human rights in the sense that it is coercively imposed upon the poor, he focuses more specifically on the oppressive nature of poverty itself as contrary to personal integrity. He argues that the way in which the global market economy operates undermines the integrity of poverty-stricken individuals who are forced to act against their will and to make decisions they would not make if their basic socioeconomic needs were met. A society that allows poverty to persist is oppressive because it severely restricts the choices of the poor. If we value personal integrity as a human right then we must recognize severe poverty as an avoidable violation of it.

Regina Kreide argues that the slow pace of mitigating global poverty is caused in part by political problems that mirror some still unresolved theoretical questions. She argues for a path between individualist theories (like Campbell's), which she criticizes for imposing overly demanding obligations on everyone while neglect- ing the structural conditions that cause poverty, and institutional theories (like mine), which she criticizes for undervaluing the utility of development aid for poverty reduction. She thus proposes an integrated view that considers features of poverty itself. In particular, she concludes that poverty is an infringement of social autonomy and in this way a human rights violation that should be eradicated.

Elizabeth Ashford finds my view that the global economic order causes a great deal of severe poverty to be compelling but also defective for supporting only negative duties. She examines the case for positive duties as supported by Kantian and utilitarian schools of thought and argues for a morally grounded human right to be free from poverty, which entails both negative and positive duties. Having argued that poverty violates fundamental human interests, Ashford concludes that there are positive and negative duties that should be borne primarily by organizations that significantly impact the poor as well as by most affluent people.

Like the previous three authors, Alan Gewirth focuses on the human depri- vations suffered while in a state of poverty. He argues that persons lose their capacity to act as moral agents because their freedom and their well-being are undermined by their lack of the means to subsistence. Efforts to reduce poverty should target all persons whose capacity for moral agency is at risk, rather than merely compatriots or other specific groups. Furthermore, Gewirth elaborates the important role democracy must play in fully realizing the basic human right to be free from poverty.

Marcelo Alegre, too, argues for the importance of democratic constitutions that include socioeconomic rights. He appeals to the fundamental human interest in freedom from poverty and argues that the case for such rights is greatly strengthened by data about how cheap it is to fulfill them. While he agrees with Campbell that the slightness of the effort required for poverty's eradication makes this a compelling goal for humankind, Alegre argues that the claim to be free from poverty flows from a principle of humanity that should be understood not as charity or simple benevolence but as a core element of justice.

Leif Wenar approaches Alegre's considerations of cost from a new angle by situating them within a comprehensive account of how we assign moral responsibility. In order to address the issue of who is morally responsible for alleviating severe poverty, Wenar sketches a general theory of assigning responsibility for averting threats to individuals' basic well-being. He does so by examining common cases in which we assign moral responsibility for averting threats and extrapolating from these the guiding principle that those who can most easily prevent threats to basic well-being should have the primary obligation to do so. This principle helps locate who is responsible for relieving the severe poverty that currently threatens so many.

Also recognizing that duties to relieve global poverty should be based on the capacity to do so, Simon Caney further argues that a human right to be free from severe poverty (HRP) is best justified by appeal to a universal human interest in eliminating poverty as an intrinsic evil. Severe poverty is bad in an unqualified sense, and it is therefore irrelevant how it comes about or whether certain parties interact in an unfair manner with the poor. As a matter of justice, humans are entitled to relief from severe poverty regardless of its cause. Accordingly, we need positive duties of justice in addition to negative duties in order to address *all* severe poverty.

Stéphane Chauvier too seeks to formulate an argument that characterizes all severe poverty as manifesting unfulfilled human rights. He presents a set of empirical conditions that poverty must satisfy in order to be considered a human rights violation. Given that poverty can be eradicated through human effort, he argues that the poor have a political claim upon their state based on the social contract, which places a positive duty upon states. Yet beyond a political right to be free from poverty, there is a natural right to the same, from which it follows that globally there is a negative duty not to violate people's right to access to essential human goods.

Arjun Sengupta examines violations of the human right to be free from poverty in both the national and global spheres. In particular, he focuses on how poverty ought to be eradicated and what this implies for states and international institutions. He argues that freedom from poverty entails a right to development: to the social, political, and economic conditions that allow the poor to thrive. His largely state-focused view emphasizes that states have a duty to formulate and implement development policies and assigns to the international community a secondary role in supporting and cooperating with these state policies.

Osvaldo Guariglia explicates the human right to be free from poverty by examining the duties it entails for different actors. In so doing, he discusses the complex relations between negative and positive rights and duties. He agrees with Sengupta that the primary duty to eradicate poverty falls upon the state in which it occurs and that the duty of the affluent countries is subsidiary to that of the developing states. Like other authors, Guariglia recognizes a responsibility for social institutions and their effects, but his discussion of this responsibility is primarily focused on domestic institutional factors involved in the perpetuation of poverty.

Roberto Gargarella examines the relationship between poor citizens and the state to which they belong. He identifies the state as the primary duty-bearer for ensuring the well-being of its citizens when it can. But rather than dwelling on what others can do for the poor, Gargarella discusses what the poor are entitled to do in light of the purpose of a legal order and of moral duties toward the disadvantaged. He makes the bold proposal that in cases where the state is a contributor to avoidable severe poverty, its poor citizens have a right to disobey laws that are systemically disadvantaging them.

The book records and reflects spirited philosophical debates among its authors about the nature of and relations among human rights, about justice, positive and negative duties and obligations, social institutions, humanity, solidarity, dignity, causality, harm, identity, and collective responsibility. Nonetheless, our disagreements are greatly outweighed by what we share. We share respect for one another's views and work as well as gratitude for the opportunity to learn from one another. And we share a sense of urgency, as academics, to help focus the attention and intelligence of humankind on the eminently solvable but stubbornly persisting problem of severe poverty, which is the key obstacle to achieving Roosevelt's four freedoms. It is more undeniable now than it was in 1941 that these freedoms can be realized 'everywhere in the world' 'in our own time and generation'. We need only the political will to realize these freedoms through a concerted effort.

1

Severe Poverty as a Human Rights Violation

Thomas Pogge[*]

Everyone has the right to a standard of living adequate for the health and well-being of himself and of his family, including food, clothing, housing and medical care. (UDHR, Article 25)

Everyone is entitled to a social and international order in which the rights and freedoms set forth in this Declaration can be fully realized. (UDHR, Article 28; see Article 22)

Freedom from severe poverty is among the most important human interests. We are physical beings who need access to safe food and water, clothing, shelter, and basic medical care in order to live well—indeed, in order to live at all.

Very poor people lack secure access to sufficient quantities of these basic necessities. This sentence presupposes a narrow, absolute, and somewhat vague definition of severe poverty which suffices for this essay. Even on such a narrow definition, which corresponds roughly to the World Bank's '$2 per day' benchmark, nearly half of all human beings alive today are living in severe poverty, with many of them falling far below the threshold.

Specifically, 2,735 (out of 6,150) million human beings are reported to have lived on less than $2 per day in 2001.[1] This international poverty line is defined in terms of monthly consumption expenditure that has the same purchasing power as $65.48 had in the United States in 1993 (Chen and Ravallion 2004: 147). By this standard, US residents would have been counted as poor only if their consumption expenditure for all of 2001 had been below $963 (www.bls.gov/cpi/home.htm).

Only one-ninth to one-third of this amount is deemed necessary to reach this poverty line in poor countries—on the ground that their currencies have much greater purchasing power than their exchange rates to the US dollar would suggest. Thus, annual per capita consumption expenditure of $240 (at market exchange rates) was generally deemed sufficient to reach the $2 per day standard in 2001.

---

[*] I am deeply grateful to the students, teachers, and practitioners who have helped shape the view here presented. If it were not part of a joint effort involving many wonderful people on five continents, my work would be pointless and unsustainable.

[1] According to Chen and Ravallion (2004: 153) who have managed the World Bank's income poverty assessments for nearly two decades. They also report that 1089 million human beings were then living on less than $1 per day (ibid.).

Those who lived below $2 per day fell 42% below this benchmark on aver-age[2] and thus had annual consumption expenditure of roughly $139 (at market exchange rates) on average. These 44% of humankind thus accounted for only 1.2% of the 2001 global product (which was $31,500 billion—World Bank 2003*a*: 235).[3] With 0.9% more, all could have lived above $2 per day. In 2001, the high-income countries accounted for 81% of the world's aggregate income and 15.6% of its population (ibid., cf. n. 27 below).

It is likely that the World Bank significantly understates the extent of global poverty when it uses purchasing power parities (PPPs) to translate its interna-tional poverty lines into other currencies. Such PPPs average international price ratios across all commodities, weighting each commodity by its share in interna-tional consumption expenditure. The poor countries tend to afford the greatest price advantages for services and other 'nontradables'. These price advantages inflate the assessed purchasing power of the local currency. But they mean little to the local poor who do and must concentrate their scarce funds on a narrow set of 'tradables', mainly basic foodstuffs—which are cheaper in the poor countries, but not as much cheaper as PPPs suggest. The number of people whose monthly consumption expenditure affords less access specifically to basic necessities than $65.48 afforded in the United States in 1993 is likely to be far in excess of the World Bank's official poverty counts.[4]

Even if this conjecture is correct, it remains true that the global poverty problem is tiny in economic terms. If it were larger by one-third than the official statistics imply, the aggregate global poverty gap in 2001 would still have been a mere 1.2% of the global product.

Much smaller than commonly assumed in economic terms, the global poverty problem is also vastly larger than most assume in human terms. It is estimated that 850 million human beings are chronically undernourished, over 1,000 mil-lion lack access to safe water and 2,600 million lack access to basic sanita-tion (UNDP 2005: 24). About 2,000 million lack access to essential medicines (www.fic.nih.gov/about/plan/exec_summary.htm). Some 1,000 million have no adequate shelter and 2,000 million lack electricity (UNDP 1998: 49). Some 781 million adults are illiterate (www.uis.unesco.org) and 250 million children between 5 and 14 do wage work outside their household—often under harsh or cruel conditions: as soldiers, prostitutes, or domestic servants, or in agriculture, construction, textile, or carpet production.[5] Roughly one-third of all human

---

[2] Chen and Ravallion (2004: 152 and 158), dividing the poverty gap index by the headcount index. Those who lived below $1 per day on average fell 28.4% short of this lower benchmark (ibid.) and thus had annual consumption expenditure of roughly $86 (at market exchange rates) on average.

[3] The 1,089 million persons below $1 per day accounted for about 18% of humankind and 0.3% of the global product.

[4] See Pogge (2004*a*), and Reddy and Pogge (2007) for detailed discussion and estimates of the errors involved.

[5] The UN International Labor Organization (ILO) reports that 'some 250 million children between the ages of 5 and 14 are working in developing countries—120 million full time, 130 million part time' (www.ilo.org/public/english/standards/ipec/simpoc/stats/4stt.htm). Of these, 170.5 million children are involved in hazardous work and 8.4 million in the 'unconditionally worst' forms of child labor,

deaths, 18 million annually or 50,000 each day, are due to poverty-related causes, easily preventable through better nutrition, safe drinking water and sewage systems, cheap rehydration packs, vaccines, antibiotics, and other medicines.[6] People of color, females, and the very young are heavily overrepresented among the global poor, and hence also among those suffering the staggering effects of severe poverty.[7]

Despite the undisputed great importance of such basic necessities for human life, there is no agreement on whether human beings have a *right*, or *human right*, to such necessities. To address this disagreement, one must distinguish between the legal and the moral question. Supranational, national, and subnational systems of law create various human rights. The content of these rights and of any corresponding legal obligations and burdens depends on the legislative, judicial, and executive bodies that maintain and interpret the laws in question. In the aftermath of World War II, it has come to be widely acknowledged that there are also moral human rights, whose validity is independent of any and all governmental bodies. In their case, in fact, the dependence is thought to run the other way: Only if they respect moral human rights do governmental bodies have legitimacy, that is, the capacity to create moral obligations to comply with, and the moral authority to enforce, their laws and orders.

Human rights of both kinds can coexist in harmony. Whoever cares about moral human rights will grant that laws can greatly facilitate their realization. And human rights lawyers can acknowledge that the legal rights and obligations they draft and interpret are meant to give effect to pre-existing moral rights. In fact, this acknowledgment seems implicit in the common phrase 'internationally recognized human rights'. It is clearly expressed in the Preamble of the Universal Declaration of Human Rights (UDHR), which presents this *Declaration* as stating moral human rights that exist independently of itself. This acknowledgment bears stressing because the distinction between moral and legal human rights is rarely drawn clearly. Many are therefore inclined to believe that our human rights are whatever governments declare them to be. This may be true of legal human rights. But it is false, as these governments have themselves acknowledged, of moral human rights. Governments may have views on what moral human rights there are—their endorsement of the UDHR expresses one such view. But even all governments together cannot legislate such rights out of existence.

---

which involve slavery, forced or bonded labor, forced recruitment for use in armed conflict, forced prostitution or pornography, or the production or trafficking of illegal drugs (ILO 2002: 9, 11, 17, 18).

[6] In 2002, there were about fifty-seven million human deaths. The main causes highly correlated with poverty were (with death tolls in thousands): diarrhea (1,798) and malnutrition (485), perinatal (2,462) and maternal conditions (510), childhood diseases (1,124—mainly measles), tuberculosis (1,566), malaria (1,272), meningitis (173), hepatitis (157), tropical diseases (129), respiratory infections (3,963—mainly pneumonia), HIV/AIDS (2,777) and sexually transmitted diseases (180) (WHO 2004: 120–5).

[7] Children under 5 account for about 60% or 10.6 million of the annual death toll from poverty-related causes (UNICEF 2005: inside front cover). The overrepresentation of females is documented in UNDP (2003: 310–30), UNRISD (2005), and Social Watch (2005).

In this essay, I am concerned exclusively with whether and under what conditions severe poverty violates human rights in the moral sense. For this to be possible at all, there must be some human right to basic necessities. The fundamental importance of basic necessities for any human life supports the claim that there is such a human right. But this claim is controversial nonetheless.

Those who contest it often argue as follows: Because rights entail duties, rights to basic necessities can be plausible only if the correlative duties are plausible as well. But it is not plausible to postulate such correlative duties. It is not plausible to hold everyone responsible for supplying basic necessities to all other human beings who need them. Nearly all of us affluent do much less than we might do toward helping persons in life-threatening poverty. Perhaps some of us do too little. But it is not seriously wrong, morally, to spend some of one's income on movie tickets and birthday presents, even when this money could be used to protect people elsewhere from starvation. It is surely unacceptable to describe people who do this as human rights violators. Hence there is no human right to basic necessities.

Arguments of this sort make two persuasive points. that rights are plausible only if the duties correlative to them are plausible as well; and that open-ended duties to supply basic necessities to any other human beings who need them is not plausible. The argument fails nonetheless because of two interrelated mistakes.

The first mistake is to assume we already know what the right in question is a right *to*. We know, of course, that we are discussing a right to basic necessities. But rights are addressed to agents and are in the final analysis rights to particular conduct (actions and/or omissions). And the brief description—'right to basic necessities'—does not specify what claims the holder of such a right has on the conduct of which other agents. This lack of specificity is shared by other human rights. Thus, consider an uncontroversial human right, such as the right to freedom from torture. Again, its brief description does not tell us what this right binds other agents to do or not to do. Presumably it obligates them not to engage in certain conduct that inflicts severe pain on others. But does it also obligate them to prevent such conduct by others (domestically, and also worldwide) or to help make such conduct illegal (under domestic and/or international law)?

The second, related mistake involves a false inference. It is true that human rights to basic necessities, on *some* specifications of them, entail implausible duties. It follows that we should reject human rights to basic necessities *so understood*. But the argument draws a stronger conclusion, namely that there is *no* (plausible specification of any) human right to basic necessities. This stronger conclusion is unwarranted, because there may be other formulations of such a human right that do not entail the duties shown to be implausible.

This is not a merely theoretical possibility. We can surely think of real-world cases where severe poverty involves the violation of a stringent moral duty. Think of a brutal monarch or dictator who, in order to improve his finances, decrees a tax that requires farmers to surrender half their produce to the state for export. As he could easily have foreseen, many of his subjects starve to death as a consequence of reduced domestic food supply and increased food prices. It is perfectly plausible to say that his conduct violates a stringent moral duty to these people. We can then find a plausible general formulation of this duty and specify a human right to basic necessities correlative to it—as a suitably qualified right not to be treated in ways that will foreseeably and avoidably deprive one of one's livelihood. So specified, the right does not entail the implausible duties considered earlier.

The main lesson from these introductory remarks is that it is inadvisable to begin with a debate about the pros and cons of accepting a human right to basic necessities. This question is too crude by assuming we already understand what the content of such a right would be. Instead, we should first think about the various dimensions in which such rights can be differently specified. Diverse specifications of human rights differ in what claims the right-holder has on the conduct of others. By examining which such claims and correlative duties are plausible, we can try to specify human rights so that they protect persons from severe poverty as far as possible without making unreasonable demands on others.

The debate about subsistence rights is often conceived and conducted as one that is about whether any such rights exist at all. But this is a misconception. Even conservatives and libertarians, who typically present themselves as rejecting subsistence rights, will recognize as human rights violations some state policies that foreseeably and avoidably produce life-threatening poverty—the tax decreed by the ruler in my hypothetical, for example, or Stalin's policies during 1930–3, which caused some 7–10 million famine deaths among peasants, mostly in the Ukraine, whom he considered enemies of his regime.

The debate is better framed, then, as one about the *range* of a human right to basic necessities. What moral claims does such a right give its holders against other agents? What correlative duties does it impose upon others? Under what conditions does severe poverty manifest a human rights violation, and which agents are then responsible for such violation? In response to these questions, conservatives and libertarians advocate a tight range. They hold that severe poverty typically manifests no human rights violation, that historically the human right to basic necessities (as they want to specify it) has been violated only rarely. Others assert a broader range for such rights. Let us try to make some progress toward resolving such disagreement.

1.1. FACTORS IN THE CAUSAL EXPLANATION OF SEVERE POVERTY

It is hard to imagine a case of torture that does not involve a violation of the human right not to be tortured. When human beings are tortured, there are torturers as well as, often, additional agents who order, authorize, facilitate, monitor, or allow the ordeal. Clearly, severe poverty is different. A person or group may encounter life-threatening poverty that no other agents have causally contributed to and no one can alleviate. The relevant analogue to torture is then not poverty, but rather a certain kind of impoverishment that other agents are causally and morally responsible for. To clarify this idea, we must discuss the possible causes of poverty and then identify the cases in which agents culpably play a causal role. There are various ways in which agents may be causally related to the severe poverty of others. Let me paradigmatically examine three types of such relations.

1.1.1. Causes of Type One: Acts (Interactional Harms)

A straightforward case of interactional harm is one where persons act in such a way that they foreseeably and avoidably deprive others of their livelihood. People living upstream pollute the river, thereby poisoning the fish on which people downstream depend for nourishment or income. One might deem this a clear-cut human rights violation, provided the people upstream can foresee the likely effects of their conduct and have a reasonable alternative (so their own survival does not require their pollution of the river).

Straightforward cases of this sort are rare in the modern age. Severe poverty in our world typically involves many cooperating causes. This complicates the picture. Even if it can be shown that some particular act caused starvation, the agent can point to other causally relevant factors without which her act would not have had this terrible effect. Thus, a supporter of the pre-2003 UN sanctions against Iraq could point out that some of the massive deprivations they caused could have been avoided had Saddam Hussein not expended much of the state's remaining wealth on palaces and the military. Similarly, Hussein could say that his expenditures would have caused no deprivations but for the sanctions.

Often the cooperating causes include not merely acts by other agents, but also the rules under which these agents operate. A bank repossesses a bankrupt farm, leaving the family who owned it destitute and homeless. Bank officials may excuse their conduct by blaming the resulting poverty on the bankruptcy laws, which permit creditors to take everything. If we do not take full advantage of the law, they may add, we cannot compete with other banks and thus would eventually go bankrupt ourselves.

The presence of many cooperating causes makes it harder to assign responsibility in another way as well: by reducing *visibility*, that is, the ability of agents to foresee the remoter effects of what they do. It is a commonplace that we now live in a heavily interdependent world in which the effects of one agent's conduct can reverberate around the globe. This is true not merely of the conduct of a few influential governments, corporations, agencies, and individuals. It holds for all those affluent enough significantly to participate in market transactions: as shoppers or investors, for example, or as employers or employees. Many of our daily economic decisions affect the livelihoods of other people: of salespeople, waiters, storeowners, or of managers and shareholders of corporations whose products we buy. These effects may be negligible, for the most part. But the impact of our economic transactions does not stop there, because these transactions also influence the *decisions* of storeowners, managers, etc., in ways that affect the liveli-hoods of yet further people. Our tastes and preferences as consumers influence which coffees, fruits, flowers, toys, T-shirts, or computers are imported in what quantities and where tourist destinations are developed abroad. Such decisions in turn affect employment opportunities in poor countries and thus can have a profound impact on the livelihoods of families there. Given the extreme vulnerability of many poor people abroad, a change in fashions in an affluent country can easily save hundreds of lives by providing desperately needed employment and can just as easily kill hundreds of children prematurely by throwing their parents out of work. In fact, it can have both effects simultaneously by shifting demand from one poor-country factory to another.

It is impossible to know which of our decisions have such effects on people in the poor countries, and what their effects are exactly. This is unknowable because, as they reverberate around the globe, the effects of my economic decisions intermingle with the effects of billions of decisions made by others, and it is impossible to try to disentangle, even *ex post*, the impact of *my* decision from this vast traffic by trying to figure out how things would have gone had I acted differently. This is impossible, because my decisions have their impact, in very large part, by affecting the later situations of other agents and the decisions they will then make (which in turn influence the situations and decisions of yet further agents, and so on). These indirect effects are not only too numerous to trace. They are also, in most cases, impossible to estimate, because one cannot deduce from what persons did in the situations they actually encountered what they would have done in the different situations they would have encountered had I acted differently.

It is highly likely that any affluent person has been involved in ordinary market transactions that have caused deaths or saved lives. This is not a comfortable reflection. We may be tempted to banish it quickly with the thought that, over time, the numbers of deaths caused and lives saved by one's ordinary market transactions probably tend to net out to zero: It comes out in the wash, as they say. But this thought cannot give much comfort when we think of those we affect as individual human beings rather than as some vast homogeneous mass. Insofar as we understand it, and feel it, the reflection remains disturbing and gives us moral reason to work for a world in which there are not hundreds of millions living on the brink of an early death from starvation or easily curable diseases.

But this reflection cannot give us moral reason to make our ordinary economic decisions in such a way as to avoid aggravating anyone's severe poverty. Endorsing this aim is pointless because we cannot possibly live up to it. In the present world it is completely beyond the capacity of affluent individuals to shape their economic conduct so as to avoid causing any poverty deaths in the poor countries. Adopting this aim could produce feelings of guilt and anxiety in us, but it could not possibly achieve its point: It could not ensure that our ordinary economic transactions cause no severe deprivations in poor countries.

In the present world, even the most important remoter effects of our conduct can often not be known—even afterwards, let alone in advance. This pervasive feature of modern economic systems shifts attention from the responsibilities of individual agents to that of other causal factors affording sufficient visibility. Among these may be larger, collective agents who have superior informational capacities and often make decisions closer to the impact of harm—multinational corporations, for instance, who operate manufacturing or resource extraction facilities in poor countries. An executive of such a corporation can find out whether pollution from its plants is causing disease, for example, or whether the wages paid to those making its products are inadequate or how vulnerable they are in the event of dismissal. The fact that such executives often do not bother to find out does not render the impact of their decisions any less foreseeable.

Suppose a corporation running a mining operation in a poor country pipes its toxic wastes into a nearby river, causing predictable severe harms downstream where people depend on this river for water and food. This would seem to be a clear-cut violation of the human right to basic necessities. Somewhat less clear-cut is the case of a corporate decision that foreseeably causes unemployment, with dire consequences, among very poor people. Thus, a corporation may close a factory to shift production to an even cheaper location, for instance, or it may buy up land while evicting existing sharecroppers. These cases are more difficult, because the corporate decision may seem like a mere omission: The corporation is not harming people, it is merely withdrawing a benefit. And the same may be said about a corporation that pays its workers so little as to render their lives vulnerable to even minor emergencies. Here too it may seem that the corporation is benefiting (surely not harming) these workers by giving them an employment option they would otherwise lack.

Yet, the larger context in which the fired workers, the evicted sharecroppers and the underpaid workers are placed may be marred by dire scarcity or grievous injustice. And this affects the moral assessment of corporate conduct. Even if there is nothing wrong with employing, on extremely ungenerous terms, someone who has other reasonable options, it may be seriously wrong so to employ someone who, because of her religion, sex, skin color, or nationality cannot find another job. By paying such a person half of what persons of different faith or sex or color or nationality get paid for the same work, the corporation would be taking advantage of an injustice. It is unclear whether such corporate conduct amounts to a human rights violation. But we may hope to get clearer about this question by examining how this notion is related to omissions and to social institutions.

1.1.2. 'Causes' of Type Two: Omissions (Interactional Failures to Alleviate)

Cases of this type were already mentioned briefly. Here some agents can act so as to alleviate severe poverty that they had no role in creating or maintaining.

Many reject a moral duty to help in such cases as absurd. If there were such a duty, would not affluent persons be required to give most of their incomes for poverty eradication efforts in the poor countries? This requirement conflicts with moral convictions that are widely shared—among those who would be subject to the requirement. However, their special position with respect to the purported duty should cast doubt on the reliability of their moral intuitions. They may well have a far more vivid sense of the burden such a requirement would impose upon themselves than they have of the much greater burdens of hunger and disease it would alleviate.

Moreover, the rejection as sketched commits the mistake exposed above (p. 14), by presenting the options in stark binary terms. Even if it is true that agents are not morally required to relieve *all* life-threatening poverty they can alleviate, they may still be morally required to relieve *some*. There are two obvious ways of limiting the demandingness of such a duty. It may be tied to some special relationship between those in severe poverty and those in a position to ease their plight. The duty may, for instance, apply only to relatives, neighbors, compatriots, or those who, immediately confronted with severe poverty, are salient in comparison to others also able to help. The demandingness of a duty of alleviation might also be limited by requiring only that one do one's fair share toward poverty alleviation (Murphy 2000). This limit works not by limiting the class of poor people one must help, but by limiting how much one must do in total.

Obviously, limits of both kinds can be combined. Thus one might say that a human right to basic necessities gives each human being in severe poverty a claim against only her more affluent relatives who must each do their fair share toward protecting her from severe poverty.

Still, even such a limited moral requirement may seem problematic. If you have relatives who are very poor through no fault of yours, and if you do nothing to relieve their severe poverty even while you have the ability to do so, can you really then be condemned as a *violator* of their human rights? Most affluent people believe that the answer is no. They hold that one is not a human rights violator merely for failing to help or protect someone whose human rights are unfulfilled or threatened. One violates human rights only if one deprives others of the objects of their human rights or actively renders their access to these objects insecure. Someone who merely fails to protect others' secure access to the objects of their human rights is not, for this reason alone, a human rights violator.

The issue is contested. Many—including some authors in this volume—argue that human rights do impose such duties to protect and to aid. Henry Shue (1996*a*), though he uses the language of 'basic rights', is an important early example of this view, as is David Luban, who writes: 'A human right, then, will be a right whose beneficiaries are all humans and whose obligors are all humans in a position to effect the right' (Luban 1985: 209).

I have considerable sympathies with both sides of this controversy. My *moral* sympathies lie with those who are appalled by how the vast majority of affluent people ignore the massive underfulfillment of human rights in the present world—even when they do not doubt that they can prevent terrible deprivations at low cost to themselves. I agree that such disregard is morally impermissible and profoundly wrong. Yet, my *intellectual* sympathies lie with those who hold that an agent's failure at low cost to protect and to rescue others from extreme deprivation, however morally appalling, is not a human rights violation.

Much of this persistent disagreement can possibly be explained, and perhaps narrowed, by distinguishing clearly two different ways in which a human right may entail a duty. The first way is direct, by correlativity: *B*'s duty not to participate in torturing *A* is correlative to, and in this way entailed by, *A*'s right not to be tortured. Here any violation of the duty is *ipso facto* a violation of the right. The second way is indirect, by presupposition: Any plausible rationale for a human right not to be tortured implies a moral duty to protect people from torture when one can do so at negligible risk or cost to oneself and others. There may well be duties that are entailed by human rights only in the second way: If torture is so horrible that one must not engage in it even when a great deal is at stake, then it is hard to deny that one ought to save a person from torture when one can do so at small cost. If this inference is indeed undeniable, then the human right entails the moral duty. But this entailment does not show that the duty is *correlative* to the human right, that any violation of the duty is also a violation of the right.

The distinction just drawn is important on the plausible assumption that any human rights violation may *in principle* be prevented by force—which means that some (not necessarily all) agents are morally permitted to use force to prevent the violation provided this can be done without disproportional harm to the would-be violator or others. Thus, if failures to prevent torture when one could prevent it at negligible risk or cost are themselves human rights violations, then it is in principle permissible to force people to prevent torture under such conditions. And likewise for failures to aid the starving. Some embrace this conclusion and applaud, for example, theft from the affluent for the relief of severe poverty (Unger 1996). But many reject this conclusion; and it is important to show them that this rejection is consistent with recognizing stringent moral duties, entailed by human rights, whose violation does not constitute a human rights violation.

To reach widely sharable conclusions about when severe poverty decidedly *is* a human rights violation, let me focus exclusively then on *negative duties* correlative to human rights: duties not to harm others in certain specific ways. This focus is consistent with affirming (or denying) that human rights also entail stringent moral duties to help and protect and with affirming or denying the in-principle enforceability of such positive duties. But my focus places these issues outside the scope of the present essay.

It is instructive, I think, to examine severe poverty in the world today under this restrictive assumption. Such an examination highlights the minimal constraints one's conduct must uncontroversially meet if it is not to be human rights violating. That these constraints are negative duties means that they require only omissions, not acts, and that they can be violated only by acts, not by omissions. Agents must refrain from (actively) causing others' human rights to be unfulfilled.

The distinction between acts and omissions is notoriously hard to make precise. An agent can behave (move her body) in many different ways, and it is hard to sort all these different possible courses of conduct into those that constitute passive omissions with regard to a certain situation and those that constitute active interference. Suppose Bob is in danger of drowning far out at sea. Jill is nearby with her boat. She sees Bob struggling in the water, but sails away. There are different ways of describing this case. On one description, Jill fails to rescue Bob and her conduct thus constitutes an omission. On another description, Jill does not remain passive, but rather actively sails the boat out of Bob's reach. Those who find the first description morally significant can say that Jill did not harm Bob because he would have died even if Jill had not been on the scene at all. Jill need therefore not be mentioned in a causal account of Bob's death. Those who see the second description as the morally significant one can say that Jill harmed Bob because he would not have died had she not sailed her boat away from him. So Jill's conduct does play a causal role in Bob's death.

How can one resolve such disputes about what might be called the appropriate *passivity baseline*? For determining which course of conduct by one agent is to count as 'remaining passive' with respect to another's predicament, can we rely on how the latter would have fared in the absence of the former? To understand this idea, we must first decide how to 'slice' the relevant agent's conduct in the time dimension. Let me illustrate this point with another case. Suppose drought is destroying your garden while you are on vacation. Your neighbor could easily water your plants, but she does nothing. Before you left, she had agreed to look after your garden during your absence (as you had looked after hers on earlier occasions). One might say that what your neighbor is responsible for is a mere omission—had she been absent from the scene, your plants would still have died. But this view depends on selecting a certain short period of her conduct for examination. Selecting instead a larger time frame that extends backward in time, we could say that she actively brought about the damage through a complex course of conduct in which she first agreed to look after your garden, causing you to rely on her, and then failed to act as agreed. Had she not been 'on the scene' in this more expansive sense, then you would have stayed home or asked someone else for this favor and, either way, your garden would have survived.[8]

This question of time frame is highly relevant to severe poverty in the poor countries. Taking a very narrow time frame, it may seem that the relation of the affluent countries and their citizens to poverty abroad is one of potential helpers who can at most be accused of failing sufficiently to alleviate severe poverty, thereby violating a merely positive duty. Taking a larger time frame, it appears that the rich countries played a significant causal role in the recent perpetuation of severe poverty by working hard to persuade and entice the political elites of the poor countries to accept the rather lopsided terms of WTO globalization. An even larger time frame would bring colonialism, slavery and genocide into the picture. Such a very large time frame is often rejected as obviously absurd: How can we hold the present citizens of affluent countries responsible for crimes these countries committed fifty-plus years ago? Surely, we do not inherit our ancestors' sins! But the same people who make this argument strangely see no problem in their inheriting the fruits of those sins. They feel quite entitled to possess and defend the wealth their ancestors acquired fifty-plus years ago through these very crimes committed against foreigners. Many societies owe the very land they occupy and all its natural resources to genocidal conquest.

---

[8] See Bennett (1995) for much more detailed discussion of such considerations.

The different ways of specifying time frames and of distinguishing acts and omissions show, one might say, that there is a conventional element in the causal explanations we give. When a toddler drowns in a shallow pond, our reports would certainly mention in an explanatory vein the presence of adults nearby who did nothing to help. When street children starve in a poor slum, our reports (if this gets reported at all) would probably not mention that the tourists in the nearby hotel regard these children as a pest and ignore their entreaties. Insofar as the conventional element in the causal explanations we give is thus informed by our moral expectations, there is the danger of circularity: We morally expect adults to help toddlers in trouble, therefore we regard the adult bystanders as a causally relevant factor in the toddler's death, and therefore we hold the adults responsible for this death. We do not morally expect tourists to help street children, therefore we do not regard the tourists as a causally relevant factor in the children's hunger, and therefore we do not hold those tourists responsible for starvation deaths among these children. What looked like a moral distinction based on an empirical one turns out to be a self-validating moral prejudice.

We have caught a glimpse of how difficult it is to make precise the intuitive distinction between acts and omissions, between positive and negative duties, in a way that is morally unbiased and thus widely acceptable to persons with different views about human rights and correlative duties. One might conclude from this difficulty that no moral weight should be placed on the distinction. On such a view, conduct should be assessed by its relative impact alone: If you behaved in a way that foreseeably led to a person's death even while you could have behaved in another way that would not have led to her death, then you are morally responsible for this death regardless of how active or passive, socially expected or unexpected, your actual and hypothetical alternative conduct may have been.

But this conclusion—defended by act-utilitarians and act-consequentialists more generally—is hard to accept. An affluent person who, in order to save $80, fails to respond to an invitation to sponsor a child in Mali with the predictable result that this child dies—such a person is not morally on a par with an affluent person who kills a child for a $80 benefit. As Wittgenstein remarked (1976: §556), 'the fact that the border between two countries is in dispute does not put the citizenship of all their inhabitants in question'. Similarly, the fact that we cannot draw an *exact* line between acts and omissions, between positive and negative duties, does not mean that we cannot apply this distinction to *any* piece of human conduct. In most cases, agreement on how to apply the distinction can be achieved in a way that sustains the near-universal conviction that detrimental relative impact of our acts is morally more significant than equally detrimental relative impact of our omissions.

Given this shared conviction, there may be significant advantages to conceiving human rights violations narrowly as breaches of negative duties. Doing so makes applications of the label more widely acceptable and also focuses attention more sharply on the kinds of misconduct it is most urgent to end. The insistence that an affluent person, in virtue of disregarding positive duties to feed, save and rescue persons caught in life-threatening poverty through no fault of their own, may be a violator of their human rights leads many to dismiss out of hand a human right to basic necessities. In fact, many who are eager to reject such a right without much thought *want* to see it formulated in this way.

Of course, a narrow conception of human rights violations brings a corresponding disadvantage: it affords less protection to the poor and oppressed. We cannot assess how big a disadvantage this is in the real world, however, without examining more closely to what extent the actual underfulfillment of human rights is due to violations of correlative negative duties, and which conduct by which agents constitutes violations of these negative duties.

Concluding this subsection, let us consider the objection that my cautions are overdone. It is widely accepted, after all, that a person's human rights impose positive duties on her government—and thereby, mediately, on her fellow citizens, who must give political and economic support to the governmental protection of human rights. It is widely accepted that citizens' human right to physical integrity gives them a moral claim against their government to operate an effective criminal justice system that prevents and deters assaults. Therefore, the objection concludes, by leaving human rights-based positive duties aside, I am conceding a point that is not seriously contested, even by most libertarians.

My response takes shape throughout the remainder of this essay. But let me offer a brief preview. Human rights are indeed widely understood as giving persons a moral claim to protective action by their government; and I certainly do not want to compromise this understanding. But why is this moral claim thought to be limited to each person's own state? What are we to make of the fact that human rights are not understood as giving persons similar moral claims against foreign governments and foreign citizens, who may be in a much better position, financially, to help underwrite a poor country's criminal justice system?

One response would hold that this common view is simply mistaken: Correctly understood, human rights do give their bearers moral claims against all human agents able to help fulfill the right. This response leads right back into the persistent disagreement discussed above which I am here trying to circumvent.

Another explanation holds that we have here a conventional division of labor built into our understanding of human rights: The positive duties correlative to human rights will be discharged more efficiently if the bearers of these duties focus their efforts within their own country. But this explanation is doubly implausible. It is plainly untrue that the fulfillment of human rights is efficiently promoted when those whose human rights are most massively and severely underfulfilled, the poor people in poor countries, are isolated from those best able to protect them. Moreover, this explanation leaves out what most would regard as highly relevant to citizens' moral claims to be protected by their government: the fact that this government subjects them to the coercive authority of its rules.

This last point suggests what I think is the best explanation: A government's positive obligation to protect the human rights of those it rules is best understood as entailed by a negative duty in much the same way as your neighbor's positive obligation to water your garden. Your moral right imposes a general negative duty on all other agents that they not make a commitment to you and then fail to honor it. Those who make no commitment to you fulfill this duty trivially. But the neighbor who made the commitment fulfills this negative duty only if she then acts as agreed. Likewise, a person's human rights impose a general negative duty on all other human agents that they not participate in imposing upon her an institutional order under which, foreseeably and avoidably, she lacks secure access to some of the objects of her human rights. Those who do not so participate fulfill this duty trivially. But those who do participate in imposing an institutional order upon her fulfill this negative duty only if they see to it that the rules they help impose afford those on whom they are imposed secure access to the objects of their human rights, insofar as this is reasonably possible.[9]

One may think that there is a significant difference between the two cases: Your neighbor consents to a task and thus to specific positive obligations. But those who participate in imposing an institutional order may not want, nor believe that they ought, to safeguard the human rights of those subjected to this order. In response, this difference is less deep than it appears. For your neighbor may neither want to, nor believe that she ought to, live up to her verbal commitment. Thus, to explain that her commitment binds her, we must invoke a moral principle whose authority and content are independent of her consent.

To dispel the doubt fully, let me present another parallel case where the feature of explicit consent is lacking. We believe that your ownership rights impose a general negative duty on all others not to use your property without permission. However, we also recognize certain emergency exceptions: I may use your car when I need it to rush someone to the hospital and I may break into your hut to save myself from a blizzard. But, when I use your property without permission in such emergency situations, I have a positive moral obligation to compensate you (for your gasoline and taxi expenses, or for any damage I caused to your hut). Fully spelled out, your ownership rights thus impose a general negative duty on all others not to use your property without permission except in emergency situations with full compensation. Those who never use your property without permission fulfill this duty trivially. But for those who, in an emergency, do use your property without permission, the negative duty entails a positive obligation whose content is independent of their consent: They must do their best to ensure that you are fully compensated (Pogge 2005c: 68–9).

I believe that, in analogy to such compensation, human rights should be understood as giving rise to minimal moral claims against those who participate in imposing social institutions. Human agents may participate in imposing social institutions only if they are also willing to help ensure that the human rights

---

[9] The last subclause indicates this qualification: Imposing an institutional order under which a human rights deficit foreseeably persists may not violate negative duties when a human rights deficit of this magnitude is either unavoidable or avoidable only at great cost in terms of culture, say, or the natural environment.

of those subjected to these institutions are fulfilled insofar as this is reasonably possible.[10]

1.1.3. Causes of Type Three: Social Institutions

Subsections 1.1.1 and 1.1.2 point to the great and increasing importance of social institutions. The discussion of omissions suggests that a very important source of positive obligations with regard to severe poverty in the modern world is our negative duty not to participate in the imposition of social institutions under which some avoidably lack secure access to the objects of their economic human rights. Our discussion of acts suggests that among the causal factors that are relevant to the incidence of severe poverty and afford good visibility, institutional factors are the most important.

The visibility afforded by institutional factors—by the rules governing economic interaction, most notably—is different, however, from the visibility enjoyed by corporations (as discussed above). When a government raises tax rates, for instance, the relative impact of this decision on the incidence of poverty and unemployment a year later may be predictable, at least roughly. ('Relative impact' here means the difference between what the incidence of unemployment *will be* at time *t* and what it *would have been* at *t* had the government not raised tax rates.) But it is not predictable which particular persons will suffer unemployment at *t* while they would have been employed at *t* if tax rates had been left unchanged. Even at *t* and thereafter it will still be unknowable who among the unemployed at *t* would be employed at *t* if tax rates had been left unchanged.

This kind of ignorance is problematic in the court room. It may be known that the people living around a polluting factory have a five times greater chance of dying prematurely from cancer than people in general and yet impossible to demonstrate of any particular cancer death that it was caused by (would not have occurred in the absence of) the pollution.

From a moral standpoint, however, this ignorance is not problematic. Even if it is unknown *which* deaths were caused by the polluting factory, it may be known roughly *how many*. And this suffices for moral assessment. Recall the rules Stalin imposed on the USSR economy in 1930–3. Even if one cannot say with certainty of any of the children, women, and men who died during this period that he or she would have survived had Stalin not imposed his noxious economic structure, it is evident nonetheless that there would have been some 7–10 million fewer deaths under feasible alternative economic institutions. It is known that Stalin's policies caused *excess poverty* and *excess mortality* from poverty-related causes, and these excesses can be quantified—albeit roughly, to be sure. This suffices for the judgment that Stalin's policies killed 7–10 million people.

---

[10] See Pogge (2002*a*: ch. 2, 2002*b*) for more detail. While I see human rights as the weightiest moral constraints on the imposition of an institutional order, I leave open here whether there are other such constraints and, if so, what they are. Different conceptions of social justice will differ on these points.

In the modern world, the rules governing economic transactions—both nationally and internationally—are the most important causal determinants of the incidence and depth of poverty. They are most important because of their great impact on the economic distribution within the jurisdiction to which they apply. Thus, even relatively minor variations in a country's laws about tax rates, labor relations, social security, and access to health care and education can have a much greater impact on poverty there than even large changes in consumer habits or in the policies of a major corporation. This point applies to the global institutional order as well. Even small changes in the rules governing international trade, lending, investment, resource use, or intellectual property can have a huge impact on the global incidence of life-threatening poverty.

Another reason why rules governing economic transactions are the most important causal determinants of the incidence and depth of poverty in the modern world derives from their greater visibility. To be sure, like the conduct of individual and collective agents, rule changes can have unintended and even unforeseeable effects. But with rules it is much easier to diagnose such effects and to make corrections. Assessing adjustments of the rules within some particular jurisdiction is relatively straightforward. One can try to estimate how a rise in the minimum wage, say, has affected the unemployment rate and per capita income in the bottom quintile. (Of course, there are other things happening in the economy besides the change in the minimum wage, so the exercise is complex and imprecise. Still, exercises of this sort can be done, and *are* done, sufficiently well in many countries.) It is more difficult, by contrast, to assess the relative impact of variations in the conduct of individual or collective agents. Such an assessment can be confined to the persons immediately affected—for example, to the employees of a corporation or to the inhabitants of a town in which an aid agency is running a project. But such a confined assessment is vulnerable to the charge of ignoring indirect effects upon outsiders. For example, when an aid agency distributes food in an impoverished town, dramatically improving the health of the townspeople, it can be claimed that the importation of free food reduces food prices in the larger region, thereby impoverishing peasants and reducing the incentives to grow food. In response to such a charge, one can try to assess the impact of the aid project upon the nutritional situation of the whole country over a period of five years, say. But within this larger frame, the aid project is a small factor whose effects are hard to discern against the background noise of many other causal factors.

A further reason why rules governing economic transactions are the most important causal determinants of the incidence and depth of poverty in the modern world is because morally successful rules are so much easier to sustain than morally successful conduct. This is so, because individual and collective agents are under continuous counter-moral pressures not merely from their ordinary self-interested concerns, but also from their competitive situation as well as from considerations of fairness. These phenomena are illustrated by the case of competing corporations, each of which may judge that it cannot afford to pass up immoral opportunities to take advantage of its employees and customers because such unilateral self-restraint would place it at an unfair competitive disadvantage vis-à-vis its less scrupulous competitors. Domestically, this sort of problem can be solved through changes in the legal rules that require all corporations, on pain of substantial penalties, to observe common standards in their treatment of customers and employees. Corporations are often willing to support such legislation (to improve the image of their industry, perhaps) even while they are unwilling to risk their competitive position through unilateral good conduct.

Similar considerations apply in the international arena, where corporations and governments compete economically. Given their concern not to fall behind in this competition and not to be unfairly handicapped through unilateral moral efforts and restraints, it is perhaps not surprising (though still appalling) that individuals, corporations, and governments have been so reluctant to make meaningful efforts toward eradicating global poverty. Most affluent countries have never gone anywhere near devoting 0.7% of their GNI to official development assistance (ODA)—a goal the UN adopted decades ago as a target to be reached by 1975. In fact, ODA shrank throughout the prosperous 1990s, from 0.33% in 1990 to 0.22% in 2000.[11] In the aftermath of the invasions of Afghanistan and Iraq, ODA is back to 0.33% in 2005,[12] but only about one-tenth of this $106 billion in ODA is spent on 'basic social services': basic education, primary health care (including reproductive health and population programs), nutrition programs, and safe water and sanitation as well as the institutional capacity for delivering these services.[13]

Again, it is possible that affluent governments and corporations could bring themselves to act much better by adopting legal norms that apply to them all and thereby relieve each of the fear that its own good conduct will unfairly disadvantage it and cause it to lose ground against its competitors. Successful efforts to reduce poverty within states exemplify this model of structural reform rather than individual moral effort. To be sure, this thought is not new, and governments have been very reluctant to commit themselves, even in joint mutuality, to serious global anti-poverty measures. Their solemn promise to halve global poverty by

[11] See UNDP (2002: 202). The United States led the decline by reducing its ODA from 0.21 to 0.10% of GNP in a time of great prosperity culminating in enormous budget surpluses (ibid.).

[12] US ODA was 0.22% in 2005—much of that going to occupied Afghanistan and Iraq and to General Musharraf's Pakistan (www.oecd.org/document/40/0,2340,en_2649_33721_36418344_1_1_1_1,00.html).

[13] See millenniumindicators.un.org/unsd/mdg/SeriesDetail.aspx?srid=592&crid=. Official spending on poverty avoidance is complemented by $7 billion in annual donations from individuals and corporations worldwide (UNDP 2003: 290). The vast majority of ODA is spent for the benefit of agents more capable of reciprocation, as is well expressed in this statement recently removed from the USAID's main website: 'The principal beneficiary of America's foreign assistance programs has always been the United States. Close to 80 percent of the US Agency for International Development's (USAID's) contracts and grants go directly to American firms. Foreign assistance programs have helped create major markets for agricultural goods, created new markets for American industrial exports and meant hundreds of thousands of jobs for Americans'.

2015 has been reiterated—in cleverly weakened formulations[14]—but has yet to result in serious implementation efforts.

This discouraging historical evidence suggests that improvements in the global institutional order are difficult to achieve and difficult to sustain. However, this fact does not undermine my hypothesis that such structural improvements are *easier* to achieve and much *easier* to sustain than equally significant unilateral improvements in the conduct of individual and collective agents. We know how much money individuals, corporations, and the governments of the affluent countries are now willing to set aside for global poverty eradication: about $18 billion annually (n. 13). This amount is very small in comparison to the harms inflicted on the global poor by evident injustices in the present global order (to be discussed in section 1.2). It is very small also in comparison to what would be required for substantial progress: The amount needed in the first few years of a serious offensive against poverty is closer to $320 billion annually.[15] It is not realistic to hope that we can achieve such a 18-fold increase in available funds through a moral change of heart of the relevant agents: affluent individuals, corporations, and governments. It is *more* realistic   though admittedly still rather unrealistic— to seek substantial progress on the poverty front through institutional reforms that make the global order less burdensome on the global poor. Accepting such reforms, affluent countries would bear some opportunity costs of making the international trade, lending, investment, and intellectual-property regimes fairer to the global poor as well as some costs of compensating for harms done—for example by helping to fund basic health facilities, vaccination programs, basic schooling, school lunches, safe water and sewage systems, basic housing, power plants and networks, banks and microlending, road, rail, and communication links where these do not yet exist. If such a reform program is to gain and maintain the support of the citizens and governments of affluent countries, it must distribute such costs and opportunity costs fairly among them in a reliable and

---

[14] At the World Food Summit in Rome, organized by the FAO in November 1996, the 186 participating governments agreed to 'pledge our political will and our common and national commitment to achieving food security for all and to an on-going effort to eradicate hunger in all countries, with an immediate [!] view to reducing the *number* of undernourished people to half their present level no later than 2015' (*Rome Declaration*, my emphasis). The *UN Millennium Declaration* proclaimed in September of 2000 commits states 'to halve, by the year 2015, the *proportion* of the world's people whose income is less than one dollar a day and the proportion of people who suffer from hunger' (my emphasis). While the old formulation aimed for a 50% reduction in the number of extremely poor people between 1996 and 2015, the new formulation—taking advantage of the 45% increase projected for 1990–2015 in the population of the poorer countries and a large 1990–2000 poverty reduction in China—aims for only a 19% reduction in this number between 1996 and 2015. See Pogge (2004*a*) for fuller analysis.

[15] See Pogge (2002*a*: ch. 8), basing this ballpark figure on the aggregate poverty gap relative to the World Bank's higher $2 per day poverty line. Amazingly, $320 billion is only 0.71% of the global product or 0.90% of the combined GNIs of the affluent countries (World Bank 2006: 289)—considerably less than annual US military spending ($466 billion in 2004) or the annual 'peace dividend' the high-income countries are still reaping from the end of the Cold War (*c*. $724 billion, cf. n. 42). Bearing its fair share of such a serious offensive against global poverty would be cheaper for the US than its current occupations of Iraq and Afghanistan.

transparent way, assuring them that their competitive position will not be eroded through others' noncompliance.

The path of global institutional reform is far more realistic and sustainable for three obvious reasons. First, the costs and opportunity costs each affluent citizen imposes on herself by supporting structural reform is extremely small relative to the contribution this reform makes to avoiding severe poverty. The reform lowers your family's standard of living by $900 annually, say, while improving by $300 annually the standard of living of hundreds of millions of poor families. By contrast, a unilateral donation in the same amount would lower your family's standard of living by $900 annually while improving by $300 annually the standard of living of only three poor families. Given such payoffs, rational agents with some moral concern for the avoidance of severe poverty will be far more willing to support structural reform than to sustain donations.[16] Second, structural reform assures citizens that costs and opportunity costs are fairly shared among the more affluent, as discussed. And third, structural reform, once in place, need not be repeated, year after year, through painful personal decisions. Continual alleviation of poverty leads to fatigue, aversion, even contempt. It requires affluent citizens to rally to the cause again and again while knowing full well that most others similarly situated contribute nothing or very little, that their own contributions are legally optional and that, no matter how much they give, they could for just a little more always save yet further children from sickness or starvation. Today, such fatigue, aversion and contempt are widespread attitudes among citizens and officials of affluent countries toward the 'aid' they dispense and its recipients.

For these reasons, I believe that the idea of severe poverty as a human rights violation should be focused, first and foremost, on social institutions—on each country's institutional order and also, and especially, on the global institutional order as well. Emphasizing this point is not meant to discourage efforts to work out what claims poor people have, in virtue of their social and economic human rights, *directly* against individual and collective agents. It is merely meant to explain why I am concentrating on the different project of working out what claims poor people have, in virtue of their social and economic human rights, on social institutions imposed upon them and thus *indirectly* against the individual and collective agents upholding these social institutions. In working on this project, I take inspiration from the Universal Declaration of Human Rights (UDHR), which does not merely postulate social and economic human rights—

Everyone has the right to a standard of living adequate for the health and well-being of himself and of his family, including food, clothing, housing and medical care (Article 25)—

but also emphasizes the relevance of such social and economic human rights to the design of the national and global institutional order:

Everyone is entitled to a social and international order in which the rights and freedoms set forth in this Declaration can be fully realized (Article 28; see Article 22).

---

[16] I owe full appreciation of the importance of this point to a discussion with Derek Parfit.

My hypothesis is that any institutional order that foreseeably produces a reasonably avoidable excess of severe poverty and of mortality from poverty-related causes manifests a human rights violation on the part of those who participate in imposing this order. In the present world, this hypothesis has important implications especially for the global institutional order and for the national institutional schemes of most countries in which severe poverty persists. In what follows, I focus on the first of these cases, on the present global institutional order, partly to complement the work of development economists who have concentrated too one-sidedly on how national institutional schemes foreseeably produce and aggravate severe poverty.

1.2. HOW FEATURES OF THE PRESENT GLOBAL ORDER CAUSE MASSIVE SEVERE POVERTY

Each day, some 50,000 human beings—mostly children, mostly female, and mostly people of color—die from starvation, diarrhea, pneumonia, tuberculosis, malaria, measles, perinatal, and maternal conditions and other poverty-related causes. This continuous global death toll matches that of the December 2004 tsunami every few days, and it matches, every three years, the entire death toll of World War II, concentration camps and gulags included.

I believe that most of this annual death toll and of the much larger poverty problem it epitomizes are avoidable through minor modifications in the global order that would entail at most slight reductions in the incomes of the affluent. Such reforms have been blocked by the governments of the affluent countries, which are ruthlessly advancing their own interests and those of their corporations and citizens, designing and imposing a global institutional order that, continually and foreseeably, produces vast excesses of severe poverty and premature poverty deaths.

There are three main strategies for denying this charge. One can deny that variations in the design of the global order have any significant impact on the evolution of severe poverty worldwide. Failing this, one can claim that the present global order is optimal or close to optimal in terms of poverty avoidance. And, should this strategy fail as well, one can still contend that the present global order, insofar as it is suboptimal in terms of poverty avoidance, is not *causing* severe poverty but merely failing to alleviate such poverty (caused by other factors) as much as it might. I will discuss these three strategies in this sequence.

1.2.1. The Purely Domestic Poverty Thesis

Those who wish to deny that variations in the design of the global institutional order have a significant impact on the evolution of severe poverty explain such poverty by reference to national or local factors alone. John Rawls is a prominent example. He claims that, when societies fail to thrive, 'the problem is commonly the nature of the public political culture and the religious and philosophical traditions that underlie its institutions. The great social evils in poorer societies are likely to be oppressive government and corrupt elites'.[17] 'The causes of the wealth of a people and the forms it takes lie in their political culture and in the religious, philosophical and moral traditions that support the basic structure of their political and social institutions, as well as in the industriousness and cooperative talents of its members, all supported by their political virtues. ... The political culture of a burdened society is all-important ... Crucial also is the country's population policy' (Rawls 1999*b*: 108). Accordingly, Rawls holds that our moral responsibility with regard to severe poverty abroad can be fully described as a 'duty of assistance' (ibid. 37–8, 106–20).

It is well to recall briefly that existing peoples have arrived at their present levels of social, economic, and cultural development through a historical process that was pervaded by enslavement, colonialism, even genocide. Though these monumental crimes are now past, their legacy of great inequalities would be unacceptable even if peoples were now masters of their own development. In response, it is often said that colonialism is too long ago to help explain poverty and radical inequality today. But consider the 30:1 gap in per capita income in 1960, when Europe released Africa from the colonial yoke. Even if Africa had consistently enjoyed growth in per capita income one full percentage point above Europe's, this gap ratio would still be 19:1 today. At this rate, Africa would be catching up with Europe in 2302.

Consider also how such a huge economic gap entails inequalities in the competence and bargaining power that Africans and Europeans can bring to bear in negotiations about the terms of their interactions. Relations structured under so unequal conditions are likely to be more beneficial to the stronger party and thus tend to reinforce the initial economic inequality. This phenomenon surely plays some role in explaining why the gap in per capita income has actually widened to over 40:1, showing that, since decolonization, average annual growth in per capita income was much lower in Africa than in Europe.[18] Rawls (implausibly) finds such entrenched economic inequality morally acceptable when it originates in earlier choices freely made within each people. But his justification is irrelevant to this world, where our enormous economic advantage is deeply tainted by how it accumulated over the course of *one* historical process that has devastated the societies and cultures of four continents.

Let us leave aside the continuing legacies of historical crimes and focus on the empirical view that, at least in the post-colonial era which brought impressive

---

[17] Rawls (1993*b*: 77)—echoing Michael Walzer: 'it is not the sign for some collective derangement or radical incapacity for a political community to produce an authoritarian regime. Indeed, the history, culture, and religion of the community may be such that authoritarian regimes come, as it were, naturally, reflecting a widely shared world view or way of life' (Walzer 1980*a*: 224–5).

[18] Data from the World Bank's WDI database (devdata.worldbank.org/dataonline). In 2005, annual GNI per capita was $745 in sub-Saharan Africa versus $35,131 in the high-income countries (World Bank 2006: 289)—at 47:1 ratio.

growth in global per capita income, the causes of the *persistence* of severe poverty, and hence the key to its eradication, lie within the poor countries themselves.

Many find this view compelling in light of the great variation in how the former colonies have evolved over the past forty years. Some of them have done very well in economic growth and poverty reduction while others exhibit worsening poverty and declining per capita incomes. Is it not obvious that such strongly divergent national trajectories must be due to differing *domestic* causal factors in the countries concerned? And is it not clear, then, that the persistence of severe poverty is due to local causes?

However oft-repeated and well-received, this reasoning is fallacious. When national economic trajectories diverge, then there must indeed be local (country-specific) factors at work that explain the divergence. But it does not follow that global factors play no role. Consider this parallel: There are great variations in the performance of my students, which must be due to local (student-specific) factors. But it does not follow that these factors fully explain the performance of my class. Clearly, 'global' factors—including the teacher, reading materials, teaching times, classroom, libraries, etc.—also play an important role. They can greatly influence the overall progress of a class—and even the distribution of this progress, as when a racist or sexist teacher impedes the learning of his black or female students.

Exposure of the popular fallacy does not yet settle the issue. Dramatic divergences in national poverty trajectories do not prove that global institutional factors exert no powerful influence on the evolution of severe poverty worldwide. But is there such an influence? It is hard to doubt that there is. In the modern world, the traffic of international and even intranational economic transactions is profoundly shaped by an elaborate system of treaties and conventions about trade, investments, loans, patents, copyrights, trademarks, double taxation, labor standards, environmental protection, use of seabed resources, and much else. These different aspects of the present global institutional order realize highly specific design decisions within a vast space of alternative design possibilities. It is incredible on its face that all these alternative ways of structuring the world economy would have produced the same evolution in the overall incidence and geographical distribution of severe poverty worldwide.

And yet this is the conclusion one may easily come to when one studies what the experts write about poverty. Across several academic disciplines, there is a vast literature analyzing the causal roles of local factors, such as climate, natural environment, resources, food habits, diseases, history, religion, culture, social institutions, economic policies, leadership personalities, and much else.[19] Advice dispensed by development economists and others is also overwhelmingly focused on the design of national economic institutions and policies while taking the global institutional context as a given. Thus, libertarian economists of the 'freshwater' school (so dubbed because its leading lights have taught in Chicago)

---

[19] Some widely read recent contributions are Landes (1998), Diamond (1999), Harrison and Huntington (2001), and Sachs (2005). But there are hundreds more.

argue that a country's best way to expel human misery is economic growth and its best way to achieve economic growth is to foster free enterprise with a minimum in taxes, regulations, and red tape. A competing school of thought, represented by Amartya Sen, contends that poverty persists because poor countries have *too little* government: public schools, hospitals, and infrastructure. Sen's favorite poster child is the Indian state of Kerala where leftist governments have given priority to fulfilling basic needs and have thereby achieved more for that population's health, education, and life expectancy than the governments of other, more afflu-ent Indian states. These hot and worthwhile debates about appropriate economic policies and social institutions for the poor countries crowd out any inquiry into the causal role that the rules of our globalized world economy may play in the persistence of severe poverty.

This research bias among social scientists is surely partly due to bad reasons: They, and their readers, are overly impressed by dramatic international diver-gences in economic performance; and they, like their compatriots, feel emotion-ally more comfortable (and careerwise more confident) with work that traces the persistence of severe poverty abroad back to national and local causes abroad rather than to global institutional arrangements their own governments are involved in designing and upholding. But there is also a good methodological reason for the research bias toward national and local causes: There being only this one world to observe, it is hard to obtain solid evidence about how the overall incidence of poverty would have evolved differently if this or that global factor had been different. By contrast, evidence about the effects of national and local factors can be gleaned from simultaneous observation of many poor countries that differ in their natural environment, history, culture, political and economic system, and government policies.

For various good and bad reasons, economists pay little attention to how the design of the global institutional order influences the evolution of severe poverty worldwide. As a consequence, we have little evidence about the relative impact of the various features of the global order. Such lack of evidence of impact is often perceived as evidence of lack of impact. But this inference is, of course, fallacious. And evidence is not, in any case, completely lacking. As will be shown, there is enough evidence to support at least rough judgments about the causal role of global institutional factors in the persistence of severe poverty. This matter is further discussed in 1.2.2 and 1.2.3.3.

1.2.2. The Panglossian View of the Present Global Order

Once it is accepted that how we structure the world economy makes a difference to the evolution of poverty worldwide, it becomes interesting to examine the present global institutional order in regard to its relative impact on severe poverty. Here it is often claimed that we live, in this regard, in the best of all possible worlds: that the present global order is optimal or nearly optimal in terms of poverty avoidance.

A commonsensical way of doubting this claim might develop a counterhypothesis in four steps: First, the interest in avoiding severe poverty is not the only interest to which those who negotiate the design of particular aspects of the global institutional order are sensitive. Any such negotiators are likely to be sensitive also to the interest of their home government in its domestic political success and, partly as a consequence of this, sensitive to their compatriots' interest in economic prosperity. Second, at least with negotiators for the more affluent states, these 'nationalist' interests are not (to put it mildly) perfectly aligned with the interest in global poverty avoidance. In negotiations about the design of the global order, particular decisions that are best for the governments, corporations, or citizens of the affluent countries are not always best in terms of avoiding severe poverty elsewhere. Third, when faced with such conflicts, negotiators for the affluent states generally (are instructed to) give precedence to the interests of their own country's government, corporations, and citizens over the interests of the global poor. Fourth, the affluent states enjoy great advantages in bargaining power and expertise. With only 15.7% of the world's population, the high-income countries have 79% of the world's income (World Bank 2006: 289) and can therefore exact a high price for access to their gigantic markets. Their advantages in bargaining power and expertise enable the affluent states and their negotiators to deflect the design of the global order from what would be best for poverty avoidance toward a better accommodation of the interests of the governments, corporations, and citizens of the affluent countries. These four steps lead to the commonsensical counterhypothesis: We should expect that the design of the global institutional order reflects the shared interests of the governments, corporations, and citizens of the affluent countries more than the interest in global poverty avoidance, insofar as these interests conflict.

There is a great deal of evidence that this counterhypothesis is true. Let me offer, for instance, this quote from *The Economist* magazine which—being strongly supportive of WTO globalization and having vilified, on its cover and in its editorial pages, the protesters against this globalization as enemies of the poor[20]—is surely not biased in my favor:

Rich countries cut their tariffs by less in the Uruguay Round than poor ones did. Since then, they have found new ways to close their markets, notably by imposing anti-dumping duties on imports they deem 'unfairly cheap'. Rich countries are particularly protectionist in many of the sectors where developing countries are best able to compete, such as agriculture, textiles, and clothing. As a result, according to a new study by Thomas Hertel, of Purdue University, and Will Martin, of the World Bank, rich countries' average tariffs on manufacturing imports from poor countries are four times higher than those on imports from other rich countries. This imposes a big burden on poor countries. The United Nations Conference on Trade and Development (UNCTAD) estimates that they could export $700 billion more a year by 2005 if rich countries did more to open their markets. Poor countries

---

[20] See, for instance, *The Economist* cover of December 11, 1999, showing an Indian child in rags with the heading 'The real losers of Seattle'. See also its editorial in the same issue (ibid. 15), its flimsy 'The case for globalisation', (*The Economist*, September 23, 2000: 19–20 and 85–7), and its remarkable lead editorial 'A question of justice?' (*The Economist*, March 11, 2004).

are also hobbled by a lack of know-how. Many had little understanding of what they signed up to in the Uruguay Round. That ignorance is now costing them dear. Michael Finger of the World Bank and Philip Schuler of the University of Maryland estimate that implementing commitments to improve trade procedures and establish technical and intellectual-property standards can cost more than a year's development budget for the poorest countries. Moreover, in those areas where poor countries could benefit from world trade rules, they are often unable to do so. ... Of the WTO's 134 members, 29 do not even have missions at its headquarters in Geneva. Many more can barely afford to bring cases to the WTO.[21]

The quote brings out how the present rules of the game favor the affluent countries by allowing them to continue protecting their markets through quotas, tariffs, anti-dumping duties, export credits, and huge subsidies to domestic producers in ways that poor countries are not permitted, or cannot afford, to match.[22] Other important examples include the WTO regulations of cross-border investment and intellectual property rights.[23]

Such asymmetrical rules increase the share of global economic growth going to the affluent countries and decrease the share going to the poor countries relative to what these shares would be under symmetrical rules of free and open competition. The asymmetries in the rules thus reinforce the very inequality that enables the governments of the affluent countries to impose these asymmetries in the first place.[24] The same rules also tend to strengthen the position of the corporate and ruling elites within countries who can exert much greater influence on the design of these rules than the rest of the population. (Protectionist measures grandfathered by WTO rules are often contrary to the interests of most citizens of

[21] *The Economist*, (September 25, 1999: 89). The three cited studies—Hertel and Martin (1999), UNCTAD (1999*b*: 143), and Finger and Schuler (1999)—are included in the bibliography.

[22] In his speech, 'Cutting Agricultural Subsidies' (globalenvision.org/library/6/309), former World Bank Chief Economist Nick Stern stated that in 2002 the rich countries spent about $300 billion on export subsidies for agricultural products alone, roughly six times their total development aid. He said that cows receive annual subsidies of about $2,700 in Japan and $900 in Europe—far above the annual income of most human beings. He also cited protectionist anti-dumping actions, bureaucratic applications of safety and sanitation standards, and textile tariffs and quotas as barriers to poor-country exports: 'Every textile job in an industrialized country saved by these barriers costs about 35 jobs in these industries in low-income countries'. Stern was especially critical of escalating tariffs—duties that are lowest on unprocessed raw materials and rise sharply with each step of processing and value added—for undermining manufacturing and employment in poor countries, thus helping to confine Ghana and Cote D'Ivoire to the export of unprocessed cocoa beans, Uganda and Kenya to the export of raw coffee beans, and Mali and Burkina Faso to the export of raw cotton. He estimated that full elimination of agricultural protection and production subsidies in the rich countries would raise agricultural and food exports from low- and middle-income countries by 24% and total annual rural income in these countries by about $60 billion (about three quarters of the global poor live in such rural areas).

[23] The Trade-Related Aspects of Intellectual Property Rights (TRIPs) Treaty was concluded in 1995. For discussion of its content and impact, see UNDP (2001: ch. 5), Correa (2000), Juma (1999), Watal (2000), Pogge (2005*b*), and www.cptech.org/ip

[24] In what follows, I use income inequalities to substantiate this point. Yet, inequalities in wealth are even greater since the affluent typically have more net worth than annual income, while the poor typically own less than one annual income.

the affluent countries adopting these measures.) The result is rising intranational inequality in most countries which also hampers poverty reduction.

The World Bank reports that GNI per capita, PPP (current international dollars), in the high-income countries rose 52.6% in real terms over the 1990–2001 globalization period (devdata.worldbank.org/dataonline). World Bank interactive software (iresearch.worldbank.org/PovcalNet/jsp/index.jsp) can be used to calculate how the poorer half of humankind have fared, in terms of their real (inflation/PPP adjusted) consumption expenditure, during this same period. Here are the gains for various percentiles, labeled from the bottom up:

+20.4% for the 50th percentile (median)
+21.0% for the 45th percentile
+21.1% for the 40th percentile
+20.0% for the 35th percentile
+18.7% for the 30th percentile
+17.2% for the 25th percentile
+15.9% for the 20th percentile
+14.4% for the 15th percentile
+12.9% for the 10th percentile
+11.9% for the 7th percentile
+10.4% for the 5th percentile
+6.6% for the 3rd percentile
+1.0% for the 2nd percentile
−7.3% for the 1st (bottom) percentile.[25]

There is a clear pattern. As trend data about malnutrition and poverty also confirm,[26] the global poor are not participating proportionally in global economic growth. And as they fall further and further behind, they become ever more marginalized, with their interests ignored in both national and international decision-making. Annual spending power of $100 or $200 per person does not command much attention when per capita incomes in the affluent countries are some 100–200 times higher.[27]

---

[25] These calculations extend the work of Branko Milanovic who reported that, for the first five years of the present globalization period, 'the bottom 5 percent of the world grew poorer, as their real incomes decreased between 1988 and 1993 by 1/4[!], while the richest quintile grew richer. It gained 12% in real terms, that is it grew more than twice as much as mean world income (5.7%)' (Milanovic 2002: 88). I am grateful to Rekha Nath and Aedan Whyatt for doing all the calculations in this paragraph.

[26] The UNDP reports annually on the number of malnourished, which has been stuck around 800 million and recently stood at 850 million (UNDP 2005: 24). For 1987–2001, Chen and Ravallion (2004: 153) report a 7% drop in the population living below $1 per day but a 10.4% rise in the population below $2 per day.

[27] Many economists find this comparison misleading, claiming that it should instead be made in terms of PPPs, which would reduce the ratio by a factor of 4. However, market exchange rates are the more appropriate measure for assessing the influence (bargaining power and expertise) that parties can bring to bear. Market exchange rates are also the appropriate measure for assessing the *avoidability* of poverty (n. 15). For comparing standards of living, market exchange rates are indeed inappropriate. But general-consumption PPPs are also problematic, as we have seen (text to note 4).

These facts should suffice to refute the Panglossian view: The present design of the global order is not, and nowhere near, optimal in terms of poverty avoidance. This value would be better served, for instance, if the poorest countries received financial support toward hiring first-rate experts to advise them how to articulate their interests in WTO negotiations, toward maintaining missions at WTO head-quarters in Geneva, toward bringing cases before the WTO, and toward coping with the mountains of regulations they are required to implement. Poverty avoidance would also be better served if these countries faced lesser constraints and handicaps on their exports into the affluent countries: The $700 billion reported annual loss in export opportunities due to rich-country protectionism is huge relative to ODA and relative to poor-country exports and GNIs. Poverty avoidance would also be better served if the WTO Treaty had included a global minimum wage and minimal global constraints on working hours and working conditions in order to constrain the current 'race to the bottom' where poor countries competing for foreign investment must outbid one another by offering ever more exploitable and mistreatable workforces. Poverty avoidance would also be better served if the Law of the Sea Treaty guaranteed the poor countries some share of the value of harvested seabed resources[28] and if the affluent countries were required to pay for the negative externalities we impose on the poor: for the pollution we have produced over many decades and the resulting effects on their environment and climate, for the rapid depletion and resulting higher prices of natural resources, for our exports of landmines and small arms, for our suppression of trade in generic medicines and seeds, and for the violence caused by our demand for drugs and our war on drugs.

Perhaps the most important example for how the global rules are designed against the interests of the poor is the current regime for rewarding and encour-aging pharmaceutical research. Under the TRIPs regime (see n. 23), inventors of new drugs are rewarded with a twenty-year monopoly. This regime causes most existing drugs to be priced out of the reach of the global poor. It also skews pharmaceutical research toward the affluent: Medical conditions accounting for 90% of the global disease burden receive only 10% of all pharmaceutical research worldwide (see Ramsey 2001 and GFHR 2004). Of the 1,393 new drugs approved between 1975 and 1999, only 13 were for tropical diseases—of which five were byproducts of veterinary research and two commissioned by the military.[29] When drug companies are rewarded with monopoly prices, they are put in a morally untenable position: to be cost-effective, they must focus their research on the health problems of the affluent and price even life-saving medications out of the reach of vast numbers of poor patients.

There are other, much better ways of encouraging pharmaceutical research. An obvious alternative is a regime under which inventors of essential medicines are

---

[28] Such guarantees were part of the initial 1982 version of the Treaty, but the Clinton administration succeeded in renegotiating them out of the Treaty just before the latter came into force in 1996 (Pogge 2002a: 125–6).

[29] Médecins Sans Frontières, www.msf.org/msfinternational/invoke.cfm?component=article& objectid=2753A561-D23D-631D-B583C5F9A9EEC3CB&method=full_html

rewarded in proportion to the impact of their invention on the global disease burden. This solution would align the interests of inventor firms and the generic drug producers. Inventor firms would want their patented inventions to be widely copied, mass-produced, and sold as cheaply as possible, as this would magnify their health impact. Many poor patients would then have access to drugs that, as things are, they cannot afford. And affluent patients would gain as well, by paying substantially less for drugs and medical insurance. This solution would also greatly expand research into diseases that, under the current system, attract very little research—hepatitis, meningitis, dengue fever, leprosy, trypanosomiasis (sleeping sickness and Chagas disease), river blindness, leishmaniasis, Buruli ulcer, lymphatic filariasis, schistosomiasis (bilharzia), malaria, tuberculosis and many more. In time, this one change in the global rules alone could halve the number of annual poverty deaths (see Pogge 2005*b*). Compared to such an alternative, the current TRIPs regime produces an unimaginable excess of suffering and death by discouraging the development of new medicines for the diseases of the poor and also by enforcing monopolies that prevent the mass-production of generic versions of life-saving drugs without shielding the global poor from exorbitant monopoly markups.

Examples could be multiplied. It is clear that there are feasible variations to the present global order that would dramatically reduce the incidence of severe poverty worldwide, far below the current, staggering figures. This order is *not* optimal in terms of poverty avoidance.

1.2.3. Is the Present Global Order Merely Less Beneficial Than It Might Be?

As the first two possible lines of defense have turned out to be indefensible, attention turns to the third: Can one say that the global institutional order, though clearly and greatly suboptimal in terms of poverty avoidance, is nonetheless not harmful to the global poor and therefore not a violation of their human rights? Let us turn to this final challenge to my view.

This challenge is especially important if one leaves undisputed, as I have here done, the narrow account of human rights violations according to which agents can be condemned as human rights violators only if they *actively* cause human rights to be underfulfilled, in violation of a *negative* duty. Appealing to this narrow account, the countries shaping and imposing the present global order could argue as follows: It is true that the incidence of severe poverty is greater under the present design of the global order than it would be if we had designed this order differently. But it does not follow that the existing global order *causes* excess poverty or excess poverty deaths, that it *harms* or *kills* anyone, or that it *violates* human rights. The design of this order is merely failing to benefit people, failing to be as protective of human life as it might be. And the same should then be said about our decision to impose the existing global institutional order rather than a more poverty-avoiding alternative: This decision does not cause excess poverty or excess poverty deaths, is not violating human rights by harming and killing people. It is merely failing to benefit people and failing to prevent human deaths. Collectively (just as individually), we are at most failing to do all we can to fulfill human rights.

This defense strategy appeals to something like the distinction between acts and omissions. Its objective is to diminish the moral significance of the rich states' decision to impose the present global order rather than a foreseeably more poverty-avoiding alternative by assigning this decision the status of a mere omission. Now the relevant countries are clearly active in formulating the global economic rules they want, in pressing for their acceptance, and in prosecuting their enforcement. This is undeniable. To be plausible, the defense strategy must then apply the act/omission distinction at another place: not to how the relevant governments are related to the global rules, but to how these global rules are related to the avoidable excess poverty. The idea must be that the rules governing the world economy are not actively causing excess poverty, thus harming and killing people, but merely passively failing to prevent severe poverty, failing to protect people from harm.

As we have seen (subsection 1.1.1), the distinction between acts and omissions is difficult enough when applied to the conduct of individual and collective agents. The application of such a distinction to social institutions and rules is at first baffling. When more premature deaths occur under some system of rules than would occur under a feasible alternative, we might say that there are excess deaths under the existing regime. But how can we sort such excess deaths into those that the existing rules *cause* (bring about) and those these rules merely *fail to prevent* (let happen)? Let us examine three ideas for how this defense strategy can be made to work.

1.2.3.1. *Invoking Baseline Comparisons*

The apparently empirical question whether 'globalization' is harming or benefiting the global poor plays a major role in public debates about the present global order and about, more specifically, the WTO treaties and the roles of the International Monetary Fund (IMF), the World Bank, the G7/G8 and the Organization for Economic Cooperation and Development (OECD). Harm and benefit are comparative notions, involving the idea of people being worse off, or better off. But what is the implied baseline to which the current fate of the global poor is to be compared? What is the alternative fate in comparison to which they are either worse off (and therefore being harmed) or better off (and therefore being benefited by globalization)?

In most cases, it turns out, the popular debate is about the question whether severe poverty worldwide has been rising or falling in the period since this globalization process began in the late 1980s. This question is hotly debated, with considerable career prizes awarded to any economists with a good story of declining poverty.

Yet, this debate is irrelevant to the moral assessment of this globalization process, epitomized by the WTO framework, which the governments of the affluent West have pressed upon the world. The moral charge before us is that governments, by imposing a global institutional order under which great excesses of severe poverty and poverty deaths persist, are violating the human rights of many poor people. The plausibility of this charge is unaffected by whether severe poverty is rising or falling. To see this, consider the analogous charges that slave-holding societies harmed and violated the human rights of those they enslaved or that the Nazis violated the human rights of those they confined and killed in their concentration camps. These charges can certainly not be defeated by showing that the rate of victimization declined (with fewer people being enslaved or killed each year than the year before). Of course, the words 'harm' and 'benefit' are sometimes appropriately used with implicit reference to an earlier state of affairs. But in the case at hand, such a historical baseline is irrelevant. For even if it were true that there is not as much severe poverty in the world today as there was fifteen years ago (but see n. 26), we could not infer therefrom that the present global order is (in a morally significant sense) *benefiting* the global poor. Drawing this inference, we would beg the whole question by simply assuming the incidence of severe poverty fifteen years ago as the appropriate no-harm baseline. Just as the claim that the Nazis violated the human rights of those they killed cannot be refuted by showing that the number of such killings declined, so the claim that the imposition of the present global order violates the human rights of those who live in—and all too often die from—severe poverty cannot be refuted by showing that their numbers are falling (see Pogge 2005*c*: 55–8).

No less inconclusive than such *diachronic* comparisons are *subjunctive* comparisons with a historical baseline. Even if it is true that there is not as much severe poverty under the present WTO regime as there would now be if the preceding regime General Agreement on Tariffs and Trade (GATT) had continued, we cannot infer therefrom that the present global institutional order is (in a morally significant sense) benefiting the global poor. Drawing this inference, we would once again beg the question by simply positing the incidence of severe poverty as it would have evolved under continued GATT rules as the appropriate no-harm baseline. By the same reasoning the military junta under Senior General Than Shwe could claim to be benefiting the Burmese people provided only that they are better off than they would now be if the predecessor junta under General Ne Win were still in power. And by the same reasoning we could argue that the regime of Jim Crow laws (www.nps.gov/malu/documents/jim_crow_laws.htm) did not harm African-Americans in the US South because they were better off than they would have been had slavery continued.

Sometimes subjunctive comparisons are presented with a historical baseline that is defined by reference to a much earlier time. Thus it is said that Africans today are no worse off than they would now be if there had never been any significant contacts with people outside Africa. In response, we should of course question to what extent there are knowable facts about such a remote alternate history. We should also, once again, question the moral relevance of this hypothetical involving continued mutual isolation: If world history had transpired without col-onization and enslavement, then there would—*perhaps*—now be affluent people in Europe and very poor ones in Africa. But these African persons and populations would be entirely different from those now actually living there, who in fact are very deeply shaped and scarred by their continent's involuntary encounter with European invaders. So we cannot tell starving Africans that *they* would be starving and *we* would be affluent even if the crimes of colonialism had never occurred. Without these crimes there would not be the actually existing radical inequality which consists in *these* persons being affluent and *those* being extremely poor.

Similar considerations also refute the moral relevance of subjunctive comparisons with a *hypothetical* baseline—the claim, for instance, that even more people would live and die even more miserably in some fictional state of nature than in this world as we have made it. In response, there are many different ways of describing the 'state of nature', and it is unclear from the received literature offering and discussing such descriptions how one of them can be singled out as the morally uniquely appropriate specification. Moreover, it is doubtful that *any* coherently describable state of nature on this planet would be able to match our globalized civilization's record of sustaining a stable death toll of 18 million premature deaths per year from poverty-related causes (see Pogge 2002*a*: 136–9). If no such state of nature can be described, then it cannot be said that the present global order is benefiting the global poor by reducing severe poverty below what it would be in a state of nature. Finally, it still needs to be shown how the claim that some people are being harmed now can be undermined by pointing out that people in a state of nature would be even worse off. If such an argument were successful, would it not show that anything one person or group does to another counts as a harming only if it reduces the latter below the state-of-nature baseline? If we are not harming the 2,735 million human beings we are keeping in severe poverty, then enslavement did not harm the slaves either, if only they were no worse off than people would be in the relevant state of nature.

Baseline comparisons do not then afford a promising ground for denying that the present global institutional order involves violations of the human rights of those impoverished under it—or, indeed, for defending any other institutional schemes from the charge that they involve human rights violations. Recall, for instance, the early decades of the United States, when men designed and imposed an institutional order that greatly disadvantaged women. The claim that the imposition of this order violated the human rights of women cannot be refuted by any diachronic comparison with how women had fared before, under British rule. It cannot be refuted by any subjunctive comparison with how women would have been faring under continued British rule or in a state of nature. What matters is whether the imposition of the institutional order in question foreseeably led to severe burdens on women that were reasonably avoidable through a more evenhanded institutional design (see Pogge 2005*c*: 61).

1.2.3.2. *Invoking the Consent of the Global Poor*

Another common way of denying that the present global institutional order is harming the poor, violating their human rights, is by appeal to the venerable precept of *volenti non fit iniuria*—no injustice is being done to those who consent. Someone physically abusing another is not harming him in the morally relevant sense if he has given prior consent to such treatment, for money perhaps or masochistic pleasure. Likewise, a social order under which excess poverty persists is not harming the poor if they have previously consented to the imposition of this order. And consent they surely did! Membership in the WTO is voluntary. Since the poor themselves have signed on to the rules as they are, the imposition of these rules cannot be characterized as harming them.

This line of argument is thoroughly refuted by four mutually independent considerations. First, appeal to consent can defeat the charge of human rights violation only if the human rights in question are alienable and, more specifically, waivable by consent. Yet, on the usual understanding of moral and legal human rights, they cannot be so waived: Persons cannot waive their human rights to personal freedom, political participation, freedom of expression, or freedom from torture. Persons can promise, through a religious vow perhaps, to serve another, to refrain from voting, or to keep silent. But, wherever human rights are respected, such promises are legally unenforceable and thus do not succeed in waiving the right in question. There are various reasons for conceiving human rights in this way: A person changes over time, and her later self has a vital interest in being able to avoid truly horrific burdens her earlier self had risked or incurred. Moreover, the option of placing such burdens on one's future self is likely to be disadvantageous even to the earlier self by encouraging predators seeking to elicit a waiver from this earlier self through manipulation of her or of her circumstances—for instance, by getting her into a life-threatening situation from which one then offers to rescue her at the price of her permanent enslavement (Pogge 1989: 49–50). Finally, waivers of human rights impose considerable burdens on third parties who will be (more or less directly) confronted with the resulting distress of people enslaved or tortured or starving.

Second, even assuming that human rights to basic necessities are waivable, an appeal to consent cannot justify the horrific burdens imposed on children: Of roughly eighteen million annual deaths from poverty-related causes, 10.6 million are children under five (n. 5 and n. 7). Does anyone really want to claim that these small children have consented to our global order—or that anyone else is entitled to consent to their horrifying fate on their behalf? Insofar as the present global order is, foreseeably, greatly suboptimal in terms of avoiding severe poverty of children, the claim that this order violates their human rights cannot be blocked by any conceivable appeal to consent.

Third, most countries containing severely impoverished people were and are not meaningfully democratic. For example, Nigeria's accession to the WTO, on January 1, 1995, was effected by its vicious military dictator Sani Abacha. Myanmar's, on the same day, by the notorious SLORC junta (State Law and Order Restoration Council). Indonesia's, on the same day, by murderous kleptocrat Suharto. Zimbabwe's, on March 5, 1995, by brutal Robert Mugabe. And that of Zaire (since renamed the Congo), on March 27, 1997, by hated dictator Mobutu Sese Seko. These rulers consented—presumably for good prudential reasons. But does their success in subjecting a population to their rule by force of arms give them the right to consent on behalf of those they are oppressing? Does this success entitle *us* to count the rulers' signatures as the populations' consent? On any credible account of consent, the answer is no. We cannot invalidate the complaint of those now suffering severe poverty by appealing to the prior consent of their ruler when this ruler himself lacks any moral standing to consent on their behalf.

Fourth, insofar as very poor people did and do consent, through a meaningfully democratic process, to some particular global institutional arrangement, the justificatory force of such consent is weakened when this consent is compelled. Thus it is doubtful that taking all your possessions could be justified by consent you gave when doing so was your only escape from drowning after a boating accident. To be sure, you are better off penniless than dead, and in this sense your consent was rational. But it remains tainted by the fact that you had no other tolerable option.

The justificatory force of consent given in calamitous circumstances is even weaker when the calamity is partly due to those whose conduct this consent is meant to justify. If your boating accident was caused by your would-be rescuer, for example, your consent to give her your possessions if she rescues you is of even more dubious justifying force. Poor countries need trade for development. They do not get fair trading opportunities under the WTO regime; but one that failed to sign up would find its trading opportunities even more severely curtailed. Any poor country is forced to decide about whether to sign up to the WTO rules against the background of other rules that it cannot escape and that make it extremely costly not to sign up. One such rule is, for instance, that the people and firms of poor countries may not freely offer their products and services to people in rich countries. This rule enables the rich countries to exact a price for whatever limited access to their markets they are prepared to grant. Part of this price is that the intellectual property rights of rich-country corporations must be respected and enforced. Poor-country governments must help collect rents for those corporations, thereby driving up the cost of pharmaceuticals and foodstuffs for their own populations. Paying this price makes sense perhaps for poor countries, given their calamitous circumstances. But this calamity is due to a rule that the rich countries impose unilaterally, without any consent by the poor.

One may think that this rule is so natural and obvious that any calamity it may entail cannot be attributed to those who are imposing it: Surely, any country is entitled to restrict access to its territory and markets as it pleases, regardless of the economic consequences for foreigners. Well, not too long ago, the rich countries proclaimed the opposite to be natural and obvious, when they forcefully insisted on their right to sell opium in China, for example.[30] And the claimed right of the United States, Canada, Australia and New Zealand to exclude outsiders from their

---

[30] In the middle of the 19th century, Great Britain and other Western powers prosecuted a series of 'opium wars' against China. The first invasion was initiated in 1839 when Chinese authorities in Canton (Guangzhou) confiscated and burned opium brought in illegally by foreign traders (www.druglibrary.org/schaffer/heroin/opiwar1.htm).

territories and markets is further undermined by the historical path on which their present occupants have come to possess them.

Let me refute here yet another popular fallacy often adduced in justification of the status quo. As elaborate empirical research shows, poor countries that embrace the new global rules perform better, economically, than countries that do not. This is taken to prove that the new global rules are beneficial to poor countries. To see the fallacy, consider this parallel reasoning. Suppose empirical research had shown that around 1940 smaller European states collaborating with the fascist alliance fared better than the rest. Would this have proved that the new dominance of this fascist alliance was good for small European states? Of course not. Drawing this conclusion, one would be conflating two separate questions: First, *given* the dominance of fascism in Continental Europe, is it better for a small state to cooperate or not? Second, is the fascist dominance in Continental Europe itself better for small European states than, say, the hypothetical dominance of parliamentary democracies? However obvious the fallacy is in this case, its analogue is endlessly adduced in the contemporary globalization debates, where many fail to distinguish the two analogous questions: First, *given* the dominance of the rich countries and of their rules and organizations (WTO, World Bank, IMF, OECD, and G7), is it better for a poor country to cooperate or not? Second, is the dominance of these rich-country rules and organizations itself better for the poor countries than, say, the full abolition of protectionist constraints?

1.2.3.3. *Invoking the Flaws of the Poor Countries' Social Institutions and Rulers*

A further popular way of denying that the present global institutional order is harming the poor points once more to the great differences among poor countries' economic performance. The success stories—such as the Asian tigers and China—show that poor countries *can* defeat severe poverty under the global order as it is; hence, that this order is not inhospitable to poverty eradication. Poor people in countries where severe poverty is not melting away therefore have only their own social institutions and governments to blame.

This reasoning involves a some–all fallacy. The fact that *some* individuals born into poverty become millionaires does not show that *all* such persons can do likewise (see Cohen 1988: 262–3). The reason is that the pathways to riches are sparse. They are not rigidly limited, to be sure, but even an affluent country clearly cannot achieve the kind of economic growth rates needed for everyone to become a millionaire (holding fixed the value of the currency and the real income millionaires can now enjoy). The same holds true for poor countries. The Asian tigers (Hong Kong, Taiwan, Singapore, and South Korea) achieved impressive rates of economic growth and poverty reduction. They did so through a state-sponsored buildup of industries that mass produce low-tech consumer products. These industries were globally successful by using their considerable labor–cost advantage to beat competitors in the high-income countries and by drawing on greater state support and/or a better-educated workforce to beat competitors in other poor countries.[31] Building such industries was hugely profitable for the Asian tigers. But if many other poor countries had adopted this same developmental strategy, competition among them would have rendered it much less profitable.

Over the past two decades, China has been the great success story, achieving phenomenal growth in exports and per capita income. So China's example is now often used to argue that the rules of the world economy are favorable to the poor countries and conducive to poverty eradication. These arguments, too, commit a some–all fallacy. Exporters in the poor countries compete over the same heavily protected rich-country markets (n. 22). Thanks to its extraordinary ability to deliver quality products cheaply in large quantities, China has done extremely well in this competition. But this great success has had catastrophic effects in many poor countries by reducing their exporters' market share and export prices. To be sure, the world economy as presently structured is not a constant-sum game, where any one player's gain must be another's loss. Yet outcomes are strongly interdependent. We cannot conclude, therefore, that the present global institutional order, though less favorable to the poor countries than it might be, is still favorable enough for all of them to do as well as the Asian tigers and then China have done in fact.

Still, could the poor countries on the whole not do much better under the present global order than they are doing in fact? And must the present global order then not be acquitted of responsibility for any excess poverty that would have been avoided if the political elites in the poor countries were less corrupt and less incompetent?

Suppose the two sets of relevant causal factors—the global institutional order and the economic regimes and policies of the countries in which severe poverty persists—were symmetrically related so that each set of factors is necessary for the current reproduction of severe poverty worldwide. Then, if we insist that the global factors must be absolved on the ground that modification of national factors would suffice to eradicate world poverty, defenders of national factors could insist, symmetrically, that these national factors must be absolved on the ground that modification of global factors would suffice to eradicate world poverty. Acquitting both sets of factors on these grounds, we would place their cooperative production of huge harms beyond moral criticism.

The implausibility of such an assessment can be illustrated through a more straightforward interactional case. Suppose two upstream tribes release pollutants into a river on which people downstream depend for their survival. And suppose that each tribe's pollutant causes only minor harm, but that, when mixed, they react to form a lethal poison that kills many people downstream. In this case, both upstream tribes can deny responsibility, each insisting that the severe harm would not materialize if the other upstream tribe stopped its polluting activity. Such a

---

[31] It also helped that the United States, eager to establish healthy capitalist economies as a counterweight to Soviet influence in the region, allowed the tigers free access to its market even while they maintained high tariffs to protect their own.

denial is implausible. Both upstream tribes are required to stop the severe harm they cause together. They can cooperate jointly to discharge this responsibility. Failing that, each has a duty to stop its pollution and each is fully responsible for any harm that would not have materialized but for the pollutants it has released (see Pogge 2005c: 63–4).

The persistence of severe poverty worldwide is importantly analogous to the harms suffered by the people downstream. It is true—as the defenders of the rich countries and of their globalization project point out—that most severe poverty would be avoided, despite the current unfair global order, if the national governments and elites of the poor countries were genuinely committed to 'good governance' and poverty eradication. It is also true—as the defenders of governments and elites in the poor countries insist—that most severe poverty would be avoided, despite the corrupt and oppressive regimes holding sway in so many poor countries, if the global institutional order were designed to achieve this purpose. This mutual finger-pointing serves both sides well, convincing many affluent citizens in rich and poor countries that they and their government are innocent in the catastrophe of world poverty. But on reflection it is clear that, while each side is right in pointing at the other, neither is right in acquitting itself. Like the two upstream tribes, each side is fully responsible for its marginal contribution to the deprivations they together produce. The 'multiplicative' cooperation of causal factors thus not merely fails to decrease, but *increases* total responsibility. This is analogous to how two criminals, if each makes a necessary contribution to a homicide, are each legally and morally fully responsible for that single death.

This response suffices to maintain the responsibility of the citizens and governments of the rich countries: They can be responsible for the severe poverty of even those people who would not be poor if their countries were better governed.

Still, by assuming symmetry between the two sets of relevant causal factors, the response is too simple, failing fully to expose the responsibility of the rich countries and of their globalization project. There is one important asymmetry. While national institutional arrangements and policies in the poor countries have very little influence on the design of the global order, the latter has a great deal of influence on the former. Yes, the social institutions and policies of many poor countries are far from optimal in terms of domestic poverty avoidance. But substantial improvement in this set of causal factors is unlikely so long as global institutional arrangements remain the way they are. The global institutional order exerts its pernicious influence on the evolution of world poverty not only directly, in the ways already discussed, but also indirectly through its influence on the national institutions and policies of the poor countries. Oppression and corruption, so prevalent in many poor countries today, are themselves very substantially created and sustained by central features of the present global order.

It was only in 1999, for example, that the high-income countries finally agreed to curb their firms' bribery of foreign officials by adopting the OECD *Convention on Combating Bribery of Foreign Public Officials in International Business*

Transactions.[32] Until then, most affluent states did not merely legally authorize their firms to bribe foreign officials, but even allowed them to deduct such bribes from their taxable revenues, thereby providing financial inducements and moral support to the practice of bribing politicians and officials in the poor countries.[33] This practice diverts the loyalties of officials in these countries and also makes a great difference to which persons are motivated to scramble for public office in the first place. Poor countries have suffered staggering losses as a result, most clearly in the awarding of public contracts. These losses arise in part from the fact that bribes are priced in: Bidders on contracts must raise their price in order to get paid enough to pay the bribes. Additional losses arise as bidders can afford to be non-competitive, knowing that the success of their bid will depend on their bribes more than on the substance of their offer. Even greater losses arise from the fact that officials focused on bribes pay little attention to whether the goods and services they purchase on their country's behalf are of good quality or even needed at all. Much of what poor countries have imported over the decades has been of no use to them—or even harmful, by promoting environmental degradation or violence (bribery is especially pervasive in the arms trade). The new *Convention* does little to curb bribery by multinational corporations[34] and banks in the rich countries continue to assist corrupt rulers and officials in the poor countries to move and invest abroad their gains from bribery and embezzlement (Baker 2005). But even if the *Convention* were effective, it would be difficult to purge the pervasive culture of corruption that is now deeply entrenched in many poor countries thanks to the extensive bribery they were subjected to during their formative years.

The issue of bribery is part of a larger problem. The political and economic elites of poor countries interact with their domestic inferiors, on the one hand, and with foreign governments and corporations, on the other. These two constituencies differ enormously in wealth and power. The former are by and large poorly educated and heavily preoccupied with the daily struggle to make ends meet. The latter, by contrast, have vastly greater rewards and penalties at their disposal. Politicians with a normal interest in their own political and economic success can thus be expected to cater to the interests of foreign governments and corporations rather than to competing interests of their much poorer compatriots. And this, of course, is what we find: There are plenty of poor-country governments that came to power or stay in power only thanks to foreign support. And there are

---

[32] The convention came into effect in February 1999 and has been widely ratified since (www.oecd.org/home).

[33] In the United States, the post-Watergate Congress sought to prevent the bribing of foreign officials through its 1977 Foreign Corrupt Practices Act, passed after the Lockheed Corporation was found to have paid—not a modest sum to some third-world official, but rather—a US$2 million bribe to Prime Minister Kakuei Tanaka of powerful and democratic Japan. Not wanting its firms to be at a disadvantage vis-à-vis their foreign rivals, the United States was a major supporter of the Convention, as was the non-governmental organization Transparency International, which helped mobilize public support in many OECD countries.

[34] 'Plenty of laws exist to ban bribery by companies. But big multinationals continue to sidestep them with ease'—so the new situation is summarized in 'The Short Arm of the Law', (*The Economist* March 2, 2002: 63–5, at 63).

plenty of poor-country politicians and bureaucrats who, induced or even bribed by foreigners, work against the interests of their people: *for* the development of a tourist-friendly sex industry (whose forced exploitation of children and women they tolerate and profit from), *for* the importation of unneeded, obsolete, or overpriced products at public expense, *for* the permission to import hazardous products, wastes, or factories, *against* laws protecting employees or the environment, and so on.

To be sure, there would not be such huge asymmetries in incentives if the poor countries were more democratic, allowing their populations a genuine political role. Why then are most of these countries so far from being genuinely democratic? This question brings further aspects of the current global institutional order into view.

It is a very central feature of this order that any group controlling a preponderance of the means of coercion within a country is internationally recognized as the legitimate government of this country's territory and people—regardless of how this group came to power, of how it exercises power and of the extent to which it is supported or opposed by the population it rules. That such a group exercising effective power receives international recognition means not merely that we engage it in negotiations. It means also that we accept this group's right to act for the people it rules. We in effect authorize any person or group holding effective power in a country—regardless of how they acquired or exercise it—to sell the country's resources and to dispose of the proceeds of such sales, to borrow in the country's name and thereby to impose debt service obligations upon it, to sign treaties on the country's behalf and thus to bind its present and future population, and to use state revenues to buy the means of internal repression. This global practice goes a long way toward explaining why so many countries are so badly governed.

The *resource privilege* we confer upon a group in power is much more than mere acquiescence in its effective control over the natural resources of the country in question. This privilege includes the power[35] to effect legally valid transfers of ownership rights in such resources. Thus a corporation that has purchased resources from the Saudis or Suharto, or from Mobuto or Sani Abacha, has thereby become entitled to be—and actually *is*—recognized anywhere in the world as the legitimate owner of these resources. This is a remarkable feature of our global order. A group that overpowers the guards and takes control of a warehouse may be able to give some of the merchandize to others, accepting money in exchange. But the fence who pays them becomes merely the possessor, not the owner, of the loot. Contrast this with a group that overpowers an elected government and takes control of a country. Such a group, too, can give away some of the country's natural resources, accepting money in exchange. In this case, however, the purchaser acquires not merely possession, but all the rights and liberties of ownership, which

---

[35] As understood by Wesley Hohfeld (1964), a power involves the legally recognized authority to alter the distribution of first-order liberty rights, claim rights, and duties. Having a power or powers in this sense is distinct from having power (i.e., control over physical force and/or means of coercion).

are supposed to be—and actually *are*—protected and enforced by all other states' courts and police forces. The international resource privilege, then, is the legal power to confer globally valid ownership rights in a country's resources.

This international resource privilege has disastrous effects in poor but resource-rich countries, where the resource sector constitutes a large segment of the national economy. Whoever can take power in such a country by whatever means can maintain his rule, even against widespread popular opposition, by buying the arms and soldiers he needs with revenues from the export of natural resources and with funds borrowed against future resource sales. The resource privilege thus gives insiders strong incentives toward the violent acquisition and exercise of political power, thereby causing coup attempts and civil wars. Moreover, it also gives outsiders strong incentives to corrupt the officials of such countries who, no matter how badly they rule, continue to have resources to sell and money to spend.

Nigeria is a case in point. It exports *each day* about two-million barrels of oil worth some $50–100 million. Whoever controls this revenue stream and associated borrowing power can afford enough weapons and soldiers to keep himself in power regardless of what the population may think of him. And so long as he succeeds in doing so, his purse will be continuously replenished with new funds with which he can cement his rule and live in opulence. With such a powerful incentive, it cannot be surprising that, during twenty-eight of the past thirty-six years, Nigeria has been ruled by military strongmen who took power and ruled by force.[36] Nor can it be surprising that even a polished elected president fails to stop gross corruption: Olusegun Obasanjo knows full well that, if he tried to spend the oil revenues solely for the benefit of the Nigerian people, military officers could—thanks to the international resource privilege—quickly restore their customary perks.[37] With such a huge price on his head, even the best-intentioned president could not end the embezzlement of oil revenues and survive in power.

The incentives arising from the international resource privilege help explain what economists have long observed and found puzzling: the significant *negative* correlation between resource wealth (relative to GDP) and economic performance.[38] Two Yale economists confirm this explanation through a regression

---

[36] See 'Going on down', in *The Economist* (June 8, 1996: 46–8). A later update says: 'oil revenues [are] paid directly to the government at the highest level … The head of state has supreme power and control of all the cash. He depends on nobody and nothing but oil. Patronage and corruption spread downwards from the top' (*The Economist*, December 12, 1998: 19). See also www.eia.doe.gov/emeu/cabs/nigeria.html

[37] Because Obasanjo was the chair of Transparency International's Advisory Council (n. 33), his election in early 1999 had raised great hopes. These hopes were sorely disappointed. Nigeria still ranks very near the bottom of TI's own Corruption Perception Index (www.transparency.org/policy_research/surveys_indices/cpi/2005).

[38] This 'resource curse' or 'Dutch disease' is exemplified by many poor countries that, despite great natural wealth, have achieved little economic growth and poverty reduction over the last decades. Here are the more important resource-rich poor countries with their average annual rates of change in real GDP per capita from 1975 to 2003: Nigeria –0.5%, Congo/Zaire –4.9%, Kenya +0.2%, Angola –1.1%,

analysis, which shows that the causal link from resource wealth to poor economic performance is mediated through reduced chances for democracy.[39] Holding the global order fixed as a given background, the authors do not consider how the causal link they analyze itself depends on global rules that grant the resource privilege to any group in power, irrespective of its domestic illegitimacy.

The *borrowing privilege* we confer upon any ruling group includes the power to impose internationally valid legal obligations upon the country at large. Any successor government that refuses to honor debts incurred by an ever so corrupt, brutal, undemocratic, unconstitutional, repressive, unpopular predecessor will be severely punished by the banks and governments of other countries. At minimum it will lose its own borrowing privilege by being excluded from the international financial markets. Such refusals are therefore very rare, as governments, even when newly elected after a dramatic break with the past, are compelled to pay the debts of their ever so awful predecessors.

The international borrowing privilege makes three important contributions to the incidence of oppressive and corrupt elites in the poorer countries. First, this privilege facilitates borrowing by destructive rulers who can borrow more money and can do so more cheaply than they could do if they alone, rather than the whole country, were obliged to repay. In this way, the borrowing privilege helps such rulers maintain themselves in power even against near-universal popular discontent and opposition.[40] Second, the international borrowing privilege imposes upon democratic successor regimes the often huge debts of their corrupt predecessors. It thereby saps the capacity of such democratic governments to implement structural reforms and other political programs, thus rendering such governments less successful and less stable than they would otherwise be. (It is

Mozambique +2.3%, Senegal −0.1%, Venezuela −1.1%, Ecuador +0.1%, Saudi Arabia −2.4%, United Arab Emirates −3.3%, Oman +2.2%, Kuwait −1.2%, Bahrain +1.1%, Brunei −2.2%, Indonesia +4.1%, and the Philippines +0.3% (UNDP 2005: 266–9; in some cases a somewhat different period was used due to insufficient data, cf. UNDP 2004: 184–7, UNDP 2003: 278–81). Despite Indonesia's exceptional performance, the resource-rich poor countries as a group did worse than their resource-poor peers and also, of course, much worse than the high-income countries whose average annual growth in real per capita income for 1975–2002 was +2.2% (UNDP 2005: 269).

[39] 'All petrostates or resource-dependent countries in Africa fail to initiate meaningful political reforms. . . . besides South Africa, transition to democracy has been successful only in resource-poor countries' (Lam and Wantchekon 1999: 31). 'Our cross-country regression confirms our theoretical insights. We find that a one percentage increase in the size of the natural resource sector [relative to GDP] generates a decrease by half a percentage point in the probability of survival of democratic regimes' (ibid. 35). See also Wantchekon (1999).

[40] Because they have collateral to offer, the rulers of resource-rich poor countries have enjoyed greater freedom than their peers to supplement their income from resource sales by mortgaging their countries' future. In 2003, the known debt service burdens of these countries, expressed as a percentage of their entire GDPs, were: Nigeria 2.8%, Congo/Zaire 2.6%, Kenya 4.0%, Angola 10.1%, Mozambique 2.0%, Senegal 3.8%, Venezuela 10.4%, Ecuador 8.9%, Oman 8.6%, Indonesia 8.9%, and the Philippines 12.8% (UNDP 2005: 280–2). Needless to say, little of the borrowed funds were channeled into productive investments, e.g., in education and infrastructure, which would augment economic growth and generate additional tax revenues that could help meet interest and repayment obligations. Much was embezzled and much expended on 'internal security' and the military.

small consolation that putschists are sometimes weakened by being held liable for the debts of their democratic predecessors.) Third, the international borrowing privilege strengthens incentives toward coup attempts: Whoever succeeds in bringing a preponderance of the means of coercion under his control gets the borrowing privilege as an additional reward.

The ongoing international resource and borrowing privileges are complemented by the international treaty privilege, which recognizes any person or group in effective control of a country as entitled to undertake binding treaty obligations on behalf of its population, and the international arms privilege, which recognizes such a person or group as entitled to use state funds to import the arms needed to stay in power. Like the erstwhile official tolerance of the bribing of poor-country officials, these privileges are highly significant features of the global order which tend to benefit the governments, corporations, and citizens of the rich countries and the political–military elites of the poor countries at the expense of the vast majority of those living in the poor countries. Thus, while the present global order indeed does not make it impossible for some poor countries to achieve genuine democracy and sustained economic growth, central features of it contribute greatly to most poor countries' failing on both counts. These features are crucial for explaining the inability and especially the unwillingness of these countries' leaders to pursue more effective strategies of poverty eradication. And they are crucial therefore for explaining why global inequality is increasing so rapidly that substantial global economic growth since the end of the Cold War has not reduced income poverty and malnutrition (n. 26)—*despite* substantial technological progress and global economic growth, *despite* a huge reported poverty reduction in China,[41] *despite* the post-Cold War 'peace dividend',[42] *despite* a 35% drop in real food prices since 1985,[43] *despite* official development assistance, and *despite* the efforts of international humanitarian and development organizations.

1.2.4. Conclusion

In just seventeen years since the end of the Cold War, over 300 million human beings have died prematurely from poverty-related causes, with some 18 million more added each year. Much larger numbers of human beings must live in conditions of life-threatening poverty that make it very difficult for them to articulate their interests and effectively to fend for themselves and their families. This

[41] The number of Chinese living below $1 per day is reported to have declined by 31%, or 97 million, and the number of Chinese living below $2 per day by 19%, or 137 million, between 1987 and 2001 (Chen and Ravallion 2004: 153).

[42] Thanks to the end of the Cold War, military expenditures worldwide have declined from 4.7% of aggregate GDP in 1985 to 2.9% in 1996 (UNDP 1998: 197) and to about 2.6% or $1,035 billion in 2004 (yearbook2005.sipri.org/ch8/ch8). If global military expenditures were still at the old 4.7% level, they would have been some $836 billion higher in 2004 than they actually were.

[43] The World Bank Food Price Index fell from 139.3 in 1980 to 100 in 1990 and then to 90.1 in 2002. These statistics are published by the World Bank's Development Prospects Group. See World Bank (2004: 277). Also at http://siteresources.worldbank.org/INTRGEP2004/Resources/appendix2.pdf

catastrophe was and is happening, foreseeably, under a global institutional order designed for the benefit of the affluent countries' governments, corporations and citizens and of the poor countries' political and military elites. There are feasible alternative designs of the global institutional order, feasible alternative paths of globalization, under which this catastrophe would have been largely avoided. Even now severe poverty could be rapidly reduced through feasible reforms that would modify the more harmful features of this global order or mitigate their impact.

Take the unconditional international resource privilege for example. It is beneficial to the affluent countries by giving us access to a larger, cheaper, and more reliable supply of foreign natural resources, because we can acquire ownership of them from anyone who happens to exercise effective power without regard to whether the country's population either approves the sale or benefits from the proceeds. Unconditional international resource and borrowing privileges are also highly advantageous to many a putschist or tyrant in the poor countries, for whom they secure the funds he needs to maintain himself in power even against the will of a large majority of his compatriots. Such privileges are, however, an unmitigated disaster for the global poor who are being dispossessed through loan and resource agreements over which they have no say and from which they do not benefit.[44]

The example illustrates the clear-cut injustice of the present global order. It also illustrates that this injustice does not consist in too little aid being dispensed to the poor. There is still so much severe poverty, and so much need for aid, only because the poor are systematically impoverished by present institutional arrangements and have been so impoverished for a long time during which our advantage and their disadvantage have been compounded. Of course, substantial funds are needed to eradicate severe poverty at a morally acceptable speed (n. 15). But such funds are not generous charity. All that is needed is compensation for the harms produced by unjust global institutional arrangements whose past and present imposition by the affluent countries brings them great benefits.[45]

Given that the present global institutional order is foreseeably associated with such massive incidence of avoidable severe poverty, its (uncompensated) imposition manifests an ongoing human rights violation—arguably the largest such violation ever committed in human history. It is not the *gravest* human rights violation, in my view, because those who commit it do not intend the death and suffering they inflict either as an end or as a means. They merely act with willful indifference to the enormous harms they cause in the course of advancing their own ends while going to great lengths to deceive the world (and sometimes themselves) about the impact of their conduct. But still, the *largest*.

To be sure, massive poverty caused by human agency is certainly not unprecedented. British colonial institutions and policies are blamed for up to a million poverty deaths in the Irish Potato Famine of 1846–9 and for about three million

---

[44] See Pogge (2002*a*: ch. 6), for an idea about how to modify the international resource and borrowing privileges.

[45] See Pogge (2002*a*: ch. 8), proposing such a compensation scheme in the form of a Global Resources Dividend.

poverty deaths in the Great Bengal Famine of 1943–44. Up to thirty million poverty deaths in China during 1959–62 are attributed to Mao Tse-Tung's insistence on continuing the policies of his 'Great Leap Forward' even when their disastrous effects became apparent. Still, these historical catastrophes were of more limited duration and even at their height did not reach the present and ongoing rate of eighteen million poverty deaths per annum.

The continuing imposition of this global order, essentially unmodified, constitutes a massive violation of the human right to basic necessities—a violation for which the governments and electorates of the more powerful countries bear primary responsibility. This charge cannot be defeated through appeal to baseline comparisons, by appeal to the consent of the global poor themselves, or by appeal to other detrimental causal factors that the present global order may merely do too little to counteract.

2

Poverty as a Violation of Human Rights: Inhumanity or Injustice?

*Tom Campbell**

The proposal that poverty be regarded as a violation of human rights and therefore abolished is presented as a new paradigm in the fight against poverty that has the potential to galvanize an effective strategy for ending poverty through an international human rights framework. In the words of Pierre Sané, Assistant Director-General Social and Human Sciences Sector UNESCO:

> If...poverty were declared to be abolished, as it should with regard to its status as a massive, systematic and continuous violation of human rights, its persistence would no longer be a regrettable feature of the nature of things. It would become a denial of justice. The burden of proof would shift. The poor, once recognized as the injured party, would acquire a right to reparation for which governments, the international community and, ultimately, each citizen would be jointly liable. A strong interest would thus be established in eliminating, as a matter of urgency, the grounds of liability, which might be expected to unleash much stronger forces than compassion, charity, or even concern for one's own security, are likely to mobilize for the benefit of others. (Sané 2003: 4)[1]

In this chapter, I explore the proposal that poverty be classified as a violation of human rights from a philosophical standpoint, examining how the proposal can be interpreted and how it might be morally and politically justified. I suggest that the moral basis for the proposal would be strengthened rather than weakened by including compassion or humanitarianism in the core of its justification, providing a morally secure basis for a universal obligation to eradicate poverty. I go on to argue that this can be done without diluting either the moral force or the radical political and legal implications of regarding poverty as a violation of human rights.

In section 2.1 of this chapter, I outline some of the practical implications of regarding poverty as a violation of human rights. I then argue for the adoption of a principle of humanity as the major basis for such a proposal, identify the

* Warm thanks are due to all who took part in the UNESCO symposium, those who commented on versions on this essay presented at the Universities of Witwatersrand, Cape Town, Stellenbosch and Rhodes, and my colleagues at CAPPE, especially Keith Horton and Seumas Miller. Particular mention must be made of the detailed advice and encouragement provided by the editor of this volume, Thomas Pogge.
[1] See also Chinkin (2001: 553–89).

distortions that arise from overemphasizing justice as the moral basis for the obligation to relieve poverty, and then deal with some misunderstandings that can get in the way of accepting the thesis that, with respect to extreme poverty— strategically and morally—we should put 'humanity before justice'.[2]

2.1. POVERTY AS A VIOLATION OF HUMAN RIGHTS

Before exploring the moral foundations of the thesis that poverty is a violation of human rights, the context of the debate may be clarified by identifying some of the possible implications of the proposal.

The categorization of poverty as a violation of human rights and talk of the abolition (rather than the eradication) of poverty may be seen at the very least as attempts to give a higher priority to the elimination of poverty as an economic and political goal (UNESCO 2003). As such it will be applauded and encouraged by everyone who recognizes the horrendous realities of widespread extreme poverty of the sort experienced by over a fifth of the world's population. Approaching poverty through the prism of human rights is to lift it from the status of a social problem to that of a moral catastrophe.

More specifically, to talk of poverty in terms of human rights violations is to endorse the parity and interconnections of basic social and economic rights with fundamental civil and political rights. Currently, while official cognisance is given to the equal importance of economic and social rights on the one hand and civil and political rights on the other, there is no doubt that, for one reason or another, social and economic rights are in practice relatively neglect.[3] Torture is held to be unacceptable, poverty merely unfortunate. The idea of poverty as a human rights violation is clearly intended to send a powerful moral message that this bifurcation of human rights is untenable.

The categorization of poverty as a violation of human rights may also be seen as a move toward bringing new mechanisms to bear on the elimination of poverty.[4] In addition to more stringent and forcefully expressed UN monitoring of state performance with respect to social and economic rights,[5] we may be led

---

[2] The provocative title of a paper written at a time when it was being asserted without contradiction that justice is, by definition, the overriding moral consideration with respect to the distribution of the benefits and burdens of social cooperation (Campbell 1974: 1–16).

[3] 'The ideal of free human beings enjoying freedom from fear and want can only be achieved if conditions are created whereby everyone can enjoy his economic, social, and cultural rights, as well as his civil and political rights' (International Covenant on Economic, Social and Cultural Rights (ICESCR) 1966: Preamble).

[4] Danilo Turk writes in the 'The Realization of Economic, Social and Cultural Rights' UN Sub-Commission on Prevention of Discrimination and the Protection of Minorities, E/CN4/Sub2/1992/16' para 184: 'the issue of whether economic, social and cultural rights can be violated in a legal sense has been answered convincingly in the affirmative', quoted in Hunt (1996: 27).

[5] Currently carried out principally by the UN Human Rights Committee. See Philip Alston and James Crawford (2000).

to contemplate extending such surveillance to the activities of non-state actors, such as multinational corporations, and bringing the focus of human rights NGOs more on to issues of poverty (Bottomley and Kinley 2002).

A further implication of regarding poverty as a violation of human rights is that we should be further developing legal remedies that empower the poor to obtain their rights. Poverty cannot be abolished, in the sense of eliminated, simply by passing laws making its persistence illegal, even if everyone were to try their best to conform with such laws. If the analogy is with the abolition of slavery, for instance, it is not easy to see what is the equivalent in relation to poverty of withdrawing the legal endorsement of treating people as property, thus legally abolishing slavery. However, the legal implications of 'abolishing' poverty could include such, possibly counterproductive, measures as withdrawing the legal recognition of debts incurred by poor people, or the enactment of a positive duty on specified individuals or organizations to provide material support for those who lack the necessities of life.

Additionally, in both domestic and international law, new remedies could be developed, such as civil liability for behavior negligently fostering poverty, or criminal penalties for knowingly implementing policies and practices, both in government and business, that avoidably increase, or fail to decrease, poverty.[6] Giving individuals or groups the right to sue for reparations on the grounds of poverty is certainly one of the principal outcomes that is anticipated from adopting the new paradigm.

Other, apparently less radical but actually more ambitious, implications involve providing a justification for some form of global taxation earmarked for the elimination of poverty, such as the Tobin Tax on international financial transactions (Tobin 1978: 153–9), or Thomas Pogge's Global Resources Dividend (GRD) (2001a: 59–77), or, more appropriately in my view, a Global Humanitarian Levy (GHL) paid by those who are sufficiently affluent to make a small contribution to poverty relief without significant hardship to themselves (see below, pp. 67–8).

Further, it may be that by treating poverty as a violation of human rights we are in effect encouraging the constitutionalization of social and economic rights, so that courts, not governments will be given the task of setting minimum welfare standards in these areas, voiding legislation that they consider increases or fails to decrease the incidence and degree of poverty in that jurisdiction, or requiring specified resources to be provided by governments or employers, or intervening when governments fail to contribute adequately to international poverty relief.[7]

Finally, a further implication of seeing poverty as a violation of human rights might be that economic sanctions, loss of access to loans, or even armed intervention may be deployed against states that culpably fail to relieve poverty in their own territory at least to the extent that these methods are utilized with respect to the protection of civil and political rights of those living under tyrannical and brutal regimes.

---

[6] A prescient model might be recent use of the ancient Alien Tort Claims Act in the United States.

[7] As, to some extent, is currently the case in the constitutions of India, South Africa, and Finland.

These possible implications of making poverty a human rights violation illustrate just how radical a proposal this could be. This presents a challenge when we turn to justifying the proposal. Here we come up against the initial difficulty that the implied scenarios may be more problematic in the case of social and economic rights, than with civil and political ones, not because widespread and severe poverty is less significant morally than deprivation of the right to vote or systematic torture, but because the causes and cures of poverty are much more elusive, much more controversial, and challenging than most other human rights deficits.

Experts disagree about the factors that produce or sustain poverty and about the economic policies that offer most hope of poverty elimination. It is generally accepted that eradicating poverty requires more than redistribution of income. If the more that is required is enabling poor people to be able to provide for their own material necessities then there may be considerable controversy over how to bring this about. Further, mechanisms do not exist for the systematic redistribution of resources throughout the world. This affects not only the problem of identifying precise human rights obligations with respect to the reduction and eradication of poverty, but also the prospect of establishing legal claims against those who are alleged to be responsible for the poverty in question.

In addition, with respect to the constitutionalization of social and economic rights, courts may lack the expertise to know which laws they should void in the interests of poverty reduction and what it is proper for them to require governments to provide by way of welfare policies and economic strategy. The legitimacy of courts having a determinative voice in such economic and financial matters may also be questioned. The more they intervene in this sphere the graver the democratic issues raised as to their legitimacy to determine economic and social policy (Beattie 1994: 321–61).

In these circumstances, it may be unjust, ineffectual, and sometimes counterproductive to contemplate legal remedies and international sanctions as responses to violations of human poverty rights or to give teeth to the idea of legally 'abolishing' poverty.[8]

These familiar objections to treating social and economic rights on par with civil and political rights are far from conclusive, but they do require clear and considered responses. The rhetoric of 'violation' and 'abolition' must be given the clarity and precision that is required to enable us to scrutinize the proposal and there may be powerful considerations in favor of one or more of the alternative implications of seeing poverty as a human rights violation.

There is no reason to exclude endorsement of some version of the tenet of the human rights movements that social and economic rights are in a mutually supportive relationship to civil and political rights. It is now well established that the logical and practical differences between justiciable and non-justiciable rights, between costless and costly rights, and between negative and positive rights have been greatly exaggerated, perhaps for ideological reasons.[9] Those social

---

[8] For an exposition and response to such critiques, see Jackman (1992).
[9] See Shue (1996a) and Holmes and Sunstein (1999).

and economic rights that are human rights cannot be left in the aspirational basket.

Nevertheless, the formidable difficulties of operationalizing social and economic rights mean that we have to work very hard to make clear the meaning and implications of regarding poverty as a violation of human rights and providing the sort of clear and convincing arguments that are be needed to give wide credibility to this thesis. A first step in carrying out this task is to consider the precise location of the violation in question. If poverty is a violation of human rights precisely of what does the violation in question consist? What precisely are the duties that are correlative to the rights of those in extreme poverty? To answer such questions we must first make clear what we mean by poverty in this context.

Unfortunately, in determining what is to count as poverty in the context of human rights, poverty is often confused with analyzing either its effects, or its causes. Thus, it is frequently noted that people living in extreme poverty are often despised and disrespected and discriminated against, so that poverty leads to a violation of their human rights in general. This assumption is frequently associated with the view that the poor are systematically excluded from society. This is one of the factors that render extreme poverty morally unacceptable. From this perspective poverty is viewed as a cause of human rights violations (Massa Arzabe 2001: 29–39). Indeed, poverty is sometimes defined as social exclusion. If this means exclusion from material powers then this is unproblematic. However, while social exclusion in a broader sense, including the absence of discrimination and the presence of political participation, is a serious consequence of poverty it is misleading to identify it with poverty itself.

Our attention is also often drawn to the fact that human rights violations themselves lead to poverty. Thus, when, in violation of peoples' civil rights they are held in confinement without justification, their families may be reduced to abject poverty. Abuse of political rights on a grand scale is a frequent cause of famine. From this perspective, poverty is viewed as the result of human rights' violations.

Perhaps because human rights violations commonly result in poverty among those abused, some analyses equate poverty with being the victim of human rights' violations. Further, many human rights violations can be in terms of making or sustaining poverty. Thus, human rights violations can be read as reducing the capacities of the right holders to lead truly human lives so making them impoverished. This approach stems from conceiving all human rights as deriving from the existence of certain human needs or, in more positive terminology, the capabilities whose absence indicates the existence of a need.[10] Thus a human life requires the capability to communicate, generating a right to freedom of speech. To be without the opportunity to communicate effectively a person may be said to be impoverished per se. In this way all human rights violations can be seen

---

[10] The project of defining poverty in terms of capabilities derives from A. K. Sen, but he does not himself use it to argue that human rights violations are a form of impoverishment. See Sen (1999: ch. 4, 'Poverty as Capability Deprivation').

as deprivations that are classifiable as impoverishments since they involve the lack of something required to live a truly human life. Poverty is then viewed as a summation of human rights deficiencies.

Such conceptual perspectives on poverty make important points and are sufficient to justify the case for seeing poverty as a human rights issue. There is no reason to doubt that the causal connections between human rights and poverty, which work both ways, have considerable factual foundations and to articulate human rights violations as a form of impoverishment has some conceptual persuasiveness. However, this does not focus adequately on the core phenomenon of poverty as severe material deprivation. If we are to argue persuasively that poverty is a human rights violation, it needs to be made clear that we are speaking of poverty in its paradigm sense of lacking the basic material provisions to support a minimally acceptable way of life. The proposal that poverty is a violation of human rights should not require manipulating the concept of poverty and must be directed at the idea that the condition of poverty is to be viewed as a distinct violation of specific human rights, such as the right to subsistence or the right to a tolerable standard of living. Such rights assume that poverty is a matter of severe material deprivation reducing below an acceptable level a person's diet, accommodation, physical comfort, and health. At base what we are talking about here is what is referred to as extreme poverty, something that international organizations, such as the World Bank, seek to define in economic terms, such as a minimum income but which may be more directly identified with malnutrition, homelessness, and the high probability of ill health and premature death.

What then is the violation when such extreme material poverty of this sort occurs or persists? It is important to note here that global poverty can be viewed in either of two rather distinct ways, according to either the extent of poverty or the degree of inequality involved. This is the familiar distinction between absolute and relative poverty. Relative poverty simply means being at the low end in the measure that is adopted to compare the holdings of those being studied. The idea of absolute poverty, however, focuses on what it is to be poor, irrespective of any comparisons that may be drawn with others. Absolute poverty is defined as a deprivation of that which is required to live a life that is worse than that delineated by standards (stating basic needs, minimum capabilities, etc.) that apply irrespective of relative holdings. Conceptually, it allows that we may all be equally poor, or that, in some unequal societies, no one is actually poor.

I am concerned in this chapter with both relative and absolute poverty, but the two interests have different foci. It is principally on the existence and persistence of absolute poverty on which I concentrate as the problem. Relative poverty is something I take up, not in determining what is wrong with absolute poverty, but in the context of determining who has the obligation to remedy this undesirable state of affairs. The basic problem at issue is poverty, not inequality as such. Inequality features only in the articulation of a solution to the problem.

Putting the issue in terms of rights, the proposition to be analyzed is that everyone has a right to the means of basic subsistence: the right to the material and social conditions necessary to remain alive, in normal health and reasonable comfort. This is a universal right (it applies to everyone everywhere), as it is undeniably an important (perhaps the most important) right, and it is something that we can individually and collectively do something about, so that it is a clear candidate for being categorized as a human right.

Yet the nature of this right remains obscure until we can identify the actual violation of human rights that is related to the phenomenon of absolute extreme poverty. Two possibilities suggest themselves. The first is that the violation occurs when the poverty is caused. More particularly, the analysis might be that poverty is a condition that is brought about by the culpable conduct of other people, and that this conduct is the violation.

Alternatively we may identify the violation, not with the causation of harm, but with the failure to act so as to enable those who are in extreme poverty to escape from that condition. On this view, the violation lies in the inactivity of those who are in a position to do something effective about it. The choice between these two readings of what the core violation of poverty oriented rights might be is at the philosophical heart of the attempt to clarify what is at stake in adopting the proposition that poverty is a violation of human rights.

Which alternative we adopt will depend on the moral basis of the claim that a right to relief from extreme poverty exists. We must, therefore, examine why we believe that such a right does or ought to exist. We have to be clear whether we are enquiring into the existence of moral human rights or positive human rights. Moral human rights are claims that we believe ought to be recognized universally (either in morality or law). Positive human rights are rights that exist in actual systems of social norms (societal rights) or posited in human legal systems, such as the International Bill of Rights (i.e., the UDHR, the International Covenant on Civil and Political Rights, and the International Covenant on Economic, Social and Cultural Rights).

Positive legal human rights do include a right to subsistence. Article 25.1 of the UDHR (which may be regarded as 'soft law' because it is unenforceable) reads as follows: 'Everyone has the right to a standard of living adequate for the health and well-being of himself and of his family, including food, housing and medical care and necessary social services and the right to security in the event of unemployment, sickness, disability, widowhood, old age or other lack of livelihood in circumstances beyond his control'. This is echoed in the International Covenant on Economic, Social and Cultural Rights Article 11.1: 'The States Parties to the present Covenant recognize the right of everyone to an adequate standard of living for himself and his family, including adequate food, clothing and housing, and to the continuous improvement of living conditions'. This is a move toward a form of hard (enforceable) law in that such covenants generate legal responsibilities on the part of the participant parties. The positive right to a decent standard of living is therefore clear and by now authoritatively expressed in international law, although there is no clear identification of the locus and nature of the correlative duties involved.

This does not settle the normative question concerning moral human rights concerning whether positive human rights (societal or legal) ought to contain such a right. Despite disagreement on the loci of the correlative duties, few people would doubt that there is a moral case for a positive right to be relieved of extreme poverty, but the (closely interrelated) questions are why this should be so, what is their form and content, and on whom the correlative obligations fall? It is to these questions that the remainder of this chapter is directed.

2.2. HUMANITY BEFORE JUSTICE

My thesis about the moral genesis of the human right to poverty relief is that the core violation of human rights that is properly associated with extreme material poverty is the failure to respond effectively to poverty by those who are able to do so. This is not an analytical but a moral thesis, but I seek to contribute philosophically to its support by examining its ingredients and its implications. The contention is that, in relation to extreme poverty, our human rights obligations derive primarily from duties of humanity (relating to benevolence, altruism, and caring) rather than duties of justice (relating to fairness, desert, and merit) and do not prioritize justice over humanity.

This rejects the thesis that the poverty that is a violation of human rights is poverty that is always the result of the culpable conduct of others (which is often the case) or that it is the abuse of human rights generally that leads to poverty (which it evidently routinely does) and holds that failure to deal effectively with the elimination of poverty when in a position so to do, is the violation. It is the failure to alleviate poverty as well as complicity in or actually causing poverty that should be regarded as violating poverty-related human rights. Inhumanity, I argue, is the more important and more fundamental, but not the only, basis for the moral status of the failure to alleviate as a violation of human rights. On this thesis, the discourse of violation is advantageous in prioritizing the alleviation of poverty in a way that focuses on failures to do something effective about eradicating poverty, and in the innovative and forceful strategies it suggests we might adopt with respect to the failure so to act.

Moreover, it is not advantageous to speak of poverty as a violation of human rights if this is linked either to the thesis that poverty is primarily caused by culpable injustice requiring compensation and reparation or that this is the primary reason why we ought to do something about it. Such an approach has the unfortunate implication that the only poverty that we should prioritize is that which results from official action or the failures of unjust social and economic systems, rather than, for instance, the product of natural disasters or in themselves innocent individual acts whose unforeseeable cumulative effects result in economic harms. We have a powerful obligation to eradicate all poverty, whatever its causes and we do not want to make this eradication dependent on how that poverty comes about, and certainly not on establishing who or what is to blame in bringing it about. The practical effect of this obligation is undermined by those who, while accepting that we have a moral obligation toward those in poverty, hold that such obligations do not correlate with the human rights of those living in poverty.

It might be argued that we can dispense with moral niceties of the sort presented in theories of international justice as to *why* the persistence of poverty is morally wrong and get on with the task of working out how to remedy what is agreed to be a morally unacceptable state of affairs, and then motivate ourselves and others to do something about it. In some ways this is correct. It is the feasibility of different corrective measures that needs most urgent intellectual attention. It is not what is wrong, but how to put it right that is the prime issue. The major practical questions are how to overcome the economic, cultural, and political obstacles to the sustainable and effective relief of widespread and devastating unnecessary poverty.

However, there is a further question that must be addressed, one which has a complex relationship to the issues of effective means and practical motivation. That question concerns *who* ought to be taking the lead or playing the major roles in doing what is necessary to correct the global imbalance of wealth. To put the matter in terms of rights: if those in remediable poverty have a right to sustenance who has the correlative duties, and what is the scope of those duties? Or, to put the matter in utilitarian terms: if the sum total of human misery can be greatly reduced, who has the duty to bring this about and what is the specific content of these duties?

At least some of the inaction over global justice has to do with the absence of agreement as to responsibility for taking remedial action, and of what sort. Disquiet about who is responsible for doing something effective about global inequality is at the very least, a contributor to general inaction. Making headway on this issue may help break this impasse and therefore have some indirect impact on resolving the problem. So it is an issue that is worth addressing. And it is an issue that cannot be addressed without having regard to the concept of global justice and in particular, why causing or acquiescing in the existence of extreme poverty is wrong, perhaps a grave wrong that should be conceptualized as a violation of human rights.

There are two broad ways into this question. There is an approach that sees poverty simply as a grave evil experienced by those who are poor. Here the focus is on suffering. The other looks at poverty mainly as the product of grave injustice deriving from the relationship between those who are poor and those who are not. Here the focus is not on the poverty itself, but on who is responsible for it. The evil in question is not simply the suffering of extreme poverty but the fact that this is the product of the behavior of other people.

On the first approach, in seeking to identify what it is about poverty that is an evil to those who are poor, the most obvious answer, and the one to which I adhere, is the suffering that lack of the means of subsistence causes: hunger, pain, misery, sickness, and death. On a utilitarian scale of values, pain and suffering are the great evils. That is why the most evident way of doing what is right to reduce extreme forms of human suffering. The relief of misery for its own sake is an impulse whose justification is a core intuition not only of utilitarian ethics but of any plausible system of moral thought.[11] That version of consequentialism called 'negative utilitarianism', perhaps better labelled 'humanitarianism', gives moral priority to the relief of pain, suffering, and distress of each individual.[12]

It is, perhaps, equally obvious that subsistence is necessary to survival, and without survival it is not possible to carry out any activities or enjoy any experiences that are deemed to be morally desirable. Subsistence is a material precondition or causal prerequisite not only of happiness but of everything that is valued by human beings. One such necessary precondition is agency. On this view agents require to be alive and in a position to think rationally and choose effectively if they are to fulfil their nature as agents.[13]

Much human rights discourse rightly centers on the idea of agency, particularly moral agency: the ennobling model of genuinely human life as a life of deliberation, moral choice, and the opportunity to act accordingly. This is sometimes held to constitute a unique and distinctively valuable aspect of genuine human existence on which the very notion of human rights is founded. It is a grounding that is said to explain why human life has such intrinsic value and marks it out as distinctive from any other sort of worthwhile being. This view, which is of obvious application to rights of freedom and democratic participation, is applied to the necessities of life by arguing that these are significant primarily as prerequisites for the exercise of moral agency.[14]

I have doubts about this way of identifying the prime evil of poverty. The loss of the opportunity to act morally is an important but secondary matter compared with the suffering involved in extreme poverty. The causal precondition approach makes the suffering involved in poverty incidental to the evil of poverty, something that is derivative (and may not actually eventuate) from the lack of such factors as agency capability. It is a different matter to rest the right to sustenance on the simple nastiness of the actual experience of living such a deprived life. When the emphasis is on the causal precondition aspect of poverty this detracts attention

---

[11] Thus, 'We cannot form the idea of an innocent and sensible being, whose happiness we should not desire, or to whose misery, when distinctly brought home to the imagination, we should not have some degree of aversion' (Smith 1976: VI.ii.3.1). The distinctive feature of utilitarianism as an ethical theory is that it makes the production of pleasure and pain the *sole* moral criteria.

[12] An approach recently developed anew in Derek Parfit, 'Equality or Priority', in Clayton and Williams (2000: 81–125).

[13] This neo-Kantian approach is exemplified in the work of Alan Gewirth. '... by virtue of being actual or prospective agents who have certain needs of agency, persons have moral rights to freedom and well-being. Since all humans are such agents, the generic rights to freedom and well-being are human rights... It is obvious that starvation is a basic harm, a deprivation of basic well-being' (Gewirth 1982: 201ff.).

[14] Thus, Article 22 of the UDHR: 'Everyone, as a member of society, has the right to social security and is entitled to realization, through national effort and international cooperation and in accordance with the organization and resources of each State, of the economic, social, and cultural rights indispensable for his dignity and the free development of his personality'.

from the independent fact of the horrible experiences that it involves and this has the effect of lessening the urgency of the moral demand for alleviating poverty. There is no question that moral agency is one of the other values at risk when there is extreme poverty, but it is by no means the only source of grave moral concern.

While these analyses (suffering per se and agency capability) generally reinforce each other and would not appear to be in competition, they are in fact rather different in content and implications. In terms of content, the former is a matter of the intrinsic undesirability of poverty as a form of suffering and the other is a matter of its causal consequences (for human agency).[15] There are, therefore, reasons to adopt a humanitarian rather than a neo-Kantian interpretation of the intrinsic evil of poverty, but this is a family quarrel within the first broad approach canvassed above, that we need not settle here, for both agree that poverty is an evil for those who experience it even although they disagree as to the reasons why this is the case.

The second approach, which takes a more radical line in explaining why extreme poverty is a violation of human rights, focuses on the concept of justice and directs our attention to those who are responsible for the production of poverty through creating an unfair social system or exploiting or abusing superior economic power. Thus, Thomas Pogge argues that 'the relevant analogue for torture is then not poverty, but rather a certain kind of impoverishment that other agents are causally and morally responsible for' (Pogge, this volume, p. 15).

Without denying that there are special duties that arise from the culpable causation of suffering and other related evils (duties that fit conceptually under the heading of justice, a discourse in which relative merits are most at home) (Campbell 2001), it is important to emphasize the existence of other, desert-free foundations of duties to relieve poverty that derive from humanity rather than justice. Such duties are not special but, prima facie, general in that they are founded on the morally uncomplicated relationship between the evil of suffering and the obligation to relieve it.

The principle of benevolence or 'humanity' (as in 'humanitarian') is based on the propriety of the elemental response of aiding another human being arising from seeing, imagining, or knowing of the suffering of that being irrespective of who is suffering or why that suffering came about. Justice looks at the matter through a more complex prism, that always at least raises the question of whether the suffering in question is merited or deserved in some way and who if anyone may be responsible for its occurrence.

At the very least, both humanity and justice are relevant to the eradication of poverty. But, perhaps humanity in relation to extreme suffering has a certain priority over justice, a priority that plays a role in blocking exculpatory rationales used to excuse people from their obligations to do something about it, such as

---

[15] It might be argued that the moral agency approach detracts from the more important evil of suffering and shields us from the more immediate moral implications arising from the facts of human suffering, but I do not pursue that line of thought in this essay.

those based on the alleged moral failures of those in dire need, or excuses based on the property rights of those who are in a position to relieve that suffering.

It is important, therefore, that in exploring the idea that poverty may be a violation of human rights, we accept that, in some spheres at least, humanity comes before justice in the sense that it has a priority over justice whereby considerations of justice seem rather unimportant. In the case of extreme poverty, humanity renders some considerations of justice irrelevant and is certainly not dependent on justice for triggering an obligation to take steps to eradicate it. This moral position cannot be excluded by definitional dogmas. Contra Rawls, justice is not by definition the overriding factor in the distribution of benefits and burdens.[16] If poverty is a violation of human rights it is primarily because of the stringency of the moral demands arising from the existence of suffering, irrespective of the special characteristics or merits of those involved. On this view, poverty is the basis of a universal, unqualified claim based on the moral relationships between those who suffer and those who can do something about it. This position is not based on a pure utilitarian claim that producing pleasure and reducing pain are the sole grounds of moral and (justified) legal obligations (Singer 1993: 218–46).[17] At its weakest it is a claim that humanity is not always to be subordinated to considerations of justice and in the stronger version that I prefer it is that the relief of suffering is capable of generating moral obligations more stringent than those of justice.[18] Thus, the duty to relieve great suffering at small cost is more stringent than a duty to refrain from causing less suffering at greater (opportunity) cost.

It is possible to take this view but to hold that such obligations do not correlate with rights, despite the fact that it is the deprivations of those in poverty that is the moral grounds for the obligations in question. In some cases the motivation for adopting this position would appear to be a lack of interest in legal compulsion or remedies for the breach of obligation (Unger 1996). However, this is not sufficient to displace affirmation of correlative moral rights. Endorsing obligations arising from humanity but excluding the recognition of correlative rights may be adopted because the right to poverty relief does not always clearly correlate with an obligation that can be laid on a particular person or group of persons. However, the discourse of moral rights can operate without such simple correlations between person A's right and person(s) B's duties. In this case, the correlative duties may be, for instance, contributing to the relief of world poverty in proportion to each person's capacity to do so, and to promote and support the creation of a system

[16] This often repeated assumption is simply stipulated in the early pages of *A Theory of Justice* (Rawls 1999a). It is related to his rejection of natural desert as an ingredient of justice.

[17] My position is similar to Singer's in that it does not place conclusive weight on the distinction between causing harm and failing to prevent or alleviate harm in extreme circumstances. Singer goes further than this in his rejection of the moral significance of the difference between acts and omissions.

[18] In the terminology often used in this context, the priority of humanity over justice is not only conceptual (in that it can be defined independently) and specificatory (in that it can be specified independently) but justificatory and moral in that it has independent moral force that in certain cases may override other moral considerations. For further discussion see Cullity (1994).

whereby effective relief is provided for those living in poverty through coordinated redistribution. These duties are not morally optional and are grounded in the correlative rights of those living in extreme poverty.

My suggestion is that subsistence rights are grounded primarily in the universal humanitarian obligation to participate in the relief of extreme suffering. The universality of this obligation is relative to the capacity of the person or collective to contribute to the reduction of extreme poverty, in that the duty of relieving world poverty falls on everybody in proportion to their capacity to do so, although it may be enhanced by any role they may have in contributing to the existence of that poverty. To effectively institutionalize this moral relationship requires that mechanisms be put in place to operationalize the causal connections between obligations and rights, but the moral basis for creating such mechanisms is an uncomplicated moral duty of humanity.

2.3. THE PRINCIPLE OF HUMANITY IN PRACTICE

The prime objections to drawing primarily on the principle of humanity with respect to the eradication of poverty is that this is assumed to be a morally weaker basis than that of justice. Humanity is thought of as 'mere charity', and dissociated in some minds from the discourse of rights and obligations. What is at issue here is to some extent a matter of moral judgment, but there is also some confusion as to the meaning and implications of the principle itself.

It is necessary to point out that what is being argued is that humanity is a basis for obligation generally, and not just the sort of moral obligations that are not legally enforceable but as a basis for the moral justification of having legal obligations. This means that my thesis is not subject to the criticism that to make the relief of poverty dependent on humanity is to rely on charity in the sense of the grace and favor of benevolent human beings. Rather, the principle of humanity is proposed as an underlying justification for creating a means of dealing systematically with poverty and establishing mandatory duties to aid and the full range of possible remedies outlined above.

Thus, the principle of humanity could be used to justify adopting radical redistributive schemes through progressive domestic taxation regimes and coercive international measures of a sort that might be adopted through the UN. One such proposal is for a Global Humanitarian Levy (GHL), which aims to capture the humanitarian basis for the alleviation of extreme poverty by instituting a universal obligation to participate in tackling poverty as a global issue through a mechanism that embodies rough proportionality with respect to capacity to assist. This might involve a 2% tax on all personal incomes over US$50,000 per year, a levy of 2% on personal wealth above US$500,000, and equivalent corporate levies relating both to profits and wealth. These levies could be imposed via national governments but would be administered globally.

The legitimacy of such levies depends on the efficient use of the funds generated for the purpose of eradicating extreme poverty. This would mean that it could not be deployed solely through the medium of governments whose efficiency, morality, and accountability are in question. Solving these political and administrative difficulties would be a precondition of the legitimacy of the scheme, as is the case with the implementation of all attempts at global redistribution and development.

Given the coercion and intervention required to establish such a universal humanitarian scheme, it fits well with the paradigm of extreme poverty in a world replete with resources as being a violation of human rights and that such poverty ought to be abolished as a matter of urgency. It has the merit of not tying this conception closely to the controversial thesis that some poverty is standardly the outcome of the injustice and of emphasizing that the violation arises foremost because of the failure to eliminate that poverty rather than complicity in causing it. The violation occurs when those with the capacity to do so fail to respond. Leaving people in extreme poverty is the affront to humanity that could justify coercive intervention in support of a GHL and in principle the full range of possible legal remedies.

A prime rationale for a GHL is the principle of humanity, that it is the obligation of those who can relieve the extreme suffering of other human beings, an obligation that is not dependent on relative merits and demerits, or identifying those responsible for the causes of poverty or suffering generally except as part of a strategy for working out how to do something effective about the evils of poverty. Such a scheme rejects the common assumption that considerations of humanity are less stringent, more discretionary, or less demanding than those of justice.

It is helpful here to distinguish the stringency and the extent of the obligation to relieve poverty. It is true that making the perpetration of harm the moral basis for the duty to aid those in poverty may result in greater amounts being contributed by those who have been shown to be culpably responsible for that poverty than the amount contributed as a result of a duty to pay an equal share in the common task of relieving extreme poverty, but this does not make the stringency of the obligation to participate with others in the eradication of poverty less powerful than the duty to compensate for the poverty that you have caused. Indeed, on account of the relatively small contribution that is required to play one's part in a common humanitarian concern, it could be argued that the obligation of humanity is more powerful and our failure to respond to its requirements more culpable to the extent that it is easier to meet the obligation than where an act of injustice causes extensive harm.

Similarly, there is no implication that justifying such obligations in terms of humanity means that what is being suggested is adopting a paternalistic attitude to the poor, or rendering them subject to the discretionary choices of those who are better-off. Rather it is the basis for asserting a moral right to poverty relief and a firm basis for the creation of legal rights to the same end.

Further, once it is accepted that there are such humanitarian obligations, then failure to fulfil these obligations does, of course, raise issues of justice. It becomes a matter of justice that such obligations are enforced and that their neglect becomes a basis for civil liability and even criminal sanctions. Having humanity rather than justice as the grounds of the obligations in question does not mean that it is not a matter of justice that such obligations be implemented. The obligations are based on the inhumanity of neglecting poverty. Justice then requires that these obligations are performed or compensation paid. The humanitarian approach to poverty can therefore generate the sort of political and legal implications identified in section 2.1 of this chapter. Indeed, they provide a basis for allocation of legal obligations and remedies on a much wider basis than is enabled by requiring complicity in the causation of the poverty in question. In this respect, there is a false antithesis between humanity and justice, for while humanity may help us identify the wrong, it is justice that requires that the wrong be put right.

Many theorists remain doubtful about the humanitarian approach to poverty. One common stumbling block is that humanitarian obligations seem to be either too demanding (in that they require that those who are not poor should give away what they have until they are themselves poor) or too undemanding (in that they are weak to the point that the 'obligations' are in effect purely optional). The first objection, that humanitarianism is overly demanding, can be met by requiring only that people contribute their share in accordance with their capacity to do so, that share being calculated by considering what their pro rata contribution would be there a global scheme to eradicate poverty in place. The second objection, that humanitarianism is not demanding enough, can be rejected as a straightforward failure to grasp the moral force of the obligation in question. Perhaps this is a point on which moral progress needs to be made, through the acknowledgment of obligations that we have hitherto failed to grasp. What I have in mind here is something comparable to the moral progress which was marked by the realization that emerged 200 years ago that slavery is an evil institution. Charity, seen in terms of humanitarian obligations, must cease to be regarded as 'mere charity'. In relation to such phenomena as extreme poverty, failure to act when you are able to do so at little cost to yourself, must come to be seen as being just as morally culpable as actually bringing it about.

Thomas Pogge, in his book *World Poverty and Human Rights*, argues that it is a mistake to rely on such developing moral insights (2002*a*). Pogge holds to a sharp moral distinction between harming and not preventing harm, between killing and letting die. For him, therefore, the violation that grounds human rights obligations with respect to poverty must be a positive act of harming others in such a way as to cause their poverty in a culpable manner. He holds that, once we have come to grips with the horrendous phenomenon of global poverty, the crucial factor is the degree to which we are all, government, citizens, and corporations, complicit in a system that causes such poverty. The evil is not so much the poverty itself as the fact that it is the result of human institutions and collective choices.[19]

---

[19] Thus, 'We should not, then, think of our individual donations and of possible institutional poverty eradication initiatives ... as helping the poor, but as protecting them from the effects of global rules whose injustice benefits us and is our responsibility' (Pogge 2002*a*: 23).

When this is established then it may seem a relatively minor step to move from talking of human rights shortfalls to human rights violations. The easy assumption is that culpable causal responsibility establishes that those so responsible have an obligation to compensate those who are in poverty as a result of that culpable conduct as well as to refrain from producing poverty in the first place. A similar, if weaker, connection is made between those who have benefited (either unknowingly or unwillingly) as the result of an economic or political regime that has reduced to or kept others in poverty.

With such relationships we can readily make sense of the discourse of compensation, perhaps enforced by courts, and criminal liability for those who deliberately or negligently take part in systems that benefit themselves unfairly to the impoverishment of others. If we consider the analogy with slavery again, the thesis is that benefits that derive from such an institution are in themselves criminal. Outlawing such benefits may not immediately eradicate the phenomenon of slavery, but the violations approach does have the effect of removing official doubt as to the legitimacy of such an institution and opening the way for appropriate remedies against perpetrators, something that may not only be immediately justified but also in the long-term more effective in eradicating the phenomenon in question.

On these grounds, Pogge proposes his GRD to raise finance for the relief of poverty by taxing the proceeds of the extraction and sale of non-renewable resources as a way of rectifying the injustices involved in the global market, a scheme that has the welcome side effect of slowing down the rate of depletion of such resources (2002*a*: ch. 8). On the same basis he argues that 'the continuing imposition of this global order, essentially unmodified, constitutes a massive violation of the human right to basic necessities—a violation for which the governments and electorates of the more powerful countries bear primary responsibility' (Pogge, this volume).

Without casting serious doubt on the thesis that the international economic system is unjust or denying that it implicates all the developed world in the outrage of global poverty, tying the rhetoric of human rights violations to this culpability/complicity analysis of the grounding of the obligation to 'abolish poverty' must be questioned. Part of that questioning goes back to the fundamental issue raised earlier about whether the moral imperatives here are exclusively or even dominantly those of justice as distinct from humanity. Other parts of the critique relate to the variety of ways in which the content and implications of Pogge's thesis may be questioned. I group these under the following headings: (1) empirical controversiality; (2) individual and collective responsibility; (3) counter morality; and (4) conceptual constrictions.

(1) *Empirical controversiality.* The empirical controversiality critique focuses on Pogge's thesis that failure to support and implement an economic and social system that would have better consequences for the poor is culpable. The objections here are not to the moral thesis but to the empirical difficulty of establishing that there was or is an attainable more just system, where justice is taken to be partly dependent on the outcomes of the system.

Take the fairly crude question as to the economic benefits or harms resulting from the attempt to instantiate the libertarian ideology of minimal government and freedom of trade. Many horror stories can be told as to the poverty deriving from the implementation of such 'economic rationalism', as the recent history of Mexico and many South American economies amply demonstrates. But how can we hope to get agreement as to whether there were better options available, either by more rigorous implementation of the libertarian model or by adopting somewhat different policies? We all have our own views on these matters, but so much depends on speculation about counterfactual situations and their likely outcomes that we must be said to lack an agreed empirical consensus, even among people of good will, to found even a probabilistic basis for an assertion about human rights violations on which it would be safe to found coercive measures.

(2) *Individual and collective responsibility.* Supposing the facts are not in doubt, and that we can agree that there were and are feasible alternatives to past and present economic orders, is this sufficient to identify those who are responsible for that order and who therefore, on the basis of justice, ought to compensate those who have been harmed by it to the point of impoverishment? The problems that arise here relate to individual responsibility for collective arrangements, arrangements that must be in many respects the unintended outcomes of uncoordinated individual choices with unforseen and often unforeseeable consequences on the part of people who are in any case powerless to change the existing order of things.

Of course, that does not mean that the existing social and economic order is not seriously unjust or that unfair advantage does not accrue to the world's wealthy minority and the elites of some developing nations, but it does suggest that the vast majority of that wealthy minority cannot reasonably be held responsible for something that they did not create and that they cannot change, at least not to the extent that it can generate an obligation to correct the moral imbalance caused by their culpability.

This does not in itself rule out drawing on the existence of an unjust domestic and international economic order as the basis for policy changes that promote fairer distribution of wealth and more equitable trading arrangements between nations, but it does suggest that the main argument for such reorderings should not be founded on an assertion of the grave moral guilt of those who have not striven to promote more just arrangements.

Considerations of moral guilt could, in principle, be more appropriately applied to those who taking a leading political and commercial role in knowingly per-petrating and supporting such injustices for personal gain. Where the chain of moral responsibility is clear and the evil of what is being done is not in serious dispute, personal, and in the case of governments and corporations, collective, liability both civil and criminal may be appropriate. Indeed this may be seen as the ultimate point of categorizing much extreme poverty as a violation of human rights and even describing it as a crime against humanity. The danger is that such reasoning will be more broadly applied to persons whose moral guilt comes nowhere near that which would license the use of such terminology. Indeed, it seems clear that the moral guilt of those affluent people who fail to give anything significant toward the elimination of poverty must be seen as greater than those who benefit from, but have not intentionally contributed to, an unfair global trading system.

(3) *Counter Morality.* One response to the dilution of moral responsibility that occurs in relation to political and economic systems is to rely, when seeking to establish the obligation to remedy unjust situations, on a very weak sense of 'participation' in such systems according to which all that is required to establish obligation is that there is a 'system' in the sense that decisions and actions taken in one place have systematic effects in another place. Thus, my purchase of tea rather than coffee, together with similar choices by millions of others, may disadvantage coffee producers and advantage tea producers in different parts of the same economic system. This 'system' may be described as an 'order' either in the weak sense that it is patterned and therefore 'orderly', or because it is the product of 'orders' in the form of rules laid down and enforced by authorities, such as the intellectual property regime under the TRIPS agreement.

I have already argued that those who act or are affected by the actions of others in such systems cannot be held to be responsible to a significant extent, if at all, for the systemic results of their actions unless we can identify them as key figures in any decisions or rule-making aspects that may be involved in them. This is true even if the results of the operations of such systems are clearly and extremely unjust. It can also be argued that such systems require to be justified in an all things considered framework that takes into account all their origins and consequences.

Thus, in relation to poverty, evaluations of the market system, or particular forms of market system, we have to see markets as economic and social mechanisms that may be necessary preconditions of the material improvements in human well-being. In this context, markets must be accepted as desirable if we accept that poverty is undesirable. As A. K. Sen points out, the prima facie moral status of markets generally must be high (1985: 1). But if market systems are the most effective way of producing the wealth that takes people out of the realm of poverty and makes available resources that may be used to alleviate poverty, it follows that being 'implicated' or 'participating' in market systems has a positive value that may be used to counter the claim that those who are so participant are responsible for the poverty of those who suffer as a result of this particular market system. It follows that it is not reasonable to criticize people for acting in accordance with the market order by, for instance, making their purchasing choices in the light of their preferences and their own priorities in spending their available resources. By so doing they contribute as they ought to the market system that generates the resources indispensable for many morally imperative ends.

This may not, of course, be intended by those who regard current market arrangements, or perhaps all market-based economies, as involving violations of human rights either because they may leave vast numbers of people in poverty or because they actually reduce almost as many to poverty. But if this is not intended, then it needs to be made clear that what is being called for is adaptations in market arrangements either to make them more fair or (and this is not necessarily the same thing) to ensure that they do not result in significant deprivations for some of those affected by it, for instance by a system of welfare redistribution. Such policy recommendations need not be based on any general criticism of market economic systems, or any culpability on the part of those involved in such systems. Indeed participation in such economic orders in accordance with their existing rules may have beneficial and laudable aspects.

Again, such considerations do not negate the morality of improving systems so that they have more and better distributed benefits, but they do suggest that identifying ordinary market players as complicit in human rights violations may be simplistic, misleading, and counterproductive. Simplistic because it ignores the overall performance of such systems in relation to generating wealth, misleading because it misascribes responsibility for existing and doubtless highly imperfect systems, and counterproductive because the flaws in the argument enable people to doubt and thence avoid fulfilling obligations that are in effect better grounded in other (humanitarian) considerations. Perhaps for this reason, Pogge tends to fall back on the culpability that arises from not rectifying the unjust economic order through engaging in effective political action.

(4) *Conceptual restrictions.* Finally, by way of a critique of what may be called the culpability approach to the abolition of poverty, I would point to certain dubious assumptions about the discourse of human rights that are involved, at least in Pogge's version. I am referring here to the thesis that human rights relate solely to claims against social institutions, particularly the state.[20] Pogge's thesis is that not all wrongs count as human-rights wrongs. If someone steals my car or locks me up that is not a violation of my human right to property or liberty, but if the state confiscates my car or locks me up, then it may be. As we have seen above, there are powerful historical and practical arguments for seeing the state as the prime focus of human rights violations and as the prime focus for the obligations to protect and promote human rights, but to view all human rights violations through the medium of coercive institutions is to mistake the contingent instrument for the evil we are seeking to curb. Excluding the harms that are inflicted or left unassuaged by business organizations, criminal conduct of individuals, and natural disasters, particularly at a time when the capacities of most states to remedy such harms has been dramatically reduced, is to underplay the potential relevance and impact of human rights discourse.

Certainly human-rights harms call for organized and systematic responses. The discourse of rights requires that we establish effective systems of rules to prevent and remedy harmful conduct. But to confine the evils that call for such remedies to those perpetrated by coercive human organizations is to diminish the potential of human rights with respect to affecting private and natural harms. It also plays a background role, I suspect, in encouraging approaches that seek to found human rights obligations entirely on identifying those who bring about or knowingly benefit from unjust systems. For, as we have seen, while this is no doubt an important part of the picture, it is only a part.

---

[20] 'We should conceive human rights primarily as claims on coercive social institutions and secondarily as claims against those who uphold such institutions' (Pogge 2002*a*: 44 f.).

2.4. CONCLUSION

In considering how to interpret and justify the thesis that poverty is a violation of human rights and ought to be abolished, there is a tactical element that intrudes into what may seem a purely conceptual or philosophical matter. Adopting this or that terminology may help or hinder the agreed objective of eradicating world poverty. Thus, the resistance to the discourse of humanity and the enthusiasm for that of justice may be based largely on what is perceived to be most forceful and therefore potentially most effective language to use. The discourse of humanity appears, to some people, to be too weak, too diffuse, insufficiently justiciable, and morally optional. Justice, on the other hand, is seen as strong, precise, legally operationalizable, and morally mandatory.

These empirical assumptions may all be challenged. Humanitarian reasoning can provide a basis for adopting strong, focused, and justiciable schemes for eradicating poverty. And the rationale it provides for so doing is uncomplicated and incontrovertible. Moreover, the discourse of humanity is not exclusive of ideas of violation, justice, rights, and remedies. We have noted that it is a gross injustice to let people off for failures to implement humanitarian obligations. Further this approach broadens the range of those to whom the obligation to work for the eradication of poverty applies. Currently, humanitarianism may be less persuasive than justice. But this does not mean abandoning the discourse of humanity for tactical reasons. Rather it suggests that we need to work for the emergence of moral progress of a kind that led to a universal acknowledgment that the once time-honored practice of slavery is morally heinous. A similar recognition is emerging as to the evil of allowing extreme poverty to continue in a world that has ample resources to see to its eradication.

In fact, most people in moments of contemplation accept such humanitarian duties in principle. The progress that has to be made is increasing awareness that failure to put this contemplative judgment into practice is a grave wrong to those who continue to suffer in consequence. While it may sometimes be a better short-term strategy to base a policy to eradicate extreme worldwide poverty on considerations of justice alone, there are tactical as well as philosophical reasons for arguing that the moral duty to help those in extreme material need is based primarily on considerations of humanity and only secondarily on justice.

3

The Moral Reality of Human Rights

*John Tasioulas**

3.1. INTRODUCTION

The elevation of the discourse of human rights in recent times to the status of an ethical lingua franca has fueled an unruly proliferation of incompatible or often just incredible rights claims. If human rights are not to fall victim to their own popularity, some principled way of distinguishing the genuine articles from the presumed spate of counterfeits is required. It is no answer to invoke the 'human rights' proclaimed as such in international treaties and declarations. To begin with, they lack the requisite universality: the instruments in which they are set out are often not legally binding and even those that are binding are not subscribed to by all states (or are subscribed to by many states subject to eviscerating reservations). More importantly, the international regime of human rights is not morally self-validating; instead, its legitimacy depends on its conformity with independent moral standards, including genuine human rights. So the intended shortcut through law and political practice rapidly leads back to our original problem.

Although philosophers disagree about whether or how the problem can be solved, many of them agree on the general character of any adequate solution. According to this standard picture, as I shall call it, which human rights exist is a *moral* question to be distinguished from the predominantly *institutional* question of the extent to which they are recognized, respected, or enforced. An uncompromising formulation of the view is given by Thomas Nagel:

> The existence of moral rights does not depend on their political recognition or enforcement but rather on the moral question whether there is a decisive justification for including these forms of inviolability in the status of every member of the moral community. The reality of moral rights is purely normative rather than institutional—though of course institutions may be designed to enforce them. (Nagel 2002: 33)[1]

* I am grateful to James Griffin, and to those who attended the seminars on human rights we jointly gave at Oxford in Trinity Term 2003, for comments on the first draft of this chapter. I also benefited from presenting versions of the paper to audiences at the University of Melbourne, the Australian National University and Monash University during my tenure of an Australian Bicentennial Fellowship in early 2004. I owe a special debt to Onora O'Neill and Thomas Pogge for their comments. My thanks are also due to Jerry Cohen, Samantha Besson, James Nickel, Dale Smith, Leif Wenar, Charles Beitz, Mark Philp, and William Twining for helpful responses to previous drafts.

[1] The standard picture is also elaborated and defended at length in Feinberg (2003).

Human rights, so conceived, have implications for the creation, modification, or abolition of institutions, but their existence is determined by moral reasoning, not by whatever institutional facts happen to obtain. Of course, institutional mechanisms—such as treaties, Bills of Rights, constitutional courts, and so on—can play a vital role in implementing human rights. In particular, they can render their content more determinate by making or reflecting an authoritative choice from among alternative eligible specifications of human rights norms. But, according to the standard picture, the rights must have a tolerably determinate content independently of any subsequent institutional specification they might receive. If they did not, there would be no warrant for treating them as human rights in the first place.

The distinction between the normative and institutional questions does not simply arise, as Nagel seems to imply in drawing no distinction between 'moral rights' and 'human rights', from the fact that human rights are morally justified. Nor is it the upshot of their moral character combined with universality of scope. These two features distinguish human rights from institutionally dependent rights that are neither morally justified nor possessed by all, such as the legal rights of slave-owners. But their moral standing does not differentiate them from moral rights that partly depend for their existence on institutional facts, for example moral entitlements arising from one's membership of an ongoing institutional scheme, such as a university or a state. Moreover, institutionally dependent moral rights are also capable of embracing all of humanity. Consider, for example, a global economic regime that assigns to every individual in the world a right of access to a newly discovered natural resource. The rights conferred by such a regime, although morally justified and universal in scope, would not count as human rights on the standard picture. Instead, what also lies behind that picture is the idea that human rights are moral entitlements possessed by all *simply in virtue of their humanity*. It seems to follow from this definition that no account needs to be taken of individuals' special relationships to persons, groups, and institutions in determining which human rights exist. And this is so even if the human *capacity* for entering into such relationships is a relevant consideration in identifying human rights.

This last point highlights the fact that there are different versions of the 'standard picture'. One rather austere version interprets human rights as 'natural rights', that is rights meaningfully capable of being possessed in a state of nature. This interpretation secures the timelessness of human rights—they can be ascribed to all human beings throughout history—but only at the apparent cost of excluding rights that require or presuppose the existence of non-universal social practices and institutions, for example, rights to political participation or to a fair trial. By contrast, I have suggested that human rights enjoy a temporally constrained form of universality, so that the question of which human rights exist can only be answered within some specified historical context. For people today and the foreseeable future, human rights are those rights possessed in virtue of being human and inhabiting a social world that is subject to the conditions of modernity

(Tasioulas 2002*a*: 86–8).[2] This historical constraint permits very general facts about feasible institutional design in the modern world, for example, forms of legal regulation, political participation, and economic organization, to play a role in determining which human rights we recognize. But this is different from making the existence of human rights turn on the specific institutional arrangements that obtain at any particular time and place.

The standard picture, if it can be vindicated, endows human rights with great critical power; this is a major source of the picture's appeal. So understood, human rights do not passively mirror the lamentable state of a world in which millions are routinely tortured, persecuted for their religious beliefs, or lack the material resources needed for a minimally decent life. Instead, they set standards to which reality must be made to conform. In view of this critical power and the widespread resonance of the language of human rights, it is unsurprising that UNESCO's strategy for eradicating global poverty is articulated within a 'human rights framework'. What more unequivocal way of condemning severe poverty than to affirm a human right to be free from it and, guided and inspired by that affirmation, to struggle for the fulfillment of that right in a world in which, as things now stand, 1.2 billion people subsist on less than $1 per day and one-third of all deaths annually are poverty-related? (Pogge, this volume).

Of course, to assert the existence of an HRP is one thing; to make good on that assertion is something very different. Let me briefly offer a highly schematic account of how an HRP might be justified within a broadly 'interest-based' theory of rights.[3] On such an account, a right exists if an individual's interest, taken by itself, has the requisite kind of importance to justify the imposition of duties on others variously to respect, protect, and promote that interest. Human rights are rights that all human beings possess simply in virtue of their humanity; on the interest-based account, they are rights grounded in universal interests significant enough to generate duties on the part of others. Although it would be pleasingly symmetrical, there is no implication that the duties must also be universal (i.e., that all persons bear the duties correlative to the human rights enjoyed by all). Some interest theorists further restrict or qualify the nature of the interests that can ground human rights. James Griffin, for example, seeks to derive human rights exclusively from the values of personhood, that is autonomy and liberty, thereby conferring a determinate sense on the idea that human rights are protections of a special status, 'human dignity'. Like Martha Nussbaum, I favor a more pluralistic

---

[2] What 'modernity' amounts to, in this connection, is a large question. For present purposes, I simply endorse Charles Taylor's characterization of it as 'that historically unprecedented amalgam of new practices and institutional forms (science, technology, industrial production, and urbanization), of new ways of living (individualism, secularization, and instrumental rationality), and new forms of malaise (alienation, meaninglessness, and a sense of impending social dissolution)' (Taylor 2004: 1).

[3] For a classic exposition of the theory, see Raz (1986: ch. 7). Note, however, that owing to an 'atemporal' interpretation of universality of the sort I said should be rejected, Raz is skeptical about the existence of human rights (or, at least, the sort of rights usually thought to be human rights), see Tasioulas (2002*a*: 86–8).

conception of the interests that can generate human rights. Unlike her, however, I am resistant to the notion that these values are best conceived as *political* in status, in a way that purports to disengage from contentious issues about their philosophical explication.[4] Now, even within an interest-based account of the sort outlined so far, there are different potential strategies for justifying an HRP. One strategy is essentially derivative. It begins by justifying certain other rights, for example a right to political participation, and then contends that the enjoyment of an HRP is necessary, whether instrumentally or constitutively, for securing the former rights. But the HRP can also be given an independent justification that does not proceed from an interest in exercising any other right, a justification to which the derivative justifications are supplementary. This independent justification would go broadly as follows:

(1) For all human beings, poverty consists in a significant level of material deprivation that poses a serious threat to a number of their interests: health, physical security, autonomy, understanding, friendship, etc.

(2) The threat posed by extreme poverty to the interests enumerated in (1) is, in the case of each human being, *pro tanto* of sufficient gravity to justify the imposition of duties on others, for example to refrain from impoverishing them, protect them from impoverishment, and assist those already suffering from severe material deprivation.

(3) The duties generated at (2) represent practicable claims on others given the constraints created by general and relatively entrenched facts of human nature and social life in the modern world.

Therefore:

(4) Each individual human being has a right to be free from severe poverty.

The HRP is meant to secure for all humans access to the means of subsistence—clean air and water, adequate food, clothing and shelter, and a basic minimum of health care—thereby enabling them to have what is needed for 'a decent chance at a reasonably healthy and active life of more or less normal length, barring tragic interventions' (Shue 1996a: 23). Nothing in the preceding argument precludes the existence of a human right to a more expansive set of resources and opportunities than those needed to secure individuals against extreme poverty. It is arguable, for example, that Article 25(1) of the UDHR—with its reference to a standard of living adequate for individual well-being rather than just subsistence—is a heftier economic entitlement than the HRP, at least if we accept the orthodox empirical measure of extreme poverty as set by the threshold of $1 per day.[5]

---

[4] For Griffin's view and my criticism, see Griffin (2001b) and Tasioulas (2002a). For Nussbaum's view and my skepticism about the Rawlsian *political* interpretation of human rights, see Nussbaum (2000: ch. 2) and Tasioulas (2002b: 390–5).

[5] 'Everyone has the right to a standard of living adequate for the health and well-being of himself and of his family, including food, housing and medical care and necessary social services and the right to security in the event of unemployment, sickness, disability, widowhood, old age or other lack of

3.2. A MERE 'MANIFESTO' RIGHT?

In this chapter, I defend the HRP against a line of attack that opposes the standard picture's separation of the normative and the institutional with respect to the identification of human rights (or, in the case of the second objection, with respect to so-called 'welfare' rights, like the HRP). Of course, skepticism about human rights generally is heavily overdetermined. One source is an outright rejection of at least some of the 'values' human rights embody as flawed or perhaps as not really values at all. This is exemplified by the familiar critique of the traditional schedule of human rights as reflecting a narrowly individualistic or masculine perspective that is sharply at odds with the so-called 'communitarian' or 'feminine' values of social harmony and care. Another variety of skepticism challenges not the values underlying human rights but rather their use as a litmus test of the legitimacy of all political communities without exception, even those whose traditions embody very different ethical orientations. Whatever their general prospects, both forms of skepticism seem implausible when pressed against the very existence (as opposed to some interpretation or other) of an HRP, since it does not obviously reflect concerns that are either distinctively individualistic or Western.

But a third form of skepticism poses a graver threat. This is the broad claim that, in the current and foreseeable state of the world, the assertion of an HRP is a hopelessly utopian gesture. It therefore has no basis in a normative reality that is, after all, supposed to inform us about what we are entitled to and from whom. Indulging in such gestures is tantamount to the harmless incantations of 'white magic' (Geuss 2001*a*: 144) or, worse, to a 'bitter mockery to the poor and needy' (O'Neill 1996: 133). These gestures are also potentially counterproductive insofar as they foster unrealistic expectations on the part of inevitably frustrated activists and would-be beneficiaries. Alternatively, if proclaiming the existence of an HRP has some value, it is the value that rhetorical pronouncements can achieve despite their falsity, such as the expressive value of manifesting a good will or the strategic value of effecting desirable modifications in individual and institutional behavior. But such pronouncements do not state any normative truth: the 'right' in question is only a political aspiration or 'manifesto right', not a bona fide right of all individuals.

My concern is with two specific forms this third objection takes when pressed against an HRP. According to the *enforceability objection*, rights are effectively enforceable claims that individuals can bring to bear against those who shoulder the correlative obligations: to make them carry out their obligations or, at least, to provide an effective remedy for their failure to do so. A condition of the existence of a right is that it is actually enforceable; it is not enough that it would be enforceable in some improved state of the world. As Raymond Geuss has put it, it is 'essential to the existence of a set of "rights" that there be some specifiable and more or less effective mechanism for enforcing them' (Geuss 2001*a*: 143).

---

livelihood in circumstances beyond his control'. See also Article 11(1) of the International Covenant on Economic, Social and Cultural Rights.

Human rights, therefore, would be entitlements possessed by all human beings that can be enforced against the relevant duty-bearers, thereby ensuring reliable access to the object of their rights or else appropriate compensation. But, in fact, there are few—if any—such universally enforceable entitlements in the world today. Indeed, Geuss goes so far as to claim that his objection is 'lethal to the whole idea of a natural or human right', showing it to be 'inherently confused' (Geuss 2001a: 146, 156). For Geuss, to assert a HRP confuses the existence of a right with a mere moral belief as to what would be a valuable state of affairs. Of course, we might eventually institute a system of enforceable claims held by all human beings, for example through the creation of an effective international legal regime of human rights. But such rights will exist because we have made them into enforceable claims; they will not have preexisted their institutional realization as grounds for assessing actual legal rights. This is because '[t]he only thing that can serve that purpose seems to be the flickering light of our variable moral beliefs' (Geuss 2001a: 144), not anything worthy of the description of 'rights'.

According to the second, *claimability objection*, rights are inherently *claimable*, if not always effectively enforceable. This means there must be specifiable agents against whom the right may be claimed, agents who bear the counterpart obligations to those rights. Some human rights, it seems, unproblematically satisfy this constraint, that is the classic 'negative' liberties, such as the right not to be tortured. This right imposes, as its key normative implication, a duty on all to refrain from torture. But a right against extreme poverty is typically thought to entail positive duties to provide its holders with opportunities and resources. Such duties are not plausibly regarded as incumbent on all human beings. As Onora O'Neill has put it: 'rights not to be killed or to speak freely are matched by and require universal obligations not to kill or not to obstruct free speech; but a universal right to food cannot simply be matched by a universal obligation to provide an aliquot morsel of food' (O'Neill 2000: 135). Instead, such rights require some sort of institutional structure to allocate duties and define their content. In the absence of institutionally allocated and defined duties, the assertion of a HRP is, yet again, another piece of rhetoric that has potentially damaging political consequences. In its place, O'Neill would favor the recognition of imperfect obligations—obligations with no correlative moral rights—to aid those with agency-threatening needs and, where appropriate, to assist in constructing institutional systems of welfare rights. But those welfare rights, which depend on institutions allocating the correlative duties, will not be human rights as understood on the standard picture. Instead, they will be institutional rights that give expression to imperfect obligations that are not, as a matter of pure moral reasoning, the counterparts of individual rights.[6]

---

[6] The upshot, on O'Neill's analysis, is that the duty to relieve extreme poverty is an imperfect duty of charity, rather than a perfect duty of justice. See O'Neill (1989: 225). This has various consequences within her theory. Most fundamentally, non-compliance with imperfect duties does not directly wrong any other person. Accordingly, such duties lack the stringency of duties of justice (those that have correlative rights), which do prohibit wrongs against specifiable others.

Both objections just rehearsed should be distinguished from a deeper criticism of the HRP as 'utopian'. This is the claim that a world in which that right is secured for all human beings is not a feasible objective given very general and ineradicable facts about human capacities and motivation, limited resources and the inexorable constraints of social life. This violation of the 'ought' implies 'can' maxim disqualifies it from being a genuine right of all human beings. Speculating in this vein, Richard Rorty in his UNESCO lecture entertained the grim prospect that 'the rich parts of the world may be in the position of somebody proposing to share her one loaf of bread with a hundred starving people. Even if she does share, everybody, including herself, will starve anyway. So she may easily be guilty ... either of self-deception or hypocrisy' (Rorty 1996; see also Geuss 2001*b*: 101–3). Now, a defender of the HRP can respond to this objection in a number of ways: by arguing that it betrays an unjustified pessimism about the available means for securing that right;[7] by relativizing what the HRP demands to those means;[8] or by insisting that the test of feasibility need only be passed by each individual's right taken singly and not by the aggregate of all rights-based claims taken as a whole.[9] Whichever response is adopted, the key point here is that the defender of the interest-based theory should accept that a feasibility constraint must be satisfied as a prelude to affirming the HRP. Its relevance was marked in step (3) of the schematic argument outlined in section 3.1. Recognition of its importance also motivates my suggestion that the existence of human rights is to be determined with respect to a specified historical context, given that any such context will enable sufficiently reliable judgments of feasibility to be reached. All this differs from the appropriate response to the enforceability and claimability objections—objections that invoke demands that may be unfulfilled even when the feasibility constraint has been met. Neither enforceability nor claimability, I argue, is an existence condition of human rights.

Notice also that, although differing significantly in the extent of their opposition to the standard picture of human rights, both the enforceability and claimability objections challenge the normative and institutional divide implicit in it. Of course, there is no necessary connection between enforceability and claimability, on the one hand, and institutional mechanisms that secure them, on the other. But in the absence of divine intervention or the workings of a reenchanted nature, enforceability is most obviously to be secured through effective institutional mechanisms (as well as various other broader cultural factors and personal qualities that ensure the good functioning of such mechanisms).[10] Similarly, claimability does not necessarily require the existence of institutions allocating the relevant duties—that was supposed to be illustrated by the example of universal

---

[7] For example, both Thomas Pogge and Peter Singer have suggested that the cost of eradicating the severest manifestations of poverty worldwide would amount to around 1% of the annual disposable income of the wealthiest tenth of mankind. See Pogge (2002*b*: 152) and Singer (2002: 194).

[8] For example, Pogge (2002*a*: 68), who suggests that one cannot be entitled to resources others need to survive.

[9] For example, Waldron (1993*b*: 207–8).

[10] See, e.g., James (2003) and Pogge (2002*a*: 62–3).

negative obligations, such as the duty to refrain from torture, generated by the right not to be tortured. But in the case of rights that ground duties requiring the active provision of opportunities, resources, etc., some institutional specification of duty-bearers seems necessary if the claimability condition is to be met.

3.3. RESPONDING TO THE ENFORCEABILITY OBJECTION

Geuss's enforceability argument depends on the contrast between an enforceable claim (a genuine right) and a moral belief, including a moral belief as to what 'enforceable claims' should exist. The standard picture of human rights, he says, offers only the latter, fobbing us off with 'a kind of puffery' (Geuss 2001*a*: 144). But why should the fact that claims about the existence of rights express beliefs about entitlements all humans have, irrespective of whether they are currently enforceable, render them rhetorical gestures in the absence of a reliable enforcement mechanism to give them teeth?

Geuss's answer is twofold: that there is radical disagreement about moral matters and that, even if it abated, this would not 'guarantee effective action' (Geuss 2001*a*: 146). But the second point merely reiterates his thesis, whereas the first generalizes well beyond rights discourse since there is no less controversy about the duties people have, what their 'true' interests are, which ideals are worthy of adoption and so on. Does it follow that, in the absence of consensus, such notions are also illusory? If so, Geuss's argument is unmasked as an all-out attack on moral thought. Moreover, it is an attack to which his own enforceability thesis is vulnerable insofar as it too is in part the upshot of a controversial moral argument. In any case, why should the very fact of deep and interminable moral disagreement have such drastic consequences? The answer, of course, is that Geuss thinks it is a basis for rejecting any form of ethical objectivity: the realm of moral belief is a realm of *mere* belief and hence of rationally intractable disagreement. As an adherent of a broadly Nietzschean perspective, he not only repudiates ethical objectivity but would likely interpret any aspiration to it as evincing the resentment of the right-claimant toward the supposed duty-bearer. On this debunking account, claims of objectivity are attempts by the weak to invoke some imaginary coercive 'force' that will back up their demands for protection.[11] But the friend of human rights who believes that they have an objective basis will have no truck with these Nietzschean moves. He will instead insist that we have good reason to disentangle the aspiration to objectivity from any claim about power, or what Rorty calls 'a noncontingent and powerful ally' who will enforce one's beliefs against transgressors. And with the possibility of objective justification in play,

---

[11]   Richard Rorty makes precisely this point in connection with human rights in his Oxford Amnesty lecture: 'We *resent* the idea that we shall have to wait for the strong to turn their piggy little eyes to the suffering of the weak. We desperately hope that there is something stronger and more powerful that will *hurt* the strong if they do *not*—if not a vengeful God, then a vengeful aroused proletariat, or, at least, a vengeful superego, or, at the very least, the offended majesty of Kant's tribunal of pure practical reason' (1993: 130–1).

why should we not understand the notion of rights as genuine entitlements that provide a critical purchase on social reality, even if they are unenforceable at any given time for the vast majority of people?

Still, we might interpret Geuss's view as expressing something less than a blanket denial of ethical objectivity. The reason why assertions of human rights constitute 'mere beliefs', in the absence of an enforcement mechanism, is that attempts objectively to justify human rights *in particular* are doomed. Geuss simply presupposes this to be so in *History and Illusion in Politics*, but more recently he has offered the following hint of an argument:

> [W]hat are sometimes called the 'normative foundations' of this theory ['natural human rights'] are anything but clear (and convincing). The suspicion immediately suggests itself that the reason for this is that the project of finding a completely secular, immanent 'grounding' for such a theory is incoherent: there simply is not any direct argumentative path from facts of nature and human psychology, as these are known to us through experience and the usual forms of scientific enquiry, the economic and commercial requirements of the kind of society in which we live, and some minimal principles of rationality, to the desired doctrine of natural human rights. (2003: 47)

There are two problems here. The first is that the sort of justification Geuss finds questionable is not one that the believer in objectively grounded human rights is bound to deliver. The notion of 'the human' or 'human interest' that is the basis of a compelling theory of human rights should not be construed value-neutrally or as reliant on a 'thin' account of rational self-interest. This ambitious characterization of what it would take to justify human rights might fit some theories, especially those of a contractarian stamp, but it does not tally with the self-understanding of leading contemporary proponents of the interest-based approach to human rights.[12] Geuss needs to do far more to substantiate his 'suspicion' about the human rights project if it is to trouble them. The second problem is that Geuss slides too quickly from the claim that human rights have no foothold in an 'objective' moral reality to the idea that the only reality they can achieve is that of being enforceable claims. But the point about metaethical status does not automatically yield that very specific normative payoff. Anti-objectivist adherents of the standard picture will plausibly insist that, although not susceptible to an objective moral justification, the existence of human rights need not be brutely institutional in that way. It may consist, instead, in their being the deliverances of a suitably refined ethical subjectivity or the presuppositions of certain social practices to which we are ineluctably committed.

Does this mean that we can discount the idea that enforceability stands in any interesting relationship to the existence conditions of human rights? Well, one conclusion we might draw is that it does, but in a very different way from that stipulated by Geuss. The point can be seen as emerging, contrary to her own intentions, from Susan James's recent attempt to build on Geuss's central thesis by elaborating on the conditions that render rights enforceable claims. According

---

[12] See, e.g., Griffin (2001*a*: 313) and Nussbaum (2000: ch. 1).

to James, it is among these conditions that duty-bearers know both *what* they are obligated to do and *how* to discharge their obligations. A further condition is a general social climate in which the right is regarded as valuable and there is support for its fulfillment through appropriate social arrangements (James 2003: 140, 143). Now, a defender of the standard picture can respond that one important technique for getting people to satisfy both conditions is by enabling them to grasp and act in the light of the moral justification for the imposition of certain duties on them. In other words, an appreciation of the case for the existence of a right as an interest that merits the imposition of duties on others helps to create the broader context of understanding and support that is essential to the genuine enforceability of rights.

But we have not yet scotched the idea of a conceptual link between rights and enforceability. Even if we give up on Geuss's uncompromising identification of rights with the power to enforce entitlements, might we not salvage from his discussion the idea that rights claims express the moral belief that certain entitlements ought to be secured through some reliable enforcement mechanism? Here, the institutional element in the existence conditions of rights would be normative, rather than reflective of actual social reality. In other words, rights will exist only if they are entitlements that *ought* to be enforced, regardless of whether they actually *are* currently enforceable. An immediate problem with this sort of proposal is the indeterminacy of the phrase 'reliable enforcement mechanism'. One popular way of making it more determinate is represented by Jürgen Habermas's thesis that 'human rights have an inherently juridical nature and are conceptually oriented toward positive enactment by legislative bodies' (Habermas 2001: 122). Those who follow this venerable line of thought defend what Joel Feinberg has aptly dubbed the 'there ought to be a law' theory of moral rights. According to this theory, 'A has a moral right to do (have or be) X' is to be understood as 'A *ought* to have a *legal* right to X' (Feinberg 2003: 45).[13]

Even this weaker thesis should, I think, be discarded. First, it fails on its own terms, since it is a notorious fact that the legal enactment of human rights is not enough to confer legal authority to enforce them, let alone the actual power to do so. To begin with, this is because a legal right can exist without any associated remedy—the right can be declaratory, for example, or enforceable only by a person or body other than the right-holder, for example, some arm of government.[14] Whether a right exists in law is a question distinct from whether it is justiciable or (legally) enforceable. This is certainly true of vast tracts of the international law of human rights. Moreover, even if the enforcement of the

---

[13] It is worth bearing in mind here O'Neill's warning against adopting any 'supposedly exhaustive contrast between that which is enforced by law and that which is simply voluntary', see O'Neill (1989: 232). There may be other versions of the enforceability thesis that are not tied to specifically *legal* enforcement. But questions will arise as to whether they are plausible or, if plausible, sufficiently determinate to be of interest.

[14] It is not clear from Geuss's discussion whether rights must be enforceable at the discretion of the right-holder, or whether it is sufficient if some third part is able to enforce them on the right-holder's behalf. I leave this issue aside in what follows.

putative right is legally authorized, the fact of such authorization may issue in no de facto power to enforce the right. Instead, the right might be effectively unenforceable due to deficiencies in the motivations and capabilities of the right-holders and duty-bearers. For instance, the former might lack knowledge of their rights or the means to avail themselves of them, while the latter might be unable or unwilling to identify or discharge their obligations. Finally, of course, many supposed human rights are enacted by cynical governments for cosmetic or strategic purposes and without any genuine intention to uphold them.

Still, these observations may simply force a slight modification to the original thesis, namely, that to claim a human right exists is to say that it ought to be an effectively *enforceable* legal entitlement. Yet even thus modified, serious problems remain. As a conceptual matter, the revised thesis does not fit the ordinary discourse of moral rights. We often speak of such rights in indicative terms as being exercised or violated even before they have become law. And we typically feel justified in asserting their existence irrespective of how things stand with respect to legal enactment. Consider the situation of slaves in America's preabolitionist era. They are naturally thought of as having possessed rights that were in fact violated. The claim that they had these rights is not equivalent to a claim about what rights to liberty the law ought to have conferred on them, although it may figure as a premise in an argument for the latter. In response, the juridical thesis might now be presented as a revisionary interpretation intended to instill some much-needed rigor into ordinary human rights discourse. But even admitting the serious imperfections of that discourse, the juridical thesis does not provide the necessary remedy. Instead, it is defeated by a number of substantive objections.

One is that the proposal to enshrine a human right in law sometimes conflicts with, and may be defeated by, other considerations (including considerations grounded in a concern for human rights). For instance, a government may all-things-considered be well-advised not to enact a right to abortion in a staunchly Catholic country if the result of doing so would be grave social unrest and a steep decline in people's confidence in the legal system. This leads to a further point: Even if legal enforcement of a specified right is not too costly in this way, it often seems far-fetched to claim that it is required if a community is to secure that right. The HRP might be effectively fulfilled in a given society through the combined influence of democratic politics, a well-functioning economy, strong familial ties, and a deeply entrenched societal ethos of respect for that right, without its figuring in the law. Moreover, as this last example shows, even where legal rights of some sort are needed to ensure the fulfillment of a human right, those rights need not have the same content as the human right (Pogge 2002*a*: 46).

Perhaps, however, some proponents of the juridical thesis have in mind the weaker claim that there is always a *pro tanto* reason for making a human right an effectively enforceable legal right. But even this weaker thesis is contestable, especially if it is interpreted as a conceptual constraint on the very idea of a human right. This is because the very nature of some human rights appears to be such as to render it *inappropriate* or *pointless* to acknowledge any reason—and, certainly not any reason tantamount to a *pro tanto* obligation—in favor of their legal enactment. For example, there are good reasons, relating to respect for privacy, against admitting any reason to enact a right to have a say in important family decisions or a right to marital fidelity, assuming both of these rights are (implications of) human rights. It is not that the positive reasons for enactment are outweighed by countervailing considerations, but that the nature of the rights themselves speak against a reason for enactment from the very start. Still, this fact in itself need not cast doubt on their status as human rights. Again, with respect to some human rights legal enactment to ensure their enforceability is pretty much pointless, because the rights concern situations in which the legal system has itself become the chief threat to human rights. An example is the right to rebel against a tyrannical government.

In the light of the complicated issues that bear on the legal enactment of human rights, we can subject the juridical thesis to the following thought-experiment. If all we knew about an otherwise unspecified right was that it is a genuine human right, would that entail the existence of a *pro tanto* reason (let alone a *pro tanto* obligation) to enact that right in law irrespective of its content and of the particular circumstances of the relevant community? I think the preceding discussion gives us firm grounds to answer 'No'.

The juridical view is just one contemporary interpretation of human rights that builds a concern with enforcement into their very nature. Another such interpretation is advanced by John Rawls, and it is precisely the enforcement-centered character of his theory that explains why his list of human rights is so drastically minimalist (Rawls 1999*b*: 65).[15] It omits freedom of expression and assembly, rights to political participation, education and health care as well as equal religious liberty. Moreover, Rawls endorses only a right to subsistence (as an implication of the right to life), but not a more demanding right that would guarantee what is necessary for a decent or adequate standard of living.[16] As Rawls conceives of human rights, they essentially belong to the segment of political morality that governs relations between political communities. Most importantly, they are conceived as norms whose violation, if sufficiently extensive and persistent, generates an in-principle justification for forceful intervention by liberal and decent peoples. In particular, given the brevity of his list of human rights and certain textual evidence (see Rawls 1999*b*: 94 n. 6), it seems that it is the in-principle justifiability of *armed* intervention in response to serious violations that serves as his criterion for identifying 'human rights proper'. Presumably, the chief benefit of Rawls's account is that it renders the notion of human rights more determinate, thereby addressing the persistent tendency to invoke it in a virtually criterionless way, while at the same time parrying accusations of ethnocentrism by distinguishing sharply between the rights of citizens in liberal democracies, on the one hand, and human rights, on the other.

---

[15] For a similar view, see Beitz (2004: 208): 'Human rights are standards for law and public policy whose breach on a sufficient scale constitutes a *pro tanto* justification of remedial international action'.

[16] I argue that Rawls's intervention-based account of human rights leads to a right to subsistence rather than to the conditions of an adequate life, and that this in turn results in an excessively weak duty of assistance to 'burdened societies', in Tasioulas (2005).

But, in the end, Rawls's revisionary view of human rights fails. It marginalizes the traditional insight that human rights are primarily protections of central human interests. As such, they provide one kind of input into the formation of principles of interstate relations, including coercive intervention. But they are not conceptually bound up with any particular form of remedy for their violation. Inevitably, Rawls's view issues in an extremely truncated schedule of human rights, but only because it conflates the existence conditions of human rights with the separate question of the conditions under which intervention by one society into another is ever justified (Tasioulas 2002*b*: 384–90). Moreover, the supposed gain in avoiding ethnocentrism turns out to be largely illusory. Rawls's doctrine certainly precludes us from criticizing some practices that are inconsistent with liberal rights (e.g., sex discrimination or deliberate failures to provide members of a society with 'sufficient all-purpose means... to lead reasonable and worthwhile lives' (Rawls 1999*b*: 114)) as violations of 'human rights'. But, at the same time, any society that discriminates on the grounds of sex or deliberately fails to secure an adequate standard of living for all its members is characterized by Rawls as at best 'not fully unreasonable', hence as defective in point of justice. Yet justice is the domain of rights, so the criticism lodged against any such society condemns its failure to respect *liberal* rights. In other words, a peculiar form of dualism results: liberal rights form part of the universally applicable principles of justice (all societies should comply with them and they are unjust to the extent that they do not), but human rights are only a subset of these rights. Co-opting the phrase 'human rights' for a subset of universally applicable liberal rights hardly defuses the fundamental problem of ethnocentrism that confronts Rawls's wider theory.

Now, some might respond that Rawls's problems partly stem from the fact that he has tied human rights to 'forceful intervention' by one society against another, and that the solution is to adopt a more expansive interpretation of that notion, so that even strongly worded protests delivered through diplomatic channels would count as 'forceful intervention'. Of course, a consequence of this proposal would be a more generous list of human rights than that endorsed by Rawls. But, leaving aside the lingering problem of ethnocentrism, at this point one might wonder whether such an attenuated notion of 'forceful intervention' is doing any load-bearing work within the theory of human rights. One is tempted to say it is scarcely doing any work at all; but, in at least one respect, it is still doing too much work. This is shown by another problem that confronts the intervention-based account of human rights, even on this expansive interpretation: it ties the concept of human rights to a particular arrangement of the geopolitical order, that is, one composed of distinct state-like entities (peoples). A bizarre consequence of this view is that it prevents us from meaningfully raising the question whether the creation of a world government can be justified on the basis of human rights protection, since human rights are to be understood as of their very nature regulating the relations between distinct political communities whose governments claim authority over defined territories. Given that the interest-based view offers a determinate criterion for identifying human rights, one suitably accommodating of many of the defensible aspirations that have been pursued by the human rights movement, why should we take the further step of subordinating the concept of human rights to contingent features of the existing global political order, thereby short-circuiting human rights arguments that bear on the desirability of precisely those features?

We should, I think, reject the juridical and the interventionist analyses of human rights. There is no a priori inference from the recognition of a human right to the even *pro tanto* conclusion that it ought to be legally enacted or that it provides a basis for armed intervention when egregiously violated. For each right, an argument needs to be made to justify its enactment or a policy of intervention in response to its violation whether in general or in any particular instance; conceptual fiat cannot take the place of such argument or generate a presumption as to its outcome. This conclusion confirms the idea that rights occupy an intermediate position in our ethical thinking, standing between the ultimate values that ground them and the normative implications they generate, including the institutions and policies that best embody and give effect to those implications. On the one hand, we should not accord rights a foundational role in ethical thought: Rights are derived from (certain of) our interests that can be specified independently of the concept of a right. Denying this derivative status is the error of human rights 'fundamentalists', like Nagel, who thereby end up shrouding in mystery the procedure for identifying human rights. Now, my objection to the juridical and the interventionist views is that they commit the converse error: understanding rights in an unduly superficial way, as essentially embodying some prescription for legal enactment or remedial measures. Human rights are now being too tightly bound up, not with fundamental ethical categories, but with specific institutions and policies. Rather than being, as they should be, potential objects of an assessment that is sensitive to the demands of human rights, these institutions and policies are imported into the very meaning of such rights.

An incidental benefit of this conceptual distancing of the existence conditions of human rights from questions of legal enactment and intervention is that it offers a further line of response to the 'Asian values' critique of human rights. Much that goes under that heading reflects the anxiety that recognizing human rights inevitably leads to the creation of an American-style culture with, among other features, a supreme court exercising judicial review, a highly litigious population and the fraying of communal bonds. By leaving it as a separate question of implementation which forms of institutional design best realize human rights in any given social context, one can partially allay such fears while still insisting on universal respect for human rights.

3.4. RESPONDING TO THE CLAIMABILITY OBJECTION

Onora O'Neill introduces the claimability objection by means of a contrast between universal liberty rights and welfare rights. The former impose 'negative' duties to refrain from harming others in various ways; the latter purport to create 'positive' duties to furnish right-holders with goods and services. Examples of 'welfare rights' are the items in Articles 22–7 of the *UDHR*, which include rights to social security, work, rest and leisure, an adequate standard of living, education, and culture. They contrast with traditional 'liberty' rights, such as the rights to physical security, political participation, and freedom of speech and religion. The description 'welfare rights', however, is not free of difficulties. First, it is not intended to imply that there are rights to welfare as such, but only to certain enabling conditions of a good life. Second, it does not necessarily imply a commitment to a 'welfare' state that secures goods and services to its citizens through redistributive policies. There may be other, and better, institutional embodiments of such rights depending on the society in question. A related contrast used in this connection is between 'first generation' civil and political rights and 'second generation' socioeconomic rights. The implied temporal ordering may reflect the history of the legal recognition of human rights, at least in the international context, but it should not obscure the venerable pedigree of rights of subsistence in Western, including liberal and political thought.

Now, in contrast to Geuss, O'Neill readily allows that rights of both sorts may exist despite being, for various contingent reasons, unenforceable at any given time or place. Moreover, to ensure their enforceability, both liberty rights and welfare rights will standardly require the creation of institutions that impose duties on certain individuals and groups to enforce the rights. Nevertheless, she insists that there is an important asymmetry between the two sorts of rights, one that has the implication that welfare rights, unlike liberty rights, cannot exist in the absence of some institutional mechanism defining correlative duties and allocating them to specifiable (if not always individuable) duty-bearers. The asymmetry concerns the *claimability* of the two types of rights: liberty rights are meaningfully claimable in the absence of the institutional assignment and specification of their correlative duties, whereas welfare rights are not. But a right only exists if the duties associated with it are claimable. Therefore, it is an existence condition of welfare rights that sustaining institutions are in place which, even if they do not ensure the enforceability of such rights, at least define and allocate the duties associated with them:

the correspondence of universal liberty rights to universal obligations is relatively well defined even when institutions are missing or weak. For example, a violation of a right not to be raped or of a right not to be tortured may be clear enough, and the perpetrator may even be identifiable, even when institutions for enforcement are lamentably weak. But the correspondence of universal rights to goods and services to obligations to *provide or deliver* remains entirely amorphous when institutions are missing or weak. Somebody who receives no maternity care may no doubt *assert* that her rights have been violated, but unless obligations to deliver that care have been established and distributed, she will not know where to press her claim, and it will be systematically obscure whether there is any perpetrator, or who has neglected or violated her rights. (O'Neill 2000: 105; see also O'Neill 1996: 131–4)

One immediate worry about this argument is its reliance on the supposed distinction between negative liberty rights and positive welfare rights, a distinction that the work of Henry Shue has taught us to treat with suspicion.[17] Even if we assume a meaningful distinction between negative and positive duties, all rights will typically have as counterparts duties of both sorts. Thus, some of the most important obligations corresponding to universal liberty rights are positive. The right not to be tortured ordinarily imposes duties on the state, for example, to establish and maintain an adequate police force, judiciary and penal system and to variously empower and constrain officials who operate these institutions to honor that right themselves, and to prevent and punish infringements of it by others. Equally, a key entailment of the HRP is a duty not to obstruct others from certain activities that would enable them to secure the means of subsistence. Among the significant causes of poverty in many less developed countries, for example, are socially imposed obstacles preventing women from undertaking employment outside the family home. Of course, this negative duty would have to be supplemented by positive duties to prevent such interference and to aid those who have already suffered from its violation. But, in this respect, the HRP is no different from the right not to be tortured.

O'Neill's argument is supposed to be compatible with the deontic pluralism of rights. Both liberty and welfare rights generate positive duties. But at least in the case of universal liberty rights, she insists, we know who bears the primary obligation of non-interference: everybody. In the case of welfare rights, however, we do not know—in the absence of an appropriate institutional scheme—*who* has the duty to provide the relevant goods and services or *what* is the precise content of that duty. This renders such rights 'radically incomplete', with the result that the process of institutionalizing them goes not just to the *enforcement* of such rights but also to their very *existence*:

> If it is not in principle clear where claims should be lodged, appeals to supposed universal rights to goods or services, including welfare, are mainly rhetoric, which proclaim 'manifesto' rights against unspecified others. (O'Neill 1996: 132)

Is this contrast sufficient to vindicate O'Neill's thesis that the existence of welfare rights is always institutionally dependent? My contention is that it is not. O'Neill, I think, takes a difference of degree—relating to how much we can typically know about counterpart obligations independently of the establishment of institutional structures—and illegitimately converts it into a difference of kind, that is that welfare rights are institutionally dependent for their very existence, whereas liberty rights are not. Relatedly, she exaggerates the significance of our preinstitutional knowledge of the duties associated with liberty rights and systematically downplays what we can know about the deontic implications of welfare rights. In other words, when it comes to discussing liberty rights, the glass looks to her half full, but when welfare rights are in question, it looks half empty.

---

[17] See the classic discussion in Shue (1996a: 35–64, 153–66). I leave aside Shue's deeper objection, i.e., that the very distinction between positive and negative duties correlative to rights is unduly simplistic, and will grant, in what follows, that some workable distinction is on hand that covers the great majority of cases.

The first point is brought out by considering the importance of the unallocated positive duties associated with liberty rights. It is central to the fulfillment of the right not to be tortured that sustaining institutions allocating positive duties are established; in their absence, the mere fact that the right will be claimable against each and every individual has limited importance. But when it comes to the issue of the *existence* of human rights, why should we be so impressed by the negative duty which is preinstitutionally allocated, as opposed to the set of no less important positive duties to implement and enforce that right, which are not? Admittedly, violators of liberty rights will be in principle identifiable, and this is no trivial matter. Reflection on it may even lead us to conclude that claimability is ordinarily a precondition for speaking in a meaningful way of *violations* of duties entailed by human rights and, in turn, of addressing questions about the blame-worthiness and punishment of this category of wrongdoers. But why should the conditions for determinate assessments of human rights *violations* be criteria for the seemingly prior and independent question of whether a human right *exists* or, for that matter, goes *unfulfilled*? The interest-based version of the standard picture encourages us to resist the conflation of these questions. According to it, a human right will exist if a universal individual interest is sufficient to generate duties to advance and protect that interest in various ways. And it will be unfulfilled if those modes of advancement and protection have not been secured to the right-holder, obstructing them from access to the object of their rights. These are important matters regardless of any concern with violations of the human right and the identifiability of their perpetrators.

Let us now turn to the way O'Neill tends to minimize unduly what we can know about the duties generated by welfare rights in advance of the establishment of an institutional scheme. The first point is that some of the duties associated with welfare rights are themselves allocated universally. The obligations relating to the delivery of the relevant goods and services may be typically unallocated and unspecified until institutionally embodied. But there is also another set of counterpart duties which, as O'Neill acknowledges, can be universally imposed obligations (1996: 103). So, it might be thought that everyone has a duty not to obstruct—and, perhaps, even in some way to facilitate, where the cost of doing so is not excessive—the setting up of an institutional framework that will enable counterpart obligations of delivery to be specified and allocated. There will also be obligations not to deprive people of resources needed to maintain them above the poverty line by, for example, actively cooperating in the maintenance of a global economic order that has the foreseeable and avoidable effect of impoverishing them—a duty whose significance in the present state of world affairs has been powerfully elaborated in the writings of Thomas Pogge.

The retort on behalf of O'Neill might now be as follows. In the case of welfare rights, the key duties are those to provide the relevant goods and services, not the negative duties to avoid the infliction of severe impoverishment or the derivative duties to assist in setting up appropriate institutional structures. For these duties of provision are the primary duties associated with welfare rights, just as the relevant forms of non-interference are mandated by the primary duties associated

with liberty rights. Thus, the duty to refrain from impoverishing others is a negative duty, and so cannot be the primary duty correlative to the HRP as that right
is commonly understood. The other duty mentioned is secondary, being parasitic
on the primary duty. It belongs to the class of duties that are modes of promoting
and monitoring compliance with the primary duties or default duties that address
the failure of the primary duty-bearers to discharge their duties.

Contrary to this line of argument, we should, I think, be reluctant to concede
that we can identify, in abstraction from specific circumstances, the primary duty
associated with any particular right. It is not far-fetched to suppose, for instance,
that the HRP might be adequately secured for the vast majority of citizens in a
wealthy and economically productive society with a strong human rights ethos,
through the widespread recognition and effective enforcement of negative duties
not to deprive others of work opportunities. But perhaps we should understand
the appeal to 'primary' duties in a different way. Liberty rights, it might be said,
can be entirely fulfilled in a world where everyone complies with the negative duty
of non-interference. But this is not true of welfare rights. The prospect of collective
action problems and 'natural' disasters, for example, means that positive duties of
provision will also need to be complied with in order to ensure the enjoyment of
such rights. Even this characterization of primacy, however, is problematic. For
instance, the right to free speech plausibly imposes on the state a duty to provide
its citizens with the opportunity to acquire basic literacy. Mere compliance with
the 'negative' duty not to obstruct free speech will not be enough to fulfill that
right. Still, let us grant, *arguendo*, that positive duties of provision have a special
salience in the case of welfare rights.

But now the response should be that we often have enough information to
know that there are duties correlative to welfare rights without the performance
of those duties being *claimable* against specifiable others. So we preserve the core
intuition that rights are correlative with duties, while abandoning the requirement
that it is an existence condition of rights that they be claimable. How can this
line of thought be substantiated? Again, the interest-based account of rights sheds
valuable light on our topic. This theory can allow for knowledge of the existence of
rights (hence of the justification of duties corresponding to those rights) without
the duties being precisely specified or allocated to particular agents.[18] Instead,
the allocation and specification is a further question, not one that needs to be
answered in order to establish the existence of the right. So, to take the HRP as an
illustration: I can know—by fleshing out the argument sketched in section 3.1—
that everyone has a right not to suffer extreme poverty and that, therefore, the
imposition of duties on others to secure that condition is justified. This is because
the interest is important enough to generate the counterpart duties given the
constraints set by human capacities, available resources, and general features of
social life. But *who* should best be assigned those duties will be a separate question
requiring further deliberation. In that process of deliberation, we have to draw on
considerations that bear on the allocation and specification of duties arising from

---

[18] See, e.g., Raz (1986: 184).

the right, including the allocation and specification of 'default' duties to cover cases where some duty-bearers fail to discharge their duties.[19]

Notice that the bracketing of these further questions in the context of asserting the existence of rights does not originate in uncertainty about whether securing those rights through the imposition of duties is feasible. If that were the case, then the very existence of the relevant rights would be doubtful, since rights ground duties and duties must satisfy a feasibility condition (this was the third objection set aside in section 3.2). Moreover, once we have separated out claimability as a further question, we can admit that a right may exist even though the allocation and specification of its correlative duties remains indeterminate. The indeterminacy arises from the fact that there will be multiple candidate schemes for allocating and rendering more precise the counterpart duties. In the case of the HRP the primary obligation might be placed on the state, or in some other circumstances on family groups, or an international poverty relief agency, or some combination of such agents. Any one of these schemes may be acceptable in principle and which, if any, is 'best' will depend on factors that are subject to considerable local and temporal variation. Often, there will be no one optimal arrangement but rather irreducibly many schemes for allocating and defining the HRP that are no worse than one another. Indeed, O'Neill admits as much when she observes that a right to food, or to work, can be 'satisfied in countless different ways', for example by earning enough money, having access to the use of land, or through membership of familial or social groups that take seriously obligations to provide the requisite support. But then she contends that 'without one or other determinate institutional structure, these supposed economic rights amount to rhetoric rather than entitlement' (O'Neill 2000: 125). Yet there are two reasons to balk at this austere conclusion.

The first is the *ad hominem* point that even positive duties of assistance can be allocated independently of any institutional structure, since principles of responsibility may sometimes adequately specify the primary duty-bearers in particular circumstances through institutionally unaided ethical reasoning. One example is an emergency-type situation where there is some agent in the position of a solitary bystander who has the capacity to take the necessary action and can do so far more effectively than anyone else and at a negligible cost. Another example is the case of the largely prosperous societies of the West, where considerations of efficiency, accountability and of the value of political self-determination, among others, combine to create a *pro tanto* obligation on states to ensure that their citizens do not fall below the poverty line. In societies that suffer from the 'weak state' phenomenon, the primary duty would lie elsewhere.[20] Granted, the cases just mentioned scarcely cover all of the situations in which people suffer from, or are threatened by, extreme poverty. So, for the most part, institutional assignments

---

[19] Obligations correlative to subsistence rights are discussed in Shue (1996a: 35–64, 153–66).

[20] See also Martha Nussbaum, who conceives of her capability theory as yielding constitutional standards with which states must comply if they are to meet a threshold of legitimacy. For criticism of this focus on an individual's state as the (primary) duty-bearer, see Okin (2003: 295).

of duties become necessary for meaningful claimability. The unpalatable alternative is to declare a generalized and ongoing state of 'emergency' with perhaps all the denizens of affluent Western societies cast in the role of duty-bound bystanders.

But now the second reply comes into play. Why should this indeterminacy—which, in any case, reflects the existence of a healthy plurality of mechanisms for securing the right rather than uncertainty as to whether there is any realistically available means of doing so—undermine the very *existence* of such rights prior to their institutional embodiment? Why is not the person's interest and the fact that it is sufficient to generate duties to respect, protect, and further it, etc., enough to warrant the existence of the right? In view of the strength of the argument for recognizing and imposing duties based on that interest, there is a strong case for regarding the issue of claimability as separate from that of the right's existence. It is an important issue, one to be addressed through further moral and empirical investigation and possibly even negotiation or formal determination within the context of democratic politics or judicial reasoning. But in addressing that issue, the existence of the right to be rendered claimable is taken as having been established by prior and independent arguments of the sort sketched in section 3.1.

The preceding line of thought is strengthened by an additional consideration, viz., that the indeterminacy of a right's deontic implications is not just a tolerable drawback of the idea that welfare rights exist preinstitutionally. Rather, it is related to another valuable feature of rights, viz., the 'dynamic' character of their normative implications.[21] The duties that a right generates are not comprehensively specifiable once and for all; instead, they can vary with changes in the nature of the agents, institutions, and social contexts in question. In order to arrive at an adequate assignment and specification of duties, one will need to engage in what Shue calls 'strategic reasoning' with respect to particular contexts (Shue 1996a: 161). Second, even within any particular context, there may be a variety of equally admissible ways of allocating the correlative duties and specifying their content. Context-sensitivity will rarely issue in a uniquely correct answer to the problem of allocation and specification. Indeed, a key function of democratic politics and legal reasoning is to provide legitimate mechanisms for arriving at decisions that take up some of the slack that is left once the resources of natural reason have been exhausted.

The consequent indeterminacy of a right's normative implications at the point at which one is entitled to affirm its existence poses no insuperable difficulty. This is because what drives the interest-based theory of rights are the interests a right protects rather than any *specific* set of normative implications they generate. The latter can undergo tremendous variation depending on changes in social conditions, and can also admit of rival specifications in the same conditions, while the right nevertheless persists throughout. But if rights are conceived in this protean way, the thesis that their very existence at any given time depends on a specific assignment of duties loses its grip on us. What is crucial to the

---

[21] The description derives from Raz (1986: 186).

existence of rights is the duty-grounding character of the underlying interests they protect, not whether a particular distribution or specification of duties has been fixed.

3.5. CONSEQUENCES OF THE DYNAMISM OF RIGHTS

Two consequences of this dynamism are worth stressing. The first is that it offers a response to Geuss's complaint that rights as standardly conceived are not only a fiction (because unenforceable), but also an 'inconvenient fiction'. And this because they supposedly foster a sclerotic political culture, one obsessed with the stability of entitlements at the expense of flexibility in adapting to changing circumstances (Geuss 2001a: 147, 152, 154).[22] In a strikingly Benthamite metaphor, Geuss contends that rights ensure that 'the ghostly hand of the present is able to throttle the future' (Geuss 2001a: 154). Now, it is rather peculiar that Geuss begins by stipulating that rights only exist if they are backed up by a settled assignment of duties and established enforcement mechanisms, and then proceeds to denounce the political ossification that is encouraged by just this stipulation. Recognition of the 'dynamic' aspect of rights enables us to deflect the accusation of conservatism precisely by exposing Geuss's linkage between rights and established enforcement mechanisms as gratuitous. The selfsame right can have greatly varying normative implications in different circumstances and may be properly enforced in a variety of ways. In a sparsely populated rural society, for example, institutional structures ensuring access to the use of land may play a fundamental role in securing the HRP. With the onset of industrialization and rapid population growth, however, the emphasis may instead fall on the provision of adequate employment opportunities for all. A due respect for rights, therefore, demands a preparedness to support radical changes in existing social practices and institutions. Geuss's strictures are properly directed only at a certain abuse to which the language of rights lends itself, one that is given comfort by his own identification of rights with effective mechanisms for enforcing entitlements. But they do not (as he supposes) call into question the value of rights themselves.

The second, and more substantial, consequence of dynamism is that it enables us to decline as false the choice between interactional and institutional conceptions of human rights. Thomas Pogge, the author of this distinction, has written:

We should conceive human rights primarily as claims on coercive social institutions and secondarily as claims against those who uphold such institutions. Such an *institutional* understanding contrasts with an *interactional* one, which presents human rights as placing the treatment of human beings under certain constraints that do not presuppose the existence of social institutions.... On the interactional understanding of human rights, governments and individuals have a responsibility not to violate human rights. On my

---

[22] This ties in with the Nietzschean hypothesis that rights discourse reflects the interests of the weak in a stable and predictable social order, see Geuss (1997: 4).

institutional understanding, by contrast, their responsibility is to work for an institutional order and public culture that ensure that all members of society have secure access to the objects of their human rights. (Pogge 2002*a*: 46, 65)

Both accounts impose *ex ante* conceptual constraints on the normative implications of rights, preempting matters best left to 'strategic reasoning' that is sensitive to the vagaries of time and place. In so doing, they contravene the dynamic character of rights and, more generally, illustrate the perils of overestimating the contribution that philosophical analysis can make to political deliberation.

Thus, the interactional account is rightly faulted for its naive assumption that each right straightforwardly entails counterpart duties on the part of particular individuals or groups. In a minimalist version of interactionism (such as libertarianism), all individuals bear the negative duty of not directly impeding the secure access of others to the object of their right. In a more maximalist version (such as utilitarianism), duties are imposed on others regardless of their causal responsibility for any deprivations. But, as Pogge has argued, the duties entailed by a right cannot simply be read off in this way from the object of the right. The chief normative implication in a particular society of the right not to be subjected to degrading treatment, for example, may be a duty to support programs to improve literacy and unemployment benefits, thereby securing that right for a large class of domestic servants (Pogge 2002*b*: 182). The assignment and specification of the duties is thus mediated by reflection on institutions, the deprivations they cause and the reforms that might prevent, ameliorate, and compensate for, those deprivations.

But rejecting the interactional account does not force us into the arms of its institutional rival. The former account was scuppered by the potential complexity (including institutional mediation) that is exhibited by the process of generating normative implications from human rights. But this does not dictate the presence of a *specific* kind of complexity in every case. In particular, it does not necessitate conceiving of human rights as, primarily, claims on coercively imposed institutional orders and, secondarily, on those who cooperate in upholding them. To demand otherwise is to impose an unnecessary restriction on our strategic thinking about the deontic implications of rights. In order for human rights concerns to be activated in any given case, is it really necessary to identify a shared institutional order that is causally responsible for the relevant deprivations? And need those deprivations have been disregarded by 'officials' within that order, as Pogge also insists?

Inevitably, a lot here turns on our considered judgments as to what should count as paradigm cases of human rights and their violation. One such case, I think, would be that of a religious community that has sought refuge from secular society in a remote corner of the Australian outback. Self-sufficient for decades, it maintains only very limited contact with the outside world. If the community's crops should fail one year, threatening its members with severe impoverishment and perhaps starvation, is it not plausible to think that the Australian government would be violating its duty to respect their human rights if it did not supply them with the aid needed to subsist, assuming it could do this at little cost? In other words, a positive duty seems to follow directly from the HRP and various facts about capacity to offer aid and the cost of doing so. Nor are the counterintuitive implications of the institutional theory confined to cases of 'positive' duties correlative to putative human rights. Another case, whose paradigmatic status Pogge would strongly contest, is that of the man who habitually inflicts serious violence on his wife and children. Why deny that he is directly infringing their human rights to physical security? Is it plausible to think that a human rights dimension enters into such a case only if his pattern of abusive behavior can be interpreted as the object of official disregard within a coercively imposed institutional scheme? Even if such institutional reasoning can be successfully carried through in intuitively compelling cases such as these— and nothing guarantees that this will be so—its precarious and circuitous nature diminishes, rather than enhances, the critical power of human rights discourse.[23] This assessment is, if anything, only reinforced by Pogge's concession that there may be universal moral rights in cases like the domestic violence scenario just described that are not *human* rights (2002*b*: 160). Presumably, both the universal moral right against physical abuse and the human right against physical abuse are grounded in the selfsame universal human interests. If so, what is gained by introducing a bifurcated system of universal moral rights, and why reserve the title 'human right' for those universal moral rights that fit the specifications of the institutional account?

It might now be objected that the institutional account is not an unnecessary encumbrance, but a powerful dialectical ploy against those—such as libertarians or adherents to O'Neill's claimability thesis—who believe that human rights (at least in the absence of institutionalization) generate only negative duties. This is a premise that Pogge shares with these opponents. On his account, all humans have a negative duty not to uphold coercive social institutions that avoidably deny others secure access to the objects of their rights. If they are implicated in any such institution, they must either desist from participating in it or else make reparation for it by working for the reform of the institution or for the protection of its victims (Pogge 2002*a*: 66). Yet it is doubtful that any dialectical advantage secured here offsets the costs incurred.

One worry is that Pogge's ploy starts by conceding too much, insofar as we have already found cause to resist as dogmatic the idea that human rights have exclusively negative counterpart duties. Second, as the domestic violence example

---

[23] Thomas Pogge has suggested (personal communication) that the outback case is covered by the institutional account, because the Australian government claims authority over Australian territory, including that piece of the outback inhabited by the imaginary community. Let us grant this claim. But what if we now alter the example, and place the community on an unclaimed island just beyond Australian territorial waters, all other salient facts held constant? Should this slight change potentially make all the difference in determining whether the Australian government bears a human rights-based obligation to render assistance? Reluctance to accept that it does ought to engender skepticism about Pogge's explanation of the existence of a human rights dimension more generally, including in the outback case.

shows, in according priority to an institutional dimension, Pogge's account arguably fails to cover paradigmatic cases of the violation of negative duties to refrain from harm. Finally, it is far from obvious that making this concession secures the advertised *ad hominem* victory. O'Neill, for example, may plausibly respond that when it comes to claimability the institutional account of welfare rights simply moves the wrinkle to a different place in the carpet. For, as Pogge acknowledges, that account entails the *collective* responsibility of all those who participate in an institutional order that causes the relevant deprivations (2002*a*: 64, 66). But it is unlikely that O'Neill would accept that the meaningful claimability of human rights is secured by identifying a collectively responsible group with a potential membership in the many millions. Instead, real claimability will require principles apportioning responsibility *within* the group, specifying exactly who has to do precisely what by way of compensation, institutional reform, and so on. Such principles will reflect a diversity of considerations: the means individuals have at their disposal, the extent to which they have contributed to, and benefited from, the maintenance of the harm-causing institutions, and so on. Presumably, there is no canonical way (or, at least, no one obvious way) of reflecting all these considerations in principles of responsibility. The irresistible upshot seems to be that the principles apportioning responsibility will themselves stand in need of institutional shaping. O'Neill's claimability objection, then, persists even on an institutional reading of the HRP: until an appropriate institutional order is in place, the right will not be genuinely claimable. What's more, her objection now generalizes to encompass all putative human rights, not just welfare rights, since liberty rights will also require a parceling out of collective responsibility through institutional mechanisms.

Of course, Pogge's institutional account deserves a more extended evaluation than I have been able to give it here. But enough has been said to motivate the suspicion that Pogge unjustifiably elevates the powerful *techniques* he has described for deriving the normative implications of human rights to the status of *conceptual constraints* on the very nature of such rights.

3.6. PUTTING RIGHTS FIRST?

Let me take up one further issue raised by O'Neill. This is her recurrent assertion that human rights enthusiasts are inclined to go wrong by putting rights 'first', whereas priority should be accorded to obligations (or, at least, that we should conceive of rights and obligations as standing in the relation of figure and ground (O'Neill 2002: 79–80; see also O'Neill 1996: 140–1). Advocates of welfare rights, in particular, are portrayed as beguiled by a grasping recipient's perspective that complacently skates over hard questions about correlative obligations. In addition, this rights-based view fails to accommodate adequately duties that lack correlative rights, leading to an impoverished understanding of morality as exhausted by principles of justice. Now, to a large extent, this critique can be endorsed by a subscriber to the view I have defended. But we need to distinguish at least three different meanings 'priority' can bear in this context.

First of all, it is clear that obligations are conceptually prior to rights. One can have an adequate grasp of the concept of an obligation, that is a categorical reason with a certain kind of exclusionary force, without having mastered the concept of a right. A right, by contrast, can only be elucidated by reference to the notion of obligation, since rights are defined as grounds for the duties that are correlative to them. Second, and at the more practical end of the spectrum, is an issue about the most effective kind of ethical-political rhetoric in bringing about desirable changes in attitudes and behavior. Here it seems to me that O'Neill is perfectly justified in rebuking those human rights activists who proclaim all manner of rights without giving any apparent consideration to the justifiability, distribution, or coherence of associated duties. This shows that rights discourse is vulnerable to abuse. But a similar vulnerability is exhibited by other forms of moral discourse, including those that prioritize the language of duty.[24] Moreover, when we do consider duties correlative to human rights, we might very well discover that (as Pogge suggests) there are significant rhetorical benefits, when addressing a Western audience, to be derived from stressing negative duties to not foreseeably and avoidably inflict harm on others. However, when it comes to priority in the order of justification, rights are prior to the duties they ground. In other words, *some* but not all duties owe their existence to the rights that are correlative to them: these 'perfect' duties fall within the domain of justice, which is one ethical category among others. In this way, proponents of the standard picture can accommodate the existence of 'imperfect' duties that lack correlative rights—duties of charity, mercy, gratitude, and so on—and thus join with O'Neill in deploring libertarians and others who squeeze such duties out of our picture of ethical life by treating rights as 'the fundamental ethical category' (O'Neill 1996: 143).[25] Moreover, even though a right is prior to the duty it grounds, it is still not *fundamental* in the order of justification. That place belongs, instead, to the interest—at least on the interest-based version of the standard picture that I have advocated. So it is one's interest in being free from extreme poverty that is the basis for the HRP and it is in virtue of its existence that duties are imposed on others. The ground floor of justification is our understanding of the human good. Of course, this last claim will not sway a Kantian, like O'Neill, who wishes to accord 'the right' or— more accurately—the realm of the deontic, autonomy from any conception of the good.[26]

This last point shows that my argument against O'Neill, or Geuss for that matter, is hardly decisive. The underlying issue is not about enforceability or claimability; instead, it implicates one's deepest moral-philosophical commitments. Both Geuss and O'Neill have profound doubts about a 'good' or 'interest' based account

---

[24] As O'Neill herself notes with respect to the 'overload' of duties problem confronting utilitarianism (2002: 78 n. 8).

[25] For an account of how duties of mercy might be defended, see Tasioulas (2003).

[26] For two powerful expressions of skepticism about the privileging of duty integral to the Kantian project, see Williams (1985: ch. 10) and Taylor (1995).

of human rights. For Geuss, these stem from a generalized ethical skepticism. O'Neill, by contrast, has serious reservations about the notion of a pluralistic human good in this context: Is there a robust conception of the good that we can stably converge on without paying an exorbitant metaphysical price? And, even if there is, how is a schedule of rights to be derived from that conception?[27] These are important questions, to which one must respond by developing a good-based account of human rights and comparing it with O'Neill's own efforts to ground rights in perfect obligations derived by means of a Kantian test of universalizability. Is it a more compelling justification of the human right not to be tortured, for example, that a policy of torture cannot be universalized without contradiction? Or would the strongest case for that right directly invoke the central human interests—in autonomy, freedom from pain, and degradation, etc.—that are at stake? Particularly important in any such comparison is the idea that the interest-based account of human rights is not necessarily to be subsumed under, hence is not immediately susceptible to the problems that beset, any form of consequentialism. Needless to say, arbitrating between the two theories is not a task to be embarked on here.

A final, diagnostic, observation. The philosophers whose skepticism about the HRP, and about the standard picture generally, I have been mainly concerned to oppose—Geuss and O'Neill—are a Nietzschean and a Kantian, respectively.[28] One might think they make unlikely allies given their otherwise radically divergent commitments. But from the perspective of an interest-based approach to human rights their collusion is unsurprising. For both the Nietzschean and the Kantian positions are skeptical about the idea of human good as understood within a broadly Aristotelian conception of ethics. Instead, they accord priority, respectively, to de facto power (hence the concern with enforceability) and duty (hence, more circuitously, the concern with the claimability of duties correlative to rights). But a presupposition of this chapter has been that, in order to 'complete the Enlightenment project' of human rights—as James Griffin has put it (2001*a*: 2)—we need to go back, beyond the Enlightenment to an Aristotelian tradition of thought about the human good and the special protection it merits. In other words, what is standardly thought of as the distinctively 'modernist' doctrine of human rights needs to be nurtured by roots that are, as a matter of intellectual history, premodern.[29] When we have gone back to the idea of the human good,

---

[27] 'Just as a shopping list will not *in itself* contain information that requires some purchases to be given priority over others, so a pluralistic account of human goods does not *by itself* require some goods to be respected at the expense of others' (O'Neill 2002: 77).

[28] And it is in the Kantian category, very broadly construed, that we can place other philosophers whose views on rights are criticized in this chapter: Habermas, Rawls, and Pogge.

[29] It is this understanding of rights that is overlooked by Alasdair MacIntyre when he famously dismisses moral rights, and in particular human rights, as 'moral fictions': 'The best reason for asserting so bluntly that there are no such rights is indeed of precisely the same type as the best reason which we possess for asserting that there are no witches and the best reason which we possess for asserting that there are no unicorns: every attempt to give good reasons for believing that there *are* such rights has failed. ... In the United Nations declaration on human rights of 1949 what has since become the normal UN practice of not giving good reasons for *any* assertion whatsoever is followed

and when we have developed the rights-generating notion that some universal human interests of individuals have the right kind of significance to justify the imposition of duties to protect and respect them in various ways, then enforceability and claimability—for all their undoubted practical significance—will cease to have a plausible claim to figure among the existence conditions of human rights. They will have been shifted to an important, but non-foundational, place in our thinking about such rights.

3.7. CONCLUSION

Our point of departure was the unsatisfactory state of contemporary human rights talk. It is understandable that theorists who aspire to clarity and rigor should instinctively recoil from this situation. Nor is it surprising that they should propose, as a remedy, conceptual constraints that tether the identification of human rights to various institutional considerations. But even real crises can provoke disproportionate responses, 'cures' worse than the disease (or worse, at least, than alternative remedies). It is as overreactions of this sort that we should understand the theories criticized in this chapter. The conceptual innovations they advocate are no substitute for sound ethical and political judgment about the duties human interests impose and the institutional structures that best embody them.

with great rigor' (1984: 60). This skepticism seems to me regrettable, not least because the general diagnosis of the deficiencies of Kantian and Nietzschean approaches to ethics sketched in *After Virtue* is otherwise congenial to the background concerns that motivate my argument in this chapter.

4

Inequality and Poverty in Global Perspective

*Álvaro de Vita**

Only a few well-known figures suffice to illustrate how significantly different life chances in the world are. About 1.2 billion people live on less than $1 per day and about 2.8 billion people live on less than $2 per day (UNDP 2000: 9).[1] The wealth of the richest 200 individuals in the world reached $1.135 trillion in 1999, in contrast to $146 billion in combined incomes of the 582 million people living in the least developed countries (LDCs) in the same year (UNDP 2000: 82). Only 25 million people in the United States, the top decile of the income distribution in the country, have a combined income greater than that of the poorest 43% of the world's population (about 2 billion people) (UNDP 2000: 19). Whereas in 1960 the aggregate income of the countries with the wealthiest quintile of the world's population was 30 times as great as that of the countries with the poorest quintile, by 1997 this ratio has soared to 74:1 (UNDP 1999: 3).[2] This picture would not be less dramatic if we shifted from income inequality to other indicators of inequality, such as infant mortality and undernourishment, life expectancy, educational opportunities, and access to basic health care. It suffices to say, for our present purposes, that 11 million children under age 5 in developing countries die every year from easily preventable or curable diseases and that the duration of life is 28 years shorter, on average, in the poorest countries than it is in the richest ones.[3]

Not only is world inequality high, but there is also evidence that it has been *increasing*. A recent (and innovative) empirical study by Branko Milanovic, which for the first time relied solely on household survey data from 117 countries, concluded that world income inequality has increased from a Gini coefficient of

* The research on which this paper is based was developed during a post-doctoral sabbatical at Columbia University from September 2001 to June 2002. I could not have done it without the grants I received from the State of São Paulo Research Foundation (FAPESP) and from the Fulbright Program. I am much indebted to Thomas Pogge for his comments and suggestions on previous versions of this paper. All responsibility for any remaining flaws or errors is, of course, exclusively mine.

[1] Figures expressed in PPP dollars of 1993.

[2] It should be noted that this estimate compares the average income of the richest countries having 20% of the world's population with the average income of the poorest countries having 20% of the world's population.

[3] UNDP (2001: 9) and UNCTAD (2002a: 254). Average life expectancy at birth is 50 years in the LDCs, compared to 78 years in OECD countries.

62.8 in 1988 to 66.0 in 1993 (Milanovic 2002: 88).[4] Milanovic's effort is one that measures (based on data taken from country surveys) income inequality across all *individuals* in the world. This is what he calls 'world inequality', and it is distinct from two other commonly used concepts of inequality between *nations* ('inter-national inequality'): The first, 'unweighted international inequality', compares mean incomes between nations, disregarding their population sizes, and the other, 'weighted international inequality', compares mean incomes between nations weighting their population sizes. The latter is the concept that generates the largest distortions, for while it weighs the population size of a country such as China, it treats all Chinese as having the same mean income. This obscures the fact that the rapid economic growth in coastal China is increasing the inequality between urban China and rural China. The same goes for urban India and rural India, and differences are widening even more between urban China and rural India (or between the former and rural areas of South Asia in general). What really matters, Milanovic argues, is to measure inequality between individuals, not between nations.

Here are some vivid illustrations of this increase in inequality between individuals: while the real income of the bottom 5% of the world decreased between 1988 and 1993 by a quarter, the richest quintile gained 12% in real terms; additionally, the ratio between average income of the world's top 5% and the world's bottom 5% increased from 78 to 1 in 1988 to 114 to 1 in 1993 (Milanovic 2002: 88–9).[5] Other findings of Milanovic's study are also relevant to the subject of this chapter. For instance, it is between-country inequality, rather than within-country inequality, that explains most of this increase in inequality (Milanovic 2002: 76–86). Between-countries inequalities—the differences between countries' mean incomes—explain 88% of world inequality (Milanovic 2002: 78).

The figures mentioned above speak for themselves, but there is no consensus among political theorists on whether global poverty and inequalities should be analyzed through the notion of *justice*. Some of the most influential Western political theorists of the present, such as John Rawls and Michael Walzer, believe it should not.[6] All the controversy on this issue arises from the fact that the existing extreme inequalities in life chances throughout the world take place both *between* countries and *within* separate political jurisdictions. From a normative point of view, the central difficulty is how to do justice, at the same time, to the causal role played by international arrangements, on the one hand, and by domestic institutions and practices, on the other, in generating such inequalities and poverty. As economic globalization and global interdependence deepen, it becomes more than an educated guess to suppose that, in tandem with the difficulty just mentioned, a central normative and institutional problem of this century will be that of striking the appropriate balance between domestic political imperatives and the

---

[4] See also Milanovic (2001).   [5] All figures adjusted for purchasing power parity.
[6] In Rawls (1999a: §58), there are only a few brief comments on this theme. Rawls made a more systematic effort to extend his theory to international relations in other works (1993b, 1999b). The most important of Walzer's texts on international justice are Walzer (1980b, 1983: ch. 2, 1995, 1997).

commitment to a tolerably just international society. It is high time to consider globalization not only as an economic issue, but also as a normative and ethical issue.

This chapter has two sections. The first section seeks to distinguish justice from humanitarian aid in the international ambit. An important related question, in my view, that has to be discussed in connection with this distinction is this: as far as international socioeconomic disparities are concerned, what is the proper focus of our moral concern? The second section of the chapter examines three different normative grounds that may perform the main role in the justification of a principle of international distributive justice, as well as some of the main objections that may be presented to them.

4.1. JUSTICE AND HUMANITARIAN AID

It seems that a preliminary theoretical complexity to sort out has to do with the distinction between justice and humanitarian aid. In the context of our discussion, what Rawls calls 'duty of assistance' qualifies as a form of humanitarian aid, whereas cosmopolitan egalitarian liberals argue that international economic disparities also involve a question of justice.[7] I use the term 'humanitarian aid' in a somewhat broad sense, to mean all forms of support, in the international context, that can be connected to a positive duty to help the poor and those under conditions of high vulnerability. Such a duty exists if the benefactor is in a position to help those who need assistance, and if he can comply with it without incurring any significant loss to his own well-being or more fundamental interests.

Now it seems to me that an aspect of this distinction is the question of what is the proper focus of our moral concern on the international level: should we be concerned only about poverty or should we *also* be concerned about inequalities of resources and power? If our moral concerns are restricted to the eradication of severe poverty, it seems to me that there is no need to be troubled with questions of distributive justice. In the following paragraphs, I discuss the two topics just mentioned in turn.

In a famous 1972 article, written during a devastating famine in the early 1970s, Peter Singer offered what is, to my knowledge, the most compelling moral reasoning in favor of humanitarian aid. The principle proposed by Singer is that 'if it is in our power to prevent something bad from happening, without thereby sacrificing anything of comparable moral importance, we ought, morally, to do it' (1972: 231). Though Singer believed this principle to be fairly uncontroversial, he went on to propose a weaker version of it, in which the expression 'anything morally

---

[7] See Rawls (1999b: 118–19), where he contrasts the duty of assistance to a 'global egalitarian principle'. Beitz (1999c) and Pogge (1989) are pioneering works on the side of cosmopolitan justice. Beitz (1999a) reviews the most significant developments in this area in the 1990s. Also akin to the cosmopolitan perspective are Barry (1989a, 1998, and 1999), Richards (1982), and Shue (1996a: 153–80).

significant' was substituted for 'anything of comparable importance' (ibid.). As an application, Singer offered the following example: 'if I am walking past a shallow pond and see a child drowning in it, I ought to wade in and pull the child out. This will mean getting my clothes muddy, but this is insignificant, while the death of the child would presumably be a very bad thing' (ibid.). Even this weaker version of the principle, Singer argued, entails that all affluent people in the world are under a moral duty to give away money to famine relief 'up to the point at which by giving more one would begin to cause serious suffering for oneself and one's dependents' (ibid.: 234).

Singer himself considered a number of objections to the way he worked out the extension from the drowning child case to the famine relief case. I do not go into a detailed discussion of these objections here, but let me just mention the issue of moral responsibility—an issue that we have to examine later in connection with the conception of justice put forward in this chapter. It could be objected to Singer that while the imputation of moral responsibility for inaction is transparent in the one-to-one relation between the potential rescuer and the drowning child, no one in particular can be held responsible for not rescuing people from starvation when there are millions of others who could have done so as well. The answer to that again makes use of Singer's simple example: If one thousand people are in a position to rescue a drowning child and none does it, the upshot is not that none of them is responsible for the child's death, but rather that they all are (Barry 1989*b*: 437). This also means that humanitarian aid to famine relief is not to be viewed as morally optional for those who are in a position to contribute to it, be it governments, companies or individuals, any more than rescuing a drowning child from a shallow pond is to be viewed as morally optional for those who are in a position to do so.

In fact, the governments of rich countries have already accepted the obligation to provide humanitarian aid for poverty reduction in the world. They have committed themselves, for instance, to gradually raise their level of Official Development Assistance (ODA) to developing countries until the target set up by the UN in the 1970s, of 0.7% of donor countries' GNP, is met.[8] More recently, they have subscribed to the goals set out by the UN Millennium Declaration, which includes objectives to be reached in the world until 2015, such as the following: to halve the proportion of people living in poverty and suffering from hunger, to enroll all children in primary school, to eliminate gender disparities in primary and secondary education, and to reduce infant mortality ratios by two-thirds (UNDP 2001: 22). Instead of consistent efforts to meet these self-imposed obligations, what we have witnessed in recent years has been a steady decrease of OECD countries' ODA, from an already very low 0.33% of their aggregate GNP in 1992 (or $74 per head of their population annually) to 0.22% (or only $62 per head annually) in 1997.[9] It is clear, however, that flouting one's own obligations cannot

[8]   The 1974 General Assembly Declaration, among other UN documents, established this target.

[9]   Figures taken from UNDP (2000: 218) and UNCTAD (1999*a*: 22). The lowest percentage of the GNP spent on foreign aid is that of the United States, only 0.1 in 1998. In spite of the country's very

be presented as a good reason to denying the existence of such obligations or to dismissing them as 'politically unrealistic'.[10] It is often said in the United States and other OECD countries that a so-called 'aid fatigue'—the decline of public support for foreign aid due to the waste of resources transferred to poor countries in objectives other than poverty reduction and famine relief—accounts for the fall in development aid. I do not think that such a claim can withstand careful scrutiny.[11] Even if it can, the proper remedy would be to design a new institutional format for dispensing aid, not to cut back aid.[12]

There is surely more to say about humanitarian aid. (I return to this topic in a later section.) At this point, the point I want to make is that even if Singer's principle provides (as I think it does) a moral justification for humanitarian aid, it covers only part of what is morally significant as far as international inequities are concerned. It applies irrespective of any institutional ties between donors and recipients and it is to be applied only to circumstances of severe poverty—and so long as these circumstances persist. Moreover, it would apply even if those circumstances had nothing to do with inequality. Now justice is not only a question of poverty and famine relief—though I hope to have made it clear that poverty relief is the most urgent and immediate moral obligation with which to comply. It is also one of rectifying unfair inequalities in resources and power generated by institutional arrangements.

To be sure, we can define justice is such a way as to equate its requirements with an absolute standard of living. David Miller does precisely that when he speaks of international justice, that is, he believes that injustice, in the international context, can only refer to a low absolute standard of living (Miller 1998, 1999). Accordingly, only the low absolute standard of living in poor countries, not (international) inequality should be the focus of moral criticism on the international level. I am not denying that, internationally, justice requires some minimal threshold defined in absolute terms. This is precisely the message we want to convey in depicting poverty as a human right violation. Nevertheless, to say that meeting basic needs of nutrition, shelter, health, and education should have moral priority over reducing relative disparities (of opportunities, power, income, and wealth) need not

---

strong economic performance in the 1990s, the US ranks behind countries that are much less rich, such as Portugal and Greece.

[10] I return to this point below.

[11] There are alternative accounts of what happened with development aid. Donor countries often decide whether to give to aid, how much, and to whom based on criteria that have more to do with their strategic interests than with poverty reduction. Fiscal austerity measures in donor countries during the 1990s, taking into account that cuts in foreign aid are the least likely to give rise to much political resistance, are another possible explanation.

[12] According to *The Least Developed Countries 2000 Report*, thirty-three of the world's forty-eight LDCs did implement a great deal of the structural economic reforms prescribed to them by the IMF during the decade of 1990. What has been not kept—and maybe that is actually what 'aid fatigue' is all about—was the commitment of donor countries to raise their ODA to the LDCs to at least 0.2% of their GNP (UNCTAD 2000: 6–7).

commit us to the very different assertion that this is *all* that justice requires.[13] I return to this question in the next section. I now want to take issue with a further implication of Miller's view. In disconnecting poverty and international inequality, Miller is in fact making two different (and controversial) claims:

(1) justice, on the international level, requires *only* some minimal threshold defined in absolute terms and specified by a more or less restricted set of basic rights *and*

(2) injustice, that is, basic rights privations in poor countries, has little to do with distributive inequalities produced by international arrangements. Such privations are due, above all, to institutional and policy failures of the poor countries themselves. Let us call this proposition 'the internal factors argument'.[14]

The combined effect of (1) and (2) is that a very low level of responsibility for basic rights privations suffered by the poor is ascribed to the international society and its most privileged members. This is the most central point at issue. A view that accepts both (1) and (2) is committed to the supposition that only weak obligations of humanity exist on the international level. How we define 'obligations of humanity' and 'obligations of justice' is not what matters most. It is the substantive disagreement, not a nominal question, which is of interest here.

4.1.1. Does Inequality Matter?

Why should we worry about international inequality? Is it not enough, morally speaking, to worry about issues of severe poverty on the international level? Let us suppose, implausibly enough as things now stand, that the countries with the richest fifth of the world's population agreed to transfer an additional 0.5% of their GNP annually, or about $100 billion, to programs of aid development and poverty reduction.[15] Additional transfers of only $80 billion annually, according to an estimate of the UN, would suffice to ensure adequate health care and basic

---

[13] This is similar to a normative stance that is very plausible domestically. Poverty is surely the most urgent problem of justice. Making it possible for the poor to escape poverty (with extreme poverty coming first) has priority over, say, reducing the distance between the bottom and the top quintiles in the income distribution. This is the reason why our conception of poverty should incorporate a large absolute core defined, for instance, by Sen's notion of basic functionings or by a notion of basic needs. Nevertheless, recognizing that should not lead us to believe that inequality of resources above this minimal threshold does not matter from the point of view of social justice. Inequalities that fall above the defined threshold do matter, morally speaking, both because they may be bad in themselves and because large inequalities of resources may make the eradication of poverty itself much harder. Both points are relevant, internationally, or so I want to argue.

[14] Though Miller does not clearly state (2), I think it is fair to consider that both (1) and (2) can be inferred from his discussion (Miller 1999: 202–4) of four ideal types of cases in which basic rights destitution may occur. Proposition (2) is strongly endorsed by Rawls in (1993*b*: especially 77) and (1999*b*: 108).

[15] This is just a rough estimate based on 1999 figures from the World Bank (2001*b*: 274).

education, and to provide monetary transfers sufficient to abolish income poverty (Hill, Peterson, and Dhanda 2001: 183). Would we be entitled to say, in that case, that as far as socioeconomic disparities are concerned, and even if the ratio between the income of the world top 5% and the world bottom 5% was kept at a very high level, no further questions of justice should arise? I do not think so. The reasons to be concerned about inequality, as something distinct from material deprivation, are similar in the domestic and international cases.

There are both moral and non-moral reasons to take world inequality as a normatively significant issue. Let me begin with those straightforwardly moral considerations. We have learned from Rawls, to mention one such reason, that the opportunities a person has to make something worthwhile of her own life should not be determined by 'morally arbitrary factors'—that is, by factors that have to do with her circumstances, not with her own choices. As mentioned before, it is nowadays difficult to find such a morally arbitrary factor that weighs as heavily on a person's life chances as the place of the world where one happens to be born. As a matter of moral argument, it is difficult to make sense of the idea that a person being born a few miles to the north or a few miles to the south of the Mexican–American border should make such a huge difference in her opportunities to have a good life. As Pogge has pointed out, the reasons to give national borders a moral status different than that of other morally arbitrary factors, such as differences in sex, skin color, or social class of origin are not, to say the very least, straightforward (Pogge 1994b: 198). National borders, after all, are institutions of human making just like any other institution—or, to be more precise, they are components of national sovereignty, which are institutions that only make sense as part of a global arrangement. One wonders why, from a normative point of view, national borders should be allowed to have such vast implications for life prospects of people throughout the world.

Moreover, there are two other relevant Rawlsian arguments showing why inequality matters. 'Significant political and economic inequalities', Rawls says, 'are often associated with inequalities of social status that encourage those of lower status to be viewed both by themselves and by others as inferior. This may arouse widespread attitudes of deference and servility on one side and a will to dominate and arrogance on the other' (2001: 131). The humiliation associated with the low social status of those who are in the least advantaged position breeds an 'excusable envy' among them and undermines their self-respect in a way that makes it hard for them to affirm their sense of justice and willingly support common institutions.[16] Let us call this argument against inequality 'the argument from self-respect'. Still another moral ground to be concerned about large socioeconomic inequalities has to do with what Rawls has dubbed 'the fair value of political liberties' (1993a: 357–63). Inequalities of wealth and income—even the level of inequality that the difference principle itself might justify—cannot be so large as to allow economic power to be converted into political power and to undermine the value of political liberties to the least privileged. If just results are to be expected

---

[16] For the idea of 'excusable envy', see Rawls (1999a: §81).

from political procedures (even from fair political procedures), socioeconomic inequalities must be kept below certain limits.[17] Let us call this argument 'the argument from the fair value of political liberties'.

Now the question arises as to whether these two anti-inequality arguments of the preceding paragraph apply not only to the domestic level but also to the international level. Charles Beitz has recently argued that they do (2001: 114–18). Insofar as this is indeed the case, they also provide reasons to reject the internal factors argument. As far as the argument from self-respect is concerned, Beitz argues that 'with the expansion and increased penetration of the global media, it cannot be held that global society is divided, as Rawls imagined a just domestic society might be, into a plurality of 'non-comparing groups' that are either unaware of or indifferent to the standards of living found in other societies' (Beitz 2001: 115). It seems implausible to argue, in the present circumstances, that people who are members of different domestic societies do not care about their relative social status. Moreover, there are global economic pressures leading to increases in wage differentials between the highly skilled and internationally mobile people, on the one hand, and the low-skilled people of poor countries against whom the barriers to immigration in rich countries mainly seem to have been designed, on the other.[18] Wide differences in wages and well-being that the most privileged may believe can be attributed to something they carry in their own brains (their so-called 'intellectual capital'), rather than to some feature of social institutions, are the most likely to generate attitudes of social superiority and social inferiority. That their belief is mistaken does not make this form of inequality tolerable for those who suffer its effects.[19]

As to the argument from the fair value of political liberties, there is an even clearer case for the application of an analogous rationale to the international level (Pogge 1989: 250). For there can be no doubt that people living in the countries that have the poorest quintile of the world's population are profoundly affected by economic and political decision-making that is mainly controlled by people and governments of countries where the wealthiest quintile of the world's population are concentrated. The governments of the wealthiest societies not only exercise a disproportionate degree of control over the decision-making in institutions

[17] Though these limits are difficult to ascertain with precision, Rawls's criticism of 'welfare state capitalism' and his remarks on his own preferred socioeconomic regime, the so-called 'property-owning democracy', make it clear that he sees the levels of socioeconomic inequality of even the most developed welfare states of the present as incompatible with the fair value of political liberties. See Rawls (2001: 138–40, 148–52).

[18] As Kapstein (1999: 104) points out, people are now no freer to immigrate than they were a generation ago and much less free to immigrate than their grandparents were.

[19] The share of the benefits of social cooperation that rewards superior skills and talents, compared with the share of social primary goods that goes to the unskilled and untalented, is of course, determined by the existing institutional arrangements. Putting international inequality aside for a moment, a significantly larger share of primary goods was available to American blue-collar workers until the early 1970s than is the case today. Almost 50 million American workers make less than $10 per hour and work 160 hours longer per year than did workers in 1973. See Steger (2002: 108). Changes in institutions (such as the tax and transfers system), not in people's brains, account for this fact.

such as the UN Security Council and the World Trade Organization (WTO), but also heavily interfere, through the IMF and the World Bank, with the domestic policies of developing countries—especially those more exposed to balance of payments problems. If economic redistribution is morally justified domestically in order (among other reasons) to block the conversion of economic power into political power, why would not a similar argument apply to the international ambit? Limiting the level of socioeconomic inequality permissible internationally is required to enhance the voice of the world's poorest in the decision-making of international organizations and institutions. This rationale would still be valid if democratic procedures were adopted in those settings.

Three moral reasons to be concerned about inequality (as something distinct from poverty) were presented in the above paragraphs: the argument from moral arbitrariness, the argument from self-respect, and the argument from the fair value of political liberties. There is still a fourth kind of argument that runs along the following lines: if you are concerned about poverty, you ought also to be concerned about inequality. The reasons why this is so are both moral and non-moral. A growing body of empirical evidence shows that high levels of inequality can reduce the pace of economic growth, which is a non-moral reason to favor greater distributive equality, and considerably weaken the poverty-reduction effect of economic growth.[20] High levels of initial inequality in assets—physical and human capital, knowledge, and access to credit—especially when coupled with high gender inequality, can be damaging to economic efficiency and, what is more important, can prevent poor people from taking advantage of economic growth when it does take place. Poor people lack the crucial assets, such as human capital, access to up-to-date technology, and adequate collateral to borrow money to start small business, that are required to profit from the new opportunities that growth provides. Only when initial inequality in assets is relatively low can economic growth really be a 'positive-sum game', as mainstream economists like to think of it, rescuing people from poverty and spreading benefits across all social groups. Saying that this is, at least in part, a non-moral reason to favor more distributive equality, what I have in mind is that such a reason appeals even to those whose sole concern is economic prosperity, not social justice. Does this mean that even rich countries have a non-moral, prudential reason to be concerned about economic prosperity in poor countries? Surely, only in a very limited sense can this be true. (I discuss this topic—what we can expect from moral and prudential reasons as far as international socioeconomic justice is concerned—in further detail below.) But it is certainly true that the most enthusiastic proponents of market-oriented globalization are not at all willing to dispose of the idea that it can foster economic prosperity everywhere in the world, not only in the developed world.[21] It could

---

[20] World Bank (2001*b*: 49–59), UNDP (2001: 16–20). See also Milanovic (2001: 58–60).

[21] In fact, a central claim of neoclassical trade economic theory is that free international trade, coupled with the 'correct' set of domestic institutions and policies in all countries, will lead to a worldwide convergence of income levels in the long run. High marginal utility of capital would make it flow to countries where there is a capital shortage. And the abundance of cheap labor would make poor countries focus on labor-intense exportable production, which in due time would lead to increasing

be argued, for instance, that economic growth in developing countries would have globally beneficial effects such as making the world as a whole a safer place to live.

One could object that these moral and non-moral reasons related to the fourth argument can and should be taken into account by domestic policy and institutional reform. This is surely correct. Nevertheless, they also provide justification for international redistribution of resources. Let us briefly consider, first, the case of the LDCs, a group of 49 countries (where 637.4 million people live) that 'contain the hard core of the problem of marginalization in the world economy' (UNCTAD 2000: 1).[22] These countries simply do not have much to invest in the enhancement of the human capital of their people and in the services and infrastructure required to make them capable of benefiting from the world economy. Their capacity to invest in their own economic and social development is made extremely difficult by a very low level of domestic savings and it is further undermined by the debt-servicing obligations to which most of these countries are currently subjected. The total debt service paid by the LDCs was above US$ 4.5 billion annually in the 1990s and some of these countries spend three to five times as much servicing the external debt as they do on basic social services (UNCTAD 2002a: 274).[23] As a result, LDCs depend crucially on external resources, such as remittances by their emigrant citizens, external aid and capital inflows to finance almost all of their investments. Moreover, even in the case of developing countries that are not subjected to such stringent conditions, the extent to which domestic policies and options are (exclusively) to blame for domestic and international socioeconomic inequalities is not clear at all. In a world of evergrowing capital mobility, domestic policies and institutional reforms geared toward distributive justice are significantly constrained by external economic forces, especially by the expectations of foreign investors (Kapstein 1999: 100–2). On the taxation side, there has been a general retreat, and not only in the developing world, from progressive taxation to an increasing reliance on value-added taxes that have particularly regressive effects. As the IMF itself acknowledges, 'globalization may be expected to increasingly constrain governments' choices of tax structures and tax rates' (IMF 1997: 70).[24] On the social spending side, fiscal austerity and adjustment programs, often pushed on the developing countries by the IMF and the

---

returns to unskilled labor. Though it is difficult for such rosy theory to be either clearly confirmed or falsified, we have already gone a long way in the implementation of neoliberal reforms and policies, both on the domestic and on the international levels, without any consistent signs of such convergence having shown up yet.

[22] The figure on population mentioned in the text is taken from UNCTAD (2002a: 253). The latter document combines three criteria (low national income, weak human assets, and economic vulnerability) to define a country as a LDC.

[23] Debt service payments of all LDCs were US$ 4.6 billion in the year 1997.

[24] The World Bank, though admitting that redistributive policies make for both equity and economic efficiency, restricts its policy recommendations to changes in the profile of government spending and market-based redistribution of assets such as land. See World Bank (2001b: 56–7).

World Bank in the 1980s and in the early 1990s under the ideological framework of the so-called 'Washington Consensus', have often led to cutbacks in the quantity and quality of state-provided education, health care, nutrition, social security, and even to the adoption of school fees in a number of countries that excluded many poor children from elementary education.

A third point worth mentioning in this context has to do with the highly uneven distribution of the gains from globalization. I do not intend to go into a detailed discussion of the political economy of globalization, a task for which I do not even have the required technical expertise. I only make a few observations in connection with the main argument of this paper. It should be noted, to begin with, that the so-called 'globalization' is not a sort of natural or inescapable economic and technological process occurring beyond human control. Though there is much debate on how far globalization has gone, many analysts single out the same set of decisions and policies as the events that have triggered and accelerated the integrationist tendencies of the world economy. To put it very briefly, one could point to the collapse of the Bretton Woods system of fixed exchange rates in the early 1970s, after Richard Nixon's decision to halt the dollar–gold convertibility in August 1971, and to the subsequent decisions and policies, carried out in the following decades, of commercial liberalization and international financial deregulation, as the main parameters of this process.[25] As a result, international trade, international financial flows, and foreign direct investments have soared to unprecedented levels in the 1990s, with their economic benefits being heavily concentrated in OECD countries and, to a degree, in a handful of developing countries. ('Developing countries' is a little misleading category, for it applies to countries ranging from the $20,000 per capita income of Singapore to the $100 per capita income of Somalia.) Foreign direct investment flows, for instance, rose to $600 billion in 1998, but about 70% of these flows went to OECD countries, and the remaining 30%, to a few developing countries (mainly China, Brazil, Mexico, and Singapore). The LDCs got almost nothing: 0.4% (UNDP 2000: 82).

As Ethan Kapstein has argued, the world leaders who erected the international institutions in the wake of World War II sought to reconcile the objectives of promoting international trade *and* social justice viewed as an international public good (1999: 88–98). The Bretton Woods system, in whose design Keynes played an important role as the key negotiator from Britain, was conceived to shield the domestic policies and institutions of the welfare state from the global financial disciplines.[26] It is true that under this system, social justice was to be pursued mainly at the domestic level. On the other hand, however, it was also widely held that international trade did have unfair distributive effects that needed correction

---

[25] For two competent analyses of this process, of contrasting political and ideological persuasions, see Gilpin (2001) and Scholte (2000). See also Held, McGrew, Goldblatt, and Perraton (1999: chs. 3 and 4) and Quiggin (2001).

[26] Crucial for that were the system of fixed exchange rates, at the international level, and the policies of capital control, at the domestic level.

by international redistribution by means of policies such as preferential tariffs, foreign aid, and transfers of technology to developing countries.[27]

It was this post-war consensus that the recent market-led globalization swept away and deliberately so on the part of decision-makers in both key countries of the North and in international organizations. It was policy change, rather than technical innovations in telecommunications and computing, that caused the growth in flows of goods, services, and capital that is often taken to be the crucial feature of globalization. And, as John Quiggin points out, instead of seeing that growth as an exogenous force pushing the implementation of the sort of market-friendly reforms favored by neoliberals at the domestic level, 'it would be more accurate to see the removal of restrictions on trade and capital flows as the international component of the neo-liberal policy program' (Quiggin 2001: 67).[28]

The political success of this program nearly erased social justice as a concern of international arrangements and institutions.[29] As a result, the distributive effects of both the international regimes, where they exist, and of the *absence* of mechanisms of global governance, can go as unchecked as ever before. The latter case is clearly illustrated by the absence of a global institution to regulate international financial flows. The collapse of the Bretton Woods system, coupled with the lift of capital controls throughout the world, have resulted in an increase in the daily turnover of international financial transactions from \$15 billion, in 1973, to the staggering amount of \$1.8 trillion in 1998 (Oxfam 1999: 1).[30] Those flows are short-term and highly speculative investments, having little to do with the production of goods or even with the international trade of goods and services.[31] Though there is talk of a 'new global financial architecture' after each new financial

[27] Critics of free trade, such as Raul Prebish and Gunnar Myrdal, argued in the early 1950s that the only way for developing countries to catch up with industrialized countries was a domestic strategy of import substitution coupled with international redistribution. Prebish's works set the stage for the later dependency theory and for the demands, put forth by the Group of 77 in the United Nations in the 1970s, of a New International Economic Order (NIEO). Though NIEO's demands were cast in terms of justice, some of its proposals, such as the idea of an international regime of commodities aimed at stabilizing the prices of raw materials, were inspired in the successful experience of OPEC and were in fact focused on strengthening the relative position of certain states of the developing world in the international system, rather than on the fate of the world's poor and international inequalities in life prospects. This is the reason why, in spite of the fact that it was the NIEO that first raised the question of international distributive justice as a political issue, today's political theory of international distributive justice cannot build on that experience.

[28] See also Steger (2002) for a criticism of the idea that market-led globalization is a kind of natural and inevitable process, for which nobody is in charge.

[29] There are some timid signs of change. The World Bank, for instance, is no longer an unqualified supporter of a Consensus of Washington position. It now recognizes—albeit rather reluctantly—that the wave of market-friendly reforms in the 1980s and 1990s hasn't made good on its promise to deliver economic growth, let alone more economic equity, to much of the developing world. According to the Bank, those 'first-generation reforms' have now to be complemented by 'a development strategy that includes investing in people through health and education services, promoting inclusive and equitable growth, supporting good governance, and protecting the environment' (World Bank 2001*b*: 192).

[30] This figure is taken from a BIS (Bank for International Settlements) paper.

[31] International exports and imports of goods and services have also soared in recent decades, but the daily amount reached by the end of the 1990s is considerably lower: \$25 billion.

crisis, such as the successive crises in Asia in 1997, in Russia in 1998, and in Brazil in 1999, there is no regime or mechanism to regulate international financial flows.

It is worth noting that, from the point of view of this study, the fact that there is no formal institution regulating an area of global concern does not mean that this absence should not count as a component of international basic arrangements. Indeed, it is a feature of the current arrangements that huge international movements of capital are left unregulated. The right thing to do is to compare the distributive consequences of the current arrangement with the distributive consequences of an alternative to it in which these flows would be regulated (and possibly taxed). It would not be difficult to show to whom the status quo is beneficial, with the American financial system ranking very highly on the list of suspects, and to whom it imposes the heaviest burdens, to wit, the developing countries that often face speculative attacks against their currencies and are constrained, in their choices of domestic policies and institutions, by the disciplines of real or threatened capital flight.[32] Unregulated financial globalization has imposed a straitjacket on the governments of these countries, in that there is strong pressure on them to practice only the so-called 'market-friendly' policies, to wit, those that show a strong commitment to price stability, low levels of public deficit and public spending, low direct taxation, privatization, and deregulation of labor relations.

International regimes, when they do exist, may also have distributive effects that contribute to international inequality. This is certainly the case of the GATT-WTO regime. It would be naive to see this regime (and other international regimes) only in terms of the promotion of economic efficiency and mutually advantageous interstate cooperation—though, of course, these more 'benign' functions are also part of the picture. Two comments are pertinent in connection with our discussion. First, although the eight rounds of negotiations under the GATT, between 1948 and 1994, reduced the average import tariff on manufactures from over 40% to only 3% in the OECD countries, the developed countries still impose high tariff and non-tariff barriers (such as import quotas, product standard requirements, and export subsidies to their own producers) on agricultural products, textiles, and other labor-intensive manufactures from developing countries. UNCTAD estimates that, in virtue of these barriers, the developing countries are losing some $700 billion of annual export earnings, and this corresponds to thirteen times the annual amount of all ODA (UNCTAD 1999*b*: IX). Strictly speaking, this is not even a question of distributive justice. Perhaps we should define it as a question of what Barry once called 'justice as requital', that is, the justice of a fair return or a fair exchange (1989*b*: 441). The remedy here is not international redistribution, but rather to make 'free trade' actually free.[33]

---

[32] According to Robert Gilpin, American governments have fiercely opposed the introduction of any form of international regulation in this area. Chief among the reasons for this are the competitiveness of the American financial system and the fact that it has much political power in the United States (Gilpin 2001: 277).

[33] Another contentious issue concerns the desirability, from the point of view of international justice, of introducing labor, environmental, and human rights standards to the international trade regime. I cannot discuss this issue properly here. But I can't help saying that, though these are legitimate

Second, there is the question of the international enforcement of property rights. This is the sort of question that makes the concern with redistribution relevant to the international context in a way that is akin to the central argument of this paper. Founded in 1995 after the Uruguay Round of the GATT, the WTO not only is endowed with more power and authority to enforce its decisions than its predecessor GATT, but also its jurisdiction extends beyond borders' barriers to topics such as the protection of intellectual property rights. Most governments of developing countries signed the 1994 Agreement on Trade-Related Aspects of Intellectual Property Rights (TRIPS), and are implementing the kind of domestic institutions required by this agreement, without actually knowing its distributive implications.[34] Research and technological development are even more greatly concentrated in rich countries than are income and wealth, and this concentration is probably the most important factor among those that make for international inequality in today's world. OECD countries account for 91% of the 347,000 new patents issued in 1998. Moreover, most research and development (60%) in these countries today takes place in multinational corporations, which are in the business of creating new products for the top one-third of the world's population who have enough purchasing power to buy them. This explains why only a tiny fraction—less than 0.6%—of the $70 billion spent on health research in 1998 was dedicated to vaccines for HIV/AIDS and malaria, two epidemics that take a heavy toll on many poor countries (UNDP 2001: 3). Some international scheme for issuing patents and for copyright protection is necessary in a market economy to provide the private sector with incentives to produce new knowledge. However, the current arrangement, enforcing strong intellectual property rights without any redistributive mechanism, will surely widen the gap in life prospects between the rich and the poor in the world.

In the above paragraphs, I pointed out reasons for rejecting the 'internal factors argument'. I only add one final comment. In the present circumstances of the world economy, in which a high international mobility for capital and highly skilled labor is combined with widespread national barriers against the immigration of low-skilled labor, it is very unlikely that *only* domestic institutions and policy change will be sufficient to significantly reduce inequality—either internationally or domestically. If we believe that inequality *is* an issue, both for moral and non-moral reasons, then there are also strong reasons for us to believe

concerns of international justice, it is far from clear whether commercial sanctions, which would surely fall on poor countries, are the best response to such concerns. As to the labor standards, Birdsall and Lawrence (1999: 143–5) suggest an alternative approach based on assistance to developing countries and non-coercive measures. What is clear, from the perspective of this study, is that these questions must be dealt with by taking into account the interests of toiling children and women in poor countries, rather than those of the AFL-CIO's constituency.

[34] A basic requirement of the TRIPS agreement is a 20-year protection period for patents. Developing countries do not have any differential treatment, except for the extra 11 years that some of them, the LDCs, have to implement this protection (UNDP 2001: 103).

that international institutions, will have to play a much larger role to guarantee distributive justice than they have been doing to date.[35]

4.1.2. Justice-Based Humanitarian Aid

Let us pause a moment for a reflection on the realism of what has been said so far. Even if, for decades to come, a significant increase in humanitarian aid is all that one can realistically hope for, this does not mean that talk of justice is idle in the international context. It should be noted that humanitarian aid is one thing when we see it as something that exhausts our moral obligations on the international level, and quite another when we see it as the least that has to be done in virtue of more demanding obligations of justice. In this latter case, the door is open for the recommendation of schemes of funding the provision of global public goods and programs of development aid on a permanent and institutional basis. Jeffrey Sachs champions reform proposals in the vein of such a justice-based humanitarian aid approach.[36] Debt cancellation for the highly indebted LDCs is one of the proposals. Even more to the point of our present concerns, Sachs also proposes a global tax on carbon-emitting fossil fuels. Such an institution would accomplish two purposes: to provide disincentives against the overreliance on fossil fuels that is deforming the world's climate and to raise revenues to fund a variety of multilateral agencies (badly underfinanced today) dedicated to development, humanitarian aid, and environmental problems.[37] Another idea in the same direction is the so-called Tobin Tax, a proposal for a levy on international currency transactions that was first submitted by the economist James Tobin in 1978. It has since then gained strong support from a variety of international non-governmental organizations (NGOs) and advocacy networks.[38] Whether it could reduce volatile capital flows and speculative attacks on currencies is debatable, but the Tobin Tax does have some attractive features in the eyes of its supporters. It is a tax 'on Wall Street, not on Main Street', it could be designed to be clearly redistributive, and even a small levy would be enough to raise a very substantial revenue. Any such scheme of international taxation no doubt would be fraught with problems of

---

[35] Developing countries' investments in education often result in a subsidy to rich countries. *The Human Development Report 2001* estimates that 100,000 highly educated Indian professionals are annually expected to take visas recently created by the United States. See UNDP (2001: 5). Indian and Chinese engineers already account for a significant proportion of Silicon Valley's highly skilled workers.

[36] *The Economist*, 1999. 'Sachs on Development: Helping the World's Poorest', August 14–20: 17–20.

[37] A related idea was put forward by Thomas Pogge some years ago (1994*a*, 1994*b*). Pogge proposed a Global Resources Dividend to be levied on those who extract natural resources or discharge pollutants. Like Sachs's proposal, the GRD would have two purposes: to slow resource depletion and pollution and to raise funds for poverty eradication.

[38] The most prominent among them are Oxfam, ATTAC (Association pour une taxation sur les transactions financiers pour l'aide aux citoyens), and the Halifax Initiative (a Canadian coalition of development, environment, faith, and labor groups). See Oxfam (1999: 14), for further references.

compliance, collection, and distribution of the tax revenue, but it seems plausible to suppose that none of these problems presents an insurmountable obstacle.[39]

Consider, for instance, the revenue distribution problem. It is sometimes objected that any such international scheme of taxation could have regressive effects—it could end up making transfers, say, from middle class Scandinavians to better-off people in developing countries. But institutional arrangements could be designed to avoid or minimize these regressive effects. This should not prove too difficult to take into account since, as Branko Milanovic points out, 78% of the world population lives with an income below the rich countries' poverty line (expressed in PPP dollars) (Milanovic 2001: 55). As Milanovic shows, there are bilateral transfers from rich to poor countries that could be made with almost zero overlap between the countries' income distributions. Those are the cases in which the representative individual in the worst position in a rich country— say, a Frenchman living on the dole—still is in a better situation than the best-off representative person in a poor country—say in rural Bangladesh (2001: 54– 6). Any scheme of redistributive taxation could start from these clear-cut cases and exclude transfers to developing countries, such as Brazil, Mexico, and Russia, whose top decile is very well-off by world standards. Though the negotiations on revenue distribution (and other relevant features of a scheme of international taxation) would surely be extremely hard; the real hurdle in the way of international redistribution is political, not a matter of regressive redistribution or practical implementation.[40]

It should be emphasized, moreover, that the point of a scheme of international taxation is not solely to transfer money from rich people to poor people, though raising the level of consumption of people living in conditions of destitution is of course necessary. Funds are also needed, on a regular and permanent basis, to face even more challenging problems, such as making science and technology address the needs of the world's poor. As mentioned before, there is no bottom line motivation for transnational corporations (TNCs) to generate the kind of knowledge that benefits the poor. In the above-mentioned proposal by Sachs, the revenues of a scheme of international taxation are necessary to provide long-term financing to such things as the development of vaccines for the epidemics that plague poor countries (mainly AIDS, malaria, and tuberculosis), to finance biotechnological research focused on the problems of agriculture in poor tropical countries, and to help poor countries adapt to the climatic changes imposed on them by rich countries (*The Economist* 1999).[41] This reminds us of something that should already be apparent at this point: the subject of social justice is the

---

[39] For further discussion see, for instance, Oxfam (1999), Quiggin (2001: 74–6); Barry (1998: 153– 6); and Milanovic (2001: 58–60).

[40] After the UNDP argued for the Tobin Tax in the 1990s, the United Nations is said to have ceased to defend the idea in virtue of the icy reception to it among American policymakers (Oxfam 1999: 13).

[41] A small step in that direction is the Global Fund recently created by the World Health Organization to raise funds and implement programs to combat with AIDS, malaria, and tuberculosis in the world.

distribution of the burdens and benefits of social cooperation, not merely the transfer of income from the rich to the poor.

It could be objected that even this more modest objective for the international society, to wit, the adoption of a justice-based approach to humanitarian and development aid, is too far-fetched to be taken seriously. Realist theorists in international relations could say that, the world being as it is, we should not bother ourselves with 'impossible' objectives such as guaranteeing a modicum of social justice on the international level.[42] According to this view, we should focus only on the 'feasible' set of alternatives. The central problem with this realist objection to the normative perspective put forth in the present study is that it makes a very ambiguous use of the word 'impossibility'. Why should we see an objective—such as instituting a Tobin Tax—as an 'impossibility'? As Robert Goodin points out in a very instructive discussion of this topic, what makes an end impossible for realists (and their considering it to be the case has the implication that the end in question should be kept off the agenda) is often merely the fact that it imposes costs on certain key political actors (Goodin 1992: 252–4). It is as if some powerful political actors—say, the governments of G8 countries—explained the impossibility of the proposals discussed above in the following terms: 'such proposals are impossible because you should not expect us to accept the costs they impose on us'. But, of course, what is at work here is not a genuine idea of impossibility—in the sense of being unable to do something—but rather an idea of *unwillingness* to bear the costs of what one is morally required to do.[43] If this is so, the least one can say is that these costs are very much a matter of public discussion, a conclusion that runs counter to the realist political theorist's suggestion of taking these issues off the agenda. As Goodin puts it, 'if the only reason the options are unrealistic is that people are unwilling to make sacrifices that they could and arguably should in pursuit of morally important goals, then those options should be very much on the table. The proper role of politics, in such circumstances, is precisely not to 'be realistic' and accept uncritically peoples' unwillingness to make morally proper sacrifices. It is, rather, to persuade them that moral ideals are worth pursuing' (Goodin 1992: 254).

I do not mean to deny that the realist argument from impossibility points to real political hurdles. Nevertheless, to suppose that it weakens the normative argument developed in this paper is humbug. The opposite, in fact, is correct.

---

[42] Realists seem to oscillate between this impossibility thesis, which amounts to denying any role to ethical ideals in international affairs, and the claim according to which the state (all states) should give an absolute priority to its national interest. This latter proposition, often attributed to Hans Morgenthau and other political realists, is a *moral* claim of the kind that can be dubbed the 'national partiality argument'. I do not examine this argument against international justice here. For discussions of realist views on ethics, see Beitz (1999*c*: 13–66), Cohen (1985), and Goodin (1992).

[43] Goodin quotes a passage from Bentham (criticizing the common law of his time) that fits in nicely with the point being made: 'True it is that under this system it is impossible, without exception impossible, ever to do justice. Nothing was ever more true. But the impossibility, whence comes it? From yourselves. First you make the impossibility, and then you plead it'. Cited in Goodin (1992: 262, n. 15).

4.2. NORMATIVE GROUNDS FOR INTERNATIONAL
DISTRIBUTIVE JUSTICE

4.2.1. Arbitrariness of the Distribution of Natural Resources

Having examined why inequality, and not only poverty, is an issue on the inter-national level, we are now able to move our discussion one step further and inquire into the question of what normative bases there may be for international distributive justice. It is also my purpose to confront each alternative that may qualify as such with the main objections that may be presented to it. This is the discussion, of a much more abstract nature, which I now go into.

In his seminal 1979 book, *Political Theory and International Relations*, Charles Beitz argued that in a Rawlsian approach there are two distinct theoretical bases for a principle of international distributive justice (1999*c*: 127–53). Beitz claimed that the morally arbitrary distribution of natural resources, on the one hand, and international interdependence, on the other, provide two distinct ways to justify a very significant redistribution of resources in the world. Even if the interdependence did not have the relevant characteristics required to justify it, the morally arbitrary distribution of natural resources would still be there to do the job. Attractive as this line of reasoning may be to supporters of international justice, I wish to maintain that, at least in a Rawlsian approach to justice, we are actually left with only one such basis; that is, the one that appeals to interdependence.[44] Let us see why this is so.

Beitz argued that the distribution of natural resources should play, in a Rawlsian theory of international justice, the same normative role that the morally arbitrary distribution of natural talents played in Rawls's theory in the domestic case. According to Beitz, even in the absence of a significant degree of international interdependence and cooperation, the parts to a global original position would adopt a resource redistribution principle in order to rectify the morally arbitrary distribution of natural resources (1999*c*: 137–8). However, as Thomas Pogge has argued, this parallel is based on a flawed interpretation of how Rawls's theory deals with natural talents in the domestic case (1989: 251). It is not the natural distribution of talents itself that has to be rectified, for no distributive effect follows from this natural fact per se. What Rawlsian justice demands is that the distributive effects of social institutions that may be heavily skewed in favor of those who happen to possess certain talents be rectified. This means that though a person's talents will always be fully hers, the benefits—her share of scarce social resources—she gets from exercising them depends on the type of basic structure adopted in a given society. It is that basic structure that needs to be justified, in particular to those who benefit least from its institutions.

---

[44] A distinct way to justify international redistribution of resources is a Lockean-Nozickian type of argument to the effect that the injustice of the original appropriation of natural resources needs to be corrected. Hillel Steiner has championed this kind of argument. See, for instance, Steiner (1987, 1992).

Likewise, what stands in need of moral justification in the international case is not the distribution of natural resources per se, but the international institution, namely, state sovereignty over natural resources. It is not a natural fact but an institution, adopted and affirmed in a variety of international documents—such as the Declarations of the United Nations General Assembly in 1970, 1972, and 1974—that belongs to the international society's basic structure (Barry 1989*b*: 449). It is not at all clear what are the distributive effects of this institution, which is, it is worth noting, fiercely defended by political leaders of both developed and developing nations. Thomas Pogge has recently suggested that the norm of state sovereignty over natural resources, interpreted as the unrestrained right a government (whatever means their leaders used to reach power) has to use the country's natural resources as it sees fit, may help to explain the so-called 'Dutch Disease', that is, the negative correlation that some economists have pointed out between rich natural resource endowment and economic development. The norm that Pogge dubs 'international resource privilege' provides, so the argument runs, strong incentives for the prevalence of predatory political elites in some developing countries that are rich in natural resources. If this argument is sound, then clear distributive effects, albeit of an indirect kind, could be imputed to the norm of state sovereignty over natural resources: in some developing countries, it would favor the perpetuation of political elites to whom the adoption of domestic institutions and policies that fight inequality and poverty reduction do not rank high in their priorities. In at least some cases, features of the global institutional arrangements would nurture the domestic factors that Rawls and other critics of cosmopolitan liberalism see as the main culprits of international inequalities.

Whether Pogge's argument of the last paragraph is correct, what we can be confident of is that there is no (positive) causal connection between the endowment of natural resources and the level of socioeconomic development of a country. A principle aimed at correcting the unequal distribution of natural resources, such as the one that is endorsed by Beitz's reasoning, could even have perverse implications: it could end up having to recommend transfers from developing resource-rich countries, such as Nigeria or Venezuela, to wealthy resource-poor countries, such as Japan. And, what is even more important to our present purposes, the morally objectionable distributive effects in question are not generated by the distribution of natural resources by itself, but rather by a norm that is part of the current global institutional arrangements. If this is so, then it is not true that the moral arbitrariness of the distribution of natural resources provides an independent normative foundation for international distributive justice.

If we want to argue for global justice within a Rawlsian approach, we are compelled—or at least that is what my argument in this section, so far, implies—to base our argument on certain normatively relevant features of the global institutional order.[45] My case for taking inequality as an issue on the international level already relied on that supposition, that is, there is such a thing as a society's basic

---

[45] To employ a Rawlsian framework in a way that Rawls himself disapproves of is to be 'more royalist than the king'. However, I see no reason to reject the label.

structure (in a Rawlsian sense) on the international level and that the distributive effects of such structure need to be addressed by a conception of justice. It also comes into play in the explanation I provided above as to why the arbitrary distribution of natural resources cannot provide an independent argument for international redistribution.

4.2.2. The Argument from Past Injustices

Before going into a more detailed discussion of objections to the central argument of this chapter, let me briefly consider a different tack one could take to justify international redistribution. It could be argued that the inequities generated by the current arrangements are not the only morally significant moral consideration to be taken into account when questions of international justice arise. Also important, so the argument proceeds, is the historical path that led to the current level of world inequality—whether it is tainted by injustices that call for compensation. Under this scheme, the citizens of rich countries today would have a moral duty to compensate the people of poor countries for all the damages inflicted on them by centuries of colonialism, slavery and slave trade, and imperialism. The supporters of the New International Economic Order (NIEO) in the 1970s, for instance, often relied on this argument to make their case for international redistribution.[46]

It is difficult to deny that there is plausibility in this argument from historical injustice. Some of the poorer areas of the world today, such as the Northeast of Brazil and sub-Saharan Africa, were subject to colonialist exploitation in the past. Nevertheless, the moral case for international redistribution that tries to make much of the compensation for past injustices is fraught with seemingly insurmountable complexities as to who should be held responsible for the damages, how much compensation would be due, and to whom (Doyle 2000: 81–2). The moral case for reparations for past injustices loses its strength as time passes— as those people directly involved in the circumstances of exploitation, or their immediate descendants, have disappeared long ago.[47]

I add two qualifications to this skeptical evaluation of what we can expect, normatively speaking, from the argument that appeals to historical injustice. The first is that, though it is true that we cannot expect to derive precise implications from this argument, it does make sense to see it as a reinforcing consideration in an argument for international redistribution that draws its strength from a criticism of the unfairness of the current institutional arrangements. Compensation for past

---

[46] On NIEO, see footnote 27 above. Some African countries have recently argued, in the 2001 World Conference Against Racism, Racial Discrimination, Xenophobia, and Related Intolerance, that the slavery and slave trade practiced by Western countries should be considered a crime against humanity (whose recognition would pave the way to demands for monetary compensation). The Conference's Declaration, however, did not endorse this stance.

[47] By contrast, the argument to the effect that the post-war generations of Germans have a moral duty to compensate the victims (and their immediate descendants) of Nazi concentration camps is straightforward.

injustices may be an *additional* reason why the governments and citizens of rich countries should accept a duty of international distributive justice. Reciprocally, to implement international institutions geared at maximizing the benefits to the world's poorest quintile—or, more realistically, to adopt a justice-based approach to humanitarian and development aid along the lines discussed above—could *also* be conceived as a form of compensation for the damages that the Western countries inflicted in the past on some of the poorest areas of today's world. At least one can say that the path on which present international inequalities have evolved cast a cloud over the legitimacy of the holdings and other advantages of the rich.[48]

Let me now qualify the qualification. This supposition of convergence would be undermined only if it could be shown that the two criteria—the compensation for past injustices and the correction of the distributive unfairness of current institutions (call it 'Rawlsian justice', for short)—would yield conflicting recommendations in a number of relevant cases. I conjecture that only in special cases, perhaps with little political significance, would this conflict show up. Here is one example, drawn from a domestic context. A Brazilian senator (Paulo Paim, from the Worker's Party) has recently proposed a bill according to which a very substantial monetary compensation (of R$ 102,000, or about US$ 35,000 in March 2004) would be due to each Afro-Brazilian (44% of the population, according to the available data) as a compensation for the centuries of black slavery in the country. In addition to it being beset by the above-mentioned difficulties that weaken any argument from historical injustice, the proposal is obviously impracticable (trillions of Reais would be required to foot the bill). However, what I want to stress now is that, even if we put all these difficulties aside, the two criteria lead to divergent recommendations in a case like the one just described. Compensation for historical injustice is always due to specific persons who can, so to speak, be known by their proper names. By contrast, Rawlsian justice seeks to correct the unfairness of institutional arrangements. For that purpose, it compares alternative institutional schemes according to the life prospects each imposes on the least advantaged group, and drives us to select that scheme in which the least advantaged are best-off. The least advantaged group, as Rawls puts it, should not be conceived as a 'rigid designator'.[49] This means that it does not refer to a specific group of persons who may happen to be the least advantaged in a given society, as Afro-Brazilian poor certainly are in the present circumstances of Brazilian society, but rather to a social position defined by the institutional distribution of benefits and burdens. What matters is the share of the benefits of social cooperation available to this social position, *whoever happens to occupy it*. Going back to the example mentioned above, let us suppose that a massive transfer of resources to Afro-Brazilians would result in an alternative scheme of social cooperation, under which the position of the least advantaged would be worse than that of Afro-Brazilian in today's status quo in Brazil. Rawlsian justice rules this move out,

---

[48] As Thomas Pogge pointed out in his comments to a previous version of this chapter.
[49] See, for instance, Rawls (2001: 59 n. 26, and 59–60).

not because it is unfeasible (which it also is), but rather because it is *unjust*.[50] If the correction of past injustices and the correction of the unfairness of the current institutional arrangement conflict, precedence should be given, so I want to argue, to the latter.

The second qualification points to a more specialized, and perhaps also more definite, normative role to the argument from historical injustice. There are issues of global concern with respect to which it is not possible to disentangle the current unfairness from past iniquity. Global warming is such an issue. For sure, the subject of justice is the distribution not only of the benefits, but also of the burdens of institutional arrangements. Let us suppose, as it is the case, that an international regime is deemed necessary to prevent a global 'public bad'—the climate change that results from the atmospheric concentration of carbon dioxide (and other greenhouse gases), brought about by the burning of fossil fuels for which rich countries have by far the greatest share of responsibility. On whom should the burdens of the proposed regime mainly fall? We cannot discuss this question from a purely forward-looking perspective, that is, a perspective that would only take into account the environmental costs of emissions of greenhouse gases from now on.[51] The process of global warming was also the process by which the industrialized countries of the North became rich and their citizens were spurred to adopt lifestyles that damaged the earth's atmosphere. While the environmental costs of such lifestyles were shouldered by everyone on the planet, particularly on those living in poor tropical countries, their benefits were of course highly concentrated.[52] The world's rich were allowed to raise their standard of living dumping some of the costs of their doing so on others who have not had any share of the benefits. This is the iniquity that a fair international regime on global climate will have to compensate for by allocating unequal burdens—and this is a case with respect to which the argument from historical injustice comes to its own.[53] It should be noticed, however, that what makes the argument from past injustice more compelling in this case is the fact that the iniquity in question is not restricted to a long-gone period. It started, say, with the Industrial Revolution and continues to the present day. Had industrial countries taken measures to cut back their levels of CO_2 emissions in the 1980s when the need to reduce the atmospheric concentration of greenhouse gases became apparent, the moral case for compensation would have been much weakened.[54]

[50] There are, to be sure, avenues of social reform in Brazil that can meet the requirements of both criteria, but monetary compensation is not one of them.

[51] This is what the so-called 'polluter pays principle', according to which the future costs of pollution should be internalized into prices, requires. See Shue (1999: 534).

[52] It seems that, among other possible negative effects, global warming may lower the productivity of tropical agriculture.

[53] The Kyoto Protocol does have this redistributive character. It imposes limits only on industrial countries and Europe's transition economies. If the regime comes into force, the burdens on industrial countries (the economic effects of the required abatement on the levels of their CO_2 emissions) will probably supersede any benefits they may derive from the provision of a global public good. This explains why it may be difficult to bring the Kyoto Protocol into force.

[54] For further discussion, see Shue (1999), Paterson (2001), and Barret (1999).

4.2.3. Distributive Iniquity of Existing Institutional Arrangements

Let us now turn to Beitz's argument for international distributive justice that appeals to global interdependence. This is the most promising line of argument, if we want to find out a solid normative foundation for a redistribution of resources that extends itself beyond what is required by considerations of humanity. Beitz asserts the following:

> The world is not made up of self-sufficient states. States participate in complex international economic, political, and cultural relationships that suggest the existence of a global scheme of social cooperation. As Kant notes, international economic cooperation creates a new basis for international morality. If social cooperation is the foundation of distributive justice, then one might think that international economic interdependence lends support to a principle of distributive justice similar to that which applies within domestic society (1999*c*: 143–4).[55]

This passage touches the point of the matter in the theoretical debate on international distributive justice. In this and in related passages of his book, Beitz argues for twin premises that are crucial to the argument in favor of extending the difference principle to the international level. First, the world is not constituted, as Rawls supposes, of self-sufficient domestic societies, each of them being a separate scheme of social cooperation. Second, the world at large should be seen as a scheme of social cooperation in Rawls's sense. To argue for these two premises, Beitz went on analyzing, in a more or less empirical fashion, some relevant features of global interdependence (1999*c*: 143–9). Beitz conceded that it is difficult to ascertain with precision what are the distributive effects of international practices and institutions, such as international trade and finance, foreign investments, international property rights regime, and regulatory structures (1999*c*: 145).[56] In spite of that, what could safely be assumed is that these institutional arrangements, largely non-voluntary for the world's least privileged, do generate large benefits and burdens that would not take place if such practices and arrangements did not exist. Moreover, there is solid evidence—much of it of the kind that I mentioned above—to the effect that these distributive effects tend to aggravate international inequality (Beitz 1999*c*: 148–9).

What some authors find disputable in this argument is not so much a question of its empirical credentials, but rather its notion of 'social cooperation' and its

---

[55] Pogge (1989: ch. 6) argues along similar lines. Nevertheless, Pogge's argument appeals more emphatically to a coercively imposed global basic structure and its effects. 'A global institutional scheme', Pogge argues, 'is imposed by all of us on each of us.... This fact is most significant in the case of the scheme's most disadvantaged participants, who are literally being forced, ultimately with resort to violence, to abide by the going ground rules' Pogge (1989: 276).

[56] Twenty-three years after Beitz's book came out, empirical studies on the distributive consequences of international institutions are still badly needed. It would be very useful, for instance, to study the WTO's rules on intellectual property from that perspective. Hasenclever, Mayer, and Rittberger (2000) have set out to do something in this fashion, taking the Nuclear Non-proliferation Regime as their test case, but they are concerned with a different kind of question, that is, the extent to which distributive fairness is a necessary condition for the stability of international regimes.

applicability to the world at large. Despite all the rapid increase in international trade, finance, regulatory structures (such as the WTO) and regimes, and despite the existence of organizations of international cooperation, such as the UN, the IMF, and the World Bank, the world cannot be conceived, as Beitz supposed it could, as a scheme of social cooperation 'in the relevant sense', that is to say, in Rawls's sense. Brian Barry was the first to voice this criticism and others, like Chris Brown and Brian Opeskin, followed suit.[57]

Let us begin by asking what a scheme of social cooperation in Rawls's sense is supposed to be like. What these three authors took—at least in the texts cited in footnote 57—to be the most relevant feature of social cooperation is something different from the reasons invoked by Rawls to reject the criticism of his own theory presented by Nozick's Wilt Chamberlain example (1974: 160–4). Let us recall that the point of Nozick's example is to demonstrate how large inequalities in scarce social resources could legitimately emerge from an initial (and hypothetical) status quo of equality of resources, through free and voluntary transactions of individual agents deciding by their own lights what to do with the equal share of resources with which each was initially endowed. Nozick's argument goes on to show that only the use of coercive power could restore the initial equality or make the distribution of resources correspond to what Rawls's difference principle would recommend. Let us briefly consider the main point of Rawls's response to this criticism. It emphasizes the need to focus on the justice of society's basic structure (something absent from Nozick's example): (*a*) because huge distributive inequalities could and do arise in society's basic institutional arrangements from individual transactions and acts that, in themselves (as in Nozick's example), were morally unobjectionable—and that is the reason why we cannot do without a notion of 'background justice' and (*b*) in virtue of 'its [basic structure's] profound and pervasive influence on the persons who live under its institutions'.[58] Now the point that I am trying to make, against Rawls's opinion, is that a similar rationale accounts for the extension of a conception of distributive justice to deal with the distributive effects of international practices and institutions. I take Beitz to have something like that in mind when he refers, in the passage I quoted above, to the 'existence of a global scheme of social cooperation'.

4.2.3.1. *First Objection: The World Is Not a Scheme of Social Cooperation*

In his 'Humanity and Justice in Global Perspective', Brian Barry argues that there is a further component in Rawls's notion of a 'scheme of social cooperation' that explains why the world at large cannot be conceived as such a scheme, that is, as the sort of social grouping to which a conception of justice is to be applied. This further feature is an idea of mutuality or reciprocity (Barry 1989*b*: 445–7). The kind of social grouping to which the requirements of justice apply, according

---

[57] Barry (1989*b*: 45–47), Brown (1992: 176), Opeskin (1996: 30). Pogge (1989: 20–1 and 263–5) also discusses this topic and responds to Barry's criticism.

[58] See, for instance, Rawls (1993*a*: ch. VII, §§3, 4, and 5).

to Rawls, is society viewed as a 'cooperative venture for mutual advantage' (1999*a*: 4). What Rawls really means with these five words is not very easy to grasp, and I hasten to add that it is not my purpose here to interpret what he meant to say. Authors of different persuasions interpreted it according to their own purposes. David Gauthier, for instance, made a lot of it, arguing that his theory of 'justice as mutual advantage' accorded more to the spirit of the idea of cooperative venture expressed in Rawls's phrase than Rawls's own theory of 'justice as fairness' (Gauthier 1986).

This is not the place to go into Gauthier's theory of justice, but it is worth noting that Barry interpreted Rawls's ideas of 'cooperative venture' and 'mutual benefit' along Gauthier's lines. The world economy, according to Barry, not only could not be viewed as a cooperative venture but also, and more importantly, the economic redistribution implied by a global difference principle could not be shown to be advantageous to rich countries. As to the latter point, Barry argued, 'the extent of increased cooperation that would really be mutually beneficial is probably quite limited.... In the foreseeable future, aid to the needy is going to flow from, say, the United States to Bangladesh rather than vice versa. The conditions for reciprocity—that all the parties stand prospectively to benefit from the scheme— simply do not exist' (Barry 1989*b*: 447). Barry's most forceful criticism against the way Beitz derives a conception of international distributive justice from Rawlsian premises is that a global difference principle cannot qualify to be mutually advantageous in this particular, Gauthierian sense.

This is an odd criticism to come from a political theorist, such as Barry, who otherwise stands resolutely for cosmopolitan liberal-egalitarian positions in his more recent work. It seems that Barry does not feel compelled to revise his earlier criticism of the way Beitz argued for international redistribution to stick to these positions.[59] In one of his recent papers, we are told that 'the demands of cosmopolitanism would, I suggest, be best satisfied in a world in which rich people wherever they lived would be taxed for the benefit of poor people wherever they lived' (Barry 1989*b*: 153). But others, perhaps more consistently, argue in the vein of Barry's 1982 essay that the absence of a global mutually advantageous cooperative venture should be taken to mean that there are no international obligations of distributive justice.

The argument that the world is a cooperative venture between five billion or so individuals, which is mutually advantageous because it produces benefits for all, is not compelling. The primary beneficiaries of international trade are multinational corporations, as Beitz himself notes, and through them the groups that comprise their stockholders. Economic gains from trade are often concentrated in the upper

---

[59] By way of justifying his egalitarian positions on the international level, Barry offers only an argument from the moral arbitrariness of the distribution of natural resources (1989*b*: 448–51), and (1998: 150). I have already criticized the supposition that such argument could provide—at least within a Rawlsian framework, which Barry otherwise subscribes to in his works on social justice— an independent normative basis for international redistribution. Moreover, I doubt that this argument could do the entire job of justifying Barry's strongly egalitarian positions with respect to international redistribution.

income elites within each state. ... Accordingly, international trade and investment may not be a firm basis for regarding humanity as a cooperative venture for
mutual advantage. I thus share the view of those who deny the existence of a global
cooperative enterprise sufficient to call for cosmopolitan duties of distributive
justice (Opeskin 1996: 30).[60]

But do global institutional arrangements and practices need to be 'mutually
advantageous', in the particular sense meant by Barry and Opeskin, for them to
qualify as a kind of social cooperation 'in the relevant sense' and to fall under the
scope of principles of justice? From the fact that international cooperation lacks
the required mutuality today—whereas people living in wealthy countries and the
upper classes of the developing world derive huge advantages from the existing
institutions and practices, the world's bottom quintile derive little benefit at all
from these arrangements—can we infer that international cooperation based on
principles of justice is neither morally required nor possible? My answer is 'no'
to these two questions. As to the first question, all we have to show, in order to
argue for a global principle of distributive justice, is that the very same (Rawlsian)
reasons that make society's basic structure the primary subject of justice in the
domestic case also apply to the effects of international institutions and practices.
As to the second question, there is a sense according to which the international
society can be a 'cooperative venture for mutual advantage' of all submitted to its
effects. But, clearly, this sense can only refer to an ideal of social cooperation based
on principles of justice, not to present-day international institutional scheme—
and certainly not to an alternative to the existing institutional arrangement that
would be mutually beneficial to all taking the distribution of advantages and
burdens of the status quo as the baseline.[61]

This last observation offers a clue to what Barry was actually going for in his
criticism of Beitz in his 1982 essay. My purpose is not to clarify Barry's ideas
for him, but to make a judgment on the damage that that criticism does to the
kind of justification of obligations of international distributive justice that I am
subscribing to in this chapter. I submit that the actual target of that criticism was
not so much Beitz's argument from global interdependence as it was of a strand of
Hobbesian moral argument that can be detected in Rawls's *A Theory of Justice*—
and that could, if taken for granted, seriously impair the extension of a Rawlsian
framework to the international level. In his works on theory of justice posterior
to the 1982 essay, Barry forcefully argued that Rawls's main argumentation in
A Theory of Justice oscillates between two very distinct and even incompatible
theories of justice: one, of a Hobbesian flavor, that Barry (after Gauthier) dubbed
'justice as mutual advantage', and the other, of a Kantian flavor, that he dubbed
'justice as impartiality' (Barry 1989*a*). This is too complex a discussion to go into
in much detail here. In the remainder of this section, I merely make an effort to

---

[60] Opeskin believes that there are only obligations of humanity requiring developed states and their
citizens to give more aid to developing countries.

[61] This is the answer that Beitz (1983: 595), gave to Barry's criticism, though he felt pressured to
concede that the case he had made for international distributive justice, in his 1979 book, presupposed
the *existence* of a mutually beneficial social cooperation.

bring out its implications for our present concerns. Also, I won't try to determine the extent to which Barry's interpretation of *A Theory of Justice* as comprising two different theories is correct.

According to the theory of justice as mutual advantage, what is at stake in an agreement to move from a point of non-cooperation (or a 'state of nature') to a scheme of cooperation is only a fair distribution of the gains from cooperation, with 'fair distribution' meaning, in this context, some kind of proportionality to the contribution each participant makes to the cooperative surplus. Distributive justice here means only that, to wit, the distribution of the cooperative surplus in proportion to the contribution that each participant makes to generate it. Since the state of cooperation is a Pareto-improvement over the point of non-agreement, and since the gains from cooperation are 'equitably' distributed among the participants, only self-interest is required for an agreement to be reached and for each participant to be motivated to comply with its terms.[62] We may say that such cooperation exhibits 'reciprocity' (or 'mutuality'), but this is so in the limited sense of everyone being disposed to reciprocate the benefits that each one gets from the scheme of cooperation. If that is what we take Rawls to mean when he says that society—that is, the unit of social life to which principles of justice apply—is a 'cooperative venture for mutual advantage', then it obviously follows that there is no social cooperation 'in the relevant sense' on the international level. What contribution does the world's bottom quintile make to the world's cooperative surplus generated by means, say, of international trade, investments, and financial operations? How could an international system of tax and transfers designed to improve as much as possible the position of the world's least privileged be thought of as 'advantageous' to people living in the richest countries? We can go some way in justifying humanitarian aid and the provision of certain global public goods on prudential or self-interested grounds, pointing to negative externalities that huge international poverty and exclusion from the benefits of globalization may generate to rich countries, such as immigration pressures, environmental damages, spread of drug trafficking and diseases, political instability in large parts of the world, and terrorism.[63] However, it is doubtful that prudential arguments can go very far when it comes to justifying the adoption of just socioeconomic and political institutions.

---

[62] This is, of course, a summary of Gauthier's view, but Barry's contention is that Rawls flirted with this position at several points of his argumentation in *A Theory of Justice*: in his argument from the original position, in which self-interested rational parties face a bargaining problem, in the ambiguous language he employs to depict his view of social cooperation (Gauthier [1986: 10–11], profited a lot from this ambiguity), and in the supposition that the motivational requirement of justice as fairness, 'reciprocity', was weaker than moral impartiality (Rawls 1993a: 16–17).

[63] There are good reasons to believe that the United States and other developed countries had better to rely on a kind of Marshall Plan to promote the socioeconomic development of Central Asia, rather than on war, to fight terrorism. Rashid (2002) provides an excellent analysis of why this region has become the home of anti-Western Islamic militancy and extremism. But this self-interested rationale for humanitarian aid doesn't apply to other areas of dire poverty and marginalization in sub-Saharan Africa and South Asia.

Now the conclusion we should draw from this discussion of a Gauthierian conception of social cooperation is not, as Barry supposed in his 1982 essay, that global interdependence cannot provide the normative basis for distributive justice. The correct conclusion is, rather, that international cooperation cannot be based solely (and perhaps even mainly) on notions of self-interest and mutual advantage. This is the point, I believe, that Barry was trying to make in his criticism of Beitz or, at any rate, the point that is worth making. The target of his criticism was, in fact, an interpretation of Rawls's theory as a version of justice as mutual advantage. As Barry himself argued in his subsequent work, justice is not a question of distributing the gains from cooperation and the difference principle is not, as Rawls may have thought in his argument from the original position, a plausible solution for a bargaining problem (Barry 1989*a*: ch. 6). Be it applied to the domestic case or to the international case, an ideal of social cooperation in which a principle such as the difference principle—or a similar principle of distributive justice—figures prominently can only be generated from the stronger moral suppositions of a conception of 'justice as impartiality'.

I am brief again. According to justice as impartiality, the ground rules of a basic institutional arrangement must be justified, by reasons that 'no one could reasonably reject', to all those who are significantly affected by its terms—including its most vulnerable participants (who have little to reciprocate for any benefits they may be entitled to) and the unborn (who cannot reciprocate at all). In this version of contractualism, a moral motive—that Barry, following Thomas Scanlon's formulation, characterizes as 'the desire to find principles which others similarly motivated could not reasonably reject'—takes the place of self-interest and mutual advantage (Scanlon 1982: 116, n. 2).[64] What principles would be generated by this contractualism is not clear, but I think that Barry is entirely correct in stressing the moral suppositions that necessarily lie in the justification of a principle of distributive justice—both on the domestic and on the international levels.[65]

It may be asked, at this juncture, if to substitute moral motive and agreement for self-interest and mutual advantage will make it any easier to persuade the beneficiaries of today's arrangements to accept the institutional reforms required by justice. This is not at all the point that I want to make. As Chris Brown has put it, Barry's position 'is not that the rich and powerful will always subject themselves to the dictates of reason, but that if they are not prepared to be swayed by a reasoned argument about the demands of impartiality there is little that moral philosophers can do about the matter' (Brown 1992: 182). Sticking to a premise of mutual advantage, at any rate, can at best only conceal the motivational and political hurdles that lie in the way of international justice.

Where Barry's argument in 'Humanity and Justice in Global Perspective' went astray, I believe, was in conflating a correct criticism of an interpretation of Rawls's

---

[64] Barry (1989*a*: 282–5, 1995: 67–72) discusses this approach to social contract theory.

[65] In the present circumstances of the world economy, there is no reason to believe that securing a Rawlsian type scheme of distributive justice will be easier on the domestic level than on the international level. While the developing world will be struggling against poverty for a long time to come, distributive inequality is on the rise also in the developed world.

theory as a conception of justice as mutual advantage with a criticism of the argument, made by Beitz and Pogge, to the effect that it is the existence of a worldwide scheme of social cooperation that makes distributive justice relevant to the international context. Indeed, it can be argued that it is in virtue of there being such a scheme—the international analogue of Rawls's basic structure—that something like Barry's contractualism can be employed to clarify the nature of social justice in the international domain. We could say, in the vein of Barry's contractualism, that the international basic structure has to be justified, for reasons that no one could reasonably reject, to all those whose life prospects are importantly affected by its distributive effects—whether they are capable of contributing to the generation of cooperative gains. To sum up, the existing distributive unfairness is what makes a concern about distributive justice sensible in the international context. But the justification of a principle and of institutions aimed at correcting that unfairness has to be based on an impartial consideration of the legitimate interests of all who stand to be affected, not on the actual degree of reciprocity of existing institutions and practices nor (solely) on ideas of self-interest and mutual advantage. Moreover, one wonders why the existing degree of reciprocity, being what it is—a function of prevailing values and institutions—could ever be taken (as Opeskin does) as the vantage point from which to judge alternatives for the international society.

4.2.3.2. *Second Objection: No Shared Meanings*

The world cannot be conceived as a scheme of social cooperation for the mutual advantage of its participants, so there are no worldwide duties of distributive justice. This is the argument examined and rejected in the previous section. Now this argument can be given a communitarian twist, to which I now turn in bringing this chapter to a close. Communitarian theorists like Michael Walzer and David Miller also argue that the world as a whole cannot be conceived as a scheme of social cooperation to which duties of justice apply. But what is lacking, for them, is not mutual advantage, a consideration entirely alien to their approach to justice. Instead, absent are shared values and a shared identity that could be embodied in common global institutions.

For both Walzer and Miller, the nation-state is the community relevant to justice. 'The only alternative to the political community', Walzer says in Chapter 1 of *Spheres of Justice*, 'is humanity itself, the society of nations, the entire globe. But were we to take the globe as our setting, we would have to imagine what does not yet exist: a community that included all men and women everywhere. We would have to invent a set of common meanings for these people, avoiding if we could the stipulation of our own values'. Later on in this book, he adds: 'there cannot be a just society until there is a society' (1983: 29–30, 313). Miller argues along similar lines. He thinks that duties of justice, corresponding to notions of equal rights and equal treatment, arise only from membership of citizens in a nation-state (1999: 189). He goes on to argue that 'although in the contemporary world there are clearly forms of interaction and cooperation occurring at the global level . . . these are not sufficient to constitute a global community. They do not by themselves create either a shared sense of identity or a common ethos. And above all there is no common institutional structure that would justify us in describing unequal outcomes as forms of unequal treatment' (Miller1999: 190).

What are we to think about this objection to international duties of distributive justice?[66] Were it to be read mainly as a realist objection, I would not take issue with it. However, Walzer and Miller surely take it to be an objection of principle to cosmopolitanism. What they mean is not only that, as a matter of fact, there are no global common institutions, but also that these institutions cannot even be created, for the common meanings and identity in which they would have to be based still do not exist. Several reasons can be pointed out as to why this normative objection should be rejected.

To begin with, let us suppose, at least for the sake of argument, that the central argument of this paper is sound. Though international political institutions similar to those of the nation-state are obviously absent, it has been argued that the existing global institutional arrangements and practices do have distributive effects that significantly contribute to world inequality in life prospects. Let us also grant, as Walzer and Miller try to make us believe, that we are deprived of 'social meanings' that could make up the normative basis of just global common institutions. If both assertions are true, what conclusion should be drawn from them—that nothing can be done with respect to those unequal distributive effects because the relevant common social meanings are still lacking? This conclusion would be acceptable only to the beneficiaries of prevailing inequalities. Moreover, the way Walzer and Miller appeal to common values and identity seems to presuppose that an agreement on principles would have to precede any efforts to set up just international arrangements. This is surely too stringent a requirement. As Henry Shue argues, we can conceive of these two things—the creation of just arrangements and the emergence of a normative consensus that underlies them— as simultaneous: 'international society and just international society can be built at the same time through the same activities. A large part of what makes a collection of people a society is, precisely as Walzer maintains, shared understandings about matters like rights and justice. Rather than waiting for a society somehow to emerge on its own before asking its members to think about what would make it a just society, one can attempt to build a society through agreement in theory or practice on just institutions'.[67] This does not amount to downplaying the hurdles in the way of reaching agreement on just international institutions and putting them into effect. Rather, it amounts to clearing the way of a normative objection to even trying to overcome them.

---

[66] We may interpret this objection as the negative part of what we can dub 'the national partiality argument', according to which our compatriots have a moral right to demand from us a special consideration for their well-being in ways that citizens from other nation-states do not. National partiality, interpreted in this way, may conflict with the liberal-cosmopolitan argument according to which a just international society should enhance as much as possible the well-being of the least advantaged on a global scale. Though this positive component of the objection examined in the text is, of course, important, I cannot discuss it now.

[67] Shue (1996a: 179).

5

Poverty as a Form of Oppression

Marc Fleurbaey*

5.1. INTRODUCTION

Can poverty be described as the violation of a fundamental human right? Human rights are usually understood in a more restrictive sense, which makes it possible to think that the glaring economic inequalities prevailing today are in theory compatible with a perfect observance of fundamental rights. If from now on poverty were to be itself perceived as a violation of these rights, the widespread self-satisfaction of the richest countries, based on the idea that their institutions represent an advanced or even the ultimate stage of respect for fundamental rights, would be completely called into question. The poverty still persisting in rich countries and their less 'developed' neighbors, would then show that, even with regard to fundamental principles, the more advanced societies have not yet reached a bearable stage.

However, it is not necessary to show that poverty *is in itself* a violation of a fundamental right in order to obtain such a calling into question of Western good conscience. It is indeed enough to prove that poverty *is always accompanied* by violations of fundamental rights, even in a restrictive definition of these rights. It is thus possible to distinguish between a strong and a weak thesis regarding the relation between poverty and fundamental rights. The strong thesis requires, for its defense, a modification of the current definition of the fundamental rights of the human person, which would incorporate into them something of the nature of a right to subsistence, to economic security, or to social integration. It thus requires a significant conceptual revision. The weak thesis rests more simply on an empirical examination of the practical conditions of exercise of human rights in situations of poverty. It does not call for a substantial revision of the concepts, but it is not less disturbing for the common idea according to which the political and legal institutions can work in a satisfactory way independently of the socioeconomic situation of the population.

Let us note in passing that the two theses encounter the same difficulty about the ambiguity of the concept of poverty. There are various definitions of poverty,

* I thank the participants at the UNESCO forum on poverty. I am also very grateful to Thomas Pogge for detailed comments on the first draft, and to Rekha Nath for useful remarks. The hospitality of Nuffield College, Oxford, where the last version was finalized, is also gratefully acknowledged.

and different ways to concretely measure its extent in a population, so that it can be difficult to specify which subpopulation is involved when examining the situation of poverty with regard to fundamental rights. One can circumvent this difficulty by slightly modifying the problem. It is indeed enough to ask whether there is a poverty line under which one witnesses a systematic violation of a fundamental right, either in an intrinsic (strong thesis) or concomitant way (weak thesis). Put in this way, the question becomes interesting even for the analysis of poverty itself, insofar as it suggests an original approach to the concept of poverty, in connection with the concept of rights violation.

The main ambition of this chapter is to show that the weak thesis can be defended in a way that makes it almost equivalent to the strong thesis. Namely that, in the usual conditions of market economy, poverty is so closely linked to an attack on the integrity of the human person, that protection against poverty should be inseparable from protection of personal integrity. To open the way to such an argument and to better put it in context, it is useful to reexamine first the libertarian approach and its egalitarian opponents with a critical eye.

5.2. THE NEGATIVE ILLUSION

The common, restrictive, concept of fundamental rights can indeed find support in the libertarian approach. According to this approach, the only legitimate rights are purely negative, that is they never make it possible to have access to the resources of others without their consent. What can be called 'the libertarian ideal' is a society in which all the material resources are allotted in full property to single owners and these individuals are free to trade, give, or bequeath their property as they see fit. The only way to come into possession of someone else's property is thus to obtain his consent, either for trade or simply as a voluntary gift.

According to this view, a poor person does not suffer any violation of his rights as long as he is not the victim of theft or violent aggression. And he is not entitled to any assistance from his fellow citizens, because this obligation would in itself be a violation of the rights of the owners concerned.

It is now well understood that this libertarian ideal is rather naive. This has been highlighted by numerous authors, including Nozick who has examined it most sympathetically.[1] Let us briefly review the problems inherent in the libertarian vision before examining how it affects the determination of a list of fundamental rights and the relation between poverty and fundamental rights.

The first problem is that a purely deontological constraint enjoining everyone to respect the property of others will in practice only produce a Hobbesian state of nature where force and violence dominate social life. A certain degree of teleological concern for the quantity of respected rights is thus inevitable. One must then

---

[1] See Nozick (1974), Nagel (1979), Cohen (1995), and van Parijs (1995), among many other references.

bypass deontology and accept certain violations of the right of property aimed at preserving, by and large, a global respect for this right. The establishment of a state financed by compulsory taxes for upholding the law is the most realistic formula to move toward the libertarian ideal; even if in itself it is an obstacle to the full achievement of this ideal.

The second problem is that the transition to the libertarian ideal would require remedying violations of rights that have occurred in the past. It is not possible to do this in a rigorous way, for experienced misfortunes cannot be erased, especially when their victims died and their descendants could not be born. It would also be necessary to think about what should be done with the people who should not have been born. All this is practically inextricable since there is very little information on the nature, and especially on the consequences, of past violations. In view of the impossibility of determining the adequate distribution of property rights for starting a libertarian society, the most reasonable option would be to make a clean sweep of the past and to seek to bring about equality in wealth. Consequently, the fight against present poverty would be a priority even for a purely libertarian policy.[2]

The third problem is that it is difficult to accept the idea that the fate of individuals is very largely determined by the wealth and goodwill of their parents. In the libertarian ideal, individuals are free to produce descendants and to bequeath to them what they want. This introduces arbitrary inequalities between individuals who are only distinguished by birth. The transfer of resources from the children of the rich to the children of the poor, in order to give everyone enough chances to have an acceptable life, seems to be a minimum requirement of equity.

The fourth problem is that the libertarian ideal ignores the existence of public goods and of externalities. However, it can be in the interest of each member of a society to institute a compulsory contribution to finance the production of a public good. The establishment of this constraint can be unanimously desired by the members of society, insofar as it constitutes the only means of guaranteeing the production of a desirable public good.[3] Prohibiting any constraint of this kind would thus hinder the achievement of the objectives of individuals relating to public goods. A sophisticated version of the libertarian ideal must thus take into account the collective dimension of certain individual projects and envisage the possibility of freely chosen constraints. The establishment of a state upholding the law and ensuring the safety of people and goods can itself be understood according to this logic; but, a more comprehensive state can result from it too.

---

[2] 'Perhaps it is best to view some patterned principles of distributive justice as rough rules of thumb meant to approximate the general results of applying the principle of rectification of injustice. For example, lacking much historical information, and assuming (1) that victims of injustice generally do worse than they otherwise would and (2) that those from the least well-off group in the society have the highest probabilities of being the (descendants of) victims of the most serious injustice who are owed compensation by those who benefited from the injustices..., then a *rough* rule of thumb for rectifying injustices might seem to be the following: organize society so as to maximize the position of whatever group ends up least well-off in the society' (Nozick 1974: 230–1).

[3] For a detailed analysis of this point, see Kolm (1985).

These last two problems combine, leading to the observation that one can hardly condemn the organization of a society whose members wish to maintain a high degree of social cohesion and remedy inequalities that they consider illegitimate; they do so even when this leads them to set up constraining mechanisms of redistribution, which restrict the right of property. In the libertarian perspective, the legitimacy of such institutions will of course depend on the explicit or tacit agreement of all citizens.[4]

Thus one can see that the fight against poverty can be legitimized in various ways, even from the standpoint of the libertarian ideal, once one seizes the naivety of this ideal in its pure form, and agrees to confront it with the historical and collective realities of social life. One can even go further and note that, from this point of view, it is possible to give to the poor a real *drawing right* on the resources of others, in the name of consensual principles of equity, as a reparation for past violence. Is this a fundamental right or a right of lower status? The question does not really arise, since this approach considers only one category of rights, whose status is sufficiently strong to be attached to the concept of fundamental rights.

However, one can consider that the aid granted to the poor within the framework of a specific policy of a community is, if sufficiently formalized, the equivalent of fulfilling ordinary rights. These rights remain non-fundamental since they are contingent and depend on the particular political agreement of a given population. However, insofar as certain principles of equity appear to be robust and universal enough to justify the elimination of certain inequalities of birth, some categories of poor people have indeed a fundamental right to public assistance. The same applies to the rectification of past injustices. One can thus conclude that, even in the perspective that is a priori the most hostile to the idea of a right of poor people to receive part of the resources of others, there are the seeds of such a right.

5.3. THE POSITIVE ILLUSION

The libertarian approach can accept the (fundamental) right of certain poor people to receive assistance, but it cannot go as far as accepting the existence of a universal right to subsistence (unless it ends up being part of the ethical principles considered to be minimal by humanity—which only amounts to repeating the question).

Some critics of libertarianism have tried to reject the restrictive concept of rights proposed by the libertarians, arguing that the priority of negative over positive

---

[4] One may think that such a consensus is hard to achieve, but Nozick has in mind the possibility to migrate to another community if one is dissatisfied somewhere. 'Utopia is a framework for utopias, a place where people are at liberty to join together voluntarily to pursue and attempt to realize their own vision of the good life in the ideal community but where no one can *impose* his own utopian vision on others' (1974: 312).

rights was untenable.[5] This strategy is ambitious, because in the event of success it would show that the right of property is neither more fundamental nor does it have a higher priority than the right to subsistence, and that its unjustified precedence is due only to the circumstances of historical evolution.

Their argument rests on the idea that the only freedom that matters is real freedom, and not formal freedom as in the libertarian ideal. This idea is very intuitive and close to common sense. It is indeed rather absurd to claim, as some libertarians do, that a poor person has more freedom than a well-paid employee who is forced to contribute to the system of social security.

They pursue their argument by asserting that human rights can be formulated in terms of access to certain real freedoms, and that the institutional forms guaranteeing this access do not matter much. In particular, the intervention of the state is not a problem in itself, because it only leads to a modification of the distribution of freedoms between individuals (the freedom of those who are taxed decreases while that of those who receive benefits increases) or between the possible activities for each individual (the minimum income increases the freedom to be idle while the income tax by which it is financed decreases the freedom to work).[6] The argumentation finally ends by noting that survival is the minimum degree of real freedom and that, if a right has priority it is certainly this one. Beyond this, one can even seek to defend the idea of a right to the equality of real freedoms.[7]

However, this line of argument is not entirely convincing. It fails to capture what makes the libertarian ideal attractive, namely the possibility for individuals to meet and sign contracts or any other form of agreement, without having to submit to the control of a third party, and without having to give part of their joint profit to a third party. This possibility is indeed a real freedom, not only a formal one, which is curtailed by the intervention of the state. It is precisely because it infringes the ordinary freedom of owners to use their property as they wish that the state requires a special justification, as the arm implementing the

---

[5] In particular Cohen (1995), van Parijs (1995), and Shue (1996a).

[6] 'Incursions against private property which reduce owners' freedom by transferring rights over resources to non-owners thereby increase the latter's freedom. In advance of further argument, the net effect on freedom of the resource transfer is indeterminate. ... The standard use of "intervention" esteems the private property component in the liberal or social democratic settlement too highly, by associating that component too closely with freedom' (Cohen 1995: 57).

[7] Dworkin (1977) claims that there is a right to equality but no real right of property. According to him, the right to equality is a fundamental right of every citizen to be treated with equal respect and concern (independently of the external preferences, favorable or hostile, of his fellow citizens toward him). It is from this fundamental right that certain specific rights, such as freedom of speech, can be derived. 'There is no such thing as any general right to liberty. The argument for any given specific liberty may therefore be entirely independent of the argument for any other, and there is no antecedent inconsistency or even implausibility in contending for one while disputing the other. ... What can be said, on the general theory of rights I offer, for any particular right of property? ... I cannot think of any argument that a political decision to limit such a right, in the way in which minimum wage laws limited it, is antecedently likely to give effect to external preferences, and in that way offend the right of those whose liberty is curtailed to equal concern and respect. If, as I think, no such argument can be made out, then the alleged right does not exist' (1977: 277–8).

collective projects of the population. There is an irreducible tension between the purely individual projects and the collective projects, whose realization requires constraints of coordination and participation. Besides, this tension does not only put individuals and the state into opposition; it also resides within individuals who, for instance, can at the same time wish to reduce poverty and seek to pay fewer taxes.

If in the name of real freedom, one can defend a fundamental right to subsistence, then one can also, in the same vein, defend a fundamental right to possess, to make contracts, and to give—in short, a fundamental right of property. The tension mentioned above resurfaces in the form of a tension between various rights, and it is not obvious how one can defend an extended right to escape poverty, not to say a right to equality, against the right of property.

5.4. THE PRIORITY ILLUSION

This tension between rights of property and 'social' rights is taken into consideration in Rawls's theory of justice (1999*a*), where it is in part dealt with by the establishment of a hierarchy not far removed from the concrete formula observed in Western societies, where the right of property lies at the heart of the institutions while poverty comes under the secondary chapter of social and economic policy.

Rawls proposes to organize society by giving an absolute priority to the fundamental rights of the person and the citizen and granting to the socioeconomic inequality issues a secondary place within the framework of the two principles of equal opportunity and difference. It is this last principle, popularized under the name of 'maximin', which concerns poverty and tackles the issue head-on, since it gives priority to the poor in the evaluation of the institutions that influence the distribution of wealth. But this priority of the poor does not arise from a fundamental right. It results from the search for equality, governed by the primordial guarantee of fundamental rights and equal opportunity in access to positions of competence and responsibility.

However, according to Rawls, fundamental rights do not include an extensive right of property, but only an elementary right to personal property, which does not include the right to invest in production or to bequeath one's possessions.[8] Rawls assigns the precise determination of the extent of the right of property to a subordinate category of political choices. Still, the fact remains that the fundamental rights, or basic liberties, which have the highest priority in the hierarchy of Rawls's principles, do not include any right to subsistence or any similar social right.[9] And yet, in normal economic conditions, it is perfectly feasible to

---

[8] 'Among the basic liberties of the person is the right to hold and to have the exclusive use of personal property... wider conceptions of the right of property... cannot, I think, be accounted for as necessary for the development and exercise of the moral powers' (Rawls 1993*a*: 298).

[9] 'Important among these are political liberty (the right to vote and to hold public office) and freedom of speech and assembly; liberty of conscience and freedom of thought; freedom of the person,

guarantee the right to subsistence to all. Therefore one cannot claim that there is a radical difference in feasibility between 'free' negative rights and 'costly' positive rights. Moreover, the political and legal institutions required by the protection of basic liberties are already very costly by themselves.

In *Political Liberalism*, Rawls writes, 'the first principle covering the equal basic rights and liberties may easily be preceded by a lexically prior principle requiring that citizens' basic needs be met, at least insofar as their being met is necessary for citizens to understand and to be able fruitfully to exercise those rights and liberties. Certainly any such principle must be assumed in applying the first principle. But I do not pursue these and other matters here' (1993*a*: 7). The right to subsistence that such a remark considers is very limited since it is linked only to the individual's ability to enjoy the basic rights and liberties, and is not designed to guarantee any broader accomplishment of human abilities. Even in this restrictive approach, it is surprising that Rawls does not explore in more detail the interaction between basic liberties and the means needed to enjoy them.

Rawls probably does not consider it necessary to put down a full-blown right to subsistence in the list of basic liberties because the priority of the poor according to the difference principle is supposed to guarantee them the most advantageous possible conditions. In a just society the social minimum would be the highest possible (taking into account the problems of incentives). One can see the limits of the relevance of a theory that outlines an ideal society but hardly guides us on the political priorities in the ordinary circumstances of a very imperfect society. A right to subsistence would not be essential in an ideal society, but could well be essential to deal with the emergencies of a strongly unequal society. Rawls's theory does not tell us anything on this subject.

It is even awkward that, in his skillfully thought-out hierarchy, the list of Rawls's principles looks very much like the order of rights and political priorities in Western societies. For, in the absence of application of the difference principle in economic and social policies, the preeminence of a restrictive list of fundamental rights, including the right of property, and the absence of a right to subsistence allows the persistence of inequalities and phenomena of social exclusion, with the consequence that basic liberties are not equally distributed and that fundamental rights, particularly in the political and legal fields, are only very partially guaranteed for the underprivileged social categories.

Besides, this contradiction of the priority of fundamental rights creating the conditions of their systematic violation at the bottom of the social scale had been considered by Rawls, in a somewhat different form, for the just society. Indeed, the application of the difference principle is a priori compatible with arbitrarily large inequalities, which can put in jeopardy the equality of political rights and the equality of opportunity. It is therefore possible that the difference principle

which includes freedom from psychological oppression and physical assault and dismemberment (integrity of the person); the right to hold personal property and freedom from arbitrary arrest and seizure as defined by the concept of the rule of law' (Rawls 1999*a*: 53).

has to be curbed in order not to exceed the limit of inequalities compatible with the first principles of justice.[10]

5.5. RIGHTS VERSUS RIGHTS

Let us summarize this. As a possible source of support for the prevailing, restrictive conception of fundamental rights, the libertarian approach encounters difficulties that, once taken into account, can lead to the legitimization of redistributive social policies, without modifying the list of fundamental rights. The extension of this list is, however, eminently plausible, but cannot be done in the sweeping way contemplated by certain defenders of the idea of equal real freedom for all, and it is necessary to acknowledge the existence of an irreducible tension between the various fundamental rights, in particular between the right of property and the right to subsistence. All in all, the strong thesis relating to a fundamental right to escape poverty is plausible, but it raises the question of coexistence between this right and the negative rights.

For the description of a just society, Rawls comes through this difficulty by giving preeminence to a minimal right of property and by giving priority to the poor in socioeconomic issues. But this skillful solution is not very useful to lay down priority orientations in an imperfect society. In particular the preeminence of a restrictive list of fundamental rights seems to result, in practice, in the undermining of the very realization of these rights, owing to the excessive inequalities that are thus tolerated. A symmetrical difficulty can be noted when the right to subsistence is put in the forefront of institutions to the detriment of the right of property: the economic difficulties of the countries that relied on central planning ended up maintaining a good part of their populations in a state of poverty.[11] In other words, when social institutions are exclusively focused on the satisfaction of negative rights, they undermine the realization of such rights for all, and similarly an exclusive focus on positive social rights may end up being counterproductive.

The tension between negative rights and social rights is thus coupled with a certain complementarity. An excessive neglect of social rights, in the guiding principles of social institutions, endangers the rights to integrity and the political rights of disadvantaged populations, and even those of the favored populations when social unrest spreads insecurity at all levels of society. Reciprocally, the neglect of negative rights creates conditions of such economic inefficiency that social rights are themselves weakened.

---

[10] 'Naturally, where this limit lies is a matter of political judgment guided by theory, good sense, and plain hunch, at least within a wide range. On this sort of question the theory of justice has nothing specific to say' (Rawls 1999a: 246).

[11] While making this observation, we do not forget that their brutal transition toward a market economy has led to an increase in poverty and inequalities without precedent in modern societies.

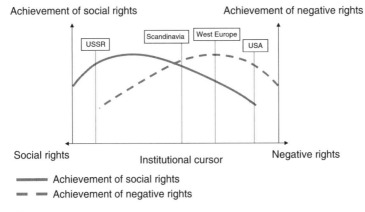

Figure 5.1.

One can thus formulate the empirical conjecture that, according to where the political cursor of the institutions is placed, between negative rights and social rights, the effective achievement of these rights for the whole of the population follows the configuration represented in Figure 5.1. The full curve describes the degree of achievement of social rights, while the curve in dotted lines describes that of negative rights. Although the negative rights are better protected in a society that gives them a certain preeminence, with the same applying to social rights, the curves are so built that an excessive neglect of one type of rights, in the design of institutions, is harmful for the achievement of all rights. One can even go so far as to include the various typical institutional configurations of modern societies in this figure.

These remarks unquestionably strengthen the weak thesis. When social rights are neglected to the point of allowing the formation of significant poverty within the population, the negative rights themselves are systematically violated, especially among the poor. The poor are the main victims of a criminality fueled by economic insecurity, and they can also not have their legal rights defended or exercise their civic rights. Subjected to criminal violence, to the arbitrary power of the police and excluded from the political arena, the poor live in a no-law zone.

5.6. POVERTY AND OPPRESSION

The weak thesis can be further reinforced by showing that poverty exerts on its victims an economic violence that is similar, in its effects, to physical violence. This phenomenon is largely ignored nowadays because on the current view of the market-based exchange it is in fact a typical example of the free union of wills.

The description of the market-based exchange that has been popularized by economic teaching since Pareto insists on the fact that the agreement between the two contractors is voluntary, which guarantees that, in normal circumstances where the contractors are fully and correctly informed, and rational, the exchange is beneficial for both. The universally beneficial nature of the market-based exchange, in the absence of external effects on third parties, is a remarkable property. This property gives us an intuitive understanding of why the market economy, in ideal conditions of information, rationality, competition, and absence of externalities, leads to an efficient distribution of resources. Any pocket of inefficiency will be systematically located by potential contractors who will spontaneously eliminate it, thus improving their own lot. This property also contributes to justifying freedom of trade in view of the possible harmful effects of public intervention, which always has a tendency, by blocking certain potential exchanges, to artificially maintain inefficient situations.

From this view, favorable to the concept of the market-based exchange, rises the now widespread idea that the best way of helping the poor is to give them better access to markets. Those who are at the bottom of the social scale will find their salvation in access to the labor market. For the 'developing' countries, international trade liberalization and the movements of capital will be seen as the best path to development.

A somewhat more comprehensive outlook on the problem of poverty, prevailing among economic theorists, consists in describing it as an insufficiency of initial endowments. The poor are those who have a limited budget set, and who consequently experience reduced freedom.[12] The difference between the poor and the rich is thus perceived as being quantitative: the poor have fewer possibilities; they can afford fewer consumer goods, etc. From this point of view it is not enough to give the poor access to the market, it is necessary to try to improve their initial endowments, or even to transfer some income to them. Assistance in initial endowments is preferable to income assistance because it does not create the same distortions of market prices, and thus generates less inefficiency. It is better to increase the human capital of the poor by developing the education system, for example, than to allot them a negative tax or a universal allowance which will tend to warp their decisions toward greater leisure and less participation in the labor market.[13]

---

[12] 'Initial endowments' are the initial possessions that the economic agent can trade on the market. This includes, e.g., the available time that a worker can trade for wages. 'The budget set' is the set of all the combinations of consumption and leisure which the individual can obtain by respecting his budgetary constraint.

[13] A universal grant or a negative income tax is typically accompanied by a marginal rate of disposable income lower than one. That is, for every dollar earned, one retains only a fraction of it and pays the rest in tax or in reduction of benefit. This does not necessarily reduce the amount of work performed by an individual, in comparison with a laissez-faire allocation. But this distortion is such that there would exist a better allocation for all individuals, in which they would work more and pay no less in taxes. Such improvement, however, is typically unattainable due to incentive constraints. It is in this sense that one can say that redistribution generates labor disincentives.

This more comprehensive view is much more satisfactory, especially in light of the conclusions of redistributive policy to which it leads. But it does not comprehend all the aspects of poverty and all its consequences, and that can also impact on issues of social policy.

Indeed, poverty is not experienced only in terms of 'less': less consumption, less leisure, reduced opportunities, etc. It is experienced in qualitatively different terms: fear of the future, shame, absence of control over one's destiny, submission to the arbitrary power of the boss or the civil servant, etc. I confine myself here to focus on a particular aspect of poverty, one that can be analyzed with the tools of economic theory. When an individual has a limited budget set, he is led to choose an option, say x, in this set that is obviously different from the one he would choose, call it y, if his budget were more favorable. The most obvious difference between these two options is that x is not as good as y in the eyes of that individual. But there can be other interesting differences. Option x can have qualitative characteristics which are missing in option y. For example, x can imply factors—working in painful conditions, a humiliating inferior position, and low wages—that do not apply to y and which would not apply to any option chosen by the individual if his budget was above a given poverty line. Or, x can also imply poor quality consumer goods, unhealthy food, bad clothing, and cheap objects manufactured under questionable conditions—things the individual would refuse to buy all these goods if his budget were above a given threshold.

The phenomenon is thus the following: poverty can lead its victims to accept types of work or consumption they would refuse in other circumstances. It remains to examine the similarity and the differences between this form of economic constraint and brutal physical constraint. The strongest difference, apparently, is that the economic constraint of poverty nevertheless leaves the poor person in a situation in which he 'voluntarily accepts' what is offered to him on the market. This difference is sometimes real, but it is often illusory. Several possible cases must be distinguished.[14] Let us consider, for instance, the problem of the acceptance of bad working conditions.

Case 1: The individual only has the choice between accepting this degrading work or sinking into misery, because all available jobs are of the same type.

Case 2: The individual could take a less degrading job but he would be paid less. The choice is thus between degrading work with a low standard of living and less degrading work, with a still lower standard of living.

In Case 1, the constraint imposed on the individual is similar to that which he would undergo if a master threatened him with the dungeon in case he refused to work. His 'acceptance' is a choice only in appearance, because the

---

[14] For a more detailed analysis, see Fleurbaey (2001).

alternative is catastrophic. The economic constraint then exerts a pressure very similar to physical violence. In Case 2, two factors combine to bring the individual to accept the degrading work. The first factor is poverty; the second is the preferences of this individual, who could choose less degrading work but who is more concerned about his income than about his working conditions. Another individual with different preferences could make another choice. This was not conceivable in Case 1.

One should further distinguish subcases of Case 2, according to the origin of the preferences of this individual. If his chief concern for income derives from his desire to ensure a minimum of education to his children, an education that represents the only hope they have to escape poverty in the future, one can consider that to be closer to a 'hard' constraint than if his preferences came simply from the wish, for example, to buy himself a more powerful motorbike.

In situations similar to Case 2, it is not easy to distinguish between the poverty factor and the preference factor. Here is a possible method for this purpose. It consists in measuring the threshold of affluence above which the individual would definitely refuse what he accepts below this level. If this threshold is very high, one can consider that the preferences of the individual play a significant role, and that the poverty factor is secondary. Indeed, in this scenario, the individual is willing to maintain his choice even when his standard of living is satisfactory. If, on the other hand, the threshold is very low, that means that the individual is eager to escape the degrading choice, and thus that the poverty factor is of primary importance. Albeit probably imperfect, this method of measurement of the degree of economic constraint provides a way to disentangle the poverty factor from the preference factor.

There are thus different possible degrees of economic constraint exerted by poverty, which is thus not always as brutal as direct physical oppression is. But direct oppression can also be more or less soft or strong, depending on the severity of punishment. When punishment is not too strong, oppression also gives a choice between submission and punishment, and the preference factor plays a role there too. But one cannot conclude from the fact that this factor can play a role that there is no physical violence. The same applies to the violence of economic constraint.

A society in which the poor are largely constrained to 'accept' degrading living and working conditions thus allows an oppression to be brought to bear on them which is close enough to physical violence for one to regard it as a violation of their personal integrity.

Although this is not directly relevant to the analysis of this point, it may be useful to underline that this oppression of the poor is not fortuitous and serves to a great extent the interests of the rich. If the poor were granted additional endowment, the comfort of the rich would be put in danger, even in the absence of any levy on their personal wealth. The profitability of companies benefits directly from the availability of a workforce ready to accept bad working conditions and low wages. Generally, the rich benefit from the presence of the poor alongside them by a pure effect of comparative trade advantage. The poor, because of their poverty, develop different supply–demand behaviors from the rich and thus offer them trade opportunities that would not exist otherwise.

Just a clarification: it is not poverty alone, but inequality in general which generates the phenomenon just described. In standard conditions, any inequality in wealth produces transactions that would be refused by the disadvantaged in the absence of inequality. It is inequality in wealth, and not poverty as such, which generates a comparative advantage between the rich and the poor, and causes induced trading. Any inequality is thus a source of oppression, at least of the Case 2 form.

Of course, as it has just been explained above, the degree of oppression is inversely related to the threshold of wealth at which the individual no longer yields to economic constraint. Therefore, a well-off individual who accepts a trade with another who is even better off is constrained in case he would refuse this trade in the absence of inequality, but much less constrained than an absolutely poor person who would refuse the trade at a much lower threshold of wealth. In that sense, poverty, as opposed to mere inequality, has a special oppressive feature, which is uniquely connected to *basic* human rights.

5.7. OFFER OR THREAT

Another apparent difference between the economic constraint of poverty and physical oppression is that the latter generally operates on a threat mode, whereas the first uses offer. A threat consists in proposing the choice between two options: x (to yield) and y (to refuse) such that y, at least, is worse than a reference situation, generally that which would obtain in the absence of threat. An offer, on the other hand, consists in proposing an option that, good or bad, leaves open the possibility of choosing to remain in the reference situation.[15]

Let us continue with the example of degrading work and consider the encounter between a potential employer and a poor person. If one takes as reference situation the one that would prevail if the poor person did not meet the employer, then it is indeed an offer because the poor person can always refuse the job even if, in the absence of a viable alternative, the reference situation meant sinking in misery. This is indeed different from the violent intervention of a lord who demands one to work or face punishment.

---

[15] The distinction between offer and threat has been the subject of an abundant literature. The definitions retained here differ slightly from the most current definitions, influenced by Nozick (1969), and according to which an offer is favorable, while a threat contains only options that are worse than the reference situation. It is more natural to extend the concept of offer to bad offers: what characterizes an offer is not the fact that it is good, but the fact that it can be refused. In the same way, a threat can, fortunately for the victim, include a favorable option (Steiner [1994] calls that 'a throffer'): what characterizes it is the impossibility to remain in the reference situation and the fact that one of the options is a punishment. How should we call the situation where a choice between two good options is offered, being forbidden to refuse both? It is neither an offer, nor a threat.

However, the role given to the particular reference situation by this difference is a little too important. Admittedly, it is very different in practice to have a good encounter (with someone who makes an offer) than a bad encounter (with someone who makes a threat). But on the scale of society, which can be regarded as responsible for the fate of its members, and therefore for the reference situation itself, the summary analysis of the offer–threat difference looks rather naive. Let us compare the three following scenarios.

Scenario 1. A lord, for some reason, requires his serfs to do additional work on his estates, under the threat of corporal punishment.

Scenario 2. A lord offers his serfs work on his estates for a salary.

Scenario 2a. For some reason, a lord levies a tax that impoverishes his serfs, under the threat of punishment. Then, he offers them work on his estates for a salary.

According to the summary analysis, Scenario 1 contains a threat while Scenario 2 contains an offer. But Scenario 2 could, if it were described more completely, correspond in fact to Scenario 2a. However, for the serfs, the combination of a tax and paid work in this scenario can be equivalent to the forced work of Scenario 1. In Scenario 2a, the lord makes an offer after having put the serfs in a position where they are forced to accept this offer. He is therefore not more generous than the lord of Scenario 1. Let us now consider another variant of Scenario 2:

Scenario 2b. A summer drought impoverishes the serfs. Then, the lord offers them work on his estates for a salary.

This time, the lord is not directly responsible for the poverty of his serfs. Nevertheless, as he is responsible for their fate in general, one can think that by making this offer to them he takes advantage of the situation, when he could give some of the contents of his granaries to them freely.

If one considers that social institutions are largely responsible for the fate of the population, then one must note that a society which imposes, under threat, degrading tasks and consumer goods to the lower classes is not very different, on a moral level, from a society which leaves the lower classes in poverty so that the degrading offers which are made to them seem acceptable to them. In the first case, the threatened individuals accept for fear of punishment. In the second, the individuals have already been punished by poverty, and are ready to accept anything. Admittedly, employers who offer bad jobs are not as violent as slave owners, just as the lord of Scenario 2b is not as violent as those of Scenarios 1 and 2a. But a society that subjects part of its population to this situation of structural dependence and submission is an oppressive society.

This type of oppression is more impersonal than physical violence, which always has a well-identified vehicle. Oppression by poverty, except in the obvious cases of theft, displacement of population, and manipulation of prices, is a form of oppression that makes it difficult to identify the oppressor. The employers who offer bad jobs, the manufacturers who offer bad consumer goods, are simply profiteers who exploit the vulnerability of their victims, but they are only part of the causal chain that keeps the poor in hardship. This is the main difficulty of positive rights. Violations of these rights are generally impersonal, anonymous, and structural. As for negative rights, they are either respected by all or violated by some; in this case there are identifiable culprits. Positive rights, on the contrary, may sometimes be respected thanks to the intervention of some individuals, but when they are violated, the community as a whole is guilty.

5.8. COERCIVE OFFERS

The controversial idea that modern society can be oppressive in spite of the apparent freedom of exchange, a thesis whose origins go back to the socialist tradition, has been the incentive of considerable recent literature devoted to offers and threats. Sections 5.6 and 5.7 summarized the analysis offered here, but it is useful to situate this analysis in the context of the main arguments, which can be found in the literature.

The controversy has focused in particular on the issue of knowing whether the workers are free to sell their working time to capitalist companies. Thus Macpherson (1973) criticizes Friedman (1962) for confusing the freedom of a proletarian to refuse a particular job with the freedom to refuse any job in a capitalist company.[16] For Macpherson, the absence of a real alternative to this kind of employment shows that the workers are not free.

For Nozick (1974) the existence of an alternative, for example a public sector capable of employing the recalcitrant workers, is secondary. According to the libertarian ideal, the determining factor is that the economic actors must respect the rights of all, in all their interactions.[17] Even though limited by poverty, the individual is perfectly free if past transactions have respected the rights of property. This leads to a view of constraint and freedom that rests on a moral reference and strays noticeably from common sense, which is rather committed to real freedom. In his former analysis of coercion, Nozick (1969) already justified the reference to a moral standard. According to him, the reference situation serving as a point of comparison to distinguish between a (non-coercive) offer and a (coercive) threat cannot simply be the status quo, or what would normally occur in the absence of intervention from the person who delivers the offer or the threat. For this status quo can itself contain a constraint. An example is that of a master

---

[16] Friedman's argument: 'co-operation is strictly individual and voluntary provided ... that individuals are effectively free to enter or not to enter into any particular exchange, so that every transaction is strictly voluntary' (1962: 14). Macpherson's critique: 'The proviso that is required to make every transaction strictly voluntary is *not* freedom not to enter into any *particular* exchange, but freedom not to enter into any exchange *at all*' (1973: 146).

[17] 'A person's choice among differing degrees of unpalatable alternatives is not rendered non-voluntary by the fact that others voluntarily chose and acted within their rights in a way that did not provide him with a more palatable alternative' (Nozick 1974: 263–4).

who beats his slave each day. One day, he offers not to beat him on that precise day provided that the slave carries out a painful task. By comparison with the status quo, it is an offer. But for the moral intuition the alternative between 'being beaten or accomplishing a painful task' has rather the character of a threat. This is possible, according to Nozick, if instead of taking the status quo as reference situation, one takes the morally normal situation, in which the slave is never beaten. As noted by Nozick, the choice of the reference situation can depend on the preferences of the victim. He offers another example to show this.[18] However, it is enough to modify this one. Let us imagine that the slave is a masochist who likes to be beaten. In this case the master's proposal looks rather like a (bad) offer.[19]

Applied to the analysis of capitalism, this view allows one to deny that the poor are constrained. Indeed, if one takes as reference situation a legitimate distribution of the rights of property, the interactions between traders are always offers, and the market-based exchange is thus free of constraint. This legitimizes the new distribution of property rights resulting from the exchange, as well as the exchanges to come. Constraint does not appear at any stage, even if economic poverty can result from the succession of these free transactions. The poor cannot thus be considered constrained when the property rights distribution used as reference for the evaluation of the offers or threats is legitimate.

Frankfurt (1973) feels that Nozick's analysis could logically lead to the conclusion that a butcher who raises the price of meat exerts a threat on his customers. Indeed, taking as reference situation the one preferred by his victims, that is keeping the initial prices, the butcher gives them, in comparison, the choice between two worse options: either buy the meat at a more expensive price or go without it (or buy it further away).[20] To avoid this conclusion, it is necessary, according to Frankfurt, to add two conditions to the definition of a threat: the victim needs what he obtains in the reference situation, and the alternative offered to him is either unjust or inappropriate. Lyons (1975) argues that these conditions are neither necessary nor sufficient, and proposes another definition of a 'coercive trade offer', which includes two modified conditions according to which, on the

---

[18] The example is that of a drug addict whose usual dealer asks, in an exceptional case, to carry out an unpleasant task in addition to the usual payment. The moral reference would be the non-supply of drug; the status quo would be the supply of drug at the usual price. According to the first reference, it is an offer, but it is a threat compared to the status quo. The victim prefers the status quo, and this, according to Nozick, is what leads us to see a threat in this example. 'It may be that when the normal and morally expected courses of events diverge, the one of these which is to be used in deciding whether a conditional announcement of an action constitutes a threat or an offer is the course of events that the recipient of the action prefers' (1969: 451).

[19] In addition, Nozick expresses doubts in cases where the moral reference includes damage inflicted by P to Q (e.g., P, a police officer, is on the point of arresting Q, a criminal). If P offers Q to spare him in exchange for a service, is it an offer or a threat? If the reference is the moral standard, it is an offer. But in reference to the situation preferred by Q (the absence of damage), it is a threat.

[20] As Frankfurt notes, the drug dealer who requires an exceptional service (see n. 18) is, after all, only increasing his prices. Nozick would undoubtedly reply to Frankfurt that keeping the price of meat constant is obviously not the relevant reference in the example of the butcher.

one hand the victim is reluctant to enter into or participate in the transaction (since his potential benefit is small), and on the other hand the victim is entitled to a better price.[21]

These two authors have in common that they follow Nozick in his use of a moral reference, and simply seek to modify its terms, moving toward an idea of just price completely alien to the libertarian approach. Many authors, on the other hand, have criticized the inclusion of morals in the definitions of Nozick, showing even that his definition of freedom and rights is a circular one, since rights are defined in terms of protection of freedom, while freedom is defined by reference to the normal situation in which rights are respected.[22] Zimmerman (1981) endeavors to build a nonmoral definition of the coercive offer, and he proposes as criteria the fact that the victim would prefer an alternative that is different from the status quo and from the offered option and that the oppressor actively prevents the realization of this preferred alternative. Applied to the problem of capitalism, this definition leads him to conclude that the job offers of capitalist companies are coercive when they satisfy two conditions: (*a*) there is another type of employment economically viable that the workers would prefer; and (*b*) the capitalists prevent the realization of this alternative.

How does the preceding analysis relate to these debates? This literature seems to ignore two theoretical possibilities, which were exploited in section 5.7. The first point is that several situations of reference can simultaneously be relevant to the evaluation of an offer or threat. According to Nozick (1969), the majority of authors have tried to give 'the' right definition of an offer and threat, by finding the right reference situation. However, Nozick himself had suggested that, depending on cases, the relevant reference situation could be the usual course of events or, alternatively, the moral standard. But none of these authors seems to have envisaged that, in complex cases where our intuition is not clear, the presence of several jointly relevant reference situations can alone provide a proper moral evaluation.[23] In the example of the beaten slave, the proposal of the master is an offer compared to the usual situation with this master (first reference situation), but it is a threat compared to the usual situation with an ordinary master (second reference situation), because in general masters do not beat their slaves every day for no reason. It is also a threat compared to the morally normal behavior of a master (third reference situation). These three situations of reference are relevant to understand an aspect of the proposal of this master.[24] In the same way, poor

---

[21] Here is the complete definition: '1. P knows that Q is rationally reluctant to give *y* to P for *x*; and 2. Either Q knows that he has a right to *x* from P on easier terms, or Q knows that P would have given *x* to Q, on easier terms, if the chance had not arisen to trade *x* for *y*' (Lyons 1975: 436).

[22] See especially Cohen (1995) and Olsaretti (1998).

[23] Zimmerman (1981) is the closest to this idea, but he seems to consider that the situation of alternative reference (that to which the victim will ultimately refer) is the only truly relevant one and above all, is unique.

[24] The second reference situation rests on a purely empirical, statistical observation. Nozick is thus wrong to believe that this example forces us to adopt a moral reference. But he is right to introduce the moral reference, because it is also relevant.

people who are offered a degrading job may consider it as an offer compared to the usual course of events, in which the unemployed sink into misery. But they may also consider it as a threat, compared to the moral standard of a just society in which everyone must have the opportunity to achieve the means to lead a decent life. These two situations of reference are relevant, and make it possible to explain why one can say at the same time that capitalist employers are less violent than feudal lords and slave owners, and that the capitalist society oppresses the poor in a way which is morally similar to what occurred in the feudal or ancient societies, since all these societies only give them the choice between humiliation and misery (or death).

The second point ignored by this literature is that a society can be oppressive toward the poor even when they do not encounter any directly oppressive inter-personal relation.[25] Zimmerman (1981) insists for example on the fact that there is oppression only if the capitalists actively intervene to keep the poor in their situation. He gives the following example. A kidnaps Q, takes him to his island where all jobs are degrading, and abandons him without resources on the beach. The following day A offers a job to Q. At the same time B, who has another factory on the same island, comes and also offers the same kind of job to Q. According to Zimmerman, only A's offer is coercive while B's is a pure offer, because A acted to put Q in this situation of dependence, whereas B is not responsible for it. But Zimmerman forgets that from Q's point of view, what happens to him is the same, regardless of whether the offer of employment comes from A or from B. Compared to the normal situation of a just society, Q is oppressed even if only B offers him a job.

Let us modify the example slightly. A terrible hurricane blows Q off his island and lands him on A's island. The following day, A offers him a degrading job. Q does not have the means to pay for his return trip, which, however, does not cost very much, and accepts the offer. According to Zimmerman's definition, there is no constraint in this example—at most exploitation by A of Q's misfortune. Yet, compared to the normal situation of a just society in which a relief fund would pay for Q's return, the job offer has indeed absolutely the nature of a threat, and can thus be considered coercive. Indeed, compared to the reference situation in which Q would be repatriated by the relief fund, the two suggested options, degrading work or misery, are clearly worse. But it is not a case of coercion exerted by A, nor of course by the hurricane, because what is at play is the failure of society, the absence of a relief fund. Coercion is thus exerted by society as a whole, A being only a cog in a structural mechanism of oppression of the victims of natural disasters. As we said in the preceding section, it is the community as a whole that is guilty, and this is what makes the oppression of the poor so easy to hide in a capitalist economy.

---

[25] On the articulation between choosing in particular institutional conditions and choosing these particular conditions, see Peter (2004).

5.9. DUTY OF ASSISTANCE AND JUST PRICE

The fact that, in a market economy, the oppression of the poor is anonymous and impersonal must not make us forget that the exploitation of their weakness results from trade relations with well-defined individuals. The stress put by Frankfurt (1973) and Lyons (1975) on the terms of trade and their distortion in favor of the already favored party, seems more relevant to describe this exploitation than to describe coercion as such. But this suggests that there may be a way to see oppression in this exploitation too.

We have seen above that the inequality of wealth was in itself enough to introduce such a distortion in trade relation that the less wealthy individual was led to accept things he would refuse were his wealth greater. He thus agrees to trade higher quantities at the current price: he would refuse to sell or buy as much at this price if his wealth was equal to that of the other.[26] One can also consider the terms of trade rather than the quantity: With equal wealth, he would agree to sell or buy as much only at a more advantageous price. It is a fact that inequality of wealth systematically tends to distort the terms of trade to the disadvantage of the weaker party.

The neoclassical, modern analysis of supply–demand equilibrium on the market has discredited the concept of just price which, in favor in the Middle Ages, has maintained itself under the denominations of 'natural price' or of 'value' among classical economists. From the contemporary point of view, the just price is the equilibrium price, whatever it may be. However, this perspective ignores the distortions of the terms of trade induced by inequalities, which may reflect a particular form of injustice. Let us propose a new definition of the 'just price': the just price is that which would be the supply–demand equilibrium price if the traders had equal wealth. Any other price, in cases of unequal wealth, is unjust if it increases the advantage of the wealthier.[27]

As an illustration, there is no need of a sophisticated analysis of the labor market to see that, if qualifications were equally distributed among the population, degrading jobs would only be filled at much higher wages than the current ones, while, under the pressure of competition, pleasant or prestigious jobs would be paid much less. The hierarchy of wages results rather directly from the unjust inequality of the initial endowments of qualifications.[28]

---

[26] Let us stress this once again: the poor buy certain lower category goods in larger quantities than the rich.

[27] This leaves the possibility for a price to be different from the just price without being unjust, when it contributes to reducing the disadvantage of the worst off. Sometimes this evaluation is ambiguous. When a price is different from, e.g., higher than, the just price, it is to the advantage of the wealthier only when they are sellers, and to their disadvantage when they are buyers. But the purpose of this analysis is not to analyze the injustice of prices, it is only to provide a sensible concept of just price.

[28] To the supply–demand pressure is added the weight of social conventions, which may explain for example the persistent inferiority of women's wages, as well as the extravagant increases in the highest salaries.

In order to eliminate injustice in a trade relation, however, it is not enough to adopt the just price, because even at this price, wealth inequality would still lead the weak party to accept what it would otherwise refuse. The only way of eliminating injustice from a trade relation is to level out the traders' wealth beforehand.[29]

In principle, this requirement of justice concerns society as a whole, and the arrangement of basic institutions. But one could nevertheless envisage turning this impersonal demand into a personal duty for all the individuals who meet on the market. Could not one say that the individuals who meet on the market should avoid trading when their wealth is unequal? Let us imagine an 'egalitarian ideal', which would, in a way similar to the libertarian ideal, dictate a clear conduct to the individuals in order to guarantee that social conditions remain just regardless of encounters and individual preferences. In the libertarian ideal, it is enough for the individuals who meet to check that the signing of their contracts is voluntary. In the egalitarian ideal, the individuals who plan to sign a contract must as a preliminary equalize their wealth. After this equalization, any voluntary contract is regarded as legitimate.[30]

In the egalitarian ideal, two poor persons who meet will equalize their poverty before making a transaction. This equalization will have a low impact on the overall inequality. But through gradual diffusion, multiple meetings between the most various individuals will lead to a general leveling of wealth, and in the long term the egalitarian ideal will maintain a very high degree of equality.

Compared to this egalitarian ideal, the exploiter who, in ordinary capitalism, takes advantage of the poverty of his trading partner fails his preliminary duty of equalization and does not respect the rights of the weak party to an equalizing transfer. The somewhat peculiar rights at play in the egalitarian ideal are positive rights, but they impose personal duties, contrary to what happens usually. Is this egalitarian ideal anything more than a theoretical curiosity? It is certainly impractical. One can imagine that, if implemented, it would make all potential contractors stay away from the less wealthy. It might also lead negotiators to incorporate the transfer in the price bargain, so that the net effect of the transfer would be nullified. But nonetheless, it might very well reveal that the dependence of the rich on the poor's labor is so strong that the community of the wealthy would be better off trading with them than not. One may also design tax incentives in order to encourage transfer-and-trade among unequal partners.

At any rate, the interest of this idea is mainly to show that, to a certain extent, the right of the poor to be helped can imply personal duties, and that their

---

[29] When the traders have special personal characteristics (handicaps, talents...), a certain compensatory inequality of wealth can be justified. This very important question is ignored here, but see Fleurbaey and Maniquet (2005).

[30] What about the encounter between an individual and a collective capital company? One can stipulate that in the egalitarian ideal, people who invest in a common business must as a preliminary make their wealth equal. This way, the owners of a company are equal. When the company plans to recruit a person, the wealth of that person must first be made equal with that of all the owners of the company (which can be done very easily by a transfer between this person and the company).

oppression therefore acquires a personal dimension: the exploiter who fails his preliminary duty of equalization is indeed an oppressor, because, compared to the reference situation in which he would do his duty, what he proposes has the nature of a threat.

Nozick was right to say that the evaluation of a proposal as offer or threat cannot rest simply on the ordinary course of things, which can include constraint. A poor person who is refused assistance and who only receives a job 'offer' is actually confronted with a threat or coercive offer, if one takes as reference the situation in which he receives assistance.

The whole question is then to know whether this reference situation has a certain moral relevance. When a poor and a rich person meet, does the poor person have a right to have part of the rich person's wealth transferred to him before being offered a job by him? If so, then the rich person who makes the offer without a preliminary transfer is not only an exploiter, but indeed an oppressor. He can be described as an oppressor even when the reference situation does not imply a complete equalization of wealth. It is enough that the moral reference implies preliminary assistance, even modest, for the fact of refusing this assistance and merely making a job offer to be analyzed as a threat.

It may be worth stressing that, even if a practical implementation of such a personal duty of equalization is out of question because of the incentive issues outlined above, this does not nullify the moral relevance of such a duty. A duty does not have to be easily implementable in order to have moral value. It is enough that complying with the duty be physically feasible, and it is certainly feasible for any pair of agents to equalize their wealth when they meet and trade. Therefore one can morally condemn the rich who trade with the poor on favorable terms to themselves, while acknowledging that the best policy is not to hope for duty compliance, but to enact tax transfers or similar kinds of public action.

5.10. CONCLUSION

The above argumentation has shown that the weak thesis is verified in a much stronger way than one could have thought at first. Two observations have been developed. First, poverty reduces the possibilities of choice to the point of exerting a real pressure on individuals 'to accept' work or consumer goods they would refuse in more normal circumstances. There is thus a factual similarity between physical violence and economic constraint, which comes basically from the fact that both reduce real freedom. Second, if one accepts the idea that the poor should normally receive more significant help from society, or even from their trade partners, then the offers made to them must be considered coercive and not very different, morally, from ordinary threats of physical violence. To the factual similarity of the condition of the poor in all types of societies is thus added a moral similarity between the old, visible violence of the masters and the apparent softness of modern employers. Formerly, the recalcitrant workers were punished.

Today, poverty acts as preventive punishment, giving to the modern threats the appearance of generous offers.

Thus, not only is poverty accompanied in practice by systematic violations of basic liberties but, more deeply, it is an element of a social mechanism that violates the integrity of the people by putting them in a condition of unduly submitting to the will of others and accepting offers that would normally be unacceptable. The poor are oppressed, and any person who, trading with them, takes advantage of their dependence is not only guilty of exploitation, but indeed of participation in this oppression.

It is not only poverty, in a strict sense, that is at the heart of such a phenomenon. Any inequality of wealth produces a similar perversion of social relations, even if the degree of gravity is of course proportional to the inequality, and is more severe when it concerns people who are below the extreme poverty line.

Viewed from this angle, the weak thesis becomes difficult to distinguish from the strong thesis. Since in all poverty (or even inequality) there is oppression, the fundamental right to personal integrity can only be respected by introducing a right to escape poverty. These two rights become almost synonymous. In the same way, physical aggression is considered to be an obvious violation of the right to integrity. However, that also depends on an empirical bond between the integrity of the person and the integrity of the body. If, as in certain video games, the individual had an unlimited reserve of bodies available, physical aggression could no longer be judged as an assault on personal integrity, and it would be comparable to jostling between pedestrians in a crowded street.

It is by discovering an empirical and moral direct bond between poverty and violation of the integrity of the person that one can condemn poverty with the same force with which one usually condemns physical aggression. If this bond is less visible in poverty, it is not less real.

6

Neglected Injustice: Poverty as a Violation of Social Autonomy

*Regina Kreide**

When discussing human rights violations, most people think of genocide, expulsion, ethnic cleansing, mass rapes, and other atrocities that violate rights to freedom, life, and property. Through the International Criminal Court, established in 2002, the international community has recognized these acts as abhorrent and sought their criminal prosecution. But the situation seems to be different when it comes to worldwide poverty. It is clearly a human rights violation if officials command the expulsion and extinction of members of their own population because the state should not intrude into the private sphere of its citizens. It is more difficult to identify a perpetrator who can be accused of having caused or sustained poverty.

Nevertheless, it is unquestionable that despite some positive developments in China, international poverty statistics are still devastating. Almost half of the world's population lives in severe poverty, which means, among other things, that they lack access to adequate shelter, clean drinking water and nutritious food, and that they are at high risk for preventable illnesses, as well as for deadly diseases such as AIDS.[1] Even in the wealthy industrial countries, the number of the 'relatively poor' is increasing: the percentage of those who earn less than 60% of their country's average net income has risen steadily in recent years.[2]

Hardly anyone denies that this is a shameful and unacceptable condition. But is poverty a human rights violation? To simply answer 'Yes' seems difficult: Who can be said to be the violator? Some believe that poverty is just the result of a weak economy, for which no specific person or group can be held responsible. Others think that poverty is at least partly brought on by people's inaction. But even if one could say that poverty violates human rights, what implications does

* I thank the participants of the UNESCO conference in Oxford (March, 2003) and those of Rainer Forst's Political Theory Colloquium at Frankfurt University (July, 2004) for their helpful comments and criticisms. Moreover, I owe special thanks to Thomas Pogge for his critical reading, written commentary and insightful suggestions. I am also grateful to Felmon Davis, Ana Garcia, René Gabriëls, Rekha Nath, Peter Niesen, and Thomas Schramme for their helpful comments.

[1] Out of 6 billion human beings, some 2.8 billion live in severe poverty, surviving on less than $2 per day. Almost 1.2 billion of them survive on less than $1 per day. See World Bank (2001*a*).

[2] World Bank (2000); for Germany see Bundesministerium für Arbeit und Sozialordnung (2001).

that have for our actions? Are we obliged to do more than distribute aid out of compassion?[3]

Engaging in poverty reduction is not a question of selfless generosity, nor is poverty usually an individual's own fault—or so I argue in this chapter. Rather, poverty is an indicator of injustice. It is a sign that essential human interests have probably been violated—even though these violations could have been prevented. Tolerating poverty contravenes universal moral rights and international law under most known conditions.

To make these assumptions more explicit, I will first turn to those human rights that are obviously at the center of the dispute regarding poverty: social and economic human rights.[4] Their justification and content is still highly contested. But for an analysis of what counts as a violation of these rights, it is necessary to make explicit how they can be justified at all. In section 6.1 of this chapter, I offer a proposal for the best way to understand these human rights. Two justifications are considered—the 'functionalist' and the 'extended freedom' justifications. This brings us then to my view, which I call the 'social autonomy' justification.

In section 6.2, I offer a detailed explanation of the 'social autonomy approach', beginning with an attempt to set out the content of social and economic rights. This can hardly be done without exploring the concept of the 'good life'. I argue for a formal conception of the good life that acknowledges that the capacities that are to be developed and the resources required for attainment of that life depend on context-specific circumstances. Nevertheless, a relativist position is vigorously rebutted. After exploring what it is that social and economic human rights entail, I turn to the question of to what extent assistance should be offered. I argue that a modest level of subsistence and a comprehensive level of health care must be guaranteed. Third, an analysis follows of who is eligible for support. Some good reasons are given—or so I hope—for why individuals should receive aid even if they can be held responsible for their fate. I also discuss whether these arguments also hold for collectives.

Despite the advantages of the social autonomy approach, when it comes to the distribution of duties, which is the subject of section 6.3 of the chapter, it turns out that this approach is unable to offer a differentiated conception of obligations. This has disadvantages for an adequate theoretical reflection on

---

[3] See Bittner (2001) who argues that because states are so complex, it is impossible to ascribe any responsibility. That is one reason why aiding the poor is a mere question of political will and not of moral obligation.

[4] I will concentrate in the following on 'social and economic human rights' and neglect 'cultural rights' that should guarantee the participation of citizens in the cultural life. This article concentrates mainly on poverty as an important indicator of international injustice, but it also acknowledges that the violation of *liberal and political rights* often exacerbates existing poverty or even causes poverty. Take, for example, the case of the peasants in Colombia whose land was sought by real estate agents. The peasants' homes were located near an attractive lagoon ripe for commercial development. When the peasants were illegally expelled from their land without compensation, they publicly protested the injustice and their new homelessness, but they were met with threats and intimidation. Some were also killed (www.fian.org 1998).

human rights violations. Therefore I discuss three different ways to justify oblig-ations, namely, through examination of the degree of relationship, expediency, and cause of deprivation. The last two turn out to be promising candidates for the distribution of duties. The 'cause principle' in particular offers new insights into duty allocation by stressing the impact of international rules on increasing and sustaining levels of poverty and deprivation. Nevertheless, the focus on causal interconnectedness between international rules and poverty is not sufficient in itself either: being expedient and having caused harm are complementary notions, and both are required for a comprehensive description of obligations. Finally, it is argued that along with states, TNCs are also duty-bearers. Section 6.4 concludes with a definition of what counts as a violation of social and economic human rights.

6.1. TOWARD SOCIAL AUTONOMY

The International Covenant on Economic, Social and Cultural Rights (ICESR), for example, which came into force in January 1976, established the legally binding rights of every individual to a decent standard of living; to a just organization of labor; to social security during unemployment, illness, disability, or old age; to employment opportunities; and to the protection of the family. Other con-ventions reinforce these rights but have a special focus: The Convention on the Elimination of all forms of Discrimination Against Women (CEDAW) details the obligations states have to abolish unfair treatment of women in public and private life, including education, health, work, and marriage. The Convention on the Rights of Children emphasizes that children are entitled to special care, protected status, and financial support. And, to mention a further important area of legislation, the International Labor Organization (ILO), founded in 1919, formulates international labor standards, and protects the rights of workers and children and the freedom of unions.[5]

One could ask whether these agreements have any positive effect on poverty reduction in the world. The Covenant on Economic, Social and Cultural Rights and some of the ILO conventions are—if ratified—binding treaties that oblige states to protect and fulfill these rights and rules as much as possible.[6] But if we

---

[5] The ILO suggested, e.g., that a so-called social clause should be integrated into the rule system of the WTO, setting core standards such as freedom for unions, abolishing forced and child labor, and banning racial and gender discrimination in the work place. At the 1996 WTO-Ministerial Conference in Singapore, it was mainly the Asian countries that turned down this proposal, arguing it was targeted to protect US and European products against cheaper products from the South. But the United States itself, despite publicly voicing strong support for the idea of social standards (Bill Clinton promoted the idea of a WTO-Social Clause in a speech given at the 50th anniversary of GATT in Geneva 1998), only ratified one core ILO convention (against forced labor) and was one of the main critics of social rights in all United Nations conferences during the 1990s.

[6] See especially Part II of the ICESR: Art. 2 (1): 'Each State Party to the present Covenant undertakes to take steps, individually and through international assistance and co-operation, especially economic

are witnessing severe deprivation day in and day out, as current poverty statistics seem to indicate, why has not more been done about it?

One reason for the slow pace in mitigating global poverty is that despite international agreements during the 1990s on the reduction of severe poverty and some progress at the political level in precisely defining social and economic human rights, current human rights legislation is still wanting in a number of respects. National governments have either failed to comply with their obligation to incorporate legislation on social and economic human rights into their national laws, or have done so only half-heartedly (Alston 1997). This situation results from, among other things, a lack of standards clearly describing under what conditions a 'social human right' is not being fulfilled. Also, mechanisms for implementation are still lacking. Furthermore, the appropriate roles at an international level for NGOs, TNCs, and citizens have yet to be clearly articulated.[7]

The extant political problems mirror some still unresolved theoretical questions. Social and economic human rights remain highly contested because of confusion regarding whom the rights address. Central questions are some of the following. Who qualifies in principle as a rights-holder or as a duty-bearer? And which duty-bearers have obligations to which specific rights-holders? Or conversely, which rights-holders have specific claims against which specific duty-bearers? Are rights' subjects only the 'near and dear', or only fellow citizens, or all those who 'need' help according to a certain standard, including strangers? And whom do these rights bind? Are nation-states, all individuals, and even private collectives like TNCs obligated to protect these rights?

Although social and economic human rights still live in the shadow of civil and political human rights, some theorists have dealt with their justification, content, and scope in detail. One prominent approach is the 'functionalist' justification of social rights through which rights are justified as instruments that guarantee important material means for the exercise of civil and political rights. Another approach, which I call the 'extended freedom' justification, accepts a non-instrumental justification and, moreover, supports a moral claim to a certain standard of living on the basis of an 'extended' notion of freedom. Finally, for those who are not satisfied with the scope of the extended freedom approach,

---

and technical, to the maximum of its available resources, with a view to achieving progressively the full realization of the rights recognized in the present Covenant by all appropriate means, including particularly the adoption of legislative measures', in Steiner and Alston (2000: Annex on Documents, 1395 ff.). Part IV formulates international measures for implementation, Art. 16 (1): 'The States Parties to the present Covenant undertake to submit in conformity with this part of the Covenant reports on the measures which they have adopted and the progress made in achieving the observance of the rights recognized herein', in Steiner and Alston (2000: 1400). See also General Comments No. 3 of the Committee for the ICESR, to be read at UN Doc.E/1991/23, Annex III, and also reprinted in Eide (1995: 442 ff.)

[7] For the historical development of the ICESR and monitoring measures, see Craven (1995); for a detailed definition of state responsibilities in relation to the right to food see Eide et al. (1995) and Künnemann (2000); see also the website of FIAN, FoodFirst Information and Action Network (www.fian.org).

there is a third justification, which emphasizes a concept of 'social autonomy' that relies on a capacity-based distribution of resources.

6.1.1. Functionalist Justification

John Rawls recently integrated a 'duty to assist other people' into what he calls the basic charter of the Law of Peoples (1999*b*: 37). This was an important step toward promoting global justice, and it demonstrated that Rawls had become aware of the importance of global poverty. The manner in which these duties were introduced, however, makes Rawls a prominent proponent of the 'functionalist' justification of international social and economic rights. The duty to offer assistance is justified as a necessary *instrument* for getting peoples to a level of development that meets certain criteria of political and juridical fairness and stability. It offers a target-related justification: assistance among peoples is justified insofar as it is an appropriate means for fulfilling other principles that are seen as their essential interests.[8] Therefore, the objects of the assistance are precisely described: one should assist those societies that do not pursue an aggressive foreign policy and that lack the material and technological means as well as the political culture to become members of the community of well-ordered societies (Rawls 1999*b*: 106). Secondly, the aim, or in Rawls's words, the 'target' of the material and technical assistance, should be to help countries to become 'well-ordered', that is, to install just (or decent) institutions. These might include educational programs (especially for women), population-control policies, reliable and independent judges, and the representation of groups or castes (even if not of individuals) in a system of political consultation that allows different voices to be heard (1999*b*: 71–8).

Rawls distinguishes his approach from those notions of global distributive justice that serves as an alternative to the 'functionalist' justification.[9] Rawls's reason for rejecting a principle of global distributive justice is that such a principle does

---

[8] Another proponent of the 'functionalist' approach is Jürgen Habermas with his legal theory. The process for the justification of human rights and their legal institutionalization is linked to the institutionalization of democratic procedures. Through the interplay between individual human rights and popular sovereignty, legal principles arose to which citizens could rationally consent. These mainly included rights to the greatest possible measure of equal liberty; rights related to membership status; the actionability of rights and individual legal protection; and political participation rights. And finally, social rights 'to the provision of living conditions that are assured socially, technologically and ecologically to the extent required to guarantee equality of opportunity with regard to the exercise of the civil rights listed' are justified as an extension of the four above-mentioned categories of rights (Habermas 1996*a*: 118nn.). Social human rights are seen as offering the necessary material and educational preconditions for exercising civil and political rights. From the perspective of a procedural justification of human rights, social rights only command attention as a precondition for the exercise of the former rights by citizens. As a legal component of the process of law making, they are of no importance. That is why they are 'justified only in relative terms' (Habermas 1996*a*: 123).

[9] He discussed this aspect in relation to criticisms of Beitz (1999c) and Pogge (1994b), who both pressed him to integrate an international 'difference principle', but which he rejected. This article discusses two other approaches ('extended freedom' and 'social autonomy') that draw on a notion of global distributive justice, but are not based on the difference principle.

not include a cutoff point; that is, it does not define when the redistribution has reached a satisfactory level. As a consequence, he fears there may be new injustices because poorer societies could demand revenue-sharing from richer societies, even if they had the same starting conditions but failed to establish a fair and efficient institutional structure (1999*b*: 117). This is not convincing, however. One can ask, first of all, why Rawls argues for a 'difference principle' without a cutoff point at the national level. Within the nation-state, he finds inequality is justified when it favors those who are worst-off and he does not require any threshold that determines the end of redistribution. He may think there exists stronger solidarity among citizens, but he does not justify this in his work.[10]

Another objection, which is also directed against the functionalist manner of justification, is that Rawls's position does not take into account those states that have undertaken measures that they thought would strengthen their economic growth but that have nevertheless failed. Countries like Thailand and Argentina followed the structural adjustment programs imposed by the IMF to the latter, but the schemes did not revitalize their economies and plunged many more people into poverty (Stiglitz 2002). These states cannot be held responsible for what they did and it seems questionable that they should not be candidates for aid.

And finally, there is a further problem. It is true that Rawls's 'duty of assistance' would require that affluent states increase their development aid and set up food and educational programs for poorer states. In the long run, this could lead to an improvement in the living situation of a huge number of people. But due to the narrowly defined assistance targets, only a portion of the needy peoples around the world would benefit. 'Burdened' societies that for cultural or political reasons aim at reducing poverty, but not at becoming well-ordered, would get no national developmental aid or credits from international financial institutions, regardless of the population's level of need. So the duty to assist would improve the living standard of peoples to very different extents, and one can imagine that the support would probably not be sufficient to satisfy the needs of a lot of citizens. This seems rather unfair as it requires the needy to become engaged in a process of institutional reform or even revolution in not-yet well-ordered societies *before* they may get any support. Citizens, however, who have to live under a dictatorial regime very often suffer economically and socially in ways that render them too exhausted or oppressed to change the situation.

6.1.2. Extended Freedom Justification

As it turns out that the Rawlsian 'functionalist' approach has its weaknesses in justifying social and economic rights, it may be helpful to turn to theorists who have offered a different method of justification, one that relies on a concept of freedom. The theorists I am grouping together under what I call the 'extended freedom' approach are unified in rejecting the traditional notion of freedom

---

[10] See also Pogge (2004*b*).

that has long-dominated the debate about human rights justification: that is, the concept of negative freedom understood as the absence of the arbitrary use of power by the state. In this case, citizens are free as long as they are not subject to arbitrary coercion by the state. As far as the classical rights are concerned, (e.g., the rights to life, personal liberty, and property), this concept of freedom provides sufficient justification.[11] But freedom is not sufficiently described through a 'negative' concept nor is this conception helpful in the case of social human rights.[12]

The chief criticism against the negative freedom concept is that it is not only external obstacles that restrict the exercise of liberty: even if I am free to go from A to B because nobody hinders me to do so, I am not actually free to undertake this trip if I do not have a car or money to use public transportation, or have any other possibilities for getting there.[13] I am not free if I lack the material requirements that allow me to proceed with my actions. And there is another issue that negative freedom does not grapple with. It is not sufficient to merely have access to the resources that meet one's needs; it is also important to have viable options—to be able to select from different, desirable resource bundles and opportunities that will assist in the pursuit of one's life plans. If my only choices are a job that does not pay a living wage or starvation, then I am not really free.[14] To have the opportunity to choose among options for fulfilling my life plans turns out to also be an important element of freedom.

Henry Shue, among others, proposes a foundation for this 'extended' notion of freedom. He does so by offering a rationale for why one should not acknowledge social and economic rights only *in relation to* the exercise of other rights—as do Rawls and other proponents of the functionalist position. Rather, he argues that one should attribute to these rights a constitutive value at the level of a legal principle.[15] Shue believes it is possible to distinguish 'basic rights' from other rights. Basic rights are those that every person must possess if he or she is to be able to exercise any rights at all. Without a right to freedom from bodily harm, to

---

[11] This notion of 'negative freedom' has been prominently defended by F. A Hayek (1960), who distinguishes between freedom as 'relation of men to other men, and the only infringement on it is coercion by men' from 'liberty as power'. Whereas in the first and preferred interpretation freedom means being one's own master and following one's own choices, the second identifies freedom with wealth and the possibility to choose among a more or less great number of options. For Isaiah Berlin negative freedom also means the absence of coercion, specified as 'the deliberated interferences of other human beings' (Berlin 1969: 122). He is less clear in rejecting economic circumstances as limitations to negative freedom. In the 'Introduction' to 'Four Essays' he proposes that resources are, of course, necessary for the exercise of negative freedom but that a claim to resources has nothing to do with the legal claim to negative freedom, which only entails the absence of coercion (Berlin 1969: 121–34).

[12] For this, see the prominent criticism of 'negative freedom': G. A. Cohen (1991) and Steiner (1974–5).

[13] See the otherwise very different approaches of Alexy (1986), Shue (1996a), Tugendhat (1993).

[14] Recently Philippe van Parijs has made this argument (1995: 22). His notion of real freedom entails three aspects: security, self-ownership, and leximin opportunity.

[15] He speaks of subsistence rights, which provide 'minimal economic security. This means unpolluted air, unpolluted water, adequate food, adequate clothing, adequate shelter, and minimal preventive public health care' (Shue 1996a: 23).

a certain minimum standard of living, and to a few civil rights and liberties, it is impossible to make use of any other rights.[16]

The basic rights are all interdependent: if one does not have a guaranteed claim to 'economic security' (which entails access to a job that is in accordance with certain labor standards such as minimum income and security at the work place) then one cannot exercise one's civil rights and liberties. On the other hand, without protection from arbitrary arrest and torture, material security is not worth much. Thus, Shue's approach goes one step further than Rawls's. While he continues to view social and economic rights as an instrument necessary for the exercise of other important rights, he does not prioritize civil rights and political liberties, but emphasizes the interdependence of the three categories of rights. Through this, social and economic human rights become valuable for their own sake: they ensure the exercise of one's freedom by formulating claims on the access to necessary material preconditions.

But this view, however, is not sensitive enough for the different personal variations that may hinder people from carrying out their plans. It fails to recognize that resources can have very different effects on the welfare of individuals and can be used by different individuals in different ways.[17] A person's standard of living cannot be determined in terms of the amount of goods she possesses in comparison to others. Which goods and the amount of goods that people require depends to a decisive degree on what needs they have and what capacities they already have and want to develop. This becomes obvious with children: they do not *yet* have the capacities to make use of the resources allocated to them, for example, for their nourishment. But also the handicapped, the ill, and the elderly often are unable to look after themselves. They may need resources to buy certain medical assistance and equipment. And they may also need the support and care of others including medical professionals, social workers, neighbors, friends, and family to develop, regain, or exercise their capabilities.

6.1.3. Social Autonomy Justification

What we have seen so far is that the 'extended freedom' approach, by recognizing the *sui generis* importance of social and economic human rights, better suits the justification of these rights than the 'functionalist approach'. It falls short, however, by characterizing these rights as rights to a universal resource bundle that is adequate for the average person rather than as rights to a variable resource bundle that can be adjusted to each person's specific needs and capacities. Social and economic human rights should make it possible for people to 'develop' themselves as they see fit, within reasonable bounds. These rights should enable them to pursue their

---

[16] See also Robert Alexy, whose theory rests entirely on the premise that the necessary preconditions must exist to make it possible for one to provide a *decent standard of living* for oneself and one's family. For this to be achieved it is argued that the corresponding material conditions must be accessible (Alexy 1986).

[17] Sen (1992, 1993: 336–64).

vision of 'the good life', even if they do not themselves possess the necessary means and capacities (Tugendhat 1993). So developing capacities demands resources adapted to the individual's needs, but it also requires the *targeted support* of others if people for whatever reason are unable to develop them by themselves. The *intrinsic value* of social and economic human rights here lies not in offering an identical resource and service bundle to fulfill conditions to act freely, as has been stated by 'extended freedom' proponents; rather, it lies in the pursuit of different activities and the development of capacities that enable the individual to pursue his or her own conception of the good. This goes beyond the concept of extended freedom in that one is no longer only speaking of spaces for action created and secured by the state through the provision of resources—this view is too narrow. Rather, a more appropriate foundation for social and economic human rights is a notion of promoting self-development. This notion includes facilitating the development of capacities that are part of one's idea of the good life, but which for whatever reason one cannot pursue independently.

The likely outcomes of this shift toward a 'self-development approach' suggest that we refer to *social autonomy*. The *autonomy* side of this concept has to be understood as self-determination in its fullest sense as one pursues his or her individual life plans as long as possible without any help and without being patronized. *Social* autonomy, however, means pursuing one's life and developing one's capacities even under conditions of constraint (e.g., illness, disability, unemployment), with the support of others. The support can take various forms, as we see later. The assistance creates conditions that allow individuals to come closer to their ideal life plan. The autonomy perspective goes further than the extended freedom approach by acknowledging the varied, individual circumstances that must be addressed in order to distribute resources and service bundles in a way that is actually equitable. It also respects individuals and requires them to handle life on their own, as long as they are able to do so. It is this theoretical shift that makes it helpful to refer to social autonomy instead of freedom, as freedom is often used in the sense of negative freedom or (although less often), in the sense of extended freedom. Introducing the concept of social autonomy underpins a paradigmatic change from addressing the needs of the average person to addressing the needs of an *individual* when she cannot pursue her life plans without external help.

This proposal for social and economic human rights is one that focuses on *moral* human rights. I cannot provide here a detailed discussion of the differences between moral and legal human rights, but some points to consider include that moral human rights have universal reach and include all human beings, whereas legal human rights have their place first and foremost in the constitutions of states and are a powerful instrument in the hands of individual citizens against illegitimate state intervention into the private sphere. Also, constitutional rights are more specific than moral human rights and are adapted to the national, sociopolitical, and cultural context; for example, there are different anti-discrimination laws in different European countries. Human rights, however, share some aspects with *moral norms*, which is one reason why human rights are sometimes seen as belonging not just to the realm of law but also to that of morality.[18] Among the commonalities between human rights and moral norms are the following three characteristics: they are universally valid (or at least that is what they claim to be); they address the individual and not a specific group; and their content is very general.[19]

Despite their similar general content, human rights (be they moral or legal) are not norms but *rights* because they typically take a legal form.[20] As such they are individual rights for which one can sue. They also leave the reasons for following them open—an individual may choose to respect the law because she is convinced that the law is justified, or she may simply wish to avoid punishment. In contrast, moral norms are grounded on obligations that we owe one another; they extend all the way to the individual's motivation for following them. A moral claim that is directed against another, asking him or her to act according to a norm, requires that the other view the duty as valid. The obligations linked to rights, however, follow from the claim to have the freedom to act arbitrarily, within the limits of not impinging on the freedom of others. Legal duties are the result of lawmaking processes that institutionalize human rights.

Although legal human rights do not have universal reach, *de facto*, most constitutional rights are valid for all citizens of the political community, regardless of their nationality. Also, some international conventions are universal and are binding contracts: the Convention on Economic, Social and Cultural Rights and the Convention on Civil and Political Rights, for example. Still, juridical means for enforcement are lacking. *Per definitionem*, moral human rights are relatively 'weak' claims and not at all actionable except through public moral blaming and shaming.[21] Nevertheless, moral human rights can play an important role in international negotiations since they can have a degree of performativity. This does not assume a causal relation between normative practice and action, but it is important to note that moral norms, as well as moral human rights, can be effective. Although it is not always or necessarily the case, moral norms and rights can influence how people live. For instance, they may trigger processes of self-reflection with the result that people perceive their situation differently—they might come to see it as unjust and act accordingly and, as a result, fight for their rights.[22] In the next section, I will further explain these assumptions on

---

[18] See also, e.g., Otfried Höffe who legitimizes human rights on the basis of political justice and the normative assumption of reciprocal waiver of freedom (Höffe 1989: 382–406).

[19] It is because of these elements that human rights claim to be valid independent of future historical developments and cultural diversity; cf. Pogge (2002a: 52–71).

[20] For this difference see Habermas (1996a: 223–5).

[21] For the distinction between moral and legal human rights see Habermas (1996a: 454–60, Post-script).

[22] On philosophy of language, J. L. Austin in *'How to Do Things with Words'* (1962) introduced the idea that when one utters a sentence like 'You're fired' or 'This meeting is adjourned' one performs an act. He calls these explicit performative utterances. The theory of speech acts, which he developed, claims that one does more things by help of words than just convey information. For the idea that normative institutions affect people's actions see Peters (1993: 325). The notion of performativity used here refers to Peters' notion: Arguments may have an effect on others, but the effect depends

the character of social and economic human rights by specifying the content and extent of these claims, and who is eligible to make them.

6.2. CONTENT, EXTENT, AND ELIGIBILITY

An initial question to consider is what does a human rights-based claim to social autonomy entail? In other words, what is the content of these rights? The second question concerns the *extent* of aid. Should there be just a *modest* level of public assistance toward the fulfillment of essential interests, but nothing above this threshold? Or does everybody have a claim to the best treatment and support possible, which would require, for example, that some people with severe illness and disability receive very expensive medical treatment? And a third unresolved problem is that of who actually is eligible to get support. Here the question is whether the 'applicant' must fulfill some conditions to actually get assistance—for example, that one is not at fault for one's situation.

6.2.1. Content of Social Autonomy-Based Claims

Let us first turn to the content of social autonomy-claims. To offer a more concrete proposal of the content of these claims, one may begin with what I call *essential* interests. They are 'essential' because they are fundamental elements of every human life. Their fulfillment cannot be denied to anybody with good reasons:[23] Nobody wants to get sick and not get medical treatment even though the know-how and medicine exists; nobody wants to starve and have no access to fresh drinking water; nobody wants to live without appropriate shelter that protects against rain, cold, heat, insects, attacks, and that allows her to carry out import social functioning such as cooking, sleeping, meeting friends; nobody wants to appear in public ashamed by their inappropriate clothes (Adam Smith); nobody wants to be in the situation of being disabled but having no equipment to move about; nobody wants to work very long hours without getting enough income to lead a decent life; nobody wants to be unemployed and without any income at all; and nobody would like to be a parentless child who has no access to the

---

on the context in which they were uttered. I illustrate the performativity of normative arguments with reference to the UDHR in Kreide (2005).

[23] This approach here rests on the assumption that what defines social autonomy-based *moral* claims in more detail, is the result of a procedure based on certain normative assumptions. See, for this, Forst (1999): Within the argumentative practice, all reasons if they fulfill the following two criteria are acceptable. They first must be reciprocally nonrejectable (Scanlon 1998), which means they must be agreeable on the basis of insight. This would prevent an author of a rule from demanding anything he or she never would submit to because he or she in fact finds the rule to be useless or inadequate. Secondly, reasons must be general, which means that they must be addressed to all those that may be affected by the norms or by the actions that follow from those norms (Forst 1999: 44).

just mentioned resources and, moreover, no access to education and personal relationships.

These interests are hardly contested. An important reason for this is that their acceptance as basic human interests has been the result of long political struggles—one can say that they have become part of a commonsense understanding of what makes a life a decent one. These interests correspond to the development of certain capacities.[24] One can distinguish between basic and advanced capacities. The former are based on the above-mentioned interests; among them are capacities such as having access to food for healthy meals or to prosthetic devices if impaired. Defining what is required within a certain context makes it necessary to turn to the individual and his or her specific conditions and needs. The development of basic capacities is a precondition for the development of more advanced ones, such as fostering a certain talent, taking part in educational programs that increase the chances for employment in a desirable field, enjoying free time, and so on. These more demanding capacities are important for most people and also form a main part of their 'good life' if their basic interests have already been fulfilled. But while a list of basic capacities can rather easily be determined, deciding on which advanced capabilities should be developed is more difficult. There is no ready moral argument that would, even under conditions of shortages, restrict the list of capacities that are part of a good life but there may be political reasons for restrictions, such as concerns about financing, management, or other priorities on the political agenda. In political negotiations about the best interpretation of social human rights, pragmatic arguments may trump moral ones. These pragmatic arguments typically include concern for the future of particular social-political programs or agendas. For example, some worry that excessive social spending constrains the 'public funds' available for investments that create jobs.

Political compromises may lead—and very often in welfare states have led—to a narrower list of capacities for which people are willing to devote funds to develop. Nevertheless, individuals do have a *strong* moral claim on the fulfillment of their *basic* capacities because their fulfillment is a necessary precondition for pursuing the good life—whatever that plan for the good life may look like. Basic capacities are not up for political discussion, and, as we will soon see, this strong moral claim also holds true for foreigners, even if conationals and the leading elite do not realize it. People have a *weak* moral claim on the realization of *advanced* capacities. Their fulfillment rests on the political will, as well as on the predominant idea of local and national needs and interests. But even within the area of essential interests, priority-setting occurs, albeit within very narrow limits. Here the priorities depend on what is judged as a very urgent matter (fighting AIDS might be very high on the political agenda in Botswana, while diminishing

---

[24] For the historical development of social claims, see Craven (1995) and Marshall (1992). Even though I claim here that these interests are accepted, I do not say that moral or legal rights related to these interests are accepted either, neither is who is obligated to fulfill these interests if people cannot do so themselves.

the incidence of heart attacks might be as important in some industrial countries).

6.2.2. Extent of Support

A further problem that has to be discussed here is whether everybody has a claim to a *comprehensive* bundle of resources and care, or whether just a *modest* level of support is morally justified. Comprehensive assistance demands that every person in need of support gets the best possible treatment and resource bundle; a modest standard entails a cutoff level in the areas discussed. Comprehensive care may lead to neglect in other fields of care: in medical treatment, for example, if huge amounts of money go to very expensive operations for few people, then there is insufficient funding for the rest. On the other hand, if modest standards are set, it may be that a poor patient does not get an expensive heart operation and has to die earlier than those who can pay for it.

It is argued here that all those who cannot help themselves have a claim to a modest standard of subsistence but to a comprehensive level of health care. As the quality of medical service literally decides between premature death and staying alive, it is hard to think of any reason why poor people should have less access to medical treatment (and to develop their good life). It is certainly permissible that a society set priorities and choose to first fight those diseases that are widespread and, only after this task is done, to provide expensive operations that cure fewer people. But there the cutoff level for services should not be defined by the point when the money for health care is exhausted; rather, the distribution should work the other way around: those who have money should continue to pay until a comprehensive level of care has been reached.

When it comes to subsistence, a modest but appropriate standard seems necessary for the development of a good life. What characterizes an appropriate standard has to be determined within the given political context. However, it is important to note that these variations do not open the door for the sort of relativist argumentation that finds that because, for example, the Republic of the Congo currently has a low standard of living, it is enough to keep up this low standard and only offer basic health care; or that because developing countries lag behind in technological development, there is no use in educating their citizens in this field. This line of thought perpetuates the existing unequal access to the fulfillment of social human rights. In any case, the diversity in needs and interests is relatively limited when what is at stake is the securing of the basic human interests mentioned above.

To sum up the last two paragraphs, with the social autonomy approach it is not possible that anybody who is in need would be denied an adequate amount of culturally acceptable resources and services to develop their basic capacities. Furthermore, it is not said that advanced capacities should never be realized in some contexts; rather, it is argued that the priority-setting should fit the actual demands and requirements. Also, even though the level of support depends on the outcome of political negotiations, this does not mean that a modest welfare level is morally sufficient. When it comes to medical treatment, people have a claim to comprehensive support, but in the case of other basic and advanced capacities, meeting moral requirements can depend on local interpretation of what counts as an appropriate standard.

6.2.3. Eligibility to Get Aid

We have seen that *in principle* everybody in need is the subject of social human rights. But what if someone has caused the situation she is in? Is she then eligible to get support? One could answer 'Yes', reasoning that responsibility is the flip side of autonomy. To further explore this, let us return to the objection stated at the beginning: It is very common to distinguish between those who are culpable for their poverty, illness, or disability, and those who are not. It is often said that only those who are not responsible for their situation should get aid. If the community pays even for those who have been lazy, ignorant, or careless, then, it is argued, there is no incentive for personal responsibility and it may become difficult to prevent this behavior in the future. A similar challenge arises at the international level with collectives. If state representatives are corrupt or unwilling to engage in building a well-functioning social security system and are therefore responsible for a country's situation, is there still a duty to aid the needy in that country? And what if a majority of the country's citizens support the regime? A common reply is that the community (whether it is one nation or the international community) should step in if those in need are not responsible for their situation. I think, however, it is problematic to connect eligibility for social assistance to an estimation of culpability. To explain this in more detail, I turn to the question of individual responsibility for one's own actions first and then turn to the collective.

Intention-based eligibility requires determining those actions and situations for which one cannot be held responsible. In most cases, however, this is difficult to accomplish.[25] Consider, for example, the people who live in the San Andreas Valley in the United States. One could argue that they alone should be held financially responsible for the disasters that result from settling in an earthquake zone. On the other hand, the area is flourishing, it is an important contributor to the entire US economy, and there has been no public warning against moving into this area. One could also refuse to cover the costs of cancer treatment for long-term smokers, or for rehabilitation for alcoholics, but very often a person has not had a real chance to become a non-smoker or non-drinker, as he or she comes from a family or community where smoking or drinking is part of the culture (Roemer 2000: 43–53). The choices, then, are to change one's habits (if one can) or to die prematurely if one gets ill and cannot afford private health care. But forcing this kind of unqualified choice is too much of an intrusion of the state into the private

---

[25] For this estimation of the problem see also Anderson (1999: 295–9).

sphere, an area that should actually be protected through the state. It is also a humiliating regulation if help is denied and one has to suffer because 'it's your own fault'. Furthermore, a 'punishing' state contravenes the idea of citizens who have rights to personal freedom.

Rather than worrying about which losses, predicaments, and injury-related disabilities that individuals should or should not be held responsible for, it makes sense to instead distinguish between those losses that can and should be compensated in any case and those that should not (Anderson 1999). The ill, for example, should not (and probably cannot) be compensated for the pain they have to bear and the joy they miss in their lives. For some disabled persons, there is no medical device or social support available that could enable them to fully take part in social interaction. And in a society where social recognition depends very much on what job one has, unemployment checks are no replacement for lost social esteem. These burdens alone are often a deterrent. They rebut the argument that if one does not distinguish between those actions and situations one is responsible for from those one is not, that then there is incentive for those who are undisciplined or just lazy to remain undisciplined and lazy at the cost of the community. Those who are (for whatever reason) in disadvantaged circumstances will only be helped to a limited extent through resources and services. They have to suffer disadvantages nobody voluntarily would like to bear.

Does this also hold for nations? Should a collective, usually a nation, receive international aid even if state representatives can be held responsible for the suffering of many people? Or even if the whole population can be held responsible because they wholeheartedly support a dictatorial regime? I think the answer is yes, for at least three reasons. First, aid should be offered with a view to the individual and not the whole collective. It is not plausible to assume that 100% of a population stands behind a dictator. If there is just one opponent, it can hardly be justified that she should be punished for the faults of others. The same is true for children who cannot yet choose to live a life of great privation. Second, from a political point of view it might make sense to increase the standard of living in a dictatorial country through aid because this can foster education, the development of a lively public sphere, and the wish for democratic self-determination. But the third and main argument is that all citizens of any country can (if they want to) call on their social and economic human rights. The only condition to be fulfilled to get legitimized support is neediness. Apart from that, social and economic human rights are unconditionally valid.

In sum, the determination of whether a claim for support should be fulfilled should depend on the indigence of the individual, regardless of whether the person who asks for assistance is at fault for his or her problems. The omission of help—I have argued—would be inhuman, especially because assistance very often cannot fully compensate for the experienced losses. In most cases, the need is obvious and uncontested. Poor people—and not only those in developing countries—suffer from multiple shortages, which augment one another: they are malnourished, which lowers their resistance to illness; and they are probably ill, which decreases their chances for employment. But even in cases where it might be unclear or debatable whether someone is eligible, one should decide in favor of the applicant.

6.3. DUTY FULFILLMENT

One aspect of social autonomy not yet discussed but of key importance for defining violations of social and economic rights arises at this point: who actually is obligated to fulfill these rights? In discussing the distribution of duties, I distinguish between three different paths to a clearer definition of individual obligations. While the first path does not lead very far, the other two are promising, and, as will turn out, complement one another. Finally, I provide some arguments for why TNCs should be included as duty-bearers.

6.3.1. Special Relationships

One variation on the notion of a *restricted* scope of obligation conveys that *special relationships* between people (be they based on kinship, neighborhood, or common citizenship) imply special responsibilities. The closer the degree of contact between two people, the more extensive are their mutual obligations. Between family members as well as between friends there doubtlessly exist more extensive obligations than between strangers. Thus we bear greater responsibility for our own children and family members than we do for other people; friends take precedence over acquaintances, one's fellow citizens over those of other countries.

The special relationship approach, however, fails to consider that close relationships are not necessarily those best-suited to providing assistance and responding to needs: very often, especially in developing countries, those close to the needy are not able to provide appropriate assistance, mostly because they themselves are lacking the necessary means to offer help. Also, a division of labor according to closeness can have a disproportionately negative impact on certain groups who might be prevented from pursuing other goals (Koller 1998). In the areas of caretaking and childrearing, for example, the lion's share of the burden of responsibility is borne by women.

In addition, in light of increasing international interdependence, it is no longer easy to determine with certainty to whom one has a special obligation, especially if one looks at the current international web of trade relations, law, and political agreements. Workers in Brazil or Colombia who produce sports articles or flowers can be 'close' to people in Europe and the United States through the producer–consumer relationship, which can be described as a special relationship. But nevertheless, consumers in wealthy countries rarely feel any solidarity on the basis of these abstract trade relations, and sometimes even workers do not. This raises the question of whether one can speak of 'special relationships' at all if people do not *feel* obligated.

Given this line of reasoning, it is not surprising that a second approach to dealing with the allocation of obligations stresses another way to justify duties.

6.3.2. Expediency

This line of argument, which I call here the expediency approach, uses anticipated efficiency and effectiveness as the basis for assigning duties.[26] When weighing expediency, those individuals that have the required knowledge and financial means are viewed as the best candidates for realizing social and economic human rights. This obviously would excessively burden some people, as it is sometimes unclear how to best coordinate, distribute, and offer assistance. Therefore, it makes sense to transfer the duty to institutions or groups that can professionally and effectively deal with the required demands. The first candidate for this role is the state, which is the first addressee for its own citizens. But the state is also the main subject of international law and is often poised to give developmental aid on a unilateral basis or to offer credits through other international organizations. States have the status of full-fledged subjects in international law, which means they are endowed with contractual capacities, the competence to conduct diplomatic relations, the right to take crimes and torts to an international court, and the burden of being held accountable for them.

Despite the clear role of the state, there may still be a feeling of unease. We have seen that those in need have a justified claim for support, and those who are able to assist have a duty to comply. But one aspect of a comprehensive notion of obligations that has been left out the discussion so far (an aspect, though, that is well-known from juridical debates on duties), is the question of who has caused poverty and deprivation, and whether or not this affects the range of responsibility and obligation. This should interest us here because usually we say that those who have caused harm are responsible and obligated to offer compensation. We have seen above that there are circumstances where it is difficult to ascribe responsibility to an individual. For example, a person's self-destructive bad habits may be the result of socialization processes that cannot be fully controlled by the individual. Also, we have seen that when someone is in need, the obligation to help has priority over the idea that the person at fault should be held responsible for any harm to herself or to others. The question we face now is whether causing poverty is a well-founded reason for imposing obligations, even though it has been argued that harming oneself compels duties on others who are able to offer support, and not on oneself.

---

[26] Goodin (1988), Shue (1988), and Koller (1998) propose a model, which integrates aspects of the *special relationship* and the *efficiency approach*. Koller, however, proceeds from the problematic assumption of the dichotomy between negative and positive duties, to which negative and positive rights respectively correspond. See also Wenar (2007), in this volume.

6.3.3. Cause

In this section I discuss this question as it relates to what I call the *'cause principle'* of duty allocation. I first point out some innovations and advantages the cause principle brings to the notion of obligations, and then I show to what extent this principle, along with a much more binding notion of obligations, should supplement the idea of basing duty-allocation on 'expedience'.

Thomas Pogge in particular has put forward two important innovations in the field of obligations (2002*a*). Pogge first introduces a change in perspective when he suggests focusing not only on a fair distribution of resources but also looking at the causes of poverty: the conditions of production, the governmental structure within a society and, especially, the international rule system. This reveals a weakness of the social autonomy approach as it has been presented so far. The social autonomy approach offers the normative tools for an economic distribution of resources and services according to human rights standards. But even if there were ideal economic distribution, this would not be sufficient to reduce poverty. Merely keeping an eye on the distribution of acquired economic goods or on *outcome distribution* neglects too much the conditions of the origin of poverty. It offers a remedy of the symptoms of poverty but does not give an analysis of the different causes and people involved. Gaining a better understanding of what causes poverty can help overcome it in the long run and helps avoid the negative side effects of a permanent foreign aid supply. Foreign aid can support or even create the development of a 'rent-seeking society' if reform proposals are not appropriately adapted by the recipient country (and not controlled by the donors).[27]

Given the interconnectedness of politics, economics, and finance, it seems also simplistic not to put a much greater and systematic emphasis on the many rules regulating international financial and cultural exchange, trade, and working conditions. Pogge highlights the fact that human beings are embedded in a world order consisting of trade and financial relations, international law, and political agreements that *affect* the social, political, and economic situations of individual citizens in such a way that results in some people being forced to live in poverty.[28] International rules can cause poverty. To mention just one example: The European Union subsidized beef exports to South Africa in 1996 to an extent that imported beef could be offered at half the price local producers could

---

[27] Tanzania is an often-cited example. It received US$13 billion in aid between 1970 and 1992, but had in 1992 a very low growth rate and its debt reached $7.5 billion in 1994 despite favorable world market prices for coffee. One important problem was that the administrative and commercial elite generally resisted bringing about a shift from a strong emphasis on personal client relations to a rational market economy. See, e.g., Rainer Tetzlaff (1996: 150). Aid to countries with 'good policies' also risks the so-called endogeneity problem: Because the recipients expect an uninterrupted flow of aid, their policies may deteriorate and administrators will become lax in their implementation. Furthermore, as recent experiences have shown, aid directed toward the government sector as a reward for 'good policies' can lead to a 'crowding out' of the private sector, which in turn diminishes economic growth (Langhammer 2002: 12–13).

[28] Pogge (2002*a*: in particular 52).

offer the African consumer. The EU replied to an official complaint of the South African government by saying that the exports were in accordance with the GATT-agricultural act and that there was no reason to discriminate against the South African importer. The economic damage caused through the price dumping was estimated at approximately US$ 100 million. Ironically, this was almost equal to the amount of Germany's developmental aid to South Africa at the time, which also included the promotion of beef production.[29] So the cheaper European beef may have benefited some African consumers, mostly those who were better off and could afford beef, but African farmers and especially their impoverished workers were hurt through these subsidies.

Incompatibilities between international rules and human rights policies make it necessary for researchers from different disciplines to help formulate a regulatory structure that is compatible with human rights. In Pogge's view, human rights, including social rights, require fair 'surroundings' for their successful implementation. Realization of social and economic human rights requires not only a fair redistribution of resources and money, but also an international rule system (as it is manifested in agreements by the WTO and organizations such as the World Bank or the IMF) that respects international human rights (Pogge 2002*b*).

The second change of perspective that Pogge undertakes is linked to the aspect just described and reveals what this change in perspective means for people's obligations to reduce poverty. The citizens of the rich Northern countries and their political representatives who take part in international negotiations and fix the international rules are not simply bystanders who maybe should do a little more for the poor because they know about their sad situation. They are the creators of these rule systems and, therefore, cooperate in a system that causes poverty and upholds it for their own benefit. To the extent we *cause* the harm to others we are coresponsible for the situation of those who are worse off.[30] This—and now we return to the question of obligations—has consequences for the notion of duties.

Pogge describes the responsibility associated with human rights first and foremost as a *negative duty*. This means that there exists a negative duty to *refrain from* participating in an organizational system that 'avoidably fails to realize human rights' (2002*a*: 166). Actions that ask for engagement in changing the current system or that entail assistance to remedy grave poverty also come into the picture, however, when Pogge admits that it sometimes 'can be better for the victims

---

[29] FIAN (1998: 121–2). There is no shortage of examples of the asymmetrical relationship in virtue of which the privileged are responsible for the poverty of others. Global organizations make decisions about international investments as well as financial and economic requirements, provide loans, and offer military and development aid, and thereby have a direct influence on the lives of people in poor countries. International agreements should therefore exclude—to mention just one of Pogge's examples—any contracts and treaties that cement the so-called international resource privilege. this privilege currently allows any group in power freely to dispose of the country's national resources—regardless of how this group came to power and of whether it is a democratic or totalitarian regime (Pogge 2001*b*).

[30] For the notion of negative responsibility see especially Pogge (2002*a*: 118).

of injustice if we continue participation while also working toward appropriate institutional reforms or toward shielding these victims from the harms we also help produce' (2002*a*: 166). So it can be the case that the best way to fulfill the negative duty 'not to participate' is by taking part in active political change of the institutional system or by undertaking some compensatory efforts toward poverty alleviation. Those actions would lead to a change of the current situation, and in turn, would improve the situation of the poor. It would suit the duty not 'to contribute to the imposition of an unjust institutional order' since it diminishes the factors that make the institutional order unjust. So active reform as well as compensatory measures let the better-off fulfill their duty toward the poor and make the situation better for them at the same time. Pogge stresses that one has a negative duty not to participate in an unjust institutional system because participating *results* in helping create or at least sustain a situation that is bad or even worse for the poor.

The priority of a negative concept of obligations suggested here provides an unambiguous and therefore strong rationale, as responsibility can be clearly ascribed: everyone who contributes to the upholding of unjust institutions and who profits from them—in other words, everyone in the world who is not poor—bears responsibility for the poor living conditions of others. In contrast, positive duties offer a vaguer notion of obligation, which requires specifying who can best provide care. When it comes to political application, this form of justification is exposed to the danger that potential duty-bearers will withdraw from their obligations by deferring to possible others who may be better equipped to discharge the required actions.

However, there is at least one decisive problem with the 'causal' approach. Refraining from participating in an unjust international system of rules, just passively desisting, can *increase* injustice. Consider a world that contains just two islands (A and B) that do not have anything to do with one another although they know of each other and the prevailing living conditions.[31] No trade relations or political agreements exist; no one has ever made his or her way to the other part of the world for any period nor have kinship relations developed. The people of Island A have built up a well-functioning infrastructure and have managed to live in some wealth, whereas people on Island B are fairly poor, troubled by natural disasters, a corrupt government, and warring guerrilla troops. Suppose furthermore that a majority on both islands tries equally hard to attain a better standard of living. Now, even if A does not inflict unfair contracts on the weaker party, B, and does not take advantage of existing 'resource privileges', which indeed would be an enormous step toward a just global order, unacceptable injustice would still remain. The problem, however, is not that the life of the inhabitants is characterized by *unequal* living conditions. The injustice, rather, is expressed by the fact that without too much trouble, some people on Island A could offer relief and make it possible for people on Island B to live a decent life. The obligations

---

[31] Gosepath also refers to an island example. He, however, uses it to demonstrate that people have a legitimized claim to certain goods without being part of a 'community of cooperation', (2002: 205).

exist because people who are unable to live a good life have a legitimate claim for support that should be addressed to all those with the potential to change the situation.[32]

We can see now why the 'expediency' and the 'cause' approaches complement each other. An indication of responsibility in the harm, poverty, or deprivation caused ('You have done this') is a stronger reason for assigning an obligation than the reference to the de facto capability to fulfill universal obligations ('You can help'). The latter reason is weaker because those who actually can offer assistance may ask why *they* should engage and not others, who, first of all may have been involved in the cause, or who, secondly, may be more able to help, or even both. But the latter reason also has the following decisive advantage: in cases where (hypothetically) no causal effects can be identified, and in cases where a clear ascription of the cause is too contested, there still exist duties to realize human rights. This is also the case if someone has obviously caused harm but is not able to bear the costs and/or offer compensation. Under these circumstances, those who can give aid or somehow change the bad situation are asked to do so.

Let us return to the obligation that the cause approach counters; that is, the claim defended above that if one has badly hurt oneself (i.e., where A [harm-producer] is also B [victim of harm]) others have an obligation to give support. A significant weakness of the cause principle in addressing this situation is that in cases of self-destruction, harm is usually unintended whereas the cause-principle presupposes intentional, direct harm or, at a minimum, toleration of collateral harm. This presupposition means that unintended but harmful side effects of an action (if in fact one can figure out which action was intended and which was not) do not raise any obligation for compensation. But this is an implausible assumption given our daily moral practices and our juridical ideas concerning liability: if I visit someone and accidentally knock over his expensive vase, it is undisputable that I should offer to compensate the loss. I think that in cases where A can be identified as having caused her own deprived situation or injury, others are obliged to offer support because she is in a state of necessity: although she caused the harm, she is unable to help herself and the principle of expediency has to be applied.

Despite the challenge raised above, the causal approach presents a change in perspective that is important for the realization of social and economic human rights. The scope of obligations is not restricted to granting support in the form of resources or services to the poor; rather, obligations extend to refraining from certain actions and monitoring international rules and their effects on people's lives. The expediency approach also includes the following obligation: those who have the most influence in international rule-setting processes are asked to use

---

[32] As has been argued in section 6.3.3, Island A has obligations toward Island B to assist the victims of natural disasters, or of famines, or of poverty as a result of war, even if a ruling elite or even if all citizens can be held responsible for those conditions. The claim to flourish, we have seen above, is legitimate regardless of whether the addressee has caused the predicament he or she is in. This is mainly because it would be cruel to deny assistance even though one could offer it without great loss for oneself. Nevertheless, if one causes harm to others and can help, one has the obligation to do so.

their power to shift negotiations toward a fairer outcome. But with the cause approach this perspective comes more to the fore; one is genuinely obligated to find out about the destructive effects and side effects of the international policies that hinder the realization of social and economic human rights.

6.3.4. Duty-Bearer

Cause and expediency are convincing criteria for the distribution of obligations. But nothing has yet been said about who the duty-bearer is. One of the main duty-bearers is the citizen, who then transfers the duty to secure and realize human rights to the state. Therefore the state has the paradoxical task of protecting citizens from human rights violations; for example, interference in the private sphere, which is usually committed through the state. Human rights violations are per definitionem carried out or are tolerated by state officials (Pogge 2002a: 59). Nation-states in general, however, have lost important decision-making competencies in many areas during recent decades whereas other agents—especially TNCs—have gained tremendous political and economic power on the international level.[33] The revenue of some exceeds the gross national product of smaller European states. And they sometimes import the whole package of labor and tax rights before making an investment and settling down in a country (Günther 2001).

A first question that arises here is what happens if the primary duty-bearer—the state—for some reason does not take charge of the carrying out of its duties. The moral claim to social autonomy does not cease to exist if social and economic rights are not integrated into a national constitutional setting or if there is no national organization that is indeed able to assure them. If those who are primarily responsible have defaulted on their duties, then those who have participated in violating human interests (even if not to the degree of the primary actor) *and* have the means to compensate for this harm, should offer effective support.[34] If there is no clear evidence that other agents are involved in committing the wrong, but are nevertheless able to offer help, they have the 'substitutional' duty to change the situation in favor of realizing human rights. And they owe this duty to the suffering population. This is similar to the argument mentioned in the eligibility discussion. The claim of the individual to lead a decent life is universal and as long as there is somebody (or some entity) that is capable of changing the situation for the better, the duty has to be carried out.

De facto, these are first and foremost the better organized and wealthier countries but it makes a difference whether the primary duty-holder is *unable* to comply or just *unwilling*. When is a state unable to comply? A criterion to decide this might be the notion of domestic sovereignty proposed by Stephan Krasner. A state has only very limited domestic sovereignty—and thus is unable to realize human rights—'either if there is no established structure of authority or the

---

[33] Perraton et al. (1998: 157); Zürn (2004).
[34] On this topic see also Wenar (2007), in this volume.

ability of its rulers to exercise control over what is going on within their own territory does not exist' (Krasner 1999: 4). Authority means here being legally accepted as a sovereign state by others. With failed states like former Afghanistan it was relatively clear that the infrastructure of the country was so completely broken down that without any external support it would take a very long time to establish a functioning welfare system, or that this might even be impossible. But in most cases, especially with resource-rich countries, the political elite and leaders are mainly interested in maintaining their power and augmenting their personal possessions, which, in turn, prevents them from respecting human rights. Here again, a reference to the approach that focuses on causes of poverty is helpful (Pogge 2002*a*). To a great extent, the wealthier countries shape the international economic and financial rules that influence the domestic structure of a society. It is in their hands to reshape the international rule system in a way that establishes incentives for realizing social and economic human rights.

A remaining question is whether collectives other than states do in fact have any human rights obligations.[35] The most prominent candidates for this burden are the TNCs. Do they have duties? And if so, how can they be justified?

From a *moral point of view* one could deny that collectives have such obligations because the members of the collective cannot be held responsible for the group's actions. And they cannot be held responsible because all collectives with an internal decision structure are more than just the sum of their members and can be distinguished from a group of people who act together but have gathered by accident.[36] This 'grammar of corporate decision-making' shapes the actions of the members of the collective. They cannot freely decide what to do, but have to submit to the corporation's or organization's purposes; in other words, they have to submit to the collective's intention. Because of the internal decision structure one can say the corporation or organization (rather than the individual members) has reasons to act in one way and not in another. I do not think it is right to remove the burden from the individuals. But even if this were convincing, the argument remains that because TNCs are so powerful internationally and can have such a tremendous effect on the lives of people, they should be treated like a moral and a legal person. In this view, TNCs must also be subject to moral and legal principles. As powerful entities, they are also very *capable* to shape their social and political surroundings according to human rights standards. They can bring about social and economic rights, for example, by offering adequate wages and leisure time

---

[35] Among the international organizations other than UN institutions there has been a discussion about the extent to which their developmental strategies should be brought into line with human rights policies. See Brodnig (2001). Within the World Bank, e.g., there are different interpretations of the Bank's Articles of Agreement. Some follow a narrow interpretation that defines as the Bank's core mandate economic and financial activities to assist the development of its members, and prohibits any political orientation and activities. Others argue that human rights issues have already become part of the Bank's engagement, as their realization is an important aspect with reference to the economic considerations that ensure development. Some go so far as to declare this instrumental view of human rights policy as the official legal position of the Bank. This is the position of the former Chief Counsel Ibrahim Shihata, according to Brodnig (2001).

[36] See for this position French (1991: 290–304).

to their workers, implementing anti-discrimination rules, guaranteeing security at the workplace, using environmental protection technology, and so on. So, the power of TNCs and their capacity to act in many arenas like states makes them candidates for becoming moral and legal persons, comparable to states.

Another position proposes that each single member of a collective—be it a biological person in a corporation or a state in an international organization—is obliged to respect human rights anyway. In the same way that human rights claims do not cease to be valid because human beings carry out a certain profession, the duties related to human rights do not cease to exist because one has a certain (economic or political) position. If the opposite were true, it would contravene the whole idea of universal human rights. Human rights are valid within every sphere of society. To comply with human rights is not a matter of 'public affairs' but of moral principles and legally binding contracts, and the collective itself also needs to adjust its intentions according to human rights standards (Brodnig 2001). So we can say that leaders of TNCs, shareholders, and workers are obliged to respect human rights even in their positions as members of an enterprise. According to their capacity to realize human rights standards, they are asked to work toward their fulfillment.

We now have two arguments for why TNCs should be subject of human rights norms. First, their power to affect the quality of life and constrain freedoms is comparable to the powers of a state, and, second, they consist of individuals who are already subject to human rights and obliged to fulfill them. Actually getting TNCs to comply with human rights codes is very difficult. Voluntary agreements require a high degree of public vigilance. Currently the most effective way to pressure international corporations and institutions is through a well-informed public that monitors human rights violations worldwide. Consumer boycotts do have some influence on the business practices of corporations because corporations are interested in maintaining a good reputation. *Naming and shaming* has become an established instrument in human rights politics. Targeted monitoring of human rights violations, its presentation in public, and the development of political strategies to prevent future violations are usually conducted through NGOs.

From *a juridical point of view* the situation is beginning to change. None of the 500 different international organizations or the 75,000 current TNCs are yet fully fledged legal subjects of law.[37] But various attempts have been undertaken to change this unsatisfying situation.[38] Recently, the United Nations

---

[37] The only exception is the UNO, which has the status of an 'international person'. This was introduced into international law after the International Court of Justice decided on the case 'Reparation for Injuries', in which the responsibility for the killing of the UN diplomat Graf Bernadotte in Palestine in 1948, was at stake. IGH ICJ-Reports 1949, see also Paech and Stuby (2001: 335). International organizations and TNCs are allowed to draw up contracts with other non-state parties or with single states according to their aims and tasks. But they cannot enforce these agreements, e.g., under Chapter VII of the UN Charter, which is a right reserved to the Security Council.

[38] The 'Multilateral Agreement on Investment' (MAI) of the OECD had the intention to strengthen the legal status of TNCs. A further prominent example for a pact between private actors (TNCs)

Sub-Commission for the Promotion and Protection of Human Rights has approved *Norms on the Responsibility of TNCs and Other Business Enterprises with regard to Human Rights*, which can be said to be the first comprehensive international human rights norms that especially address TNCs and other business entities.[39] They lay out the responsibilities of companies to respect, secure, and promote the fulfillment of human rights with a special focus on consumers' and workers' rights, environmental protection, and national sovereignty. One result of the Commission's meetings was to define TNCs as legal persons. This is analogous to the status of natural persons in that these entities then have both rights and obligations (Weissbrodt 2000). However, in this document, the status as a legal person (whether it is an entity or an individual) depends on the approval of the state. It is the state's task not to tolerate those people or organizations that do not respect and protect human rights. This is a weak but as yet the only control mechanism available.

6.4. VIOLATION OF SOCIAL AND ECONOMIC HUMAN RIGHTS

In conclusion, it is now possible to come to an approximate answer to the question raised at the beginning; namely, whether poverty is a human rights violation. Human beings, so it has been argued, have a strong interest in developing basic capacities (among them leading a healthy life, which includes having healthy meals, fresh drinking water, and adequate shelter and clothing) as well as advanced capacities (developing talents and enjoying free time), and they have this interest even if disabilities or age hinder them from developing these capacities on their own. Some of these essential interests are expressed in the 'right to social autonomy'. This entails a modest, culturally specific but adequate level of subsistence and economic security, as well as a comprehensive level of health care. Even though the concrete content of these claims depends on the context-specific interpretation within a political community, it should not fall beneath a minimum

and the United Nations is the so-called *Global Compact*, brought to life by Kofi Annan in January 1999. Besides the UN High Commission for Human Rights, the Labor Organization (ILO), and representatives of the UN Environmental Program, about 50 corporations take part, among them Nike, Shell, BP Amoco and Rio Tinto. The deal is that the corporations have to go public on the Global Compact Internet site by describing their progress in implementing human rights standards. In turn they are allowed to use UN logo on their advertising. NGOs fear that the prestige of the UN will sustain damage if its name is closely linked to corporations that have not respected human rights in the past. Besides this, corporations also agreed to voluntary *codes of conduct,* some even subject to external control. See for this debate, among others, S. Prakash Sethi who criticizes group-based company codes and suggests instead individual codes (Sethi 2005), whereas Ralph G. Steinhardt argues that there is a potential for a slow development of a new *lex mercatoria* that links market incentives directly with corporate social responsibility (Steinhardt 2005).

[39] The full text of the approved 'Norms' is available at: www.unhchr.ch/Huridocda/Huridoca.nsf/ (Symbol)/E.CN.4.Sub.2.2003.12.Rev.2.En?Opendocument. See also Hillemanns (2003) who gives a good overview of these latest developments.

standard, or so it has been argued. Poverty is an indication that one or some actors have neglected their duties. Every instance of neglect is a violation of social and economic human rights. To make this explicit, I come, in the end to a more detailed proposal of duties, which correspond to social and economic rights.

It has become very common to distinguish between three different kinds of duties for *states*: States—so it has been proposed by the Committee of the ICESR—should respect, protect, and fulfill human rights. In more detail it says the following:[40]

1. With regard to social and economic human rights the obligation *to respect* requires states not to intervene in the private sphere in any way that hinders the enjoyment of social and economic rights. This precludes, for example, that the state engage in forced eviction that deprives people of their necessities of life.

2. The obligation *to protect* demands from states that they prevent violations by third parties, for example corporations that do not respect basic working standards.

3. And finally, states should work toward the *fulfillment* of these rights by implementing budgetary and judicial measures as well as the creation of appropriate legislation that guarantee social security for a stable period of time. (*Maastricht Guidelines* 1998: paragraph 19, 698)

Following our discussion, this list of duties can be complemented with the acknowledgment of three additional dimensions: agents of duties, the distribution of duties, and 'substitutional' duties.

4. All non-state agents who *affect* people's essential interests have enduring duties to respect, protect, and fulfill social and economic human rights *within their functional domain of influence*. For TNCs, to respect these rights means that the establishment of their production sites and the pursuit of their enterprises should not destroy local, essential living conditions, nor obstruct access to economic and social rights. Protecting economic and social human rights means that TNCs have an obligation to prevent third parties—mainly their subcontractors—from violating these rights. And finally, TNCs should contribute toward fulfilling economic and social human rights by, for example, respecting international labor laws and/or participating in voluntary agreements on labor standards.

---

[40] The first three obligations are also described in the *ICESR*, which were further specified in the *General Comments of the Committee on Economic, Social and Cultural Rights No.3*. The main task of the Committee for ICESR that came into being in 1987 is to control the state's report. It also formulates so-called General Comments that specify single aspects related to the protection of ESC rights. The General Comments No. 3 can be read at UN Doc.E/1991/23, Annex III, and it is also reprinted in Eide (1995), 442ff. A further interpretation of these obligations is developed in the *Limburg Principles on the Implementation of the ICESR*. The *Limburg Principles* have been issued as an official UN document, adopted 8 Jan. 1987, and reprinted in Human Rights Quarterly 1987. Meanwhile the discussion has continued and found its expression in the *Maastricht Guidelines on Violation of Economic, Social and Cultural Rights*. These guidelines are the result of a workshop in early 1997, on the tenth anniversary of the *Limburg Principles* intended to strengthen the monitoring of the ICESR. See the informative article by Dankwa, Flinternan, and Leckie (1998). For the three-part duties see also Henry Shue who already in 1980 had proposed to distinguish between duties to avoid deprivation, duties to protect deprivation, and duties to aid the deprived (1996a: 52).

5. Those agents who have *caused* harm and are capable of offering compensation in accordance with the realization of these rights have a strong duty to do so—again, within their functional area. If a direct causal involvement for whatever reason cannot be identified, those who are *capable* of realizing social and economic human rights have an equally strong duty to comply.

6. All the above-mentioned duties have to be fulfilled even if a state fails to comply with its duties. 'Substitutional' duties are to be taken over by any other states that are able to fill the gap, or by the community of states, even if a state's leader is capable but unwilling to comply. Part of fulfilling these 'substitutional' duties may be to urge the state to comply through economic sanctions or incentives.

This list is not intended to be comprehensive; rather it needs to be supplemented and made concrete in different political contexts. But the monitoring of human rights violations needs to be done by another international agent. While it is still weak and is an increasingly threatened instrument, especially when fighting terror entails constraining citizens' freedoms, a vigilant public can be a detector that tracks down violations of human rights.

7

The Duties Imposed by the Human Right to Basic Necessities

Elizabeth Ashford[*]

7.1. INTRODUCTION

There is a compelling case for the claim that there is a human right to basic necessities, given the devastating impact the lack of them has on persons' interests and the threat it poses to their lives. Moreover, there has been widespread international acknowledgment of such a right. A right to basic necessities is a claim right, and it therefore entails corresponding duties. This means that genuinely acknowledging this right requires specifying and enforcing those duties. However, there has been very little agreement about what they are and who has responsibility for fulfilling them. More than a billion people currently live on less than $1 per day international poverty line (specified at purchasing power parity 1993) below which 'a minimum, nutritionally adequate diet plus essential non-food requirements are not affordable' (UNDP 1996: 222).[1] Therefore, depending on what duties are in fact imposed by the human right to basic necessities, this situation could constitute one of the largest-scale deprivations of a basic human right there has ever been, both in absolute terms and in terms of the percentage of the population affected.[2] I argue that on each of the two main rival accounts of the grounding of human rights, the human right to basic necessities imposes both negative and positive duties. I also argue that ultimate responsibility for implementing both kinds of duties lies largely with citizens in affluent countries.

It is uncontroversial that the human right to basic necessities imposes a negative duty not to deprive persons of access to basic necessities. Nevertheless, as

[*] I am grateful to Simon Caney, Roger Crisp, Rowan Cruft, Brad Hooker, Susan Mendus, David Miller, Derek Parfit, and John Tasioulas for their helpful comments. I am particularly grateful to Thomas Pogge, Christopher R. Taylor, and Leif Wenar for their extremely astute and extensive comments on several drafts.

[1] There is strong argument that the official World Bank figure underestimates the actual number; see Reddy and Pogge (2007).

[2] Of course, huge numbers of people have lacked basic necessities throughout history, but, as I argue, whether this lack constitutes a human rights deprivation depends on whether agents have causal responsibility for this situation and on the ease with which persons' access to basic necessities could be secured.

Thomas Pogge argues in this volume and elsewhere, wide-scale violations of this negative duty have not been adequately acknowledged (Pogge 2002*a*). I argue that part of the reason such violations tend not to be sufficiently recognized is because they generally do not conform to our commonsense conception of a human rights violation, but that there are compelling reasons for revising this conception.

I then turn to the question of whether the human right to basic necessities also imposes a positive duty to protect persons' opportunity for earning a subsistence income and to provide basic necessities to those unable to provide them for themselves. I argue that on a Kantian deontological account of the grounding of human rights, as well as on a utilitarian account, the human right to basic necessities also imposes positive duties.

In section 7.2, I discuss the concept of human rights, and in light of this, in section 7.3, I briefly consider the groundings of human rights. In section 7.4, I discuss the negative duties imposed by the human right to basic necessities. I then argue in section 7.5 that the human right to basic necessities imposes positive duties.

7.2. THE CONCEPT OF HUMAN RIGHTS

Human rights are a set of urgent and rock bottom moral claims against others that every human being has simply in virtue of their humanity. Moral rights are held by the right-holder in virtue of the right-holder's moral status. I am taking human rights to be distinguished from other moral rights in three principal respects: first, they mark out those rights that are particularly morally urgent and basic; second, they ought to be enforced; and third, they are rights that are held by everyone in virtue of the universal moral status of human beings.

Thus, the only underlying assumption behind the claim that there are certain human rights is that each person without exception has moral status and can therefore justifiably demand not to be treated in ways that are fundamentally incompatible with that moral status. As Henry Shue argues, basic rights designate the 'lower limits on tolerable human conduct', the 'morality of the depths' as opposed to exalted ideals (Shue 1996*a*: 18).

Most important rights are at their core claim rights, which conceptually entail corresponding duties: they are justified claims to something, and they are justified claims against some duty-bearer(s) to perform or refrain from some action.[3] A human right to basic necessities will be in this category. Specifying a particular claim right therefore requires specifying both the object of the right (i.e., what it is a right to) and the duties it generates. It should be noted, though, that while claim

---

[3] It is plausible that all basic rights include duties as at least one of their second-party correlatives. For example, the right to vote is at its core a liberty right, but it also imposes negative duties not to threaten or interfere with persons' voting and positive duties to enable the right-holder to exercise the right by, e.g., providing registration forms and ballot papers.

rights conceptually entail corresponding duties, identifying which duties a claim right imposes is a substantive question that cannot be determined by conceptual analysis of the right alone.

Human rights claims are claims of basic justice. Each person is entitled to the objects of their human rights and can justifiably insist on them as their due. These claims ought to be institutionally guaranteed, but since human rights are grounded in fundamental moral principles they are independent of established institutional standards. For this reason, a central function of human rights is to evaluate existing social institutions: a test of whether any institution is minimally just is whether it acknowledges human rights. For example, societies that legalized slavery clearly failed that test and were fundamentally unjust.

However, it is a disputed question whether human rights are claims only on social institutions. Pogge has helpfully introduced a distinction between what he terms 'the institutional' and 'the interactional' conceptions of human rights. According to the institutional conception, human rights are claims on social institutions. It should be stressed that on the institutional view human rights do impose duties on private individuals, since, as Pogge argues, claims on social institutions are also indirectly claims against those who participate in upholding those social institutions (Pogge 2002*a*). On the institutional view, though, these duties are held in virtue of the duty-bearer's belonging to the same institutional scheme as the right-holder.

According to the interactional conception, human rights are claims directly on the conduct of individual and social agents, and these claims apply even in the absence of a common institutional background. The interactional conception will hold, though, that social institutions have a uniquely important practical role in enforcing and implementing the duties imposed by human rights, and that, conversely, they tend to have the greatest power to violate persons' rights.

The two accounts agree, therefore, both that social institutions play a crucial role in securing or violating human rights and that private individuals as well as officials have responsibility for fulfilling the duties imposed by human rights. Where they differ is over whether this responsibility is always based on the duty-bearer's belonging to the same institutional scheme as the right-holder.

It is not plausible to build into the concept of human rights that they are claims only on social institutions. If we took it to be a conceptual constraint on human rights that they are addressed only against institutions, then an isolated incidence of severe domestic violence or of parents starving their children could not qualify as a human rights violation. However, many would consider these to be human rights violations, and do not seem to be misusing the term 'human rights'. Moreover, it is possible to combine the institutional and interactional accounts of human rights. I argue for such a combined account: I argue that human rights are claims directly on private individuals as well as social institutions, but that the institutional account provides a particularly perspicuous account of the nature of many of the duties generated by human rights.

7.3. THE GROUNDINGS OF HUMAN RIGHTS

Human rights, then, are a set of rock bottom moral claims that every human being can justifiably insist on in virtue of the moral status they have as human beings.[4] The UDHR reflects this when it asserts the equal moral value of every human being. In order for a theory of justice to capture the notion of human rights, therefore, it must base them on a credible account of the universal moral status of human beings.

The two most plausible grounds for this universal moral status are, first, each person's capacity for well-being or suffering, and, second, each person's dignity in virtue of their rational autonomous agency. Appeals to fundamental human interests and to human dignity and autonomy have therefore played a prominent role in human rights documents. However, in order to specify and justify the human rights that are grounded in these values, we need to look at the basic moral principles that underlie such human rights. First, these grounds of human rights need to be made more specific; the notion of human dignity, in particular, is too vague to determine the content of human rights. Second, in order to establish the duties imposed by human rights, we need to examine questions of responsibility and of what constitutes a reasonable obligation.

I focus on the two main rival impartial moral theories, utilitarianism and Kantianism, founded on each of these two grounds of the universal moral status of human beings, respectively. These are the two theories historically most closely connected with the human rights tradition. They are the most famous representatives of the two main accounts of the functions of rights, the interest theory and the will theory. (Though given that both interests and autonomy play a central role in both theories' accounts of human rights, as I shortly discuss, these labels for them are perhaps rather misleading.) The interest theory of human rights takes their role to be to protect persons' basic interests, and the will theory takes their role to be to protect the right-holder's control and liberties. Most importantly, utilitarianism and Kantianism are also the dominant representatives of the two main rival moral frameworks, consequentialism and deontology, which offer the most straightforward and in my view the most plausible versions of the two main theories of the justification of human rights, instrumentalist and status theories. Instrumentalist theories take human rights to be valuable because of their role in promoting and protecting core interests. Status theories by contrast take them to be intrinsically valuable because they express the value of each person as a rational autonomous agent and an end in himself or herself; according to status theories, to respect a person's right is to respect that person's sovereignty and inviolability.

---

[4] According to both the utilitarian and the Kantian accounts of human rights, the term 'human' refers to persons rather than to members of the species *Homo sapiens*. Moreover, according to utilitarianism the moral status of persons is grounded in their capacity for well-being and suffering, and since this capacity is shared in varying degrees by every sentient being, moral status is not unique to persons (though persons have a special moral status in virtue of their particularly rich capacity for well-being and suffering, and human rights correspondingly have a special moral urgency).

My own view is that the most credible theory of human rights integrates a utilitarian and Kantian account of them, since persons' moral status is most plausibly taken to be grounded both on the moral importance of their interests and their dignity as rational autonomous agents, and each of these features calls for a distinct moral response; well-being calls for concern to promote it, while persons' dignity and sovereignty calls for respect. What I want to argue here, though, is that both of these theories, despite being the main representatives of the two main rival moral frameworks, lead to the same conclusion about the duties imposed by the human right to basic necessities.

While utilitarianism and Kantianism are the most famous representatives of the interest theory and will theory, respectively, both interests and liberties play a central role in each theory's account of human rights. Choosing one's own course through life is a central component of a plausible conception of human well-being. Utilitarians therefore emphasize the essential role that safeguarding liberties will play in protecting persons' basic interests. On Mill's view, liberties are in fact necessary conditions for the realization of the higher pleasures that fulfill our natures 'as progressive beings', and these higher pleasures trump lower pleasures. Conversely, since respecting persons as rational autonomous agents involves both respecting the rational ends they have set themselves and ensuring the preconditions for their successful pursuit, and since basic interests are universal human ends or are preconditions for the pursuit of any ends, this will centrally involve protecting such basic interests.

The core difference between the two theories lies, then, with their different accounts of the justification of human rights. Utilitarianism takes human rights to be valuable as protections of persons' basic interests. Accordingly, utilitarianism takes autonomy to be morally important in virtue of being a central component of persons' well-being, which, along with other core interests, should be protected and promoted. Kantianism, on the other hand, takes human rights to express the intrinsic dignity and sovereignty of persons as rational autonomous beings. It takes autonomy to be the ground of human dignity, and takes the appropriate response to this dignity to be respect.

The most significant normative implication of these different justifications of human rights concerns the debate over whether human rights impose positive as well as negative duties. Within this debate, the distinction between positive and negative duties is generally drawn in terms of the distinction between the duty to actively aid someone and the duty to refrain from interfering in someone's life in such a way as to cause them to be significantly worse off than they would have been without the agent's intervention. Positive duties, then, require the agent to take certain positive actions, whereas negative duties are duties to forbear from initiating a threatening causal sequence of events. Deontological accounts tend to draw a sharp distinction between the moral urgency of positive and negative duties, on the ground that active harms express greater disrespect than do failures to provide assistance. By contrast, a central feature of consequentialist moral theories is that there is no intrinsic moral distinction between positive and negative duties, given that their consequences, which may be identical, determine their moral value.

The deontological conception of human rights is much more in line with the traditional conception, according to which human rights are taken to be, most fundamentally, claims against being harmed in certain serious ways (being killed, assaulted, and so on). I should therefore briefly discuss why utilitarianism can nevertheless be viewed as also offering a forceful account of human rights.

Utilitarianism holds that agents must take as much responsibility for harms they allow as for harms they cause, given that their impact on persons' interests is the same in both cases. It takes human rights to be protections of the right-holder's basic interests. Since these basic interests may be just as threatened by omissions as by actions, utilitarianism takes human rights to comprise protections against omissions just as much as against active harms. This is one of the most important challenges utilitarianism presents to the traditional conception of human rights, which takes them to generate primarily negative duties.

On a utilitarian analysis, human rights are particularly heavyweight contenders against rival moral claims but are not immune to trade-offs. Given the importance of the interests they protect, it will take them to be resistant to trade-offs. On a credible conception of measuring well-being, moreover, there is discontinuity in value between basic interests and relatively trivial interests.[5] This means that one person's human right could never be outweighed by any number of others' trivial interests. However, according to utilitarianism, human rights are not immune from trade-offs, on the ground that the basic interests protected by human rights could be outweighed by the comparably serious interests of several others. From the utilitarian point of view, such trade-offs between different persons' interests cannot be avoided, given that we have to take just as much responsibility for harms we allow as for harms we ourselves actively cause. The importance of protecting one person's basic interests must therefore always be weighed up against the cost this would impose on others, since we have to take full responsibility for that cost.

Utilitarianism accordingly holds that the specification and justification of a human right must depend not only on the importance of the interests it would protect but also on the cost that protecting these interests would impose on others. The question of what human rights there are will be determined by examining how much sacrifice would be required from how many for the sake of how much gain for how many. The utilitarian will argue that it is for this reason that it is not plausible to think there is a general human right to life, if we specify such a right as a universal claim on others to ensure that one's life be preserved. While it is not hard to show the importance of the content of such a right, there are situations in which it would be so costly for society to do whatever was needed to try to keep some persons alive that these duties would not be reasonable, such as, for example, if they were suffering from very rare medical conditions that would be so expensive to research and treat that this would impose significant costs on a

---

[5] This is still compatible with taking the moral goal to be maximizing overall well-being, though it will not take such maximization to consist in promoting the greatest net sum total of welfare; see Griffin (1986).

huge number of others. Given the small number of people affected by this kind of medical condition and the large cost to others of treating it, these persons might not have a human right to such treatment. The utilitarian will also argue that for the same reason the right to life must impose positive as well as negative duties when the cost of saving someone's life is small.

By contrast, since Kantian accounts of human rights take them to be expressive of persons' dignity, they tend to hold that there is an important distinction between the moral urgency of positive and negative duties, on the ground that failure to comply with negative duties expresses greater disrespect than failure to comply with positive ones when the impact on the interests of the person affected is the same in each case. I argue, though, that on a Kantian as well as a utilitarian account of human rights, positive duties to secure persons' access to basic necessities are sufficiently morally urgent to constitute human rights claims. I also discuss Onora O'Neill's influential Kantian argument that rights to assistance, unlike traditional negative rights not to be actively harmed in various ways, cannot be genuine until institutional structures are in place that specify and allocate their corresponding duties. I argue that in the absence of just institutions, many of the most important negative duties imposed by human rights are in fact imperfect in nature in just the same way as positive duties of aid, and that this undermines the sharp distinction O'Neill draws between rights to assistance and negative rights.

We can now turn to the human right to basic necessities. Since specifying a particular claim right requires specifying both the object of the right (i.e., to what it is a right) and the duties it generates, justifying such a right correspondingly also has two components. First, it requires establishing the importance of the object of the right. Second, it requires showing that the duties generated by the right can reasonably be imposed on agents.

The importance of the object of the human right to basic necessities is indisputable. When people lack secure access to basic necessities their lives are drastically impoverished and stunted. Chronic poverty imposes very severe restrictions on the range of options they can pursue. It may undermine their most central goals and commitments that are absolutely integral to their ability to live out their conception of a decent life, such as their goal of raising flourishing children if, for example, they are unable to provide their children with the food or basic medical care they need for health or even survival. Malnutrition can cause chronic lethargy, which restricts persons' ability to pursue any activity. It can moreover cause brain damage and so permanently impair persons' rational autonomous faculties, and it can cause other permanent debilities. It can also cause extreme physical pain (from hunger or disease) and mental pain (e.g., through the preventable death of several close family members). Lack of basic necessities can therefore preclude a minimally decent and autonomous life. It can also deprive people of their lives themselves: chronic severe poverty is currently the cause of eighteen million deaths per year.

The key moral questions, however, concern what duties might be imposed by the human right to basic necessities, and who has responsibility for fulfilling those duties. The human right to basic necessities can be divided into a negative right not to be actively deprived of access to basic necessities, and a positive right to be guaranteed access to basic necessities to a reasonable level of security. I discuss the plausibility of the negative right and the positive right in turn. In section 7.4, I discuss negative duties not to deprive people of their means of subsistence, and in section 7.5, I turn to the question of whether the human right to basic necessities also imposes a positive duty to promote and protect persons' access to basic necessities.

7.4. NEGATIVE DUTIES

It has been widely argued that persons' lack of secure access to basic necessities results principally not from famine or other natural disasters, but from their coming to be actively deprived of any realistic chance of earning a subsistence income. This deprivation tends to involve a complex web of causal factors, including in particular the operation of unjust social institutions under which persons are deprived of access to a fair share of natural resources and of adequate economic entitlements. Moreover, it is uncontentious that a minimal acknowledgment of the universal moral status of human beings entails acknowledging certain constraints against inflicting very serious harms on anyone. For example, it is uncontroversial that every human being has a right not to be enslaved, nor to suffer a physical assault that causes brain damage or other permanent serious injury, nor to be killed. Given the impact on persons' lives of lacking access to basic necessities, the harms inflicted on them by actively depriving them of secure access to basic necessities are as serious as those inflicted by slavery, grievous physical assault, or genocide: as we have seen, lack of basic necessities can preclude a minimally decent and autonomous life, can cause brain damage and other permanent debilities, and leads to eighteen million deaths per year.[6] It is therefore clear that minimal acknowledgment of the moral status conferred on each person by the importance of their interests and their dignity as rational autonomous agents entails the negative duty not to deprive persons of access to basic necessities, and that violations of this duty can constitute human rights violations. What is more controversial is the implication of acknowledging this negative duty.

   This will depend first on views about who has primary responsibility for persons' coming to be deprived of secure access to basic necessities. There is a widespread view that corrupt and non-democratic leaders have primary responsibility for such deprivations. However, there are compelling arguments that the role played by these leaders is in fact only a part of the causal story, and that the global

---

[6] WHO (2004: 120–5). Admittedly, causing a huge number of deaths may not fit the legal definition of genocide as denoting the intentional extermination of a certain racial group. However, when term 'genocide' is applied in the context of assessing the moral gravity of human rights violations, so as to decide what political action is called for, the most important notion is that of mass killing. In this context, disputes over whether an instance of mass killing fits the more technical definition of genocide can seem beside the point.

institutional order also plays a crucial causal role in the current level of chronic severe poverty (see Pogge 2002).

Second, though, it will also depend on our conception of the nature of a human right violation. The causal chains that lead to particular individuals' coming to be deprived of access to basic necessities are generally extremely complex, and for that reason diverge considerably from our paradigm conception of a human right violation. According to this paradigm, the negative duties imposed by human rights are taken to be specific, clear-cut prohibitions on certain kinds of actions (duties not to kill, assault, and so on). Allocating responsibility for the violation of a negative right is seen as a matter of identifying the perpetrator(s) of that violation, where the perpetrator is taken to be the agent or agents who violated such a prohibition and so can be singled out as solely or primarily responsible for inflicting a specific harm on a particular victim. I conform to this standard usage of the term 'perpetrator'.

It follows from this conception of a human rights violation that in order for a harm to count as a human rights violation it must be possible to identify the perpetrator(s) of that violation: there must be a particular agent or agents who can be assigned primary causal and moral responsibility for the serious harm suffered by the victim. It also follows that when we assign responsibility for a human rights violation, we ought to focus largely or even exclusively on those perpetrators.

The causal chains that lead to a particular farmer's coming to be deprived of any realistic chance of earning a subsistence income are so complicated that it is often hard or even impossible to trace responsibility for a specific person's coming to lack secure access to basic necessities to any particular agent. These causal chains therefore do not fit our paradigm conception of a human rights violation, and it is for this reason, I suggest, that we tend not to view them as constituting a human rights violation. If a victim's death or permanent debility results from a particular agent's (or agents') violating a clear-cut prohibition against murder or assault then we do recognize this harm as a human right violation. However, when a victim's death or permanent debility results from an extremely complex causal chain culminating in that person's coming to be deprived of their subsistence income, we generally fail to recognize the harm as a human right violation. It is also because of the influence of the paradigm, I suggest, that where we do recognize violations of the human right to basic necessities, it tends to be by virtue of our assigning responsibility for such violations to corrupt leaders in poor countries and identifying them as the perpetrators, because their causal role in the chronic poverty of their citizens tends to be particularly salient, even when it is in fact only a part of the causal story.

I argue, however, that there are compelling reasons for revising our paradigm conception of a human rights violation. This paradigm was appropriate to settings in which most agents' behavior had an impact only on the small group of individuals with whom they personally interacted, but it is now outmoded and ill-suited to the modern context of our behavior. Increasingly, many of most serious and prevalent harms to persons' basic interests and autonomy result from extremely complex causal chains in which the actions of millions of agents are implicated, few or none of whom can be singled out as responsible for a specific serious harm to a specific victim.[7]

I argue that there can be clear cases of violations of negative human rights in which the causal chains that lead to the harms are such that none of the agents who contribute to them can be singled out as solely or primarily responsible for a serious harm to any specific victim. In such cases, then, direct responsibility for a human rights violation lies exclusively with agents who cannot be identified as the perpetrators of it, in the standard sense of the word. I therefore claim that when we assign direct responsibility for a human rights violation, our focus should often be much broader than identifying the perpetrator.

I then argue that when it comes to assigning overall responsibility for a human rights violation, we should often focus not only on the agents who are directly responsible for the violation but also on those who share indirect responsibility for it. Even if it is possible to identify specific individuals as the perpetrators of a human rights violation, other agents may have made an important indirect contribution to these violations, by, for example, supporting social institutions within which such violations are encouraged or even play a systematic role. Furthermore, as Pogge's institutional account of human rights makes clear, there is a central aspect of human rights violations that cannot be captured in terms of specific harmful actions performed by specific agents at all. Rather, the violations are also constituted by a system of laws and other social institutions. This means that if we exclusively focus on the perpetrators of specific harmful actions in assigning responsibility for human rights violations, we will fail to acknowledge altogether a central aspect of these violations. I further argue that when serious harms result from the operation of unjust social institutions, the content of the negative duties that these unjust social institutions impose on those who participate in them is often neither obvious nor specific.

If we do revise the paradigm, we should be open to the possibility that the complex causal chains that ultimately lead to millions' being deprived of secure access to basic necessities constitute a violation of an urgent negative right on a vast scale, and that responsibility for this violation is shared by millions of agents who causally contribute to it, either directly or indirectly. However, in order to establish that these agents' behavior does in fact constitute a human rights violation, it must be shown, third, that it is reasonable to hold them morally responsible for their causal contribution to the harm. I argue that on both the institutional and interactional accounts of human rights, a huge number of agents can reasonably be held to share moral as well as causal responsibility for the current high level of chronic poverty, including, to some extent at least, most citizens in affluent countries. I should stress, though, that the various agents who contribute to the causal chains have very different degrees of moral responsibility, and that the

---

[7] Along similar lines, Samuel Scheffler argues that we ought to revise our commonsense conception of moral responsibility in Scheffler (2001). See in particular ch. 2, 'Individual Responsibility in a Global Age' (originally published in Scheffler 1995).

behavior of almost all of them is far less blameworthy than that of those who perpetrate paradigmatic human rights violations; in fact, I argue that we should move away from the conception of human rights violations as necessarily or even standardly reflecting an unusual and vicious character.

As I argue, utilitarianism strongly supports this revision of our paradigm conception of a human right violation. Nevertheless, a common Kantian conception of the duties imposed by human rights is very much in line with the traditional paradigm conception. This is the Kantian conception that Onora O'Neill, for example, appeals to in her famous Kantian critique of welfare rights. I argue that this conception is based on an overly narrow view of the relations between agents and victims that focuses on the relations between a specific agent and a specific victim, and overlooks relations between a large group of agents and a large group of victims. While the former focus is appropriate to small-scale social settings in which the agent is directly interacting with a few individuals, it is inappropriate to the much more complex relations between agents and victims that now form the backdrop of much of our behavior. I argue that a plausible version of Kantian deontology needs to accommodate these more complex relations between agents and victims, and that when it does, this will lead to a Kantian account of the negative duties imposed by human rights that is much broader than the one O'Neill assumes. Moreover, on this broader account, many negative duties imposed by human rights will be seen to be close in nature to positive duties, and, as I argue in section 7.5, this undermines the contrast Onora O'Neill draws between positive and negative rights.

In section 7.4.1, I discuss the primary causes of the current level of chronic poverty. I then (in section 7.4.2) discuss why I take our commonsense paradigm conception of a human rights violation to be inadequate, once the complexity of the causal chains that lead to many of the most serious and prevalent contemporary harms is addressed. Third (in section 7.4.3), I discuss the question of whether the agents who contribute to the causal chains that lead to chronic severe poverty should be held morally responsible for this contribution. Finally (in section 7.4.4), I turn to the implications of this revision of the paradigm for the utilitarian and Kantian accounts of the duties imposed by human rights.

7.4.1. The Primary Causes of Chronic Severe Poverty

It has been forcefully argued that the global institutional order plays a crucial causal role in the current level of chronic severe poverty. Thomas Pogge points out, for example, that the International Resource Privilege as it is currently defined, which guarantees rich countries a cheap supply of resources, also greatly encourages and facilitates the exercise of non-democratic power that is so closely correlated with chronic severe poverty (Pogge 2002*a*). This privilege accrues to anyone holding effective power, however undemocratic and repressive they are, entitling them to sell off their country's resources. Non-democratic rulers have a strong incentive to compete with other markets to sell off their country's resources cheaply in order to gain as much short-term profit as possible and to spend the money on buying off the military and their cronies and strengthening their power base. By contrast, these leaders tend to have little incentive to distribute the resources to poor, powerless citizens, to ensure they have opportunities to make a living, and to conserve their country's resources for the sake of its long-term financial interests, since they are not democratically accountable. The privilege can also destabilize struggling democracies because it provides a constant, very strong financial incentive for the undemocratic takeover of power. Pogge suggests specific measures to limit the anti-democratic incentives the privilege generates. The arms trade is another factor that significantly affects the capacity of non-democratic rulers to drain their country's resources and to hold onto power through internal repression, while bringing huge revenue to affluent countries.

There is therefore a cogent case for the claim that a predictable result of the conjunction of all these kinds of factors is that the chronically poor are largely forcibly deprived of their fair share of the benefits of natural resources and of fair opportunities to make a living, while a grossly disproportionate share of those benefits is funneled to Third World elites, oppressive governments, and affluent countries and corporations. Another predictable result is that the chronically poor are deprived of their democratic rights that would enable them to effectively demand a subsistence income. Furthermore, while the affluent get most of the benefits of exploiting natural resources, the chronically poor who are largely excluded from those benefits often suffer the worst effects of the resulting pollution.

While these empirical claims may be contested, it is important to examine what follows from accepting them, given their potential moral significance. I therefore now explore the moral implications of assuming these empirical claims. I begin by arguing that we should revise our paradigm conception of a human rights violation.

7.4.2. The Inadequacy of the Commonsense Paradigm Conception of a Human Rights Violation

I now argue that in assigning direct responsibility for a human rights violation, it may be the case that we should not focus primarily or even at all on agents who can be identified as perpetrators. I examine two common kinds of causal chains such that for many or even all of the agents who contribute to them, these agents cannot be singled out as individually responsible for any specific serious harm to any specific victim and so identified as perpetrators: causal chains that involve additive and multiplicative harms. In both cases, the behavior of each individual agent on its own does not cause a serious harm to any individual. I argue that both cases can nevertheless constitute human rights violations.

I then argue that the other respect in which a focus on the perpetrator(s) is too narrow in assigning overall responsibility for a human rights violation is that it overlooks the extremely important role played by those who have indirect responsibility for the violation, by supporting institutional structures that foreseeably lead to high levels of such violations or themselves constitute a human rights violation. Finally, I turn to the other feature of our paradigm conception of the negative duties imposed by human rights, according to which the content of these duties is obvious and specific, and argue that many of the most important negative duties imposed by human rights lack this feature.

7.4.2.1. *Direct Responsibility for Human Rights Violations*

Additive Harms

In some cases, for many or all the agents who contribute to a causal chain that leads to a serious harm, the effect of each of these agent's behavior is very thinly spread over millions of victims and therefore does not in itself cause a serious harm to any particular victim, even when the cumulative effect of the behavior of all these agents is an extremely serious harm to a huge number of victims.

In this kind of case, we cannot single out any agent as specifically responsible for any particular victim's suffering a serious harm. It might be argued that, for precisely this reason, such cases could not qualify as human rights violations. We think of human rights violations as crimes that can be prosecuted in a traditional criminal court, but this involves attempting to identify who is solely or primarily responsible for the serious harm that the claimant has suffered. Certainly, in current criminal courts we need to be able to identify the victim and the violator.

The problem with this argument, though, can be illustrated with a thought experiment that is a variation of Derek Parfit's 'harmless torturers' example (Parfit 1984: 80–1). Consider 'The Torturers' Union': a group of torturers fear they may one day be prosecuted for human rights violations. They therefore arrange a new system whereby they act together in such a way that the electric shock each administers is spread out over a huge number of prisoners and so causes only a very small incremental amount of pain to each of the prisoners, though the total quantity of pain inflicted by each torturer and suffered by each prisoner remains the same as under the previous system. Since the pain any one of the agents causes to any particular prisoner is very small, it is not possible to allocate responsibility for the extreme pain any of the prisoners suffers to any particular agent. This is not just the epistemic problem that it is hard to discover which victim is affected by the behavior of any particular agent. Rather, none of the agents is responsible for a serious harm to any one of the victims. Moreover, if any one agent withdrew from participating in the causal chain, none of the victims would suffer significantly less. It is therefore impossible even in principle to identify a particular agent as causally responsible for any particular victim's suffering a human rights violation. Nevertheless, clearly the behavior of these agents should still be classified as torture and as a human rights violation.

I now consider some further variations of the example. Suppose, first, there are many more agents inflicting the pain than victims, so that the total quantity of pain each agent administers is very small. This does not plausibly prevent these agents' behavior from counting as a human rights violation; just as, if a large number of agents beat to death a single victim, their behavior counts as a human rights violation even if the harm each agent administers, taken in isolation, is not very serious.

Suppose now that there is the same number of agents inflicting the pain as victims, but some of the agents deliver a much smaller amount of shock than the others, so that the total amount of pain these agents administer is very small. Again, it does not seem plausible to deny that these agents are guilty of a human rights violation, though in this case they should be assigned a smaller degree of responsibility for it than the others; just as, again, if a group of agents beat someone to death, one of the agents cannot plausibly appeal to the fact that others inflicted much more serious blows than she did in order to deny that she shares responsibility for the human rights violation, though she can plausibly hold others to be more responsible for it.

In the cases I have been considering so far, the overall harm is the deliberate action of an organized group. The agents have coordinated their action so as to inflict severe pain on each of the prisoners. It might be argued that it is only for this reason that each of the agents involved can be held responsible for the overall harm they together cause. I therefore consider some variations on the example, to examine the degree of deliberate coordination among a group of agents that is required if we are to hold members of the group responsible for an additive harm.

Let us therefore consider a further variation of the example, and suppose that those administering the electric shock have not set up the arrangement them-selves, and work in isolation from each other. The arrangement has been set up that way by other people in order to minimize the psychological impact of the job and so encourage recruitment and retention. Let us assume that those administering the electric shocks do not like to see themselves as torturers and do not intend the serious pain the victims suffer, and are able to do the job because they are each rightly told that their individual job does not cause anyone a significant amount of pain. Nevertheless, the overall harm the prisoners suffer is clear.

It is still plausible to hold each of them responsible for their share of the overall harm they are together causing because the harm results from an ongoing practice in which they are each participating. Although in this case they are not aiming at the harm or deliberately coordinating their actions to cause it, to hold them responsible for the harm it is enough that it foreseeably results from the ongo-ing practice of which they are members, and that they each could have avoided participating in that practice.

I finally consider one further variation, in which the causal chain that leads to the victims' pain is even more complex. In this case the agents are each allo-cated responsibility for manufacturing or maintaining different components of the torture equipment, and the actual infliction of the pain is done by robots. Moreover, the manufacture of different components is done in different factories. Let us suppose that the agents each focus their attention on the technical details of the functioning of a particular component part and are not actually aware of the overall harm the equipment causes, though they have strong reason to suspect it, and there are human rights organizations directed at providing information about the harms these kinds of jobs cause. Let us suppose they remain willfully ignorant because it is a well-paid job, and it would be hard to find alternative employment.

Although in this case the agents are not acting as a coordinated group, and none of them is directly inflicting any pain at all, it still does not seem plausible to deny that this counts as a human rights violation. Again, it is enough that they are each participating in an ongoing practice that foreseeably leads to the serious harm to a large number of victims, and that they each ought to be aware of the harm they are together causing by maintaining the machinery, and each could have acted otherwise.

These examples indicate that it is not plausible to claim that serious harms can only count as human rights violations unless we can identify the agent or agents specifically responsible for any particular victim's suffering from such a harm. Rather, if a large number of agents contribute to a complex causal chain that ultimately leads to very serious harms, this can constitute a human rights violation provided the agents either know about those harms or are culpably ignorant of them. Although usually we can identify perpetrators of violations of the human right not be tortured, the Torturers' Union et al. examples indicate that the status of torture as a human right violation does not depend on our being able to identify the perpetrators.

I now turn to the second kind of case in which the agent's behavior leads to a serious harm only in conjunction with the behavior of another agent or agents: multiplicative harms.

Multiplicative Harms

In the case of multiplicative harms, the main effect of a contributing causal factor is to magnify the harm caused by another agent or agents. On its own, it would not cause a significant harm. Furthermore, there might be circumstances under which it would even be beneficial. However, when it operates in conjunction with that other agent or agents it is predictable that the combined effect will be an extremely serious harm.

Pogge gives an example that illustrates the implausibility of denying that multiplicative harms constitute human rights violations (Pogge 2005a: 48). If a factory negligently causes pollution that predictably leads to wide-scale death and severe health problems among the local population, the factory owner is likely to be held responsible for a human rights violation. Let us now suppose that there are two factories pouring pollutants into the same river, where the two kinds of pollutant mix. The pollution produced by either of the factories in isolation would not cause any harm at all. However, the two kinds of pollutants in combination form a lethal cocktail that, as with the previous example, leads to wide-scale death and severe health problems. Consequently, for each of the factory owners it is entirely predictable that if they both pollute the river, the overall result will be devastating. If it counts as a human rights violation for one factory to cause such harms, it is not plausible to deny that it counts as a human rights violation for the two factories in conjunction to cause them. Again, then, this behavior counts as a human rights violation even though no serious harm can be traced to the behavior of each agent considered in isolation.

In the case we have considered so far, the harm to individual victims each factory owner causes, given that the other factory owner is also releasing a pollutant, is so serious that it is still plausible to hold each of them responsible for causing very serious harms to specific victims. It therefore may be possible to identify both of them as perpetrators of human rights violations. Nevertheless, this is an important departure from our traditional paradigm conception of a perpetrator, given that each agent's responsibility for the human right violation is based not on the harm that can be attributed to his own behavior in isolation but on the predictable overall impact of his behavior when conjoined with the behavior of the other agent. (As Pogge points out, a common argument for the refusal to accept responsibility for contributing to the high level of chronic poverty is to point out that the poverty would not have occurred if it were not for other causal factors.)

Moreover, when multiplicative harms occur in large-scale contexts, those responsible for such harms diverge even more significantly from our paradigm conception of perpetrators. Let us now turn to a case in which multiplicative harms are a large-scale phenomenon. Let us suppose the pollution is caused by a huge number of factories. Suppose too that the pollution they each cause in isolation causes no serious health problems. Nevertheless, it is entirely predictable that when all these pollutants mix their chemical combination will have the same devastating effect on the local population. Those whose lives are devastated by the serious health problems that they are suffering and by the deaths of their relatives caused as a result of the pollution can plausibly complain that their negative rights are being violated. However, in this case, while we can identify the group of factory owners as sharing responsibility for all the human rights violations, the causal effect that any one of these factories in isolation has on any particular victim is not salient or significant enough to identify them as the perpetrator of that particular victim's right's violation. In the absence of institutional arrangements to determine how the shared responsibility for the harm is allocated among the factory owners in order to redress the claims of those harmed, it is indeterminate against which particular agent or agents a particular victim has a claim. All we can say is that this victim, along with all the other victims, has a claim against the whole group of factory owners.

I conclude that direct responsibility for human rights violations may be very broadly shared, and need not lie solely or at all with agents who can be identified as perpetrators. The level of responsibility for a human rights violation held by the agents who causally contribute to it in such cases is a complex issue and is very much a matter of degree. It should be stressed, though, that moral responsibility does not simply distribute in such cases. For example, the fact that two persons planned and executed a murder together does not entail that each bears less moral responsibility than a single-handed murderer would bear. Aggregate moral responsibility can thus be superproportional to aggregate harm.

7.4.2.2. *Indirect Responsibility for Human Rights Violations*

The other respect in which an exclusive focus on the perpetrators of human rights violations is too narrow is that it ignores the central role played by those who indirectly contribute to such violations. First, even if we consider cases in which we can identify specific individuals as the perpetrators of a human rights violation, it is not adequate to limit our focus to them in assigning overall responsibility for such violations. Let us consider the example of torture. When this right it violated, it is generally easy (in principle at least) to identify the perpetrators of the violation: the agents who actually commit the torture. However, the duty not to perpetrate torture is not the only negative duty generated by this right. The human right not to be tortured is most plausibly taken to be a claim to a reasonable level of security against being tortured. If so, then it must generate a negative duty not to reduce persons' security against being tortured.

This centrally includes a duty not to support institutional arrangements that foreseeably lead to a high incidence of torture. We therefore need to look at the political structures within which torture is encouraged or even plays a systematic role. It is worth noting in this context that some victims of torture have subsequently described their torturers as themselves the victims of a system, on the ground that these torturers had been systematically brutalized and indoctrinated.

This negative duty therefore implicates international institutional features that support such structures, such as the International Resource Privilege in conjunction with the arms trade, or, even more directly, the substantial 'security' aid given to regimes known to commit systematic torture. It also implicates institutional cultures in which torture is encouraged or ordered. We therefore need to address the broader institutional factors that reduce persons' security against such violations. Those who collaborate in and support these institutional factors share indirect responsibility for the perpetrations of human rights violations that occur.

Second, human rights violations may not just consist in specific harmful actions but may be importantly constituted by social institutions themselves. The plausibility of this can be illustrated with the example of slavery. The interactional account of human rights is correct, in my view, to hold that private individual agents who owned slaves were in so doing directly committing a human rights violation, independently of their belonging to the same institutional scheme as their slaves. (In the same way, I suggest, if a group of bandits operating completely outside the law were to enslave members of a remote island with no institutional links with the outside world, it would not be plausible to deny that this constitutes a human rights violation.) However, as the institutional account makes clear, neither is it plausible to think of the human rights violation of slavery as just comprising specific wrongs against slaves committed by their owners. As Pogge argues, slavery was not simply a popular crime committed by specific individuals. It also comprised a set of laws and social arrangements under which slaves were classified as property.[8]

---

[8] Pogge discusses this example in *Realizing Rawls* (1989: 27), and in 'O'Neill on Rights and Duties', (1992*b*: 233–47).

Responsibility for these laws lay with the citizens who sustained them. Therefore the human right not to be enslaved imposed on citizens a negative duty not to collaborate in the imposition of these laws, over and above the duty not to own slaves themselves. A wealthy citizen in the mid-nineteenth century United States, for example, was likely to have been deeply implicated in slavery even if he avoided owning slaves. His prosperity would have probably been dependent on the economic opportunities afforded by living in a society that relied on slave labor. Furthermore, in his everyday activities such as buying a cotton shirt he would be both supporting and benefiting from slavery. Thus by freely participating in that society and failing to oppose its economic and social laws concerning slavery, he could reasonably be held to have been complicit in the social institution of slavery, and to have shared indirect responsibility for the harms it caused. Although it would not have been reasonable to have held him to be directly responsible for all the specific harms to individual slaves he was causing in his everyday behavior (such as the harms resulting from his purchases of products of slave labor if those products were essential and there were no available alternatives[9]), it would nevertheless have been reasonable to have held him to share responsibility for the social institution of slavery itself, if he had collaborated in it.

Again, the degree of indirect responsibility for unjust social institutions varies considerably among different citizens; in the case of slavery, for example, a wealthy and influential citizen would have had a far greater responsibility for institutional reform than a small-hold farmer.

I now further argue that if we consider the content of the negative duty not to support and collaborate in unjust social institutions, we can see that it is generally not specified.

7.4.2.3. *How the Content of the Negative Duties Imposed by Human Rights May Be Unspecific*

This can again be illustrated with the example of slavery. Given the extent to which the social institution of slavery structured so many of the daily activities of a citizen in that society, it might not have been feasible for him to withdraw his involvement in that social institution. Doing so might have required leaving the society altogether, which might not have been a realistic option. Moreover, this social institution very much circumscribed the options for action available to him. It would therefore not have been possible for him to avoid complicity in the social institution of slavery simply by avoiding going out of his way to harm anyone. Fulfillment of the negative duty not to collaborate in the social institution of slavery required citizens to support reform of that social institution in order to minimize the extent of their collaboration, and to provide recompense for the harms they had caused through their participation in that social institution.

---

[9] In fact, an important part of the abolitionist movement was an attempt to encourage people to boycott products of slave labor and to make available alternative products.

Agents who freely participate in unjust social institutions are under a shared duty to reform those institutions. However, no single member can accomplish the duty of achieving institutional reform, and the shared duty has not been parceled out among members. The duty of individual members is therefore not a perfect duty with a specific content that can be fully discharged. Until institutional reform and coordinated shared action has been achieved, it is largely indeterminate how to prevent the right not to be deprived of access to basic necessities from being violated. The onus is on individual agents to decide how to implement their share of the corresponding negative duty.

There could perhaps also be cases in which the content of the negative duty not to directly contribute to such harms allows some latitude. For example, if the agent is contributing to a large number of additive harms, in certain circumstances it might be plausible that, rather than having a perfect duty to withdraw from all these chains, the agent has flexibility over which of the harms she is causing she should focus her energy on trying to prevent or compensate for, given that in such cases the harm the agent causes is so thinly spread that none of the victims would suffer significantly less if the agent withdrew from the causal claim.

I suggest, then, that our paradigm conception of a human rights violation should be revised. According to this revision, direct responsibility for human rights violations need not lie solely or even at all with agents who can be singled out as the perpetrators, but may be very broadly shared by a huge number of agents, few or none of whom can be singled out as individually solely or primarily responsible for a specific serious harm to a specific victim. Moreover, we should also examine the agents who have indirect responsibility for human rights violations, either by encouraging such violations or by supporting social institutions that themselves constitute a human rights violation. Finally, the content of many of the negative duties imposed by human rights may not be fully delineated. The negative duties imposed by human rights do not simply consist in clear-cut prohibitions that have an obvious and specific content and can easily be fulfilled simply by going out of one's way to harm anyone. The onus may be on the individual agent to take the initiative both in accepting her share of responsibility for the violations and in deciding how to implement these negative duties.

In order to address the implication of this revision of the paradigm for considering violations of the human right to basic necessities, the key question is whether the agents who causally contribute to the complex causal chains that lead to persons' coming to lack secure access to basic necessities can reasonably be held morally responsible for those harms, and it is to this question that I now turn.

7.4.3. Moral Responsibility for Deprivations of Basic Necessities

Some of the ways in which we individually contribute to the complex causal chains that ultimately lead to such high levels of chronic poverty are foreseeable and avoidable, in that we are either aware of the harms we are causing or could reasonably be expected to find out about them, and we could refrain from causing them. In such cases, we can plausibly be held to be directly morally responsible for the harms caused by our individual behavior.

Some of our individual causal contributions to the causal chains, on the other hand, are unforeseeable or unavoidable, or both. The harms we individually cause largely result from our participation in social institutions (in particular, the financial rules that govern persons' economic entitlements) that govern many of our everyday activities, along with those of millions of other agents. In such cases, it is often not possible to identify the harms caused by our own individual behavior (such as our individual economic transactions). In other cases we can identify the harms we are individually causing, but cannot feasibly avoid them, given that these social institutions highly constrain the options for action available to us, and given that they pervade so many aspects of our lives that it may not be viable to withdraw from them. However, the institutional account of human rights offers a powerful explanation for why we may still be plausibly held to share responsibility for a human rights violation.

The focus of the institutional account of human rights is the harm resulting from the operation of social institutions. It is much easier to identify the harms caused by the social institutions in which we freely participate than the harms we individually cause. This means that even when we cannot identify the harms caused by our individual behavior, we can often reasonably be expected to be aware of or find out about the harms caused by the social institutions of which we are members. In addition, even when we cannot avoid the harms directly caused by our individual behavior in virtue of our participation in these social institutions, it is plausible to hold us responsible for collaborating in them—for freely participating in them and benefiting from them without working toward their reform—as was illustrated with the example of slavery.

7.4.4. Violations of the Human Right to Secure Access to Basic Necessities

I suggest, then, that the complex causal chains that ultimately lead to millions lacking secure access to basic necessities constitute a violation of a basic human right on a huge scale, and that millions of agents share direct or indirect responsibility for this violation, though various agents will have very different degrees of responsibility. Although the role played by corrupt and non-democratic leaders in high levels of deprivations of access to basic necessities among their citizens does tend to be particularly salient, it is often only a part of the overall explanation. Direct responsibility is often shared by millions of agents who make a contribution to these causal chains, generally in the course of their everyday behavior.

Even where it is plausible to assign these corrupt leaders primary responsibility for the chronic poverty suffered by citizens and identify them as the perpetrators of violations of the human right to basic necessities, it is important to consider the global institutional factors that support and encourage the non-democratic rule under which such violations are predictably prevalent. Moreover, global social institutions under which the chronically poor are not entitled to a fair share of the benefits of natural resources and of fair opportunities to earn a subsistence income can themselves plausibly be seen as constituting a violation of the human right to secure access to basic necessities. Like slavery on the plantations, social and economic laws that increase the wealth of already wealthy nations and corporations and of Third World elites, at the expense of keeping or pushing others below the international poverty line, involve the pursuit of greater wealth at the cost of others' capacity to lead minimally decent and autonomous lives. Again, millions of agents share indirect responsibility for the harms caused by such global social institutions, in virtue of collaborating in them.

Human rights violations that do fit the paradigm tend to have far more impact on the moral consciousness of the agents involved than do cases in which the causal chains involve additive or multiplicative harms, or in which the agent plays an indirect role in the violation. The agent's role in bringing about a harm tends to be much more salient when the agent has sole or primary direct causal responsibility for a specific harm to a specific victim than when no serious harm to an individual victim can be traceable to that agent's behavior considered in isolation. Thus, complex causal chains that ultimately lead to millions of poverty-related deaths and cause millions more to lead severely impoverished lives tend to have much less impact on our moral consciousness than do simple causal chains in which we are solely or primarily responsible for a much less serious harm to a particular individual. However, as I have argued, we have strong reason to revise the paradigm and to take these causal chains as constituting a violation of a basic human right on a huge scale.

I should stress, though, that for most of the agents involved in the causal chains, their behavior is far less blameworthy than that of those who commit paradigmatic human rights violations. The view that human rights violations result from the specific deliberate actions of malicious individuals is, I suggest, another important respect in which our paradigm conception of the nature of human rights violations needs to be revised. Again, if we are to adequately address the nature of prevalent contemporary threats to persons' basic interests and autonomy, we should acknowledge that increasingly they result from the operation of social institutions that govern the routine behavior of a huge number of agents, none of whom intend the result. The motivation of the agents involved, far from being that of malice, tends to be a refusal to accept personal responsibility for their contribution to the harms. This largely results from the complexity of the causal chains that lead to the harms, which tends to lead agents not to feel individually responsible for them.

7.4.5. The Implications of the Revision of the Paradigm for the Utilitarian and Kantian Understanding of the Duties Imposed by Human Rights

As I have argued, violations of the negative duty not to actively deprive persons of their subsistence income are incompatible with the most minimal concern for persons' basic interests and respect for their dignity as rational autonomous agents. Both utilitarianism and Kantianism, founded as they are on concern for persons' interests and respect for their dignity, underscore the claim that this duty is sufficiently morally urgent to constitute a duty of basic justice imposed by a human right. I have also argued that the fact that this duty diverges from our paradigm conception of the duties imposed by human rights is no reason for denying that violations of it constitute human rights violations. Nevertheless, while utilitarianism strongly supports the revision of our paradigm conception of the nature of the duties imposed by human rights that I have argued for, a common Kantian deontological conception of these duties is very much in line with our traditional paradigm conception of them. I argue that this conception is based on focusing on the relation between a specific agent and a specific victim, and considering what harms to that victim can be attributed to that particular agent. When the focus is broadened to accommodate the more complex relations between agents and victims that form the backdrop of much of our contemporary behavior, this has significant implications for a Kantian deontological understanding of the duties imposed by human rights.

According to utilitarianism, the evaluation of agents' behavior is based simply on its foreseeable overall impact on persons' interests. There are several respects in which this utilitarian focus underscores the challenges to our paradigm conception of the nature of the duties imposed by human rights that I have been discussing. First, the harm the agent causes may not be intended. As long as the harm is foreseeable and avoidable, the agent must take full moral responsibility for it. Utilitarianism therefore challenges the view that human rights violations are generally intended. Second, the agent's most significant overall causal impact on the total consequences may be through the way in which her behavior interacts with the behavior of others. The utilitarian approach, then, does not focus on harms that can be attributed solely or primarily to the behavior of that particular agent. Third, the overall impact of the agent's behavior might not be immediate; long-term consequences of the agent's behavior are just as important as short-term consequences. Fourth, the agent's overall contribution to the consequences might be thinly diffused over a large number of victims. Even if the agent's impact on a particular person is very small, the overall aggregate impact of that agent's behavior may be very serious, where the total consequences to which her behavior is contributing consist in a threat to the basic interests of a large number of persons.

According to Kantian deontology, by contrast, the moral evaluation of an agent's behavior is not based on the consequences of that behavior, but on the nature of the relation between the agent and the victim. A common Kantian deontological conception of duties of justice focuses on the relation between a specific agent and a specific victim. The agent is responsible for violations of negative duties of justice because a serious harm to a specific victim can be attributed solely or primarily to that agent.

This conception underlies Onora O'Neill's discussion of positive and negative rights in her Kantian critique of welfare rights. She takes the negative duties entailed by human rights to consist in specific prohibitions on certain kinds of actions (duties not to kill, assault, and so on). The content of these duties is obvious and specific, and whoever violates such an obligation can be singled out as responsible for the serious harm the victim has suffered and identified as the perpetrator of the violation. Allocating responsibility for the violation of a negative right is a matter of finding the perpetrator:

> ... when a liberty right is violated, then, whether or not specific institutions have been established, there are determinate others to whom the violation might be imputed (no doubt, perpetrators are often unknown and can't be brought to book when institutions are inadequate). (O'Neill 1996: 132)

However, as I have argued, the relations between agents and victims that underlie many of the most serious contemporary harms tend to be far more complex. Serious harms that result from the interaction of the behavior of a huge number of agents can clearly constitute human rights violations, even though it is not possible even in principle to single out the agent or agents specifically responsible for the serious harm any particular victim has suffered and so assign particular perpetrators to particular violations. In these kinds of cases, we cannot identify the nature of the human right violation by considering the relation between a specific agent and a specific victim.

Let us consider, for example, the deontological claim that an important feature of negative duties is that when such duties are violated, the agent is introducing the threatening causal sequence of events, rather than allowing a preexisting threatening causal sequence to continue. In both of the kinds of causal chains examined in this section, no specific individual agent can be held solely or primarily responsible for introducing the serious threat to the victim. In the case of additive harms, moreover, if we focus on the impact of the behavior of each agent in isolation, the threatening causal sequence of events will be seen to be already in place for each of the victims. If we consider the Torturers' Union case, for example, we can see that for each agent, if the other torturers are already administering the shocks, there is a preexisting serious harm to each of the victims, and if the agent contributes to the causal chain, she will not significantly increase this harm for any individual victim. Conversely, if she fails to show up to work one day, or even leaves the job without being replaced, none of the victims will suffer significantly less. It is only the group of agents acting together that can be clearly held to be introducing the threat to the victims. Therefore the nature of the violation can only be addressed if we consider the relations between the group of agents and the group of victims. If the agent focuses on the impact that can be attributed to her behavior in isolation, she will miss altogether her share of moral responsibility for a human right violation.

As I have argued, many of the most pressing negative duties imposed by the human right to basic necessities are most plausibly thought of as shared duties that have not been specified and allocated among agents, any more than positive duties of aid. In such cases, we can say that a group of agents is responsible for a large number of human rights violations, but we cannot single out the perpetrator of a particular victim's right's violation. Moreover, as I have also argued, when unjust institutions are in place, the content of many negative duties imposed by human rights is not specific.

Given the urgency of these negative duties from a Kantian as well as a utilitarian perspective, it is not plausible to deny that they constitute duties of justice, the fulfillment of which each person can justifiably demand. I suggest, then, that Kantian deontology needs to accommodate relations between groups of agents and groups of victims, and that when it does, this leads in turn to a more expansive conception of the nature of the negative duties imposed by human rights. Moreover, as I argue in section 7.5, on this broader conception of the negative duties imposed by human rights such duties can be close in nature to positive duties of aid, and this undermines O'Neill's critique of rights to assistance.

This brings us to the question of whether there is a positive right to be guaranteed access to basic necessities to a reasonable level of security.

7.5. POSITIVE DUTIES TO PROTECT PERSONS' ACCESS TO BASIC NECESSITIES

I now turn to the question of whether the human right to basic necessities imposes a positive duty to protect persons' access to basic necessities to a reasonable level of security. This will comprise duties to provide the opportunity to earn a subsistence income and to provide basic necessities for those who are currently unable to provide them for themselves. I focus only on the question of whether the human right to basic necessities imposes positive duties to assist those who lack access to basic necessities through no fault of their own, and I set aside cases in which persons could provide for themselves but refuse to do so. When I refer in short to the duty to secure persons' access to basic necessities, this limitation in its purview should be understood. I argue that on both a utilitarian and a Kantian account of human rights, this positive duty is imposed by the human right to basic necessities.

7.5.1. The Utilitarian Account

Utilitarianism takes human rights to be protections of persons' fundamental interests. According to utilitarianism, the justification of a human right depends both on the importance of the interests that would be protected by acknowledging the right and the number of people this would benefit, and on the total burden such acknowledgment would impose on others. The burden imposed by acknowledging a human right depends on factors such as the level of wealth and available resources. What we have a human right to will therefore increase as our wealth and capability increases. In order to establish whether there is a human right to basic necessities that imposes positive duties, we need to compare the importance of the interests this would protect and how many would be benefited with the total cost imposed on others by protecting those interests relative to the overall amount of available resources.

Let us first consider the importance and scale of the interests at stake. Chronic severe poverty currently leads to eighteen million deaths each year, and leads many more millions to have drastically benighted lives. The protection of this interest requires the fulfillment of positive as well as negative duties: it requires protecting persons against being deprived of access to basic necessities and assisting those who have already suffered such a deprivation or who lack access to basic necessities because of natural circumstances such as severe disability.[10] It follows that on a utilitarian account of human rights, the human right to basic necessities must impose positive duties, provided these duties would not impose an unreasonable total cost on the duty-bearers.

Let us now examine the burden that would be imposed by implementing the positive duty to secure each person's access to basic necessities. According to utilitarianism, the only satisfactory way of implementing this positive duty would be via social institutions, and it would involve a redistribution of wealth from rich to poor countries through measures such as tariff and subsidy reform, compulsory taxation, and so on.[11] Institutional measures would be far more efficient than the actions of private individuals. This would also be the only way of enforcing compliance with the duties and so of ensuring both that the interest in basic necessities were protected and that the burden of protecting that interest were distributed in such a way as to minimize the cost to duty-bearers.[12]

In considering the total cost this would involve, it is important not to extrapolate from the inefficiency of past-aid projects by western governments. First, aid would be vastly more effective if the level of oppression, corruption, and warfare in poor countries was lower; and as we have seen, there are powerful arguments that establishing minimally just global social institutions would first and foremost require reform of features, such as the International Resource and Borrowing Privileges, that support and facilitate the exercise of non-democratic power and the warfare that are so closely linked to chronic poverty.[13] Second, much government

---

[10] For a subtle account of these duties see Shue (1996*a*).

[11] Of course, many of these measures might also be seen as fulfilling a negative duty to stop harming the global poor or to compensate for harms we are causing, but my focus here is on whether there is a positive duty of justice to redistribute wealth independently of whether rich countries are causally responsible for the level of chronic poverty.

[12] Given diminishing marginal utility, on a utilitarian analysis the best way of distributing the positive duty would involve imposing the bulk of the cost on the richest countries, and within them imposing graduated taxation. It would also involve compensating those initially hardest hit by tariff and subsidy reforms, such as small cotton farmers in the United States.

[13] Indeed, Thomas Pogge has made a strong case for the claim that fulfilling the negative duty to implement such reforms alone would eliminate most chronic poverty.

aid in the past has been tied to domestic commercial or strategic interests, rather than being primarily targeted at tackling chronic poverty as efficiently as possible.

Determining the exact cost of eliminating chronic poverty is of course a highly complicated matter. However, given the enormity of the current disparity in wealth, we can reasonably assume that the cost imposed on affluent countries of removing chronic poverty would be extremely small relative to their overall amount of wealth. Those who fall below the International Poverty Line do so by on average \$36 per year.[14]

The aggregate cost to the welfare of agents in affluent countries of implementing the positive duty would therefore be trivial in comparison with the vast amount of extreme suffering or death it would prevent. On a utilitarian analysis, the situation could hardly be more gratuitous. Given the importance of the interests at stake and the cheapness of protecting them, failing to protect those interests is incompatible with even a minimal acknowledgment of the moral importance of persons' basic interests. According to utilitarianism, therefore, such protection must be among the rock-bottom moral claims every human being can reasonably demand in virtue of their capacity for well-being and suffering. While it is hard to determine precisely the extent of the measures that can reasonably be demanded to protect persons' basic interests, when such interests are threatened because of a daily income shortfall of on average around ten cents, this has to count as a failure to uphold human rights.

Since utilitarianism takes justice to be grounded in the protection and promotion of basic interests, it holds that responsibility for fulfilling the positive duties imposed by the human right to basic necessities ultimately lies with any individual who is in a position to protect the interests at stake at a reasonable personal cost. This includes most citizens in affluent countries. Ideally they ought to implement these duties via institutions, since this would be far more efficient than if they act individually. They therefore ought to endeavor to create and support such institutions. In the meantime, however, they are also in a position to protect the basic interests of the chronically poor by donating to aid agencies and, according to utilitarianism, they have a duty of justice to do so.

I now argue that Kantian moral theories also take the human right to basic necessities to impose positive duties. I begin by discussing the dominant neo-Kantian account of justice, Kantian contractualism, and I then turn to arguments from a more traditional Kantian perspective, focusing in particular on Onora O'Neill's influential objection to welfare rights.

---

[14] The international poverty line is currently specified at an annual per capita income of \$394 at Purchasing Power Parity (henceforth 'PPP') 1993. Those who fall below the line do so by on average 30%. \$394 PPP 1993 is a little over \$500 PPP per year today, which corresponds to about \$120 in typical poor countries. The average shortfall per person is therefore about \$36 per year. Thomas Pogge estimates that a redistribution of just 1.13% of GDP of richest countries would be enough to raise each person above both the one dollar a day international poverty line and the two dollar a day line, which may be a more realistic estimate of the amount needed for secure access to basic necessities.

7.5.2. Kantian Contractualist Accounts

Kantian contractualism is based on Kant's core claim that each person's moral status is grounded on their dignity as a rational autonomous agent, capable of setting their own ends and of acknowledging and acting on moral reasons. The central idea behind Kantian contractualism is that the moral acceptability of principles for individual conduct or social institutions depends on whether each person could rationally endorse them under certain specified conditions, or could not reasonably reject them. One of the most prominent and sophisticated developments of this idea is found in Thomas Scanlon's *What We Owe to Each Other*, and I focus on his formulation. On his account, an action is right if and only if it is not prohibited by a set of moral principles for the general regulation of behavior that no one could reasonably reject (Scanlon 1998).

There are two central features of what counts as reasonable rejection. First, the only reasons for and against a principle that are eligible for judging whether it can be reasonably rejected are 'single individuals' reasons for objecting to that principle and alternatives to it' (Scanlon 1998: 209). Second, whether a principle can be reasonably rejected depends on the comparative strength of different individuals' reasons for and against a principle.

Often 'gains and losses in well-being (e.g., relief from suffering) are clearly the most relevant factors in determining whether a principle could or could not be reasonably rejected' (Scanlon 1998: 277), and this will most obviously include cases in which persons' basic interests are at stake.[15] As with utilitarianism, therefore, the impact candidate principles would have on individuals' basic interests plays a central role in assessing such principles. However, according to Kantian contractualism, the underlying ground of acceptable principles is not the promotion of persons' interests, but respecting each person affected by the principles as a rational autonomous agent by ensuring that those principles are ones to which each person could reasonably agree. This is the rationale behind allowing only single individuals' complaints in the assessment of proposed principles, which rules out appealing to aggregate welfare in order to justify a burden that is individually unacceptable.

It is clear that a principle according to which affluent agents have some kind of a duty to aid the chronically poor cannot be reasonably rejected. The most important objections to consider in assessing such a principle are the burdens imposed on affluent individuals by a duty to give the help and the burdens imposed on destitute individuals by not being helped. The cost to destitute individuals of lacking secure access to basic necessities is that their vital interests are threatened, and their lives are drastically stunted and impoverished. This will clearly outweigh the cost to affluent agents imposed by at least some kind of duty of aid. The central question here is whether this duty of aid should be seen as a duty of benevolence

---

[15] The burden a principle imposes on someone is a function both of that person's absolute level of well-being under acceptance of the principle and of the amount by which that person would be worse off under acceptance of the principle than under acceptance of some alternative principle.

or a duty of basic justice to which the chronically poor are entitled as a human right.

I first discuss the features of duties of benevolence and duties of basic justice and then argue that a principle that characterizes the duty of aid as a duty of basic justice cannot be reasonably rejected. I then argue that both destitute individuals and affluent agents have strong objections to understanding the duty of aid as a duty of benevolence.

7.5.2.1. *The Features of Duties of Benevolence and Duties of Basic Justice*

If the duty to protect persons' access to basic necessities were taken to be a duty of benevolence, each affluent agent would have a duty to help some chronically poor individuals some of the time. Unlike duties of justice, duties of benevolence are not ones that ought to be enforced, so there is likely to be widespread non-compliance with the duty of aid. Even if there were widespread compliance, there would be no guarantee that each person would have reasonably secure access to basic necessities. For particular individuals suffering chronic poverty, their being helped would be treated as morally optional; it would be one of many possible opportunities for affluent agents to give help, and those agents could permissibly choose to help others in need instead. Any particular destitute individual would not be entitled to be helped and could not justifiably demand this. Therefore if the duty of aid is taken to be a duty of benevolence it is highly probable that some individuals will continue to lack access to certain basic necessities, and none of the chronically poor can be said to have *secure* access to basic necessities.

As I argued in section 7.3, the distinctive features of the duties of basic justice imposed by human rights are that they are particularly morally urgent and basic and enforced by minimally just institutions, and that they are owed to every human being in virtue of their universal moral status. If the duty of aid were understood as a duty of basic justice, there would be a shared obligation to ensure that each person has reasonably secure access to basic necessities all of the time. Just institutions would specify and enforce the duties that must be implemented in order to achieve this and so to guarantee each person's access to basic necessities to a reasonable level of security; and in the meantime, as long as any individuals lacked reasonably secure access to basic necessities, those individuals could justifiably complain that they were being deprived of what they were entitled to as a matter of basic justice.

To see why a Kantian contractualist would have to treat the duty as one of justice, we need to consider first the comparative burdens that duties of justice and benevolence would place on destitute and affluent individuals.

7.5.2.2. *The Burdens Imposed by Construing the Duty of Aid as a Duty of Benevolence*

An individual suffering chronic poverty can object to a set of principles under which his or her being secured access to basic necessities is treated as morally optional, and can propose an alternative set of principles under which it is considered to be an enforceable duty of justice. As we have seen, if the duty of aid is taken to be a duty of benevolence, there will be some individuals who lack access to certain basic necessities. These individuals can object that this undermines their capacity to lead a minimally decent and autonomous life and threatens their very survival. Acceptance of an alternative principle under which the duty of aid is taken to be a duty of justice would transform their lives, and so the sacrifice imposed on them by rejection of that principle is also huge. In addition, all those suffering chronic poverty can object to the burden imposed on them by having only insecure access to basic necessities. They can complain against the impact this has on their 'planning and on the organisation of their lives' (Scanlon 1998: 203), since it will drastically impinge on their ability to form and pursue long-term plans and projects.

The cost to individual affluent individuals of providing the help needed to secure each person's access to basic necessities if this duty were institutionally enforced and implemented is, as we have seen, very small. It is not only far less than the cost to destitute individuals of not being helped, it is not even comparable. Clearly, therefore, if we consider the comparative burdens imposed by a principle under which the duty of aid is taken to be a duty of justice, we can see that it cannot be reasonably rejected.

Moreover, affluent agents too can reasonably reject a principle under which the duty of aid is taken to be a duty of benevolence. As we have seen, a principle according to which there is a duty to aid the chronically poor cannot be reasonably rejected. Affluent agents therefore have to acknowledge a duty of aid. The only remaining candidate principles are one that characterizes the duty of aid as a duty of benevolence and one that characterizes it as an enforceable duty of justice. As I now argue, affluent agents have a very strong objection to its being specified as a duty of justice.

As I have argued at length elsewhere, the duty to aid those who lack secure access to basic necessities is extremely onerous for individual agents in circumstances in which there is widespread non-compliance with this duty.[16] A conscientious agent can object to the unfairness of having to give more than her fair share of aid to the chronically poor. However, if she gives only her fair share of aid in circumstances of widespread non-compliance with the duty of aid, there will be chronically poor individuals who are not helped, and whom she would help if she gave more than her fair share of aid. These individuals can object to her giving only her fair share of aid. Given the extremity of their plight and given that their lives would be transformed if the agent helped them, their complaint at not being helped by her is likely to outweigh her complaint at having to give more than her fair share of aid until the point that her duty of aid is very demanding indeed.

The only way of ensuring that the burden of implementing the duty of aid is fairly distributed among affluent agents and that the cost to individual

---

[16] For a fuller argument about the demandingness of Kantian contractualist duties of aid, see Ashford (2003).

duty-bearers is minimized is by enforcing widespread compliance with the duty. Morally conscientious affluent agents therefore have strong reason to prefer the duty of aid to be characterized as a duty of justice that ought to be enforced. And given that the non-compliers are under a duty to give their fair share of aid, complaints they have at being compelled to fulfill this duty either have no legitimacy or at any rate will certainly be outweighed by the complaints of the conscientious agents.

I finally discuss a further objection a chronically poor individual can raise to any set of principles under which his or her being secured access to basic necessities is considered morally optional. This objection concerns the role of principles in expressing persons' moral status.

7.5.2.3. *The Expressive Role of Principles*

As Scanlon points out, moral principles have an important role 'in defining [persons'] standing', able to 'enter into relations with others as an equal' (1998: 204). As he argues, 'because principles constrain the reasons we may, or must, take into account, they can affect our relations with others and our view of ourselves in both positive and negative ways' (1998: 203–4).

Such is the difference between the burden imposed on the chronically poor by not being helped and the burden imposed on affluent agents by meeting a shared obligation to ensure that each person has reasonably secure access to basic necessities that a principle under which the chronically poor are not entitled to or guaranteed such access allows an inequality so extreme as to be degrading. This principle is so far from being justifiable to chronically poor individuals as to constitute a flagrant disregard for their standing as rational autonomous agents. Likewise, for those individuals to accept this principle would be completely incompatible with self-respect to the point that, as Henry Shue puts it, it would amount to 'submissively withering' (Shue 1996*a*: 129).

According to Kantian contractualism, the underlying basis of moral principles is to recognize each person's moral standing as a rational autonomous agent. Their status as moral principles is contingent on whether any person could reasonably reject them. Hence, if principles that take the duty of aid to be anything short of a duty of justice could be reasonably rejected, then only the principle that takes it to be a duty of justice is consistent with recognizing the moral status of those in desperate need. But we can say more than this. If affluent individuals' complaints at acceptance of the principle are massively outweighed by complaints from chronically poor individuals at its rejection, then refusing to acknowledge and act on this principle is inconsistent with even a minimal recognition of others' moral standing. As I claimed in section 7.3, it is this that makes a duty of justice one grounded in a human right.

I conclude that according to Kantian contractualism, the positive duty to secure persons' access to basic necessities is a duty of basic justice. It might be argued, however, that on Kant's original theory there is an important distinction between the moral urgency of positive and negative duties, and that Kantian contractualism cannot adequately accommodate this central feature of Kant's theory. I now turn to some arguments along these lines.

7.5.3. Kantian Deontology

Kantian contractualism largely focuses on the recipient's perspective. From this perspective what has primary importance is how that person's interests are likely to be affected by various proposed principles. However, it might be argued that Kant's original theory focuses on the duty-bearer's perspective, and that from this perspective we can see that violating a negative duty tends to express more disrespect and to constitute a greater affront to persons' moral status than violating a positive one even when it has the same impact on the interests of the recipient.

The key question here, though, is whether the positive duty to protect persons' access to basic necessities is sufficiently morally urgent to constitute a human rights claim. Kant's moral theory may offer a forceful account of why negative duties are more morally urgent than positive ones when holding constant what is at stake for the recipient, but that is of course compatible with the claim that some positive duties are extremely morally urgent, when what is at stake for the recipient is sufficiently drastic and the cost to the duty-bearer of fulfilling the duty would be minimal. The positive duty to secure persons' access to basic necessities is an obvious candidate, given the extremity of what is at stake for the recipient, and the cheapness of implementing the duty. Access to basic necessities is a precondition for sustained autonomous action. To allow persons to be precluded from leading minimally autonomous lives or even suffer brain damage as a result of a daily income shortfall of, on average, ten cents hardly seems compatible with respecting the priceless value of each person's dignity as a rational autonomous agent and end-setter. This indicates that the most minimal respect for persons' dignity requires protecting their access to basic necessities, in which case such protection must be among the rock-bottom moral claims each person has in virtue of their universal moral status.

Nevertheless, it might be argued that Kant's original theory drew a further important distinction between positive and negative duties in virtue of which positive duties should be seen as duties of benevolence rather than duties of justice that correspond to human rights: the distinction between perfect and imperfect duties. Onora O'Neill has raised an influential objection to welfare rights along these lines. I now in section 7.5 turn to her objection.

7.5.4. Onora O'Neill's Objection to Welfare Rights

7.5.4.1. *A Summary of O'Neill's Argument*

Onora O'Neill argues for the view that there is an important asymmetry between positive rights to assistance, which includes the right to basic necessities along with other welfare rights, and negative rights not to be actively harmed. The asymmetry, she claims, is that welfare rights, unlike negative rights, are not claimable in the absence of institutional structures that specify and allocate the duties they impose. Since genuine rights must be claimable, she concludes that welfare rights do not qualify as genuine unless such institutional structures are in place.

She stipulates that in order for a right to be claimable the right-holder must be able to identify (at least in principle) both the precise content of the corresponding duties and the specific agents responsible for fulfilling them. Perfect duties are claimable, because their content and the agents responsible for fulfilling them are both specified. Imperfect duties on the other hand allow the agent discretion over both the content and the recipient of the duty, and so are not claimable.

She points out that positive duties of aid are imperfect in nature unless there are institutional structures in place to specify and allocate them. This is because unlike negative duties, they require the expenditure of resources, such as time and money. For this reason the agent cannot owe a duty of aid to every destitute person. Unless there is some special relation between the agent and a particular victim, there is nothing to pick out any particular person as the appropriate recipient of the aid. This means that the duty of aid leaves the agent with latitude over which destitute individuals to help. The agent also has latitude over what kind of help to give. These duties are therefore, she argues, not claimable: an individual in need is not able to identify which particular agents are responsible for helping her specifically, and what kind of help they ought to give. The only way in which the duties could become claimable is through establishing special relationships between obligation-bearers and right-holders. This requires an institutional specification of the obligations of aid and allocation of responsibility for fulfilling these obligations to particular agents. In the meantime, welfare rights are not claimable and are therefore not genuine. Moreover, given that welfare rights depend on institutional structures for their existence, even when such structures are in place these rights cannot be said to be universal rights owed to every human being simply in virtue of their moral status as human beings. Strictly speaking they are special rights, which arise through relationships established by institutions (O'Neill 1996: 130, cf. 133).

By contrast, she assumes that the duties imposed by negative rights are perfect in nature 'even when institutions are missing or weak'. That assumption is based on her conception of these negative duties as consisting in specific, clear-cut prohibitions on certain kinds of actions (killing, assaulting, and so on) that are always incumbent on every agent; every agent is prohibited from performing such actions on any occasion. She argues that since the fulfillment of the negative duty just requires abstaining from these kinds of actions, it can easily be completely fulfilled toward everyone. The content of the duty is clear, and it is clear to whom it is owed—everyone—and which agents are responsible for fulfilling it—all of them.

O'Neill's argument, therefore, relies on two assumptions. First, she assumes that the negative duties imposed by rights are perfect in nature even in the absence of just institutions. Second, she assumes that imperfect duties are not claimable. She concludes that there is an important asymmetry between positive and negative rights, in that positive rights, unlike negative rights, require institutional structures to be claimable and therefore genuine.

However, as I argued in section 7.4, many of the most urgent negative duties imposed by human rights are imperfect in nature in just the same way as positive duties. While O'Neill's account of the negative duties imposed by human rights applies to small-scale interactions where a specific agent can be singled out as responsible for assaulting or killing a specific victim, it fails to apply to cases in which someone suffers permanent debility or death as a result of the interaction of the behavior of a huge number of agents. As I argued, there can be clear cases of violations of negative rights where it may not be possible even in principle to identify the perpetrators of the violations. The negative duties corresponding to these rights may be shared duties that have not been specified and allocated among agents. In such cases, while we can identify a group of agents as sharing responsibility for a large number of violations, we cannot match up specific victims to specific violators and single out the agent(s) specifically responsible for a specific victim's violation. Moreover, the content of many of these negative duties is not specific. These negative duties are therefore not claimable, on O'Neill's account of claimability.

It therefore follows from O'Neill's argument that not only welfare rights but in addition many negative rights not to be actively harmed in extremely serious ways are not in fact genuine. In particular, there is no human right not to be actively deprived of access to basic necessities, where that deprivation results from the operation of unjust social institutions. It is more plausible, I suggest, to reject O'Neill's assumption about claimability, and to accept a broader account of claimability and of the duties imposed by human rights. I now argue for such a wider account.

If we accept this wider account of claimability, then the fact that rights to assistance require institutional structures in order to specify and allocate their corresponding duties is no reason for denying that they are genuine rights before such structures are in place. As I argue, in the case of both the positive right to be secured access to basic necessities and the negative right not to be actively deprived of access to basic necessities, institutional structures are essential to the realization of the rights but not to their existence, and the degree of the injustice of the behavior of agents and of the operation of social institutions is measured by the extent to which these rights remain unrealized. I argue, then, that the duty to seek an institutional specification of the duties that would lead to the realization of the rights should be taken to be a demand of basic justice imposed by the rights themselves, rather than taking such an allocation to be a condition of the rights' existence as O'Neill claims.

An Alternative Account of Claimability

O'Neill is assuming a picture of claimability according to which the victim has a claim against a specific agent or agents to act or refrain from acting in a certain specific way. In the case of the negative rights, the victim has a claim against a particular identifiable perpetrator or perpetrators. In the case of positive rights, institutional structures match up specific agents to specific addressees.

This picture cannot acknowledge cases in which responsibility for human rights violations is very broadly shared by a huge group of agents and the duties not to contribute to such violations have not been specified and allocated among particular members of the group. When serious harms are the result of the operation of unjust social institutions, I suggest that the right not to suffer these harms is a claim against the vast group of agents who participate in these social institutions. When these agents cannot avoid the harms they individually cause, victims have a claim against them that they take action to reform the system and to mitigate the harms it causes. The task of reforming the system is a shared one that has not been allocated among agents. The onus is on individual agents to take the initiative in deciding how they should do their part in bringing about institutional reform. Agents therefore have considerable latitude in how they fulfill this duty. Nevertheless, the claim that can be made against them by victims of the system is not empty. It is a claim that for their sake they do take this initiative, and each accept their share of responsibility for the harms caused by the system and take action accordingly, rather than continuing to collaborate in it. This is genuine claimability, because it articulates a demand each victim can make against all those who participate in the system that harms them and who fail to take enough action toward reforming it. Where agents can be held directly responsible for the harms they individually cause, but their actions are implicated in extremely complex causal chains that lead to serious harms only in conjunction with the actions of a huge number of other agents, the right not to suffer these harms is a claim against these agents that they each take personal responsibility for their contribution to these causal chains, and either withdraw from them or seek to coordinate with others to stop them.

The shared duty not to deprive anyone of secure access to basic necessities does not depend on any institutional allocation of responsibilities. Rather, in the modern world, such an institutional allocation is the most plausible objective of this duty: we are best able to realize the right not to suffer this deprivation by collaborating with others in effecting institutional reforms that tighten up the allocation of responsibility for fulfilling this shared duty. (These reforms involve carefully analyzing and specifying the ways in which the operation of existing social institutions, together with the behavior of a huge number of agents and agencies, in conjunction contribute to the high level of chronic severe poverty, and examining what measures need to be taken to avoid this contribution. In the light of this analysis, the negative duty could be made specific and enforced, and responsibility could then be allocated for violations of the duty.) It is therefore not true that an institutional specification of duties is a condition of the right's existence. The right exists, and imposes corresponding obligations, even in the absence of any institutional allocation of duties. In particular, it imposes (in the absence of such an institutional allocation) the corresponding duty to coordinate with others to bring about an institutional allocation of duties that realizes the right, insofar as this is reasonably possible.

The right not to be deprived of secure access to basic necessities owes its existence to the universal moral status of human beings. It exists independently of current institutions, and serves as a test of the justice of those institutions: if they fail to specify and enforce the corresponding negative duties, those institutions are fundamentally unjust. It is the right that explains why it is important to specify and enforce these duties; it is not the institutional specification of the duties that generates the right.

In the same way, people possess the human right to secure access to basic necessities before the positive duty to guarantee this right has been institutionally defined and allocated. In the absence of just institutions, again, the onus is on individual agents to take the initiative in deciding how to implement their share of this duty and to seek to institutionalize the task. And again, the right-holders' claim is a claim against every agent who is not doing enough to implement their share of the shared duty. The right exists independently of the institutions that define and allocate the duty of aid. It exists in virtue of the universal moral status of human beings, and again, serves as a test of whether existing institutions are minimally just: as long as they fail to guarantee the right for every human being, and such failure is reasonably avoidable, they are judged to be unjust.

In each case, minimally just social institutions will specify and allocate the duties needed to fulfill the shared obligation not to deprive anyone of secure access to basic necessities and to guarantee each person's access to basic necessities, respectively. Institutional structures therefore play just as central a role in realizing both kinds of rights. Before just social institutions are in place, the negative right not to be deprived of access to basic necessities and the positive right to secure access to basic necessities are equally genuine, and they ground a demand of basic justice that we find a way of specifying and allocating their corresponding duties.

7.6. CONCLUSION

I conclude that on a Kantian account of human rights as well as a utilitarian account, the human right to basic necessities imposes both positive and negative duties. Failure to recognize and implement either kind of duty is fundamentally incompatible with acknowledging the universal moral status of human beings, whether we take that moral status to be grounded on the moral importance of persons' basic interests or their dignity as rational autonomous agents, and whether we take human rights to be justified as protections of basic interests or as expressive of persons' dignity. I have argued that we tend not to recognize our role in bringing about violations of the human right to basic necessities because such violations do not conform to our paradigm conception of a human rights violation. However, we need to revise this paradigm. Moreover, once we do, we can see that the positive and negative duties imposed by human rights are often closer in nature than we tend to think. In particular, until just institutions have been brought about that specify and enforce both kinds of duty, the onus is often on individual agents in affluent countries to take the initiative in accepting responsibility for fulfilling these duties and in deciding how to do so.

8

Duties to Fulfill the Human Rights of the Poor

*Alan Gewirth**

Many human beings still live in conditions of severe poverty, with insufficient and uncertain access to food, water, clothing, shelter, basic health care, and elementary education. What may they expect from those better off? Few would deny that the more affluent should do something to help the poor. But most well-to-do persons understand this 'should' in a weak sense. They see such aid as beyond the call of duty, as supererogatory or, at best, as provided pursuant to an 'imperfect duty' of charity, humanity, or solidarity, which leaves it to donors' discretion as to how much they give and to whom. It is good to help, but the poor have no right to be helped.

However commonly held, this view may not be correct. We must examine the alternative possibility that the poor have a moral right to be assisted in achieving the basic necessities of life. The Universal Declaration of Human Rights (UDHR) postulates such a right, most clearly in Article 25: 'Everyone has the right to a standard of living adequate for the health and well-being of himself and of his family, including food, clothing, housing and medical care'.

Moral rights impose correlative duties: not imperfect duties of charity, humanity, or solidarity, but perfect, stringent, and in principle enforceable duties of justice. The alternative view to be developed here thus faces two important questions. First, how can we plausibly specify, and identify bearers of, the perfect, stringent, and in principle enforceable duties that are correlative to a human right to basic necessities? That is, what moral claims do the poor, in virtue of this human right, have upon the conduct of other agents, and of which other agents? And second, how can we justify the postulated human right together with the specific duties it entails?

I. I will open my inquiry with some basic questions about the foundations of justice. What are its central requirements and, especially, what is it about justice that underlies or explains its mandatoriness: why is it that justice is regarded as so

* This essay is adapted from my keynote address to the XXI World Congress of Philosophy, delivered on August 17, 2003 in Istanbul, Turkey.

morally necessary that any violation of it calls for the most severe condemnation and correction?

We may begin by noting that justice has traditionally had two different meanings. One meaning, which goes back at least to Aristotle, is *formal*, or *comparative*; it holds that justice consists in treating equals equally and unequals unequally. Thus, for example, if worker A deserves a wage of $X because his work has quality Q, then worker B also deserves a wage of $X if his work also has quality Q. This argument relies on a principle of *universalizability* or *generalization*: if A has X *because* A has quality Q, where this 'because' signifies a sufficient condition or reason, then every other entity B, C, and so forth that has quality Q must also have X. So this pattern of argument is based on the concept of sufficient condition or reason.

This formal conception of justice, taken by itself, obviously has severe limitations, for it leaves out the substantive content of what is the quality Q that justifies having X. Let us call this the *anchor* or the *independent variable* that specifies what is the *content* of the justifying quality Q. The formal conception of justice is therefore at most a requirement of consistency, and it can be used by any partisan who wants to uphold some quality Q as a sufficient justifying condition or independent variable for having some other quality R. A Nazi who says that some person A should be killed because he is a Jew would satisfy this condition of justice if he were to go on to say that all other persons B, C, and so forth should also be killed because they too are Jews. So the justificatory or validating force of the formal conception of justice, taken by itself, is severely limited. To apply it in a morally right way we would need a further, independent, morally right criterion for the justifying sufficient condition Q.

Despite these limitations, the comparative conception of justice can carry important justificatory weight as a principle of fairness where it is understood to counteract unjustified self-partiality. If I claim some good for myself because I have some justifying quality or independent variable Q, then fairness as well as logic requires that you also are entitled to that good if you also have Q. In this specific kind of case of quality Q, the comparative or formal conception of justice can serve to ward off an egoistic overriding of the comparative merits of other persons, including especially women and blacks; and as we shall see, it has a vital place in the argument for universal human rights. So what is crucially needed here is a way of specifying the anchor or content or independent variable that fills in the argument.

Let us now consider a second, more substantive conception of justice. According to this, which goes back to Plato, justice consists in rendering to each person his or her *due*, that is, what he or she has a *right* to. So on this view, justice consists in rights: to do justice is to uphold or protect rights, where rights are understood to be important interests that ought to be fulfilled on behalf of persons and groups. This conception has the same formalist difficulty as besets the comparative conception, for it leaves open the substantive question of the anchor or independent variable that specifies its content of *who has rights to what*.

Let us now tie these considerations to the issue of *human rights*, understood as rights that are had equally by every human being. This is the most important example of the substantive conception of justice, a conception of what human beings minimally owe one another. But human rights cannot be simply invoked as having justificatory validity; it must itself confront the problem of the independent variable. Is there any way of proving that there are human rights? How, if at all, can it be proved that all humans have certain moral rights? In what way, if any, can one logically justify the movement from 'A is human' to 'A has certain moral rights'? To what substantive content or independent variable can we appeal to justify this movement? And how far does the justification of human rights extend?

We may divide the answers that have traditionally been given to the question of the independent variable of human rights into two sorts: intuitive and argumentative. According to some thinkers, carrying on to the present day, no argument is needed here, for it is *self-evident* that there are human rights: as Jefferson said, 'We hold these truths to be self-evident, that all men are created equal, that they are endowed by their Creator with certain unalienable rights....'

The trouble with this appeal to self-evidence is its lack of universal firmness: what is 'self-evident' to one person may not be self-evident to others; some may, in fact, regard it as moronic or worse.

Let us then turn to some arguments that have been given for the thesis that all humans have certain moral rights. These arguments are of two sorts: religious and secular. Some thinkers hold that the justifying basis of human rights is to be found in the consideration that all humans are children of God, and hence all have a certain sacredness that grounds their having moral rights. Such an argument, however, would not convince a non-believer. Secular thinkers, including Kant and John Rawls, have tried in various ways to ground human rights in certain procedural considerations. Rawls's method of reflective equilibrium is the most famous of such recent attempts, but it does not succeed in establishing a firm and sound basis for human rights.

I now want to deal with this problem of the justification of human rights in a more systematic way. In order to do this, we must move back a few steps, to examine the objective *context* in which the concept of rights has its chief and necessary justifying basis. In other words, the question is: when we say that someone has a right to something, what is the more general conceptual area or independent variable to which we are appealing in justification of this claim?

I now want to suggest that this conceptual area is *human action*. It is the concept of action that underlies and justifies the invocation of rights. To see this, we must note that the concept of a right is a moral concept before it is a legal one; and the general context of all moralities is *action*. For all moralities, amid their various conflicting contents, require that persons *act* in certain ways. The specific kinds of action that are upheld are, of course, very different, especially as concerns the root principles to which they appeal: thus the religious moralist differs from the atheist moralist, the communist moralist differs from the libertarian, the aesthete differs from the Benthamite utilitarian, and so forth. Nevertheless, all these different moralities agree in setting forth requirements for *action*. It is from the necessary conditions of action that moralities come to prescribe rights.

To this focus on action it may be objected that some moralities center not around action, but around virtues. Their cardinal precept is not '*Do* this' but rather '*Be* this'. Since, however, virtues are dispositions to *act* in certain ways, the concept of action figures centrally in virtue moralities as well.

How does the concept of action serve as the anchor or independent variable for all rights? The answer is that action in the relevant sense has certain necessary conditions, and it is the necessary conditions that provide the general contents that justify the move from 'A is human' to 'A has certain moral rights'.

What are these necessary conditions of human action? To get at them, we must note that the actions that are prescribed in moralities, amid their varying contents, all have two generic features in common. One feature is *voluntariness* or *freedom*. When requirements for action are set forth, it is assumed that the persons thus addressed have autonomy whereby they can control their behavior by their unforced choice while having knowledge of relevant circumstances, so that their behavior is *voluntary* or *free*. The other generic feature of action is *purposiveness*, or *intentionality*, which at its fullest successful extent I call *well-being*. When requirements are addressed to agents, it is assumed that they act with some end in view, some purpose they want to achieve. This purpose may not be fully explicit or definite, but it has at least the aspect of trying to accomplish something, achieve some purpose. Well-being consists in having the abilities and conditions that are at least minimally needed for all successful action. It is these two generic features of freedom and well-being that constitute the necessary conditions of human action, that we were looking for to serve as the independent variables for all rights.

There are three different levels of well-being. First, there is *basic well-being*, which consists in having the elemental abilities and conditions that are needed for any purposive action at all; it includes having life, physical integrity, and mental equilibrium. Second, there is *non-subtractive well-being*, which consists in having the abilities and conditions that are needed in order to maintain undiminished one's level of purpose-fulfillment; it includes not being lied to, not having promises to oneself broken, and so forth. And third, there is *additive well-being*, which consists in having the conditions and abilities that are needed for increasing one's level of purpose-fulfillment; it includes education, self-esteem, and other conditions of making progress in one's abilities of agency. It is these three levels of well-being together with freedom that constitute the abilities of human agency to which all humans have rights.

How do we get from these necessary conditions of action to the agent's necessary claiming of rights? The answer to this question may be laid out in greater or lesser detail, and I have elsewhere provided a very detailed answer.[1] To put it briefly: Every agent must regard his freedom and well-being as necessary goods for him, since without freedom and well-being he would not be able to act either at all or with general chances of success in achieving his purposes. From this it

---

[1] See Gewirth (1978), Gewirth (1982), and Gewirth (1996).

follows that the agent must hold that he has rights to freedom and well-being. For if he were to deny that he has these rights, then he would be in the position of holding that it is permissible for other persons to interfere with his having freedom and well-being, so that it is permissible that he not have freedom and well-being. But this would contradict the agent's previous acceptance that his freedom and well-being are necessary goods for him, so that as an agent he must have freedom and well-being. So, to avoid this contradiction, the agent must accept that he has rights to freedom and well-being. And since it is as a prospective purposive agent that he claims these rights for himself, he must accept, on pain of contradiction, that all prospective purposive agents have these rights. By this social universalism, the rights in question are now moral rights. Since all humans are actual, prospective, potential agents, what this argument establishes is the existence of human rights. So this argument for human rights is based on the formal conception of justice whereby similar cases must be similarly treated.

It is from the necessity for action of freedom and well-being—that is, in virtue of their status as necessary goods of action—that the argument establishes the existence of human rights within the general context of agency. It is the necessity for action that provides the justification we were looking for in the movement from 'A is human' to 'A has rights'.

Let us put this point in a related way more briefly as follows. What is meant by 'a right' here? At a minimum, a right is an important interest of a person that ought to be fulfilled, and controlled by him as his normative property. It is this concept of a right that figures in the principle of substantive justice that I cited above as 'render to each person his rights'. Since freedom and well-being, as the generic features and necessary goods of action, are obviously important interests of the agent, it follows from the concept of rights that, from within his own context of purposive action, any agent must claim to have rights to them. And since claim-rights entail correlative duties, each agent must also hold that other persons are the respondents who have duties to respect his having these necessary goods. Governments are the main but not the only respondents. The nature of this respect may vary in different situations, as we see. The correlative duties are an intrinsic part of claim-rights. Without the duties to implement them, rights are ineffectual. Because of the importance of their objects, rights make demands that certain interests of persons be fulfilled. These demands set duties to fulfill them. In the case of human rights, the duty-bearers or respondents are, in theory, all human beings; but in practice it is mainly governments that serve as their representatives.

So I have here argued from goods being necessary for action to the claiming of rights to these goods. It must be emphasized that, since this whole argument proceeds on the basis of reason, the necessary goods that figure in it must be truly necessary for the agent; they are his intrinsic abilities of agency. Thus, one cannot say, 'I must have a ten-speed bicycle; it is a necessary good for me, so I have a right to it'. The argument is confined to the necessary and universal goods of purposive action; and the agent, in claiming rights to these goods, is indicating that they are truly important interests, his abilities of agency, that must be fulfilled if he is to act in pursuit of any purposes. If he were to deny that he has rights to these necessary goods, then he would be saying that it is permissible for other persons to interfere with his having them, and thus would contradict what he regards as the normative necessity of his having them.

Let us now consider this objection. Against the thesis that the agent must claim rights to the generic features of action, it may be objected that this claim of rights is pointless. For the agent cannot help having the generic features of action, his abilities of agency, since, as an agent, he necessarily has them; hence, it is pointless for him to claim a right to them.

There are two replies to this objection. First, although regularly successful action is indeed characterized by freedom and well-being in all of its dimensions, not all actions are successful. Some actions do not manage to attain non-subtractive and additive goods, and their agents may lack the abilities and conditions that are required for such attainment. Since well-being in its full scope consists in having these non-subtractive and additive abilities as well as the basic ones, the agent in claiming a right to well-being does not claim a right to what he necessarily has *already*. Second, the objection fails even with regard to freedom and basic well-being. Although these necessarily pertain to every agent, a person is not always an actual agent. He claims the right to freedom and well-being not only as a present or actual agent but also as a prospective agent; and in the latter capacity he does not necessarily have freedom and well-being. There is always the possibility of interference with his agency and hence of his lacking the freedom and well-being that agency requires. It is within this broader, prospective context that he, even as an agent, claims the right to have freedom and well-being.

As for human beings who are so deficient mentally or physically that they cannot engage in full-fledged purposive agency, this can be taken care of by a principle of proportionality, which I do not have the space to spell out here.

In this way, then, we have arrived at human rights as the substantive concept of justice. The main point is that human rights are normatively mandatory on two grounds: first, on the substantive ground that their objects, what they are rights to, are the necessary goods of action; and second, on the formal ground that any attempt to violate them involves the agent in self-contradiction, for he is then in the position of denying that his victim, as a prospective purposive agent, has the same generic rights he must claim for himself.

We may also call this principle of human rights the *principle of generic consistency* (PGC) because it combines the formal consideration of consistency with the substantive consideration of the generic features and rights of action. It is this principle that underlies the moral requirements both of human rights and of global justice.

What has emerged from this argument about human rights is that they are rights on the part of every human being that his necessary needs for freedom and well-being be fulfilled. This involves that his abilities of agency are to be developed and exercised in ways that are compatible with a similar development for all other human beings. In this way, then, we have attained to the rational foundations of human rights as the central conditions of justice.

Let us now look briefly at a related objection. It is sometimes held that human rights are not sufficient conditions of moral rightness because they are concerned with protecting only the interests of individuals. As such, they are held to conflict with 'Asian values' because the latter are concerned with the common good or the good of the community. Thus, for example, when the government of Singapore imposed quarantines and other intrusive legislation to ward off the impact of severe acute respiratory syndrome (SARS), and some civil libertarians protested these draconian measures, a Singapore official commented: 'In your country individual rights always take precedence over community rights. In our country it is the other way around'.[2]

This comment raises the question of what is this community whose rights take precedence? Is the community distinct from the individuals who compose it? If it is their vital health and basic well-being that is being protected, the real issue concerns not the subjects of the rights—the community as against the individual, but rather the objects of the rights, the kinds of interests that are in question. If the interests involved in 'community rights' are life and basic health, while the interests involved in individual rights are privacy and convenience, then it is a plausible reaction to suggest that the latter interests should give way to the former. This reaction relies on a general thesis about degrees of needfulness for action, which may be stated as follows: when two rights are in conflict and they cannot both be fulfilled or moderated, that right should take precedence that is more needed for action. Thus, to take some traditional examples, when the right not to be lied to conflicts with the right of an innocent person not to be murdered, the former right should give way to the latter because not being murdered is more needed for action than is not being lied to; or when the right not to starve conflicts with the right to private property, the latter right should give way to the former. Many alleged conflicts between individual rights and group or community rights can be dealt with in this way, rather than focusing on who, as such, have the rights. When the subjects are held to be of central importance, as in family or national rights, it is still the objects, the relevant interests, that must be appealed to.

These considerations bring out that what is of central importance about human rights is their objects, the necessary interests to whose fulfillment persons have rights. But it must also be recognized that the rights aspect itself—the nature of rights, what being a right consists in—is also of central importance. When we consider that an interest is fulfilled, protected, or promoted, there remains the question of what, if anything, is added when we say that a person has a *right* to this fulfillment? There are different theories on this question, but a main one, the will theory, emphasizes that, to have a right to X involves that a person should have personal control and autonomy over his having X, so that X is his personal

---

[2] 'In Singapore, 1970's Law Becomes Weapon Against SARS', *New York Times*, June 10, 2003, Section D ('Science Times'), D5, National edition.

normative property. This point can be accepted as giving added weight to the idea of individual human rights as against community or group rights, but it does not remove the essential focus of human rights on the interests of agency that they serve and fulfill.

What has emerged from the above line of argument is that human rights are based on the necessary conditions of human action. It is this normative necessity that explains the mandatoriness of human rights.

II. Let us now consider some of the applications of the PGC. These applications are of two main kinds: *direct* and *indirect*. In the direct application, individual agents act toward their recipients with due consideration for their freedom and well-being. This due consideration may be negative—that is, not violating their generic rights—or positive, in which agents help their recipients to have some aspects of freedom and well-being, though this help may largely proceed through appropriate institutions.

In the indirect applications, the actions of agents proceed through morally justified institutions. These institutions are morally justified insofar as they are based on the freedom of agents to act in accord with the PGC, or as they enable such agents to advance their well-being along one or another of their three levels, with due consideration for the recipients' own generic rights.

It is especially in these indirect, institutional applications that we find a severe challenge to the general theory of human rights sketched above. The challenge is this: How can the moral necessity, the normative mandatoriness of human rights, be extended to the complex empirical contexts in which human rights are to be applied and implemented? These contexts are in important respects immoral, rights-violating. They comprise in large part systems of oppression and impoverishment that are diametrically opposed to the general freedom and well-being that are upheld in the fundamental theory of human rights.

The challenge to human rights, then, is this: How can the moral necessity of human rights be upheld in the face of the wrongful contingencies, the rights-violations of the actual world? Indeed, these wrongs have been so widespread throughout human history that they may themselves be regarded as necessities—not moral but empirical. But in any case there have also been stalwart defenders of freedom and well-being on a universal or at least social scale. In these contingencies the moral necessity of the PGC can at least serve as a model of an ideal to be aimed at, although this must not be confused with the empirical realities. Still, morality, including human rights, can serve as a stimulus to moral struggle for human rights.

It is indeed true that one may react to the widespread morally pathological situations by urging that they be replaced by regimes of freedom and well-being. But these, as counsels of perfection, may be ineffectual at best, especially if they provide no means of moving from the ideal theory to the actual practice. So if discussion of the applications of the PGC is to be at all relevant to the actual world, we must take due account of the limitations of human rights as purported guides to social policy in the empirical circumstances that provide the actual context of practice.

The regime of human rights can provide at least two related ways of circumventing these empirical challenges. One way is by an appeal to the self-interest of the wrongdoers. If they can be made to see that action in conformity with human rights advances their self-interest more than do violations, such conformity can be promoted. This may sometimes work, but then again it may not.

A second related way of meeting the empirical challenge is by the threat or actual use of force. After all, force was used in the historical antecedents of human rights in the appeals to 'natural rights' in the modern English, American, and French Revolutions. As we shall see, power underlies all the main segments of human rights. The use of force or power is not at all precluded by the status of human rights as highly valuable norms for action. Human rights need not be empirically ineffectual; on the contrary, it is permissible to threaten or actually to use force in order to advance what is morally justified. To be sure, the use of force should not make things worse for the victims of rights-violations; but this is a matter of empirical calculation, not of moral prohibition. A fuller understanding of human rights must include these empirical complexities.

Let us now begin this more contextual analysis. The institutional applications of the PGC as kinds of human rights are often divided into political-civil rights and social-economic rights, with further rubrics of cultural or group rights, as well as developmental rights. While these divisions according to objects have some prima facie plausibility, it is important to recognize that all these kinds of rights, including economic rights, are focused on or derivative from political rights, because they crucially involve institutional relations of power. The hunger, malnutrition, disease, poverty, and illiteracy that plague millions of human beings throughout the world reflect distributions of power that are unjust because of their severe negative impact on the rights of agency and their drastically crippling inequalities. Amid the great values of deliberative democracy, it is largely the power of the dominant groups of agents that generates and solidifies these injustices. The question of what is to be done about them, what duties they impose, thus comes down to an issue of the power of agents as individuals, as groups, and as institutions. And this involves the abilities of agency both as what interests are to be protected and as institutional steps taken to provide this protection. So the abilities of agency figure here both as ends and as means.

This thesis about power and the centrality of political rights is not to be confused with the oft-disputed doctrine that social and economic rights do not belong within human rights at all. Rather, it is a thesis about the scope of social and economic rights within the general sphere of human rights.

Economic rights are intensely controversial partly because they threaten the libertarian or free-market principles that are upheld by advocates of economic globalization. For such advocates, the economic provisions of the Universal Declaration of Human Rights (UDHR) and the International Covenant on Economic, Social and Cultural Rights, which propose to protect basic abilities of agency, are dangerous threats to economic freedom and the power it brings to the wealthier segments of society. These provisions are redistributionist; far from letting the free market take its course in determining economic outcomes, they intervene to protect and promote the agency rights of the most vulnerable persons.

The aim of human rights in this context is, in important part, to equip human beings with the abilities of agency that derive from the generic features of action and that give them the power to ward off the hardships of political oppression and severe economic deprivation and to attain their opposites. For this purpose there must be social institutions of various kinds, including political, legal, and economic, and these institutions must be global in scope because it is the essential interests of all human beings that are at stake. But ultimately all these institutions must be systems of power and, as such, they are instrumental to the fulfillment or implementation of human rights. In this regard they are themselves included among human rights.

The central question of economic justice is: how can the human right to basic economic well-being—whose objects include food, shelter, and medical care—be implemented in the face of the opposition to change on the part of dominant groups and the extreme poverty and consequent suffering that afflict millions of human beings in all parts of the world? At least two assumptions underlie this question. One is that mass global poverty is a violation of human rights because it involves a humanly generated lack of the necessary goods of action, with severe constrictions of the abilities of agency. Hence, the duty that is called for is not merely compassion or charity, valuable though these may be, but rather a way of preventing and overcoming the violations, including therein the system that allows or fosters them. To overcome them is to fulfill the rights of agency that are thus violated, so that the rights are implemented as a matter of substantive global justice. A second assumption is that, despite the arguments of Malthusians, social Darwinians, and others, the impacts of poverty can to a large extent be removed by the actions of appropriate institutional respondents.

The UDHR sets forth, as the respondents or duty-bearers of the rights, both private individuals or groups on the one hand and governments on the other (Preamble). As respondents, they seek to control or determine how the objects of the rights are to be distributed.

Following up this distinction, let us begin with a policy of self-help as a way of dealing with the economic needs. The 'self' in self-help may refer to a large variety of potential respondents, ranging at one extreme from a solitary individual to, at the other extreme, a whole society viewed as providing for its own needs as against relying on the help of other groups or societies. Despite attempted idealizations on the model of Robinson Crusoe, there are sharp limits to what the hungry, malnourished, disease-ridden individual can do for himself without outside help to develop his abilities of successful agency. Much will depend on his intelligence and determination as well as on his external circumstances. It is far more likely that he will have to have the help of others to provide for his basic agency needs. These others may range from a cohort of fellow-sufferers to organized groups, including NGOs and governments (Nickel 1996:171–85). This, then, presents a severe challenge to the efficacy of human rights. Let us, then, turn to governments as potential providers.

In approaching governments for this economic purpose, we must consider a preliminary caution about political power. Will the ruling authorities in a state agree to have their prerogatives diluted by the groups or parties of the poor, including when they invoke the equalities of human rights? Won't they regard this as an attack on their sovereignty? There is a long history of hindrance and sabotage on the part of governments when the poor parties they are supposed to serve seek to fulfill their human rights by participating in decisions affecting them. Moreover, if the government in its 'political culture' is corrupt, may not similar corruption attach to the poor when they, in order to implement their rights, must group themselves into politically effective organizations? May not these organizations be subject to the same conflicts over ethnic and other divisive features as characterize their governments? These questions indicate the empirical obstacles against global justice as serving to implement economic human rights. Nevertheless, the drastic imperatives for basic well-being set by hunger, malnutrition, illness, ignorance, and so on can lead the poor to focus on policies that address their basic needs. They can make at least partly effective appeals for assistance to sympathetic organizations that would contribute to effectuating the needed reforms in the distribution both of political power and of necessary economic goods.

Let us now consider governments as the respondents or duty-bearers of economic human rights. Amid the limitations of governments indicated above, should each government take care only of its own citizens' basic economic needs, or should the responsibility be spread around so that a government is responsible for helping the citizens of other countries as well as its own? Let us call the former position *internalist* and the latter *externalist*. Problems of universalism and national sovereignty are involved in this alternative of policy, the externalist being closer to the universalization of human rights. Even apart from the issue of what particular governments can afford, the internalist–externalist debate raises questions about applications of global justice and international obligations.

A large part of the background of the internalist position bears on the causal explanation of the deprivations that are violative of economic human rights. These explanations are themselves either internalist or externalist. The internalist explanation holds that the causes of these deprivations lie entirely within each country's policies, so that what is required to avoid or rectify the deprivations is mainly to remove those internal causes. Thus, in specific regard to the causation of famines, John Rawls held that this causation rests not with the non-availability of food in the affected counties; rather, in Rawls's summary, 'The main problem was the failure of the respective governments to distribute (and supplement) what food there was' (1999*b*:109). More generally, Rawls wrote: 'The causes of the wealth of a people and the forms it takes lie in their political culture and in the religious, philosophical, and moral traditions that support the basic structure of their political and social institutions, as well as in the industriousness and cooperative talents of its members, all supported by their political virtues' (1999*b*:108). In a similar vein, Jean Drèze and Amartya Sen wrote that, with regard to the responsibility for famine prevention, 'the initiative and responsibility of entitlement protection efforts rested squarely with the government of the affected country' (1989: 159). Sen and Drèze uphold the internalist position more fully as follows: 'The agents of change in conquering hunger can come from inside or outside the country in question.... the focus of this book has been primarily on forces that operate from *inside*.... We have indeed mainly concentrated on what can be done through public action *within* the country to eradicate hunger'. The authors acknowledge that 'international help' can be useful in this regard, but as supplementing the internal forces: 'We do believe that both famine prevention and the eradication of endemic undernutrition call for leadership and coordination coming from inside rather than outside the country...' (1989: 273 [emphasis in original]). So this involves a particularist limitation on the universalism of human rights, and a corresponding restriction on the use of abilities of agency.

Both the internalist and the externalist positions involve relations of power. The internalist position by withholding aid to poor countries leaves them subject to exertions of power. The externalist position leaves the alien poor countries in the position of powerless petitioners.

The internalist causal explanation represents, at least in part, a damning empirical and moral indictment of the countries in question. The explanation is not that the respective governments lack the resources to prevent mass hunger, but rather that they are corrupt or incompetent or lack the will to prevent the calamities of starvation or famine. This would strongly suggest that power may be used to force government authorities to mend their ways or be overthrown in favor of a government that fulfills its moral obligations of economic human rights. Here a certain kind of self-help is called for where the suffering masses take their fate into their own hands to stop the violations of their basic human rights and at least start the process of fulfilling their rights. It is to this reversal that the internalist position on governmental responsibility may appeal.

There are several interrelated reasons for the avowed preference for the internalist position. Drèze and Sen point out that the governments of affected countries are 'able to draw at short notice on extensive networks of information, administration, communication, transport, and storage'. Political pressure within the affected countries can also be helpful 'in galvanizing the national government into action' (1989: 159). Such statements may take a too optimistic view of the effectiveness of popular protests in curbing the lethal violations committed by governments. And they leave unexplored the question of whether these internalist advantages can also be brought to bear on behalf of foreign countries. But the internalist arguments indicate that basic economic rights are requirements of political power, so that there is no separation of social-economic rights from political-civil rights.

The internalist may also hold that there is greater security in relying on internal forces rather than in steps to be taken from outside the country. In this regard, the internalist position focuses on self-reliance rather than on passive dependence upon other countries. Of course, the nature of the 'self' here may vary in important ways. For a government or country to rely on 'itself' is not necessarily the same as for the citizens or subjects of that government to have self-reliance; they may be passive dependents of 'their' government, without the latter being democratic.

The internalist position also incurs serious difficulties. It assumes two important points about the governments of the affected countries. First, if the governments are not democratic, they cannot be counted on to manage the production and distribution of food and other necessary commodities in a way that takes adequate account of the equal human rights of all their inhabitants, especially women. As is usually the case, the ruling oligarchies in the respective countries may be at best indifferent and often inimical to the food needs of their impoverished masses. There are important reasons for overthrowing such governments or at least intervening to rectify their policies in a more democratic direction. The vexed issues of 'humanitarian intervention' arise here. But second, even if they have some modicum of democracy, the governments, and indeed the entire country, may be so subjected to foreign power centers, political and economic, that they cannot do what is required to get food to those who need it most. Or else their democratic institutions may be too feeble to provide the needed corrections. More on this below.

The internalist position also incurs other difficulties. On the moral side, it suggests that wealthier countries have no moral obligations to meet the demands of human rights by warding off famine and other basic harms that afflict other poor countries. Blame for incurring such harms is to be directed against the poor countries themselves; if they would only correct their deficient 'political culture', all would go well with them. So, even in the face of massive poverty, richer countries, on this view, have no responsibility to intervene. This disregard for the requirements of human rights is a glaring situation of social and, indeed, global injustice.

This matter of moral responsibility also has an empirical or causal side. Is it really the case that, as the internalist view strongly suggests, a country's severe poverty and other acute hardships derive solely from within its own society and can be adequately dealt with solely from within such a country's resources? As one writer puts it: 'This [internalist] view clearly underplays the vulnerability of developing societies to global markets, a situation which economic liberalization, whatever its benefits, has inevitably increased. It neglects the degree to which the emergence over time of the 'unfavorable conditions' that afflict poor societies has as much to do with external and global factors as with internal ones; and it ignores the extent to which national economic policy is shaped by international economic institutions and powerful states. How can a developing country be held responsible when the content of its economic policy is shaped by external pressures and by policy injunctions enforced by far-reaching commonalities? . . . there is enough evidence of the importance of external influences and of the impact of the global system to suggest that the idea of coresponsibility should act as the overall guiding principle' (Hurrell 2001: 46).

This criticism from the externalist position is augmented when we consider some of the internalist position's specific recommendations. When the internalist holds that systems of public employment can be established to remedy massive poverty, the question arises of how the impoverished government can pay for such a policy.[3] If it has the resources to cover these expenses, then it is already a long way past the endemic poverty that afflicts it. Public employment may indeed produce new wealth, and with it the benefits of economic exchange. But it is more likely that there must be an initial base to cover the start-up expenses of government-funded employment. An important possibility is that richer parts of the society would be taxed to pay for the work of the poor classes, so that while the position is still internalist, the society has segments that are differentially related to the economic process.

The distribution of power within a country has an important effect on its ability and willingness to provide the kinds of redistributive policies that public employment may support. But this distribution, especially as part of a country's 'public culture', may inhibit rather than support the relief of widespread poverty.

These empirical difficulties of the internalist position may lead to acceptance of an externalist view: that impoverished or developing countries should rely on help from richer countries as respondents or, to put it otherwise, that richer countries have a moral obligation to help relieve the severe poverty of developing countries. This has been a chief emphasis of the global justice movement: richer countries should transfer some of their great wealth to poorer countries, at least to the extent of enabling the latter to overcome their impoverishing disabilities. This would mean that the basic economic rights of persons would no longer be violated in the poor countries of the world.

While this is the most widely held position on 'foreign aid', it has serious difficulties. Since the giving of help is to be unconditional, this may encourage a kind of dependence on the power of others that saps the initiative and productive agency of the receiving countries. It may solidify and increase the very endemic suffering and inequality of wealth that constitute the problem of poverty.

According to the externalist position, government should provide long-term aid to the groups or individuals of other societies as well as their own when the persons in these other societies are suffering from the lack of fundamental well-being, including food, shelter, health care, and similar basic goods. This provision of long-term or short-term aid is to be unconditional, except perhaps that the receiving countries, if they can, are to buy the products of the donor countries. To provide such otherwise unconditional aid, income taxes and similar redistributive policies should be imposed by the donor government—all with a view to remedying the severe lack of basic well-being in other countries. The burdens thus imposed are to be cosmopolitan or global, taking no account of the diversities of states or nations except insofar as they reflect the radical contrasts of wealth and power between rich and poor countries.

This decrying of dependence may seem to contradict the widely held thesis that human rights are so inherent in all humans that they do not have to be 'earned' by

---

[3] For the difficulties of the employment creation policy, see Drèze and Sen (1989: 115 ff.).

one's labor or particular merits of accomplishments. Hence, 'dependence' is ruled out in any case of a human right: the non-dependence is a necessary condition of receiving the benefits of human rights. There is no contradiction, however, if the thesis is understood as holding that while the benefits of human rights belong to their holders unconditionally, what those benefits are may vary with different circumstances. A partial parallel is the case of criminals: by committing crimes they lose some of their human rights (such as freedom of movement) but still retain others.

In view of the difficulties of the internalist and externalist positions, let us turn to a third position, which I shall call *agency-empowering*. Unlike the internalist position, the agency-empowering government provides basic assistance for the impoverished persons in countries other than its own. But unlike the externalist position, while assistance is to be provided for poor persons regardless of location, this assistance is not to be unconditional or open-ended; rather, it is to aim at empowering the individuals and groups in the poor countries in order to enable them to develop their own human capital, their own abilities of productive agency so that they can provide for their own needs.

I have here sketched a way of overcoming world poverty that combines the internalist and externalist positions. In view of the drastic empirical difficulties, there is of course no absolute assurance of success in this enterprise, but it involves at least some major steps toward overcoming world poverty. This process is strongly augmented when we take account of the position I have called agency-empowering. The development I have traced has not been merely an increase of economic wealth; it has also involved a learning process whereby persons come to have greater control over their fortunes; they recognize much more fully how they can use self-help to develop their abilities of agency. So instead of being passive recipients of the actions of other persons, they are active agents in their own behalf. This is a vital contribution that derives from the implementation of the PGC that the whole process exemplifies.

The positions I have sketched have involved the receipt of assistance from governments, although in different ways. But all reflect the grounding of social-economic rights as civil-political rights. The chances of success in coping with world poverty thus depend heavily on what kind of government is to be invoked here. It is natural to conceive of this government as democratic, especially because of the agency-empowering position's emphasis on mutually developing and apply-ing the abilities of agency on the part of each individual. Although 'democ-ratization' is often invoked as a key to progress in the developing countries, its success is often hindered because of a lack of understanding on this vital matter. Democracy is not only instrumentally useful as helping toward the ful-fillment of social-economic rights; it has important value in its own right as assisting toward the fulfillment of human rights that are specifically political and civil.

In this specific scope, political democracy has three important aspects. They bear on the *source* of political action, the *limits* of power, and the *ends* of power. These yield three different kinds or aspects of political democracy. *Electoral* democracy is a system of universal suffrage in which the required majority or plurality of equally counted votes deriving from the abilities of agency serves to determine who are to be the holders of political authority. *Constitutional* democracy sets limits on political power; it requires protection of basic human rights, including the civil liberties of expression and association, and the rule of law, including equal protection of the laws, whereby political authority is bound by antecedent, general, predictable rules set by previously agreed-upon precedents, so that the abilities of agency are protected in regularized patterns. *Social* democracy bears on the ends of political authority. While these may be quite diffuse, they serve to bring together most directly the civil-political rights and the social-economic rights discussed above. The rights of social democracy especially require protection of basic economic well-being, including that equal educational opportunities be provided for the development and exercise of the abilities of agency. Here, the political and civil rights merge into the social and economic rights.

While each of these kinds of democracy can exist without the others, the full development of political democracy requires all three. All three are concerned with equally developing and applying the abilities of agency that are central objects of human rights. All three can provide for deliberation and mutual consultation.

Of these three aspects of political democracy, the first, bearing on the source of political authority, is the most familiar. It involves a principle of consent: as a matter of human rights, political authority must rest on the consent of the governed. It is not easy, however, to be clear about what this consent involves. John Locke declared that 'no one can be . . . subjected to the political power of another, without his own consent' (1988: II. 95). This individualist conception of consent opens the way to anarchy: if the individual's consent is the necessary condition of political obligation, then all one needs to do to evade one's obligation to obey laws one dislikes is to withdraw one's consent. Here is not the place to trace Locke's tergiversations on this issue, ultimately in his appeal to 'tacit consent'. Consent, as a matter of human rights, must be viewed rather in dispositional or systemic terms as involving an institutional method and deliberative framework whereby consents and dissents are counted equally to arrive at majority or plurality votes. The majority or plurality party wins the election and takes on governmental authority.

The method of consent is a political application of the generic human right of freedom of action. Although political freedom is not the same as freedom of action, the two are closely related. Freedom of action consists in controlling one's behavior by one's informed choice, and political freedom is a system for controlling the actions and policies of the governmental officials as they impinge on one's freedom and well-being.

The principle of electoral democracy is given this succinct statement in Article 21 of the Universal Declaration of Human Rights (UDHR): 'Everyone has the right to take part in the government of his country, directly or through freely chosen representatives. .... The will of the people shall be the basis of the authority of government; this will shall be expressed in periodic and genuine elections, which shall be by universal and equal suffrage and shall be held by secret vote or by equivalent free voting procedures'. The method of consent provides for active participation of all citizens in the electoral process of debating and advocating one's preferred policies. This active participation is a fundamental value of the human right to electoral democracy: it involves that persons are not mere passive beneficiaries of the actions of others, but are rather active determinants who are in control of their own destinies. By exercising their abilities of agency, they can make their views known forcefully and vociferously, especially calling attention to their vital economic needs. One is reminded of Amartya Sen's striking statement that famines have not occurred in democracies with a free press (1999: 152).

The method of consent, however, also has well-known dangers that graphically indicate the empirical limitations of human rights. Despite its equal counting of votes, the method allows for great departures from effective equality: groups that are wealthier and hence more powerful are able to control the policies of government with a view to their own, often inimical, interests. The method may therefore fail to take account of the vital needs of the majority in fields like work conditions, housing, health care, and education. In a different relation, a majority may vote its prejudices to oppress a disliked minority; it may win an election and then become electorally undemocratic and violate the method of consent.

The requirements of constitutional democracy can make a valuable contribution here, by imposing limits on what a majority may do in oppressing the minority; for example, the majority may not remove or diminish the electoral influence of a minority or impose on it drastically unequal conditions such as slavery. But there is a strong possibility of conflict here between electoral and constitutional democracy. There is much to be said for forcibly imposing constitutional limits that prevent such violations of constitutional democracy. The non-violence of consent may here have to give way to the coercion of constitutional guarantees, although this coercion may itself be favorably voted on by electoral democracy.

The inequalities of effective political power allowed by electoral democracy have a deleterious effect on the abilities of governments to cope with the searing traumas of world hunger and poverty. Two kinds of empirical attempts at remedy are relevant. One is the growth of international institutions like the United Nations and the European Union, which seek to impose certain standards of human rights for morally justified policies. What may be called 'moral globalization', in symmetry with economic globalization but with a substantive focus on moral policies and institutions, is dedicated to implementing such moral policies on a worldwide basis. Second, there is the emphasis on the empowerment of individuals and groups whereby they develop and use their abilities of agency to implement their human social and economic rights. These abilities are of central importance in the attempts to overcome world poverty.

Many of the above considerations have emphasized the importance of avoiding undue idealizations of human rights. The claims made by human rights must be moderated in various empirical contexts, including where their mutual conflicts are dealt with in their varying degrees of needfulness for action, their circumscription by realities of power, their division into internalist and externalist duties of governments, the difficulties of electoral democracy, and so forth. Despite these practical limitations, human rights can be fundamental factors in the civilizing and moralizing of human life.

9

Extreme Poverty in a Wealthy World: What Justice Demands Today

*Marcelo Alegre**

9.1. INTRODUCTION

In this essay I defend the validity of a human rights approach to the problem of global poverty, emphasizing one characteristic of the prevailing indifference toward extreme deprivation—its gratuitousness. Some of the predominant views about the problem are based on obsolete factual assumptions (that poverty eradication is impossible or very costly). Removing these false assumptions is an important part of a pro-poor strategy.

I briefly expose some of the reservations that the UN Millennium Goals provoke from a human rights perspective, both for their wording and their substantial omissions. Poverty alleviation should be understood as more than a 'goal' and the aim should be its eradication, not its administration.

I then examine the relation between justice and a humanity principle interpreted in a different way from the libertarian and utilitarian readings of this principle. I argue that humanity is not well understood as simple compassion, or as a requirement that falls outside of the realm of justice. On the contrary, humanity, I claim, sets the lower bound for the operation of fairness considerations.

Finally, and turning into the national context, I consider the case for the constitutionalization of a right to freedom from poverty (especially in the intranational context) and some of the consequences of such constitutionalization.

9.2. POVERTY IN A RICH WORLD

A right to subsistence has been aptly named by Henry Shue (1996*a*) a basic right. This right is basic in the sense that enjoyment of other rights depends on the

* I am most grateful for illuminating and detailed comments generously made to a previous draft by Thomas Pogge. Thanks also to Paola Bergallo, Eugenio Bulygin, Ricardo Caracciolo, Leonardo Filippini, Roberto Gargarella, Ricardo Guibourg, Pablo Navarro, Rekha Nath, Eduardo Rivera López, to the assistants to the workshop organized by UNESCO on this subject in the University of Sao Paolo, Brazil, May 6–7, 2003, to the assistants to the Legal Philosophy Seminar held at Vaquerías (Argentina) in September 2004, and to the assistants to the Seminar on Practical Ethics (UBACYT Project) directed by Florencia Luna at the Sociedad Argentina de Análisis Filosófico.

enjoyment of this one. I think the basic character of this right also is strengthened by the peculiarity of the corresponding duties, particularly by the minor cost of satisfying this right. Extreme poverty today is inextricably linked to extreme inequality, and the necessary redistribution of resources needed from the wealthy would not affect them substantially.

A human rights claim usually means that the interests at stake are so crucial that other goals or preferences must be subordinated to the fulfillment and respect of those interests. An extra weight (in some cases an absolute one) is attached to such rights. A hard case arises when rights are in conflict or competition with one another. But even when they compete merely with social preferences and aggregate utility, there are issues of policy, democratic legitimacy, and stability, which are not always easily solvable. But the case of extreme poverty seems different in that its abolition under present circumstances is not in conflict with *anything of comparable value*. In other words, attainment of a right against extreme deprivation does not require significant sacrifices.

Awareness about the factual basis of our reflections is particularly necessary in this terrain. Much of the common sense opinions in relation to severe poverty is based on false empirical claims, the most influential being that eradication of poverty is impossible, or at least very costly. Richard Rorty (1996), for example, says that poverty eradication is a chimera. To him, it is like requiring a person to share a loaf of bread with a hundred starving people: all would end up starving.[1] This view ignores some proved facts about severe deprivation, mainly the extraordinary levels of global inequality, which entails that the transfers from the wealthy portion of humanity to the poor one, required to wipe out indigence, do not amount to nothing near an important burden. A right to basic necessities emerges more clearly once some of those falsities are removed. The point is not merely rhetorical: the moral force of a right is greater when its satisfaction does not demand extreme or even significant sacrifices and, conversely, the moral evil of violating a right increases when there is no relevant cost involved in stopping the violation.

The consideration of the subject has been dominated by the idea that the duties correlated with a right to basic necessities entail some relevant sacrifices or costs. Framing the issue of extreme poverty as a human rights problem was, in this context, extremely important, because it provided a strong moral justification for the efforts and sacrifices needed for the eradication of severe deprivation. Rights are focal interests deserving special protection and a strong priority in the public agenda and the public policies. In the same way that respecting civil and political rights may entail sacrifices for third parties (having to tolerate expressions we deeply dislike, for example, is a sacrifice required by the respect of freedom of speech), and economic sacrifices too (think of the massive budgetary provisions needed to sustain a system of courts), the burdens imposed by a principled commitment to end extreme poverty are amply justified by any decent conception of society that recognizes human beings' dignity and inviolability. Accordingly,

---

[1] Pogge (2004*a*) shows the inadequacy of Rorty's view.

the costs incurred by an anti-poverty policy—from slowing economic growth to underfunding artistic enterprises—are just the price a civilized order must pay to gain legitimacy.[2] This is also true, of course, at the global level—even a war fought for a just cause must not be won at the cost of terrorizing civilians or torturing prisoners. A right to basic necessities is correlated with global duties, duties of states and of individuals. The fulfillment of *global rights* may also trump the pursuit of *global goods* or benefits.

Well before the end of the twentieth century, it was clear that humanity could put an end to extreme poverty, although this would entail—it was assumed—significant global, national, and/or individual efforts. But it seems that we are in a different stage today, one in which severe deprivation is a particularly monstrous kind of human rights violation. Given the actual state of affluence of the developed countries, it is not the case that in order to remove extreme poverty it is necessary to embark on policies requiring significant sacrifices.[3] If properly implemented with the full cooperation of the governments of the rich countries, eradication of extreme poverty will not have a significant negative impact on wealthy individuals and nations.

On the one hand, a powerful anti-poverty policy would not need an extra financial effort, but could instead be based on the reallocation of part of what now is being spent on other issues, like military resources and self-defeating protectionist policies (shown in Pogge 2002*a*). On the other hand, the eradication of poverty would mean the inclusion of one billion more people into the global economy, which means greater consumption and consequently growth, and in turn, more profits for the central economies, which are the best positioned to take advantage of an increase in global demand.

This is not to say that the eradication of poverty is the policy that best satisfies the self-interest of the wealthy. It means that eradication of poverty is consistent with the self-interest of the privileged portion of humanity, that it does not threaten our comfortable position, and that this makes our indifference toward the global poor more unjustifiable. Now, even if eradication of poverty advanced

---

[2] Some of the sacrifices needed to alleviate global inequality were suggested in 1998 by the UNDP *Human Development Report*, as reported by Crossette in 'Kofi Annan's astonishing facts!', *New York Times*, September 28, 1998: 'Americans spend $8 billion a year on cosmetics—$2 billion more than the estimated annual total needed to provide basic education for everyone in the world. Europeans spend $11 billion a year on ice cream—$2 billion more than the estimated annual total needed to provide clean water and safe sewers for the world's population. Americans and Europeans spend $17 billion a year on pet food—$4 billion more than the estimated annual additional total needed to provide basic health and nutrition for everyone in the world. It is estimated that the additional cost of achieving and maintaining universal access to basic education for all, basic health care for all, reproductive health care for all women, adequate food for all and clean water and safe sewers for all is roughly $40 billion a year—or less than 4 percent of the combined wealth of the 225 richest people in the world'. If I am right, no cut on these trivial expenditures, or any taking of the property of the referred billionaires, is needed to eliminate extreme poverty.

[3] Pogge (2002*a*: 2) explains that the poorest '2,800 million people together have about 1.2 percent of aggregate global income, while the 903 million people of the 'high income economies' together have 79.7 percent. Shifting merely 1 percent of aggregate global income—$312 billion annually—from the first group to the second would eradicate severe poverty worldwide' (internal footnotes omitted).

the selfish interests of the rich persons, states and corporations (a stronger claim than the one I am making here) it would not be surprising that they refrain from voluntarily changing the status quo. Schools, hospitals, and roads also improve the situation of all, but we do not expect them to be built by market forces. Eradication of poverty is on a par with these public goods—private agents acting separately face coordination problems that call for a transnational commitment of efforts. Another popular view about poverty, related to the first one (that poverty is ineradicable or, if solvable, only at an exacting cost) is that we should not focus first on poverty, but on development. This view plays the similar function of serving to undermine the requirement of direct and urgent actions to alleviate destitution. Yet the view that poverty will be reduced only as a result of economic growth has proven to be too simplistic. Dani Rodrik (2000) shows that implementing the right anti-poverty policies does not impede but rather accelerates economic growth. Bruno, Ravallion, and Squire (1998) show the inefficiency of the credit constraints affecting the poor, which slows economic growth. They also explain that redistribution of assets through land reform contributed to economic growth in Japan, Taiwan, and South Korea. In the same way, Eckstein and Zilcha (1994) show that compulsory schooling (a crucial tool in poverty eradication) affects growth positively. The context of high inequality that often surrounds extreme poverty also produces a disproportionate influence of the rich on the public policies, favoring particularly tax policies (Persson and Tabellini 1994) and monetary policies (Laban and Sturzenegger 1992) that generate slower growth.

Poverty is not unavoidable, its eradication is feasible at low cost, and pro-poor policies accelerate and do not slow development. If this is right, this means that in 2005 the human right of subsistence is correlated with duties involving no relevant costs, which in turn means that the violation of human rights implied by extreme poverty is particularly egregious because it is gratuitous and irrational. More than one billion human beings are being wronged not just by being treated as mere means to some useful social end (say, the preservation of the economic basis of modern democracies, or the accumulation of capital that would make poverty eradication possible in the future). That would be wicked enough, but, even worse, they are being denied their rights for no important reason whatsoever, given that implementing policies aimed at wiping out destitution would not significantly affect (and perhaps would advance) the interests (including the crude economic interests) of the rest.[4]

Once the urgency of the needs is established, and the unfairness of global political and economic institutions (I will say more about the core of this unfairness) enters into the picture, the fact that what the privileged would forgo in a more just global arrangement is superfluous or even amounts to nothing, further

---

[4] Would not it also be objectionable to achieve poverty eradication motivated by the reward of having one billion of additional consumers? I am aware that from some Kantian quarters it could be claimed that this would be just another way of treating the poor as means. Yet I am not praising the moral value of actions by individuals who are motivated by self-interest alone, but defending the legitimacy of institutions and policies that take advantage of those motivations. (I thank Ignacio Mastroleo for helpful discussion of this point.)

strengthens, in my view, the stringency and force of a global right to be free from extreme poverty.

This fact also forces us to reflect on problems of irrationality and lack of collective coordination which transcend the bare domain of justice. I do not know whether it would be more effective to challenge the prevailing indifference toward the global poor for being immoral or for being just irrational, but I certainly believe the second route deserves some attention, for it speaks in the language of national and individual self-interest that dominates the conversations of the powerful.[5]

It seems plausible to think there is a lag in the informational basis informing public opinion on this issue. Maybe the predominant reactions in wealthy societies regarding the problem of global extreme poverty are informed by wrong information—wrong because obsolete. For example, a great proportion of well-educated citizens in the wealthy countries perhaps shares Rorty's claim that the aim of eradication of poverty is utopian because it would throw the affluent people of the developed democracies into destitution. If this is so, then it seems crucial to spread the word how cheap it is to drastically reduce extreme poverty—this would erase one of the sources of resistance to change.[6] This is part of, among others, academics' responsibility on this issue.

If poverty were not a main global problem, but an insolvable tragedy, then it would be less objectionable for the non-poor people to turn our backs to the issue. Even if it were not considered a tragedy without solution, if the efforts needed to overcome it were enormous, this would also explain (though not justify) the predominant attitude of indifference. But if extreme poverty is acknowledged to be fixable, through a modest redistribution of resources and through intelligent policies, then ignoring the problem is more than simple rational avoidance—it becomes unforgivable complicity.

A caveat: I do not claim that transfer of resources is the only means to eradicate severe poverty—this would be plainly wrong.[7] But I do assume that a shift of resources is necessary and those who believe in the impossibility or the extreme

---

[5] Against this it could be argued that, from the standpoint of the privileged, providing one billion victims of inequality with a modicum amount of resources would threaten the interest of the rich because it would imply empowering the poor to struggle for justice on a more secure footing. It is difficult to imagine this idea being phrased in the public discourse of civilized people, but it should be certainly considered when assessing the rationality of the resistance to eradicate severe deprivation. Another point often made is that global environmental problems would intensify if the present poor also became significant consumers of depletable resources and producers of pollution. But this ignores that population control is easier in the absence of extreme poverty.

[6] Another source of resistance that deserves attention (at least in the United States) is the false belief that huge amounts of money are actually spent on foreign aid that contributes to poverty relief.

[7] Heredia (1996) lists seven structural roots of poverty: Lack of democracy, lack of access to means of production and resources, lack of adequate mechanisms for savings and distribution, national economies not being oriented to local needs, weak government role regarding social services, overexploitation of resources and pollution, policies favoring monopolization and thus, polarization. Good democratic governance—local and global—is the key to resolve the problem. Economic transfers make sense as part of it.

difficulty of poverty eradication have in mind this redistributive aspect of strong anti-poverty policies. My argument addresses those views.

From a human rights perspective, the feasibility of poverty eradication removes two obstacles in the defense of the protected interests. First, consequentialist arguments, second, self-interested motives. A right trumps both, and so does the right to minimum resources, but having consequences count in favor of pro-poor policies makes it easier to achieve its fulfillment. Also, the fact that the efforts required are not heavy, should be publicized in order to erode self-interested sources of resistance. The human rights strategy, then, should be careful to make clear that this right has the particular feature of not colliding with consequentialist reasons and of not pressing too hard on self-interested motives.

Before speculating on the philosophical grounds of the right to be free from extreme poverty, I would like to note that a human rights approach to the issue of extreme poverty that would take into account the previous observations, cannot be but critical of the Millennium Goals, unanimously approved by the member states of the United Nations, which read, in relation to extreme poverty, as follows:

Target 1: Halve, between 1990 and 2015, the proportion of people whose income is less than one dollar a day.

Target 2: Halve, between 1990 and 2015, the proportion of people who suffer from hunger.

The Millennium Goals have been criticized for their lack of ambitiousness, and for the way in which they measure poverty.[8] In my view, under a human rights approach the Goals deserve several objections. First, there is the problem of the use of the language of 'Goals'. As we saw, rights are more than just desirable objectives. They entail a kind of priority that is watered down by talking of goals. We could certainly use the word goal trying to mean 'imperative goal' or 'overriding goal', in order to convey the idea—entailed by the notion of rights—that respecting or fulfilling them is not just an objective among others, but a reason to postpone other goals and objectives. Governments have lots of goals, and because they cannot attain all of them, they practice some sort of balance among them, ideally putting more weight on the more urgent goals and less into the less imperative ones. There are innumerable excuses often used to postpone respect for rights, and in the case of poverty the list of excuses tends to be long. One of the most common excuses places the 'goal' of alleviating extreme deprivation on the same footing as other 'goals', like those of guaranteeing security, or stability, or the need of fostering capital accumulation, or of supporting a system of incentives, and so on and so forth. 'The Millennium Goals' wording is unfortunate because it fails to transmit the urgency and crucial significance of the problem of extreme poverty. There has been a gradual erosion of the stance taken at the 1996 FAO World Food Summit in Rome, where 186 governments joined to condemn it as 'intolerable that more than 800 million people throughout the world, and particularly in developing countries, do not have enough food to meet their basic nutritional

---

[8] See, e.g., Reddy and Pogge 2007. Ravallion (2002) wrote a response to this critique, followed by a rejoinder from Reddy and Pogge (2002).

needs'.[9] The erosion is not wholly unrelated with the fact that, having endorsed this Declaration, the US government then went out of its way to explain that 'the attainment of any "right to adequate food" or "fundamental right to be free from hunger" is a goal or aspiration to be realized progressively that does not give rise to any international obligations'.[10]

Second, the Goals might be criticized for aiming at halving the proportion of people living under extreme poverty instead of at eliminating extreme poverty. Aiming at halving the proportion of extreme poor does not show respect, to say the least, for each of the victims of this global injustice. Extreme deprivation is not just a problem to be administered and, in time, reduced, but also a moral shame on humanity, to be eliminated as urgently as possible. Human rights have an individualistic feature: they derive from the unique and inviolable character of each human being. Given this individualized attribute, any policy attempting to rectify violations of human rights must take into account that each victim implies a distinct and separate, non-fungible loss. It has been pointed out that given current demographic trends, even if the Goals were accomplished, in 2015 nine million people would annually die from poverty-related causes (Pogge 2002*a*: 10). The Goals communicate the idea that extreme poverty is some sort of intractable issue, which we should hope to control and reduce, like an extended illness whose cure we have not yet discovered. If instead the international leaders had acknowledged that poverty is the result of unjust institutions, they would have agreed on the goal to terminate it and they would have set a shorter deadline. In any case, that a deadline for the elimination of extreme poverty has not been set at all or even discussed is startling and tacitly fosters the idea that eliminating poverty in the short run is an unrealistic objective, or that this is simply not so important.

Third, there is also the risk that a global target, because imperfectly built, condones an unacceptable aggregation of steps forward and steps back. As has been shown repeatedly, a strong reduction of poverty in China and India has, naturally, a great impact on the global numbers, which may serve to hide the fact that extreme poverty is not being reduced at all in other regions, like Latin America and sub-Saharan Africa.[11] Therefore, by not linking in its very formulation the objective of diminishing global poverty with national benchmarks, the Millennium Goals allow for an unacceptable aggregation of advances and retreats. The Goals give place to a monitoring process that releases pressures toward poverty alleviation in those areas that are described as being 'on track', as if there were reason for rejoicing while large numbers of people remain condemned to living below acceptable conditions and to dying prematurely. The status quo in each country should have been taken as a reference point in order to prevent that increases in poverty or lack of progress in anti-poverty policies in some places were balanced with improvements in other regions.

---

[9] http://www.fao.org/wfs/index_en.htm. See Pogge (2002*a*: 10).

[10] The whole document can be seen in the Web page of the United State Department of Agriculture-Foreign Agricultural Service, http://www.fas.usda.gov/icd/summit/interpre.html

[11] As shown in Report of the Secretary General of the United Nations General Assembly (2003). The data for Latin America is from World Bank (2003*b*).

If extreme poverty is a violation of human rights, then global policies should start by aiming at its eradication, not at its reduction to 'acceptable' levels. The best developments in some countries demonstrate it is possible to achieve elimination (not just halving) of extreme poverty in the near future. While pressing for the fulfillment of the Goals we must insist that the 'good trends' in some regions demonstrate that much more could and should be achieved much sooner.

Now this right to basic necessities could be understood as obliging only local governments and compatriots. On the contrary, I take this right as correlated also with global duties, especially duties of affluent states and individuals. Here the 'cheapness' of poverty eradication policies reinforces backward- and forward-looking arguments in favor of a cosmopolitan view. First, there is the backward-looking consideration to the effect that the way in which the current generation distributes the enormous accumulated capital labored by previous generations is arbitrary. In other words, there is no reason to exclude anyone from access to at least a small portion of what humanity has achieved throughout its history. It is plausible to think that radical inequality in the access to abundant resources, is morally worse than injustice in the distribution of very scarce resources. Second, 'cheapness' makes the case of extreme poverty a case falling into the Rescue Principle, the familiar forward looking consideration that makes it morally mandatory to support the extremely needy when this support entails little costs.[12]

In the next section, I explore some ways of grounding this global right to be free from severe deprivation.

9.3. HUMANITY, CHARITY, AND UNBOUNDED UTILITY

Do duties to eradicate poverty emanate from justice or from compassion? Tom Campbell has defended the view that a principle of humanity (or 'compassion')

---

[12] Scanlon (1998) provides this contractualist version of the Rescue Principle, which 'could not reasonably be rejected': 'if you are presented with a situation in which you can prevent something very bad from happening, or alleviate someone's dire plight, by making only a slight (or even moderate) sacrifice, then it would be wrong not to do so' (224). Recall the formulation, in Peter Singer (1972), of a stronger and a weaker variant of the principle to prevent famine in his famous piece ('if it is in our power to prevent something bad from happening, without thereby sacrificing anything of comparable importance, we ought, morally, to do it'; and, 'if it is in our power to prevent something very bad from happening, without thereby sacrificing anything morally significant, we ought, morally, to do it') (231). The empirical assumption that poverty eradication is not costly would make the moral obligation to support that policy fall into the weaker formulation. Singer claims, however, that his second formulation would imply 'that we all ought to give away half our incomes' (237), that it would require 'a great change in our life', and that it would 'ensure that the consumer society...would slow down and perhaps disappear entirely' (241). (Singer saw these effects as not necessarily bad.) Now if none of these actions or consequences (which could scare other people) are required to wipe out extreme poverty, then 'morally significant' in the less demanding variant of the principle could be interpreted in a much more conservative way than the one proposed by Singer himself, weakening the second formulation even more.

should be distinguished from claims of justice.[13] Now Campbell's point rests on the assumption that justice in turn depends on considerations of merit and desert. If we believe people are entitled to certain things irrespective of their merit or desert, then, according to Campbell, we should seek support outside the domain of justice. For Campbell, humanity (or compassion, or utility, or beneficence,[14] which he uses interchangeably) 'may properly be regarded at least on equal footing with (and perhaps as overriding) justice in the determination of our moral priorities for the distribution of benefits and burdens' (1974: 6).

According to Campbell, humanitarian duties somehow compete with justice. I want to endorse a different approach. I will distinguish three readings of a principle of humanity, and then try to defend the third one. The first is the libertarian reading, according to which humanity means compassion, and calls for a supererogatory, non-enforceable obligation. (I call this reading 'libertarian' not because it is accepted by mainstream libertarianism, but for the weaker reason that this is the most that some of them could come to accept.) This view has been traditionally attacked for leaving untouched (discursively and in deed) the injustice of underlying social and economic structure, and for transmitting a demeaning message to the receivers depicted as beggars who should be grateful to the donors and not as victims of extreme forms of inequality (Nagel 1977).

A second reading is the utilitarian one. Utilitarians tend to accept (on certain Humean variants) a link between compassion and duty, but they favor a more stringent and demanding version of a humanity principle, one that should be legally recognized, for example. They interpret this principle in terms of an unconditional duty to relieve suffering.

These two readings have been criticized by liberal egalitarians who reject, in general, the libertarian understanding of humanity for being too weak and quietist, and the utilitarian version for not providing restrictions to the kind of things that must be done to alleviate suffering or to maximize utility. Yet I share the utilitarian aspiration of unconditionality—the claim that people are entitled to a certain minimum without further investigations on their desert, merits, or the causes that led them into destitution. (I say 'aspiration' because, in fact, utilitarianism does condition poverty alleviation to the requirement that this would maximally improve some empirically measurable factor, like utility or preference satisfaction. A 'prioritarian' approach would place the claims of the poor in a safer status—they are preferentially entitled to resources or benefits even if that allocation results in a lower aggregated utility.)

I want to propose a third reading of the principle of humanity, one that may also be acceptable from non-utilitarian quarters, like the Rawlsian or liberal egalitarian perspectives. Humanity—the principle that all humans must have a guarantee of basic necessities—may be construed under a fairness approach, thus strengthening the unconditionality of the utilitarian version. The idea is that in order to act as givers of justice, people need to be above a certain level of material resources.

---

[13] Tom Campbell (1974 and this volume). Iglesias Vila (2004) agrees with this approach.
[14] See Campbell (1974: 1 and 6; this volume: 2).

This interpretation makes sense even on a narrow reading of what justice is. Even if we take justice to be the domain of distributive considerations ruled by desert and merit, a principle of humanity plays the important, though negative, role in setting the limits of the playing field—it sets the lower bounds below which nobody is allowed to fall, whatever the antecedent merits of his or her conduct.

This humanity principle is, in my view, the core idea grounding the human right to be free from extreme poverty. This does not mean that claims of causal responsibility are superfluous. Knowing which practices actually work to enslave people into poverty, which rules discriminate against the global weak, and which groups and persons take advantage of these unjust institutions is the best way to know what to do to stop these trends, and to single out who should be principally charged with the duties to end the violation of the basic rights at stake. But the humanity principle does entail that the core injustice of global institutions consists in their denial of a universal guarantee of basic necessities for all. All other factors of unfairness pile up on this nuclear injustice.

The fact that a principle operates as a condition (or as a limit) for other considerations of justice does not mean that this principle is outside the realm of justice. After all, the base of a building is part of the building. In this case, this principle of humanity serves as a guide for basic institutions and for public policy, its violation seems sufficient to deem a society unjust, it has significant distributional implications, and so on and so forth. What else should be shown to convince anyone that this *is* a principle of justice?

Some time ago, Nagel (1977) described extreme poverty as an issue of 'radical inequality' and proposed a principle of humanity as a matter of justice:

> One consequence of the view that radical inequality is an injustice arising from the economic system is that aid should be truly humanitarian. By this I mean it should be directed at the impoverished purely in virtue of their humanity and not in virtue of their special relation to the donor. Everyone at the bottom deserves help.

It is important not to confuse this controversy with a merely linguistic one. What is at stake is not the proper use of the term 'humanity'. This discussion is not about words, but ideas—in particular if an unconditional, universal duty to protect people from severe deprivation is grounded on justice or not. I called that duty a humanitarian one, but it may be named differently, of course. The issue is whether that duty (whatever its label) is to be understood as just the product of a sympathetic concern with the fate of the poor, or of a generous response to the pull exerted by the suffering of deprivation and hunger, or whether, as I claim, it should be considered a core element of justice, that is, of those set of considerations which should ultimately guide the functioning of institutions. Sympathy, generosity, and fraternal love are too contingent a base for a right to basic resources, and it seems difficult to translate them into institutional responses. This is not to deny that these sentiments may play a fundamental role in a global strategy against poverty. On the contrary, according to a conception of humanity-as-justice they gain a stronger footing: they are the proper attitudinal response to the unfairness of the current state of affairs regarding the access to basic goods.

Therefore, I think Pogge (2002*a*) is right when he says that our duties to the global poor arise from the obligation not to impose an unjust system on others. I think the claim should be considered right even by someone who rejected in total or in part Pogge's plausible causal claims. Even if someone could find (or imagine) a place in the world where extreme poverty could not be causally attributed to the working of the unfair global rules, or a history of oppression and violence, it would remain true that we are imposing an unjust system on the poor living there, by our refusal to guaranteeing basic necessities to them, when that guarantee would be insignificantly costly for us and most probably beneficial. An objector could ask us to imagine two societies on separate continents, and not connected by trade or travel. If the rich one refuses to help erase poverty in the poor one, is that enough, the objector could ask, to say that it is 'imposing an unjust system on the poor living there'? How could the rich be 'imposing' anything if they are just refusing to be related or connected with the poor society to start with? I would respond that the rich society is imposing injustice by excluding the poor society from resources it is entitled to as a society of humans, given that those resources could be transferred without affecting significantly the rich society's welfare. The same reasoning would apply if the isolated continent were affected by a genocide, or a disease for which the rest of the world knew the cure. The victims there would be entitled to international intervention or to access to the formula for curing the disease, independently of the existence or absence of past connections. It would not be controversial to say that, from the standpoint of the victims, we would be imposing on them an unjust system if we did nothing to stop the genocide or refrained from sharing our medical knowledge with the inhabitants of the unfortunate continent. A system that makes it possible for a genocide (or a preventable epidemic) to occur when it would be avoidable is unjust, and those who have effective control over the relevant outcomes are indeed imposing this system on those who suffer under it.

Now it may be objected that the point is merely academic and that, given the world as we know it, there is no need to appeal to an unconditional right to resources as a way of showing that the rights of the global poor are being systematically violated. But I think that the point is significant, and that there are potent political reasons in favor of the humanity approach. First, a humanity principle provides a safer ground for the claims of the poor in the sense that it is less dependent on empirical claims. It is not implausible to think that some of the poverty in the world does not originate in the unfairness of global rules. If a humanity principle is included in what fairness requires, as I think it should be, even this hypothetical set of people would be entitled to redistribution. Second, I suspect that it is more realistic to believe that even in a world of open markets and without tyrannies there will be people that could be excluded from the benefits of economic progress, just because markets imply winners and losers, and democracies may well create and sustain hard conservative coalitions. A principle of humanity should be included in any defense of the rights of the poor based on fairness, if the latter is to have a universal and less contingent foundation.

I want now to turn to one institutional implication of a right to freedom from extreme deprivation.

9.4. THE RIGHT TO FREEDOM FROM POVERTY AS A CONSTITUTIONAL ESSENTIAL

The right to subsistence has, in my view, a global scope—it bounds powerful states and individuals beyond national borders. But a right to subsistence also has intranational implications. One of them is that it deserves to be recognized as a constitutional essential—it must be included among the fundamental legal considerations of constitutional democracies.

From what I said about the transnational character of this right, it follows that freedom from severe poverty should also be considered a constitutional essential at the global level—it should be included among the fundamental norms-binding behavior at the global level. Though I will not be focusing here on this global aspect I think the constitutional importance of a right to subsistence in the international domain may and should be used to justify exceptions to patent requirements in relation to HIV drugs and vaccines, to force drastic reductions on sovereign debts of developing countries, or to challenge, politically and legally, subsidies and tariffs that perpetuate poverty worldwide. What I said about the cheapness of poverty eradication at the global level makes the case for considering a right to subsistence a constitutional essential of international law even stronger than in the intranational plane.

The number of countries adopting a written constitution including a list of rights is continuously increasing.[15] It may be thought that constitutionalizing a right to freedom from extreme poverty would have little significance in very poor countries characterized by situations of extreme scarcity. The claims of societies submerged into destitution, as suggested before, are rightfully conceived as focused primarily on the governments of richer countries. But a minimal duty of equality holds everywhere, and a constitutional recognition of a right to basic necessities serves to highlight the very urgent among the urgent.

Now even in the context of more developed countries, the constitutionalization of rights has been widely criticized (e.g., Waldron 1993*a*, 1999). Is there something especially problematic with constitutionalizing socioeconomic rights, and in particular a right to be free from extreme poverty, that is, some particular difficulty that could be added to the list of objections to constitutionalizing rights *generally*? And, then, which are the consequences of constitutionally entrenching this right?

In many countries there is an important difference between the predominant interpretation of equality at the political level, on the one hand, and of its requirements at the socioeconomic level, on the other hand. The first type of equality is indisputably embodied in legal rights, at least in most democratic regimes. The

---

[15] More than 60% of states, encompassing nearly 60% of the world population, live under constitutional democracies, according to Diamond (1997) and Freedom House (2004).

basic claims of justice at the moral and political level are, at the same time, true propositions of law. Accordingly, denials of basic moral equality or of political equality are, in modern democratic orders, violations of the law. But the same is not the case regarding even basic requirements of socioeconomic equality (like a right of freedom from destitution), at least in many countries. Rights to minimum welfare, health, housing, and the like, are not commonly seen as legal requirements. Rather, they are perceived as connected with the political agenda of the left and, as such, to be decided in the legislative arena. The idea behind this way of conceiving of essential socioeconomic rights seems to be that there is no univocal connection between moral and political equality and economic equality. In other words, the rejection of essential economic rights does not amount to a violation of moral and political equality, or a violation of a similar importance. The denial of a right to minimum income, or the access to health care or housing does not incur—according to the prevailing view—the moral wrong (if at all) of discrimination or second-class citizenship that violations of moral or political equality are deemed to bring about. This seems, then, to be the principal challenge for those defending a human rights approach to the problem of severe deprivation: to present their claims as true propositions of law.

Recall arguments successfully used to debunk moral subjectivists (Dworkin 1996; Nagel 1997). Subjectivists tried to preserve their commitments to certain values and convictions, and at the same time deny the truth of those values and convictions. They were told they could not—their 'meta-ethical' claims just implied the negation of their first-order, moral claims. They were not allowed—in the name of consistency—to believe and to not believe at the same time. The moral—first order—level dominates any attempt at metaethical detachment. We may try to reason in a similar way regarding institutions, trying to make our moral convictions dominate our constitutional convictions as they dominate metaethical reflections. In this way, our belief in the truth of a right to subsistence would be incompatible with our denial of a constitutional status to those rights, in the same way it is incompatible with a skeptical theory about moral rights. In other words you cannot believe both in a basic right to be free from extreme poverty and that this right should be granted, if at all, at the discretion of a prevailing political force. There are two ways of trying to defend the constitutional status of a right to be free from severe deprivation. The first is to defend the idea that democratic constitutions *should* incorporate these rights. The second, maybe more imaginative, way, is to claim that socioeconomic rights are entailed by the very idea of a constitutional democracy, and if so, that any sound interpretation of a democratic constitution needs to assume the constitutional status of those rights. This second strategy would not require constitutional amendments, but a reinterpretation of the actual constitutions of modern democracies. While determining which of the two strategies is more convenient depends on context, it seems plausible to suggest that all democratic constitutions should be read as including some reasonable protection against severe deprivation, as a precondition for the exercise of legitimate authority. Even the most proceduralist view of a constitution, presenting it as a mere set of rules to elect public officials, must presuppose some minimum access to the conditions that make democratic elections and political discussion possible. The point is not about constitutional interpretation but about legitimacy. If the constitution just says that everyone has a right to vote, it would be excessive to interpret this sentence as also guaranteeing persons rights to basic necessities. Still, it remains true that any authority lacks legitimacy if it purports to enforce such a radically unequal distribution as one denying basic necessities to some.

I defend here the claim that justice requires that socioeconomic rights be included in a democratic constitution. I address some objections and describe some consequences of constitutionalizing socioeconomic rights.

Among the reasons offered against the inclusion in a constitution of socioeconomic rights, the two that deserve greater attention, in my view, may be classified under the rubric 'Watering Down' and 'Non-Essentiality'. The Watering-Down argument relies on the idea that an inflation of rights would devaluate the weight of rights, much as excessive emission of currency decreases its value. According to this objection, a constitution including too many rights would be a manifesto, not a legal document. This argument is general and unspecific, because it does not entail that this or that concrete right should be included or removed from the constitutional list. It says that few are better than many. This general argument has been directed against constitutionalization of socioeconomic rights because, as it happens, they arrived late to the constitutional party, as it were. Against this objection we may respond that, while it is certainly true that the constitutional language should tend to be austere rather than exuberant, it is not true that displaying a broader list of rights is a disservice to the cause of human rights. Rather, it seems that the opposite is the case—a partial, narrower account of rights runs the peril of making the constitution appear as an ideological and biased instrument instead of an inclusive commitment to preserve the dignity of human beings. In any case, one could easily accept the general argument that a constitution should include a short rather than a massive list of rights, but insist that a right to be free from deprivation, being a basic and fundamental one, may not be excluded from any short or modest bill of rights.

While the Watering-Down objection is an instrumental one (pointing to rhetorical and political risks), the Non-Essentiality objection goes deeper, because it does not just claim that it is unwise to have too many rights in the constitution, but that these particular rights (socioeconomic rights) do not deserve constitutional status—that they should be included in the democratic agenda, not removed from it.

This was Rawls's position regarding the difference principle. Now we should be careful not to extrapolate Rawls's view on this issue to the discussion around the constitutionalization of a right to subsistence. The difference principle is far more ambitious than a right against destitution. In fact, Rawls defended the view that a right to subsistence should be regarded either as included in his first principle of equal liberty or as an independent principle, prior to the first principle of justice, and both interpretations would lead to the constitutionalization of a right against extreme poverty. Nevertheless, I think it may be useful to examine Rawls's opposition to the constitutionalization of the difference principle, because the reasons Rawls directed against viewing the difference principle as a constitutional essential are usually repeated against the incorporation into the constitution of any socioeconomic right (even the very modest version of an anti-destitution right) (Rawls 1993*a*: 7).

Rawls mentions two difficulties, which justify according to his view, considering the difference principle a matter of legislative discussion. These are, first, the problem of disagreement ('...the question whether legislation is just or unjust, especially in connection with economic and social policies, is commonly subject to reasonable differences of opinion'), and second, the problem of information ('The application of the difference principle in a precise way normally requires more information than we can expect to have and, in any case, more than the application of the first principle'). Do these difficulties threaten the constitutional protection of a right to freedom from extreme deprivation (1999*a*: 174–5)?

Regarding the first problem, it may be subject to the criticisms directed against moral conventionalism: social agreement on a certain moral principle does not constitute its validity; otherwise, those who opposed that principle would be wrong merely as a result of their disagreement with the majority. The second difficulty is no better, because the information problem is much more manageable for a right to be free from extreme poverty than for Rawls's difference principle.

What institutional conclusions would, then, best fit with the reasonable part of the two difficulties, that is, the fact that there may be reasonable disagreements on the best ways to realize the difference principle, and that there are obvious informational difficulties in knowing its full and detailed implications? I think it is clear that the answer consists in the constitutionalization of the right against poverty, leaving the bulk of its implementation to the decision of the democratic institutions. Democratic discussion and everyday politics would then be constrained to discussing the implementation of the principle, but not the principle itself, and in some clear cases of violation, judges could step in, as they do in reference to other constitutional rights and rules. A sense of dignity plays an important role here. Protection against poverty by an institutional framework means a strong recognition of an entitlement to receiving one's (minimally) fair share of social resources. If this were true, then receiving basic resources in application of a constitutional agreement would be more in accord with the dignity of the disadvantaged. The resources the poor receive in this context are even less contingently dependent on a particular political decision or temporary public consideration.

I conclude that it would be wrong to try to find support in Rawls's theory for opposing the constitutionalization of a right to be free from extreme poverty. This would be wrong, first, for the obvious reason that Rawls explicitly defends a right to subsistence as a constitutional essential. And it would be wrong, second, because his objections to the constitutional entrenchment of the more ambitious difference principle cannot be extrapolated to the more modest right to basic necessities. Therefore a right to subsistence, much less demanding than other socioeconomic demands entailed by the difference principle, belongs in the constitution of any well-ordered society.

In the case that a principle of freedom from extreme deprivation is to be included in the constitution, concerning the ways of achieving the principle, should the democratic organs have the prominent role? Obviously yes, because they are the ones that are in the best conditions to produce and analyze the relevant information. A provision regarding the special competence of the democratic organs in this respect could be part of the clause.

Now how can constitutional entrenchment contribute to the satisfaction of basic needs? There are three main ways in which constitutionalization would advance the interests of the poor: It would block arguments against pro-poor policies and institutional arrangements, it would mandate such policies and arrangements, and it would protect the poor from certain legal claims or requirements.

As an example of the first type of consequences of constitutionalizing a right against poverty, think of the institutional arrangement of mandated political representation for the poor as practiced in India, which reserves some political spaces for disadvantaged minorities. Pande (2003) shows that this mechanism has been successful in increasing transfers to groups represented in that way. This policy, however, could be opposed from the perspective of the principle 'one person one vote'. A constitutional right to freedom from poverty would at least force to balance an argument based on electoral equality with considerations of constitutional nature about the material requisites of such equality. The judges would be obliged to assess on new terms the constitutionality of norms passed in accordance with the right to freedom from destitution and challenged for supposedly contradicting other standards. The constitution could not be used *against* policies in favor of the victims of inequality.

The second effect of constitutionalizing a right against poverty (making pro-poor policies mandatory) calls for a distinction between constitutionalization of a right to subsistence and its judicial review. Constitutionalization of a principle does not automatically make the judiciary the ultimate authority on the issue (Sager 1978). However, there is much to say in favor of a different role for judges, that allows them some control over the other branches of government. In case certain statutes or government measures are *clearly* incompatible with this constitutional right, they should be able to declare it unconstitutional. There is no particular difficulty in the judicial review of socioeconomic rights vis-à-vis other rights. In those societies where the poor constitute an isolated minority, majority rule could be an insufficient device for the defense of their rights. However, the constitutionalization and judicial enforcement of socioeconomic rights should not ignore the difficulties that the objectors have presented, mainly objections based on the democratic and technical weaknesses of the judiciary. They could be taken into account in the following ways: (*a*) Courts should be deferential (though not absolutely, of course) in their assessment of whether these rights are being respected or transgressed; (*b*) Courts' level of scrutiny should be directly proportional to the urgency of the needs involved;[16] (*c*) Courts should favor or

---

[16] As an example, consider Grootboom and others v. Government of the Republic of South Africa and others (CCT38/00) 2000 (11) BCLR 1169; 2001 (1) SA 46; [2000] ZACC 14 (21 September 2000).

force participatory ways of resolving these conflicts, in accordance with the idea that denials of socioeconomic rights are linked with denials of political voice and effective participation.[17]

The third consequence of constitutionalization of a right to basic necessities is that it would make the poor a legally protected group. Tax norms, property rights, contract regulations, excuses in criminal law, etc., should be read through a more humane interpretation of the law. An important issue that may be influenced by the constitutional status of a right to freedom from extreme deprivation is the way in which a democratic state ought to deal with social protests, especially when linked to the injustice and exclusion of the poor.[18] Many people appeal to rule of law arguments to defend the formalistic use of the criminal code as the unique response to social and political struggles. Constitutionalizing a right to basic necessities would make it clear that it is not always the case that the struggling victims of exclusion are the violators of the law. Often they are just fighting for their rights. This might be a crucial consideration, because it supports a different approach to social conflicts, an approach based on mediation and dialogue (i.e., aiming at inclusion, which is what the protesters have been seeking all along) instead of repression and punishment.

Irene Grootboom and another seven hundred adults and children were evicted from two places where they were living in inhuman conditions. While sheltered in a sports field they initiated an action on the grounds of the constitutional right to access to housing (recognized in section 26 of the South African Constitution), and the rights of children. While the Court rejected the claims made on behalf of the children's rights, it ultimately issued a declaratory order mandating the government to comply with section 26 of the Constitution and take 'reasonable measures to provide relief for people who have no access to land, no roof over their heads, and who are living in intolerable conditions'. The key for the decision was the way in which the Court interpreted the reasonability requirement of the measures that the Constitution orders the state to take. According to the Court, these measures should be understood in a way that gives weight to the needs of the worse off. The measures 'cannot exclude a significant segment of society', and it is not enough to show that the measures tend to a 'statistical advance in the realization of the right'. It must 'respond to the needs of the most desperate', because 'the Constitution requires that everyone must be treated with care and concern'. The government's program did not meet that standard, because 'it failed to make reasonable provision within its available resources for [the homeless] people in the Cape Metropolitan area'.

[17] Cécile Fabre (2000) offers a detailed defense of the inclusion of economic rights in a democratic constitution. She claims that a constitution should entrench a right to 'a minimum income, health care, education and housing', that judges should be entrusted to protect them, along with some special body like a Human Rights Commission, in what she calls 'a dual system of protection'. While I agree with her practical recommendations I have some reservations about how Fabre grounds these rights in the ideas of autonomy and well-being (I think they are best understood as entailed by an idea of equality), about her purely procedural view of democracy (I think, following Beitz (1989) that a democratic system must include some non-procedural elements), and about her rejection of the view (which I favor) that the constitutionalization of socioeconomic rights is best defended as serving the ideal of equal citizenship.

[18] See Gargarella (this volume). I am less prone than he seems to be to seeing cases of resistance like those described in his work as morally justified violations of the law or resistance to the law. I see most of these actions as *legally* justified, through an appeal to some basic constitutional rights. Civil disobedience may well be a way, though untidy, of advancing the legality of a social order.

Many countries have constitutional texts including in some way or another, a right to minimum needs. The governments of many of these countries, however, fail to fulfill this right. Recognition of the constitutional relevance of a right against poverty is a step forward toward justice, but of course not a sufficient one. But it is important to note that once the morally basic character of a right to basic necessities is accepted there are no sound arguments to deny them the same legal hierarchy of other fundamental rights.

9.5. CONCLUSION

A right to be free from extreme poverty is supported by the basic character of the interests it refers to, but also by the cheapness of its fulfillment. A case could be made that the denial of justice to the global poor is also a problem of irrationality, given that poverty eradication does not significantly affect, and perhaps enhances the national and individual self-interests of all. A right to basic resources trumps, as any other right, consequentialist and self-interested preferences, but this does not mean that, in practice, consequentialist considerations contradict pro-poor policies. On the contrary, eradication of poverty would most probably increase aggregate global welfare, and would certainly not imply an important sacrifice for anybody.

Given that poverty violates a basic human right, the Millennium Goals fail to fully capture the principled character of this problem.

The right to basic necessities derives from a principle of humanity, understood not as charity or simple benevolence, but as a nuclear element of justice, even if justice is narrowly understood as dealing with merit and desert.

Institutionally, a right to be free from extreme poverty deserves constitutional standing, and arguments based on democratic disagreement and informational deficits must be rejected. Directly, such a right commands judges to enforce it if the democratic branches fail to do so. Indirectly, it justifies a more responsive approach to legal problems, in particular those arising from alleged violations of other legal standards (like mandated political representation) and the resistance of the victims of extreme inequality.

10

Responsibility and Severe Poverty

*Leif Wenar**

Human rights define the most fundamental responsibilities of those who hold power. In the cases of the Holocaust, or of the Rwandan massacres, we do not need a theory to tell us who was responsible for the violations of human rights. The violators were those who authorized and carried out the atrocities, who failed so conspicuously in their duties toward the humans that became their victims.

The subject of this volume presents a more difficult question: Who, if anyone, is morally responsible for acting to alleviate severe poverty? Here our convictions are less steady. Are impoverished people responsible for improving their own condition? Or are the leaders of their countries also responsible, or the leaders of rich countries, or we ourselves as individuals? When considering these questions, we tend to have the kinds of reactions—avoidance of the topic, brief enthusiasm, nagging guilt—that indicate that we perceive several strong pulls on our reasoning, but are unsure how to order our thoughts so as to reach a firm conclusion. Here is where a philosophical account of responsibility might help. What we want to know is how to determine who, if anyone, has moral responsibility for ensuring that each person's human right to an adequate standard of living is secured. What we need is a general theory that tells us how to locate responsibility for averting this type of threat to individuals' basic well-being.

In developing such a theory, we will begin not with contested questions about human rights, but with familiar cases in which we are certain where to locate responsibility for averting threats. There are after all many threats to our well-being in everyday life. In everyday life we face threats from traffic accidents, house fires, knives, guns, and toxic household chemicals. For each of these threats we are confident that we know who is responsible for making sure that the threat does not harm us. Moreover, we are surrounded by very young, very old, and very sick people who would not live long if they had to take care of their basic needs themselves. And again, we are certain that we know how to locate responsibility for taking care of these people who cannot take care of themselves. In these familiar cases we know without thinking who must take responsibility for averting threats to basic well-being. If we can find a theory that explains how we go about assigning responsibility in these familiar cases, we will have a theory of responsibility to

* I would especially like to thank Thomas Pogge, Ulrike Heuer, Fabian Freyenhagen, and Henry Richardson for their help with this essay.

draw on when ordering our reflections about who is responsible for responding to severe poverty.

When we reflect on how we assign responsibility in everyday cases, I believe we find that a single principle is guiding our reasoning in almost every instance. We appear to rely on this principle to locate responsibility in a wide range of situations in which there are threats to basic well-being. It is striking to discover that a single principle can explain so much of our thinking about responsibility. Yet the main benefit of finding this principle is not theoretical; it is practical. The main benefit comes from a better understanding of where we should place responsibility for securing each human's right to an adequate standard of living.

10.1. RESPONSIBILITY IN EVERYDAY CASES

If you are responsible for something, then in the sense we are interested in it is *up to you* to take care of it. If you do take care of it, you have discharged your responsibility. If you do not, you may be subject to blame or punishment. When we blame or punish someone we do so because he has done something that he was responsible for not doing, or because he has not done something that he was responsible for doing. Yet how do we know where we should locate responsibility for any particular task? How do we determine, that is, who should see to what? Since we are ultimately interested in severe poverty, we can ask a more focused question: How do we determine who should be responsible for preventing a serious threat from damaging the basic well-being of some particular person?

Let us begin with an ordinary example of legal responsibility: the legal responsibility for averting automobile accidents. Two cars are traveling down the expressway in the same lane, one in back and one in front. Whose responsibility is it to keep the two cars from colliding? Who is it 'up to' to prevent this kind of accident? The obvious answer is that it is the responsibility of the driver of the car in back, not the driver of the car in front, to keep the two cars from colliding. If there is a collision, the driver of the car in back will be cited, and his insurance company will be the one who pays for damages. Yet the ease with which we answer the question of responsibility in this ordinary case does not mean that the answer explains itself. Why after all should we locate responsibility in the trailing driver, instead of in the lead driver—or perhaps in someone else entirely?

The thought that it is the trailing driver who will have *caused* the accident will not help us here, at least if we stick to a philosopher's definition of 'cause'. To a philosopher, the causes of an event are, roughly, all of the factors that contribute to the event occurring. In this philosopher's sense, there is no way to pick out the actions of the trailing driver as especially significant. In a particular case, perhaps the accident would not have happened if the trailing driver had not edged so close to the car in front of him. Yet it may also be the case that the accident would not have happened had the lead driver not slammed on his brakes. In fact, if we seek out everything that contributed to this accident occurring, we will quickly collect a huge number of causal factors. It could be that the accident would not have occurred if the baby in the car in back had not been crying, or if a rabbit had not jumped out onto the expressway in the path of the car in front, or if the trailing driver had not gotten the last-minute phone call that made him late for his appointment. When we say that the driver of the car in back 'caused' the accident, we are not intending this philosophical sense of causation. We are scanning a large number of causal factors and picking out the actions of the trailing driver as where responsibility for the accident lies. The question is why we pick out this factor— the actions of the trailing driver—and say that this is the 'cause' of the accident in the sense that we use to assign legal responsibility.

When we reflect on why we hold the trailing driver responsible for an accident in a case like this, we will arrive at the following explanation: the trailing driver is the person who can most easily keep the collision from occurring. It would be senseless, we think, to assign responsibility to the driver of the car in front— because it is much harder for drivers in front to avoid accidents with cars behind them. The kinds of things that lead drivers would have to do to avoid such accidents—constantly checking their rear-view mirror, suddenly speeding up or changing lanes—would greatly increase their risks of getting into accidents with other cars. It is much easier, we think, for trailing drivers to ensure that they keep their distance from the cars that are, after all, right in front of them. This is why we assign responsibility for avoiding these accidents to trailing drivers.

The hypothesis here is that we place responsibility for preventing traffic accidents on the party who could most easily prevent the accident. This hypothesis seems fruitful: it appears to explain many 'rules of the road' for cars, and for vehicles besides cars as well. International maritime codes, for example, specify that more manoeuvrable vessels must keep out of the way of less manoeuvrable vessels. The captains of more manoeuvrable vessels, such as power-driven boats, are responsible for avoiding less manoeuvrable vessels, such as sailing ships, and ships engaged in fishing, and vessels not under command.[1] It is easier for power-boats to avoid hitting sailing ships than vice versa. Aviation codes are based on the same principle. The right of way of the sky ranks craft in order of the ease with which they can be controlled. Airplanes in normal operation, which are the most easily manoeuvred aircraft, have the lowest priority in right of way. Airplanes refueling other aircraft, which are less easily manoeuvred, have a greater right of way than airplanes in normal operation. Balloons, which are still less manoeuvrable than airplanes refueling other aircraft, have a higher priority right of way. Finally, aircraft in distress have the highest priority right of way of all— which makes sense by our principle, since what it is for an aircraft to be in distress is for it to be very difficult or impossible to control.[2]

---

[1] United States Coast Guard 1999. Transportation Rules—International, Inland. Washington, DC: Department of Transportation.

[2] See Section 91.113 of the 'Federal Aviation Regulations', www.airweb.faa.gov/ Regulatory_and_Guidance_Library/rgFAR.nsf/MainFrame?OpenFrameSet

The general hypothesis is that responsibility for averting threats to basic well-being should be located in the agent who can most easily avert the threat. This hypothesis, when tested more broadly, appears to organize many of our thoughts about responsibility. The world is after all full of potential threats. It appears that we think that the fairest and most efficient way to allocate responsibility for these potential threats is to put the burden on the agent who can most easily bear that burden.

Consider the threat of guns. We could say that it is the responsibility of each person to avert gun deaths by always wearing a bullet-proof body suit. Yet this would be burdensome, to say the least. We instead assign responsibility for averting gun deaths to the people who are holding the guns in their hands. These after all are the agents who can most easily avert the potential threats of death that are posed by the guns that they are holding. It is easier to avoid shooting someone than to avoid being shot.

The idea that responsibility for averting serious harm should be located in the agent who can most easily avert the harm also explains one of our firmest and most general convictions about the location of responsibility. This is the conviction that, in a wide range of cases, competent adults should be responsible for taking care of themselves. If a competent adult edges too close to a cliff edge in broad daylight, or falls asleep while smoking in bed, or leaves the drain-cleaning fluid where he normally puts his mouthwash, we will say that he had no one to blame but himself for the harms that result. We could assign responsibility for averting these kinds of harms to other agencies, but we do not. Each competent adult is responsible for avoiding a great many threats to his own well-being because he is the agent who can do so at the least cost.

There are of course exceptions to the general rules about responsibility that we have just been discussing. Yet even these exceptions appear to follow the 'least-cost' principle. A driver is in most cases responsible for keeping his car off of the sidewalk, because in general the driver is the person who can most easily control the car. However, the driver is not blamed if his passenger suddenly lunges over and wrenches the wheel toward the pedestrians. This is because it is easier for the passenger to keep himself from wrenching the wheel toward the pedestrians than it is for the driver to stop the passenger from doing so. These kinds of exceptions to our general judgments about who is responsible for controlling threats are in fact not exceptions to our principle. They are themselves responsive to our judgments about who is most easily able to control a threat in the circumstances.

10.2. EXCESSIVE BURDENS

Our ultimate aim will be to apply this hypothesis concerning the location of responsibility to the case of severe poverty. While we are not ready to address severe poverty at this early stage, we can see the general principle at work when we study our reactions to Peter Singer's famous example of saving the drowning child (Singer 1972: 229–43). In Singer's example, you notice a child drowning in a shallow pond nearby, and realize that you could save the child by wading into the pond and grabbing him. You have, we think, a responsibility to wade in and keep the child from drowning. You can, after all, save the child's life, and you need only get your trousers muddy to do so. Saving the child is your responsibility.

Why is saving the child up to you? You have the responsibility to save the child from drowning because you are the person who can most easily keep the child from drowning. Here, as before, the least-cost hypothesis explains our reasoning.

Yet our reactions become less settled when Singer attempts to make a parallel between the pond case and our responsibilities toward people starving in Bangladesh (Singer was writing in 1971). When Singer makes us feel that helping starving Bangladeshis is just as easy as saving the drowning child, we are drawn to the idea that we do have a responsibility to avert the threat of starvation that is endangering those Bangladeshis.[3] While Singer has believing that we can very easily save people from starving, we are pulled toward believing that we must do so. Yet in the back of our minds, or perhaps in the front, is a concern that perhaps we are not the people who can *most easily* avert the threat of starvation. Perhaps primary responsibility for alleviating the famine does not lie with us. Perhaps there are people closer by who should help instead, or perhaps there are people around us for whom the sacrifice required to help the Bangladeshis would be less costly than it would be for us. The thought that we may not have primary responsibility for responding to poverty in Bangladesh, and the question of whether we have some responsibility to these people nevertheless, are topics to which we will return.

Reflecting on our reactions to Singer's famine example also reveals a new thought, and an important qualification to our central idea. Perhaps, we think, Singer is simply wrong about the costs of aid. Perhaps we are indeed the people who can most easily act to alleviate the famine. Yet perhaps it would very expensive for us to do anything that could help. If the costs are very high, it might seem unfair to burden us with the responsibility for alleviating the famine, even if we are the people who could most easily do so. Responsibility, we appear to think, can be negated if costs are too high. If it would be too hard for the people who can most easily avert a threat to avert it, then we will not hold these people responsible.

This is an important qualification to the central idea about assigning responsibility, and we can see it at work even in Singer's case of the drowning child. You are responsible for saving the child if you are the person who can most easily do so— unless trying to save the child would put you at serious risk of drowning yourself. In a situation where attempting the rescue is itself very dangerous, we will not hold you responsible for making the attempt. Of course we have not said how much difficulty or danger will count as 'excessive costs'. Presumably, this depends

---

[3] Singer says, 'Expert observers and supervisors, sent out by famine relief organizations or permanently stationed in famine-prone areas, can direct our aid to a refugee in Bengal almost as effectively as we could get it to someone in our own block' (1972: 232).

on the magnitude of the threat in the circumstances at hand. Nevertheless, we are often very clear about what level of cost counts as excessive. In the drowning child example, we are clear that you are not required to put your own life at risk in order to attempt the rescue.

We can find this qualification for 'excessive costs' at work in all sorts of cases. Imagine you are spending the night in a remote cabin in the wilderness. A strange man, obviously dehydrated and seemingly delirious, appears at the fence. If the man calls for water, you might well believe that it is your responsibility to provide for him at least enough water to sustain him for the night. After all the man clearly needs water, you have a fair amount of water, and there is no one else around even if you had a telephone to call for help. Yet now imagine that you leave a bottle of water outside for the man, and he proceeds to pour it on the ground and call for more. Here you might think that your responsibility to help the man has run out. The thirsty man appears to take no interest in meeting his own basic needs, and leaving water out for him has not proved an effective way to help him do so. In this situation it might still be true that you are the person who can most easily ensure that the thirsty man gets rehydrated. But what you would have to do to secure his health—capturing him, restraining him, forcing him to swallow the water— would be too risky to expect you to do it. You have 'done enough' here, and may bear no further responsibility to assist the man, at least while he remains in his delirious state.

These core ideas—about who can most easily avert threats, and about whether averting a threat would be too costly—form the backbone of our judgments about where (if anywhere) responsibility for averting threats should be located. The simple principle that lies behind our thinking about averting threats to basic well-being is that the agent who can most easily avert the threat has the responsibility for doing so—so long as doing so will not be excessively costly.[4] In section 10.3, I distinguish two different ways in which this principle is elaborated in our reasoning about responsibility for averting threats to well-being.

10.3. ROLE RESPONSIBILITY

In the cases of the drowning child and the thirsty man we apply the principle of responsibility directly. There is a threat to the basic well-being of some individual A, and we assign responsibility to that individual B who can at that moment most easily act so as to avert this threat (so long as this is not too costly for B). In other cases, we apply the principle of responsibility not directly to individuals, but to individuals based on the general description that they fall under. For example, consider again the traffic case where one car is traveling behind another on the

---

[4] The principle suggested here would have to be stated more precisely to be fully adequate; for example, it seems to apply only to threats to innocents. This qualification will not affect the discussion here, but would need to be explored in a discussion of, for instance, the prevention and punishment of wrongdoing.

expressway. In our legal system, responsibility for preventing an accident always lies with the person falling under the description of 'trailing driver'. The trailing driver is always legally responsible for avoiding collisions with cars in front of him, even if in some specific, unusual case it would be easier for the lead driver to avert the accident. If there is a collision involving two cars where one was trailing the other, the authorities will not try to determine which driver could most easily have averted that particular accident. Rather, the authorities will always hold the person responsible who falls under a certain general description—'trailing driver'—whatever the particular facts of the case at hand. In this kind of situation, we assign responsibility based on the general description, not based on the actual costs to individuals at a given moment.

It is easy to see why we sometimes assign responsibility based on general descriptions. General descriptions help to define simple and public rules of who must take care of what. Having these simple and public rules makes it easier for people to coordinate their actions, and so reduces everyone's risks. Driving at high speed on the expressway in the middle of a group of cars is potentially an extremely dangerous activity. The risks of driving on the expressway would be many times greater if each driver, at each moment, had to try to determine whether he or another driver was responsible for avoiding a collision between their two cars. Traffic rules such as 'the trailing driver is responsible for avoiding collisions with the car in front of him', make it easy for each driver to know what he must do, and so reduce the risks of driving on the expressway to a tolerable level.

How then do we assign responsibility based on general descriptions when we create roles? The answer follows from the hypothesis that we have already framed. We assign responsibility according to the principle of 'least cost', this time based on costs in the general case. For each type of situation where someone will predictably face a threat to basic well-being, we ask who in the general case will be most easily able to avert that threat (without being excessively burdened by doing so). In the expressway situation, we have determined that it is generally easier for trailing drivers to avoid accidents with lead drivers than vice versa. So we assign responsibility to trailing drivers. Similarly, we think that it is generally easier for airplanes in normal operation to stay out of the way of balloons than vice versa, so we assign responsibility to the operators of airplanes. And so on.

The traffic-law cases are good examples of how we assign responsibility based on general descriptions. The least-cost principle can also explain assignments of responsibility that define some of our most important social roles. Consider, for example, the care of young children. We know that children will face any number of threats to their basic interests during their early years, from lack of adequate nutrition to accidental self-injury. Moreover, we know that young children will be incapable of avoiding many of these threats themselves. On whom, then, should responsibility fall to protect young children against the dangers they will predictably face? There are a variety of individuals and groups who could bear responsibility for children. Yet the most popular answer to this question, across many different societies, is that it is the biological parents of a child who should bear most of the responsibility for averting threats to the child.

The ascription of responsibility to biological parents reflects an assessment of relative costs in the general case. Biological parents are assigned primary responsibility for taking care of their children's basic needs because they are, in general, the people who will bear the least costs in carrying these responsibilities through. Biological parents, after all, often seek out the kind of relationship with the child where they are responsible for protecting the child's interests. And even in cases where the biological parents have not sought out this kind of relationship with the child, we tend to think that the parents will be less burdened by the responsibility than others would be, because humans have strong innate desires to protect their own offspring. Of course our rules for the care of children are more complex than simply 'biological parents must assume responsibility', and later we will consider how some of these complexities can be explained. Yet on the first pass, reasoning about relative costs appears to be the basic explanation of why we turn the neutral general description 'biological parent' into the socially and legally responsible role of 'parent'.

The example of assigning responsibility to biological parents brings out another benefit of applying the least-cost principle to people as they fall under general descriptions, instead of case by case. Defining roles make it easier to know what one has to do both in order to take on, and in order to avoid, bearing a certain responsibility. This can be very useful for planning. For many people taking responsibility for the care of a child does not fit into their immediate (or even their ultimate) life plans. With roles constructed as we have them, people know exactly what they must do in order to avoid having responsibility for caring for a child. They must simply avoid coming under the description 'biological parent'. Knowing what one must do in order to avoid burdensome responsibilities at any given time can be very helpful in arranging one's activities so as to reach one's goals.

Of course not all social roles are avoidable. A nation under military attack will draft its young men to be soldiers—it will place primary responsibility for averting the most dangerous threats from the enemy onto those who fit the general description 'able-bodied young male'. These young males will typically have little choice in the matter. The least-cost principle explains why it is that young males are selected to fight: they are generally best suited to perform aggressive, physically demanding tasks; they are easier to fit into the bottom of rigid command hierarchies; and they are less likely than older males to have families and careers in progress. This example shows that we sometimes assign responsibility in such a way that it is unavoidable. It also shows, we might notice, that in cases of extreme threat we expect people to bear very heavy burdens of responsibility. When there is a military invasion, the 'get-out clause' for excessive costs is very hard for young males to activate.

We have been examining how we assign responsibility to agents falling under general descriptions, instead of assigning it case-by-case. As we broaden our perspective, it becomes clear that we deal with many serious threats by constructing not just single roles, but systems of roles. For instance, consider how we deal with the standing threat of house fires. A case-by-case assignment of responsibility for putting out house fires based on least cost would be burdensome to everyone. Imagine the disruptions and dangers in your life were you responsible for responding to fires whenever you were the person nearest to the fire. The role-based system of responsibility that we have set up is much more effective. In our system, we apply the least-cost principle to a series of roles, so that each group does what it can most easily do. Those who have income and wealth are responsible for paying taxes to fund the fire service. Those who work in city government are responsible for using these funds to train and equip firefighters. Firefighters are responsible for fighting the fires. The system of dividing responsibility among roles is effective in meeting the threat posed by house fires, the system of roles meeting this threat in such a way that each group of role-bearers faces a relatively low burden.

In modern societies, almost all roles that we create to avert serious threats are parts of systems of roles. This is in fact true even of the roles of 'driver' and 'parent'. Drivers have many responsibilities for averting accidents, but government officials also have responsibilities for maintaining and patrolling the roads so that accidents are prevented. Parents have immediate responsibility for feeding their babies, but officials have responsibility for running the economy in such a way that parents are able to procure food to feed their babies. When we examine these systems of roles, we will find the least-cost principle always at work. In a good system, each role will be assigned to the group of people that can, because of the general description they fall under, bear the burdens of that role better than could other groups that might be singled out.

Of course, there is a certain amount of indeterminacy in the application of the least-cost principle. There are many roughly equivalent ways to set up traffic laws, child-care arrangements, and fire prevention schemes. Between any two possible systems of roles it may not be easy to tell which one imposes the least costs on its participants. What is crucial for all serious threats is that there be some system in place that meets the threat, and that this system is not obviously worse than some other feasible system would be. Serious threats to well-being must be averted, and it is the responsibility of the people who can avert the threats to settle on one system or another for responding to them.

10.4. PRIMARY AND SECONDARY RESPONSIBILITY

We have examined the ways in which we assign responsibility for averting threats to basic well-being. We have found that we assign responsibility where it can most easily be borne, except when this would be excessively burdensome. With some 'one-off' threats, like children drowning in ponds, we apply the principle directly—whichever person is closest must help. When we face a more predictable type of threat, we set up a system of roles whereby people falling under certain descriptions are made responsible for what they can do at lower cost than others.

The least-cost principle guides our reasoning about distributing responsibility, both immediately and systematically.

What about when the person responsible fails? What if the person responsible for averting a threat does not, for one reason or another, do so? If we examine our judgments in these types of situations, we will find that the least-cost principle continues to work. If the person with primary responsibility is unwilling or unable to carry through on his responsibility, we assign the responsibility—'secondary responsibility'—to the person *besides him* who can most easily bear the burden (so long as it would not burden this person excessively). If the person with this secondary responsibility then fails, we look for the person besides him who can next most easily shoulder the costs, and so on. We keep 'stepping back' levels to find bearers of responsibility, until (if ever) we reach a level where fulfilling the responsibility would impose too great of a burden.

We can see this 'stepping back' reasoning in action by modifying Singer's child-in-the-pond example. While walking to work you see a child drowning in a shallow pond not far away. At the edge of the pond, between you and the child, a man sits on a park bench watching the drowning child with an impassive expression. This man is obviously not going to help, although being closer to the child it appears that he could do so more easily than could you. The distribution of responsibility here is still clear. The man on the bench has primary responsibility for wading in and grabbing the child. It is in the first instance up to him to perform the rescue. Yet since the man is not, apparently, going to lift a finger, the responsibility of rescue 'steps back' to you. Indeed your secondary responsibility here seems to be just as strong as if the impassive man were absent from the scene.

We reason in the same 'stepping back' manner when assigning responsibility to roles. Biological parents have primary responsibility for averting threats to the basic well-being of their children. Yet what if the biological parents prove unwilling or unable to discharge their responsibilities? For instance, what if the parents die? What is the general description of the people who can now most easily look after the child? If there are guardians who have signaled their desire to take the child in these circumstances, the guardian will be assigned responsibility. Beyond this there are no hard and fast rules, but we know where to look. We will look for people who know the child, who are more likely to have some emotional attachment to him or her, who may have experience with raising children, and whose life plans are likely to be least disrupted. We are obviously looking for a family relation, and in our culture grandparents fit the bill. In other cultures, where extended families are bound more closely together, aunts, uncles, and more distant relations might also be called on. Nor do we stop with family members to bear responsibility for children. If we do not find a family member willing or able to care for the child, we then step back one more level to vest responsibility for the child in the state.

Now it might appear that this explanation of how the least-cost principle bears on secondary responsibility has failed to register an important distinction. I have said that secondary responsibility vests whenever the primary responsibility-holder is 'unwilling or unable' to do what they ought. Yet it may seem to make a big difference whether the primary responsibility-holder is not *willing* to do what they should, or whether they are actually not *capable* of doing it. 'Unwilling' seems unlike 'unable'. This is correct—it can make a big difference to us whether the primary responsibility-holder is unwilling or, rather, unable. But the difference it makes concerns only the appropriateness of blaming or punishing the person with the responsibility. We blame and punish those unwilling to discharge their responsibilities; we excuse those who are unable. Yet the appropriateness of blame and punishment makes no difference to the assignment of secondary responsibility. Whether a primary responsibility-holder is blameworthy or not, or deserves punishment or not, we will still locate secondary responsibility in the person who can next most easily bear that responsibility. You are just as responsible for rescuing the drowning child whether the man on the park bench is callous, or whether he is rather disabled.

The least-cost principle relocates responsibility whenever the holder of primary responsibility fails. It can also happen, of course, that this process works in reverse. Sometimes people become more capable of averting threats. Should the now-more-capable person become the person who can most easily avert the threat, then responsibility will shift to him. This 'reverse' shifting of responsibility can be seen in cases where a person regains responsibility for himself after a period of incapacity. The host of the party who gives the guest's car keys back when the guest has finally sobered up is shifting responsibility for averting traffic accidents back onto the guest himself. We can also see this reverse process at work in our example of parenting. Initially the parents are primarily responsible for the main conditions and actions necessary to ensure, for example, that their child has adequate nutrition—for purchasing the food, preparing the food, cutting up the food, putting the food in the child's mouth, and so on. As the child grows up, it becomes successively easier for him or her to perform these tasks, and so the child takes over primary responsibility for performing them.[5]

Indeed there are two basic strategies for fulfilling one's responsibilities to avert a threat. The first is to avert the threat oneself; the second is to make it easier for someone else to avert the threat. The second strategy is in many cases preferable. For example, consider again the case of house fires. It would, as we have noticed, be very costly for each person to be obliged to respond to the fires that break out around him. It is far better to set up a system whereby a certain small group of persons deals with the immediate threat, while everyone in the larger group is responsible only for ensuring that the small group of persons has adequate resources to do their job. In setting up this system, the majority shifts

---

[5] First the parents teach the child how to put food in his own mouth, then how to use utensils, and so on. Once the child is able to perform these basic tasks, the parents no longer have primary responsibility for performing them. During this process, the parents must still ensure that the general conditions exist which allow the child to carry through on these responsibilities by himself. The parents must, for instance, continue to provide the food that the child then prepares and eats. Ensuring that these conditions obtain is still their primary responsibility, because they continue to be the agents who can most easily ensure that these conditions necessary for maintaining the child's basic nutrition are met.

responsibility for responding to house fires onto a small, specialized group. We use the same strategy when it comes to crime. It would be hard for each of us to police the area around us; so instead we shift many of these responsibilities onto a police force that deals with criminal activities. Individuals shift their responsibilities onto a smaller and better-trained group, and retain responsibilities only to pay taxes and to alert the police to crimes that they witness in the course of their normal activities.

Of course, attempting to shift responsibility to another party is only defensible if one reasonably believes that this will be an effective strategy for averting the threat. One may not slip out of one's responsibilities by shifting them to a party that one knows will never act to avert the threat, or by shifting them to a party that one knows will shift them right back. Once again, threats to basic well-being must be met, and the imperative in situations containing threats is that those responsible put in place some system that they believe will be effective in meeting those threats.

10.5. THE NATURE OF OUR RESPONSIBILITIES

We have found the principle of least cost guiding our thinking about responsibility wherever we have looked. We can take a moment to reflect on the nature of this principle before applying it finally to the case of severe poverty.

On reflection, it appears that our reasoning about responsibility is in one way expansive, but is in the main rather conservative. Our reasoning is expansive in that it recognizes *in principle* no outer limit to the responsibility that one person may have for another. It is conceivable that—should all intermediate responsibility-holders fail—one individual could become responsible for the basic needs of another who lives very far away and whom he has never met. This potential expansiveness in our reasoning is what gives Singer's examples their punch. You may be responsible for wading in to save a drowning child, even if you have never seen the child before. If you really are the person who could most easily keep a child from starving half-way around the world, then you may have the responsibility to do so even though the physical distance between you is great and your social connection is zero.

Yet our reasoning about responsibility, though potentially expansive, is also conservative in two ways. First, we acknowledge a 'get-out clause' for excessive costs. We do not assign responsibilities to individuals or roles when it would be too costly to carry out such responsibilities. Passersby, for example, are not responsible for disarming knife-wielding psychopaths, however much these psychopaths are threatening themselves or others. A sister is not legally required to donate a lung, even when doing so is the only way to save her brother's life.

Second, our reasoning is conservative because it tends to press responsibility for sustaining an individual's basic needs inward, toward the individual himself. This is the result of the general fact that individuals—and after them those physically and socially closest to those individuals—are often better able than others to take care of their own basic needs. Moreover, relatively 'distant' agents can frequently discharge their responsibilities by empowering those closer to the threat in a way that shifts responsibility toward them.

If we are looking for a capsule summary of what we have discovered about responsibility so far, we will find one in the adage: 'With power comes responsibility, and with great power comes great responsibility'. Any kind of agent who becomes more powerful also becomes more capable of averting threats, and thereby more responsible for making sure that those threats are defused. For example, as a child grows more capable, he becomes more responsible for taking care of himself. Similarly, a nation that builds up its military for self-defense becomes stronger, but it also becomes responsible for ensuring that its new troops and weapons do not harm (and even that they are available to rescue) the innocent. Citizens who build up institutions of government in order to provide themselves police protection may find that these institutions have become efficacious enough that they must now also be used to provide basic health and unemployment insurance to all. Even technology plays a role in locating responsibility, as it lowers costs and so increases power. The advent of mobile phones has made it easier for people to report serious crimes and accidents, and so has increased people's responsibility to make these reports. You are, after all, more blameworthy for failing to report an accident that you see on the motorway if you have a phone in the car than you are if the nearest phone is five miles behind you.

We should notice also that our reasoning about where to locate responsibility is uncontaminated by distinctions between 'positive' and 'negative'. Least-cost reasoning explains why trailing drivers are responsible for avoiding the cars in front of them, why adults are responsible for not tipping over cliffs, why parents are responsible for taking care of their children, why hosts are responsible for taking keys from (and can eventually return keys to) their intoxicated guests, why taxpayers are responsible for funding the fire service, and why owners of mobile phones are responsible for reporting accidents. Attempting to draw a line between 'negative' and 'positive' responsibilities in these examples, even where this is possible, would be attempting to separate responsibilities with a single rationale. It may be that on particular occasions it would be easy for one person to keep from harming another, but excessively costly for that person to help the other. In this case the first person would have a responsibility not to harm, but no responsibility to help—a 'negative' without a 'positive' responsibility. Yet this separation is not an exception to what we have discovered about responsibility. It is simply an application of the least-cost principle in a particular type of situation.[6]

---

[6] It might be thought that a responsibility-holder must face greater costs to activate the 'get-out' clause of excessive costs when negative responsibilities are at stake—that he must face more costs to excuse harming than he must to excuse not helping. This is a larger topic than can be addressed here.

Indeed the striking fact about least-cost reasoning is that it appears to give a unified explanation of where to locate responsibility for averting threats to basic well-being. It appears to account for our assignments of responsibility wherever we look. If we do find cases that appear to be counterexamples, they will typically involve one of two kinds of mistakes. The first kind of mistake is to think that least-cost reasoning must always be applied directly, ignoring the fact that assigning responsibility to role-bearers is often a more effective long-term solution. Why, for example, is Bill Gates not responsible for paying for the police and fire services that protect everyone in his country—or responsible for paying at least up to the point where he is no longer the richest man in his country? The last clause contains the answer to the question. An economic order in which the richest person was responsible for paying to avert threats to everyone up to the point where he is no longer the richest person would be a much less productive economic order than one with a system of progressive taxation. Such an order would be one in which the police and fire services would be worse at meeting the threats that they will predictably face.

The second kind of mistake is to imagine that least-cost reasoning must be applied within roles. When we divide up responsibility for averting fire deaths, we assign the responsibility for fighting fires to a small professional group. Because of their training and willingness to take the job, this is the group that can fight fires at the least cost to themselves. Yet we do not of course think that whenever a fire alarm sounds it is always the most skilled, most energetic, and most enthusiastic firefighters that have the responsibility to respond. We would lose much of the efficiency that we gained by setting up a fire service if firemen had to determine for each call who within the group could most easily go. Moreover, always sending the most skilled and willing firemen to fight the fire might just be unfair. We assign responsibility to role-bearers based on relative costs between groups; but using least-cost reasoning to divide responsibility within a group would often be either counterproductive or simply wrong.

10.6. THE PRINCIPLE OF COMPENSATION

There is, however, one significant exception to our general reliance on least-cost reasoning. There are, that is, cases in which we assign responsibility for averting a basic threat to well-being to an agent who is not the agent that can most easily avert the threat. These are cases that fall under the principle of compensation. Compensation is required when one person has harmed another, and the harm to the victim constitutes a continuing threat to their basic well-being. Say I cause a traffic accident that puts you in the hospital with failed kidneys. I may then have primary responsibility for paying for your long-term care, regardless of whether I am the person who can most easily do so. I am responsible for the care that averts the threat to your well-being because I caused the harm that now threatens your life.

The principle of compensation is important in our reasoning, and we apply it beyond those situations in which basic well-being is threatened. I am responsible for compensating you, for example, whether an accident I cause breaks your ribs or breaks only the front grille of your car.

Yet the principle of compensation governs our reasoning in a rather restricted class of cases of threats to basic well-being. Moreover, even when the principle of compensation does apply, it is surrounded by least-cost reasoning on all sides. The principle of compensation is limited in at least five ways.

First, the principle of compensation only applies when a threat to well-being arises because there has been a harm. But most threats to well-being (from cars, weapons, poisons, and cliff edges) do not arise because one person has harmed another. In these cases, the idea of compensation can do no work in locating responsibility.

Second, even when there has been a harm, it is least-cost reasoning that will determine who is responsible for having caused the harm in the morally or legally relevant sense. Recall from our earlier discussion of drivers on the expressway that least-cost reasoning enables us to pick out the actions of trailing drivers as the 'cause' of certain accidents. We pick out the cause of harms by least-cost reasoning, and then hold the harm-causer responsible for the further threats to the victim's well-being that have arisen from that harm (e.g., for the injuries from the accident).

Third, the principle of least cost overrides the principle of compensation in emergency situations. Say that I fire an arrow far off into the distance, into the park, and when it comes down it goes through the shoulder of the person walking next to you. Who at this moment has primary responsibility for trying to stop the bleeding and getting the victim to the hospital? It is you, because you are closer to him than I am. I am responsible for compensation only after the emergency is over.

Fourth, the principle of compensation, even when we do apply it, is a shallow or one-leveled principle. Compensation can only locate primary responsibility. If the person who owes compensation is unwilling or unable to compensate, we will as always turn to least-cost reasoning to find the persons or groups who can most easily bear secondary responsibility for helping the victim.

Finally, the principle of compensation becomes less important in our reasoning the less sure we are who is responsible for causing a harm, or indeed whether there has even been a harm at all. Attempting to apply the principle of compensation to this volume's topic, severe poverty, would raise extremely complex questions. A variety of factors usually contribute to any given individual's poverty, and it is often very difficult to judge what would have happened had some person acted differently or had particular institutions been differently structured. Moreover, it is likely that many of the people who have contributed to an individual's poverty are no longer alive to do any compensating. Because of these complexities the principle of compensation appears to play little role in our thinking about responsibility for severe poverty. We can therefore focus again on the least-cost principle, since it applies most fully to the case of severe poverty which is our central concern.

10.7. RESPONSIBILITY FOR ALLEVIATING SEVERE POVERTY

There is one principle, we have found, that explains our beliefs about responsibility for averting threats to basic well-being in almost all cases. We rely on this principle when writing 'the rules of the road', when assessing emergency situations, and when constructing our most basic social roles. Indeed with one limited type of exception, we apply this principle everywhere. The least-cost principle—with the qualification for excessive burdens, with the distinction between direct and role-based responsibility, and with the provision for stepping back to secondary responsibility—guides our reasoning about responsibility in almost all everyday examples of threats to basic well-being.

We are now in a position to apply what we have discovered to the difficult question of alleviating severe poverty. Severe poverty is a major threat to basic well-being, and in our world poverty threatens the lives of billions of people. The question we face is who bears what responsibility for ensuring that this threat to these individuals is averted.

Who, then, has primary responsibility for averting the threat of severe poverty? The answer, as we have seen, will depend on the circumstances. The least-cost principle says that, in good conditions, a great deal of this responsibility will rest with the individual himself (or, in the case of children, with the individual's parents). When resources and opportunities are generally available, each person has primary responsibility for doing what he can to provide himself with adequate food, clothing, shelter, and so on. Each individual is responsible for taking care of his basic needs because, in good conditions, he is the person who can most easily do so.

In many places, however, conditions are much less than good. Individuals are unable to secure for themselves an adequate standard of living, or can only do so with the greatest difficulty. In these kinds of situations, we should expect our reasoning to 'step back' to the next level, as in the everyday cases above. If an individual becomes destitute and unable to provide for himself, then that individual's family becomes responsible for his care. If a family becomes destitute and unable to provide for itself, then the local community becomes responsible for making sure the family has enough to live on. In each case here we are stepping back to find the agent who can bear the responsibilities at the least cost.

What if a local community is unwilling or unable to take responsibility for averting the threats of severe poverty to some or all of its members? This is, unfortunately, all too common a state of affairs. Here we step back again to the level of the national government, and so arrive at the level of human rights. Human rights specify the responsibilities of those who hold power, especially state power. One responsibility of those who control the state is to ensure that each resident of their territory is protected against the dire threat of severe poverty. This is the responsibility of securing each resident's human right to an adequate standard of living.[7]

---

[7] Universal Declaration of Human Rights, Article 25.

So state officials are responsible for ensuring that every person in the territory can attain an adequate standard of living. When residents of a territory are faced with the threat of poverty, officials can take either of two courses of action for fulfilling their responsibilities. These two courses of action will be familiar from what we have already seen. First, officials can act to avert the threat directly. For example, if people are starving, officials can simply make more food (or the means for securing more food) available. Alternatively, officials can attempt to improve general economic conditions so that people are empowered to provide for their own needs. Officials taking this latter course might, for example, work to improve the country's economy so that famines are alleviated and then prevented. Indeed, the two courses of action are not mutually exclusive. Officials can supply food to avert the immediate threat of starvation, while also working to improve the economy so as to avert the threat of famine in the longer term.

The government of each state has a responsibility for ensuring that the conditions are in place so that the basic needs of each person in the territory can be met. What if the government fails in its responsibility? Should a government be unwilling or unable to carry out its responsibilities, secondary responsibility then falls to the citizens of that country to install a new government capable of meeting the obligations of holding state power. The responsibility to reform a state wherein people cannot meet their basic needs rests in the first instance on the shoulders of the citizens of that country, because in general they are the people who can most easily make these reforms.

Yet there are many cases in which the citizens of a state are unable to institute such reforms, or where it would be excessively costly for them to do so. In some countries it has proved extremely difficult for citizens to put into place a government that will meet its basic domestic responsibilities. In these circumstances, the responsibility for sustaining the conditions in which the basic needs of the citizens of this country can be met shifts again to the next level out. This is the level of foreign governments and the 'international community'.

The outward expansion of the assignment of responsibility that we have seen so far appears plausible, and there is no principled way to contain the momentum of the argument so that it applies only to conationals. The conclusion that states can have responsibility for securing citizens of other countries against severe poverty is the clear consequence of the principle of responsibility that has accounted for our firm beliefs in other cases. Some, however, have tried to keep the argument from extending this far. The government of the United States, for example, has never accepted that it might have responsibility for helping to ensure that the citizens of other countries maintain a decent standard of living. The severe poverty of foreigners, according to the US government, generates not responsibilities, but at most aspirations.[8]

---

[8] See, e.g., 'Statement of the United States of America to the 59th Commission on Human Rights; Item 10: Economic, Social, and Cultural Rights', delivered by Richard Wall of the US delegation to the UN Commission on Human Rights. April 7, 2003—usembassy.state.gov/nigeria/ wwwhp040703a.html

Yet the United States and other countries cannot consistently refuse responsibility for acting to secure the rights of foreigners to an adequate standard of living. For the United States and other countries have long accepted that they can bear responsibility for averting threats to the basic interests of foreign nationals. Consider, for example, the right to asylum. The right to asylum is by definition a right that obliges governments to protect foreign citizens when certain of the foreigners' basic interests are being threatened by their own governments. All states, including the United States, have acknowledged the right to asylum, and have acknowledged that this human right places them under corresponding duties. So the US government, and all other governments, have already granted the principle that they can have responsibility for meeting threats to the basic well-being of foreign citizens. Furthermore, the right to asylum itself follows from least-cost reasoning, since it is the government of the country of asylum that can most easily avert the threat to the asylum-seeker's life.

Nor is it likely that the United States can succeed, as it has often tried to do, in making a fundamental distinction between 'civil and political' human rights and 'economic and social' human rights, or in its claim that the former are in some way more genuine than the latter. There have been many attacks on the coherence and significance of this distinction, and we can now see why these attacks have tended to be effective. Our reasoning about responsibility contains no fundamental rationale for making this distinction. The least-cost principle does not differentiate among types of threats, or among the actions that are required for averting these threats. The political/economic distinction has no more weight in our reasoning about locating responsibility than does the positive/negative distinction. In principle, these distinctions mean nothing.

Moreover, the United States and others cannot plausibly resort to blaming the local government in order to avoid their responsibilities. In some poor countries, government officials may be unable to act to ensure that their citizens' basic needs are adequately secured. In other countries, government officials may be ignoring the basic needs of their citizens and feathering their own nests. The corrupt officials in the second case are certainly reprehensible, and likely deserve blame and punishment for the suffering they are causing. Yet the distinction between unwilling and unable officials makes no difference to the argument about the responsibilities of the international community. As we have seen, whether a primary responsibility-holder is unwilling or unable to carry out their responsibilities can make a difference as to whether or not blame or punishment are appropriate. But it has no bearing on the assignment of secondary responsibility. The assignment of secondary responsibility always goes to the agent or agents who can next most easily bear the costs of averting the threat in question. In this case, secondary responsibility lies with the international community—whether the local government is blameworthy or not.

Of course, it may be that it is more costly for governments to help avert severe poverty in foreign countries than it is for governments to accept some asylum-seekers. We have found that considerations of cost do indeed play a basic role in our reasoning about responsibility, so there is some room for political leaders to allege that meeting the costs of averting severe poverty in our world would be excessively burdensome. One version of this allegation would be the claim that developed countries have tried conscientiously but unsuccessfully to alleviate severe poverty in poor countries, and that trying harder would be simply too costly. (Recall here the thirsty man who pours out the water.)

In general, these pleas of excessive costs are not compelling. There is almost certainly some international economic and political system that is now available to us in which no individual would face a high risk of severe poverty, and in which no party was burdened by excessive costs. There is, that is, some feasible system for averting severe poverty where no one is excessively burdened by the responsibility to secure the human right to an adequate standard of living. In fact, it is likely that the problem is less that there is *no* feasible and effective system for dividing responsibilities, than that there are *too many* possible systems.

There are many ways of dividing up responsibility among the actors in the international community that could avert severe poverty. For example, one scheme might place more emphasis on regional political solutions, which would require governments to attend more closely to the governance of those countries in their vicinity. Another scheme might place more emphasis on global economic solutions, which would require, for example, more equitable tariff and subsidy levels between developed and developing countries. Another scheme might require major development efforts to be funded by countries proportionately to the size of their national products. No doubt there are other kinds of schemes, and schemes that contain 'mixed' strategies. The costs of moving to any particular one of these schemes for dividing responsibility would not be excessive, but for each scheme the costs would be significant and would fall differently on different parties. Each government prefers the schemes that would be less costly for its own country. This is why we get the kind of finger-pointing and delay on the issue of severe poverty that have become so familiar. The governments of rich countries will together continue to say that the governments of poor countries should bear more responsibility for fighting corruption. The US and Europe will continue to advance proposals for reducing farm subsidies that each knows will be unacceptable to the other. Every country will favor a different scheme, knowing very well that the lack of coordination will mean that no satisfactory scheme will be put in place.

There are, no doubt, many people who are to blame for this state of affairs, but as always allocating blame is not our main concern. What is important is that the threat of severe poverty, which harms so many, be averted. When someone is drowning, it is no good for the people nearby to begin an argument about who can most easily perform the rescue. The important thing is that something be done so that the person is saved. The leaders of the international community have a responsibility to ensure that some definite scheme be put in place that averts the threats of severe poverty for all. An adequate standard of living is the right of each person, and the international community bears the responsibility for ensuring that—in one way or other—each person's right be secured. Leaders may choose to act more directly—for example, by sending food aid to avert the famines that arise. Or they may, with greater likelihood of success, choose to revise the system of international political and economic institutions so that the threats of severe poverty do not arise in the first place. Or they can opt for some combination of these strategies. What is important is that they decide upon some system that will enable the international community to discharge its responsibility to avert the threat of severe poverty.

10.8. INDIVIDUAL RESPONSIBILITY FOR SEVERE POVERTY

The location of secondary responsibility in the leaders of the international community returns us to the adage that with power comes responsibility, and with great power comes great responsibility. Responsibility falls on developed countries because these countries can help without bearing excessive costs. The costs to these nations are not excessive because these nations have been economically and politically successful. States which have been successful find themselves with the resources necessary to assist those states which have been unable to create (or have been prevented from creating) the conditions wherein they can provide for their own needs. The price of success is to ensure that others can also succeed.

Of course, the momentum of the argument does not stop here. We must admit to ourselves that our own political leaders have repeatedly proved themselves either unwilling or unable to discharge their responsibilities for averting the threat of severe poverty around the world. And there is still one level left to which we can step back. This is the level at which we act as individuals. We have seen that in principle there is nothing in our reasoning about responsibility that will keep one person from being responsible for averting threats to any other person, no matter how unrelated or far away. Singer's arguments tried to draw on this fact to reach conclusions about our responsibilities, yet his arguments left out the intermediate steps. We have now traced responsibility back, step by step, until it rests again with us as individuals. This is a conclusion that we must accept if we are to remain true to our most basic principles about the assignment of responsibility.

We are, then, as individuals responsible for doing what we believe will be effective in alleviating and preventing severe poverty. We are responsible for doing this up to the level where it would impose excessive costs for us to do more. As always, these responsibilities can be discharged either directly or by empowering those closer to the problem. We can act to alleviate severe poverty directly by giving our resources to organizations that we believe will be effective in helping those threatened by poverty. Or we can give our political leaders incentives to carry through on their own responsibilities by making it clear that leaders who shirk their responsibilities will pay costs in political support. Or we can combine both strategies. What is important is that each of us actively assume the responsibilities we have for averting the dangers of severe poverty that threaten so many. We must carry out these responsibilities in order to live up to the principle of responsibility in which we already believe. If we do not abide by our own principles, we will not live up to our own convictions about what it is morally up to us to do.

11

Global Poverty and Human Rights: The Case for Positive Duties

*Simon Caney**

The moral seriousness of the existence of global poverty is hard to dispute. According to recent UN figures, 1.2 billion people have to survive on less than $1 per day (UNDP 2000: 8). Furthermore, 790 million people are in hunger and cannot readily obtain food (ibid.). The same report records that 'More than a billion people in developing countries lack access to safe water, and more than 2.4 billion people lack adequate sanitation' (UNDP 2000: 4). Some political leaders have recognized the moral urgency of this situation. The United Nations Millennium Development Goals, for example, include as their first goal a commitment to 'Eradicate extreme poverty and hunger' where this requires commitments to 'Reduce by half the proportion of people living on less than a dollar a day' and to 'Reduce by half the proportion of people who suffer from hunger' (www.un.org/millenniumgoals/ index.html). These were agreed on by the UN, IMF, and World Bank at the United Nations Millennium Summit, held in September 2000.[1] Also, importantly, these meetings were followed by discussions of what practical policies should be adopted to achieve these goals, most notably at the International Conference on Financing for Development held in Monterrey in Mexico on March 18–22, 2002.[2]

People may condemn the existing global poverty for a number of different reasons. Some, for example, may think that we ought to alleviate global poverty out of a duty of charity or philanthropy. They might think that it would be callous and selfish not to help the needy. My aim in this chapter is to motivate some

* An earlier version of this chapter was presented at the UNESCO symposium on 'Poverty as a Human Rights Violation' at All Souls College, Oxford, on March 16–17, 2003. I am grateful to all the participants for their suggestions and to Leif Wenar in particular for his helpful written comments. I owe a special debt to Thomas Pogge for his extensive illuminating and probing written remarks on two drafts of this chapter. I am grateful too to Rekha Nath for her close reading of the text and her helpful editorial suggestions. This chapter was written while I held a University of Newcastle Research Fellowship and I am grateful to the University for this support.

[1] For further details see the United Nations Millennium Declaration: www.un.org/millennium/ declaration/ares552e.pdf. See also the United Nations' 'Road map toward the implementation of the United Nations Millennium Declaration' at www.un.org/documents/ga/docs/56/a56326.pdf

[2] For further details see: www.un.org/esa/ffd

support for the idea that there is a human right not to suffer from poverty. On such an account, people are entitled not to be subject to poverty and can claim relief as a matter of justice. Having sought to defend this claim, I aim to address a serious and pressing challenge raised against this proposed right, namely the challenge that there cannot be a human right not to suffer from poverty because one cannot give an adequate account of who is duty bound to protect this right.

11.1. THE RIGHT NOT TO SUFFER FROM POVERTY

How might one ground a human right not to suffer from poverty? The best argument for such a human right would, I think, make two claims. The first maintains the following:

(1) An adequate account of human rights must rely on, and be informed by, an account of persons' human interests.

(1), note, does not claim that an account of human interests entails a set of human rights and, as such, it is not vulnerable to the objections directed against that claim. It makes the more modest claim that interests are a necessary feature of an argument for a specific set of human rights and it is not committed to the claim that the former are sufficient to ground human rights.[3]

(1) is, I think, hard to dispute. It might be supported by two considerations. First, it draws support from the recognition that the language of human rights is invariably employed to refer to rights to protect fundamental and important interests. The standard lists of human rights bear this out, referring always to interests (such as the interest in being able to practice one's religion or associate with others) that we deem valuable. Second, we might note that it is hard to see how one can derive any specific content for any human rights without drawing on an account of persons' interests. Notions like 'respect for persons' or 'treating persons as ends in themselves' are far too thin to yield specific human rights. As James Griffin points out, '[w]e cannot begin to work out a substantive theory of rights—what rights there actually are—without a substantive theory of goods. We need to know what is at the center of a valuable human life and so requires special protection' (1986: 64, ch. XI in general). What we need, if we are to generate a concrete account of particular human rights, is an account of persons' interests.

The next step in the argument is:

(2) Persons have an interest in not suffering from poverty.

This view is hard to dispute. Persons vary, of course, profoundly in terms of their conception of the good but common to all of them is the belief that poverty is bad. This point can be illustrated in numerous ways. Poverty, of course, simply

---

[3] For a canonical discussion of the relationship between rights and interests see Raz (1986: ch. 7 in general and 166 in particular).

and straightforwardly restricts someone's ability to pursue his or her conception of the good. Furthermore, since the poor cannot afford an adequate diet, this frequently leads to poor health. In addition to this, it leads to vulnerability and a susceptibility to exploitation for it undermines their bargaining power. We might also note, in support of (2), that it enjoys ecumenical appeal. That is, one does not need to arbitrate between competing accounts of persons' interests to evaluate it because they all condemn it whether one's account of persons' interests is, say, the Rawlsian notion of the two moral powers (the capacity for a sense of justice and the capacity to form, revise and rationally pursue one's conception of the good) (2001: 18–24) or Sen (1993) and Nussbaum's notion of the capability to function (2002).

At this point in the argument, a critic might dispute (2), arguing that some persons do not think poverty is bad. Such a critic might cite the example of religious ascetics (ranging from St Francis of Assisi to Buddhist monks) to show that many do not think of poverty as an evil. Several points might be made against this kind of objection. First, it is of negligible relevance in the context of contemporary global poverty. Second, on a more philosophical level, one can address this concern by modifying (2) to state:

> (2*) Persons have an interest in having the opportunity not to suffer from poverty.

(2*) recognizes that for almost all poverty is an evil, but it also recognizes that some may not wish to take up the opportunity to avoid poverty. The point is well made by Martha Nussbaum who, when faced by the claim that food is not a human interest because some choose to fast, replies: '[t]he person with plenty of food may always choose to fast, but there is a great difference between fasting and starving, and it is this difference that we wish to capture' (2002: 131, see more generally 131–2).

Now (1) and (2*) together provide some support for the following:

> (3) An adequate account of human rights will include the human right not to suffer from poverty (where this refers to the right to avoid poverty).

Hereafter this right shall be referred to as HRP. The preceding discussion is, of course, very cursory and more needs to be said. My aim, though, is to indicate a rationale for it and then to respond to a powerful objection to the HRP.

11.2. ASCRIBING DUTIES

One of the commonest, and most serious, objections to the claim that there is a human right not to suffer from poverty is voiced by Onora O'Neill. O'Neill objects that this kind of claim is misconceived because it does not, and cannot, provide an adequate account of who is duty bound to uphold this right. O'Neill employs the language of negative and positive rights, arguing that one can easily identify who is at fault when a negative right is violated. There is, however, no easy or obvious answer, she claims, to the question of who has the duty to protect positive rights.[4] This defect is not simply a theoretical one for it also has severe political ramifications. The failure to specify who is duty bound to protect the human right to avoid poverty has, she argues, contributed to a lack of progress. Unless one can specify who is duty bound to do what, it is hard to see how one can make any practical contribution to the matters at hand (O'Neill 2001, especially 185–6).

My aim in the rest of this chapter is to address this pressing issue and to provide an account of who is duty bound to protect this right. To do so it is useful to consider three accounts of the duties to ensure that persons enjoy the human right not to suffer from poverty (hereafter duties$_{hrp}$):

Account I: the Nationalist Account: this maintains that the duty to ensure that a person's human right not to suffer from poverty is met falls on his or her fellow nationals.

Account II: the Institutional Account: this maintains that the members of an 'institutional scheme' have a responsibility for the justice of this scheme and hence that the duty to ensure that a person's human right not to suffer from poverty is met falls on the other members of his or her 'institutional scheme'.

Account III: the Interactional Account: this maintains that the duty to ensure that a person's human right not to suffer from poverty is met falls on all other persons who can help (whether they are conationals and whether or not they are members of his or her 'institutional scheme').

Before proceeding further we should note that the concepts employed to characterise Accounts II and III (namely the terms 'institutional' and 'interactional') were coined by Thomas Pogge (2002a: especially 45, 64–7, 170–2, 174–6).[5] We also need to flesh out what is meant by what Pogge calls an 'institutional scheme' (1989: 8). As Pogge employs this term, it refers to systems of interdependence. Institutional schemes refer to existing schemes of trade, production, consumption, law, and interaction in general. An institutional scheme is, I think, equivalent to what Rawls terms the 'basic structure': it denotes those economic, political, social, and legal institutions that structure people's lives (Rawls 1999a: 6–10). Two other points should be borne in mind. First, we should note that the concept of an 'institutional scheme' is not to be understood in a communitarian sense as a group of people with a common cultural identity for Pogge explicitly rejects this (2002a: 176). Second, we should also note that membership of a common institutional scheme requires more than that people are aware other people's existence. Institutional schemes, to repeat, refer to systems of economic interdependence.

---

[4] This is a long-standing aspect of O'Neill's work. She presses it in *Faces of Hunger* (1986: ch. 6, especially 101–3, 118–20); *Toward Justice and Virtue* (1996: 129–35); *Bounds of Justice* (2000: 134–6); and 'Agents of Justice' (2001).

[5] For earlier discussions see Pogge (1994c: 90–8 especially 90–1; 1995: 113–19). Both chapters have been incorporated into Pogge (2002a). For other earlier discussions of the distinction see also Pogge (1992a: 90–101; 2000a: 51–69).

With these clarifications in mind, let us now consider each of the accounts, starting with the Nationalist Account.

11.3. THE NATIONALIST ACCOUNT

This is affirmed by David Miller in *On Nationality*. Miller holds that although there is a human right not to suffer from poverty this does not entail that each person is duty bound to ensure that all persons can enjoy this right. Rather the duty$_{hrp}$ should be ascribed to people's fellow nationals (1995: 75–7; 1999: 200, 202). Why should this be so?

One answer to this question proceeds as follows: first, it maintains, persons, in virtue of their membership of a nation, acquire special duties to their fellow nationals. This is, moreover, a duty of justice (1995: Chs. 3 and 4, especially 83–5 and 98). The argument then claims that since persons have special duties of justice to their fellow nationals this entails that they have a responsibility to ensure that their fellow nationals can exercise their human rights. As Miller puts it:

Who has the obligation to protect these basic rights? Given what has been said so far about the role of shared identities in generating obligations, we must suppose that it falls in the first place on the national and smaller local communities to which the rights-bearer belongs. (1995: 75)

Hence the duty$_{hrp}$ accrues to one's fellow nationals.[6]

This line of reasoning is problematic for a number of reasons. First, it is far from clear that persons *do* have special obligations to fellow nationals. Whether persons have obligations to other people who belong to the same group as them should surely depend, in part, on the moral decency or otherwise of that group. We cannot think that morality demands that anti-Semites are bound by moral duties to put the interests of fellow anti-Semites above others. But then, given this, we need an argument to establish that a nation is a morally decent institution before we are entitled to conclude that persons have a duty to their fellow nationals (Caney 1996). Second, suppose that we concede that persons have special duties to their fellow nationals. This is insufficient to support Account I. We need also to be shown that these duties are duties of justice and, in particular, duties$_{hrp}$. Many

---

[6] In addition to the argument in the text, two reasons might be given in defense of Account I. Consider a nation, A, that contains people who are in dire need. First, according to one common argument, to ascribe a duty$_{hrp}$ to all people would sanction intervention in A. It then objects that such intrusion into a nation is prima facie wrong, and hence, the duty to ensure that the members of A do not suffer from poverty should fall on their fellow nationals (Miller 1995: 77–8). Second, it is sometimes argued that since A is responsible for its own decisions the duty to ensure that impoverished members of A are granted their HRP should not be ascribed to foreigners. Rather, since A makes the decision, the members of A should pick up the bill (Miller 1995: 108; Miller 1999: 193–7; Rawls 1999*b*: 117–18). Certainly non-members should not have to bale them out. For a critique of the first argument see Caney (2000: 135–9) and for a critique of the second argument see Caney (2002: 114–17; 2003: 301–5).

duties that arise from our membership of groups are not obligations of justice at all. We are bound by duties of love and community and it often misrepresents some of our duties to other members of our communities to construe them as duties owed as a matter of justice that others can demand as a right. Given this, we need further reasoning to show that the duties yielded by our membership of nations are duties of justice (Caney 1999: 128–33). Let us suppose, however, that persons have duties of distributive justice to their fellow nationals. Even this does not yield the conclusion, for a third problem with Account I is that it contains a mistaken inference. Just because X has a right to a and I have a duty (of justice) to X, does not show that I have a duty to provide X with a (Caney 2001: 983). Consider, for example, a person's right to medical care and consider a specific individual. Let us focus on an individual who is an academic. We would say that academics have special duties of justice to their departmental colleagues. It does not follow, though, that the duty to ensure that an academic enjoys the right to medical care falls on his or her departmental colleagues. He or she cannot plausibly say to his or her colleagues: 'You have a duty of justice to ensure that I possess the right to health care: you owe me this'.

A fourth problem with the Nationalist Account is evident if we ask why nationality should play the privileged role that Account I ascribes to it. Let me explain. The nationalist position maintains that a person's cultural identity leads to duties to other members of this cultural group. But given this premise it follows that members of religious communities have duties to fellow members of their community; members of a class have duties to fellow members of their class and so on. But then, given this, why can we not equally conclude that the duty$_{hrp}$ falls on members of a person's religious community, class, etc.? Why should the duty$_{hrp}$ be allocated to those belonging to a person's nation instead of being allocated to those belonging to that person's class, ethnic community, caste, region, profession, and so on?

The final problem with Account I is that it is radically incomplete. Consider an impoverished country A. According to Account I, the duty to ensure that the members of A enjoy the human right not to suffer from poverty should be attributed to other members of A. But, of course, given its impoverished nature, the members of A are likely not to be sufficiently wealthy to ensure that the right is met. This then entails that if the human right is to be honored duties must fall on non-nationals. Account I, thus, needs to be supplemented for we need an account of who has the duty to uphold the human right if fellow nationals cannot.[7] Is it everyone else? Or those who are part of the same socioeconomic system? Or some other group of people?[8]

---

[7] Miller himself notes that Account I is incomplete stating that if a nation's government 'cannot send relief [to its impoverished people], then there is a good case for saying that outside agencies have a duty of justice to supply it)' (1995: 77 n. 30). He does not say which 'outside agencies' are duty bound. He examines the question of who (outside a nation) has the duty to ensure that people enjoy the HRP in a later work (1999: 201–4).

[8] Someone might query this last point, arguing that the latter assumes, without warrant, that if human rights can be protected then there is a duty on the part of some people to protect this human

11.4. THE INSTITUTIONAL ACCOUNT

With this in mind, let us turn now to Account II. This position has been developed and defended by Pogge. For Pogge, principles of justice apply to systems of economic interdependence. Duties of justice extend to those who are members of the same scheme of trade, cooperation, and economic interdependence in general (2002*a*: especially 45, 64–7, 170–2, 174–6). This claim about the scope of justice is then combined with a second, empirical, claim, namely that the world we live in is a global system of interdependence (2002*a*: especially 13–26, 111–17, 139–44, 172–5: cf. also 1998*a*: 504–10, especially 504–7). This yields the conclusion that the duty$_{hrp}$ falls on all persons.[9]

Institutional accounts are also affirmed by many other thinkers. Rawls, notably, is committed to it although, of course, he does not think there is a global institutional scheme in the strong sense that thinkers like Pogge maintain (1999*a*: 6–10).[10] Thomas Scanlon (1985: 202) and, more recently, Darrel Moellendorf (2002: 30–40, 43, 48, 53, 62, 72) too both adopt an institutional approach. They both maintain that justice applies within systems of interdependence and that there is a global system.[11]

Prior to evaluating Account II, it is essential to distinguish between two versions. According to one version, all the duties of justice that one has are owed only to fellow members of one's institutional schemes. This view adopts what might be termed a wholly institutional approach. According to a second version, some, but not all, of the duties of justice that one has are owed only to fellow members of one's institutional schemes. This adopts what might be termed a partially institutional approach. It allows that one may have some duties of justice to persons whether there is interdependence or not.

In what follows, I construe Account II as affirming a wholly institutional approach. I also argue that a wholly institutional approach is implausible. My aim is to show that we should accept some duties of justice to all persons—including duties of justice to eradicate poverty—whether everyone is a member of a universal institutional scheme. But I am not disputing the claim that there

right. To reply: My final objection to Account I does indeed make this assumption. However, I believe it can be justified: for if human rights are to be more than idle and empty promises as to what people are entitled to do then it must be the case that others act in such a way as to enable the rights-holder to be able to exercise the capacities the right promises to protect.

[9] We should note that Pogge defends an institutional approach only as an account of our duties of justice. He would thus allow that one can have 'a positive duty of beneficence' to aid those outside one's institutional scheme (2002*a*: 198). See further (1992*a*: 91; 2002*a*: 170).

[10] Although critical of the language of rights, O'Neill, like Pogge, thinks that duties of justice apply among persons who are interconnected: O'Neill (1996: 105–6, 112–13). Also, like Pogge, she maintains that the scope of justice in our world is global or pretty much so: O'Neill (1996: 113–21, especially 121).

[11] Charles Beitz is a more complicated case. He maintains that some global principles of distributive justice (such as a principle governing the distribution of natural resources) apply even without there being a global institutional structure (1999*c*: 136–43). However, he also maintains that some other global principles of distributive justice (such as a global difference principle) apply only if there is a global institutional structure (1999*c*: 131, 143–54).

are some duties of justice that pertain only to members of schemes. My position is therefore compatible with a partially institutional approach. The following section completes the analysis by adducing further considerations in support of an interactional approach according to which there are positive duties of justice owed to all persons independently of the existence of global interdependence. To show that a wholly institutional approach is unfounded I wish to make five points.

(1) First, we can begin our inquiry by asking why membership of institutional schemes should bear on one's duty to eradicate poverty. What reason do we have for thinking that membership of institutional schemes generates duties of justice? The most powerful and sophisticated answer to these questions comes from Pogge. His argument relies on the distinction between positive and negative duties: it contends that, as a matter of justice, persons have a negative duty not to participate in an unjust socioeconomic structure. Relying on this, Pogge maintains that persons are bound by justice to distribute resources to the needy in their own scheme because not to do so would be to impose an unjust system on them. Persons, he writes, have a '*negative* duty not to uphold injustice, not to contribute to or profit from the unjust impoverishment of others' (2002a: 197; cf. also 1989: 276–8; 1994c: 92–9; 2002a: 13, 66–7, 133–9, 144–5, 172, 197–8, 201, 203, 204, 210, 211). Membership of institutional schemes, some of whose members are impoverished, is morally significant because through one's membership one supports an unjust regime and thereby violates a negative duty.

This is an ingenious and appealing argument. What is worth noting for our purposes, though, is that it is insufficient to establish a wholly institutional approach. What it can show—using the idea of negative duties—is that persons are under some duties of justice that they owe only to other members of their institutional schemes (the duty not to perpetuate unjust structures). In itself, however, it does not show that there can be no positive duties of justice that are owed to all persons regardless of whether all are interlinked by global economic-social-political relations. Nothing it says gives us reason to reject an interactional component to a political morality. Put otherwise, it is an argument for an institutional component, not a refutation of an interactional component.[12]

(2) Consider now a second different defense of a wholly institutional approach. Many argue that duties of justice apply within systems of economic interdependence because such systems have a tremendous effect on people's lives. Their claim is that principles of justice (including a principle condemning poverty as unjust) apply to the 'basic structure' because the latter exercises a profound

---

[12] On this point see Caney (2005a: 113–14). I should stress that my argument is not (and is not intended to be) a criticism of Pogge for he does *not* reject the claim that there are positive duties of justice. His central claims, rather, are: that persons are under negative duties of justice that are owed to other members of their institutional setup; that these include a duty to eradicate global poverty; and that, given this, we do not need to invoke positive duties of justice to combat global poverty. He is, therefore, neutral on the question of whether there are positive duties of justice. I argue below that we should not be neutral on this question and must, if we are to eradicate global poverty, embrace positive duties of justice.

impact on individuals' lives. Institutional schemes have moral significance because of their effects on people's interests.[13] Let us call this the Outcomes Argument.

The problem with this argument as a defense of a wholly institutional approach stems from its starting assumption that what is of fundamental importance—what really matters—is that people can exercise their abilities and further their interests. For if this *is* what matters does it not generate duties on everyone even if they are not part of any common association? The criterion being invoked to justify the moral significance of an institutional scheme is concerned with outcomes, in particular, the capacity to act and to pursue one's conception of the good. But if this is the case, parties external to an institutional scheme also equally have moral responsibility because by omitting to act in certain ways they too affect outcomes within that scheme. An outcome-inspired rationale cannot vindicate a wholly institutional account of the duties$_{hrp}$.[14]

(3) Having seen how neither of the arguments considered can support a wholly institutional account of who is duty bound to uphold the human right not to suffer from poverty we may now also observe three additional problems it encounters. First, one puzzling feature of a wholly institutional perspective is evident if we consider a point commonly made by institutionalists themselves about what constitute morally arbitrary influences on people's entitlements. One institutionalist, for example, writes that '[s]ince one's place of birth is morally arbitrary, it should not affect one's life prospects or one's access to opportunities' (Moellendorf 2002: 55; cf. also 79).[15] But, if we accept this (and it is a pow-erful line of reasoning) it causes problems for an institutional perspective. Can someone not equally persuasively argue that 'one's life prospects or one's access to opportunities' should not depend on 'morally arbitrary' considerations such as which institutional scheme one comes from? Moellendorf's own institutional approach contradicts its own guiding principle by penalizing some on the basis of their 'place of birth'. If someone is born into an impoverished system that has no links with the rest of the world, a wholly institutional account must maintain that members of the latter have *no* duties of justice to the former—thereby penalizing them, depriving them of the very means to live, simply because of their 'place of birth'. Put otherwise, if it is arbitrary that some face worse opportunities because

---

[13] For examples of this kind of reasoning see Jones (1999:7–8); Moellendorf (2002: 32–3, 37–8); and, most famously, Rawls (1999*a*: 7; 2001: 55–7).

[14] For an earlier statement of this objection to the Outcomes Argument see Caney (2005*a*: 112). For another instance where the outcome-inspired justification of why the basic structure has ethical significance does not sustain the intended conclusion see G. A. Cohen's important discussion. Cohen argues that if (like Rawls) one deems the basic structure to be significant because of the outcomes it generates then one must (contra Rawls) not define the basic structure in narrow legal-coercive terms: (Cohen 2000: 136–40). The upshot of Cohen's argument is that a theory of justice should employ a broader notion of the basic structure. The upshot of my argument, by contrast, is that a theory of justice should take into account causal factors other than, and external to, the basic structure. (For a response to Cohen's argument see Pogge (2000*b*).)

[15] Again: '[t]he underlying idea is that one cannot claim to deserve things such as place of birth and education, race, or parents' privilege. Hence, these things should not be the basis of a distribution' (Moellendorf 2002: 79, my emphasis). See also Pogge (1989: 247).

they come from one nation rather than another, is it not equally arbitrary to penalize some for coming from one institutional scheme rather than another? The logic of the intuition underpinning cosmopolitanism thus subverts a wholly institutional perspective.[16]

(4) A further problem with a wholly institutional approach is that it generates malign incentives. If the duty$_{hrp}$ applies only to those linked by interaction then this gives the wealthy and powerful an incentive to disassociate themselves and disconnect themselves from the disadvantaged thereby avoiding being bound by the duty$_{hrp}$. It thus generates incentives for people to lighten their load by eschewing interaction with the impoverished. One must be cautious in making this objection against Pogge for he makes exactly the same type of argument against those who limit justice to political communities. In his illuminating 'Loopholes in Moralities' he objects to any scheme that makes political–legal borders the borders of schemes of distributive justice on the grounds that it provides some with an incentive to create new borders, with themselves on one side and the poor on another in what is now a new country, and thereby no longer have obligations of distributive justice to the poor (cf. 2002*a*: 71–90 in general; and 80–2 in particular).[17] Given this, we should be wary in arguing that Pogge is vulnerable to exactly the same objection.

Consider two replies that might be made. First, it might be argued that it is not *possible* for people to disconnect themselves from the existing global schemes of economic interaction. So, while it is possible to create new political borders and thereby transform former co-citizens into foreigners, it is simply not possible to divorce oneself from the global economy. It is interesting to record, here, that in a different context Pogge himself maintains that it is impossible for the wealthy to disassociate themselves from the rest of the world:

whether the members of different societies can or cannot avoid mutually influencing one another is, though an empirical matter, surely not up to them. At this stage of world history we cannot realistically avoid international interaction, and so the members of rich societies have no incentive to exploit the fact that the criterion of global justice would not apply if societies were self-contained. (1989: 241 n. 3; cf. also 263)

Pogge's remark is not directed to the objection that I am making. Nonetheless, one might affirm his empirical claim in order to undermine the thesis that a wholly institutionalist position would generate malign incentives.

However, this first kind of response is unpersuasive for two reasons. First, it is surely possible for some to weaken their links to some extent with the rest of the world. On any plausible view, the extent to which people are obligated will vary depending on how extensive the interdependence is.[18] But, bearing this in

---

[16] My argument here draws from Caney (2005*a*: 111–12).

[17] For an earlier succinct statement of the argument see Pogge (1989: 253–4).

[18] Note that the defenses of a wholly institutional perspective that have been considered above at (1) and (2) support the view that the extent of one's obligations to others should increase proportionately with the level of interdependence (what we might term 'the variable view'). According to the first argument considered, the more interdependence there is the more that the plight of some can be said

mind, we can see that a wholly institutional account can generate incentives for people to minimize their obligations to the impoverished. Even if it were true that they could not sever all ties completely they could decrease the extent to which they are connected to others and thereby decrease their duties$_{hrp}$ to the needy. Second, this reply does not get to the heart of the matter for it concedes that if it were possible for people to leave the global economic system then they could permissibly immunize themselves from duties of justice to assist those dying of starvation, malnutrition, and so on. The fact that in theory it would sanction it (even if this does not obtain at the moment) should, I think, cast severe doubt on it. The first response thus fails.

A second response to the 'malign incentives' objection is that we need much more information about how the wealthy in the example obtained their wealth before we can conclude that a wholly institutionalist position can be indicted for fostering incentives for the wealthy to disconnect themselves.[19] To see this consider some possibilities. Suppose, for instance, that the wealthy acquired their wealth through exploiting members of their own scheme. Here it seems entirely reasonable for an adherent of a wholly institutionalist position to say that the wealthy are under a duty to compensate the unjustly treated for this exploitation and are disallowed from simply removing themselves and their unjustly acquired monies. And if this is the case, a wholly institutionalist position would not generate the malign incentive.

In reply: This is a plausible response for a case in which the affluent gain their wealth through unjust means. However, suppose that the affluent acquire enormous wealth because the land they own is tremendously bountiful. Or, suppose that they acquire great wealth because of their talents. In such cases, the second response is powerless. Persons who acquire great wealth through either of these mechanisms would, in a world governed by a wholly institutionalist approach, have an incentive to disconnect from their existing institutional scheme. The charge thus remains: a wholly institutionalist position generates malign incentives,

to have been produced by the imposition on them of an unfair system at (1). Similarly, according to the Outcomes Argument, the more interdependence there is then the more the global economy will affect individuals' lives. Neither argument, then, supports an institutionalism that states that the barest interaction generates the same extensive principles of justice as profound interdependence (what we might term 'the invariable view').

See, in this context, one of Liam Murphy's arguments against institutionalism. He remarks that it would be very strange to think that the smallest contact has such an enormous ethical significance (1998: 274). This, I think, is correct but it applies only to the invariable view and not to the variable view. For further critical analysis of institutionalism see Murphy (1998: 271–5).

Charles Beitz has also argued that a small amount of international trade does not justify the adoption of an expansive global distributive programme (1999*c*: 165). He thus rejects the invariable view. But he does not endorse the variable view. Rather he argues that a global difference principle applies if, and only if, global economic interaction reaches a certain 'threshold'. His view maintains then that: (i) below the designated threshold the global difference principle does not apply but (ii) once the threshold has been met the global difference principle applies and it applies whether the economic interaction is of a just-above-the-threshold-level or is much more extensive than that (1999*c*: 165–7). For a critical discussion of this claim see Caney (2005*b*: 396–7).

[19] I owe this point and the ensuing development and elaboration of it to Thomas Pogge.

giving the rich an incentive to leave and thereby immunize themselves from the duty$_{hrp}$.

To make the case stronger yet, consider another distinct kind of incentive effect encouraged by a wholly institutional approach (one against which, again, the second kind of response is powerless). The above analysis has noted how a wholly institutional account induces the wealthy to disconnect themselves from the impoverished. Note, however, that it also generates a second unattractive kind of incentive, for it encourages the wealthy not to connect with the impoverished in the first place. An example may illustrate the point:

> Example I: A ship from a wealthy country sees two remote islands. Island 1 has no natural resources, is generally impoverished, and its population is on the verge of starvation. Island 2, by contrast, is blessed with wonderful natural resources (and its population is well-off). Now, knowing that under a wholly institutional approach, one is obligated to all with whom one is linked by trade and economic interaction, the ship goes to island 2 and avoids contact with island 1.

A wholly institutional position thus encourages the wealthy not to make contact with the impoverished because that would lead to some duty$_{hrp}$. Moreover, what is especially paradoxical is that island 1 is penalized *because* it is poor: the factor that would normally make us think that it should receive aid (its poverty) in fact under a wholly institutional approach is the very reason why it receives none.

(5) A fifth consideration that tells against a wholly institutional account of the duties$_{hrp}$ concerns its implications for civil and political human rights. Imagine the following:

> Example II: An isolated island is run with ruthless cruelty by a tyrant who, because of his possession of weaponry far superior to the other islanders, is able to persecute them, slaughtering enemies, torturing suspects, and so on. Suppose, further, that we are aware of this island and could easily assist the persecuted and bring about a more tolerant peaceful society.[20]

Now my point in creating this example is to bring out and emphasize the point that persons' most basic *civil and political rights* would also be sacrificed if we adopted a wholly institutional perspective. If someone is to adopt a wholly institutional account of duties$_{hrp}$ they must not only conclude that we have no duty of justice to protect the welfare rights of remote individuals: they must also abandon any idea that we have a duty of justice to protect the fundamental civil and political human rights of remote individuals. And this, I think, casts a wholly institutional perspective in an even more unattractive light.[21]

---

[20] Charles Jones makes a similar point (1999: 13). However, by doing so he undermines his own institutionalism (1999: 7–8).

[21] One response to this is that although institutionalism would not affirm duties *of justice* to aid those whose civil and political rights are imperilled in the example given in the text it need not object to the claim that there are duties of morality to aid them. Hence, a world given by institutionalist

11.5. TOWARD AN ALTERNATIVE ACCOUNT—THE
HYBRID ACCOUNT

Having criticised Account I and argued that a wholly institutional version of Account II is incomplete, let us turn now to Account III. According to Account III, a theory of global justice should begin by addressing the question of people's rights and entitlements. These have moral primacy. With these in mind one can then address the question of how we can ensure that people enjoy their entitlements (Shue 1996*a*: 164–5). This is where Accounts I, II, and III come into play. Account III maintains that the duty to ensure that people can enjoy their human rights (including the right not to be impoverished) falls on all persons who can help.[22] All persons have a duty to bring about and maintain institutions that ensure that persons can enjoy their human rights.[23] This may, of course, involve setting up new institutions which bring all into a common institutional structure but this does *not* mean that it collapses into an 'institutional' position for the point is that the obligation that justifies the creation of the institution precedes the creation of the institution. The key point is that persons (independently of any interdependence) have obligations to ensure that all persons can enjoy their human right not to be impoverished.[24] So whereas an institutionalist position sees (international) institutions as a source of (international) duties of justice, the position I am sketching sees them as a possible means for implementing people's duties of justice (Shue 1996*a*: 164–5).

In the last section we saw various ways in which a wholly institutional account of the duty$_{hrp}$ was unsatisfactory. My aim in what follows is not to argue that Account III be put in its place. It is not, that is, to defend a wholly interactional position, which treats all duties of justice along the lines specified by Account III, for I think that Pogge has made a compelling case for thinking that there are

principles need not be as bad as the argument in the text suggests. I respond to this kind of move in section 11.6.

[22] This position is a version of what Pogge terms 'maximalist' interactionalism (2002*a*: 64). There are other kinds of interactionalism. A notable and unorthodox example is Nozick's brand. In his interesting analysis of the question of whether social cooperation is necessary for distributive justice, Nozick famously asks whether ten isolated Robinson Crusoes are bound by justice to redistribute their wealth (1974: 185). Working on the assumption that they are not, he sees in this support for his own individual entitlement theory on the grounds that such isolated persons provide the clearest instance where an individual can claim to be solely entitled to the resources they own. Economic interdependence is, thus, not on his view a necessary condition for principles of economic justice and entitlement (1974: 185–9).

[23] My account, here, is indebted to Shue (1988: especially 695–8 and 702–4; 1996*a*: 17, 59–60, 159–61, 164–6, 168–9, and 173–80). See also Jones (1999: 66–72 especially 68–9). Both, however, may disagree with the way I develop this account.

At this point we should note that there is some dispute as to whether Shue's position is accurately described as an interactional one. Pogge once claimed that it was (1994*c*: 118 n. 5). Shue has, however, queried this (1996*a*: 224 n. 21; cf. for further comments 1996*a*: 164–6 and 225 n. 27 and n. 29). See, finally, on this issue Pogge (2002*a*: 226 n. 98, and n. 249 n. 271). None of this affects my position which follows Shue's in several ways but explicitly includes an interactional component.

[24] For a defense of this claim see also Ashford's chapter in this volume.

negative duties of justice generated through persons' membership of an institutional scheme. My aim, rather, is to argue that a comprehensive account of
the duties$_{hrp}$ should include not just an institutional account (as outlined and
defended by Pogge) but also an interactional account and the positive duties that
that account yields. I am defending, then, what I term a Hybrid Account. Stated
very roughly, this may be characterized as follows:

> Account IV: the Hybrid Account (the General Version): this maintains that
> (a) persons have a negative duty of justice not to foist an unjust global
> order on other persons (the institutional component); and (b) persons have
> a positive duty of justice to eradicate poverty that does not arise from the
> imposition of an unjust global order (the interactional component).

In what follows I give both general reasons as to why we need to add the interactional component and also outline the nature of the positive duties of justice
generated by the HRP.[25]

(1) Before drawing attention to the main considerations in defense of adopting
an interactional element it is worth noting three misconceptions about interactionalism.

First, we should record that the examples employed to discredit an interactional
approach often load the dice against it by building into it features that are not
integral to it. Let me explain. It is interesting to record that many critiques of
interactional perspectives employ science fiction examples. For instance, both
Onora O'Neill and Jonathan Wolff use this kind of example to motivate support
for Account II and against Account III. O'Neill employs an example referring to
'the aliens of an inaccessible planet' (1996: 105) and Wolff employs an example
containing 'a creature in human form from an alien planet which is desperately
short of water' (1996: 269).[26] These kinds of examples, however, muddy the water
by introducing a separate question: namely, what are our obligations of justice
to aliens? To judge an interactional account fairly one should think of examples
involving human beings on the same planet. We should focus our attention on
cases involving, say, a remote people living in grueling poverty on an island with
no trade or political or environmental links with the rest of the world.

Second, one might think that persons only have a duty$_{hrp}$ to other people
when the former are aware of the latter. This claim—what one might term the
'knowledge' principle—insists that one cannot ascribe a duty$_{hrp}$ to others if they
are unaware that the others even exist. Now drawing on this one might infer
from this that a wholly institutional view is correct and that interactionalism is
false. To reply: the 'knowledge' principle has some plausibility but, even so, it is

---

[25] Pogge, note, does not commit himself to the rejection of approaches which, like the Hybrid
Account, marry institutional and interactional components. See, e.g., 2002a: 170.

[26] See also what Pogge terms 'the Venus argument' (1998a: 503). The latter attacks interactional
theories by asking whether we would have obligations of justice to persons on Venus. Pogge, note, is
careful to refer to persons (not aliens or undefined 'creatures').

separate from and does not entail a purely institutional approach.[27] For example, it is entirely possible that I know of a remote island struck by disease and famine even though I am not a part of its institutional structure.

Third, interactionalism might seem implausible and be rejected on the grounds that it is incompatible with the claim that duties$_{hrp}$ can only be attributed to those who are able to contribute to the alleviation of poverty. This claim—let us term it the 'can help' principle—is hard to dispute. Note again, however, that this principle is distinct from, and does not entail, the rejection of interactionalism. Consider someone who flies over a remote island suffering from famine. They cannot be said to be part of the same institutional structure and yet they know about the famine and it is possible that they can easily assist the needy (dropping supplies from the airplane). The 'can help' principle, then, does not entail anti-interactionalism but might reasonably be confused with it.

(2) The preceding points note how interactionalism is mischaracterized but do not give us a positive reason to incorporate an interactional component into a theory of justice. For the main reasons why a Hybrid Account is more plausible than Accounts I and a Wholly Institutional Version of II we should return to the objections to Account II for they do not simply show the limitations of a wholly institutional approach. They also support adding an interactional component.

Consider, first, the Outcomes Argument for the moral significance of 'institutional schemes'. Since this maintains that membership of a basic structure is ethically significant and generates duties to others because of the basic structure's impact on people's lives it must ascribe duties to anyone who is able to affect people's lives whether those others belong to the same basic structure (point (2) on p. 282). Anyone who gives the Outcomes Argument in order to show the moral significance of the basic structure is, then, committed to positing positive duties of justice to those external to the basic structure who can make a difference. As such it provides support for the Hybrid's Account's ascription of interactional positive duties$_{hrp}$ to people.

Second, one central point in favor of my proposed hybrid is that, unlike Account II (understood in the Wholly Institutional sense), it does not penalize persons because of wholly arbitrary considerations such as their place of birth (point (3) on p. 283). Unless we ascribe duties$_{hrp}$ to all persons (whether they are all members of a shared institutional scheme) we may end up condoning situations in which some, such as the inhabitants of isolated islands, avoidably live in grueling poverty and die prematurely. And if we do this we allow some to suffer from grinding poverty and needlessly so, even though we can help, for no reason other than

---

[27] Note that I am not claiming that the 'knowledge' principle is correct. We might wrongly be led to think so if we did not distinguish carefully between the issue of whether someone has an obligation and the issue of whether one may criticize someone for not complying with an obligation. Of course, it would be entirely wrong to criticize someone for not complying with an obligation to assist A if that person did not know that A even existed (and their ignorance is not culpable). But this does not show that that person does not have the obligation. We can make perfect sense of someone having moral rights of which they are unaware, so why can someone not have moral duties of which they are unaware?

that they have the misfortune to be a member of an impoverished institutional scheme disconnected from the modern world. The Hybrid Account, by contrast, is committed to eradicating such poverty as a matter of justice and it entails that the affluent have a duty of justice to aid the impoverished in question.

Third, we should observe that by including positive duties of justice to protect persons' rights, the Hybrid Account avoids the malign incentive effects generated by a wholly institutional account (point (4) on p. 284). The point here is that under the Hybrid Account persons cannot liberate themselves from a duty to ensure that others do not die of poverty by making sure that they do not belong to the same scheme as those impoverished others for they will have duties to them (including the duty$_{hrp}$) anyway. It is true that if the Hybrid Account is put into practice they may still have incentives to have less dealings with some people, such as people from whom they can gain little in terms of trade. So even under the Hybrid Account they may have incentives not to build up economic links with those with little to offer. But the crucial point is that they are unable to act in such a way that they will not have duties of justice to eradicate global poverty because under the Hybrid Account they have these duties whether there is interdependence. By ascribing positive duties of justice to eradicate poverty, then, the Hybrid Account is not vulnerable to the objection that it induces malign incentive effects that disadvantage the global poor.

And, fourth, and finally, of course, the Hybrid Account is able to say that we have obligations to protect the civil and political human rights of those oppressed by distant local despots (point (5) on p. 286). For as long as persons can help they have a duty of justice to protect those whose human rights are violated no matter where they live or who they are.

In short, each of the shortcomings of a wholly institutional approach chronicled in the last section is remedied by combining an institutional approach with an interactional component in the way that the Hybrid Account proposes.

(3) The case for adding an interactional component can be strengthened further by exploring the causes of global poverty. Moreover, in doing so we can not only underscore the need for adding an interactional component: we can also identify which positive duties of justice are required to address global poverty. At present the Hybrid Account is stated at a high level of generality and does not indicate what specific positive duties of justice are required. Through an analysis of the causes of global poverty we can remedy this and arrive at a more detailed statement of the particular positive duties of justice needed to overcome the limitations of a wholly institutional position.[28] As such it enables us

---

[28] The argument that follows is indebted to Miller (1999) in two ways. First, Miller suggests that our account of the duties to eradicate poverty should be informed by an analysis of the causes of poverty. Second, he considers four causes of poverty, prescribing different obligations in the different instances. The four causes of poverty that he considers are the lack of a state, the existence of a corrupt government, an unpropitious global economic environment, and the lack of natural resources (1999: 201–4). My typology overlaps with his. It does, though, differ in some important respects. I have argued elsewhere that his typology is too narrow and that his account of the appropriate duties in the different cases is implausible: see Caney (2003: 305–7).

to provide a comprehensive statement of the duties of justice generated by the HRP.

Let us begin then by listing the possible causes of global poverty. These include:

   (i) global variables: that is, an unfair global economic and political order,
  (ii) local variables: that is, an oppressive élite (or, in a variation on this, a well-meaning but incompetent élite),
 (iii) poor natural resources, and
 (iv) physical and/or mental infirmities.

Pogge's institutional approach can clearly deal with the poverty that arises from (i). But what of poverty that arises because of factors (ii), (iii), and (iv)? Let us consider each in turn.

Consideration (ii) What of poverty that arises because the government of a state is corrupt and uninterested in the plight of its people? What of poverty that is brought about by government inefficiency and incompetence? *Ex hypothesi*, such poverty does not stem from the global order and hence arises even if members of the latter do not violate their duty not to impose unjust global institutions on others.[29]

One might make a number of responses to this argument. First, one might argue that (ii)-like scenarios are rare or, perhaps, non-existent. What appear to be local variables are often themselves the product of some global variables.[30] But while this may sometimes—perhaps often—be the case, I can see no a priori reason for thinking that this applies in all circumstances. To claim that the global system is one significant causal factor is a credible one but to claim that it is the only cause of existing global poverty is implausible. It might, perhaps, *sometimes* be the case that the poverty of some people is *wholly* explicable in terms of global considerations. It might even *always* be the case that the poverty of people is *partly* explicable in terms of global considerations. But for this first (empirical) reply to succeed it must be the case that global factors are *always* the *sole* explanation of poverty. Wherever *part* of the causal explanation of poverty concerns local variables, the first response fails and leaves the door open for an argument for positive duties.[31]

---

[29] This point is the economic analogue to the argument in section 11.4 invoking civil and political rights abuses committed in a far-off land.

[30] Pogge persuasively argues that it is often shortsighted to explain poverty as a product of corrupt governments because the global order tends in various ways to encourage corruption (2002*a*: 22, 112–16 and 146–67; herein: 24).

[31] Pogge, I think, acknowledges that local considerations can constitute part of an explanation of global poverty. He makes a variety of claims of differing strength. First, and most modestly, he denies that 'the existing global economic order is not a causal contributor to poverty' (2002*a*: 14), and this is consistent with allowing that local variables may also be causal contributors (2002*a*: 14, 22, 49–50, 112, 208, 214–15). His keenest aim, under this heading, is to deny the 'purely domestic poverty thesis' (herein: 30–3). Note, one of Pogge's own analyses of how institutions cause poverty—that of starvation in the USSR in the 1930s—invokes a local (non-global) variable, namely Stalin's collectivization programme (herein: 15 and 25). Second, more strongly, he claims that 'the existing global order

A second reply would be to say that even if we grant that poverty arises from (ii)-like causes, this does not undermine Pogge's institutional claim that poverty arises because people violate their negative duty of justice not to foist unjust institutions on others. It is just that the violators in this kind of scenario are not global actors but the local political authorities and their members. The latter have a negative duty of the kind specified by Pogge. Therefore we do not need to ascribe positive duties of justice to non-members. To reply: this has some force but suppose that these local political authorities, as is often the case, do not comply with the duty$_{hrp}$. We are faced then with a world in which people will face profound poverty. In such circumstances, surely the appropriate response—if we are committed to the human right not to suffer from poverty—is to maintain that non-members have a positive duty of justice to protect these peoples' HRP.[32] For if we do not accept this then we must resign ourselves to the conclusion that a world in which some people face dehumanizing and life-threatening poverty because they have the misfortune of living in certain countries is not an unjust world.[33]

Having considered poverty that arises because of (ii), let us turn now to (iii).

Consideration (iii) What of poverty that arises from poor natural resources? What of people who live in barely habitable lands or lands devoid of natural resources? Since some poverty stems from these natural causes, an institutional theory of justice that contains only a negative duty not to impose unjust institutions on people is unable to justify measures to eradicate such poverty. This said, it is important not to overstate the importance of this variable as a cause of global poverty for much research has shown that poverty often does not stem from poor natural resources. Indeed much research has shown that some of the poorest societies have considerable natural resources (Ross 1999).[34] Nonetheless it would be rash to assume that it never plays a role in causing poverty and it should be included in any complete account of the duties needed to ensure people can exercise their right not to suffer from poverty.

This leaves one final causal variable.

---

plays an important role' in the existence of global poverty (2002a: 208). Third, he downplays the role of local variables by arguing that local variables may explain where poverty arises but not necessarily the amount of global poverty (1998a: 506).

[32] For a contrary position see Miller (1999: 201–2). There Miller argues that external bodies have a negative duty not to collaborate with the corrupt state but he excludes there being a positive duty of justice. And in an earlier work he explicitly states that outsiders are under a 'humanitarian' duty to eradicate poverty stemming from an unjust government but they are not under a duty of justice to do so (1995: 77 n. 30).

[33] Again we should, of course, note that someone may reply that although there is no duty of justice to deal with (ii)-like causes there is nonetheless a non-justice-based duty to do so and hence that a proponent of institutionalism is not saddled with the unattractive conclusion that we have no duties to help people in (ii)-style scenarios. I deal with this response shortly: see point 3 on p. 298.

[34] For further analysis see Atkinson and Hamilton (2003). See, further, Michael Ross's analysis of how opulent natural resources can contribute to civil war (2004): given that civil war frequently leads to poverty and famine, bountiful natural resources can contribute via civil war to severe poverty.

Consideration (iv) It seems reasonable to suggest that some are poor because they are physically or mentally unable to secure a sufficient standard of living. They might suffer from sickness or disease or be handicapped in some way. Now if we are to combat poverty it follows that those who are capable are obligated to ensure that people do not suffer from poverty because of such human frailties. And this requires attributing to them positive duties of justice. A system of negative duties is unable to prevent the afflicted from suffering impoverishment.

How might one respond to this argument? It is hardly credible to claim that poverty never arises because of people's physical or mental infirmities. This argument can not then be undermined on empirical grounds. Someone might, however, challenge it on normative grounds. Consider two points they might make. First, they might argue that people are only under a duty of justice to eradicate poverty that they have caused. A person can be obligated (as a matter of justice) to help only if other people's poverty results from his or her action. If it does not then the person can ask, 'why should I do this? It is not my fault they are impoverished. I did not bring it about'. Let us call this the Causation Assumption. To this claim they might also, second, add that one might have positive duties of charity and benevolence to aid people. It is just that one does not have a duty of *justice* to provide assistance.

Before evaluating this response we should note that the Causation Assumption, if true, does not just undermine those who claim that there is a positive duty of justice to eradicate poverty stemming from natural and physical frailties. For if it is correct, then it also undermines the above analysis of considerations (ii) and (iii).

The main problem with this response is simply that we are rarely given any reason to accept the Causation Assumption. It is certainly not self-evident. Why should we ascribe duties of justice to persons only if and when they have caused some disadvantage? Unless a defense of the Causation Assumption is given we have no basis on which to reject positive duties of justice to eradicate poverty stemming from people's infirmities. The argument for a positive duty of justice to eradicate poverty that arises because of mental or physical infirmities thus stands.

Now in light of the analysis of considerations (i), (ii), (iii), and (iv), I wish tentatively to suggest that we develop the Hybrid Account so that it claims that the following duties are generated by the human right not to suffer from poverty:

Account IV: the Hybrid Account (the Expanded Version)

Principle 1: in (i)-type cases there is a Poggean negative duty of justice on everyone to secure persons' HRP;

Principle 2: in (ii)-type cases there is a Poggean negative duty of justice on the members of the local élites to secure persons' HRP;

Principle 3: in (ii)-type cases, where members of local élites do not comply with their Poggean negative duties, then those outside of their 'scheme' have a positive duty of justice to secure persons' HRP;

Principle 4: in (iii)-type cases there is a positive duty of justice to secure persons' HRP; and

Principle 5: in (iv)-type cases there is a positive duty of justice to secure persons' HRP.

This Expanded Version, note, conforms to the structure laid out by the General Version of the Hybrid Account. It includes both institutional duties (Principles 1 and 2) and interactional duties (Principles 3, 4, and 5).[35]

The critical point that the Hybrid Account (in both the general and expanded versions) brings out is that negative duties of justice are not enough. If we are to eradicate poverty and to assure people of the human right not to suffer from poverty we must accept a scheme of positive, as well as negative, duties of justice. In particular, the positive duties of justice enunciated by Principles 3, 4, and 5 are needed to address the poverty that a wholly institutional position would allow to persist.[36] The Hybrid Account seeks to safeguard the human rights of *all* (whether isolated poor people or people whose poverty stems in part from local causes or natural calamities and so on). It recognizes and is responsive to the fact that some suffer deprivation that is not caused by us and that it is our duty to prevent this.[37]

(4) It should, of course, be immediately conceded that Account IV needs far more development. First, it does not say how the duties$_{hrp}$ should be distributed. One particularly pressing issue in this context is how the duty$_{hrp}$ should be distributed when some do not do what is required of them.[38]

Second, it does not indicate how Principles 1, 2, 3, 4, and 5 are to be ranked. One neat and tidy way forward would be to group together all the principles that fall under one heading (say all instances of 'Principle 1') and state that this category of principles always takes priority over all the principles that fall under a second heading (say, all instances of 'Principle 2') and so on. This category-based approach (or type-based approach) would be relatively easy to employ when making decisions as to what one should do. One would rank the different

[35] For an earlier account with which mine has much in common see Shue's analysis: (1996*a*: 51–64, especially 55–60).

[36] Pogge is aware of this. He writes that his account of human rights 'afford[s] less protection to the poor and oppressed' (herein: 23). As he rightly adds, 'we cannot assess how big a disadvantage this is in the real world, however, without examining more closely to what extent the actual underfulfillment of human rights is due to violations of correlative negative duties' (herein: 23). This is clearly an absolutely critical issue. The question of how to respond to the global poverty that remains once we have factored out that which issues solely from violations of global negative duties constitutes one major site of disagreement between proponents of positive duties of justice and their critics.

[37] My position echoes that taken by Allen Buchanan: 'if the reasons why they [individual human beings] should not be treated in certain ways have their source in the nature of persons as persons, rather than in the fact that they are our fellow citizens or fellow members of a cooperative scheme (a global basic structure), then why are we not obligated to help ensure that all persons, no matter where they are, are included in institutions that protect their basic rights?' (1999: 72). See also Beitz's perceptive discussion (1983: especially 593 and 595–6).

[38] See Derek Parfit's pioneering discussion of 'collective consequentialism' (1984: 30–1) and Murphy's extended discussion of this issue (2000).

categories of principle (so that, e.g., all instances of Principle 1 take priority over all instances of Principle 2, and/or that all instances of Principle 2 take priority over all instances of Principle 3) and then when deciding what to do one would just examine which category a principle falls into. From this one could then read off which principle takes priority. Unfortunately, while neat and tidy, it is implausible (especially given the grounding of human rights in persons' interests canvassed in section 11.1) for it is possible to have cases where a violation of Principle 1, say, would result in less damage to persons' interests than a violation of, say, Principle 5. And in such cases it would be perverse to rank all instances of Principle 1 higher than all instances of Principle 5.

This point suggests that we do not rank actions/omissions by what type they fall into: for example, are they an instance of Principle 1 or 2 or 3, etc.? Instead we examine the individual tokens. So we would ask, for instance, whether we should reform this particular international treaty which imposes a minor injustice on disadvantaged persons (a Principle 1 issue) or whether we should instead spend our time and effort distributing resources to handicapped persons abroad which could have a major impact on their lives? (a Principle 5 issue) This points to the need for some kind of cost-benefit analysis of different principles in terms of their impact on persons' lives. However, this option is not straightforward either for it is not clear how we factor into the cost-benefit analysis intuitive convictions like, for example, the conviction that the violation of a negative duty which results in a harm X is worse than the non-compliance with a positive duty which also results in a harm X. The challenge here is to arrive at a way of factoring such convictions into a quantitative analysis. In short, then, a type-based approach (which ranks all instances of Principle 1 as higher than all Principle 2 etc.) is simple to employ but issues in implausible decisions. A token-based approach (which compares particular instances of each principle against particular instances of other principles) avoids the problem which afflicts the type-based approach but runs into the problem of how to quantify valuations that are not based on the amount of harm. A fully adequate elaboration of the Hybrid Account must thus make progress on this front.

Third, it should be noted that the above sketch is also silent on the important practical question of how duty-bearers should fulfill their duty. As Shue has pointed out, this is likely to require that persons create and support political institutions that would be charged with securing the human right not to be impoverished,[39] but a great deal more work needs to be done as to what this requires in practice. The account defended must then outline what institutions, if any, should be brought into existence and/or how current institutions should be reformed.[40] The key point is that negative duties of justice are not enough.

---

[39] See, again, Shue (1988: especially 695–8 and 702–4; 1996a: 17, 59–60, 159–61, 164–6, 168–9, and 173–80).

[40] The Commission on Global Governance, e.g., proposed the creation of an 'Economic Security Council' to coordinate existing institutions and bring about a fairer world (1995:153: cf. further 153–62).

11.6. THREE OBJECTIONS CONSIDERED

Many, however, have misgivings about theories of distributive justice that ascribe positive duties of justice to others and so I wish to supplement the above analysis by addressing three queries or concerns.

(1) One concern is that the Hybrid Account, by including positive duties of justice, is too concerned with the 'recipients' and accords too little respect to the 'duty-bearers'.[41] In maintaining that persons who suffer from poverty because of natural calamities or the oppression of despots or because of their own physical frailties are entitled to receive support it is, it might be said, overly concerned with the beneficiaries and insufficiently concerned about those who are burdened with the responsibility to eradicate poverty.

The appropriate reply to this worry is to note that there are a number of different ways of according respect to duty-bearers. One way focuses on the *type of duties* one posits. It avers that one shows respect to duty-bearers by telling them that they must honour negative duties of justice but that they are not constrained by positive duties of justice. It asks persons only that they comply with negative duties of justice. There are, however, other ways of accommodating the legitimate concerns of duty-bearers. A second distinct way of respecting duty-bearers focuses on the *demandingness of any duties*. It maintains that one respects duty-bearers by limiting the amount that one may permissibly require of individuals. This distinction is of considerable importance for it is open to a proponent of the Hybrid Account to respond to the challenge by adopting this second account. The idea, then, would be to include all persons within the scope of distributive justice (affirming both positive interactional duties of justice and negative duties of justice) but ensuring that the principles selected are not unduly onerous on the relevant duty-bearers.[42] Accommodating the 'duty-bearer' perspective does not then require abandoning positive duties of justice and it does not therefore require the rejection of the Hybrid Account.

(2) A second concern one might have about the Hybrid Account is that it lacks the strategic advantages of a purely institutional approach. Let me explain. One great virtue of Pogge's institutionalism is that many people accord negative duties a very great weight and rank them higher than positive duties.[43] By showing that members of advanced capitalist societies are violating a negative duty because they are imposing unjust institutions on other members of the global order, Pogge's

---

[41] See in this context Pogge (2002a: 13, 174). Shue also makes this distinction, referring to 'duty-bearers' and 'rights-bearers', in his illuminating discussion of institutional and interactional accounts (1996a: 164–6).

[42] Here I am in agreement with Shue, see his pertinent discussion: Shue (1996a: 164–6; 1996b, especially 117, 119, and 126). See also his analysis of the demandingness of the duties imposed by global principles of distributive justice (1983: 600–8).

[43] Pogge, himself, maintains that negative duties have 'special moral urgency' (2002a: 201: cf. also 130, 132, and 211); see further (2002a: 134–5).

institutionalism has great strategic appeal.[44] With this in mind a critic of positive duties of justice might say:

it may or may not be true that there is a positive duty of justice to protect the HRP of some people but in the contemporary context this is a misplaced strategy. Given the common belief that negative duties have overriding weight it is better to challenge the anti-HRP position on its own terms (we only have negative duties) rather than rely on a controversial notion such as a positive duty to protect the human right not to suffer poverty.

To this I would make two comments. First, I believe that what is central to prevailing attitudes toward negative and positive duties (to the extent that there is a consensus on this) is *not* that it is wrong to include any positive duties of justice at all. It is, rather, that one should recognize that there are negative duties of justice; that they are of very great weight; and that they normally take priority over positive duties. Thus defined the commonsense view does not run counter to the Hybrid Account. For the latter affirms weighty negative duties of justice in the form of Principles 1 and 2. It can, moreover, rank negative duties as being more weighty than positive ones (although it need not be committed to such a ranking—cf. above). The Hybrid Account is, thus, not at loggerheads with common attitudes toward negative duties. It is simply that it also adds three positive duties of justice as well. This would be a liability only if one thought that commonsense moral thinking also rejected positive duties of justice but we do not, I think, have any reason to think that this is the case.

A second reply follows from some of the points made above, namely that a 'negative duty' approach is insufficient to eradicate global poverty (point (3) on p. 290). For people may comply with the negative duty not to impose unjust global institutions on others and we might still have a world of dire poverty in which people are unable to exercise the HRP. So even if the introduction of positive duties of justice is controversial that is insufficient reason to abandon them for relinquishing them comes at a cost—namely an acquiescence in a state of affairs in which grueling, debilitating poverty persists and claims the lives of many. The negative duty approach is most appealing when it is sufficient to deal with all poverty. Where it is not (as I have argued above) we face a choice between, on the one hand, addressing all poverty but doing so by relying on potentially controversial ideals or, on the other hand, relying on less controversial ideals but failing to eradicate all serious poverty.[45] Furthermore if we are persuaded by the

---

[44] See, in this context, Pogge (herein: 20). The argument in this paragraph is in keeping with Pogge's overall strategy of trying to build a case for global justice that is realistic and that seeks to work, so far as is possible, within the parameters of the modern world.

[45] We might also note one cost of the 'negative duty' approach. The advantage of the latter is that it relies on a duty that people think is of fundamental moral importance. Ironically, this strength may also, in some instances, be a weakness in a strategic sense. Let me explain. By arguing that our duties of justice to the globally impoverished are negative duties, the negative duty approach ups the stakes. It entails that those who do not comply with it are guilty of a serious moral offence (more serious than non-compliance with a positive duty). Now this in itself may lead some people to resist the negative duty approach for they resist the idea that they are guilty of such a serious moral offence (although they might accept that they could do more and hence might more readily accept the existence of positive

defense of a human right not to suffer from poverty adduced in section 11.1 then, so I have argued, we should embrace the first option.

(3) Let us turn now to a third query. Someone might argue that the case for the Hybrid Account is incomplete, for there is an alternative that possesses all the desirable aspects enjoyed by Account IV and which arguably enjoys an extra advantage that the Hybrid Account cannot possess. Let me explain. Consider a fifth account of our duties$_{hrp}$ that mirrors the Hybrid Account in all respects except that where the Hybrid Account refers to 'positive duties of justice' this fifth account refers simply to 'positive duties'.[46] The fifth account would thus read as follows:

Account V: the Alternative Hybrid Account

Principle 1: in (i)-type cases there is a Poggean negative duty of justice on everyone to secure persons' HRP;

Principle 2: in (ii)-type cases there is a Poggean negative duty of justice on the members of the local élites to secure persons' HRP;

Principle 3: in (ii)-type cases, where members of local élites do not comply with their Poggean negative duties, then those outside their 'scheme' have a positive duty to secure persons' HRP;

Principle 4: in (iii)-type cases there is a positive duty to secure persons' HRP; and

Principle 5: in (iv)-type cases there is a positive duty to secure persons' HRP.

Thus Principles 1 and 2 are unchanged and Principles 3, 4, and 5 are revised to refer to 'positive duties' (as opposed to 'positive duties of justice'). Note that this account might either be silent on the question of whether these positive duties are duties of justice or it might, more strongly, expressly deny that these positive duties are duties of justice. I leave this choice open for what follows is unaffected by whichever of these versions we adopt.

Now with this conception in mind someone might make two points against my argument so far. First, they might claim, Account V has all the attractive properties that Account IV possesses. Their reasoning proceeds as follows: Account V would not penalize persons because of wholly arbitrary considerations such as their place of birth; it would not generate malign incentive effects because those who set up a new scheme are still bound by positive duties of morality to ensure that people do not suffer from deprivation. It would, moreover, also provide protection to those whose poverty stems from an unjust government and/or poor natural resources

---

duties of justice). Of course, some people may not react in this way, but if, as I speculate, some do then the negative duty approach incurs a strategic cost. This point is made not to discredit the use of negative duties of justice to ground global principles of justice, but rather to show that we should not uncritically accept the idea that it is a strategic advantage to press the case for global duties of justice in terms of negative duties.

[46] The objection was prompted by some comments of Thomas Pogge on an earlier draft of this paper. He, though, should not be held responsible for the way I have spelt it out or sought to motivate support for it.

and/or human infirmities. If this is true it shows that the case for the Hybrid Account is incomplete. Our choice is underdetermined since, for all that has been said so far, we have no reason to prefer Account IV to Account V. But we can go further. A critic might argue, and this is the second point, that Account V enjoys an advantage over Account IV, namely that it is less contentious because it does not affirm positive duties of justice. A proponent of Account V might, that is, reintroduce strategic considerations. She might reason that by eschewing the controversial notion of positive duties *of justice* and by relying simply on the notion of positive duties (where these might be positive duties of morality or human decency) we avoid estranging those who deny positive duties of justice. So the argument here is that we can get all that we need from Account V and, moreover, Account V will win over more adherents than Account IV because it is not reliant on contentious moral premises.

This, note, is a stronger challenge than that discussed at point (2) above (p. 296), for by explicitly affirming positive duties it attempts to avoid the charge that it would acquiesce in the kinds of poverty that a moral theory that affirms only negative duties of justice would condone.

This challenge to Account IV can, however, be met. Three points can be made in reply. First, while on first inspection it seems reasonable to claim that Account V possesses all the attractive properties that Account IV does, when we analyze it more closely we find that this is not the case. The key to seeing why is to note that (positive) duties of justice are duties that would and should be enforced whereas (positive) duties of morality would not necessarily be enforced. This difference means, for example, that Account V is more vulnerable to the charge of malign incentives than Account IV. Under the latter, the wealthy who disconnect themselves from the impoverished are under an *enforceable* duty to protect the HRP of people outside their own institutional schemes. Under the former, by contrast, the wealthy are not compelled to protect the HRP outside their own institutional schemes: they are under (and are told that they are under) a positive duty to protect the human rights of others, but it is not an enforceable one. This point can be made more generally: whereas Account IV states that Principles 3, 4, and 5 are enforceable Account V would not enforce the corresponding principles. Given this, there would be less compliance and hence more poverty. More concretely, Account IV, unlike Account V, would seek to make persons comply with their duty to protect others' HRP in cases where the latter is threatened by unjust government (Principle 3), poor natural resources (Principle 4) and personal disabilities (Principle 5). Hence a world governed by Account V would result in poorer protection of the HRP than would one governed by Account IV.

The second, and decisive, point in favor of Account IV over Account V is that the argument for the human right not to suffer from poverty outlined in section 11.1 leads naturally to Account IV rather than Account V. Let me explain: the justification of the HRP is built around the value of securing some preeminent interests. From these interests we can then derive negative duties of justice—duties of justice not to violate these interests. However (and this is the key point), given that the interest-inspired approach suffices to entail negative duties of justice, it is hard to resist the conclusion that the positive duties that it also entails (and Account V, recall, does not deny that it does entail positive duties) are also, by the very same token, positive duties *of justice*.[47] The justification adduced in defense of negative duties of justice logically requires us to accept positive duties of justice as well. It thereby gives no support to Account V. Put otherwise, Account V operates with an asymmetry in that it affirms 'negative duties *of justice*', on the one hand, and 'positive duties', on the other. Hence any defense of Account V must supply an explanation of this asymmetry. Yet the argument that I have given in support of negative duties of justice cannot provide this kind of explanation: it is unable to ground (or make sense of) the asymmetrical treatment of positive and negative duties that Account V affirms. The reasoning it employs, thus, impels us to adopt Account IV in preference to Account V; and the differentiated duties affirmed by Account V are alien to the rationale adduced for the HRP. Account IV is, thus, for that reason superior to Account V.

Let us turn now to the strategic consideration that has been mooted in support of Account V—namely the claim that Account V's asymmetrical treatment of positive and negative duties is justified because by referring to 'positive duties *simpliciter*' rather than 'positive duties *of justice*' it is capable of garnering wider support. The appropriate reply to this argument for Account V is that these strategic considerations are the wrong kind of reason.[48] In the light of my second point there needs to be a rationale explaining why it is incorrect to deduce positive duties *of justice* from the interests that justify the HRP whereas it is correct to deduce negative duties *of justice* from these very same interests. And the argument that 'positive duties of justice' are more contentious is not the right sort of reason. It does not, and indeed cannot, show why it is inaccurate to describe the positive duties as duties *of justice*. It fails to reveal a mistake in the derivation of these duties and it does not establish that their claim to be a requirement of justice is false.

To gain a fuller understanding of the issue at stake it might be useful to distinguish between what we have reason to believe, on the one hand (level-1), and what we have reason to say in the public realm, on the other (level-2). The reasoning given above has, I believe, established that the rationale for the HRP gives us reason to believe that Account IV is correct and that Account V is mistaken. The reasoning logically entails Account IV—not Account V. Now the strategic considerations adduced in support of Account V simply do not engage at this level (namely, level-1). Rather, they make the (level-2) point that to campaign in public for Account IV would be impolitic and since Account V

---

[47] Compare with Ashford (herein) and Wenar (herein). Neither, though, is addressing the precise issue I am addressing, namely that of showing why it is implausible to claim that the negative duties generated by the HRP are duties of justice whereas the positive duties generated by the HRP are not duties of justice.

[48] I am grateful to Andrew Williams for a discussion of the issues that follow. He set me thinking along these lines and the argument of this paragraph and the next two paragraphs is indebted to him. He, though, should not be held responsible for the way in which I have presented the ensuing line of reasoning.

is more likely to win more converts it should be adopted as part of a political campaign.

This, however, puts the strategic considerations in an unattractive light. For when making the case for our account of duties$_{hrp}$ it is essential that we are able to give a publicly available account of our reasons for thinking Account V is superior to Account IV.[49] And this requires that we state publicly the reasons for, on the one hand, affirming negative duties of justice and positive duties, and, on the other hand, eschewing positive duties *of justice*. Put otherwise, it requires—if we are to show respect to persons—that we show a flaw in the reasoning adduced in support of Account IV. To see why this is problematic suppose that one is trying to persuade the public of the merits of Account V and that someone asks:

What is the case for these positive duties? And what reason do you have for thinking that these are not duties of justice? What is the argument for thinking that we have negative duties of justice but not positive duties of justice? How do you justify this asymmetry?[50]

It would seem thoroughly implausible (and unconvincing as an answer to one's interlocutor) to reply:

My reason for holding this is that positive duties of justice are contentious. I do not have an argument that shows that the derivation of positive duties of justice is mistaken but I eschew them all the same because to affirm them is politically costly.

That is not the right kind of answer. The questioner wants a *reason* as to why we should not believe in positive duties of justice and a *reason* why the argument for positive duties of justice adduced above is incorrect: the strategic considerations, however, do not speak to this question.

In short, then, the problem with Account V is that it would result in avoidable life-threatening global poverty and deprivation; the argument for the HRP entails Account IV and provides no support to Account V; and strategic considerations do not give us a reason for affirming 'positive duties' rather than 'positive duties of justice'. The Hybrid Account remains intact.

11.7. CONCLUSION

As is evident from the above much more remains to be done. My aim, in this chapter, has been to provide a critique of several accounts of the duties generated

---

[49] The importance of 'publicity' and 'public justification' is, of course, a key theme in much recent liberal political philosophy, in particular that of John Rawls: see his discussion *in A Theory of Justice* (1999a: 397–8) and *Political Liberalism* (1993a: 66–71). The argument in the text employs a very minimal, and hopefully uncontentious, notion of publicity. Another relevant influence here is Bernard Williams's discussion of 'Government House Utilitarianism' (1985: 108–10).

[50] Of course, it is unlikely in the extreme that someone would ask such fine-grained questions. But that is irrelevant. I take publicity to require being able to provide (and actually providing) a full account of the reasons supporting one's views and the reasons one rejects other views (even if people do not actually ask for the full rationale).

by the right not to suffer from poverty (notably Accounts I, II, and V) and to have motivated some support for an alternative account—what I have termed the Hybrid Account. In doing so I have sought to rehabilitate the idea of positive duties of justice owed to the impoverished and to have fleshed out the particular duties that the HRP would entail. Only if these duties are honoured will we live in a world in which persons' rights not to suffer from poverty are respected.

12

The Right to Basic Resources

Stéphane Chauvier

Poverty, like disease, is an absolute and not a relative state. Its opposite is not wealth, which is a relative concept, but what one could call vital security. A person living every day in the fear of not finding food or shelter, but who, by fortunate coincidence, manages to find a roof and sufficient food each day, would still be considered poor in spite of his good fortune, because poverty contains a subjective dimension: it is not only characterized by a low level of resources, but also by a vital insecurity, namely the absence of a foreseeable and reliable access to the resources that are essential to life.

The fact that poverty is an evil, and an absolute evil, is thus as obvious and indisputable as the fact that disease is one. However, the fact that something is held to be evil by every human being does not necessarily imply a *human right* to the corresponding good. It is likely that being loved by the person we are in love with is universally considered as a good, however one could hardly, unless rhetorically, assert that every human being has a right to the love of the person he loves. The evil suffered by someone who is spurned by the person he loves is indeed caused by the one he loves, but the latter cannot be said to be violating the right of the lover, by not loving him.

This suggests that, in order to assert that poverty is a *human rights* violation, it is not sufficient to assert that poverty is a *human evil*. For if every human good is not necessarily the core content of a human right, then every human evil can not be regarded as the violation of a human right. But this also suggests that it is not sufficient to reconstitute the causal genealogy of poverty and to show that certain human beings are responsible, if not for the creation of this human evil, at least for its persistence. For, if every human evil cannot be considered as the violation of a human right, then every *author* of such an evil cannot be considered as a human rights *violator*.

It is true that inflicting intentionally a serious evil to a person, and, especially, acting deliberately to impoverish a person, to deprive him from his basic resources, is immoral as well as illegal. But except in certain pathological cases that we mention at a later point, the main part of the massive severe poverty that exists today in the world is much more the result of the absence of a general will to reduce it than of a malevolent will to cause it. Poverty is less something intentionally created than something that persists and spreads over because people are not concerned enough with reducing it. Now, if it is decisive, in this context, to call upon the language of rights, and specifically of human rights, it is because the existence of a human right has as a corollary the existence of a universal and *enforceable* duty. It is indisputable that because poverty is a human evil of a particular severity, it challenges our humanity or our virtue. But asserting that severe poverty is a human rights violation is very different from calling upon our virtue or our charity. Such an assertion implies an enforceable duty to provide a reliable and durable access to basic resources to those who are deprived from them. And this does not require individual acts of charity or benevolence, but substantial institutional changes and, consequently, a political commitment in this direction.[1]

One can thus understand the importance that the use of the language of human rights holds in this context. It is because, in most of the cases, we cannot speak of an intentional and malevolent causation of severe poverty that we have to call upon the language of rights and enforceable duties if we want to trigger a global commitment into the fight against severe poverty. But, in my view, it remains true that the obvious evilness of severe poverty, and even the obvious existence of a human responsibility in the persistence of this state of affairs do not imply by themselves the existence of an HRP. There is no direct transition from the naturalistic concepts of goods and evils to the normative concepts of rights and duties. A conceptual or philosophical job must also be done to establish that severe world poverty has to be regarded *as* the violation of a human right to a secure and regular access to basic resources.

My chapter is divided into two sections. In section 12.1, I try to show that, in order to assert that poverty is a human rights violation, it is indeed at least *necessary* to validate certain empirical assumptions relating to the nature and causes of poverty. Poverty must be of a certain nature and have certain causes if it has to be viewed as the violation of a human right. But, in section 12.2, I try to show that, because these empirical assumptions are not *sufficient*, we have to show *independently* that there exists a human right to a reliable and durable access to basic resources. However this demonstration inevitably encounters a well-known difficulty: a right of this kind seems to imply an enforceable duty not only of non-interference, but also of assistance or action, and such a duty may seem incompatible with a minimal understanding of individual freedom and independence.[2] Therefore, I also try to show that, even with a 'libertarian' constraint imposed on the concept of right, it is possible to maintain that there is a human right to a reliable and durable access to basic resources, but that this can be done by calling upon two different types of philosophical arguments whose political consequences can generate what I call a risk of denial.

---

[1] The distinction between enforceable and unenforceable duties is a reformulation of the classical distinction between perfect and imperfect duties and of the Kantian distinction between duties of right and duties of virtue. cf. Kant (1968b: 239): 'All duties are either duties of right (*officia juris*), that is to say duties for which an exterior legislation is possible, or duties of virtue (*officia virtutis s. ethica*), for which such a legislation is not possible'. In the language of Kant, the problem we are dealing with amounts to whether the fight against poverty is a duty of virtue or a duty of right.

[2] The *locus classicus* here is Nozick (1974: 175).

12.1. THREE EMPIRICAL CONDITIONS

First, I would like to show that there are certain empirical conditions that must be met before it is even *possible* to consider poverty as the violation of a right. I have claimed that neither the nature nor the causes of poverty imply by themselves that poverty is a human rights violation. But while no empirical characteristics of poverty are sufficient conditions for poverty to be considered as a human rights violation, some are necessary. I would therefore like to set apart three crucial assumptions concerning the nature and the causes of poverty which it is necessary to validate before we can envisage a human right to non-poverty.

12.1.1. The Universal Accessibility of Non-poverty

Let us imagine a world in which all the inhabitants are equally poor. It is not obvious whether, in such a world, the mere concept of poverty would be conceivable. One is tempted to say that, since no contrast would be perceptible in the material situation of people, there would be no way to characterize a fate common to all. However, since poverty has a subjective dimension, since it is as much a state which is experienced as an objective situation, a concept expressing this state could emerge, if only because of the capacity of the mind to consider desirable, though unreal, states, as illustrated by the word 'mortal'.

In any case, it is obvious that the problem of knowing whether poverty is the violation of a right would not arise in a world in which all the inhabitants, without past or present exceptions, were equally and inescapably poor. Indeed, for a given situation to be perceived as the violation of a right, it has to be possible to consider an alternative situation as both *accessible* and *desirable*, and its non-realization as the result of an *accidental difficulty*. It makes no sense, even from a theological point of view, to wonder whether being mortal is the violation of a right, as this would amount to supposing that the situation is accidentally imposed on persons who, at the same time, have an accessible and universally desired alternative. It therefore means that the question of knowing whether poverty is the violation of a right can only arise because non-poverty is a state that is considered as accessible and universally preferred to poverty.

Now, at this point, the first difficulty arises and the first empirical assumption must be validated. Though the existence of non-poverty in the world proves that it is *possible* to live outside poverty, it does not follow that this possibility can be universally achieved. The fact that in each race there is a winner proves that it is possible for a person to run faster than the others, but it is logically impossible that everyone can run faster at the same time than the others. Admittedly, in the case at hand, there seems to be no logical impossibility in the concept of a world where no inhabitant is poor. This is the reason why the problem is purely empirical and economic: do the available resources and the economic way in which they are exploited make a universal emergence from poverty possible for all the inhabitants of the Earth, at this point in the demographic evolution of humanity?

Clearly, the answer to this question is not obvious. But, on the other hand, it seems certain to me that it must be positive if poverty is to be perceived as the violation of a right. If it were not economically possible, in the present and future demographic context, to eradicate poverty completely, it would clearly be impossible to hold poverty as a human rights violation, for a human right is, by definition, a right for every human being. One could say that universalizability is a constraint inherent in the concept of human right: something accessible only to certain lucky human beings and not to others cannot be the core content of a human right. In order to consider that poverty is the violation of a right, it must be economically possible for the nine billion people who will live on Earth by 2050 to be free from poverty.[3]

I contend that this goal can be met economically, even though it is likely that it cannot be reached with a constant growth rate, except by creating negative side effects at an exorbitant cost to the environment and public health. *Global* development is, in fact, one of the facets of the economic problem of *sustainable* development.

12.1.2. The Non-responsibility of the Poor with Respect to Their State of Poverty

I now come to a second empirical condition, which must be satisfied for poverty to be perceived as the violation of a right.

Let us imagine that philosophical knowledge is a good in itself and suppose that we live in a society that enables each one of its members to acquire philosophical knowledge. If in that society there were persons suffering from not possessing this philosophical knowledge, simply because they had not done anything to acquire it, their situation would not pose any particular ethical problem. Their philosophical ignorance could not be perceived as the violation of a right, because they would be *responsible* for their ignorance. According to the Latin formula *volenti non fit iniuria*, what one does voluntarily or for which one is responsible cannot injure or prejudice his rights.

Applied to the case at hand, this idea means that poverty should not be attributable to the poor themselves. If poverty could be attributable to the poor themselves, there would be no sense in wondering whether it is the violation of a right. For poverty to be considered as the violation of a right it is conceptually necessary that the poor be subjected to it, that poverty be imposed on them.

This purely conceptual point thus leads to a second empirical thesis that needs to be validated if poverty is to be perceived as the violation of a right: it must

---

[3] But the following situation is, however, possible: something would be the core content of a human right because it would have been possible for every man, in the past, to enjoy that right. But now, for demographic reasons, it would no longer be universally accessible and humanity would be condemned to tragic sacrifices. This would be a far more complicated case, which could probably only be solved by a utilitarian calculus. For the sake of simplicity, we prefer to assume that the eradication of poverty is still universally accessible.

be true that the millions of people who live in poverty do not owe it to their own actions or their own omissions or, for children, to the actions or omissions of their parents or guardians.

In a sense, this condition is self-evident: except on the grounds of mystical motivations, one can no more wish for poverty than disease, and there is even something indecent in considering that the poor owe their poverty only to themselves. But in another sense, this empirical assumption can cause difficulty. Some empirical theories of the causes of poverty, like that of David Landes call upon historical and cultural factors (Landes 1998). But how should these historical and especially these cultural factors be situated in the theory of responsibility? Is culture the result of external determinism or of mutual consent and if so does it, for this reason, belong to the realm of subjective responsibility? Moreover, there are situations of poverty, in Western societies, for which it is difficult to say whether they are due to fate or to lack of will. The causes which lead people to live in the streets are numerous and among these causes there can be acts, if not of will at least of non-resistance. Finally, it is known that poverty can foster behaviors that help to maintain or perpetuate it.

I think however that these reservations cannot call into question the idea that, in general, people are in no way responsible for their poverty and that they are subjected to it. However, since poverty is not homogeneous in its causes and since it is itself able to generate, in the poor themselves, behaviors which perpetuate it; it is necessary to introduce a restriction or to be more specific: it is only the kind of poverty that satisfies the condition of non-responsibility which can be perceived as the violation of a right. This condition of non-responsibility is, like the preceding one, that of the universal accessibility of non-poverty, an empirical condition that is necessary for poverty to be perceived as a human rights violation.

12.1.3. Poverty as a Negative External Result of Economic Activities

To these two conditions it seems necessary to me to add yet a third one, which is in a sense much more significant or, in any case, much more a matter of controversy when one seeks to put the details together.

Let us consider a situation in which there would be poor people who, though they might not be poor, would at the same time not be responsible for staying poor. For their situation to be perceived as the violation of a right, a condition of a causal nature would still be necessary. Let us suppose that all people that are poor are so because they live in a land and a climate which do not make it possible to ensure their vital security, but that this is not the case for all lands and all climates of the world. Let us also imagine human nature a little different from what it is: people born in a place are naturally tied to that place, perhaps magnetized to it, and are unable to move except within a very small area. The two preceding conditions, the accessibility of non-poverty and the involuntary character of poverty, would then be met but there would be no sense in talking about the violation of a right. The reason is that the cause that would prevent the poor from ceasing to be poor would be natural. If it makes no sense, for example, to call disease a human rights violation, it is because it has a natural cause.[4] In the same way, if all men living in a certain country are tortured by the wind that blows there, there would be no sense in saying that the wind, by torturing them, violates their rights, unless the wind were a conscious and responsible agent. It is a point of a purely conceptual nature: the concept of violation of a right presupposes a human interaction, so that a given situation can only be perceived as the violation of a right if a human agent is causally implicated in its creation. It is thus conceptually necessary that poverty be imposed on the poor or that they are prevented from ceasing to be poor by other persons, in order to regard their poverty as the violation of a right.

However, this conceptual point leads again to a difficulty that is, this time, of an empirical nature. There is indeed one sense in which this assumption concerning the human causes of poverty, though perhaps not extravagant, is at least irrelevant: it would be to say that poverty is caused intentionally, that it is the goal that certain persons seek to achieve. It is true that, if this were the case, if some persons acted with the aim of making other persons poor, the problem which we consider would, from a conceptual point of view, be easy to solve: causing harm intentionally is obviously morally reprehensible in any moral system. Consequently, if poverty were intentionally caused by some human agents, the ethical problem posed by poverty would be, conceptually at least, easy to solve: those causing this evil intentionally should at the same time repair its effects and be institutionally prevented from satisfying their sadistic vice or from reaching their ends by such inhuman means. But, the fact is that things do not generally happen this way. One could indeed quote some cases of policies deliberately aimed at impoverishment, for instance in Khmer Rouge's Kampuchea or, probably, in today's North Korea. But it seems difficult to claim that the bulk of today's world poverty is the result of such policies of impoverishment. Once again, if that were the case, it would not be necessary to ask whether poverty is a human rights violation: it would be an obvious enforceable duty to desist from such universal sadism or to act against it.

Therefore, if it is conceptually necessary for poverty to be caused by human acts in order to be perceived as the violation of a right and if it is empirically false that the main part of today's severe poverty is intentionally caused by human acts, there remains in my view only one solution which makes it possible to perceive poverty as the violation of a right: it is to regard poverty as a *negative externality* or a *negative side effect* of certain human acts. Someone who travels by car knows that he contributes to increasing air pollution and perhaps to generating lung diseases or cancers. But it is clear that he does not use his car *in order* to increase air pollution. However, in order to bear responsibility for an increase in pollution,

---

[4] One has to distinguish between health and health care. Disease, except when it has social or economical causes, cannot be the violation of a right. But the lack of access to health care, when it is available, can be viewed as the violation of a right. Strictly speaking, there can be a right to health care, but not a right to health.

it is enough for him to know that pollution is a foreseeable side effect of his intentional activity and that his activity has produced this effect. In the case at hand, the argument goes roughly as follows: economic agents or their political leaders can foresee that, by engaging in certain forms of economic activities, they will cause poverty as a negative externality. Poverty is certainly not for them an intentional goal: they do not work to create poverty in the world. But they work in a way that contributes either to creating poverty or at least to not making it cease.

This is, in my view, the third empirical assumption, which though it does not imply that poverty is the violation of a right, is nevertheless likely to legitimize this view. If one accepts on the one hand that poverty must have a human cause in order to be regarded as the violation of a right and if one accepts on the other hand that it is not very realistic to suppose that some persons have the intentional goal of causing poverty in the world, then the assumption should be made that poverty is a negative consequence of certain human activities, an external consequence of which the human agents are aware, though it is not their intentional objective. Negative external causality is the only case of unintentional human causality, which is compatible with a certain form of responsibility.

Now, while this assumption on the cause of poverty can rather easily be validated, it raises an important problem. It is related to a possible competition between two types of human activities which both, one is tempted to say, have poverty as a negative side effect. The first type is that of the political activities of governments. We have claimed that, except in some pathological cases, no government considers poverty in its own country as a political goal.[5] But the fact is that certain governments act in such a way that their actions foster poverty or (at least) do not contribute to reducing it, although that is not their goal. A state in which the government diverts its oil revenue or does not ensure the safety of investments carries an obvious responsibility in the poverty of the populations that are in its political purview.

There is, however, another possible scenario, another kind of possible human cause of poverty, which is today at the heart of the debates on globalization. In the context of a global economy, the slightest individual economic decision, of a consumer or an investor, can indeed create, in an unintentional way, poverty at a distant point in the system. Neither global markets, through which the effects of individual decisions propagate, nor international economic organizations are designed to generate poverty. However (though this is perhaps more debatable), they are also not designed to alleviate or eradicate poverty.[6] Their effects on

---

[5] It is true that a government may consider poverty in another country as a political goal and, for instance, organize an economic embargo. And, if such a conduct can be condemned as a human rights violation, it can also, more classically, be condemned as a form of Machiavellism. But, as a matter of fact, it is false that the main part of today's world poverty is due to such Machiavellian foreign policies.

[6] Even those who hold that globalization has some positive consequences on poverty cannot maintain that market globalization aims at eradicating poverty. The soul of the market, if we can call it a soul, is profit. The impact of globalization on poverty can then only be a side effect, be it positive or negative.

poverty, positive or negative, are therefore external. One can thus think, when talking about the human causes of poverty, of a causality that can be called systemic. It would not be the mode of action of governments, but the mode of organization of human economic activities on a global scale that would create or foster poverty as a negative external effect.

I assume, in what follows, that it is legitimate to speak of a global responsibility for the existence or persistence of poverty. But we can see that, accepting such a level of responsibility is likely to result in underevaluating the responsibility, though more direct and individual, of certain governments in the poverty of the populations of which they are in charge.[7] This is what I call the risk of denial of responsibility. This risk is serious, because it can result in shifting the responsibility for this state of affairs to those who contribute only marginally to its creation.

I reconsider this question of the shared responsibilities in the conclusion of this chapter. For now, as a conclusion to this first part of the argument, I would like to underline the fact that by asserting that poverty is a human rights violation, one undoubtedly embarks on defending a substantial thesis, not only on the nature of rights but also on the nature and causes of poverty. By suggesting that poverty should be perceived as a human rights violation, one attributes to poverty itself a certain nature, which can be summed up by three properties:

(1) It must have a global remedy, including within the demographic context we are now considering.

(2) It must be involuntary, in the sense that the poor should be neither directly nor indirectly responsible for their situation.

(3) Finally, it must be involuntary not because it is the result of a natural situation, nor because it is intentionally imposed on the poor, but because it is a negative side effect of the political and/or economic activities of the nonpoor.

Combined together these three properties lead to the following thesis on the nature and cause of poverty: poverty is a contingent external effect of the mode of organization of human economic activities.

It seems to me that it is this synthetic thesis on the nature and the causes of poverty that is implied by the idea that severe world poverty is the violation of a human right. If poverty were to have no global remedy, if it were partly attributable to those who suffer from it, or if no causal link could be made between the mode of organization of economic activities and poverty, then it could not be the violation of a right. Of course, not all the forms of poverty that can be found in the present world satisfy these three conditions, especially the second and the third one. But this only means that these conditions can be viewed as discriminating conditions:

---

[7] However, it may be assumed, as suggested by Thomas Pogge, that the global system maintains the national political causes of poverty, especially through the international borrowing privilege and the international resource privilege (Pogge 2002*a*: ch. 6).

they isolate the part of world poverty for which there is a sense to ask whether it is the violation of a human right.

12.2. IS THERE A RIGHT NOT TO BE POOR?

The problem now is that, even if we assume that these empirical conditions are satisfied by the bulk of today's world poverty, we have not established that severe world poverty is a human rights violation. For the only thing we have established is that poverty is a remediable negative side effect of some human activities. However, it is clearly false that the concept of negative externality and the concept of human rights violation are identical. Admittedly, the existence of any negative external effect raises, in theory, a problem of social ethics. But it is clear that social life, by its very nature, generates all kinds of negative external effects, which are not infringements of the rights of the people. A person driving a car generates noise, but it seems difficult to say that this noise violates a right of those who are subjected to it. For, though silence is preferable to noise, it seems difficult to speak of a right to silence, in general. In the same way a mayor who, in order to support employment, allows a hideous industrial zone to be built at the entrance of his city, causes, as an external effect, the sensitive traveller to suffer aesthetically. But there again, one could not say that the traveller's rights have been violated. For, even if the beautiful is preferable to the ugly, it seems difficult to speak of a right to see only what is beautiful. One can say, in a general way, that any negative externality consists in imposing on others an option that they would not have chosen, had the choice been offered to them. Those who are subjected to the traffic noise would have chosen silence if the choice had been offered to them. Those subjected to the sight of a hideous city entrance would have chosen to see different buildings, or none at all, if the choice had been left to them. It can thus be said that any negative side effect consists in imposing an evil on others. But it is obvious that not all evil inflicted on others, as a negative side effect of social activities, can be held as the violation of a right.

12.2.1. Causing an Evil and Violating a Right

Could we say, however, that even if there is no identity between the concept of a negative side effect and the concept of a violation of a right, the particular severity of a negative externality must, in contrast with the cases we have considered above, be viewed as a human rights violation? Is poverty a violation of a human right *because* it is an externality of a special *severity*? One could envisage three complementary criteria for identifying side effects of a particular severity.

First, the evil inflicted on others must be *inescapable*. Those who cannot put up with the noise generated by traffic can seek a withdrawn or quiet place to live. They do not necessarily have to be exposed to the evil from which they suffer. Of course, the option that is imposed on them, to stay or to leave, has a cost that should be compensated, but the main point is that they are not physically constrained to suffer the negative effects of the activities of others.[8] The poor, on the contrary, cannot remedy by themselves their state of poverty.

Second, there must be no possible *compensation or negotiation* for the inflicted evil. Someone can agree to endure the noise of traffic for a proper compensation or if he can judge that the evil he suffers is compensated for by the fact of also being able to use his car. But conversely, one cannot imagine that anything can compensate for the evil which poverty constitutes. It is this that makes it an absolute evil, or an evil whose compensation would have an infinite cost.

Third, the evil suffered must deprive the person of an option that, in one way or another, is *an essential need*, either to live or to live as a human being. One can obviously live with the traffic noise and even live humanly, since a broad range of possibilities remain unaffected. On the other hand, poverty is precisely the deprivation of the possibility of satisfying, in a regular and assured way, the needs that are essential to life and to the dignity of life.

However, is it sufficient that the side effect of an activity prevents a person, inescapably and in a non-negotiable way, from engaging in an activity which is essential in order to live and live humanly, for that activity to constitute the violation of a right?

It is undeniable that when a social activity has such a side effect, something *must* be done to remedy its pernicious causality. But the reason why we have that duty is not, or is not necessarily, the fact that our activity is violating a human right. Indeed, the same properties—no possible escape or compensation and the frustration of an essential need—apply, for instance, to some of the severe diseases generated by human industrial activities and yet we do not call upon the language of rights. The language of risks, of acceptable and unacceptable risks, and the utilitarian language of global compensation between goods and evils, can apply to such cases. We have then, in such cases, the duty to remedy these side effects—for instance, to remedy industrial pollution. But this duty does not have the urgency it would have had if we had introduced the language of human rights.

It can also be suggested that the number of people affected by such an external effect may be relevant to what constraints or limitations should be imposed on the activity responsible for this effect. Yet, to the contrary, numbers should play no role in human rights issues. Let us suppose that the whole of the economic and political activities of all human beings have the negative side effect of forcing a single person to remain poor all his life. And let us suppose that the way in which these activities are carried out satisfies all the agents optimally. It is doubtful that the particular gravity of the effect suffered by this sole person could morally

[8] I do not mean, in a Hobbesian fashion, that the only human right is the right to escape! I only mean that the absence of an escape option rules out any redeployment of the individual rights. A person does not lose his right to live where he wishes because somebody, in the neighborhood, entertains an activity that he cannot stand. Social life implies flexibility (i.e., negotiability) of the rights, or else the only way to enjoy our rights would be to live in the middle of the desert.

compel all of the other agents to modify the way in which they live and act. On the other hand, if we think that the right of this person not to endure such an effect is fundamental, then we will be morally obliged to modify the whole system, even if it is optimal to all of the others.

It is then unquestionable that when our activity is responsible for a side effect of a particular severity, we have the moral duty to remedy that effect. But the concept of right adds something more to the simple idea of the severity of an effect: it precludes any idea of compensation, it can impose sacrifices on the better off, it requires that we remedy without any delay its violation, and it calls into question the legitimacy of the responsible activity itself.

The massive character of poverty, combined with its extreme gravity, thus plays an obvious role in prompting us to do something about it. However, the only thing that would be able to compel us in an enforceable way to remedy it, without any delay and calculation, is the fact that poverty is the deprivation of a human right. But neither gravity, nor the massive character of poverty is sufficient to imply that every person has a right to a guaranteed and permanent access to basic resources. The existence of such a right must then be *independently* established.

12.2.2. Negative and Positive Claims

Let us consider now how we could argue in favor of such a right. The pure concept of a right not to be poor faces an important conceptual difficulty that I first try to characterize. Let us consider the case of an activity that, as an external effect, would deprive others of their freedom of movement. We can say that if this activity did not take place, people would exert their freedom of movement. They are thus clearly prevented from doing something. But one can be prevented from doing something in two different ways: either by being physically prevented from acting or by being deprived of the necessary means to act.

Let us consider freedom of thought, generally considered to be a right. Let us put aside the all too simple case of a government that would intentionally seek to prevent its citizens from exercising this freedom, and let us rather imagine the case of a social activity which would have the destruction of all printed matter as an external effect, so that there would no longer be any books, or newspapers. I think that we could clearly say that this social activity would violate a right, not in the sense that it would intentionally aim at reducing freedom of thought, but in the sense that it would deprive the citizens of the necessary means of exercising this freedom, that is books and newspapers. We would naturally conclude that this activity should either cease or that a remedy must be found for its external effect in order to continue.

This suggests that it is not possible to establish a clear-cut distinction between freedom-rights and claim-rights or right *to do something* and right *to something*. Or, more exactly, the expression 'right to something' may have two meanings and one of these meanings is analytically implied by the single concept of a freedom-right. It is indeed obvious that to have the right to do something is also to have a right to *use* the necessary means to do it. If someone has the right to go where he pleases, he also has a right to use the appropriate means of transport, so that he would be equally deprived of his right, either if he was locked up in his house or if he was deprived of the means of transport necessary for the exercise of this right. In the same way, if someone has the right to develop his mind as he wishes, he also has a right to use the means that are necessary to develop his mind, that is books, newspapers, etc. In that sense, we can say that the right to do something implies a right to the means of doing it.

But there is another aspect of the problem: the content of a right cannot be determined independently of the obligations that *the others* may have. For if some person has a right, then the others have an obligation not to violate this right. These are two sides of the same reality: one person's right is an obligation for the others to respect it. However, it is crucial to underline that this obligation is essentially negative: it consists in a prohibition, the prohibition to do anything which would deprive someone of his right, of the exercise of his right. If someone has the right to develop and exert his capacity to think, the others then have the obligation not to infringe on this right. They have in particular the obligation not to deprive him of the essential means necessary to develop and exert his mind. Concretely, they cannot bar him access to books and to the various means of forming and exerting his mind.

However, and this is the decisive point, they do not have the obligation *to provide* him with these means, nor to place at his disposal the means to develop and exert his mind. If I have a right, others have an obligation not to prevent me from exercising it. But they do not have the obligation to make its exercise possible. They have the obligation to not deprive me of the means to exercise my right, *when these means exist and are at my disposal.* But they do not have the obligation to provide me with them *if they do not exist.* I have a right to do something, I have also a right to the *existent* means that are necessary to do that thing, but if others cannot deprive me from these means, it does not follow that they have the duty to provide me with means that do not exist.

It is true and it is a frequent objection to this distinction, that there can be empirical cases where it is difficult to say whether one person deprives another of the means of action or whether he does not provide him with them. But first, we must set aside the case of the state which, as we see, has *a contractual* obligation, not only to not deprive its members, but also to provide them with the means of exercising their subjective rights. We are only speaking here of the obligations which derive from subjective rights *outside any kind of contract*, in other words in what philosophers call a 'state of nature'. Second, it is known that the difficulties of the application of a concept in certain borderline cases, in soritical cases for instance, do not ruin the meaning and value of the concept. There is a clear conceptual difference between depriving someone of what is at his disposal and not providing him with what he would like to have. But this conceptual difference is enough to specify the nature of the obligations implied by subjective rights: a subjective right creates a negative obligation, an obligation not to prevent, but it does not create a positive obligation of assistance or collaboration.

Where is the proof? One can ask. What proves that a subjective right creates a negative obligation of non-prevention, and not a positive obligation of collaboration? The answer is that it is simply the definition of a subjective right or, more exactly, the existence of a link between the concept of subjective right and the concept of individual freedom. One could indeed very well imagine an entirely different ethical and legal system from the one I have just described, a system based on the idea that it is not the rights but the enforceable *natural duties* of men to act for the good of others which are preeminent, so that each person would be entitled to have other persons do certain things for him. For example, each person could be entitled to have the others communicate their thoughts to him so that he could exert his own thoughts. Or each person could have the right to the assistance of the others in case of need, the right to be provided with aid or resources by them. But one sees at once that such an ethical and legal system would be incompatible with the concept of self-ownership, which is admittedly one of the foundations of the concept of a human person. For such a system would imply that every man would be at the disposal or in the ownership of all the others since every person would have reasonable grounds to require from every other person to do or to provide him with certain things, whatever his projects for life or his preferences were. Every person would then be defined in natural law by his obligations toward the others and his freedom would merely consist of what he would not be obliged to do for the others.

This system of reciprocal alienation is certainly not contradictory in itself, but it is not compatible with the concept of self-ownership, which seems to me to be a plausible philosophical version of the modern concept of subjective freedom.[9] The alternative to this system of enforceable natural duties is thus precisely the system of subjective rights. To say that men are free is to say that there are certain things that the others should not do to them or should not prevent them from doing.

From this I conclude that if it is equivocal to distinguish between freedom-rights and claim-rights, it is on the other hand necessary to distinguish between two types of claims on others. One can say that all a subjective right gives its holder is *a negative* claim on others. He is entitled to the right that certain things should not be done to him either intentionally or as an external effect of the activities of others. But a right does not give its holder a *positive* claim on others, that is the right to have certain things done for him, either privately or politically by others; for instance, improving institutions in his favor. Admittedly, there are positive claims, but they can only arise from an agreement of the wills, in other words

---

[9] 'The ... right of self-ownership is the right not to (be forced to) supply product or service to anyone.... Failing to help another person cannot be construed as interfering with his right to use himself as he wishes, and not being required to help others leaves everyone with more rights over their own powers than they would have otherwise' (Cohen 1995: 215). I cannot argue here in favor of the relevance of the concept of self-ownership. Cohen scrutinizes the problems raised by this concept in Chapters 9 and 10.

from a contract, but not from the mere existence of a subjective right. By signing a contract, I acquire a positive claim on the other person, a right to see certain things done for me. But it can only be an *acquired* right, a right resulting from an agreement of the wills.

It can thus be said that, in a sense, each right is a claim on others, but a distinction must be made between claims that are negative and original, and claims that are positive and derived, in other words between rights that are natural and original, and rights that are contractual and derived.[10]

12.2.3. Poverty as a Shortcoming of the State

Let us now apply these distinctions to the case at hand. Under what conditions can poverty be the violation of a right?

Let us simplify the situation by imagining a social system consisting of three people, A, B, and C, working in such a way, that owing to the fact that two of these three people, A and B, have economic exchanges of a certain kind, it follows that the third, C, is reduced to a state of poverty. C's poverty is thus an external effect of the activity of A and of B. It is not the purpose of A and B to make C poor, but because of the nature of their economic exchanges and the rules which govern them, C is reduced to poverty. The question is to know whether A and B violate C's rights.

A first answer, which I believe is the most traditional in the history of political and legal philosophy, consists in calling upon the existence of a *positive and derived* claim from C on A and B. A and B violate C's rights because, by leaving him in poverty, there is something that A and B are not doing for C that they are *by contract* obliged to do for him. A and B fail to honor their commitments and, as a result, the *acquired* right of C is violated.

To give meaning to this idea, it is enough to call upon the traditional social contract theories. It is indeed enough to suppose that A, B, and C are bound by a social contract under which terms each one is at least committed to ensure that no other person finds himself in a worse situation than he was in the state of nature, so that, by leaving him in poverty, A and B violate the acquired, contractual right of C. The social contract indeed gives everyone a positive claim on all the others, the right to require that other people ensure that his situation is not worse than what it would have been in the state of nature. It is on the basis of this commitment, this *minimal* commitment, that men form a state. One can imagine that the contractors as a whole have delegated to the state apparatus the task of carrying out their joint obligations on their behalf. Poverty can then appear as the violation of a derived or acquired right, the right of each member of a state to obtain from the other members that they do not place him in a worse state than the one in which he would have been in a state of nature.

---

[10] This is obviously only an outline, for there can also be negative contractual rights, concerning, for instance, the use of natural common goods.

It seems to me that this line of reasoning can be easily documented. For instance, Rousseau wrote in the *Social Contract* that 'any man is naturally entitled to that which is necessary for him', but it is only in the state that his natural right become a 'real right', for, through the social contract, each contracting party commits itself to ensure that no one lacks the essentials (1964: 365). In the same way, Kant wrote, in his *Philosophy of Law*, that 'the universal will of the people has in effect united into a society which must always maintain itself and which has consequently submitted to the internal public power, in order to give assistance to the members of society who are not able to support themselves' (1968*b*: 326).

In this line of reasoning, poverty is the violation of the right—held by everyone in a state against the others and against the state that represents them—to be provided with the basic necessities insofar as he would otherwise be without them. The existence of poverty thus implies, in this line of reasoning, that the state has not fulfilled its obligations and that the right derived by all from the contract is violated. Poverty is a violation of the social contract. In every society where there is poverty, a social contract has been violated.

There is a consequence to this way of thinking that must be emphasized: it is that the responsibility or the coresponsibility for poverty is defined by the scope of the social contract, that is it is aimed at the fellow countrymen and political leaders. Everyone has the right not to be left in poverty by his fellow countrymen or his government, but this claim can only be made on his fellow countrymen or on the state to which he belongs.[11] The right to the assistance of others is less a universal human right than a political right or a right that results from the political contract. But let us suppose, as is often the case nowadays, that a state is not doing what it should, that its leaders do not take the necessary actions to put an end to poverty. Can one say that the members of other states are also jointly responsible for this situation? Obviously not. The poor, in this line of reasoning, have the right to require that the state behave toward them in a certain way, but they have no right to require that all men provide them with resources which they need in order to live. If two people E and F are bound by a contract and if one of them, E, does not respect his contractual obligations, it is difficult to maintain that any third person G, should have to force E to carry out his obligations or, even more so, that G should have to replace E and fulfill his obligations in his place.

The philosophical concept of social contract thus gives a sense, it seems to me, to the idea that poverty is the violation, by the state, of the right of every citizen to have whatever is necessary for his subsistence. However, it restricts at the same time the scope of responsibility and thus does not really allow the introduction of a human right not to be poor. For, as we have said earlier, there is a constraint of universalizability inherent in the concept of human rights.

---

[11] One must remember that we are only speaking of enforceable duties (duties of right), not of unenforceable duties (duties of virtue). For there is a natural duty of assistance, which concerns every human being, but this duty is a duty of virtue, not a duty of right or a duty based on a right.

12.2.4. Poverty as Deprivation

There is, however, another philosophical possibility, which I would now like to present. Let us again consider our three persons A, B, and C and let us this time ask ourselves under what conditions the violated right of C would not be a right acquired by contract, but rather a *natural* right, an authentic *original human* right.

That would be the case if, by their economic activities, A and B *prevented* C from being able to enjoy his right to vital economic resources. Indeed, let us come back to the distinction that we made previously between an obligation of non-prevention and an obligation of service. To say that A and B violate *the natural* right of C does not mean that A and B *do not provide* C with vital resources. For, as we have seen, the corollary of a natural subjective right is a negative claim, not a positive one. It is the right not to have something done to us by other people and not the right that they do something for us. To assert that C's poverty constitutes a violation of his natural rights by A and B, it is thus necessary to admit that, in the absence of A and B's activity, C *would have had access* to vital resources of which he is deprived because of their activity.

From a strictly logical or conceptual point of view this is, in my opinion, the only way to give sense to the idea that A and B violate C's *natural rights*. C is poor because he is barred access to resources to which he would have had access if A and B had acted differently. Poverty can be the violation of a right only if interpreted as a deprivation of access to resources to which everyone is originally entitled and which would indeed be accessible to them in the absence of this deprivation.

This line of reasoning can also be historically documented. The most appropriate reference here is, in my view, Thomas Paine's essay *Agrarian Justice* (Vallentyne and Steiner 2000: 81–98).[12] Paine contrasts what he calls the state of civilization to the state of nature. In the state of civilization there are two situations that are unknown in the state of nature: affluence on the one hand and poverty and forfeiture on the other. Paine's argument goes as follows: in the state of nature, each man is the joint owner of natural resources, so that each one has a right of access to and of use of these resources. The state of civilization brought with it the institution of private property. However, according to Paine, it is unjust for men to be in a worse condition in the state of civilization than they would have been in if they had remained in the state of nature:

The first principle of civilization ought to have been and ought still to be that the condition of every person born into this world, after a state of civilization commences, ought not to be worse than if he had been born before that period. But the fact is that the condition of millions, in every country of Europe, is far worse than if they had been born before civilization begin.... (2000: 84)

---

[12] We could also refer to Chapter 6 of François Huet, *Le règne social du christianisme* (1853): see Vallentyne and Steiner (2000: 99–123).

Paine concludes from this that justice dictates that a tax should be raised on the transmission of land, a tax corresponding to the value of the natural resource, and whose product should be equally divided among the members of society.

I leave aside the solution for compensation imagined by Paine.[13] The central point, for our purpose, is the idea that poverty is not simply a defect of civilization, but the violation of a natural human right by the non-poor or, more exactly, the property owners. And if there is a human rights violation, it is not in the sense that the non-poor fail to provide the poor with resources with which they should provide them. It is in the sense that they deprive them of resources to which every human being has an original natural right. The mode of organization of human 'civilization' should have ensured that no one finds himself in a worse situation than he would have been in a state of nature, where he would have enjoyed free access to the resources of nature. Leaving the state of nature is legitimate, not on the condition that everyone enjoys equal treatment but on the minimal condition that no one is thereby worse off—in other words if it is Pareto-efficient. Poverty, on this view, is the violation of what one could call a 'pact of civilization'. For Paine, the poor do not have a positive claim on the non-poor, in the sense that they should be entitled to be provided with resources by them. But they do have a negative claim on them: they are entitled to not be deprived of the resources to which they would have had access and right of access if the non-poor had not deprived them of this free access as a result of the institution of private property. The problem is not to abolish the latter, but to make its existence compatible with the 'pact of civilization'.

One can obviously object that, if this line of thinking is the only way of validating the idea according to which poverty is, in an intrinsic way, a violation of a natural right, of a natural and original human right, then this right rests on a rather fragile basis, or, in any case, on too philosophical of one. The idea of a situation where every one would normally have had access to sufficient basic resources is certainly a possibility that one can imagine, but it is difficult to base a real right on a possible state of things. However, it is possible to formulate Paine's idea in a way that reconciles it with facts. In real terms, Paine's idea comes down to saying that the Earth and its resources must be conceived of as a *res communis* whose economic exploitation is submitted, because of its common character, to a constraint of equity: since some men are de facto excluded from this use, they are entitled to a compensation and, more deeply, they have a right to the establishment of an institutional system which would not doom them to this situation of exclusion. If a man who is born on the earth cannot find resources to live in a decent way, this is not due to the earth itself but to the other men who have, however, no right to exclude him from the use of the earth.

This line of reasoning remains in my view, the only philosophical way of validating the idea according to which poverty is, in an intrinsic way, a violation of

---

[13] To which we could compare the 'Global Resources Dividend,' imagined by Thomas Pogge (cf. esp. 2002a: ch. 8).

a natural right, a natural and original human right.[14] Poverty is the violation of a right if it deprives the poor of resources to which they are entitled. However, saying that they are entitled to these resources does not mean that they have a right to be provided with them by others (this is the 'libertarian' constraint on the concept of natural right). It rather means that they have a right not to be deprived of them by other people. But to say that the poor are deprived of resources, means that in the absence of a social interaction violating their rights, these resources would have been at their disposal. It thus means that originally everyone could access the natural resources that are necessary for life and that this access is a right. It is thus only by calling upon such a natural right of access to the resources which are necessary to subsistence that poverty can be regarded as the violation of an original natural right. And that idea means that the earth must remain, in spite of its private exploitation, a *res communis* which imposes on every man an enforceable duty to let the others have access to natural resources or to provide them with equivalent capitalistic resources.[15]

This line of reasoning has in my view two remarkable consequences, which I would like to stress before concluding. The first is that its scope is universal, or global. Indeed, what ends the state of nature, and makes natural resources inaccessible to the poor, is the fact that the state of civilization covers the entire earth. Let us come back to our initial example. Let us admit that A and B, because of their relationship, force C into poverty. If A, B, and C are the sole inhabitants of the earth, then C's poverty is not without remedy. It would be enough for him to move away. It is thus only because C can no longer move away, and because the entire planet is inhabited and 'civilized' that C's right is violated. Therefore, from this point of view, there is a global, planetary responsibility, with regard to poverty.[16]

Another consequence of this line of reasoning is that, as Thomas Paine suggests, the violation of the rights of the poor creates an obligation of compensation for the non-poor: 'It is not charity but a right, not bounty but justice, that I am pleading for' Paine wrote (2000: 91). In our example, A and B have an obligation to ensure that C is not in a worse state than he would have been in the state of nature so that, while they are not obliged to share the ownership of the resources, they must share the value of the corresponding properties. This is clearly a legal duty, not

---

[14] One could argue that we have a right to what we need. But I cannot see how such a view could not imply that the others have an enforceable duty to provide each human being with what he needs. And in that case, we would no longer be the owners of ourselves, for good or evil. There would no longer be responsible individuals, but a human community unified by a web of enforceable positive duties of all men toward each other. There is no inconsistency in that view, but it is a philosophical contingent view.

[15] Viewing the earth and its resources as a *res communis* is not only a mere idea which serves to justify, from a philosophical point of view, a global solidarity with the very poor. This kind of global communism could also have a legal and institutional implementation when applied to the concrete exploitation of natural scarce resources, even in a market economy. On this point, see Chauvier (2006: ch. 6).

[16] We can see, incidentally, the crucial role of the right of immigration. For a discussion of the role of this right in a theory of global justice, see Chauvier (1999).

a moral one, and a duty that falls on whoever is the owner of natural resources. However owing to the fact that these resources are built in into all the things that we possess, this legal duty weighs on each and every one of us in a global way.

12.3. CONCLUSION: THE RISK OF DENIAL

It is thus clearly possible to see in poverty, not an inevitability calling upon our virtue, but the violation of an authentic human right. Even when imposing a libertarian constraint on the concept of right and trying to keep it compatible with the axiom of freedom as self-ownership, it is possible to argue that poverty, as an external effect of social activities, is the violation of a right.

There are, however, two interpretations of the word 'right' which, at the same time, are compatible with the axiom of freedom and imply that poverty is the violation of a right. The first, it is that of rights acquired by contract, in which poverty can be seen as the violation of the right of every citizen to expect that the state organizes social life in such a way that at least no one is deprived of the capacity of living decently. Poverty, in this interpretation, is a violation of a political right and it is a human rights violation only because, indirectly, every political right is a human right. But the second interpretation of the word 'right' implies more directly that poverty is a human rights violation. It is the natural rights interpretation, which, in this case, implies giving sense to the idea of a natural right for each human being to have access to the resources essential for his subsistence. It is this natural human right that poverty violates.

The point I would like to make in conclusion is that these two interpretations have different practical consequences and that it is crucial not to see them as alternative answers to world poverty. The contractual line of argument tends to focus moral attention on the political leaders of each country by imposing upon them at least a duty of good governance. By contrast, the second line of reasoning emphasizes the obligation of each property owner worldwide to compensate those who are deprived of access to vital resources—an obligation that can be put to work for instance through global tax transfers (public aid) or though an artificial adjustment of market prices (fair trade). The availability of these two lines of reasoning can then create what we might call an ethical ousting effect. Suppose that, in some country, we find poverty and bad governance and, plausibly, poverty partly due to bad governance. If we stress only the global responsibility in regard to poverty, then we risk sidelining the local leaders' duty of good governance. It is true that perfect justice and efficiency in the fight against world poverty require both global measures and domestic good governance. Nonetheless, global measures can alleviate poverty in a country that is still badly governed. Fair trade can alleviate poverty at least in some areas of a country, for instance, even while its government remain unreformed. And this may nourish the temptation to emphasize the global responsibility with regard to world poverty, to see it as primarily a problem of global governance.

But if world poverty is truly a global problem that engages the responsibility of all property owners worldwide, then good governance at the domestic level is required not only for reasons of efficiency, but also for reasons of justice. This means that, if a global responsibility toward world poverty must be realized and accepted, this must be done in a way that does not cause, by globalizing responsibility, an effect of ethical denial from which, to the greatest misfortune of their people, the failing political leaders would profit. Though taxpayers and political leaders of rich countries must feel themselves under a duty of justice with regard to world poverty, no measures against poverty that are to be not merely effective, but also just, can ignore the requirements of good governance. The 'pact of civilization' binds all human beings, but the obligations it imposes should not displace those that arise from the domestic social compact.

13

Poverty Eradication and Human Rights

Arjun Sengupta

13.1. INTRODUCTION

In this chapter, we examine the proposition that 'poverty is a violation of human rights', which has been put forward by UNESCO and some other human rights activists to mobilize international public opinion in the fight against poverty. It will hopefully lead to the adoption of an international strategy aimed at the abolition of poverty, in the same way as describing slavery as gross violation of human rights could have led to the abolition of slavery (UNESCO 2003).

Whether this proposition can effectively galvanize people and policymakers throughout the world will depend on the interplay of political forces as well as the stage of economic development in different countries. There is a view that slavery could be abolished only when the economics of slavery lost out to the economics of wage labor in terms of productivity and cost, and support for the call for abolishing slavery gathered momentum without much effective opposition from vested interests. In a similar vein it can be argued today that the world economy has developed sufficiently, not only to abolish poverty everywhere but also actually to benefit from that abolition, thanks to feedback from expanding markets and improvements in the quality of human capital. It may therefore be the opportune time to arouse international public opinion by means of an appropriate moral appeal to work out acceptable strategies for abolishing poverty.

These are interesting issues of political economy very much worth thinking and writing about. But we do not propose to deal with them in this chapter. We instead confine ourselves to discussing the logical implications of the proposition that poverty is a violation of human rights, and whether there is an acceptable and plausible interpretation of the proposition, in a human rights framework, that improves the chances of implementing a strategy for the abolition or eradication of poverty.[1] An affirmative answer to this would be the first step toward calling for a human rights approach to the eradication of poverty. The chapter does not examine in much detail any particular strategies for poverty eradication. It is presumed that such strategies exist, and that at least some of them are amenable to a human rights treatment; that is, they can be designed and implemented in

---

[1] Much of this chapter builds on, criticizes, extends, and disagrees with the arguments of the excellent study of Thomas Pogge on this subject. See Pogge (this volume).

a manner consistent with human rights standards to achieve the eradication or alleviation of poverty as a human rights objective.[2] The economics and, possibly, the politics of poverty eradication can be regarded as separate subjects of research. Here they will be touched on only to illustrate some points. Instead the chapter focuses on how poverty can be viewed as a human rights violation, precisely, in terms of the definition and content of those human rights and what would be the added value of pursuing a human rights-based strategy for eradicating poverty.

In section 13.2, we discuss the concept of human rights as it relates to poverty and corresponding obligations. In section 13.3, we try to identify the nature of the right the violation of which is associated with poverty and who are the right-holders. In section 13.4, we discuss the obligations of those who bear the duties corresponding to the right identified in section 13.3, duties that must be fulfilled if the right is to be effectively realized.

13.2. HUMAN RIGHTS AND POVERTY

Poverty has always been considered a degradation of human dignity, extreme poverty a form of extreme degradation: Poor people cannot lead a life commensurate with the standards of civilized existence. They are afflicted with hunger, malnutrition, ill health, unsanitary housing and living conditions, and often lack education. They do not have the resources to overcome these afflictions. Nor does society provide the means for them to overcome these afflictions. They lose their self-respect and ability to participate in any kind of fulfilling social life. In short, poor people lack the freedom to lead a life with dignity.

Poverty in this sense has existed throughout human history, and removing or alleviating poverty—helping the poor and improving their living conditions— has been recognized as a universal moral value in practically all societies. In every religion and civilization, fellow human beings had a bad conscience about other fellow human beings, suffering the indignity of poverty. So, Gods and saints were supposed to look after the poor, good kings were expected to protect the poor, and all virtuous people were enjoined to help the poor. In spite of all that, poverty persisted and moral values alone were not sufficient to motivate a society to take the required steps to remove poverty. The contradiction between such professed

---

[2] It may be noted that a human rights activity is concerned not only with the outcome or the consequences of the activity, but also with the way the activity is carried out. For example, if hunger is considered as a violation of human right, it cannot be eradicated, say, by throwing food at the hungry, but only by ensuring availability of food with dignity and sustainability, through employment, income, or commodity-support programs. I have discussed the related issues in my reports to the Human Rights Commission at Geneva, as the Independent Expert on the Right to Development (1999, 2000*b*, 2001, 2002*b*). (First Report Ref. No. E/CN.4/1999/WG.18/2 July 27, 1999. Second Report Ref. No. A/55/306, August 17, 2000. Third Report Ref. No. E/CN.4/2001/WG.18/2, January 2, 2001. Fourth Report Ref. No. E/CN.4/2002/WG.18/2, December 20, 2001.)

values and the actual performance of society in the removal of poverty became more and more glaring with the growth of prosperity in many countries and in the world economy as a whole. Poverty has persisted, but not because there are insufficient means to eradicate it. The level of wealth in developed societies and, more broadly, of the international community, is more than sufficient to eradicate poverty from the face of the earth. If there had been a political will to translate the relevant moral values into practical social arrangements, even if only over the last few decades of the twentieth century, there would be very little poverty today.[3]

It is against this background that one can fully appreciate the appeal of the concept of poverty as a violation of human rights, and the removal of poverty as a method of fulfilling human rights. If that claim was accepted, it would raise the cause of poverty eradication to a status equivalent to that of protecting the foundational norms of a society, which human rights are recognized to provide. Human rights have emerged from a long history of people's actions—from the days of the Magna Carta, the American War of Independence, and the French Revolution right up to recent efforts—to convert moral values into rights as claims on those in authority and power in a society. Human rights are claims that set the standards of achievement of a society—on the basis of which societies are formed. Meeting these claims lends legitimacy to the authorities governing the society. If human rights are violated, people can legitimately demand a change in the government or a repeal of the constitution.[4] As early as 1776, the American Declaration of Independence declared that the government was instituted to secure certain inalienable rights, and 'whenever any form of government becomes destructive of these ends, it is the Right of the People to alter or to abolish it'.

After World War II, human rights came to be incorporated in intergovernmental instruments, such as the UN Charter and the UDHR, which formed the basis of the new international order. These instruments, together with the UN Covenants of Economic, Social and Cultural Rights, and Civil and Political Rights (adopted in 1966, entered into force in 1976) recognized human rights in international law. They reflected 'the spreading conviction that how human beings are treated anywhere concerns every one, everywhere' (Henkin 1989: 129). All individuals, anywhere in the world, were recognized to have some indispensable human rights and fundamental freedoms, the protection and promotion of which was the purpose and concern of all states and institutions in the international society of nations. Fulfilling human rights became the obligation not only of the nation-states, but also of the international community. A violation of these rights

---

[3] Thomas Pogge, in a very thorough recent study, has estimated that an income transfer of $300 billion a year, in 2001, would eradicate poverty of all the 2,800 million people in the world living below $2 per day, which is a higher poverty line than $1 per day that is more generally used for such calculations. This amount is less than 1% of world income and is much less than some comparable figures, such as the US defense budget ($400 billion) or the affluent countries' estimated annual 'peace dividend' resulting from the end of the Cold War ($477 billion). See Pogge (2002a: ch. 8).

[4] An overview of the history of the evolution of the concept of human rights was presented in my paper on 'Realizing the Right to Development' (Sengupta 2000a).

would, in theory at least, attract international reprimand and calls for appropriate remedial action in accordance with the relevant provisions of the aforementioned instruments. So if poverty can be shown to be a violation of human rights, the removal of that poverty will become a binding obligation on all states that desire to be members of the international society, bound by international law, and with parallel obligations of assistance and cooperation toward other members.

All this goes to show the attractiveness of approaching the problems of poverty from a human rights perspective, whereby the eradication of poverty can be equated with the prevention of a violation of human rights. But they still do not establish how this can be done, whether such an equation is meaningful, whether one can specify certain rights whose denial can be described as poverty, whether those rights can be regarded as human rights, whether there can be correlative duties that are binding on identified duty-bearers, and whether their duties are plausible in an appropriate sense of the term. All these issues are problematic, and if these cannot be resolved both in theory and practice, the notion of poverty as a violation of human rights cannot be taken as more than an empty and ineffective slogan.

To begin with, let us assume that poverty can be identified with the absence or denial or violation of one or more human rights. What would that imply for the set of actions or social arrangements that can be adopted toward fulfilling those rights and removing poverty? This would depend very much on what we mean by 'human rights' and how the recognition of a claim or an object of value as a human right would bind the different agents in the society to specified obligations of duty. Who would be those agents and what specific obligations would they have with respect to that right?

All rights entail obligations—that is how rights are defined as distinct from any other claim or object of desire. If there is a right 'R' which can be claimed by an agent 'A', then there is some obligation 'O' of at least one other agent 'B' (and possibly additional agents, C, D, E . . .) to enable the realization of the right, when the agents are members of the society that recognizes the right.[5]

The binary relation between rights and obligations cannot be appreciated without relating them to the binary relation between right-holders and duty-bearers. The same right when claimed by different right-holders may entail different kinds

---

[5] This is an extension of the definition of rights as claim provided by Feinberg and Raz, building on Hohfeld, when someone having a right is to have a claim 'to' something (objects of value or interest) and *against* someone, who is under an obligation to act in such a way as would enable its fulfillment (Feinberg 1973: ch. 4; Hohfeld 1964; Raz 1984).

It may be noted that in terms of this definition, while for every right there is a corresponding duty or obligation, there need not be for every duty a corresponding right. A duty may be called for or performed, for many reasons, and not necessarily because an agent has a right to call for that. But a right on the other hand cannot be a valid claim, if it is not matched by a corresponding duty. Accordingly a 'valid right' can be defined as a valid claim both to an object and against another subject. A valid claim to an object has to be justified and procedurally legitimate. A valid claim against a subject has to be 'plausibly' assignable to some duty-bearer, whose actions could satisfy the right.

of obligations depending on who bears the obligation.[6] For example, the right to food claimed by someone who is extremely poor would call for actions different from what would be required if someone of middle income made the same claim. The actions to be taken will also be different for different duty-bearers—states, international institutions, and other agents. Recognizing a right would therefore imply recognizing a 'right-holder', who is in a position to claim the right. It would also imply specifying some actions or policies that enable the fulfillment of the right being carried out as an 'obligation' or 'duty' by identified duty-bearer(s).[7]

When a right is created by law or contract, the right-holder, the agent 'A', can be an individual, a group of individuals, or a legal personality, and the claim of the right is justified by the legal system. When it is recognized as a human right, it is justified by a system of values that bind a society and are accepted as 'the norms of behavior' or 'the standards of achievement' of all social agents. They may in due course be incorporated into that society's legal system and institutional arrangements, but the justification of the claims does not depend on such incorporation. It depends on their relation with the notions of human dignity, liberty, happiness, and well-being whose promotion is supposedly the purpose of societies. Therefore, the right-holder must be an agent whose improved realization of the right would improve the overall social values or aggregate happiness and well-being. That is why the agent 'A' claiming a human right has to be an individual, or a collective that behaves like an individual, because only an individual can have a sense of dignity or happiness. Only then is it possible to order different states of social arrangement in terms of overall improvement in welfare.[8]

---

[6] It is usual in the human rights literature to treat the terms 'obligation' and 'duty' interchangeably, although philosophers following Rawls, often, distinguish between general duties (e.g., to keep one's promises) and specific obligations (e.g., to keep some specific promise one has made). However, human rights, recognized as law, would call for specified obligation, which would be binding and therefore would have very little scope for any general duty until it is related to specific duties. That is why usually no distinction is made between these terms, and we follow the same practice in this chapter. (I am grateful to Thomas Pogge for drawing my attention to this point.)

[7] Thomas Pogge aptly describes rights as 'addressed to agents and, in the final analyses, ... rights to particular conduct (actions and/or omission)'. The agent B, who has the obligation of satisfying the right, cannot just gift it to the right-holder, but has to take some actions or adopt some policies (P)—perform a 'conduct'—to enable the right to be enjoyed. As we argue later, all policies involve incurring costs, in terms of alternative opportunities foregone, which must be taken into account in fixing obligations.

[8] Only an individual can be described as happier in one state of affairs than another, unless specific rules are laid down for such assessment of the improvement of welfare of a collective, in which case it functions like an individual. That is why the notion of a 'people's' right in the human rights instruments would imply either that it is enjoyed individually, but exercised collectively, or that it refers to a notion of well-being of a collective, which cannot be disaggregated into the wellbeing of distinct individuals but has accepted procedures for indicating its improvement. In the first case, policies to fulfill the right would apply to the collective of all individuals who are in a position to claim the right. That is the case with most rights, such as to food, health, education or culture, religion, freedom of expression, or information. There must be a mechanism to ensure that the benefits of the right can be enjoyed individually. In the second case, which is more of an exception than a rule, such as the right of self-determination or the cultural identity of indigenous people, the right refers to the privilege or advantage of a whole group, treated as a unit in itself. A people's right is sometimes erroneously

Besides specifying the right-holder A, it will also be necessary to establish an indicator of the right 'R'. An improvement in the value of R can be taken as an improvement in the enjoyment of the right. Such an indicator must be 'objective'—that is independent of the subjective preferences of the right-holder and expressed as a function of some determinate objects, which combine to yield that right. In that sense, the rights can be described as determined by the access to and availability of goods and services, of technology and institutions, of time, and of scarce resources. An indicator of a right can be built on the measures and values of these determinants. The indicator of the right to food, for example, has to be constructed out of the indicators of the access to and the availability of food, and the right to food of the poor can reflect quite distinctive characteristics of the problems of access and availability, very unlike the problems that concern the not-so-poor or the relatively rich in a particular country.

The identification of the right, whose violation can be regarded as poverty, besides being described as a function of the access and availability of corresponding goods and services, would involve laying down a procedure, such that if steps were taken to improve the right or remove its violation, the benefits would be enjoyed by all individual members of the group identified as 'poor'. For instance, if the right to food is regarded as an essential element of the right whose violation can be described as poverty within a country, the international community sending food aid to that country would not remove that violation, unless a mechanism was set up in that country to make that food accessible to all the poor people in a non-discriminatory manner consistent with human rights standards. Further, it will also be necessary to identify the members of the group of the 'poor' who could use that mechanism if they wished to claim the right.[9]

The 'obligations' corresponding to human rights are usually addressed to the state or the sovereign authority of a country, in whose jurisdiction the right-holders reside. That is how human rights have evolved through history, out of movements and struggles of peoples asserting their rights against authorities. But logically, human rights, which are foundational norms of a society, entail obligations for all agents or members of the society, whose actions can have an impact on the fulfillment of the rights. In the human rights instruments of the UN, the state has been described as the 'primary duty-bearer', recognizing the paramount importance of the action of the state either by directly impacting the rights or indirectly by influencing other agents' behavior and coordinating their actions. The state has the authority to enact legislation to frame rules and regulations and to enforce them with penal powers over all the agents functioning within its

---

described as a state's right. Unless the state is not only fully representative of all the people in its jurisdiction, but also automatically transfers the benefits of the right to all individuals, the state cannot have a human right. For all this, see Sengupta (2002*a*). On the significance of group rights, and on the subject of states asserting the human right to development see also Salomon and Sengupta (2003).

[9] If a class of people whose per capita income or expenditure is less than a specified amount, say $1 in PPP terms is defined as 'poor', then the statistical size of that class can be reasonably determinate. But it still may be extremely difficult to identify each individual member of that class who can be given a coupon or ration card to claim the benefits of the poverty-alleviation mechanism.

jurisdiction. It is also the agency that mediates with international institutions and other states, whose cooperation may be essential for a state to succeed in delivering the rights. Such coordination and mediatory functions of the state must build on the obligation of all the agents within the international community to do what they can to enable the fulfillment of the right. As members of the international society, who recognize human rights and ratify the related treaties and covenants, all such external states and institutions take on the obligation of ensuring these rights and cooperating with the states where the right-holders reside.

Just as there are several duty-bearers, there may be a number of different duties that each duty-bearer may perform, where duties refer to actions taken or specific measures adopted, to enable the enjoyment of the right. These duties may be categorized as 'direct' duties, 'indirect' duties, and 'contingent' duties. Direct duties directly impact the enjoyment of the right by the right-holder. Indirect duties impact through the duties or policies carried out by other duty-bearers. Contingent duties are to be adopted by a duty-bearer in response to actions taken by others or to unforeseen changes in the situation. For example, the right to food of the poor can be ensured directly by the state through public distribution of food, or by enabling the poor to earn more, and indirectly by helping increase production of food and cheapening the price. Contingent duties of the state may consist in taking special measures if there is a drought or protecting poor employees if they lose their employment. The international institutions may carry out their obligation: by directly providing food aid to the destitute, indirectly through the local authorities for distribution, or by supporting an international trading system that allows either the cheaper import of food or higher incomes of the poor through exports (or both), and contingently by protecting the terms of trade of primary products during a world recession. Similar duties can be specified for non-governmental corporate sectors and other individuals who might help the poor earn more income by expanding production and employment or by paying more taxes to enable their government to increase aid or income transfers to the poor.

It is important to identify all the different duty-bearers and specify their duties to ensure the fulfillment of any particular human right. Even if the state is the primary duty-bearer, it cannot deliver the right on its own without taking into account the actions of all concerned social agents. A society consists of a large number of interacting agents, with the actions of each of them having an impact on the actions of others. Economists like to talk about a general equilibrium system of production, but the logic is equally applicable to any complex social order. The result of the action of any single agent depends on the actions of others, taken autonomously or in response to others' behaviors or some specific contingencies. The extent of the impact of any agent's action—or the marginal product in terms of the final result—would vary for different activities and for different agents. But an assessment has to be made of this interactive process before judging whether a right can be fulfilled and what steps should be taken to fulfill it and by whom.

The identification of the obligations of the different agents and their specific duties so that a right can be realized is an essential condition for determining the feasibility of the right. Passing the test of feasibility or, as Maurice Cranston would put it, 'the test of practicability' is in turn an essential condition for the admissibility of the right. If a right is not feasible, no duty of any agent can realize the right (1973: 65–71). But even when one can identify a set of actions or policies that enable the realization of a right, assigning those actions or policies as duties to different agents in the society may not be straightforward. It will be necessary to assign these duties within a human rights framework so that if they were carried out consistently with human rights standards, then the right will be, with a high probability, realized. It is in that sense that specifying the relevant duties and obligations would demonstrate thefeasibility of the program to realize the right.[10]

If it is accepted that a human right should be a 'feasible' right—to go beyond the status of a 'manifesto' right and become a 'full-fledged right'—and if poverty eradication is to be identified with the fulfillment of a specific human right, it will be necessary to design a program to be implemented by the state and other agents to realize that right. But 'feasibility' does not mean that the right would be actually realized, immediately, under present circumstances, and for everyone, without limiting the rights to a very few in number.[11]

First, the actions taken or the policies adopted by any duty-bearer, if they are appropriate, can at best be described as having a high probability of producing the outcome of realizing the right. There is seldom a one-to-one correspondence between a policy P and the outcome R, especially when one is talking about a social system with interacting agents. This is true of all rights, economic and social or civil and political, especially if they are human rights, applicable to all individuals, in all circumstances. So even if the policy P is adopted and the obligation is fully carried out by the state or any other duty-bearer, there will always be some probability that the right may remain unrealized because of unforeseen disturbances.

Second, very few rights can be realized immediately within the given circumstances. They need to be progressively realized over time, because policies take time to work themselves out with all agents adjusting to the changes. Even freedom from torture cannot be secured immediately after legislation is adopted. It requires time not only to build up the institutions that will enforce the observance of rights, but also to allow the legislation to be absorbed in the social structure. This is even truer if all members of society are to enjoy freedom from torture, not just from the state but from all other social agents.

---

[10] In a similar vein, Feinberg has talked about a 'full-fledged' right, when a valid claim to a right derived from some accepted norms is matched with a valid claim against some agents, who have specific duties to make the right practicable. He calls a right a 'manifesto right' when the valid claim to the right has not yet become practicable on a scale to be matched with a valid claim against duty-bearers (Feinberg 1970: 254–6).

[11] This has been the argument used by many authors to challenge the validity of the economic and social rights, by denying their 'feasibility', and if this argument is correct, poverty eradication can never be achieved as realizing any human right. The untenability of the argument has been clearly demonstrated by Amartya Sen (2003).

Third, a human right is supposed to motivate social change, the reformation of institutions, the amendment of laws and convert its in-principle feasibility to actual realization. To say that until it is actually realized it cannot be regarded as a human right is to deny its essential character and its role in social transformation. The UDHR proclaimed itself as 'a common standard of achievement for all peoples and all nations', to which end 'every individual and every organ of society...shall strive by teaching and education to promote respect for the rights and freedoms and by progressive measures, national and international, to secure their universal and effective recognition and observance'. Human rights are both realizable standards of social behavior to be enshrined in a country's legal system and social institutions, and also a guide to social change and public action, moving beyond 'feasibility' to actual implementation of those standards.

There are two other aspects of the rights–obligation relation that need to be clarified before linking poverty with a human right violation. The first is related to the question of whether a human right is a legal right or a moral right, also raised by Pogge before he decided to treat the subject only as a moral right: 'whether and under what conditions severe poverty violates human rights in the moral sense' (Pogge, this volume).

Human rights, according to the human rights movement and international human rights laws, are legal rights, with binding obligations on the duty-bearers, who are primarily the states. They are supposed to be accountable for any failures to carry out their obligations and are expected to take remedial action if their non-compliance with their duties is determined by an appropriate independent mechanism. It is this legality of the rights and the binding nature of their obligations that is the main attraction of claiming human rights. It improves unquestionably the likelihood of fulfilling the rights and also monitoring, restraining, or promoting, as the case may be, the actions of all the parties that impact the realization of the rights.

The crucial feature of legal rights is their binding obligation and not necessarily that they are justiciable in a court of law. If appropriate legislative measures or laws can be adopted to incorporate those obligations in the legal system, then the courts may be able to settle the disputes according to law. But monitoring and arbitration, including enforcing remedial action can be done via other mechanisms also, such as administrative systems, treaty bodies, executive and legislative authorities, local government agencies, peoples' committees, civil-society organizations, and village elders or bodies upholding customs and conventions. Given the way the judicial systems function in most developing countries, there is no reason to believe that the courts of law would always be a better adjudicating mechanism than others. It is the acceptability of the binding obligations by the society and the social pressure on the duty-holders that ultimately determines the extent of compliance.[12]

Moral philosophers, on the other hand, would regard human rights essentially as moral rights, where some universal moral values derived from notions of

---

[12] For a discussion on the nature of legal rights, see Henkin (1990).

human dignity are claimed as rights by human beings irrespective of their class, religion, language, or ethnicity. As rights they will have corresponding obligations but they will be moral obligations on duty-bearers who *should do* their duties, so that the corresponding rights *should* in practice be realized. Even if these may not be legally enforceable, these obligations are no less binding on moral agents as constraints on their behavior. If these rights can be institutionalized and made into binding legal rights, they probably will be more regularly realized. But even if they are not, and even if such rights are not always actually realized, the importance of moral rights claims would remain as grounds for public action and for making people do what they should do according to their obligations. Those obligations may be legally non-binding if they cannot be perfectly specified, but there are still ethical grounds for carrying them out.[13]

Moral rights, accordingly, have a very powerful appeal for establishing standards of behavior of social agents. The chance of poverty eradication would improve if poverty were seen as a violation of specific moral rights. But this appeal will fall far short of the reach and the force of the human rights claimed as legal rights, especially against the authorities of the state to which the people claiming these rights belong and other states who recognize them as international law.

All human rights, claimed as legal rights should qualify also as moral rights, justifiable in terms of acceptable norms of a universal moral order.[14] That is necessary to establish the legitimacy of the rights, particularly when the human-rights label elevates a right to the status of a foundational norm of a society. But then, they have to go beyond that and get converted into legal rights, creating binding obligations on agents who are in a position to enable the fulfillment of the right. In

---

[13] Amartya Sen is one of the strong protagonists of this view. For this, he invoked the Kantian notion of 'imperfect obligation', which relates to situations when the obligations related to a right cannot be perfectly specified, either in terms of the duties to be performed or the duty-bearers who are supposed to perform them. Without such specification, it may be difficult to make the rights legally binding. Still these would remain 'imperfect obligations' on agents or duty-bearers, who are in a position to help to realize the right and therefore should help, under such obligation as a moral responsibility. The view that, if they can help to fulfill a right they have a duty to help is clearly brought out in his paper: 'Consequential Evaluation and Practical Reason' (2000).

[14] For a legal positivist, it is not necessary that a justification as a moral right must precede its recognition as a legal right. If a claim is recognized through an appropriate norm creating procedure and accepted and ratified as a legal right, then it becomes a legal right irrespective of whether the moral arguments behind the legal right are recognized. There is no reason to believe that human beings are born with some inherent moral rights. It is good enough if these rights are bestowed on them by some legal order to have all the force and appeal of human rights. If there is no legal recognition, there may be social traditions or moral reasons to support some norms or advance some claims, but they cannot be regarded as rights with binding obligations.

For protagonists of moral rights, this argument breaks down when one considers questions such as the following: What if governments are *not* bestowing such legal rights, what if, say, to take an extreme case, the Nazis had won World War II? Would in that case, human rights not exist and the Nazi atrocities would not have violated anyone's human rights? Moral rights precede legal rights with binding moral obligation, which would disallow such atrocities; when some of these rights are derived, from some paramount, universal moral values, they can be raised to the status of human rights, not necessarily because they belong to human beings, but because they are justified morally and procedurally.

Sen's language, such rights must have identifiable and specified correlated duties, which can be regarded as perfect obligations, as well as the duty-bearers. These can be complemented by general duties of all members of the society, national or international, that recognize that human right.

In terms of our classification of duties, the 'direct' duties are equivalent to 'perfect obligation' of the different agents, especially of the state because the outcome of the right and performance of the duty are positively correlated, and if the duty is not performed, the outcome is negatively affected. Non-performance of the duty would be equivalent to a violation of the right.[15] The 'indirect' duties and the 'contingent' duties would be more akin to 'imperfect obligations', as the exact relationship between the duty and the outcome is uncertain and cannot be specified until other duties are specified and performed. But if the state or any other designated agency works out a program, taking into account all these indirect and contingent duties, assigning them to specific duty-bearers, to complement the direct duties performed by the state and other concerned 'agents', these 'imperfect' obligations can be converted into perfect obligations, which would be binding on those identified as duty-bearers. In that case, any agent in a position to improve R—including foreign governments, or wealthy individuals or corporations—would be human rights violators for failing to raise R, if their obligations can be specified, and their initially imperfect obligations are changed into perfect obligations to make them binding.[16]

---

[15] If R is the indicator of the right, P stands for performance of a direct duty, then this relationship is expressed as $\delta R/\delta P > 0$, and $P \neq 0$, implying that not taking any action is also a policy or performance of a duty. A 'non-performance' is negative performance $(-P)$ which would reduce the value of R. Not allowing P to take a value '0' implies that for an agent like the state, there is no such thing as 'non-action', because everything the state does, including not taking any action is a decision that has a cost, in terms of alternative values lost. For instance, consider the right not to be tortured. It is usually considered to be costless by writers who are bent on distinguishing between the so-called negative and positive rights—negative rights are supposed to be 'costless' and positive rights 'costly'. The state deciding 'not to torture' can fulfill the right without spending any resources. But this argument is faulty, because if the state practices 'torture', and if the state is not irrational or pathological, it must expect some 'value' to result from the torture. It may get some information, or some special service, or some other objectives. If the state has to stop practicing torture, as that violates a human right, it has to adopt some other 'positive' policies, such as incentives, bribes, or institutional changes, all of which cost resources. So not torturing would also involve spending resources for the state in terms of such opportunity costs. To this must be added costs of administering the policy and ensuring others in the society, and not just the state, refrain from torturing under pain of imprisonment. All these would blur the conventional difference between the 'negative' and 'positive' rights.

[16] Making the obligations binding does not mean making them 'legal' in the narrow sense of being 'justiciable'. Some of them may possibly be made a part of law, adjudicated by different institutions to which we have referred above. For our purpose, it is sufficient if it can be demonstrated that the obligations are binding enough to be enforceable. It is the enforceability that is linked to the notion of feasibility we have talked about that makes the right a 'valid' or 'full-fledged' concrete right. If the institutions of enforcement are weak, it may not actually be enforced. But that does not make it any less 'binding' or 'valid', because actual 'enforcement' is concerned with issues separate from the logic of 'enforceability', which is essential for cogency of the right. Even for 'legal' rights, Maurice Cranston distinguishes between 'positive' legal rights, which are enjoyed by everyone under a given jurisdiction and 'nominal' legal rights which are not enforced but still play a role in realizing some major rights. See Cranston (1973: 19–20).

This takes us to the other issue, referred to by Thomas Pogge as the 'plausibility' of duties (Pogge, this volume). According to him, if poverty is to be identified with the absence, denial, or violation of a human right, then that right is 'plausible' if the correlative duties are plausible as well. But how do we judge that 'plausibility'? Can we lay down some principles, which can decide that plausibility as a general rule, without changing them according to subjective judgments about the morality of the rights? I have said elsewhere that for an object of claim to qualify as a right, it must satisfy the tests of legitimacy and coherence, described as Sen's test of admissibility of rights.[17] If a right passes these tests, then that should be sufficient for it to be considered plausible. The legitimacy test involves the moral judgment that a right is of paramount importance and thus raises it to the level of a human right. The procedures to be followed would make such moral judgments largely, if not universally, shared, and not arbitrarily advanced. The 'coherence' test links it to the duties whose plausibility depends on (*a*) whether performance of these duties enhances the likelihood of realizing the right—the higher the likelihood the more plausible the duty; and (*b*) the opportunity cost of these duties should not be too high, in the sense that the alternative values that are sacrificed by performing these duties should not be generally unacceptable. The example given by Pogge of an affluent person asked to contribute $10 to save a child in Mali can be used to explain this point. If that affluent person is a member of a society that recognizes the universal right of a child to live, wherever he lives, he has at least an 'imperfect' obligation to help if he can. However, if that helping means he has to sacrifice a lot of income and give up a lot of alternative 'values', it may not be plausible, not because the beneficiary is some unknown child from Mali, but because that obligation is not 'enforceable', with a high probability of leakage or diversion to other uses, even if a law is enacted for that purpose. However, if the state of that affluent person, equally obligated to help realizing the right, provides a substantial amount of aid to Mali, which would save a large number of such children there, and asks that affluent person and others in a similar position to pay a cess or tax of $10 only per head to finance that aid, they should be 'perfectly' obligated to help, because what a single $10 contribution by each of them could not do, the totality of contributions from all would do. This is basically the argument for redistributive taxation within a nation-state for the rich helping the poor, and the human rights commitments extend the argument beyond the borders of the state. The plausibility then depends entirely on the ability of the duty-bearers to

---

[17] Qualifying for these tests is an effective answer to the charge about proliferation of human rights. Unless a claim is put to these tests, it should not be admissible for being treated, with all the policy implications, as a human right. These are built on Sen's notions of 'the legitimacy critique' and 'the coherence critique' of human rights (Sen 1999: 228–33). To sum up the arguments, it can be said that, for a claim to be regarded as a right, it has to be justified, normatively and procedurally, and it is this that provides legitimacy to the right. It should also be possible to identify the correlative duties, assignable to different duty-bearers, which would enable the realization of the right and which would lend 'coherence' to the right. See Sengupta (2004).

design a program of realizing the human right, at a reasonable cost, if that right is recognized by the society.[18]

13.3. IDENTIFICATION OF THE RIGHT, THE RIGHT-HOLDERS, AND THE OBLIGATION

In this section, we consider the issues related to the identification of the right whose violation can be regarded as poverty. There are many characteristics of poverty that provoke different sentiments, such as a sense of indignity and intensity of anguish. Our aim is to define the right in a way that has the maximum chance of being fulfilled by removing the violation and actually eradicating poverty in the shortest possible time. The purpose is to look for a practical way of solving the problem of poverty and not entering into the polemics of the historical origin of poverty or injustices of the current global system.

The right has to pass the tests that determine which are human rights. That means its moral and procedural legitimacy should be universally accepted and that the obligations associated with that could be specified and assigned to all the duty-bearers: the nation-states, the international community, corporate sectors, individuals, and tax payers. The duties should be not only practicable but also reasonable in terms of costs and efforts. More importantly, the right should be, as far as possible, composed of or derived from internationally recognized human rights. It should not be necessary to campaign for launching a new human right in international law through a long-winded procedure of intergovernmental negotiations. It is of course not essential to get this right recognized in international law, because as we have seen, a moral right accepted universally could have a far-reaching binding power for its obligations and for effective enforcement. But its appeal would fall short of the force of a legal right, because then the obligations for its fulfillment are backed by remedial actions and other disincentives, raising the likelihood of its realization.

Seen from this perspective, defining poverty as 'lack of secure access to sufficient quantities of basic necessities, such as food, water, clothing, shelter and minimum medical care' or sufficient income or purchasing power to have a command over these basic necessities, would only be the first step toward the recognition of such

---

[18] The reasonableness of the cost, reckoned in terms of alternative values foregone, should be, logically, limited to the loss of other human rights, because human rights are supposed to trump over other priorities or values. If paying for fulfilling a human right costs so much that it sacrifices values other than human rights, such as armament expenditures or extravagant luxuries that should give way to funding a program for human rights, inside or outside the boundaries of the nation-state. Here the logic of the human rights action and the political practicality of the program have to be balanced, not on principle, but on the basis of realpolitik. The same logic applies to individuals: They must contribute to the fulfillment of human rights, domestically and abroad, in preference to any and all 'other priorities or values'.

lack as a violation of human rights. Lack of these basic necessities would create conditions of existence without any dignity, self-respect, and freedom, or in short without any human rights. But availability of these would not necessarily fulfill human rights. It is the access to these necessities in a manner consistent with human rights standards of equity, non-discrimination, participation, accountability, and transparency, together with availability, that make them satisfy human rights. A society of slaves having all these basic necessities will not be reckoned as enjoying human rights, not just because they lack the right to liberty but because those necessities are not provided in a rights-based manner. Any program of action aimed at providing these necessities as human rights must be formulated to conform to these human rights standards.

It is important to highlight this point to distinguish a purely economic program of supplying the basic necessities from a program for fulfilling human rights, which can be regarded as foundational objectives of a society. They command the first claim on resources and efforts of all agents within that society and in the outside international community. It would therefore be more appropriate to define poverty not just as the lack of sufficient quantities of basic necessities, but as the lack of or the violation of the right to these basic necessities such as the right to food, the right to health, the right to education, and the like. These rights have in effect all been already recognized in international law through the convention on the economic, social, and cultural rights. When these necessities are claimed as rights, it is implied that they are to be fulfilled in a rights-based manner. It may be necessary to have some consensus about the notion of 'basic' or 'minimum' that can be physically or culturally determined and once that is done, the right to different basic necessities can be fairly clearly specified. It should be possible to extend the notion of the right to basic necessities to some of the civil and political rights, since these are essential to ensuring the eradication of poverty as a fulfillment of human rights. Poverty can then be described as the violation of the rights to basic necessities and the rights to some basic freedoms.

But who would be the right-holder in this context? In a general human rights framework, everybody should have rights to basic necessities and freedom. But that cannot be the basis of an anti-poverty program. It should be targeted at a group of people, identified or defined as 'poor' or 'extremely poor', otherwise it will be 'open-ended'. Suppose it is argued that the right to basic food needs to be satisfied with the provision of free food; it will be unmanageably expensive if everybody is supplied with that provision (although in this case it *will* mean that the poor will receive the food they need).

It is possible to invoke in this context the conventional definition of the poor in terms of per capita income or expenditure, such as people living on below $1 per day (as extremely poor) or $2 per day (as poor); that is, in terms of the purchasing power parity value of the currency. There is a lot of debate about the appropriateness of this poverty line, and ultimately it has to be decided by some kind of a consensus about the minimum income that separates the poor from the non-poor. Whatever may be the consensus or the acceptable definition of it, the category of the people identified as 'poor' can then be described as the right-holder whose right is to be free from poverty; that is to be free from the violation or absence of the right to basic necessities.[19]

Clearly the right whose violation is regarded as poverty in this sense is a composite right, constituted by all the different rights to basic necessities, and plausibly also by rights to basic freedoms. But how does one determine that the composite right has been violated, when some of the component rights have been successfully promoted while one or two of them have actually regressed or deteriorated? What kind of rules would need to be formulated to compare the progress or regress of different rights when human rights by definition do not admit any trade-off? If poverty has to be regarded as the violation of all the rights to basic necessities, its incidence will be rather limited. If poverty is taken to be the violation of even a single such right, even if other rights are fulfilled, the scope of poverty can be unreasonably large.

Furthermore, these rights can be realized mostly over a period, progressively, as described in the human rights literature, because of the resource constraints and also because of the time taken for the institutional adjustments. How does one assess the intermediate stages, when rights have not been fully realized, but are in the process of progressive improvement? Suppose having x amount of food grains for all the people identified as poor is a necessary condition of fulfilling the right to food for them, and the country has reached a stage when three-quarters of the poor compared to half of them previously have that amount of food: is the right to food still violated or is it being increasingly realized?

These issues are important when we move from expressing anguish at the prevalence of poverty to the stage when policies are actually designed and implemented to remove poverty. As we mentioned earlier, it is the policies or the conduct of the duty-bearers, which is the main concern of the claimants of human rights.[20] There is a good deal to gain just by fulfilling the obligations of conduct, in terms of ensuring appropriate policies are in place and, even if the desired outcomes of these policies are not fully realized. In fact, it is possible to argue that in many cases where the realization of the right may take a long time, but policies exist that have a high likelihood of producing the right, that those policies themselves can be claimed as a right, that carries with it the duty of assigning the responsibilities of carrying out those policies to appropriate agents and setting up proper mechanisms for monitoring and remedial action.[21]

---

[19] The human right of a category of people called 'poor' is no less a universal right than any other human right. Universality means any human being who is in a position to claim the right, can be a right-holder, irrespective of caste, creed, or citizenship. The obligations corresponding to that right are also universal, meaning all agents have obligations, perfect or imperfect, to fulfill the right. Only the category of people qualified as poor will be in a position to claim that right.

[20] These issues have been discussed extensively by the International Law Commission, in terms of 'obligations of conduct' and 'obligations of result', International Law Commission, UN Doc. A/CN.4/Sev.9/1996.

[21] Amartya Sen talked about a meta-right, while discussing the right not to be hungry or the right to food, which it may not always be possible to guarantee for all persons in a country in the near future, though 'policies that would rapidly lead to such freedoms do exist'. So a right to x, such as not to be hungry, or the right to adequate means of livelihood, may be an abstract background right. But the

From that perspective, the right whose violation is regarded as poverty, or more simply the right to poverty eradication may be much better tackled in terms of appropriate development policies that are most likely to remove or eradicate poverty and which can be claimed as rights in themselves. These rights can be formulated more effectively in terms of the right to development, a right which has been recognized as a human right by the international community through the Declaration on the Right to Development of the UN (1986), followed up by the Vienna Declaration of 1993.[22] This is the right to a process of development in which all human rights and fundamental freedoms are realized, a process that is seen as an evolving social arrangement and international order that facilitates the realization of, and actually realizes, in a progressive manner, all those rights. It is a composite right, of incremental realization of all its constituent rights and it is a process, in the sense that these rights are interdependent, over time, with changing social and institutional arrangements. The composite right is increasingly realized if one or more of its constituent rights are themselves more fully realized, while no constituent right regresses or is violated. It is regarded as development, because development means expansion of freedoms and rights that improve the well-being of all people.

The obligation corresponding to the composite right is a development policy adopted and implemented by the primary duty-bearer, the state, coordinating the various policies relating to each of the constitutive rights with an overall policy of economic growth that lessens resource constraints and adjusts the institutions that facilitate the realization of all or most of these rights. Such a development policy would have a high likelihood of realizing these rights, but may not always be able, within a short period, to actually realize all of them. In that case that development policy can be treated as the obligation corresponding to the right to development or as a meta-right, with all the characteristics of a real right, and which can be claimed by the people who are the right-holders of the identified human rights (i.e. the recognized economic, social, and cultural rights, as well as the civil and political rights).[23]

---

right to demand that policy be directed toward securing the objectives of making the right to food or the right to adequate means of livelihood a realizable right—this right to $p(x)$, as a meta-right to x, will be a real right (Sen 1984).

[22] See Declaration on the Right to Development, adopted by General Assembly resolution 41/128 on December 4, 1986 (www.unhchr.ch/html/menu3/b/74.htm) and the Vienna Declaration, adopted by the World Conference on Human Rights on June 25, 1993 (www.unhchr.ch/huridocda/huridoca.nsf/(Symbol)/A.CONF.157.23.En?OpenDocument). See also Sengupta (2002*a*).

[23] If D^* is the process of development that can be claimed as a human right, then $D^* = (\Delta R_1, \Delta R_2, \ldots, \Delta R_n, \Delta Y^*)$, where ΔR_i is improvement in the realization of the ith right represented by increment in the indicator of that right and Y^* is the rights based growth of income, that does not increase inequality and discrimination and is participatory and accountable. Such economic growth enters the argument, both as an instrumental and a substantive variable. Without such growth, a sustained realization of all the rights, all of which consume resources, is not possible, and for the purpose of enabling the rights to be realized following human rights standards, it must be rights-based itself. It has also a substantive value, because technically all other objectives of development not captured by the fulfillment of rights are represented by that growth. It is also because most developing

Poverty then can be described as the absence or the violation of the right to development of the category of people identified as 'poor'. Removing poverty would then imply adopting policies to raise the level of income of the poor above the poverty line and to enable the realization of the rights to basic needs, such as food, health, shelter, and education, to the extent they are considered necessary. Together, they or these policies would expand the capability of the poor and the policies would contribute to the removal of both income poverty and capability poverty. This approach is much more realistic and flexible than being fixated on satisfying targeted amounts of basic needs. The concern would be with creating conditions for removing poverty, in terms of both capability and income poverty, progressively over a given period. The policies that should be formulated to suit the specific economic and social context of each country would have a high, if not the maximum, likelihood to achieve the results. But as there is not a one-to-one correspondence between any specific policy and the targeted outcome, or between the obligations of conduct and the obligations of result, the rights may not be fully realized as intended. The trends will be firmly set and the social arrangements established to achieve the results and realize the rights as early as possible.

We need not get bogged down in controversies about whether such a right is a moral right or a legal right or whether non-fulfillment of a right is a violation or a denial of a right. A legal right entails legal obligation, and if that obligation is not carried out, it is an act of violation for which the duty-bearer is reprimanded or penalized, whether the policies that should be formulated are directly causing non-fulfillment of the right. A moral right entails moral obligation, and a duty-bearer is expected to do what he or she should do, but is not legally bound to do so. He or she would not even be morally bound to that obligation, unless it can be shown that not carrying out that obligation causes the non-fulfillment of the right, in which case it would be a case of 'violation' for which the duty-bearer would be held accountable and morally reprimanded. These issues lose their relevance in the case of a human right, which begins as a moral right but ends up as a legal right, or a 'binding' right which is enforceable either by the judicial system or by different administrative and institutional measures. The relevant issue is not whether the non-performance of the duty causes the non-fulfillment of the right or a violation of the right; but whether the obligation is 'perfect' when the duty can

countries consider economic growth that is equitable and just as desirable in itself. The ΔR_i represent all recognized rights, civil, political as well as economic, social, and cultural rights and those recognized later. The constraints imposed on them for inclusion in the overall index of the right to development is that they have to be non-negative. Some of the rights may not improve while others do, but none can regress; i.e., no right can be violated. For all these, see Arjun Sengupta et al., 'The Right to Development and Human Rights in Development', presented in the Nobel Symposium, Oslo, October, 2003.

Development policy, which is the corresponding obligation, primarily of the state, but coordinating with other duty-bearers, can be formulated by fixing all the ΔR_i, as targets, following the obligation of results, and by adopting policies for sectoral developments and overall economic growth with both internal consistency and respect for human rights standards, fulfilling the obligations of conduct. (The *Maastricht Guidelines* [1998] spell this out: 'The obligation of conduct requires actions reasonably calculated to realize the enjoyment of a particular right...The obligations of result requires states to achieve specific targets to satisfy a detailed substantive standard' [paragraph 7, 694].)

be specified and the duty-bearer identified, whether that duty has a 'direct' impact, and the size of the impact is significant on the fulfillment of the right. In a complex interdependent system with 'indirect' and 'contingent' duties of the different duty-bearers, accentuating or neutralizing the direct impact of any action, it would be difficult to identify any activity as directly causing the violation of the right, unless the size of the direct impact is sufficiently large to clearly establish the case of a violation.

As we discussed earlier, the distinction between the violation of a right and the denial of a right would get blurred in such cases. If a policy or action P has a large positive impact on the right R, and a non-action $(-P)$ leads to a regression of the right $(-R)$, then such non-action would be equivalent to violation, provided of course the duty-bearer is aware of that effect. Suppose there is a famine going on in a country A, and its neighbor, country B, could, without much difficulty, mitigate the famine through food distribution efforts. If the government of country B is aware of its ability to relieve the famine, then if it does not act to distribute that food there, it will be responsible for a violation of the human right of freedom from hunger. It does not matter whether that government is responsible in any way for causing the famine in the first country. The crucial relation that determines the obligation is whether the other agent, the government of the neighboring state, can adopt any policy that impacts the famine of the first country, and to what extent it can do so.

To sum up, therefore, poverty can be regarded as a violation of human rights, provided the content of those rights can be properly identified, such as our notion of the right to development of a group of people defined as 'poor', and provided that corresponding obligations can be properly specified and assigned to different duty-bearers.

13.4. THE DUTY-BEARERS

Who are these duty-bearers who have the obligations corresponding to the rights whose violation is regarded as poverty? What kinds of duties are to be assigned to the different duty-bearers to realize the right to development of the poor? In this section we take up these issues to wrap up our discussion on poverty as a violation of human rights.

It is the state that is the primary duty-bearer of this right, just as it is with all other human rights. The state or the government of the country to which the poor belongs would have the responsibility of formulating and implementing a development policy, because it has the power and authority to frame laws and regulations and adopt policies that affect all individuals in its jurisdiction. The policies can be carried out in practice by respecting the views of all parties that have some role to play in fulfilling the right. As the right to development is a composite right of at least the basic or core rights to food, health, shelter, and education, the state has to formulate sectoral policies for ensuring rights-based access to and availability of corresponding goods and services, and then coordinating them in a program that promotes overall economic growth benefiting the poorest sector of society. Such growth secures sufficient increased income of the poor to allow them to rise above the poverty line and remove the resource constraints in the individual sectors.

The state's adoption of this role does not imply that the markets are not going to play their role in resource allocation with efficiency and over time. It is a misunderstanding of the human rights principle to think that it promotes an interventionist or dirigistic state as opposed to the market mechanism. Human rights are addressed to the state, because that authority can directly violate or promote the different rights and help or prevent other agents from promoting or violating them. In playing that role, the state must work with the existing relationships between all the actors in an economic, political, and social system. For removing poverty or promoting development the state must build on the market forces that govern economic relationships, as an objective reality. If a free-market mechanism can achieve the rights-goals, it must protect and promote free markets. If achieving those goals calls for channeling and influencing market forces in a particular direction, the state must do so, without denying the reality of market interrelations. The state has to operate on those relations, leveraging them and intervening on the margin, and occasionally restructuring them, but never trying to replace them as that has very little chance of success. The development programs that we are talking about for realizing a right to development are very different from the earlier central planning-based programs, not only because it cannot do without operating with the market mechanism to have a real chance of success, but also because it has to be participatory, with decentralized decision-making and popular accountability in order to be consistent with the human rights standards.

One implication of this is to appreciate that to ensure the fulfillment of rights, the determinants of demand and supply of goods and services, incomes and purchasing power, or the entitlements of those who are claiming the rights have to be assessed dispassionately before ascribing specific roles to different agents to carry out their obligations.[24] This would be very complex, and more often than not it may not be possible to ascribe to any agent the responsibility of 'causing' the non-fulfillment of the right. But nevertheless it should be possible to work out a program, influencing various agents to play specific roles, singly and together, to realize that right. Once those roles are specified, the agents that do not play their

---

[24] See Sen (1995), where he warns against any instant economic or simple explanation in terms of vested interests and calls for serious examination of the problems of 'acquirent' and 'entitlement' to food of different persons to work out a program for a 'freedom from hunger'. For a flavor of the complexities, just consider the following statement: 'A person has to starve if his entitlement set does not include any commodity bundle with enough food. A person is reduced to starvation if some changes either in his endowment (e.g., alienation of land or loss of labor power due to ill health) or in his exchange entitlement mapping (e.g., fall in wages, rise in food prices, loss of employment, drop in the price of the goods he produces and sells), make it no longer possible for him to acquire any commodity bundle with enough food'.

roles can be determined, in terms of our analysis, to have violated that right. The state as the primary duty-bearer and sovereign authority over divisions within its jurisdiction will have to be responsible for designing the program and specifying the roles of others.

The issues are much more complex when we consider the role of other states and institutions such as members of the international community, who are also duty-bearers for an international human right, such as the right to development or the composite of the rights to food, health, education, and standard of living. All of them operate within an international framework of rules and procedures, and all of them have a responsibility either through 'direct' actions or through 'indirect', and 'contingent' measures to enable the fulfillment of the right.

In the international legal system of sovereign states, international relations are based on a horizontal interstate system, that is the states deal with other states, while the human rights of the citizens pertain to a vertical relationship between a state and its subjects. Even though the human rights are accepted as universal, irrespective of the citizenship of the right-holders, implying that a denial or violation of a human right anywhere is the concern of all agents, everywhere, it is only rarely that states get into a diagonal relationship with individuals in other states facing a gross violation of human rights.[25] In such a situation, if there is a violation of a human right of an individual or a group of individuals (such as the poor), the international community can intervene to remove that violation mostly through the intermediation of the states. Similarly, if the international community is to be held responsible for that violation, the role of the intermediary state has to be shown as neutral or ineffective in the transmission of the effects of action of the international community on the individual right-holders within the concerned state.

A closer scrutiny of the issues will bring out how difficult it is to hold the international community responsible for the violation of human rights in a given country, if violation is linked to causation and not, as we have defined it, as non-performance of a positive action that could prevent poverty. It is of course possible that the external activities of a state may have human rights effects on citizens of other states, and it may therefore have obligations to mitigate or compensate those effects. These may pertain to effects on environment, trade, technology, or security. The adverse effects may be so blatant or so one-sided that the intermediary states where the affected people live cannot or do not have any reason to do anything to neutralize those effects. The obligations of the states to prevent these human rights effects would be clear-cut enough to call for a remedy, but still may not be clear enough to be linked to the aggravation of poverty.

In most other cases of external effects of a state's activity, there would be a complex relationship with the activities of the other concerned states. For example,

---

[25] See Skogly and Gibney (2002) and Rosas (1995). Except in cases of humanitarian intervention and economic sanction or in the use of 'optional protocols', no state can usually intervene in another state directly in favor of a third party suffering from a human rights violation. On the responsibility of the international community of states to protect human rights see also Salomon (2003).

take the case of the opening up of international trade under globalization or the protection of intellectual property rights. The international rules governing these transactions may cause severe adverse effects on many developing countries. But still the states of those countries might often through international negotiations agree to these rules, expecting returns in other areas or through a greater quantity of benefits in some other period, or to protect the interests of some special groups or lobbies more powerful in these states. Who should then be held responsible for those adverse effects? Unfortunately, that has been mostly the reality of interrelation, or negotiations on international trade, between developed and developing countries. Only when it can be established that the developing countries were helpless and had little option but to acquiesce to the dictates of the richer nations, can the latter be held directly responsible for the unequal and often unjust rules that affect adversely the overall development of a developing country. The governments of the developing countries who negotiate and interact with the other developed country's governments often represent special groups and not their whole people or the poorer sections of the people. So even when alternative negotiating strategies or policy programs exist that would make most of their people better off, they choose the option which is inferior in terms of the interests of the majority of the people, but more suited to smaller special groups.

The point to note is not that the developing country governments, which are sometimes neglectful of the interests of the majority of their people, are always guilty of complicity in a relationship with the richer states. They may or may not be representative of all people, particularly the poor people. They may or may not have the flexibility of pursuing a course that would be most beneficial to them. Even when the trade and investment rules allow their economic growth to increase and production structure to change for a sustainable and substantial improvement of the whole economy, they may fail to protect, promote, and fulfill the human rights of the poor and thus remove poverty. In all such cases, to consider that the international community is responsible for continuing poverty, without considering the role played by the intermediary nation-states where the poor live, will not be reasonable.

When, in the 1970s, the developing countries were calling for an NIEO, they were talking about equity in the decision-making process, the sharing of benefits of international transactions with the industrial countries, and the right to development of the governments of the developing countries. That was a logical step in an international relation between nation-states with horizontal equity, all states having equal rights. It was possible to argue that international law should concern itself with a just and fair relationship between the states, and the vertical relationship between the states and their citizens should be treated separately through constitutional reforms within the sovereign states. But when the claims of equality of relationship are advanced in terms of human rights, such as the right to development, those vertical relations also come within the purview of discussions. It would then be essential for the developing countries to show that their states were truly representative of all their people; that mechanisms existed to translate the fulfillment of rights to benefits for the individuals who were the effective claimants of those rights. In a similar vein, if poverty is described as the violation of the right to development of the poor people of a country, whose eradication is the obligation of all agents in the international community, it will be essential to demonstrate that mechanisms exist to transmit the benefits of international action to fulfill the right actually for the poor people of a country.

For all these reasons, it is much better to look for effective mechanisms of international cooperation, which is the term that has been used in the international covenants and also the UN Charter. According to that, the international community is to cooperate with the national state authorities to fulfill the right to development, and for poverty eradication (the right to development of the poor people in those countries). There are certain steps that the international community must take that enable the developing countries in general to have freer trade, better terms of investment, technology transfer, and foreign aid that directly affect all people of the developing countries. This would forge a 'diagonal' relationship between the developed countries and the people of the developing countries. These policies have to be complemented by direct international cooperation with the state authorities, indirectly impacting on the citizens of these countries, together with different contingency facilities available to those states in case they need to resort to them. This relationship may be conceived in terms of a development compact. If the developing country governments set up a program for rights-based development that eradicates poverty and fulfills the core rights to basic needs, to food, health, education, etc. as we have discussed above, then the industrial countries should enter into commitments of international cooperation, as the need may be, of aid, trade, debt, and finance which would facilitate the developing country governments to carry out their programs.

From this perspective, the obligations of the international community can be clearly defined. If such programs exist and if developing countries can implement these programs through appropriate mechanisms that clearly transfer benefits to the poor, then the industrial countries have an unequivocal obligation to play their roles. If they do not play these roles, they violate the human right to be free from poverty.

14

Enforcing Economic and Social Human Rights

*Osvaldo Guariglia**

14.1. INTRODUCTION

The various international covenants and declarations on human rights include two kinds of rights, which are usually described as 'civil and political rights', on one hand, and 'economic and social rights', on the other. Typical of the former is the statement in Article 3 of the *UDHR*, which asserts 'Everyone has the right to life, liberty and security of person'. An example of the latter is Article 25, according to which, 'Everyone has the right to a standard of living adequate for the health and well being of himself and of his family, including, food, clothing, housing and medical care and necessary social services, and the right to security in the event of unemployment, sickness, disability, widowhood, old age, etc.' (see also Article 11 of the *International Covenant on Economic, Social and Cultural Rights*).

This division of human rights into two separate groups has brought about two very different theoretical stances; particularly as regards the validity and status of each type of rights. On the one hand, *libertarianism* holds consistently that the only existing rights are civil ones. They ground their opinion on the plausible reason that civil rights are the only ones that entail a corresponding obligation on the part of everyone else toward the holder of the right insofar as they *must refrain from depriving* him or her from any of the items included in the right in question: be it life, liberty, or property (Nozick 1974: 28–35). Seen in this light, civil and political rights protect people's integrity and liberty, and they are basically *negative* since they defend each individual from coercive interference by everyone else and, in particular, by the State. Due to their general character, civil and political rights have met with much faster and more adequate enforcement through relevant legislation than have the second category of rights. In fact, as noted by lawyers who endorse this point of view, only negative rights fall within the ambit of courts of justice because both the damage and its reparation or sanction can be clearly established. On the other hand, they hold that *positive rights* are subject to a variety

* An earlier version of this chapter was read at the XXI World Congress of Philosophy (Istanbul, August 10–17, 2003). I am grateful for extensive observations and corrections of my poor English to David Crocker and Thomas Pogge. The remaining faults are, of course, mine.

of circumstances that elude the ruling and competence of judges (Steiner and Alston 2000: 275–6).

A maximalist philosophical line has developed in opposition to the former, minimalist one. It contends that there is a strict parallel between these two types of rights and describes both as basic. In fact, as Henry Shue has asserted in his already classical work, 'the same considerations that establish that security rights are basic for everyone also support the conclusion that subsistence rights are basic for everyone. It is not being claimed or assumed that security and subsistence are parallel in all . . . respects. The only parallel being relied upon is that guarantees of security and guarantees of subsistence are equally essential to providing for the actual exercise of any other rights' (Shue 1996a: 25–6). Despite that, economic and social rights—regarded as *positive* insofar as they acknowledge that the subject of those rights holds a valid demand to have some particular basic rights satisfied (such as to food, medical care, etc.)—have not received equal sanction by laws in developing countries, let alone in so-called poor countries, as they have in developed ones. On the other hand, in some of the most powerful nations the protection the state offers through these rights to their least favored groups is currently endangered by the enactment of policies that cut taxes that should finance such protection.[1]

In what follows, I focus on those features of economic and social rights that cause them to receive such scant consideration both in the domestic level and, especially, in the international or transnational field. Having said that, I must first describe briefly how I classify the different types of rights and in what way they are connected to various kinds of obligations.

14.2. ECONOMIC AND SOCIAL HUMAN RIGHTS

How should we define the formal concept of an economic or social human right? This type of right asserts in each case a demand that must be satisfied—with respect to food, for instance, or clothing, housing, medical care, and the like. Nevertheless, human rights, formally considered, cannot go beyond this overall general statement, since the actual and precise extent of whatever may be regarded as a basic right to be satisfied will depend on each national, regional, and even communal context. An additional controversial point is whether this rights claim or demand has in each case a particular addressee, since it is not usually a simple matter to identify a particular agent's precise obligation corresponding to the claim set forth by the holder of the right. Of course, one may think that the primary addressee is always the relevant state, or some of its institutions or agencies. Even if this is admittedly the most straightforward answer, some not easily surmountable obstacles immediately crop up. For example, what happens when the state is so weak that it is unable to note in a precise and orderly manner the

---

[1] See Paul Krugman, 'Stating the Obvious', *New York Times*, May 27, 2003.

basic demands of its population, let alone to satisfy them? Numerous countries in Central America, the Caribbean, and sub-Saharan Africa are cases in point. Would economic and social human rights cease to exist for that part of the population that requires—with the greatest urgency—that they be taken into account? What is at stake here is the very notion of a 'human right' and its status both as a moral and a legal right. We must therefore examine briefly this question.

If some person A has a *right* to some state of affairs a, he or she has a *claim* against any other person B, that the state of affairs a obtains. In the case of civic and political human rights, it is easy to see how this formula applies; for example, pursuant Article 5 of the *Universal Declaration* asserts that 'No one shall be subjected to torture or to cruel, inhuman or degrading treatment or punishment'. The state of affairs a obtains for A so long as he or she is not subjected to torture or any kind of degrading treatment. So, if some person A has a right to some state of affairs a, he or she has a claim against any other person B that B not act in ways that make it the case that the state of affairs a does not obtain. It is also clear why this article proclaims a moral and at the same time a legal right, providing its infringement is punished by law. What would happen if the right stated by Article 5 was not protected by law in a given state? Obviously, the claim not to be tortured does not cease to exist for A, but it is only a moral constraint wanting its legal enforcement (Thomson 1990: 36–43, 70–8). Similarly, since social and economic rights are also moral rights, they are usually claimed 'only when not protected by legal rights efficiently acknowledged' (Nino 1989: 48 n. 37). In other words, the moral validity of the demand and, along the same lines, its universal appeal persists counterfactually, especially wherever the state does not fulfill its task of legal enforcement. However, the question remains open: how is it possible to allocate responsibility for fulfilling positive rights? Who are its secondary addressees? Without an answer to this question, the rhetoric of human rights can easily become empty.

Undoubtedly, a detailed approach to the situation of economic and social human rights in the world at large is not only impossible but also useless, seeing that their status varies in each country and even in regions within the same country. Accordingly, I confine my chapter to an overview of the current situation in countries with an intermediate level of development, such as Argentina, Brazil, Uruguay, and others in South America. Among other shared features, they have been living under fully democratic governments for the past two decades, after an extended and troubled period of military coups and authoritarian regimes.

14.3. NEGATIVE AND POSITIVE RIGHTS

For the sake of delineating the perspective from which I examine the obstacles and possibilities of enforcing socioeconomic human rights, it will be convenient to set up a classification of both negative and positive rights, with their corresponding duties. We stress the peculiar characteristics of each, as well as their implications.[2]

In the first place, we must point to a feature in the distinction between *negative and positive duties* which, though repeatedly noted, is not often duly taken into account. My point is that, insofar as they are obligations, both kinds of duties are equally constraining. Their difference lies, rather, in the material contents of the obligations. The first kind gives a detailed description of a type of action the agent is under obligation to avoid. There may be no gradation in fulfilling the obligation since it is simply a question of letting the same situation prevail for the other agents, as was the case before the omission. In the case of positive obligations, on the other hand, the content of the obligation is constituted by an aim that differs from the natural flow of the state of things prior to the action. This end can be indicated only vaguely, since both its enforcement and its results will be subject in each case to the peculiar characteristics of the situation. An additional feature of the distinction is the scope of each kind of duty. While negative ones are almost exclusively *general* duties, positive duties are almost exclusively *special*. This implies that the duty holder of the latter must possess some requisite *ability or other characteristic* in order to be able to discharge his or her obligation. For example, if someone has a heart attack in front of you, the positive duty of attempting to save her life with all means at your disposal is a special one if you are a doctor; if you are not, you are only required to seek help for her.

That said as regards duties, we must note that there is no clear-cut correlation between rights and duties of the same sign (i.e., positive or negative), as assumed by libertarians. In fact, negative rights are correlated not only to general negative duties—that is, we all have the obligation to respect the life and integrity of others—but also to the *special positive* duties that concern government agents and leaders. They are under the obligation of foreseeing and enforcing every measure guaranteed or likely to prevent and repair damage attributable to actual or possible violations of negative rights. The original ground of the very claim for security and integrity of the person is a negative general right, which is undoubtedly closely connected to a perfect negative duty we all have. Furthermore, public agents and judges have a special *positive* duty to protect and ensure people's security and integrity. Therefore, the *positive right* to have the security and integrity of citizens' lives protected by public powers is a supplementary positive right, which derives from the negative general right originally grounding the claim.

In conclusion, though the methodological distinction between negative and positive rights must be taken as conceptually founded, the actual web of negative and positive rights shows that, when it comes to enforcement, they are both combined in order to guarantee the actual protection of their holders. It is thus impossible to comply with one set, negative rights in this case, without admitting

---

[2] See Shue (1988: 688 f.; 1996a: 18–64), Gewirth (1996: 33 f.), Fabre (1998: 263 f.), Guariglia (2002: 123 f.), and Pogge (2002a: 52–70).

at the same time the necessity of the other set—that is positive rights—to the protection of each person's security (Gewirth 1996: 34–8; Shue 1996*a*: 37–40).

14.4. POSITIVE RIGHTS AND DUTIES: WHO OWES WHAT TO WHOM?

Let us now consider original positive rights, that is, those grounded in a claim of the right holder, whose aim is the satisfaction of a basic need. Prima facie, two substantial queries crop up when it comes to reaching an adequate understanding of these rights and, consequently, their future enforcement. The point is to establish who are directly concerned (*a*) as the holders of the right in question; and (*b*) as the bearers of the obligation's burden.

The first question—(*a*) who are the relevant holders of positive rights—may be solved in general terms by answering that, potentially, all members of a given society qualify. For, either they have citizenship rights in the corresponding state, or they are foreign residents legally acknowledged as such by the state. At present there is a group of philosophers and economists who favor the adoption of a *universal basic income* for every citizen and resident of a given country—following a minimum period of residency—regardless of other sources of income and civil status. The discussion fostered by this proposal is not only interesting, in my opinion, but also most relevant for the issue under study. Nevertheless, it has an intrinsic limitation that curtails its analysis on a worldwide level: it requires a previous accumulation of wealth in both material and human resources that can only be found in highly developed countries.[3] I mention this proposal in order to show that those involved as holders of positive rights can, in fact, be *all* the members of a given society. In view of the fact that resources are limited, however, it is imperative to establish some kind of hierarchy among potential beneficiaries. This will require selecting—as a guiding criterion—a minimum set of basic needs that must be satisfied.

It has been rightly objected that it is impossible to determine beforehand the scope and characteristics of basic needs in each individual society since its culture, and economic and technological development decisively influence both variables. That notwithstanding, it is actually possible to establish a sufficiently exact, albeit flexible, indicator to determine a set of basic needs—and these would include food, housing, education, and medical care. I am referring to the typical needs

---

[3] See van Parijs (2001: 43–4). Pogge disputes this last affirmation arguing that 'with the social product of the rich countries at $26,000 billion annually, the world could easily sustain a basic income provision in the amount of $600 billion annually. This is $100 per year per person. In most developing countries, this would be worth around $400–$600 in purchasing power, and this would more than double the incomes of the poorest half of the human population'. Actually, I do not disagree with such proposal, but I must observe that my contention regards in first place enforcement of the human right within a national state, and in second place, at international level between the states. This is the reason why I call my position 'a weak cosmopolitan view'.

of a person of either sex required in order to attain sufficient control of his or her capacities and abilities, ensuring the potential for full use of his or her *autonomy*.[4] The magnitude of the resources necessary to guarantee the fulfillment of such a minimum set of needs will largely depend on the stage of social development achieved not only by a particular country, but also by the various regions within it. Thus, whoever falls below the minimum line, established according to regional, even communal, parameters and is unable to provide subsistence for himself or herself by his or her own means, due to temporary or permanent impairment, temporary or chronic unemployment, or whatever other reason—will be a primary beneficiary of economic and social rights.

The second issue is more complex: (*b*) who must bear the burden of providing the necessary resources to meet the needs of others? This is basically the point that exercises libertarians. They argue that positive obligation to meet needs would imply using some people—the bearers of the obligations—as means and not as ends in themselves (Nozick 1974: 32–3). At first sight, it looks like a peculiar objection since it uses a Kantian argument to oppose all types of legally enforced solidarity among citizens of a given society. In its most basic form, it aims at denouncing an unequal distribution of burdens, for example by means of direct taxation, because, if taxes were exacted in proportion to income, it would appear to be a case of negative discrimination against the wealthiest. But the cost of respecting a universal right—so goes the libertarian objection—should also be universally borne. The objection, however, collapses as soon as we note that this positive duty to contribute to the maintenance of the state—which, in the long run, will fund the distribution of public resources—falls, in some way or another, on every member of society. Besides, this duty concerns the maintenance of police and security forces that are indispensable for the protection of negative rights for, as was powerfully argued by Holmes and Sunstein, 'property rights depend on a state that is willing to tax and spend... [A] state that could not, under specified conditions, take private assets could not protect them effectively, either' (Holmes and Sunstein 1999: 61, see also 71–2). In other words, the question is not about the burdens to be imposed for the maintenance of the state, since they would have to exist anyway. Rather, the point is the range and quality of the services to be provided by the State; this is in fact the main concern of libertarians, who insist on cutting down to a bare minimum the public goods to be supplied by it. Seen in this light, the objection no longer holds in its original formulation because it has shifted to the hierarchy of priorities that each democratic state, in view of its sovereignty, chooses as the ends of its political action.

From the point of view of obligations, therefore, the combination of negative and positive duties is analogous to that of negative and positive rights. And that is so because every member of a given state has a negative general duty not to harm anybody else's security as well as to refrain from contributing through his

---

[4] See Guariglia (1992: 23–33; 1996: 173–4), Gewirth (1996: 51–2), Fabre (1998: 267–8), and O'Neill (2000: 29–49, 137–8).

or her own actions to worsen the already precarious situation of those who are worst off. (This may be done through works that degrade the quality of water or soil or by corrupt practices that will contribute to the decline of services provided by the state in its various fields.) Besides, everyone must fulfill a special positive duty of contributing to the upkeep of the State according to his or her relative income. This will allow the state to have the resources necessary to ensure the security of the population as well as to provide for the basic needs of the worse off. Before we proceed with the analysis of one of the crucial issues connected to the enforcement of economic and social rights, namely the role to be fulfilled in this task by the different powers of the State, there is something we must note. Up to now, I have only considered what, following the Kantian distinction, we can term *perfect duties*, which are mutually related to the rights binding citizens within a particular State and vice versa. The more controversial issue about the existence of *imperfect duties* connected to economic and social rights will be dealt with later. In my opinion, these duties imply two essential features: (*a*) the active participation of every citizen in the public sphere in order to promote the actual fulfillment by governments of economic and social rights; and (*b*) each one's responsibility for the satisfaction of basic needs beyond national boundaries.

14.5. DUTY-BEARERS AND THE ENFORCEMENT OF RIGHTS

We must now cope with another complex topic, entailed by the fulfillment and actual enforcement of economic and social rights. I am referring to the need to determine the primary duty-bearers who are responsible for fulfilling this category of human rights. There is no doubt that the primary duty-bearer is the State on its various levels, from the broadest—national or federal—to regional, provincial, municipal, or communal levels. In fact, we can posit the existence of special duties that concern governments and political agents of the State as correlative to general positive rights held by every inhabitant of a country, although the object and magnitude of such rights can scarcely be established legally and taking them to courts of justice is a difficult matter. This latter point poses one of the toughest obstacles for the enforcement of such rights. The difficulty may be asserted as follows: What happens when national, provincial, or municipal governments cease to satisfy basic demands, be it through corruption, negligence, or sheer impossibility? The first response to the question is to examine if and how there is a judicial procedure appropriate for taking the case to court whenever and wherever rights-bearers are being deprived of the substance of their rights.

I refer to a particularly acute example relating to the current situation in Argentina. I allude, specifically, to the demand that the State should provide unemployment insurance to all citizens who cannot find either temporary or stable employment. This right, stipulated in Article 9 of the *ICESR*, was included in the *Constitution of the Argentine Republic* in 1994. Although it has been part of the Constitution since that date, no legislative measure has been taken to enforce it, either in periods of crisis, such as the current one, or during times when the State was reasonably affluent. Why is it that in situations like the one mentioned it is not possible to force a state by judicial means to fulfill the obligations agreed on in international covenants? Needless to say, the usual objection to such a demand points at the impossibility of seeing to the needs of a large percentage of the population (between 18 and 20%) plagued by unemployment. And furthermore, the scarce fiscal resources of the federal government must be used to comply with other, previously undertaken obligations. It is also objected that, if judges were to determine priorities in the distribution of budgetary resources, we would face a situation incompatible with a democratic state. It would not be the elected representatives in the Executive Branch or Congress, but the judges, not directly chosen by the citizens, who would claim for themselves the competency to establish the goals of social policy.

A possible reply to this objection is connected to a feature of the relation between rights and duties mentioned above. As has been rightly observed, duties associated with certain rights do not come singly but in waves, that is, they are interconnected (Waldron 1989: 509–11). Therefore, granting judges competence to warn the other two powers about the existence of unfulfilled positive duties, which the State is committed to through international covenants, and to assert that carrying out that duty is linked to the actual enforcement of other duties—to abstain from spending or cutting taxes for purely electoral purposes, for example—is in no way synonymous with substituting democratic political agency by a tyranny of the judges. Judges would in fact be confined to the non-political task of setting restrictions on the powers enjoyed by the other two Branches. Thus, judges would be limited to establishing the priority of the goals to be attained in accordance with the Constitution, rather than having the capacity to set other priorities, which would remain within the sphere of politicians.

In broad terms, my thesis runs as follows: satisfying socioeconomic rights, as positive rights of citizens, necessarily entails a restriction on those in power politically with respect to the distribution of fiscal resources and, generally speaking, the economic policy of the state. There are prior social goals that must be met before any others—such as, say, tax cuts on profits or total exemptions from income tax—that politicians may have included in their programs. In more abstract terms, this means that the interrelatedness of duties we mentioned above generates a definite consequence for public policy. Its implication may be stated as follows: the first obligation of those charged with special positive duties to see to the satisfaction of the social and economic rights of citizens, is to *refrain from taking any measure that will presumably worsen the existing, and already precarious, situation of the worst-off.* In this way, just as negative citizens' rights create supplementary positive rights—namely, the preservation of the life and integrity of persons—and public officials' special positive duties, so we now have the opposite figure. Citizens' positive rights give rise to supplementary negative citizen rights, which are correlative with the specific negative duties of those in power, particularly in the economy. Such duties include halting any economic or social action that will cancel the exercise of positive rights by a large majority of citizens, aggravating already bad situations. On account of their very nature, these supplementary negative duties are more likely to be considered justiciable by a tribunal, with appropriate expert advice. The tribunal should deal with those cases in which there is an overall impoverishment of a population or in which it is predictable that there will be a sudden worsening of life conditions such as those caused by huge financial deals, embezzlement of social security funds, and the like.

Finally, what has been said above shows how both kinds of rights—the civil and political ones as well as the economic and social variety—are closely and inseparably linked. A demand for the actual fulfillment of economic rights by the executive or legislative powers can only be put forward if it is backed by an independent judiciary that will see to the protection of civil rights. These include, among others, the rights of free association, the right to petition and demand for the protection of rights, and the right to hold and express opinions and to inform the public about the existence of situations of extreme poverty or destitution in a given country, region, or province. Summing up, the actual enforcement of social and economic rights must not be used, as is often the case, as an excuse for overlooking compliance with an active protection of civil and political rights. On the contrary, it presumes that both kinds of rights are necessarily fulfilled and must be simultaneously respected.

14.6. IMPERFECT DUTIES

As stated above, up to now I have been referring to perfect duties, negative and positive, and in particular to those concerning political positions and judges within a given state. This description of the problems connected to economic and social rights would not be complete, however, if I did not address, all too briefly, the more general and diffuse responsibilities that may normally be ascribed to all the members of a political society. These duties concern the respect for rights within one's own state and, in the case of citizens of rich countries, they concern their duty to contribute to the alleviation of situations of poverty and destitution in poor countries. This issue of duties beyond borders has been widely discussed of late, particularly after the publication of John Rawls's lecture and subsequent book, *The Law of Peoples*. In my opinion, what is being argued here has two different dimensions according to whether the starting point chosen is that of the individual members of a given national state, on one hand, or their national representatives among other countries in the community of nations, on the other. For the sake of brevity, I concentrate exclusively on the first case and steer clear of the technicalities that complicate the second.

First, it is convenient to explain why I term these duties 'imperfect', in accordance with Kant's distinction in the *Metaphysics of Morals* between legal duties and purely moral ones regarding others. In fact, when we strive to establish precisely who must be legally responsible for failure in meeting the economic rights of citizens, we are actually trying to attribute primary responsibility to government officials whether in the executive branch or legislators. The purpose of this ascription is to make sure that each official's political agenda will be subject to the kind of legal control that will warn him that he must refrain from carrying out a given policy if it is detrimental to protecting internationally established and covenanted human rights. None of this is either possible or advisable in the case of common citizens, removed from government or judicial functions. At the other extreme, we should not label the actions of common citizens aimed at the fulfillment of economic and social rights exclusively as 'supererogatory acts of beneficence'. On the contrary, such actions, in my view, should be considered morally obligatory *actions* and omitting to do them would count as an indisputable moral flaw (O'Neill 2000: 136–42). I describe two cases which I classify as instances of imperfect duties borne by all the members of a society: (*a*) within the boundaries of their own country; and (*b*) as citizens of the more developed countries in regards to less developed ones. Since my purpose is to prove the existence of these imperfect duties, I have selected those that I deem minimum duties.

14.6.1. Duties within Developing Countries

One of the most pernicious consequences of a country's lack of social and economic development is the constant decline in educational achievement. This entails a consequent fall in the capabilities that would allow a significant sector of the population to join the labor market with greater opportunities. In turn, this fosters the conditions that will turn a large percentage of the population into a permanently unemployed mass of people. In the absence of a system of unemployment insurance and training to sustain them, they will unavoidably depend for their survival on the gifts granted by the political elite in power. That is how a web of clientelism is spun. Its maintenance requires drawing on fresh funds outside the legally sanctioned budget and this dependence in turn demands a parallel network of negotiations where bribe-money often flows. In this way, corruption seeps into all social structures, including those at the center of political power, and carries in its wake two regrettable consequences for the enforcement of human rights in a country. On one hand, the political party that has come to power through this client system becomes so strong that it turns into a hegemonic party, practically unbeatable in democratic elections. On the other hand, it disrupts the principle of equality for all citizens, since those closer to power shall have privileges that place them beyond any sort of competition with others on the basis of merit, efficiency, honesty, and so forth. Consequently, the political regime gradually becomes less of an open and transparent democracy and turns into some sort of plebiscite oligarchy.

Such a situation, fairly common in developing countries, imposes a broad duty on its citizens, who may avail themselves of a wide array of actions. They range from the purely negative act of turning down any demand for bribes in their relations with the various departments of public administration up to the forthrightly positive action of demanding that every governmental action be publicly accountable, and publicly exposing any witnessed instance of corruption. In view of the fact that in this kind of situation individual action is normally ineffective, a positive action like the one we have just described will naturally lead to new ways of association between citizens in order to challenge and denounce public officials. Such citizen actions will not be limited to controlling the administration but will also be capable of forcing the government to open up to debate on the priorities established by its policies. The imperfect duty of eradicating corruption will thus turn gradually from a purely negative duty to a positive one of widening and deepening the quality of the political regime until it becomes a deliberative democracy.

14.6.2. Duties within Developed Countries

It has lately been asserted that neither economic and social rights nor the duties they impose are restricted by the boundaries of the national state in the midst of a world where all sorts of transnational agents are at work: corporations, financial markets, the IMF, the Internet, migrations, and so forth (O'Neill 2000: 115–19; Pogge 2002a: 91 f.). In fact, on one side the power of the national state has gradually decreased in the face of external factors, ever more oppressive and demanding. On the other, as national frontiers have become more and more blurred, the effects of political, commercial, and financial decisions taken in some of the centers of power of the developed world have an immediate and frequently fateful impact on developing countries. In not a few cases, their aftermath gives rise to real humanitarian catastrophes. Nevertheless, it is not my intention to shift the entire burden of responsibility for the fulfillment and enforcement of economic and social rights in poorer countries to the citizens of the richer nations. Several governments of the former have frequently done precisely that in order to water down or evade their own responsibility and that of their agents and businessmen in the face of the critical woes that plague their population. That notwithstanding, it is impossible to overlook the minimal duties that may be attributed to the elites and citizens of developed countries with respect to the fulfillment of human rights in developing countries and poorer nations.

Again, these duties do not concern in the same way those who occupy positions of power, be it political or economic, and mere citizens. In the first place, the greatest contribution that political and financial leaders and businessmen in the developed world can make is also, albeit at the international level, to *refrain from taking any measure that will presumably worsen the existing, and already precarious, situation of the worst off.* Should this maxim be followed, a wide range of measures would automatically be discontinued on account of their proven deleterious impact on both developing countries and the poorest nations on the planet. A case in point would be the maintenance of trade barriers and subsidies applied by the European Union, the United States, and Japan in order to protect their own farmers. Such protectionism causes an artificial decrease in the price of those goods in world markets thus condemning producers in poorer countries to perpetual poverty.[5] A long list of similar examples could be added, such as those reported by Joseph Stiglitz in his recent book on globalization (Stiglitz 2002: 196–206). But the case of rich-country protectionism should suffice to illustrate my main point: that, applied to governments of the developed countries, the suggested maxim (not to take measures that worsen the situation of the worst off) has significant implications that, in special cases like this, are tantamount to a perfect duty not to harm.

Focusing on the greater potential contribution that leaders of the developed world could make by following this negative maxim also indicates a path for plain citizens in developed countries to become conscious of their own responsibility. After all, it is they who choose their representatives to carry out such selfish and exclusive policies. In this case too, the aim of a wide duty that no human being can overlook is to contribute to enlighten a society lulled by its own well-being, so that it will not be deceived about the cost that such well-being imposes on poorer nations.

14.7. ENFORCEMENT OF SOCIOECONOMIC RIGHTS AT THE INTERNATIONAL LEVEL

Finally, as purely moral obligations are insufficient where there is strong resistance against any reform that will entail a relative loss in benefits, an effective enforcement of economic and social human rights should include the possibility of an international regulation of financial and commercial relations. It is important to note that whereas pursuant to the 1976 *Optional Protocol* to the *International Covenant on Civil and Political Rights*, the Human Rights Committee has been vested with the authority to hear individual claims of violations by states accepting this protocol of any right set forth in the *ICCPR*, there is no equivalent enforcement mechanism in relation to the rights enshrined in the *International Covenant on Economic, Social and Cultural Rights*. The idea of establishing a similar type of body in relation to these latter rights has generated significant controversy in contemporary human rights discussion. To further stress the asymmetry between these categories of rights, the International Criminal Court, created by the 1998 Rome Treaty, attributes individual criminal responsibility in cases that entail serious violations of certain civil and political rights. An international tribunal focused on the defense of social and economic rights should not, however, be

---

[5] See A. Toumani Touré and B. Compaoré, 'Your Farm Subsidies Are Strangling Us', *New York Times*, July 11, 2003.

primarily oriented toward penal law. Rather, it should control, and eventually sanction states or international unions and corporations that violate those rights or fail to enforce the enactment of such rights within reasonable periods of time. Financial and commercial relations would then be subjected to a normative accountability at an international level. Judges would be able to settle disputes impartially, with the greatest possible independence from the power of the parties involved.

14.8. CONCLUSION

In conclusion, I have merely tried to indicate the problems that come up when economic and social rights are seriously examined from a *weak cosmopolitan* perspective. I have suggested some of the potential solutions that may be posited for them to be appropriately enforced, without weakening in any way their status as human rights. This argument makes it imperative to overcome national boundaries and think open-mindedly about the world at large, in spite of the present darkness of its political and economic situation.

15

The Right of Resistance in Situations of Severe Deprivation

Roberto Gargarella

Since the end of the 1990s, and following a decade of severe economic programs of structural adjustment, Latin America has experienced numerous popular revolts. These revolts involved massive popular manifestations over a period, and high levels of verbal and physical aggression against politicians, judges, and public officers in general. The protests included, for example, picketers blocking the traffic on national or state highways demanding employment, food, or subsidies, and noisy demonstrations or 'cacerolazos' (pots and pans demonstrations). Aggressive action aimed at public authorities reached their homes and properties, and also the public buildings where they work (government offices, the legislatures, and the courts). Among other things, these protests forced the resignation of President Raúl Cubas in Paraguay, in 1999, President Alberto Fujimori in Peru, in 2000, President Jail Mahuad in Ecuador, in 2000 (as well as the removal of President Abdala Bucaram, in 1996); President Sánchez de Lozada in Bolivia, in 2002, and President Bertrand Aristide in Haiti, in 2004. In Argentina, these protests culminated in a profound crisis that saw five different presidents in office in less than two weeks. Of course, these protests were triggered by different circumstances. Some of them were more legitimate than others; some were more 'spontaneous' or 'genuine' than others; some were more powerful and enduring than others. However, all these differences should not prevent us from recognizing the similarities that united these events, similarities that reflect the type of crisis that is affecting many contemporary legal orders.

15.1. INTRODUCTION

The premise according to which poverty is a human rights violation is powerful and carries with it powerful implications. In this chapter I want to explore some of these implications, with regard to the idea of law. The question that guides my work is whether those who have to live in conditions of severe and systematic poverty have a duty to obey the law. For them, the law has not been a means for gaining freedom or achieving self-government but rather, more often than not, an instrument that has decisively contributed to their oppression. As a consequence—we should wonder—is it justifiable for them to challenge and even to resist the law?

These claims may sound radical at the present time, although surprisingly or not they represented the common sense among legal thinkers during hundreds of years. Taking this fact into account, I first examine this long-standing legal tradition that connected severe violations of basic human interests with the right of resistance. I then explore whether it may yet be reasonable to maintain that assumption. I want to examine this topic out of the conviction that all of us, and particularly those interested in the protection of human rights, should rethink both about the purposes of having a legal order and about our immediate moral duties to the most disadvantaged. My analysis may also be helpful to test, in an exercise of 'reflective equilibrium', the strength of our adherence to the premise of this anthology.

15.2. A MISSING RIGHT

One of the striking notes of contemporary constitutionalism is the lack of discussion around the right of resistance, which was deemed one of the main concepts of constitutionalism for almost four centuries. The idea of resisting the authority of government has been an important object of study to all those interested in philosophical problems of politics and jurisprudence, at least since the Middle Ages. Such reflections upon resistance took on special significance during the Reformation, the successive confrontations between Roman Catholics and Protestant reformers, and above all, the ensuing possibility that religious duties were in deep tension with duties of obedience to political power (Linder 1966: 125–6). Notably, and by dint of being consistent with their reasoning, authors coming from rigid conservative backgrounds started to tear open their own dogmas. Who, they wondered, should we obey if political authority eventually ceases to coincide with the religious authority? On the other hand, and step by step, many authors began to challenge the extraordinarily influential teachings of St Paul on the people's unconditional duties of obedience;[1] St Augustine's claims that rulers should be respected as God's representatives even if they did not fulfil their political duties properly; and particularly, as time went by, even important sectors of Lutheran doctrine, which backed the power of absolute monarchies, founding it on the people's inability to recognize God's mandates.[2] Thus, the idea of resistance to

---

[1] In Romans 13, St Paul famously wrote that 'we should obey the powers that be [because] they are ordained of God and that whosoever resisteth the power resisteth the ordinance of God, and they that shall resist shall receive to themselves eternal damnation'.

[2] It is important to emphasize, however, the significant theoretical developments that took place within Lutheranism itself, which helped to gradually undermine its apparently solid structures. These developments were launched by studies such as those carried out by Philip de Hesse at the beginning of the XVIth Century. Then, Hesse advanced interesting reflections about the Lutheran notion according

authority grew until it arrived at a central place within constitutionalism by the end of the eighteenth century.

By that time, thanks to John Locke, resistance to authority appeared as one of the four ideas that, I think, distinguished constitutionalism. Thus, the idea of resistance tended to appear together with the concept of the inalienable character of certain basic rights; the idea that authority was legitimate as long as it rested on the consensus of the governed; and the idea that the first duty of any government was to protect the inalienable rights of the people. In such a context, it was held, the people could legitimately resist and finally overthrow the government in the event it did not give due respect to those basic rights.[3]

Remarkably, these four constitutional principles, all of them founded on the basic idea of the essential equality of all individuals, were later adopted by the two great revolutions of the eighteenth century, the American and the French revolutions. They were first picked up by Thomas Jefferson and incorporated almost unmodified into the American *Declaration of Independence*, written in 1776. Strictly following Locke, the *Declaration* stated its adherence to the following 'self-evident truths':

... [T]hat all men are created equal, that they are endowed by their Creator with certain unalienable Rights, that among these are Life, Liberty and the pursuit of Happiness. That to secure these rights, Governments are instituted among Men, deriving their just powers from the consent of the governed, that whenever any Form of Government becomes destructive of these ends, it is the Right of the People to alter or to abolish it, and to institute new Government, laying its foundation on such principles and organizing its powers in such form, as to them shall seem most likely to effect their Safety and Happiness.

The *Declaration of the Rights of Men*, passed by the French National Assembly on August 26, 1789, followed the previous example closely. Thus, for instance, it proclaimed the existence of 'natural, imprescriptible, and inalienable rights'; it asserted the basic equality and freedom of each person (Article 1); and held that the main object of all political association was to preserve the imprescriptible and natural rights of man, which are the rights to 'freedom, property, security, and resistance to oppression' (Article 2). The popularity of the idea of resistance reached many new independent nations, some of which decided to include it into the text of their new Constitutions.

---

to which all powers derived from God; about the possibility that the Emperor achieved an alliance with the Catholic majority; and about the unexpected case that it became necessary to resist its authority through the use of force. Other jurists of the Lutheran formation, such as Martin Bucer, emphasized the duties of magistrates in the defense of Lutheran religion, and denied the Emperor's capacity to rule according to his discretionary will and against the needs of the people. In such extreme cases, Bucer affirmed, inferior magistrates could not be expected to obey the commands of the sovereign.

[3] Locke developed these ideas in his polemic with Robert Filmer's work, and *Patriarcha* in particular, where Filmer defended a 'patriarchal' view of power. According to this view, the king was authorized to exercise his power without attending to the will of the people, as the father could with his children (Filmer 1991).

15.3. LEGAL ALIENATION AND THE JUSTIFICATION OF THE RIGHT OF RESISTANCE

During the many centuries when it was alive, the right of resistance was defended by theorists with different backgrounds and different ideals. All of them, however, seemed to share a common assumption, namely that resistance becomes defensible in what I will call situations of *legal alienation*. In situations of legal alienation, the law begins to serve purposes contrary to those that, in the end, justify its existence.[4] This is what most of the defenders of the right of resistance seemed to claim by asserting, in different ways, that the norms that were supposed to guarantee the people's liberty and welfare, were working against the people's fundamental interests.

Of course, there were many different readings—many different conceptions— of this implicit concept of legal alienation. Originally, some authors focused their analysis on the offenses committed against the people's objective interests, *substantive reasons*, while in modern times *procedural reasons* acquired more significance at the time of defining the concept of legal alienation. Among the first defenders of the right of resistance, natural law theorists like Francisco Suárez justified tyrannicide out of the principle that 'force may be met with force' and the conviction that the State needed to be preserved (Copleston 1963; Hamilton 1963). At the bottom of both claims was the assumption that 'the state, as a whole, is superior to the king, for the state, when it granted him his power, is held to have granted it upon these conditions: that he should govern in accord with the public weal, and not tyrannically; and that, if he did not govern thus, he might be deposed from that position of power' (Suárez 1944: 855). In other words, for people like Suárez legal alienation meant a situation where the ruler used his powers against the basic interests of the people that he was supposed to serve. It must be noted, however, that for Suárez, as for the majority of the Thomist theologians, the possibility of resisting the tyrannical behavior of a ruler of legitimate origin was subject to the previous authorization of superior religious authorities (Copleston 1963: 61–3; Hamilton 1963: 220–2). Only they could certify that the ruler's actions were unacceptably offensive.

Most other theorists in the Middle Ages adhered to similar principles. For the Swiss Pierre Viret, a personal friend of Calvin and considerably influential in France, resistance to power was justified for religious reasons as much as for social and economic injustices committed against the people on the part of the ruler (Linder 1966). The Scottish Calvinists justified resistance through still more radical claims (Rueger 1964; Skinner 1978: vol. 2). John Ponet, for example,

---

[4] This notion of alienation—a notion of alienation that is objective rather than subjective—is related to the one defended by Karl Marx, e.g., in his analysis of work and its products. According to Marx, 'the object that labor produces, its product, confronts it as an alien being, as a power independent of the producer ... [the] externalization of the worker in his product implies not only that his labour becomes an object, an exterior existence but also that it exists outside him, independent and alien, and becomes a self-sufficient power opposite him, that the life that he has lent to the object affronts him, hostile and alien ... the worker becomes a slave to his object' (2000: 86–7).

considered that there existed a duty (and not simply a right) to resist anytime the sovereign betrayed his country, or committed any kind of abuse of his position. For Christopher Goodman, resistance was justified in all those situations in which rulers became the oppressors of their people. Rulers, held Goodman, had not been placed in their privileged position to act according to their judgment, but *to act in benefit of their subjects*. That is why, he concluded, when rulers violated their duties they became equal to any other citizen, and could be resisted by any of their peers.[5] Again, in most of these cases among Calvinists, the right of resistance depends on the finding of severe offenses, which had to be previously so defined by the main religious authorities.[6]

John Locke's justification of the right of resistance was undoubtedly based on these antecedents. However, in his view, the concept of legal alienation seemed more clearly related to the betrayal of the people's will. The people's acquiescence, their *tacit consent*, implied their approval of the government, as their rebellion manifested that the government was beginning to act abusively. Locke spoke, thus, of 'a long train of abuses', an idea that was later directly incorporated into the American *Declaration of Independence*, related to the tyrannical and capricious use of power. More specifically, Locke referred to situations where the government promised one thing and did the opposite, used chicanery to elude the law, or employed its unique powers against the welfare of its people—situations where arbitrary actions followed one after another (Dunn 1969: 179; Locke 1988: II. 225). In such cases, he assumed—and these are the final lines of his *Second Treatise on Government*—'the People have a Right to act as Supreme, and continue the Legislative in themselves, or erect a new Form, or under the old form place in the new hands, as they think good' (1988: II. 243). Now, the people, acting collectively, spontaneously and extra-institutionally, had the final say regarding the rulers' violation of basic human interests.

At the time of the American Revolution, the justification of the right of resistance acquired its more robust form, combining substantive and procedural reasons. Resistance was justified, on the one hand, out of the commission of substantive harms—harms that, it was assumed in this case, the people could identify and discuss collectively. The long list of 'grievances' included in the *Declaration of Independence* illustrates the types of harms I am considering here, and the way in which they were collectively addressed. Not surprisingly, here the most serious grievances seemed to be the violation of basic procedural rights derived from

---

[5] In a similar sense, Georges Buchanan held that the power that the people had yielded at one time could be retaken at any other: to do so was not to go against the institution of the king, but against the person that coincidentally filled that position at the moment (Rueger 1964).

[6] John Mair, e.g., connected the overthrow of the sovereign with a duty of prudence that he left in the hands of the highest spheres of society: without their careful deliberation, there was the risk that such a serious decision was the result of the mere passions of the few. Jacques Almain held a similar position (Skinner 1978: vol. 2). However, it is also true that this elitist epistemology began to change toward the end of the sixteenth century, particularly through the work of some of the Scottish Calvinists. People like John Knox, for example, began to defend a different position, more closely associated with philosophical anarchism than with philosophical elitism. Now, every person had a more significant role in defining whether substantive offenses were present (Knox 1994).

the people's basic right to self-government. Violating the people's right to self-government, the British put all the Americans' human rights under serious risk. Thus, the *Declaration* faulted the British authorities for offenses such as not having approved (or having prevented the approval of) laws necessary for general welfare, having offended the representative bodies, having obstructed the performance of justice, having fostered dependency in the judiciary, having created a multitude of unnecessary positions, having privileged military power over civil power, having set taxes without the consent of the people, and having deprived the people of the benefits of a jury. These were all demands that the people presented and defended during the revolutionary years, and that the British government systematically ignored. The British authorities were faulted for the dramatic deterioration of the Americans' welfare. Preventing the locals from taking control over their own affairs, they had transformed the law into an instrument of oppression, rather than an instrument of freedom. The people were thus becoming the victims of the very legal order that was supposed to serve the improvement of their lives. This was, again, a dramatic case of legal alienation that came to justify direct challenges to the law.

During those years, Thomas Jefferson developed one of the most interesting views on the topic, which he made explicit not only in his draft of the *Declaration of Independence*, but also and most importantly, in other writings and letters where he clarified the view of self-government that lay behind his defense of a right of resistance. His notion of a *self-governing republic* appeared as the opposite of what we called a situation of legal alienation.[7] A self-governing republic meant, in his view, 'purely and simply ... a government by its citizens in mass, acting directly and personally, according to rules created by the majority'. For him, governments were '*more or less republican, as they have more or less of the element of popular election and control in their composition*' (Jefferson 1999, emphasis added). Self-government, then, implied a situation where the community was able to decide in all the things that mattered to it, through representatives that it chose and controlled. In situations where self-government was denied, resistance appeared to be justified. Jefferson's preference for a self-governing republic became also apparent in his defense of 'external' or 'popular' controls over 'internal' ones; in his proposal for calling a popular convention each time it were necessary to correct breaches of the Constitution (a proposal that Madison fiercely criticized in *Federalist Paper*, no. 49); or in his repeated criticisms of the judiciary and its final interpretative powers.[8] In the end, and through these debates, Jefferson as well as other early modern constitutionalists were defining the necessary conditions for a legal system to be worthy of respect. The concluding idea seemed to be that the legal order was not worthy of respect when its norms inflicted severe offenses on the members of the legal community—substantive condition—and were not

---

[7] Exploring alienation and self-government as opposite concepts, see Elster (1985).

[8] Thus, e.g., in his letter to judge Spence Roane, September 6, 1819, he claimed that the Constitution could become 'a mere thing of wax in the hands of the judiciary, which they may twist and shape into any form they please' (Jefferson 1999: 379).

the result of a process in which that same legal community was meaningfully involved—procedural condition. *When these substantive and procedural conditions were present, resistance was in principle justified.*[9]

15.4. LEGAL ALIENATION TODAY: FROM THE RIGHT TO RESISTANCE TO CIVIL DISOBEDIENCE

After centuries of being one of the key concepts of constitutionalism, the idea of resistance virtually disappeared from our political and legal discourses.[10] There are many factors that may help us explain this disappearance, and I only refer to some of them.

Within contemporary democratic regimes, the idea of resistance seems to be less possible, practically speaking, and less reasonable. This seems to be so, among other reasons, as a consequence of some dramatic changes that took place in the last two centuries. First of all, political power seems to be far more atomized now than centuries ago. Of course, decentralization of power does not preclude the emergence of situations of political oppression. However, even when oppression exists, the sources of domination tend to be multiple and dispersed, which make resistance more difficult. The question is, whom should the deprived fault for their misery: The police who prevent them from acceding to food and shelter? The capitalists who do not guarantee their right to work? The local authorities who do not satisfy their needs? Their inactive representatives at the national Congress? The judges who dismiss their claims? The situation was very different, centuries ago, when all political power was concentrated in one single powerful figure—the king or the tyrant—and the people had the chance of easily identifying who was responsible for their suffering. Now, the fact that power has become decentralized not only makes political oppression less visible, but also makes it less conceivable to overcome it. Centuries ago, the oppressed had the illusion that a single heroic act allowed them to completely change their destiny and facilitate the birth of a new regime. For good or for bad, this illusion certainly has now disappeared.

Another important factor that distinguishes the present from the past concerns the fragmentation of society, which mirrors the existing fragmentation of political power. Most contemporary societies are divided into numerous groups, some of which are better off than others. This fragmentation makes resistance less

---

[9] One could maintain that the presence of only one of these conditions should be sufficient to declare the legal system illegitimate. However, as I explain later, both conditions tend to go together: e.g., the fact that certain rights are systematically violated (i.e. when certain groups have been systematically deprived of food and shelter) tends to be an indication that the other condition is also present.

[10] Contemporarily, we find obvious examples of situations of legal alienation in dictatorial governments, which still abound around the globe. Facing these terrible threats, many modern Constitutions have incorporated specific clauses calling for a right of resistance in case a military coup occurs. The cases in which I am interested, however, are those related to democratic regimes (I here assume a minimalist notion of democracy [Dahl 1989]).

conceivable because now there are groups that, first, do not suffer from oppression and, consequently, tend to counteract and block any attempt at rebellion by the oppressed. Centuries ago, we may reasonably assume, political oppression affected the entire society, or at least large sections of it, which made it thinkable for a rebellious movement to gather active or passive support from the majority of society.

The previous factors mainly refer to the possibility conditions of the right of resistance, and help us understand why resistance is less imaginable or feasible today than before. However, these factors say very little about whether it could be justified to engage in an act of resistance. In other words, we still have not explored whether what seemed to justify resistance, namely legal alienation, continues to be a distinctive factor in present societies. Now, some of the crucial innovations that democracy brought with it may move us to think that some fundamental changes have definitively been introduced in our institutional system, making resistance totally unreasonable.

First of all, the present institutional organization, which among many other things includes the division of power among different branches of government and systems of checks and balances, reduces the risk that the law becomes oppressive. In addition, and equally significant, this system includes numerous tools for facilitating or promoting peaceful and ordained political changes, even radical ones. The mechanism of periodical elections, in particular, seems to be decisive in this discussion, signaling a crucial difference between our time and the time when resistance was a key political concept. Some time ago, the right of resistance was the only mechanism available for making the authorities in power accountable, and to prevent political abuses. As John Locke maintained, the right of resistance was simply the only instrument in the hands of the people to avoid excesses on the part of the rulers. Resistance was seen, then, as the opposite of the ordinary positioning of the people with respect to the government, which consisted of a mix of passivity and *tacit consent* (Seliger 1991: 603). From this perspective, the coming of periodic elections seems to make all the difference: in fact, where would be the sense in using physical force to overthrow or eliminate an abusive ruler when it is possible to displace him by the force of votes?

We can advance similar considerations regarding the mechanisms for constitutional reform that we find in all modern constitutions. Through these mechanisms, in effect, each community has the chance of radically reviewing the merits of the entire system of government. Considering this extreme possibility, it is reasonable to ask ourselves, again, about the sense of resorting to a violent mobilization of the population to achieve ends that can be achieved much less dramatically through a civilized constitutional assembly.

The coming of these new political possibilities makes the disappearance of the right of resistance more understandable. Now, it is assumed, legal integration, rather than legal alienation, widely prevails. Legal integration would also explain why in present times we began to think about *civil disobedience* or *conscientious objection* as the most extreme forms of challenging the law. In effect, and according to the most common definitions of civil disobedience and conscientious objection, those who get involved in these actions are willing to suffer the penalties that the law reserved for their actions, because even they, as objectors, accept the general validity of law. In other words, these acts of disobedience came only to question very specific aspects of the law, rather than the law as a whole, which is considered worth obeying.[11] As a consequence of these changes, the law should no longer be considered (and it is not generally considered) a mere instrument of oppression. We may occasionally be in fundamental disagreement with some of its specific dispositions, but we generally recognize its value and importance. We assume that we are *legally integrated*, rather than legally alienated, even if, occasionally, we radically oppose some particularities of the law.

15.5. LEGAL ALIENATION IN SITUATIONS OF SEVERE DEPRIVATION

In spite of what was suggested in section 15.4, there still seems to be ample space between situations of complete legal alienation and situations of complete legal integration. In this sense, both the right to civil disobedience and the right to object to a particular law by reasons of conscience may be unable to cover other, more dramatic situations that characterize contemporary societies. The limits of these new rights become clearer when we think about situations where *certain specific groups* (although not the entire society, as it could have happened centuries ago) face systematic difficulties regarding the *law as a whole* (and not simply regarding certain specifics of the law, as it happens in situations of civil disobedience or conscientious objection). It should not surprise anybody that there are still groups that face serious problems satisfying their most basic needs, problems making their viewpoints available to others, problems successfully demanding the introduction of changes to the law, problems reproaching their representatives for their actions and omissions, etc. The situation these individuals face seems to be

---

[11] According to a rather standard definition of civil disobedience, given once by Hugo Bedau (1961). In his opinion, 'Anyone commits an act of civil disobedience if and only if he acts illegally, publicly, non-violently, and conscientiously with the intent to frustrate (one of) the laws, policies, or decisions of his government'. Authors like John Rawls—who rely on the classical analysis by H. Bedau for their definitions of civil disobedience—hold that civil disobedience 'arises only within a more or less just democratic state for those citizens who *recognize and accept the legitimacy of the constitution*' (Rawls 1999a: 319, my italics). It is because of this acknowledgment that those who get involved in civil disobedience (or conscientious objection) actions are willing to suffer the penalties law has in store for them—there is an ultimate acceptance of the general validity of law, which is questioned only in some specific respect (Cohen 1972). The differences between these cases of civil disobedience and those under examination here are, therefore, significant. Conceptual distances are even wider if what we compare are these cases of resistance with conscientious refusal. According to John Rawls, conscientious refusal implies 'noncompliance with a more or less direct legal injunction or administrative order' (Rawls 1999a: 323). Unlike the case of civil disobedience, there is no appeal here to the community's convictions of justice, but to the individual's. There is no attempt in this case (at least primarily) to call upon 'the majority's sense of justice', or to act, necessarily, from political principles (Rawls 1999a: 324).

far graver, in depth and width, than that faced by conscientious objectors or civil disobedients. The philosopher John Rawls, for example, admits this possibility in his analysis of civil disobedience. For him, there are groups that, given the dire circumstances in which they live, have reasons to believe that the legal order is severely unjust, or that it 'depart[s] ... widely from its own professed ideals'.[12] For them, it seems reasonable to advance 'a more profound opposition to the legal order'. This is so, as Rawls affirmed, because 'to employ the coercive apparatus of the state in order to maintain manifestly unjust institutions is itself a form of illegitimate force that men in due course have a right to resist' (Rawls 1999a: 342).

Now, although we may all agree, at a very general level, upon the existence of situations of extreme socio-legal exclusion, we may find problems reaching agreement on how precisely to characterize these situations or define the group of those marginalized by society and its legal norms. This lack of agreement is certainly troublesome, because it makes it more difficult for us to think thoroughly about issues of the utmost importance, related to the law and social exclusions. However, we could make some (provisional) progress in this discussion if we accept (as I propose we accept) one among the different 'objective' standards that have been proposed for defining situations of extreme social exclusion, such as the international poverty line. This line refers to 'that income or expenditure level below which a minimum nutritionally adequate diet plus essential non-food requirements are not affordable'.[13] This metric would be significant for our purposes, given that the presence of situations of severe poverty would signal to us the existence of both 'massive underfulfillment of social and economic human rights' and 'underfulfillment of civil and political human rights associated with democratic government and the rule of law' (Pogge 2001b: 8, 2002a).[14]

Taking this (or a similar) metric seriously, we should be able to presume that those systematically deprived of certain basic human goods are living in a situation of legal alienation. The reasons that would justify this presumption reside in the presence of substantive and procedural conditions such as those that modern constitutionalists found as constitutive of situations of legal alienation. Clearly, those who have been systematically deprived of an adequate shelter, those who suffer from hunger, those who experience systematic violence, and so on, face the most

---

[12] Rawls advances these opinions when reflecting on what he calls 'militant action[s]', to which he refers in his study of civil disobedience. For him, a 'militant action ... is not within the bounds of fidelity to law, but represents a more profound opposition to the legal order. The basic structure is thought to be ... unjust or else to depart ... widely from its own professed ideals' (Rawls 1999a: 322–3).

[13] I take this definition, proposed by the UNDP in 1996, from Pogge (2001b: 7).

[14] Alternatively, we could also accept Martha Nussbaum and Amartya Sen's approach about human capabilities and examine the situation of those groups that fall below the threshold of what they call basic human capabilities. The capability approach that they propose is interesting, among other reasons, because it provides us with a useful metric, which may also function as a meeting point for different normative theories concerned with these issues (Nussbaum 2000). According to this analysis, '[if] people are *systematically falling below the threshold in any of* [*the included*]*core areas*, this should be seen as a situation both unjust and tragic, in need of urgent attention—even if in other respects things are going well' (71, emphasis added).

serious grievances a person may face (substantive condition). At the same time, these offences, and particularly their systematic character, point to the existence of grave procedural deficiencies—deficiencies that belong to an institutional system that proves to be incapable of repairing the existing evils. In these situations it is very difficult not to fault the law for what has happened and continues to happen to members of the most disadvantaged groups. Remember that these disadvantaged groups are deprived of goods that, as philosophers such as Amartya Sen, Martha Nussbaum, and John Rawls affirmed, are basic for every possible life plan, and consequently irrational to reject. Then, the fact that they have been systematically excluded from the enjoyment of these goods appears to be an indication of persistent and grave institutional failures (procedural condition). In fact, these systematic offences tell us that the affected groups are experiencing serious political problems either in transmitting their demands to their representatives, or in making them accountable for their faults. Moreover, the persistent difficulties that they face point towards the grave judicial problems that they confront, both in acceding to the judiciary and in forcing judges to guarantee their violated basic rights. In this situation, we may conclude, the law is either blind to these people's deprivations, deaf to their main claims, or unwilling to remedy the humiliations that they suffer. In this sense, the law can be made responsible for the deprivations that these groups suffer—responsible as a result of its actions, its omissions, or both. As Amartya Sen and Jean Drèze have put it, in their work on hunger:

When millions of people die in famine, it is hard to avoid the thought that something terribly criminal is going on. The law, which defines and protects our rights as citizens, must somehow be compromised by these dreadful events. Unfortunately, the gap between law and ethics can be a big one. The economic system that yields a famine may be foul and the political system that tolerates it perfectly revolting, but nevertheless there may be no violation of our lawfully recognized rights in the failure of large sections of the population to acquire enough food to survive. The point is not so much that there is no law against dying of hunger. That is, of course, true and obvious. It is more that the legally guaranteed rights of ownership, exchange and transaction delineate economic systems that can go hand in hand with some people failing to acquire enough food for survival. (Dréze and Sen 1989: 20)

15.6. THE RIGHT OF RESISTANCE REVISITED

In previous pages I have maintained that those who suffer from systematic and severe poverty could be listed among those who live in a situation of legal alienation. Then, if we accept the teachings of the legal theorists that preceded us, we should be able to conclude that these disadvantaged groups have no general duty to obey the law, because the legal order affords them no protection against the severe harms they are suffering and often even sanctions the imposition of these harms. Insofar as the law is causally and morally implicated in their suffering, certain forms of resistance to the law should in principle be morally permissible to them.

Now, what forms of resistance should be deemed acceptable? Let me distinguish between two types of resistance, which I call *passive resistance* or non-cooperation, and *active resistance* or confrontation. The former refers to omissions to act in the way prescribed by the State (a refusal to comply with its commands), while the latter refers to actions that challenge certain legal prohibitions. I propose that both forms of resistance (which are obviously associated) should be prima facie admissible. First of all, the oppressed are morally free to disobey those orders that tend to reinforce their situation of oppression. Of course, in many cases we will disagree regarding 'what causes what': some will consider that certain laws do not affect the fundamental interests of the disadvantaged, while some others will maintain that there are no laws that, directly or indirectly, do not contribute to the suffering of the least favored. Yet there are certain 'clear cases' with which we can start our analysis. Think for example about the attitudes of the first colonists in America, who refused to pay taxes that they deemed unjust and that were not the product of their creation (a clear case of what we called legal alienation). In a similar way, I believe, the oppressed of our time could decide not to support a tax system that they have not designed and that, in addition, disfavors them. Similarly—and only to include an additional example—the disadvantaged could decide not to take part in the military and expansionist projects promoted by the state (i.e., refusing to serve as soldiers in those initiatives). Why should they so serve? Black victims of severe racism in the United States, during World War I, for example—offered their lives to the state when public authorities had systematically ignored their most basic interests and claims?

Second, the oppressed should be able to defy existing legal prohibitions, when these challenges could reasonably serve to put an end to their extreme suffering. For example, and only to illustrate this claim, we could say that the disadvantaged should be able to occupy empty lands, or use unused property in order to ensure their family and themselves the basic rights (in this case, food and shelter) that the state is not guaranteeing.[15] Similarly, they should be able to explore non-traditional venues of protest (e.g., block traffic in national or state avenues in support of their demands for employment or food, as many disadvantaged groups do in Latin America), in order to force the State to attend to their fundamental interests—interests, again, that the state has been systematically ignoring.

Now, there are a few points that I would like to mention to support these claims and begin to justify their scope and limits. Let me refer to these points.

First of all, I would mention one point about causality. The general presumption that we accepted in favor of all those who fall below the threshold of a certain level of welfare (a presumption according to which this deprivation is provoked by the prevailing legal order) should be open to revision. On many occasions it would be unreasonable to fault the state for the misery of the most disadvantaged.

---

[15] We find a contemporary example of this type of active resistance in the actions of the *Landless Workers' Movement (MST)* in Brazil.

Most importantly, it may well happen that the state finds no better alternative at its disposal for ensuring that no groups are systematically deprived of certain basic goods. If this is the case, the state should not be considered unjust, and its commands should not be resisted. In addition, it may happen that certain groups fall below the minimum threshold of well-being exclusively through their fault (i.e., as a result of their obsession with gambling), while having good alternative options at their disposal. It is a different question how we should act in all these cases (i.e., whether we should yet do all that is possible to ensure the satisfaction of the basic needs of these individuals). Taking into account these considerations, it may be reasonable to qualify the above-mentioned presumption, considering it a *general but refutable presumption*.

Second, there is an issue about mutual respect. The idea is that even if the state were responsible for the extreme suffering of the disadvantaged, this would not give the latter a carte blanche to act as they please against public authorities or other individuals. The fact that the disadvantaged groups are alienated from the law may indeed imply that, in principle, they have no duty to obey the legal order. However, this presumption would not exempt them from fulfilling certain basic duties with regard to others. We may call these basic duties of humanity (related to what John Rawls called 'natural duties', [1999*a*: §§19, 51]), which are non-legal moral duties, associated with the ideas of respect and reciprocity (these moral duties, of course, may overlap with some legal duties, e.g., in the case of murder).[16]

Third, there is the question of linkage. The question is that those lacking basic human goods have fewer reasons to cooperate with the law in those areas directly linked to the disadvantages that they suffer. That is to say, it may be reasonable for them not to pay the taxes that will be used to maintain a legal order that works to their disadvantage, but unreasonable to cross a street with a red light, when doing so has no relation to the injury they have suffered at the hands of the State.

Fourth, there is an issue of proportionality. Already, most legal systems refuse to punish those who steal food for their own consumption, when they are on the verge of starvation. The above discussion could justify other more significant breaches of the law (e.g., the occupation of unused land or houses) in similarly extreme cases. However, this reconceptualization of the law should not prevent

---

[16] However, one should also take into account that the perpetuation of situations of extreme injustice within a society does not only speak about the responsibility of public authorities in the shaping of that situation. It must always be acknowledged that in normal circumstances the disgrace of certain groups is linked to the advantageous situations of most others. The latter may be directly or indirectly favored from that situation in many different ways, (e.g. by the low wages that they are allowed to pay, by the existence of a large group of unemployed that help them to maintain that structure of low wages, by the low taxes that they are allowed to pay, etc.). In addition, there are many things to be said about a collectivity that continues to vote in favor of politicians that do not take immediate steps for repairing the dramatic offenses that are still present in their society; and about a group of citizens that do not use their privileges to force the adoption of changes in favor of the most disadvantaged. Thomas Pogge analyses our collective responsibilities towards the maintenance of situations of severe poverty in the international context; see, e.g., Pogge (2001*b*: 14).

us from taking into consideration questions of proportionality. Typically, the decision to severely hurt someone who denies their right to occupy empty land, or the decision to destroy the shop from where they obtained food should be seen, in principle, as unjustifiable. The disgrace that they suffer does not justify their imposition of unnecessary sacrifices upon the rest of society. Their challenges to the law should harm others as little as possible.

15.7. A FEW LAST WORDS

In this last section, I want to address a few additional relevant questions. First of all, do these comments about the right of resistance say something regarding the cases with which we opened this work? Surely not much, given the need to refine our historical and political knowledge about each of the specific cases that were mentioned. However, even at this early stage of our analysis it should be possible to advance a few suggestions. Above all, I believe that our previous analysis encourages us to look at our cases differently. Thus, it might be said, we would be looking at them wrongly if we obsessively focused on the details of the different crises and ignored the complete social picture within which these crises took place. We would go wrong if we simply paid attention to the protesters' specific claims (e.g., their claims against a particular privatization process, or their claims against the banks), disregarding the institutional implication of those protests (i.e., their difficulties in promoting certain political changes through the use of legal means). We would also miss something important if we insisted on looking at the law from the perspective of well-integrated citizens, rather than from the viewpoint of the least advantaged (as John Rawls has suggested). Finally, we would act wrongly if we dismissed the worth of the protests as a consequence of the 'evil' or self-interested motivations of some of their leaders, ignoring the fact that there are also legitimate interests at stake, which are seriously and systematically affected.

Second, after having seen the consequences of classifying severe poverty as a human rights violation—consequences that may include the right to resist the law—should we still think that severe poverty should, under certain conditions, be so classified? I believe so. In confidently answering in this way, I follow John Locke's and Thomas Jefferson's healthy attitude of *trust* toward their fellow citizens—an attitude that was associated, in both cases, with their egalitarian assumptions about human nature. I do not hesitate to give an affirmative answer to the question posed because, like Locke and Jefferson, I do not share the view that considers all violations of the law as if they were performed by individuals who simply want to take advantage of others' efforts. In sum, I do not believe that, after recognizing the people's right to disobey the law in situations of severe poverty, the people will start doing what they do not have a (moral) right to do. To the contrary, I believe, with Locke, that if the government were sincerely committed to respecting the people's rights, the latter would tend to recognize and honor these efforts (Locke 1988: II. 225).[17] Also with Locke, I believe that the people are 'more disposed to suffer' than to engage themselves in acts of rebellion against the government (Locke 1988: II. 230). Similarly, I share Jefferson's view on the topic, as expressed in the US *Declaration of Independence*, which maintains that 'all experience hath shown that mankind are more disposed to suffer, while evils are sufferable than to right themselves by abolishing the forms to which they are accustomed'. I believe that these empirical claims, which are temporally and culturally related claims, might still represent sound assumptions and good points of departure in our discussions on the topic.[18] It makes sense to begin such discussions assuming that those who live in situations of extreme poverty want, above all, to live with dignity (and not that they are mainly 'free riders' who use their situation of deprivation to obtain unfair advantages).

Because of the attitude of trust that distinguished their work (and also because they recognized that most people would do everything they could to become integrated to the legal order), both Locke and Jefferson looked at these actions of legal disruption with an open mind. Both of them understood these situations as signaling the profound deficiencies that characterized the political life of their communities and, as a result of that, they tried not to simply restrict themselves to condemning these breaches of the legal order. Jefferson, in particular, advanced this view at a time when there already existed institutional tools for peacefully promoting changes of the law. For him, these disruptions of the legal order were on the one hand unfortunate because of the costs they carried, but at the same time significant because they kept the government within its boundaries and citizens involved in the decisions of matters pertaining to them. In this sense, he described them as a 'medicine necessary for the sound health of the republic' (Jefferson 1999: 108).[19] Jefferson's argument in favor of the restriction of the use of the coercive state apparatus against those who resisted authority was then based on the public significance of such acts. This was due to the value of having good active citizens (and therefore the importance of not discouraging that activism by means of penalties), the need for keeping the government under constant criticism, and the need to have public officials accept the most thorough responsibility to the citizens.[20]

Of course, it has never been easy to follow authors like those examined in their discussions upon the limits of the law. On the one hand, it is likely that in the gravest situations, those where legal alienation is pervasive, the conditions

---

[17] According to Locke's analysis, it was conceivable that some 'turbulent spirit', eager to change the order of things, would become involved in a violent action against the government. But, as he foresaw, such cases tended to result in the adventurer's 'ruin and perdition' (Locke 1988: 417–8).

[18] Although it is still more important, as John Rawls claimed, to build a culture in which these attitudes are always true.

[19] Jefferson affirmed that these uprisings could occasionally be founded on barely acceptable reasons. But even so, he added, the reaction of the government must be measured: severe punishment was a real mistake, since it implied 'suppressing the only safeguard of public liberty' (1999: 153).

[20] In this sense, his view was similar to the one that Rawls defended in his analysis of civil disobedience. For him, civil disobedience 'is one of the stabilizing devices of a constitutional system' (1999a: 336, see also 337–8).

for individual and collective deliberation will be least likely to appear, given the lack of adequate collective forums and the extent to which money and political power can interfere with transparent public communication. On the other hand, the question of 'how the state should react' to these difficult issues is obviously problematic: could one reasonably 'propose' that state authorities adopt more respectful and open attitudes toward these problems, when they are supposed to be part of the problem? Nevertheless it is within this framework that we must operate. We know, at the very least, that the first legal theorists that reflected upon the issue of resistance, like many of our contemporaries reflecting on civil disobedience, recognized the possibility of these radical difficulties, and tried to develop at least tentative views on how to react in such cases. Today, we are again obliged to confront serious social difficulties. But we have an important advantage over our predecessors, which consists in their teachings and the theories they developed through all these centuries.

Bibliography

Aiken, Will and Hugh LaFolette (eds.) (1996). *World Hunger and Morality*. Upper Saddle River, NJ: Prentice Hall.

Alexy, Robert (1986). *Theorie der Grundrechte*. Frankfurt: Suhrkamp.

Alston, Philip (1997). 'Making Economic and Social Rights Count: A Strategy for the Future', *Political Quarterly*, 2: 188–95.

—— (ed.) (2005). *Non-State Actors and Human Rights*. Oxford: Oxford University Press.

Alston, Philip and James Crawford (eds.) (2000). *The Future of UN Human Rights Treaty Monitoring*. Cambridge: Cambridge University Press.

Anderson, Elizabeth (1999). 'What is the Point of Equality?', *Ethics*, 109: 287–337.

Ashford, Elizabeth (2000). 'Utilitarianism, Integrity and Partiality', *Journal of Philosophy*, 97: 421–39.

—— (2003). 'The Demandingness of Scanlon's Contractualism', *Ethics*, 113: 273–302.

Atkinson, Giles and Kirk Hamilton (2003). 'Savings, Growth and the Resource Curse Hypothesis', *World Development*, 31(11): 1793–807.

Austin, J. L. (1962). *How to Do Things with Words*. Oxford: Oxford University Press.

Baker, Raymond (2005). *Capitalism's Achilles Heel*. New York: John Wiley and Sons.

Barret, Scott (1999). 'Montreal versus Kyoto: International Cooperation and the Global Environment', in Kaul, Grunberg, and Stern (1999).

Barry, Brian (1989*a*). *Theories of Justice*. Berkeley and Los Angeles: University of California Press.

—— ([1982] 1989*b*). 'Humanity and Justice in Global Perspective', in *Democracy, Power and Justice: Essays in Political Theory*. Oxford: Clarendon Press.

—— (1995). *Justice As Impartiality*. Oxford: Clarendon Press.

—— (1998). 'International Society from a Cosmopolitan Perspective', in David Mapel and Terry Nardin (eds.), *International Society*. Princeton, NJ: Princeton University Press.

—— (1999). 'Statism and Nationalism: A Cosmopolitan Critique', in Ian Shapiro and Lea Brilmayer (eds.), *Nomos XLI: Global Justice*. New York: New York University Press.

Barry, Brian and Robert E. Goodin (eds.) (1992). *Free Movement: Ethical Issues in the Transnational Migration of People and of Money*. University Park, PA: Pennsylvania State University Press.

Barry, Christian and Thomas Pogge (eds.) (2005). *Global Institutions and Responsibilities: Achieving Global Justice*. Oxford: Blackwell Publishers.

Beattie, David (1994). 'The Last Generation: When Rights Lose Their Meaning', in David Beattie (ed.), *Human Rights and Judicial Review*. Martinus Nijhoff, pp. 321–61.

Bedau, Hugo (1961). 'On Civil Disobedience', *Journal of Philosophy*, 58: 653–65.

Beitz, Charles (1983). 'Cosmopolitan Ideals and National Sentiment', *Journal of Philosophy*, 80(10): 591–600.

—— (1989). *Political Equality*. Princeton, NJ: Princeton University Press.

—— (1999*a*). 'International Liberalism and Distributive Justice', *World Politics*, 51: 269–96.

—— (1999*b*). 'Social and Cosmopolitan Liberalism', *International Affairs*, 75(3): 515–19.

—— ([1979]1999*c*). *Political Theory and International Relations*, 2nd edn. with a new afterword. Princeton, NJ: Princeton University Press.

—— (2001). 'Rawls's Law of Peoples', *Ethics*, 110(4): 669–96.

Beitz, Charles (2004). 'Human Rights and the Law of Peoples', in Chatterjee (2004).

Beitz, Charles, Marshall Cohen, Thomas Scanlon, and John A. Simmons (eds.) (1985). *International Ethics*. Princeton, NJ: Princeton University Press.

Bennett, Jonathan (1995). *The Act Itself*. Oxford: Oxford University Press.

Berlin, Isaiah (1969). 'Two Concepts of Liberty', *Four Essays on Liberty*. Oxford: Oxford University Press.

Birdsall, Nancy and Robert Z. Lawrence (1999). 'Deep Integration and Trade Agreements', in Kaul, Grunberg, and Stern (1999).

Bittner, Rüdiger (2001). 'Morality and World Hunger', in Pogge (2001c).

Bottomley, Steven and David Kinley (eds.) (2002). *Commercial Law and Human Rights*. Aldershot, UK: Ashgate.

Brodnig, Gernot (2001). 'The World Bank and Human Rights: Mission Impossible?', The Carr Center for Human Rights Policy, Working Paper T-01-05, fletcher.tufts. edu/praxis/xvii/Brodnig.pdf

Brown, Chris (1992). *International Relations Theory*. New York: Harvester Wheatsheaf.

——(1993). 'International Affairs', in Robert E. Goodin and Philip Pettit (eds.), *A Companion to Contemporary Political Philosophy*. Oxford: Blackwell Publishers.

——(2000). 'John Rawls, "The Law of Peoples", and "International Political Theory"', *Ethics and International Affairs*, 14: 125–32.

Bruno, Michael, Martin Ravallion, and Lyn Squire (1998). 'Equity and Growth in Developing Countries: Old and New Perspectives on the Policy Issues', in Vito Tanzi and Ke-young Chu (eds.), *Income Distribution and High-quality Growth*. Cambridge, MA: The MIT Press.

Buchanan, Allen (1999). 'Recognitional Legitimacy and the State System', *Philosophy and Public Affairs*, 28(1): 46–78.

Bundesministerium für Arbeit und Sozialordnung (2001). *Lebenslagen in Deutschland*. (*Armuts und Reichtumsbericht der Bundesregierung*). Bonn, www.bma.bund.de/de/ sicherung/armutsbericht/ARBBericht01.pdf

Campbell, Tom (1974). 'Humanity before Justice', *British Journal of Political Science*, 4: 1–16.

——(2001). *Justice*, 2nd edn. London: Macmillan.

Caney, Simon (1996). 'Individuals, Nations and Obligations', in Simon Caney, David George, and Peter Jones (eds.), *National Rights, International Obligations*. Oxford: Westview Press.

——(1999). 'Nationality, Distributive Justice and the Use of Force', *Journal of Applied Philosophy*, 16(2): 123–38.

——(2000). 'Global Equality of Opportunity and the Sovereignty of States', in Tony Coates (ed.), *International Justice*. Aldershot, UK: Ashgate.

——(2001). 'Review Article: International Distributive Justice', *Political Studies*, 49(5): 974–97.

——(2002). 'Survey Article: Cosmopolitanism and the Law of Peoples', *Journal of Political Philosophy*, 10(1): 95–123.

——(2003). 'Entitlements, Obligations, and Distributive Justice: The Global Level', in Daniel Bell and Avner de-Shalit (eds.), *Forms of Justice: Critical Perspectives on David Miller's Political Philosophy*. Lanham, MD: Rowman and Littlefield.

——(2005a). *Justice Beyond Borders: A Global Political Theory*. Oxford: Oxford University Press.

——(2005b). 'Global Interdependence and Distributive Justice', *Review of International Studies*, 31(2): 389–99.

Center for the Study of Human Rights (1994). *Twenty-five Human Rights Documents*. New York: Columbia University.

Chatterjee, Deen (ed.) (2004). *The Ethics of Assistance: Morality and the Distant Needy*. Cambridge: Cambridge University Press.

Chauvier, Stéphane (1999). *Justice internationale et solidarité*. Nîmes, France: Jacqueline Chambon.

——— (2006). *Justice et droits à l'échelle globale*. Paris: Vrin/EHESS.

Chen, Shaohua and Martin Ravallion (2004). 'How Have the World's Poorest Fared since the Early 1980s?', *World Bank Research Observer*, 19: 141–69. Also at wbro.oupjournals. org/cgi/content/abstract/19/2/141

Chinkin, Christine (2001). 'The United Nation's Decade for the Elimination of Poverty: What Role for International Law?', in M. D. A. Freeman (ed.), *Current Legal Problems*, 54: 553–89.

Cohen, G. A. (1988). *History, Labour, and Freedom*. Oxford: Clarendon Press.

——— (1991). 'Capitalism, Freedom, and the Proletariat', in David Miller (ed.), *Liberty*. Oxford: Oxford University Press.

——— (1995). *Self-Ownership, Freedom and Equality*. Cambridge: Cambridge University Press and Paris: Maison des Sciences de l'Homme.

——— (2000). *If You're an Egalitarian, How Come You're so Rich?* Cambridge, MA: Harvard University Press.

Cohen, Marshall (1972). 'Liberalism and Disobedience', *Philosophy and Public Affairs*, 1(3): 283–314.

——— (1985). 'Moral Skepticism and International Relations', in Beitz, Cohen, Scanlon, and Simmons (1985).

Commission on Global Governance (1995). *Our Global Neighbourhood*. Oxford: Oxford University Press.

Copleston, Frederick (1963). *A History of Philosophy: The Revival of Platonism to Suárez*. New York: Image Books.

Correa, Carlos (2000). *Intellectual Property Rights, the WTO and Developing Countries: The TRIPs Agreement and Policy Options*. London: Zed Books.

Cranston, Maurice (1973). *What are Human Rights?*, 2nd edn. London: Bodley Head.

Craven, Matthew (1995). *The International Covenant on Economic, Social and Cultural Rights: A Perspective on Its Development*. Oxford: Oxford University Press.

Crocker, David (1998). *Florecimiento humano y desarrollo internacional*. San José: Editorial de la Universidad de Costa Rica.

Crocker, David and Toby Linden (eds.) (1998). *Ethics of Consumption: The Good Life, Justice, and Global Stewardship*. Lanham, MD: Rowman and Littlefield.

Cullity, Garrett (1994). 'International Aid and the Scope of Kindness', *Ethics*, 105(1): 99–127.

Dahl, Robert (1989). *Democracy and Its Critics*. New Haven, CT: Yale University Press.

Dankwa, Victor, Cees Flinterman, and Scott Leckie (1998). 'Commentary to the Maastricht Guidelines on Violations of Economic, Social and Cultural Rights', *Human Rights Quarterly*, 20(3): 705–30.

Dasgupta, Partha (1993). *An Inquiry into Well-Being and Destitution*. Oxford: Oxford University Press.

de Greiff, Pablo and Ciaran Cronin (eds.) (2002). *Global Justice and Transnational Politics: Essays on the Moral and Political Challenges of Globalization*. Cambridge, MA: The MIT Press.

de Vita, Álvaro (2000*a*). *A justiça igualitária e seus críticos*. São Paulo, Brazil: Editora Unesp-Fapesp.

de Vita, Álvaro (2000*b*). 'Individual Preferences and Social Justice', *Brazilian Review of Social Sciences*, special issue, 1: 95–109.

Devetak, Richard and Richard Higgott (1999). 'Justice Unbound? Globalization, States and the Transformation of the Social Bond', *International Affairs*, 75(3): 483–98.

Diamond, Jared (1999). *Guns, Germs, and Steel: The Fates of Human Societies*. New York: W. W. Norton & Company.

Diamond, Larry (1997). *The End of the Third Wave and the Global Future of Democracy*. Vienna: HIS.

Doyle, Michael (2000). 'Global Economic Inequalities: A Growing Gap', in Paul Kevin Wapner and Lester Edwin Ruiz (eds.), *Principled World Politics: The Challenge of Normative International Relations*. Lanham, MD: Rowman & Littlefield Publishers.

Drescher, Seymour (1986). *Capitalism and Antislavery: British Mobilization in Comparative Perspective*. Oxford: Oxford University Press.

Drèze, Jean and Amartya Sen (1989). *Hunger and Public Action*. Oxford: Clarendon.

_____ (eds.) (1991). *The Political Economy of Hunger*. Oxford: Oxford University Press.

Dunn, John (1969). *The Political Thought of John Locke*. Cambridge: Cambridge University Press.

Dworkin, Ronald (1977). *Taking Rights Seriously*. London: Duckworth.

_____ (1985). *A Matter of Principle*. Cambridge, MA: Harvard University Press.

_____ (1996). 'Objectivity and Truth: You'd Better Believe It', *Philosophy and Public Affairs*, 25: 87.

Eckstein, Zvi and Itzhak Zilcha (1994). 'The Effects of Compulsory Schooling on Growth, Income Distribution and Welfare', *Journal of Public Economics*, 54: 339–59.

Eichengreen, Barry, James Tobin, and Charles Wyplosz (1995). 'Two Cases for Sand in the Wheels of International Finance', *Economic Journal*, 105 (428): 162–72.

Eide, Asbjorn (1995). 'Economic, Social and Cultural Rights as Human Rights', in Eide, Krause, and Rosas (1995).

_____ Catarina Krause, and Allan Rosas (eds.) (1995). *Economic, Social and Cultural Rights: A Textbook*. Dordrecht, Netherland: Kluwer.

Elster, Jon (1985). *Making Sense of Marx*. Cambridge: Cambridge University Press.

Fabre, Cécile (1998). 'Constitutionalising Social Rights', *Journal of Political Philosophy*, 6: 263–84.

_____ (2000). *Social Rights Under the Constitution*. New York: Oxford University Press.

Feinberg, Joel (1970). 'The Nature and Value of Rights', *Journal of Value Inquiry*, 4: 254–6.

_____ (1973). *Social Philosophy*. Englewood Cliffs, NJ: Prentice Hall.

_____ (2003). 'In Defense of Moral Rights', *Problems at the Roots of Law: Essays in Legal and Political Theory*. Oxford: Oxford University Press.

FIAN (1998). 'Food First. Mit Menschenrechten gegen Hunger' Bonn, www.fian.org

Filmer, Robert (1991). *'Patriarcha' and Other Writings*, Jóhann P. Sommerville (ed.). Cambridge: Cambridge University Press.

Finger, J. Michael and Philip Schuler (1999). 'Implementation of Uruguay Round Commitments: The Development Challenge'. World Bank Research Working Paper 2215, econ.worldbank.org/docs/941.pdf

Fleurbaey, Marc (2001). 'Forced Trades in a Free Market', Mimeo: Université de Pau.

Fleurbaey, Marc and Francois Maniquet (2005). 'Compensation and Responsibility', in K. J. Arrow, Amartya Sen, and Kotaro Suzumura (eds.), *Handbook of Social Choice and Welfare*, 2. Amsterdam: Elsevier.

Follesdal, Andreas and Thomas Pogge (eds.) (2005). *Real World Justice: Grounds, Principles, Human Rights, and Social Institutions.* Dordrecht, Netherland: Springer.

Forst, Rainer (1999). 'The Basic Right to Justification: Towards a Constructivist Conception of Human Rights', *Constellations*, 6(1): 35–59.

Frankfurt, H. G. (1973). 'Coercion and Moral Responsibility', in Ted Honderich (ed.), *Essays on Freedom of Action.* London: Routledge & Kegan Paul.

Freedom House (2004). 'Democracy's Century: A Survey of Global Political Change in the Twentieth Century' at www.freedomhouse.org/reports/century.html

French, P. A. (1991). 'The Corporation As a Moral Person', in P. A. French (ed.), *The Spectrum of Responsibility.* New York: St. Martin's Press.

Friedman, Milton (1962). *Capitalism and Freedom.* Chicago, IL: University of Chicago Press.

Gallagher, Kevin (2000). 'World Income Inequality and the Poverty of Nations', in Frank Ackerman, Laurie Dougherty, Kevin Gallagher, and Neva Goodwin (eds.), *The Political Economy of Inequality.* Washington, DC: Island Press.

Gauthier, David (1986). *Morals by Agreement.* Oxford: Oxford University Press.

Geuss, Raymond (1997). 'Nietzsche and Morality', *European Journal of Philosophy*, 5: 1–20.

——— (2001a). *History and Illusion in Politics.* Cambridge: Cambridge University Press.

——— (2001b). *Public Goods, Private Goods.* Princeton, NJ: Princeton University Press.

——— (2003). 'Outside Ethics', *European Journal of Philosophy*, 11: 29–53.

Gewirth, Alan (1978). *Reason and Morality.* Chicago, IL: University of Chicago Press.

——— (1982). *Human Rights: Essays on Justification and Applications.* Chicago, IL: University of Chicago Press.

——— (1996). *The Community of Rights.* Chicago, IL: University of Chicago Press.

GFHR (Global Forum for Health Research) (2004). *10/90 Report on Health Research 2003–2004.* Geneva: Global Forum for Health Research 2004. Also at www. globaforumhealth.org/pages/index.asp

Gilpin, Robert (2001). *Global Political Economy. Understanding the International Economic Order.* Princeton, NJ: Princeton University Press.

Goodin, Robert (1988). 'What Is So Special about Our Fellow Countrymen?', *Ethics*, 98: 663–86.

——— (1992). 'Commentary: The Political Realism of Free Movement', in Barry and Goodin (1992).

Gosepath, Stefan (2002). 'Die globale Ausdehnung der Gerechtigkeit', in Reinold Schmücker and Ulrich Steinvorth (eds.), *Gerechtigkeit und Politik—Philosophische Perspektiven, Deutsche Zeitschrift für Philosophie, Sonderband* 3. Berlin: Akademie Verlag.

Gosepath, Stefan and Georg Lohmann (eds.) (1998). *Philosophie der Menschenrechte.* Frankfurt: Suhrkamp.

Green, Duncan and Matthew Griffith (2002). 'Globalization and Its Discontents', *International Affairs*, 78(1): 49–68.

Griffin, James (1986). *Well-Being: Its Meaning, Measurement, and Moral Importance.* Oxford: Clarendon Press.

——— (2001a). 'Discrepancies Between the Best Philosophical Account of Human Rights and the International Law of Human Rights', *Proceedings of the Aristotelian Society* CI: 1–28.

——— (2001b). 'First Steps in an Account of Human Rights', *European Journal of Philosophy*, 9: 306–27.

Guariglia, Osvaldo (1992). 'El concepto normativo de "persona" y los requisitos mínimos de justicia distributiva en una sociedad democrática', *Desarrollo Económico*, 32(125): 23–33.

Guariglia, Osvaldo (1995). *Universalismus und Neuaristotelismus in der zeitgenössischen Ethik*. Hildesheim, Zürich, and New York: George Olms (Philosophische Texte und Studien, Bd. 40).

_____ (1996). *Moralidad (Ética universalista y sujeto moral)*. Buenos Aires: Fondo de Cultura Económica.

_____ (2002). *Una ética para el siglo xxi: Ética y derechos humanos en un tiempo posmetafísico*. Buenos Aires and México: Fondo de Cultura Económica.

Günther, Klaus (2001). 'Rechtspluralismus und universaler Code der Legalität: Globalisierung als rechtstheoretisches Problem', in Klaus Günther and Lutz Wingert (eds.), *Die Öffentlichkeit der Vernunft und die Vernunft der Öffentlichkeiten: Festschrift für Jürgen Habermas*, Frankfurt: Suhrkamp.

Habermas, Jürgen (1996*a*). *Between Facts and Norms, Contribution to a Discourse Theory of Law and Democracy*. Oxford: Oxford University Press.

_____ (1996*b*). *Die Enbeziehung des Anderen*. Frankfurt: Suhrkamp.

_____ (2001). *The Postnational Constellation: Political Essays*. London: Polity Press.

Hamilton, Bernice (1963). *Political Thought in Sixteenth-Century Spain*. Oxford: Clarendon Press.

Harrison, Lawrence E. and Samuel P. Huntington (eds.) (2001). *Culture Matters: How Values Shape Human Progress*. New York: Basic Books.

Hasenclever, Andreas, Peter Mayer, and Volker Rittberger (2000). 'Is Distributive Justice a Necessary Condition for a High Level of Regime Robustness?', *Tübinger Arbeitspapiere zur Internationalen Politik und Friedensforschung*, paper number 36, www.uni-tuebingen.de/pol/taps/tap36.htm

Hayek, F. A. (1960). *The Constitution of Liberty*. London: Routledge and Kegan Paul.

Held, David, Anthony McGrew, David Goldblatt, and Jonathan Perraton (1999). *Global Transformations: Politics, Economics, Culture*. Stanford, CA: Stanford University Press.

Henkin, Louis (1989). 'International Human Rights As "Rights"', in Morton E. Winston (ed.), *The Philosophy of Human Rights*. San Diego, CA: Wadworth.

_____ (1990). *The Age of Rights*. New York: Columbia University Press.

Heredia, Carlos (1996). 'The World Bank and Poverty', in Peter Bosshard et al. (eds.), *Lending Credibility: New Mandates and Partnerships for the World Bank*. Washington, DC: World Wildlife Fund.

Hertel, Thomas W. and Will Martin (1999). 'Would Developing Countries Gain from Inclusion of Manufactures in the WTO Negotiations?', ideas.repec.org/p/gta/workpp/397.html

Hill, Ronald Paul, Robert M. Peterson, and Kanwalroop Kathy Dhanda (2001). 'Global Consumption and Distributive Justice: A Rawlsian Perspective', *Human Rights Quarterly*, 23: 171–87.

Hillemanns, C. F. (2003). 'UN Norms on the Responsibilities of Transnational Corporations and Other Business Enterprises with Regard to Human Rights', *German Law Journal*, 10: 1065–80. Also at www.germanlawjournal.com

Höffe, Otfried (1989). *Politische Gerechtigkeit, Grundlegung einer kritischen Philosophie von Recht und Staat*. Frankfurt: Suhrkamp.

Hohfeld, Wesley N. ([1913, 1917] 1964) . *Fundamental Legal Conceptions As Applied in Judicial Reasoning*. New Haven, CT: Yale University Press.

Holmes, Stephen and Cass Sunstein (1999). *The Cost of Rights: Why Liberty Depends on Taxes*. New York and London: W. W. Norton & Company.

Hunt, Paul (1996). *Reclaiming Social Rights*. Aldershot, UK: Dartmouth.

Hurrell, Andrew (2001). 'Global Inequality and International Institutions', in Pogge (2001*c*).

Hurrell, Andrew and Ngaire Woods (eds.) (1999). *Inequality, Globalization, and World Politics*. Oxford: Oxford University Press.

Iglesias Vila, Marisa (2004). 'Poverty and Humanity: Individual Duties and the Moral Point of View', www.giuri.unige.it/phd/paper/iglesias.pdf

Ignatieff, Michael (2003). *Rights As Politics and Idolatry (The University Center for Human Values Series)*. Princeton, NJ: Princeton University Press.

ILO (International Labor Organization) (2002). *A Future Without Child Labour*. Geneva: ILO. Also at www.ilo.org/public/english/standards/decl/publ/reports/report3.htm

IMF (International Monetary Fund) (1997). *World Economic Outlook*. Washington, DC.

International Covenant on Economic, Social and Cultural Rights (ICESCR), adopted by General Assembly resolution 2200A (XXI) of 16 December 1966, www.unhchr.ch/html/menu3/b/a_cescr.htm

International Law Commission (1996). 'UN Document A/CN.4/Sev.9/1996', www.un.org/law/ilc/reports/1996/96repfra.htm

Jackman, Martha (1992). 'Constitutional Rhetoric and Social Justice: Reflections on the Justiciability Debate', in Joel Bakan and D. Schneiderman (eds.), *Social Justice and the Constitution: Perspectives on a Social Union for Canada*. Ottowa: Carelton University Press.

James, Susan (2003). 'Rights As Enforceable Claims', *Proceedings of the Aristotelian Society*, CIII: 133–47.

Jefferson, Thomas (1999). *Political Writings*. Cambridge: Cambridge University Press.

Jones, Charles (1999). *Global Justice: Defending Cosmopolitanism*. Oxford: Oxford University Press.

Juma, Calestous (1999). 'Intellectual Property Rights and Globalization. Implications for Developing Countries'. Science, Technology and Innovation Discussion Paper No. 4, Harvard Center for International Development, www2.cid.harvard.edu/cidbiotech/dp/discuss4.pdf

Kant, Immanuel (1968*a*). 'Grundlegung zur Metaphysik der Sitten', *Kants Werke, Akademie Textausgabe*, IV. Berlin: Walter de Gruyter.

——(1968*b*). 'Metaphysik der Sitten', *Kants Werke, Akademie Textausgabe*, VI. Berlin: Walter de Gruyter.

Kapstein, Ethan (1999). 'Distributive Justice As an International Public Good', in Kaul, Grunberg, and Stern (1999).

Kaul, Inge, Isabelle Grunberg, and Marc Stern (eds.) (1999). *Global Public Goods: International Cooperation in the 21st Century*. Oxford: Oxford University Press.

Kersting, Wolfgang (1993). *Wohlgeordnete Freiheit (Immanuel Kants Rechts und Staatsphilosophie)*, 2nd edn. Frankfurt: Suhrkamp.

Knox, John (1994). *On Rebellion*. Cambridge: Cambridge University Press.

Koller, Peter (1998). 'Der Geltungsbereich der Menschenrechte', in Gosepath and Lohmann (1998).

Kolm, S. C. (1985). *Le contrat social libéral*. Paris: Presses Universitaires de France.

Krasner, Stephen (1999). *Sovereignty—Organized Hypocrisy*. Princeton, NJ: Princeton University Press.

Kreide, Regina (2005). 'Deliberation or Negotiation? Remarks on the Justice of Regional and Universal Rights Agreements', in Follesdal and Pogge (2005).

Künnemann, Rolf (2000). 'Neuere Entwicklung beim Recht auf Nahrung', in Gabriele von Arnim, Volkmar Deile, et al. (eds.), *Jahrbuch Menschenrechte*. Frankfurt: Suhrkamp.

Kuper, Andrew (2000). 'Rawlsian Global Justice: Beyond the Law of Peoples to a Cosmopolitan Law of Persons', *Political Theory*, 20(1): 38–52.

——(ed.) (2005). *Global Responsibilities. Who Must Deliver on Human Rights?* New York: Routledge.

Kuttner, Robert (1996). *Everything for Sale : The Virtues and Limits of Markets*. Chicago, IL: University of Chicago Press.

Laban, Raul and Federico Sturzenegger (1994). 'Distributional Conflict, Financial Adaptation, and Delayed Stabilizations', *Economics and Politics*, 6: 257–76.

Lam, Ricky and Leonard Wantchekon (1999). 'Dictatorships As a Political Dutch Disease', Working Paper 795, Yale University, www.nyarko.com/wantche1.pdf

Landes, David (1998). *The Wealth and Poverty of Nations: Why Some Are So Rich and Some So Poor*. New York: W. W. Norton & Company.

Langhammer, R. J. (2002). 'Halving Poverty by Doubling Aid: How Well Founded Is the Optimism of the World Bank?', Kiel Working Paper No. 1116, Kiel Institute for World Economics, Kiel, www.uni-kiel.de/ifw/homeeng.htm

Limburg Principles on the Implementation of the International Covenant on Economic, Social and Cultural Rights (1987). *Human Rights Quarterly*, 9: 122–34.

Linder, Robert (1966). 'Pierre Viret and the Sixteenth-Century French Protestant Revolutionary Tradition', *The Journal of Modern History*, 38(2): 125–37.

Linklater, Andrew (1999). 'The Evolving Spheres of International Justice', *International Affairs*, 75(3): 473–82.

Locke, John (1988). *Two Treatises of Government*, cited by volume and section. Cambridge: Cambridge University Press.

Luban, David (1985). 'Just War and Human Rights', in Beitz, Cohen, Scanlon, and Simmons (1985).

Lyons, Daniels (1975). 'Welcome Threats and Coercive Offers', *Philosophy*, 50: 425–36.

Maastricht Guidelines on Violations of Economic, Social and Cultural Rights (1998). *Human Rights Quarterly*, 20(3): 691–704.

MacIntyre, Alasdair (1984). *After Virtue: A Study in Moral Theory*, 2nd edn. Notre Dame, IN: University of Notre Dame Press.

Macpherson, C. B. (1973). *Democratic Theory*. Oxford: Oxford University Press.

Marshall, Thomas (1992). *Citizenship and Social Class*. London: Pluto Perspectives.

Marx, Karl ([1976] 2000). *Selected Writings*, 2nd edn., David McLellan (ed.). Oxford: Oxford University Press.

Massa Arzabe, Patricia Helena (2001). 'Human Rights: A New Paradigm', in Willem van Genugten, Camilio Perez-Bustillo, and Mary Robinson (eds.), *The Poverty of Rights: Human Rights and the Eradication of Poverty*. London and New York: Zed Books.

Milanovic, Branko (2001). 'World Income Inequality in the Second Half of the 20th Century', info.worldbank.org/etools/bspan/EventView.asp?EID=89

——(2002). 'True World Income Distribution, 1988 and 1993: First Calculation Based on Household Surveys Alone', *The Economic Journal* 112(1): 51–92. Also at www.blackwellpublishers.co.uk/specialarticles/ecoj50673.pdf

——(2005). *Worlds Apart: Measuring International and Global Inequality*. Princeton, NJ: Princeton University Press.

Miller, David (1995). *On Nationality*. Oxford: Clarendon Press.

——(1998). 'The Limits of Cosmopolitan Justice', in David Mapel and Terry Nardin (eds.), *International Society*. Princeton, NJ: Princeton University Press.

——(1999). 'Justice and Global Inequality', in Hurrell and Woods (1999).

——(2000). *Citizenship and National Identity*. Cambridge: Polity Press.

Moellendorf, Darrell (2002). *Cosmopolitan Justice*. Oxford: Westview Press.

Muguerza, Javier (1989). 'La alternativa del disenso (en torno a la fundamentación ética de los derechos humanos)', in de G. Peces-Barba (ed.), *El fundamento de los derechos humanos*. Madrid: Debate, pp. 19–56.

Murphy, Liam (1998). 'Institutions and the Demands of Justice', *Philosophy and Public Affairs*, 27(4): 251–91.

—— (2000). *Moral Demands in Nonideal Theory*. Oxford: Oxford University Press.

Nagel, Thomas (1977). 'Poverty and Food: Why Charity Is Not Enough', in P. G. Brown and Henry Shue (eds.), *Food Policy*. New York: Free Press.

—— (1979). *Mortal Questions*. Cambridge: Cambridge University Press.

—— (1997). *The Last Word*. Oxford: Oxford University Press.

—— (2002). 'Personal Rights and Public Space', in *Concealment and Exposure & Other Essays*. Oxford: Oxford University Press.

Nickel, James (1987). *Making Sense of Human Rights*. Berkeley, CA: University of California Press. Also at homepages.law.asu.edu/~jnickel/msohr%20welcome.htm

—— (1996). 'A Human Rights Approach to World Hunger', in Aiken and LaFollette (1996).

Nino, Carlos (1989). *Ética y derechos humanos*, 2nd edn. Buenos Aires: Astrea.

Nolan, Brian and Christopher Whelan (1996). *Resources, Deprivation and Poverty*. Oxford: Oxford University Press.

Nozick, Robert (1969). 'Coercion', in Sidney Morgenbesser, Patrick Suppes, and Morton White (eds.), *Philosophy, Science, and Method: Essays in Honor of Ernest Nagel*. New York: St Martin's Press.

—— (1974). *Anarchy, State, and Utopia*. New York: Basic Books.

Nussbaum, Martha (1996). 'Patriotism and Cosmopolitanism', in Joshua Cohen (ed.), *Nussbaum with Respondents, For Love of Country: Debating the Limits of Patriotism*. Boston, MA: Beacon Press.

—— (2000). *Women and Human Development*. Cambridge: Cambridge University Press.

—— (2002). 'Capabilities and Human Rights', in de Greiff and Cronin (2002), pp. 117–49.

Nussbaum, Martha and Amartya K. Sen (eds.) (1993). *The Quality of Life*. Oxford: Oxford University Press.

Okin, S. M. (2003). 'Poverty, Well-being, and Gender: What Counts, Who's Heard?', *Philosophy and Public Affairs*, 31.

Olsaretti, Serena (1998). 'Freedom, Force and Choice: Against the Rights-based Definition of Voluntariness', *The Journal of Political Philosophy*, 6: 53–78.

O'Neill, Onora (1985). 'Lifeboat Earth', in Beitz, Cohen, Scanlon, and Simmons (1985).

—— (1986). *Faces of Hunger: An Essay on Poverty, Justice and Development*. London: Allen and Unwin.

—— (1989). *Constructions of Reason: Explorations of Kant's Practical Philosophy*. Cambridge: Cambridge University Press.

—— (1996). *Towards Justice and Virtue: A Constructive Account of Practical Reasoning*. Cambridge: Cambridge University Press.

—— (2000). *Bounds of Justice*. Cambridge: Cambridge University Press.

—— (2001). 'Agents of Justice', *Metaphilosophy*, 32(1–2): 180–95.

—— (2002). *Autonomy and Trust in Bioethics*. Cambridge: Cambridge University Press.

Opeskin, Brian (1996). 'The Moral Foundations of Foreign Aid', *World Development*, 24(1): 21–44.

Oxfam G. B. (1999). 'Time for a Tobin Tax? Some Practical and Political Arguments', Policy Paper, May (1999), www.oxfam.org.uk/what_we_do/issues/ trade/trade_tobintax.htm

Paech, Norman and Gerhard Stuby (2001). *Völkerrecht und Machtpolitik in den internationalen Beziehungen*. Hamburg: VSA-Verlag.

Paes de Barros, Ricardo, Ricardo Henriques, and Rosane Mendonça (2000). 'Pobreza e desigualdade no Brasil: retrato de uma estabilidade inaceitável', *Revista Brasileira de Ciências Sociais*, 15(42): 123–42.

Paine, Thomas (2000). 'Agrarian Justice', in Vallentyne and Steiner (2000), pp. 81–97.

Pande, Rohini (2003). 'Can Mandated Political Representation Increase Policy Influence for Disadvantaged Minorities? Theory and Evidence from India', *American Economic Review*, 93(4): 1132–51.

Parfit, Derek (1984). *Reasons and Persons*. Oxford: Oxford University Press.

——(2000). 'Equality or Priority', in Matthew Clayton and Andrew Williams (eds.), *The Ideal of Equality*. London: Macmillan.

Paterson, Matthew (2001). 'Principles of Justice in the Context of Global Climate Change', in Urs Luterbacher and Detlef Sprinz (eds.), *International Relations and Global Climate Change* (*Global Environmental Accord: Strategies for Sustainability and Institutional Innovation*). Cambridge, MA: The MIT Press.

Perraton, Jonathon, David Goldblatt, David Held, and Anthony McGrew (1998). 'Die Globalisierung der Wirtschaft', in Ulrich Beck (ed.), *Politik der Globalisierung*. Frankfurt: Suhrkamp.

Persson, Torsten and Guido Tabellini (1994). 'Is Inequality Harmful for Growth?', *American Economic Review*, 84: 600–21.

Peter, Fabienne (2004). 'Choice, Consent, and the Legitimacy of Market Transactions', *Economics and Philosophy*, 20(1): 1–18.

Peters, Bernhard (1993). *Die Integration moderner Gesellschaften*. Frankfurt: Suhrkamp.

Pogge, Thomas (1989). *Realizing Rawls*. Ithaca, NY: Cornell University Press.

——(1992a). 'An Institutional Approach to Humanitarian Intervention', *Public Affairs Quarterly*, 6(1): 89–103.

——(1992b). 'O'Neill on Rights and Duties', *Grazer Philosophische Studien*, 43: 233–47.

——(1994a). 'Uma Proposta de Reforma: Um Dividendo Global de Recursos', *Lua Nova*, 34: 135–61.

——(1994b). 'An Egalitarian Law of Peoples', *Philosophy and Public Affairs*, 23(3): 195–224.

——([1992] 1994c). 'Cosmopolitanism and Sovereignty', in Chris Brown (ed.), *Political Restructuring in Europe: Ethical Perspectives*. London: Routledge.

——(1995). 'How Should Human Rights be Conceived?', *Jahrbuch für Recht und Ethik*, 3: 103–20.

——(1998a). 'A Global Resources Dividend', in Crocker and Linden (1998).

——(1998b). 'The Bounds of Nationalism', in Jocelyne Couture et al. (eds.), *Rethinking Nationalism, Canadian Journal of Philosophy*, Supplementary Volume 22: 463–504.

——(1999). 'Human Flourishing and Universal Justice', *Social Philosophy and Policy*, 16(1): 333–61.

——(2000a). 'The International Significance of Human Rights', *The Journal of Ethics*. 4(1): 45–69.

——(2000b). 'On the Site of Distributive Justice: Reflections on Cohen and Murphy', *Philosophy and Public Affairs*, 29(2): 137–69.

——(2001a). 'Eradicating Systemic Poverty: Brief for a Global Resources Dividend', *Journal of Human Development*, 2(1): 59–77.

——(2001b). 'Priorities of Global Justice', in Pogge (2001c).

——(ed.) (2001c). *Global Justice*. Oxford: Blackwell Publishers.

_____ (2001*d*). 'Rawls on International Justice', *The Philosophical Quarterly*, 51(203): 246–53.

_____ (2002*a*). *World Poverty and Human Rights: Cosmopolitan Responsibilities and Reforms.* Cambridge: Polity Press.

_____ (2002*b*). 'Human Rights and Human Responsibilities', in de Greiff and Cronin (2002).

_____ (2004*a*). 'The First UN Millennium Development Goal: A Cause for Celebration?', *Journal of Human Development* 5(3): 377–97; reprinted in Follesdal and Pogge (2005).

_____ (2004*b*). 'The Incoherence between Rawls's Theories of Justice', *Fordham Law Review,* 72(5): 1739-59.

_____ (2005*a*). 'Real World Justice', *Journal of Ethics*, 9(1–2): 29–53.

_____ (2005*b*). 'Human Rights and Global Health: A Research Program', in Barry and Pogge (2005).

_____ (2005*c*). 'Severe Poverty As a Violation of Negative Duties', *Ethics and International Affairs*, 19(1): 55–84.

Quiggin, John (2001). 'Globalization and Economic Sovereignty', *The Journal of Political Philosophy*, 9(1): 56–80.

Rachels, James (1979). 'Killing and Starving to Death', *Philosophy*, 54: 159–71.

Ramsey, Sarah (2001). 'No Closure in Sight for the 10/90 Health-Research Gap', *Lancet*, 358: 1348.

Rashid, Ahmed (2002). *Jihad: The Rise of Militant Islam in Central Asia.* New Haven, CT: Yale University Press.

Ravallion, Martin (2002). 'How *Not* to Count the Poor? A Reply to Reddy and Pogge', www.socialanalysis.org

Raventós, Daniel (ed.) (2001). *La renta básica.* Barcelona: Ariel.

Rawls, John (1993*a*). *Political Liberalism.* New York: Columbia University Press.

_____ (1993*b*). 'The Law of Peoples', in Shute and Hurley (1993).

_____ ([1971] 1999*a*). *A Theory of Justice*, Revised edn. Oxford: Oxford University Press.

_____ (1999*b*). *The Law of Peoples: With 'The Idea of Public Reason Revisited'.* Cambridge, MA: Harvard University Press.

_____ (2001). *Justice As Fairness: A Restatement*, in Erin Kelly (ed.). Cambridge, MA: Harvard University Press.

Raz, Joseph (1984). 'On the Nature of Rights', *Mind*, 93(370): 194–214.

_____ (1986). *The Morality of Freedom.* Oxford: Oxford University Press.

Reddy, Sanjay and Thomas Pogge (2002) (August 15, 2002). 'How *Not* to Count the Poor! A Reply to Ravallion', www.socialanalysis.org

_____ _____ (2007). 'How *Not* to Count the Poor', in Sudhir Anand and Joseph Stiglitz (eds.), *Measuring Global Poverty.* Oxford: Oxford University Press. Also at www.socialanalysis.org

Richards, David (1982). 'International Distributive Justice', in J. R. Pennock and J. W. Chapman (eds.), *Nomos 24: Ethics, Economics and the Law.* New York: New York University Press.

Rodrik, Dani (1998). *The New Global Economy and Developing Countries: Making Openness Work.* Washington, DC: Overseas Development Council.

_____ (2000). 'Institutions for High-Quality Growth: What They Are and How to Acquire Them', *Studies in Comparative International Development*, 35(3): 3–31.

Roemer, John (2000). *Equality of Opportunity.* Cambridge, MA: Harvard University Press.

Rome Declaration on World Food Security (1996). www.fao.org/wfs

Rorty, Richard (1993). 'Human Rights, Rationality and Sentimentality', in Shute and Hurley (1993).

Rorty, Richard (1996). 'Who Are We? Moral Universalism and Economic Triage', *Diogenes*, 173: 5–15.

Rosas, Allan (1995). 'State Sovereignty and Human Rights: Towards a Global Constitutional Project', *Political Studies*, 43.

Ross, M. L. (1999). 'The Political Economy of the Resource Curse', *World Politics*, 51(2): 297–322.

——(2004). 'How Do Natural Resources Influence Civil War? Evidence from Thirteen Cases', *International Organization*, 58(1): 35–67.

Rousseau, Jean Jacques (1964). 'Du contrat social' in *Œuvres complètes*, t. III. Paris: Gallimard, 'Bibliothèque de la Pléiade'.

Rueger, Zofia (1964). 'Gerson, the Conciliar Movement and the Right of Resistance', *Journal of the History of Ideas*, 25(4): 467–86.

Sachs, Jeffrey (2005). *The End of Poverty: Economic Possibilities for Our Time*. New York: Penguin Press.

Sager, Lawrence (1978). 'Fair Measure: The Legal Status of Under Enforced Constitutional Norms', *Harvard Law Review*, 91: 1212–64.

Salomon, Margot (2003). 'Globalization of Responsibility: Interdependence and Cooperation in the Protection of Human Rights in International Law' PhD Dissertation London School of Economics and Political Science, December 2003.

Salomon, Margot and Arjun Sengupta (2003). 'The Right to Development: Obligations of States and the Rights of Minorities and Indigenous Peoples'. Minority Rights Group International.

Sané, Pierre (2003). 'Poverty, the Next Frontier in the Struggle for Human Rights', paper presented to an International Seminar on 'Poverty and Inequality in Brazil', Brasilia, 8–9 May 2003, p. 4.

Scanlon, Thomas (1982). 'Contractualism and Utilitarianism', in Amartya Sen and Bernard Williams (eds.), *Utilitarianism and Beyond*, Cambridge: Cambridge University Press.

——(1985). 'Rawls' Theory of Justice', in Norman Daniels (ed.), *Reading Rawls: Critical Studies of A Theory of Justice*. Oxford: Blackwell Publishers.

——(1998). *What We Owe to Each Other*. Cambridge, MA: Harvard University Press.

Scheffler, Samuel (1995). 'Individual Responsibility in a Global Age', *Social Philosophy and Policy*, 12 (1): 219–36.

——(2001). *Boundaries and Allegiances: Problems of Justice and Responsibility in Liberal Thought*. Oxford: Oxford University Press.

Scholte, Jan Aart (2000). *Globalization: A Critical Introduction*. New York: Palgrave.

Seliger, Martin (1991). 'Locke's Theory of Revolutionary Action', in Richard Ashcraft (ed.), *John Locke: Critical Assessments*, 3: 598–621. New York: Routledge.

Sen, Amartya (1981). *Poverty and Famines*. Oxford: Oxford University Press.

——(1984). 'The Right Not to be Hungry', in Philip Alston and Katerina Tomasevski (eds.), *The Right to Food*. Netherlands: SIM.

——(1985). 'The Moral Standing of the Market', *Social Philosophy and Policy*, 2:1–19.

——(1992). *Inequality Reexamined*. Cambridge, MA: Harvard University Press.

——(1993). 'Capability and Well-being', in Nussbaum and Sen (1993), pp. 30–53.

——(1995). 'Food, Economics, and Entitlements', in Jean Drèze, Amartya Sen, and Athar Hussain (eds.), *The Political Economy of Hunger: Selected Essays*. Oxford: Oxford University Press.

——(1999). *Development As Freedom*, New York: Alfred Knopf.

——(2000). 'Consequential Evaluation and Practical Reason', *The Journal of Philosophy*, 97(9): 477–502.

_____ (2003). 'Human Rights and Development', the paper presented at the Nobel Symposium on the Right to Development, Oslo, October 2003.

Sengupta, Arjun (1999). 'Reports to the Human Rights Commission at Geneva, As the Independent Expert on the Right to Development', Reference Number E/CN.4/1999/WG.18/2, 27 July 1999.

_____ (2000*a*). 'Realizing the Right to Development', *Development and Change*, 31(3): 553–78.

_____ (2000*b*). 'Reports to the Human Rights Commission at Geneva, As the Independent Expert on the Right to Development', Reference Number A/55/306, 17 August 2000.

_____ (2001). 'Reports to the Human Rights Commission at Geneva, As the Independent Expert on the Right to Development', Reference Number E/CN.4/2001/WG.18/2, 2 January 2001.

_____ (2002*a*). 'The Theory and Practice of the Right to Development', *The Human Rights Quarterly*, 24(4): 837–89.

_____ (2002*b*). 'Reports to the Human Rights Commission at Geneva, As the Independent Expert on the Right to Development', Reference Number E/CN.4/2002/WG.18/2, 20 December 2001.

_____ (2004). 'The Human Right to Development', *Oxford Development Studies*, 32(2): 179–203.

Sengupta, Arjun, Asbjorn Eide, Stephen Marks, and B. A. Andreassen (2003). 'The Right to Development and Human Rights in Development' presented in the Nobel Symposium, Oslo, October 2003.

Sethi, S. Prakash (2005). 'Corporate Codes of Conduct and the Success of Globalization', in Kuper (2005).

Shue, Henry (1983). 'The Burdens of Justice', *Journal of Philosophy*, 80(10): 600–08.

_____ (1988). 'Mediating Duties', *Ethics*, 98: 687–704.

_____ (1996*a*). *Basic Rights: Subsistence, Affluence, and U.S. Foreign Policy*, 2nd edn. Princeton, NJ: Princeton University Press.

_____ (1996*b*). 'Solidarity among Strangers and the Right to Food', in Aiken and Lafollette (1996), 113–32.

_____ (1997). 'Eroding Sovereignty: The Advance of Principle', in Robert McKim and Jeff McMahan (eds.), *The Morality of Nationalism*. Oxford: Oxford University Press.

_____ (1999). 'Global Environment and International Inequality', *International Affairs*, 75(3): 531–45.

Shute, Stephen and Susan Hurley (eds.) (1993). *On Human Rights: The Amnesty Lectures of 1993*. New York: Basic Books.

Singer, Peter (1972). 'Famine, Affluence, and Morality', *Philosophy and Public Affairs*, 1(3): 229–43.

_____ (1993). *Practical Ethics*, 2nd edn. Cambridge: Cambridge University Press.

_____ (2002). *One World: The Ethics of Globalization*. New Haven, CT: Yale University Press.

Skinner, Quentin (1978). *The Foundations of Modern Political Thought*, vol. 2. Cambridge: Cambridge University Press.

Skogly, Sigrun and Mark Gibney (2002). 'Transnational Human Rights Obligations', *Human Rights Quarterly*, 24: 781–98.

Smith, Adam ([1759] 1976). *The Theory of Moral Sentiments*, in D. D. Raphael and A. L. Macfie (eds.). Oxford: Clarendon Press.

Social Watch (2005). *Roars and Whispers. Gender and Poverty: Promises vs. Action*. Montevideo: Social Watch 2005.

Steger, Manfred (2002). *Globalism: The New Market Ideology*. Lanham, MD: Rowman and Littlefield.

Steiner, Henry and Philip Alston ([1996] 2000). *International Human Rights in Context: Law, Politics, Morals*, 2nd edn. Oxford: Oxford University Press.

Steiner, Hillel (1974–75). 'Individual Liberty', *Proceedings of the Aristotelian Society*, 75: 33–50.

—— (1987). 'Capitalism, Justice, and Equal Starts', *Social Philosophy and Policy*, 5: 49–71.

—— (1992). 'Libertarianism and the Transnational Migration of People', in Barry and Goodin (1992).

—— (1994). *An Essay on Rights*. Oxford: Blackwell Publishers.

Steinhardt, Ralph G. 'Corporate Responsibility and the International Law of Human Rights: The New Lex Mercatoria' in Alston (2005).

Steward, Frances and Albert Berry (1999). 'Globalization, Liberalization, and Inequality: Expectations and Experiences', in Hurrell and Woods (1999).

Stiglitz, Joseph E. (2002). *Globalization and Its Discontents*. New York: W. W. Norton & Company.

Suárez, Francisco (1944). *Selections from Three Works*. Oxford: Clarendon Press.

Tan, Kok-Chor (2000). *Toleration, Diversity, and Global Justice*. University Park, PA: Pennsylvania State University Press.

—— (2004). *Justice Without Borders: Cosmopolitanism, Nationalism and Patriotism*. Cambridge, Cambridge University Press.

Tasioulas, John (2002*a*). 'Human Rights, Universality and the Values of Personhood: Retracing Griffin's steps', *European Journal of Philosophy*, 10: 79–100.

—— (2002*b*). 'From Utopia to Kazanistan: John Rawls and the Law of Peoples', *Oxford Journal of Legal Studies*, 22: 367–96.

—— (2003). 'Mercy', *Proceedings of the Aristotelian Society*, CIII: 101–32.

—— (2005). 'Global Justice without End?', *Metaphilosophy*, 36(1–2): 3–29.

Taylor, Charles (1995). 'A Most Peculiar Institution', in J. E. J. Altham and Ross Harrison (eds.), *World, Mind, and Ethics: Essays on the Ethical Philosophy of Bernard Williams*. Cambridge: Cambridge University Press.

—— (2004). *Modern Social Imaginaries*. Durham and London: Duke University Press.

Tesón, Fernando (1995). 'The Rawlsian Theory of International Law', *Ethics and International Affairs*, 9: 79–99.

Tetzlaff, Rainer (1996). *Weltbank und Währungsfonds—Gestalter der Bretton-Woods-Ära*. Opladen, Germany: Leske and Budrich.

Thompson, Paul and Doug MacLean (eds.) (1992). *The Ethics of Trade and Aid: US Food Policy, Foreign Competition, and the Social Contract*. Cambridge: Cambridge University Press.

Thomson, J. Jarvis (1990). *The Realm of Rights*. Cambridge, MA: Harvard University Press.

Tobin, James (1978). 'A Proposal for International Monetary Reform', *Eastern Economic Journal*, 4(3–4): 1153–9.

Tugendhat, Ernst (1993). *Vorlesungen zur Ethik*. Frankfurt: Suhrkamp.

UDHR (Universal Declaration of Human Rights), approved and proclaimed by the General Assembly of the United Nations on 10 December 1948, as resolution 217 A (III).

UN Millennium Declaration, General Assembly Resolution 55/2, 2000, www.un.org/millennium/declaration/ares552e.htm

UNCTAD (United Nations Conference on Trade and Development) (1999*a*). *The Least Developed Countries Report 1999*. New York and Geneva: United Nations Publications.

—— (1999*b*). *Trade and Development Report 1999*. New York: United Nations Publications.

—— (2000). *The Least Developed Countries Report 2000*. New York and Geneva: United Nations Publications.

—— (2002*a*). *The Least Developed Countries Report 2002*. New York and Geneva: United Nations Publications.

—— (2002*b*). *Trade and Development Report 2002*. New York and Geneva: United Nations Publications.

UNDP (United Nations Development Program) (1996). *Human Development Report 1996*. New York: Oxford University Press.

—— (1998). *Human Development Report 1998*. New York: Oxford University Press. Also at hdr.undp.org/reports/global/1998/en

—— (1999). *Human Development Report 1999*. New York: Oxford University Press. Also at hdr.undp.org/reports/global/1999/en

—— (2000). *Human Development Report 2000*. New York: Oxford University Press.

—— (2001). *Human Development Report 2001*. New York: Oxford University Press. Also at hdr.undp.org/reports/global/2001/en

—— (2002). *Human Development Report 2002*. New York: Oxford University Press. Also at hdr.undp.org/reports/global/2002/en

—— (2003). *Human Development Report 2003*. New York: Oxford University Press. Also at hdr.undp.org/reports/global/2003

—— (2004). *Human Development Report 2004*. New York: UNDP. Also at hdr.undp.org/reports/global/2004

—— (2005). *Human Development Report 2005*. New York: UNDP. Also at hdr.undp.org/reports/global/2005

UNESCO (2003). 'Abolishing Poverty through the International Human Rights Framework: An Integrated Strategy', Working Paper.

Unger, Peter (1996). *Living High and Letting Die: Our Illusion of Innocence*. New York and Oxford: Oxford University Press.

Unger, Roberto (1998). *Democracy Realized: The Progressive Alternative*. London: Verso.

UNICEF (United Nations Children's Fund) (2005). *The State of the World's Children 2005*. New York: UNICEF. Also at www.unicef.org/publications/files/SOWC_2005_(English).pdf

United Nations (2003). 'Implementation of the United Nations Millennium Declaration. Report of the Secretary General', www.un.org

Universal Declaration of Human Rights, Approved and Proclaimed by the General Assembly of the United Nations on 10 December 1948, as resolution 217 A (III).

UNRISD (United Nations Research Institute for Social Development) (2005). *Gender Equality: Striving for Justice in an Unequal World*. Geneva: UNRISD/UN Publications. Also at www.unrisd.org

Vallentyne, Peter and Hillel Steiner (eds.) (2000). *The Origins of Left-Libertarianism*. Basingstoke: Palgrave.

van Parijs, Philippe (1995). *Real Freedom for All: What (if anything) Can Justify Capitalism?* Oxford: Clarendon Press.

—— (2001). 'Una renta básica para todos', in *Raventós*: 43–62.

Waldron, Jeremy (1989). 'Rights in Conflict', *Ethics*, 99: 503–19.

—— (1993*a*). 'A Right-based Critique of Constitutional Rights', *Oxford Journal of Legal Studies*, 13: 18–51.

—— (1993*b*). *Liberal Rights*. Cambridge: Cambridge University Press.

—— (1999). *Law and Disagreement*. Oxford: Oxford University Press.

Walzer, Michael (1980*a*). 'The Moral Standing of States', *Philosophy and Public Affairs*, 9: 209–29.

―― (1980*b*). *Just and Unjust Wars*. Harmondsworth: Penguin Books.

Walzer, Michael (1983). *Spheres of Justice*. New York: Basic Books.

―― (1995). 'Response', in David Miller and Michael Walzer (eds.), *Pluralism, Justice, and Equality*. Oxford: Oxford University Press.

―― (1997). *On Toleration*. New Haven, CT: Yale University Press.

Wantchekon, Leonard (1999). 'Why Do Resource Dependent Countries Have Authoritarian Governments?', Working Paper, Yale University, www.yale.edu/ leitner/pdf/1999-11.pdf

Watal, Jayashree (2000). 'Access to Essential Medicines in Developing Countries: Does the WTO TRIPS Agreement Hinder It?', Science, Technology and Innovation Discussion Paper No. 8, Harvard Center for International Development, www2.cid.harvard.edu/ cidbiotech/dp/discussion8.pdf

Weissbrodt, David (2000). 'Principles Relating to the Human Rights Conduct of Companies', E/CN.4/Sub.2/2000/WG.2/WP.1, 25 May 2000, www.unhchr.ch/Huridocda/ Huridoca.nsf/0/4c9f4b9319945428c125691b00438fdf/ $FILE/G0013862.pdf

WHO (World Health Organisation) (2004), *The World Health Report 2004*. Geneva: WHO Publications. Also at www.who.int/whr/2004

Williams, Bernard (1985). *Ethics and the Limits of Philosophy*. London: Fontana.

Wittgenstein, Ludwig (1976). *Zettel*. Berkeley, CA: University of California Press.

Wolff, Jonathan (1996). 'Rational, Fair, and Reasonable', *Utilitas*, 8(3): 263–71.

World Bank (2000). 'Country Reports on Health, Nutrition, Population, and Poverty', Washington, DC, www.worldbank.org/poverty/health/data

―― (2001*a*). 'Global Poverty Monitoring', www.worldbank.org/research/ povmonitor

―― (2001*b*). *World Development Report 2000/2001: Attacking Poverty*. Oxford: Oxford University Press.

―― (2003*a*). *World Development Report 2003*. New York: Oxford University Press.

―― (2003*b*). 'Preliminary Report on Inequality in Latin America and the Caribbean', worldbank.org

―― (2004). *Global Economic Prospects 2004: Realizing the Developing Promise of the Doha Agenda*. Washington, DC: The World Bank.

―― (2006). *World Development Report 2007*. Washington, DC: The World Bank.

Wright, G. H. (1963). *Norm and Action*. London: Routledge and Kegan Paul.

Zimmerman, David (1981). 'Coercive Wage Offers', *Philosophy and Public Affairs*, 10: 121–45.

Zürn, Michael (2004). 'Global Governance and Legitimacy Problems', *Government and Opposition*, 39 (2): 260–88.

Index